CW00925876

The Captain Cook Encyclopædia

The Captain Cook ENCYCLOPÆDIA

Written and Edited by
JOHN ROBSON

CHATHAM PUBLISHING
LONDON

STACKPOLE BOOKS
PENNSYLVANIA

Half-title: A Hei tiki, a pounamu Māori ornament collected in New Zealand on the second voyage. Pounamu, or greenstone, is a highly prized material used for ornaments. The tiki, possibly once a fertility symbol, today has protective and positive connotations. (Forster Collection, Pitt Rivers Museum, Oxford)

Frontispiece: The replica bark *Endeavour*. (Jenny Bennett)

Contributors

Vanessa Agnew
D E Anderson
Rosalin Barker
Tim Beaglehole
Ian Boreham
Julia Bruce
Jeremy Coote
Andrew David
Michael Goldsmith
Adrienne Kaeppler
Pieter van der Merwe
John Morris
John M Naish
Wayne Orchiston
Alwyn Peel
Julia Rae
Tom Ryan
Victor Suthren
Clifford E Thornton
Christopher Ware
Glyndwr Williams
Lawrence Worms

First published in Great Britain in 2004 by
Chatham Publishing
Lionel Leventhal Ltd
Park House
1 Russell Gardens
London NW11 9NN

And in North America by
Stackpole Books
5067 Ritter Road, Mechanicsburg
PA 17055-6921

British Library Cataloguing in Publication Data
Robson, John, 1949-
The Captain Cook Encyclopaedia
1. Cook, James, 1728–1779 – Encyclopaedias 2. Discoveries in geography – History – Encyclopaedias 3. Pacific Area – Discoveries and exploration – Encyclopaedias
I. Title
910.9′0

ISBN 1 86176 225 9

Printed and bound in China by Imago

Contents

Foreword and Acknowledgements

IT SEEMS remarkable that among the thousands of books that have been written about James Cook over the years there has never been an encyclopaedia devoted to him. It was, therefore, not before time when Chatham Publishing decided to prepare a *Cook Encyclopaedia* as a companion to its earlier excellent Nelson volume, compiled by Colin White. It was, though, a surprise and an honour when I was asked to compile the Cook work.

Having jumped at the offer by Julian Mannering, reality began to set in as I realised the enormity of the task ahead. Cook is of interest to a large range of people, some of whom are researching at an academic level while others only want a general introduction. The range of subjects touched upon by Cook and his voyages is enormous. A multi-volume encyclopaedia seemed to be in order though a single volume was being proposed. How, therefore, to include everything and provide sufficient space to do justice to them all.

The final list of topics owes much to suggestions by friends and colleagues. Especially, I would like to thank Cliff Thornton, Ian Boreham and Alwyn Peel, members of the Captain Cook Society, for their contributions and encouragement. Realising my knowledge was limited in certain quarters, I approached several experts, asking them to contribute short essays on topics in their field. I am very grateful that most of them agreed and their excellent credited pieces are scattered through the *Encyclopaedia*. To them all, many thanks.

Chatham indicated from the start that the work would be well-illustrated and they have done a sterling job securing images from around the world. Many Cook books contain the same somewhat tired illustrations and, for this work, I wanted to use some different ones. Obviously, some core pictures, such as the portraits of Cook, must be used but we have been fortunate to arrange some new ones. I would like to thank Herb Kāne, Robin Brooks, Nigel Brown, and Raymond Massey for generously granting permission to reproduce their work. Ron Ravneberg in the USA has been particularly helpful in arranging images from early volumes for reproduction while libraries and museums in Australia, New Zealand and the UK have also provided illustrations. Thanks also to Mark Adams and Dave Fisher for providing photographs.

Max Oulton, who computerised the maps for the earlier work, *Captain Cook's World,* was again ready to assist and worked on the maps included. In addition to others mentioned elsewhere, several people critically read and made valuable suggestions. Thanks to Herb Kāne and Larry Robbins for covering most of the pieces about Hawai'i and things nautical respectively. Any errors persisting are all mine.

As stated above, no Cook encyclopaedia has appeared before. I trust that this work succeeds in filling that void. It was realised that a published book would not be large enough to carry all the information that had been assembled and various items, especially pieces produced for the appendices, would have to be left out. To offset that disappointment, I have initiated a *Captain Cook Encyclopaedia* website where extra material will be displayed, as and when it comes to hand. There will also be the opportunity to correct errors and spelling mistakes that have sneaked through. The url is http://www.captaincookencyclopaedia.com/. Please use the email listed there to contribute or let me know of errors.

Julian Mannering, as Commissioning Editor, has been a wonderful colleague from the start. Supportive and encouraging, he gave me virtual free rein in subject content, yet has remained quietly in control, ensuring that wild fancies never eventuated, deadlines were met and the final work bears some resemblance to what was planned. It has been a pleasure to work with him and I thank him greatly for the opportunity he offered me.

Finally, I thank my corgis again. Once more, the three dogs, Oscar, Cullen and Hector, have quietly watched without complaint while all my free time has been given over to reading and writing for the Encyclopaedia. The work is dedicated to the boys.

John Robson
Hamilton, New Zealand, May 2004

Introduction

THE EXPLORER, James Cook (or Captain Cook as he is generally known), has been described as a man who was concerned principally with facts. On that basis I hope he would have approved of this Encyclopaedia, which aims to bring together a mass of facts and information to do with Cook, his life and his voyages.

With Drake and Nelson, James Cook makes up the trio of British maritime heroes whose names are known beyond naval circles. Nelson remains the archetypal naval military hero, who died during his greatest action at Trafalgar, while Drake, the privateer, is synonymous with daring, especially against the Spanish. Cook's fame is based on more peaceful activities and he is closely associated with the development of the British Empire through his explorations and charting of unknown seas. Cook's fame, though, is universal and not restricted just to British history. Like Christopher Columbus and Marco Polo, Captain Cook is a name associated throughout the world with exploration. It is interesting to note that Cook only held the rank of captain officially from 1775.

Since Cook's death in 1779, his fame has spread throughout the world. Cook has become a name known to many even if they cannot state exactly what he did or achieved. His current standing can be summed up by an event that happened to me in 2000. My book *Captain Cook's World* had just appeared and I was walking home across the fields of the University of Waikato campus when I was stopped by a Māori student, wearing dreadlocks and tino rangitanga (Māori sovereignty) colours. During our conversation, he said 'I really enjoyed your book. He's part of all our histories'.

Thousands of book and articles have been written about him and his exploits, and not only in English. In recent years, books have been published in Estonia, Iran and Italy. In 1991, Greg Dening wrote a foreword for a book of poems by the Australian poet, Alex Galloway. In it Dening, a respected Pacific historian, wrote: 'I do not find it strange that Alex Galloway should choose to write a poem about James Cook. In the 212 years since Cook's death in Hawai'i, there has hardly been a year that has not seen another poem, play, ballet, pantomime, novel or history written of him and his "discoveries".'

In 1974, a biography of Cook, written by J C Beaglehole, was published. Beaglehole, who had died the previous year, had spent most of the previous 25 years researching all aspects of Cook's voyages and the Hakluyt Society had published his monumental edition of Cook's journals. With the appearance of the biography, there were some who felt there was little else to be written about Cook as Beaglehole had covered everything. In reality the opposite happened. More has been written in the last 35 years than in the previous 200. It would probably have been better had many of those books never been published. Many have been poorly researched and have simply rehashed material from earlier works. In doing so, they perpetuated errors. One aim of this volume is to bring together as much verified information about Cook as possible in one place for future researchers.

People approach Cook from many different angles and at different levels of prior knowledge so another aim of the Encyclopaedia is to provide different access points for a study and understanding of the explorer. The range of articles is designed to help everyone from a person wanting a general introduction to Cook to someone else requiring detailed information about a specific aspect of the voyages. While many of the articles deal directly with places, people and events in Cook's life, others have been included to provide background to the times and conditions in which Cook operated. 'Lunar distance method', 'Logs' and 'Cats' are among the topics covering sailing and the Navy at the time while 'The Seven Years War', 'The Enlightenment' and 'Quakers' are examples of topics illustrating the eighteenth century. Other pieces, somewhat lighter in tone, such as 'Philately', 'Wallpaper and stained glass' and 'Space, Cook in' cover subjects influenced by Cook's legacy and reputation.

That reputation, however, has suffered in recent years. For 200 years, his deeds went largely unquestioned and his immense achievements were applauded. 1969 and 1970 marked the 200th anniversaries of Cook's first visits to New Zealand and Australia respectively. The European histories of these two countries effectively dated from Cook's arrival and he had become a hero in both of them. Cook celebrations were many, conferences were held, music composed, plays written, and Cook was hailed as a founding father. As the 1970s progressed, however, they paralleled an awakening in indigenous societies around the Pacific and a questioning of what Europeans had contributed, with Cook's role coming into question. By 1979, at a conference in Vancouver, academics were beginning to reappraise Cook's work.

The general reappraisal has continued since then, though some of the initial criticisms applied to Cook have been modified. It is now felt that while not everything he did or achieved had beneficial outcomes for all involved, especially the peoples of the Pacific, it is accepted that Cook was a man of his times and to apply the hindsight of 200 years is not particularly fair. As a man of his times, Cook was for the most part, a most humane and moderate person. He was acutely aware of the problems such as venereal disease that Europeans had brought with them to the Pacific. In the piece on Australian Aborigines, it is noted that 'Captain Cook' has become a term synonymous with European and, in blaming Captain Cook, people are blaming Europeans in general for the perceived wrongs done to them. The negative points of Cook's actions have been included here as well as the positive.

In recent years, there has also been reassessment of other matters and persons associated with Cook. His role in finding a prevention for scurvy continues to cause debate while Beaglehole's negative attitude towards the Forsters has been questioned. It is acknowledged that Reinhold

Forster was an irascible man who made enemies on the second voyage but it is now felt that Beaglehole was unnecessarily critical of Forster's overall contribution. Another long-held myth now largely discredited was Alexander Dalrymple's supposed animosity towards Cook after Cook was chosen to lead the *Endeavour* voyage.

Cook's death has given rise to one of the major debates in anthropology, which has been conducted through the 1990s. Marshall Sahlins and Gananath Obeyesekere have polarised the anthropology community on the matter of whether Cook was seen by the Hawaiians as a manifestation of the god Lono or whether this was something concocted by Europeans later in order to raise Cook's standing. Articles in the Encyclopaedia summarise the argument in which Cook himself is largely a bystander.

The journals of Cook's voyages continue to be worked over by academics from varied backgrounds. They provide source material on contact between cultures and first-hand descriptions of Pacific societies, as well as information for meteorologists and for medical historians. Even the language of the journals itself is being studied to show the development of ships' narratives. Ethnographers are beginning to unravel the many collections of artefacts sitting in museums incorrectly identified and attributed and use them to provide further insights into the Pacific. The whereabouts of the final resting places of Cook's ships continues to involve marine archaeologists. The list of current Cook studies is long and varied and it seems fairly certain that conferences, books and journals will continue to feature Cook-related subjects for many years to come.

Cook set new standards on his voyages. They became the benchmarks against which all later expeditions were measured. The observations of Cook and his colleagues played an important role in botany, zoology, astronomy and oceanography. They also helped to give birth in the next century to the new disciplines of ethnology, anthropology and hydrography. Cook's three voyages of discovery have provided people with unprecedented information about the Pacific Ocean, and about those who lived on its islands and shores. He brought order to what was known of the region, replacing vagueness and uncertainty with accuracy and, in doing so, drew the modern map of the Pacific.

There is a vast reservoir of information available on Cook and his voyages. I hope the *Captain Cook Encyclopaedia* is able to reproduce much of that reservoir and can answer most questions on anything to do with James Cook. Where it cannot and for people who require more in-depth information, I trust it can point them in the right direction. Cook remains a fascinating subject at the beginning of the twenty-first century. As Greg Dening, in his foreword for Galloway's poetry book, concluded: '. . . this man James Cook and his deeds are as deep as the ocean he crossed and as unfathomable. The furrows he made on the waves do not seem to disappear. They last forever.'

James Cook (1728–1779)

Captain James Cook, painted by William Hodges. 1776. Long thought lost, this portrait resurfaced in 1986 in Ireland. (National Maritime Museum, London)

JAMES COOK is universally known yet only part of his life is well documented. Unfortunately, his early and middle life are poorly recorded while the last ten years, covering his three great voyages, are very well documented. We are fortunate that Cook himself maintained comprehensive logs and journals on all of his three voyages of exploration to the Pacific. However, while we now have intricate detail of where he went, what he saw and whom he met, we still know little about Cook the person from these records. He offers opinions and occasionally shows his feelings, but his character and personality remain somewhat elusive.

We are left little the wiser as the result of writings by others, as, unfortunately, there are no long and detailed descriptions of Cook by persons who knew him. Joseph Banks for one, who probably knew Cook better than anyone, left nothing about his friend. Nor do Banks or Cook's widow appear to have been interviewed by Andrew Kippis, who wrote the first biography of Cook, a work which concentrates on the voyages and is sadly lacking in information about the man. It is perhaps to be regretted that James Boswell, Samuel Johnson's friend and scribe, did not travel with Cook on the third voyage, an action he expressed a desire to do at one time. No doubt Boswell would have given us a proper and full report. He met Cook several times in 1776 and wrote: 'Cook...was a plain, sensible man with an uncommon attention to veracity. My metaphor was that he had a balance in his mind for truth as nice as scales for weighing a guinea.... I talked with him a good deal today, as he was very obliging and communicative. He seemed to have no desire to make people stare, and being a man of good steady moral principles, as I thought, did not try to make theories out of what he had seen to confound virtue and vice'.

One of the few men who did sail with and write about Cook was James Trevenen. A few lines of verse, attributed to him, describe the end of an excursion in one of the small boats with Cook ('Toote' was a Polynesian name for Cook):

'And pulling 'gainst tide, or before the wind spooning,
Sometimes were shooting and sometimes surveying,
With pleasure still watching, with pleasure obeying,
Till pleased with our efforts, thy features relax,
And thou giv'st us thy game to take home on our backs.
O day of hard labour, O day of good living,
When TOOTE was seized with the humour of giving –
When he clothed in good nature his looks of authority,
And shook from his eyebrows their stern superiority.'

So we are left to piece together a biography and draw conclusions about Cook from scattered sources, an action Cook would have not approved if Boswell is correct in his statement above. It took nearly 200 years before a good biography of Cook was published. This appeared in 1974 as a result of research when editing Cook's journals and J C Beaglehole's work will probably remain the definitive biography. Even Beaglehole was unable to unearth much about Cook's early life. Since then, Clifford Thornton (on the childhood in Cleveland) and Julia Rae (on Cook in London) have added considerably to what we know.

James Cook was born in Marton in Cleveland, north-east England, in 1728. He was the second of eight children of James and Grace Cook. James Cook was a farm labourer, originally from Scotland, while Grace was a local woman from Thornaby. In 1736, the Cooks moved a few kilometres south to Great Ayton where James attended the local school for four years. His father's employer, the lord of the manor, Thomas Skottowe, arranged a job for Cook, working in a shop at Staithes, on the North Sea coast. The work did not suit Cook but Staithes had introduced him to the sea. His employer, William Sanderson, knew a family of ship operators in Whitby and terms were agreed whereby Cook became an apprentice (or servant) with the Walkers.

Cook would spend the next few years until 1755 working on the colliers sailing in the North Sea coal trade. It marked the apprenticeship stage in his life during which he learned seamanship and navigation skills along the east coast of England with its treacherous shoals and uncharted shallows. It also instilled in him the knowledge that only through application and hard work would he achieve anything. To this end he was prepared to do the hard physical work demanded of a seaman but he also put in many hours of study reading books on navigation and mathematics in the Walkers' house where he stayed when not at sea. Cook realised at this time the need for discipline and structure both in his own life and on board ship, a discipline that he applied to his commands in the Pacific. It also helped his cause later that the ship chosen for the first voyage to the Pacific, the *Endeavour,* was originally a collier, the type of vessel on which he had learnt his seamanship.

The trade involved carrying coal from the Tyne to the Thames and so marked an introduction for the young man to London, especially Wapping and Shadwell near London Bridge where the coal was unloaded. Cook formed a close friendship with his employer John Walker and continued to correspond with him after he left his service. However, it was Cook's ability and record that saw him promoted to mate on Walker's ships and being offered his own command of a collier in 1755. To everyone's surprise though, Cook declined the offer and enlisted as an able seaman with the Royal Navy at Wapping in June 1755. The reasons for this move remain unknown. War between Britain and France had been simmering and was about to break out formally so perhaps Cook felt it offered a new challenge or perhaps he simply wanted a change.

From 1755 until 1767, Cook served with the Royal Navy and it marked the proving stage in his career. He had received a basic grounding in the North Sea and now he could build on it and prove himself in the Navy. Cook would spend time on patrols in the English Channel and took part in the capture of several French ships. Cook, serving on HMS *Eagle,* quickly was promoted to master's mate and in 1757 passed the examinations to become a ship's master. His captain during the later months on *Eagle* had been Hugh Palliser, who became a friend and helped

Cook's career. As master, Cook began on HMS *Solebay,* off Scotland before, in October 1757, he was shifted to the *Pembroke.* In May 1758, Cook and the *Pembroke* were sent as part of the war effort against the French in North America and Cook would spend the next ten years in Canadian and Newfoundland waters.

He took part in the siege of Louisbourg in 1758, and the capture of Quebec the following year. It was during this time that he developed the surveying and cartographical skills that would serve him so well in the Pacific. Cook met Samuel Holland, a military surveyor, at Louisbourg and with the encouragement of his captain, John Simcoe, he learned surveying techniques from Holland. Cook quickly developed a capacity for compiling charts and sets of sailing directions, and for taking plans and views. Cook joined HMS *Northumberland* after the battle of Quebec and spent time based in Halifax, Nova Scotia. In 1762, the British, including Cook, rushed to Newfoundland to recapture St John's, recently taken by the French. It began five very important years of association with the island of Newfoundland for Cook. However, Cook returned to Britain in late 1762 for the first time in four years and promptly married Elizabeth Batts in Barking on 21 December 1762.

Thomas Graves, the Governor of Newfoundland, appointed Cook as surveyor of the island to chart the lengthy and complex coastline. Cook began his duties in 1763 and was assigned a small schooner, the *Grenville,* and a small crew. Over the next five summers, Cook produced a set of charts of the highest quality, remarkable for their precision, comprehensiveness and consistency. Cook, given the responsibility of command, showed himself determined and a natural leader. He applied his ideas on discipline but realised that fairness, openness and consistency were required when dealing with his men. He also saw that a healthy and contented crew was essential and to this end insisted that beer was brewed at every opportunity for the men to drink. Cook's friend, Captain Palliser from the *Eagle,* had become Governor of Newfoundland and their friendship developed. Cook also had direct dealings with the Admiralty back in London and his reputation there grew apace. The Secretary to the Board, Phillip Stephens, was another influential person who became a friend.

Over the years Cook had added astronomy to his list of skills so, in August 1766, he was able to observe a solar eclipse while on the south coast of Newfoundland. He submitted the results to the Royal Society of London. The same Royal Society had been petitioning the British government and the Admiralty to send astronomers and a ship to observe a Transit of Venus scheduled for 1769. A pattern of accurate observations at points around the globe would help to determine the distance of the earth from the sun. The Admiralty agreed and acquired an ex-collier, renamed HM Bark *Endeavour*, for the expedition to Tahiti in the South Pacific, which had been deemed the best location to observe the transit. Before Cook could complete the Newfoundland survey he was appointed in April 1768 to command this expedition. His appointment met with

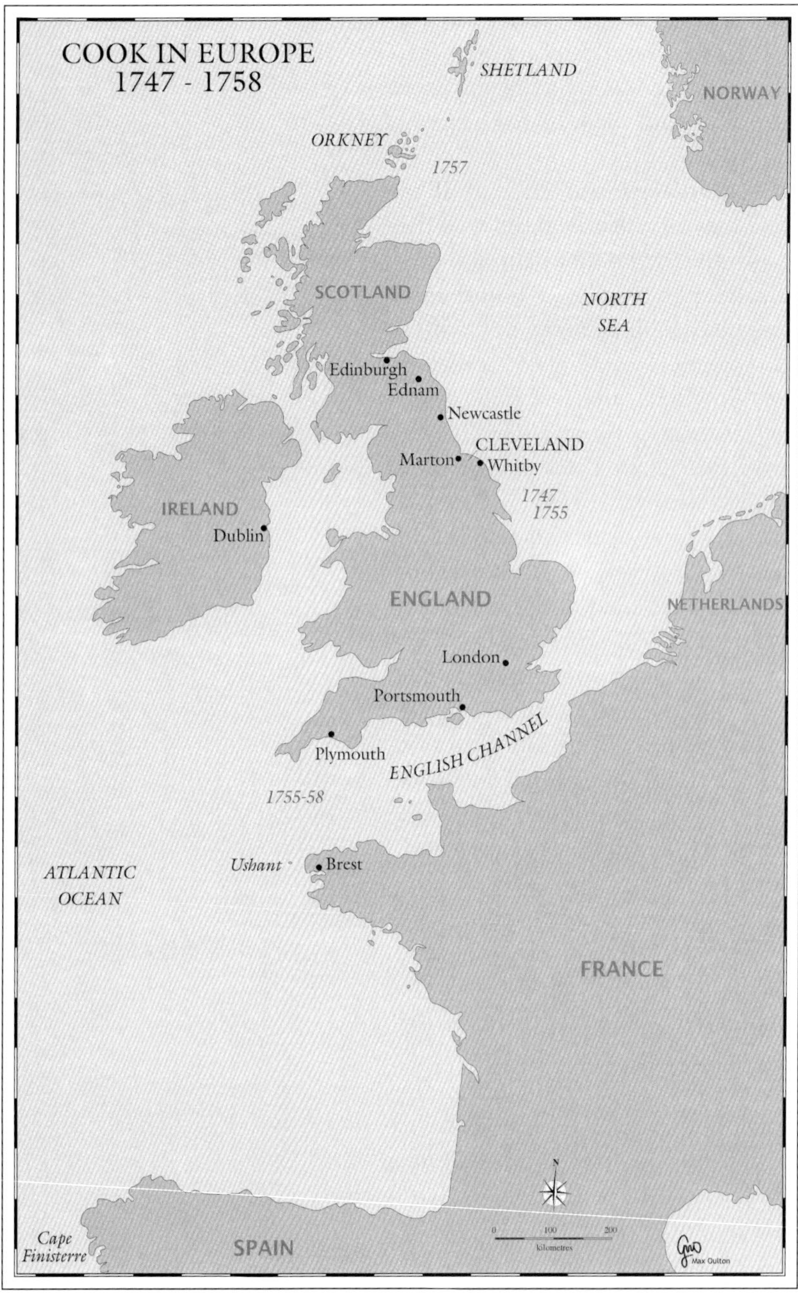

the approval of the Royal Society as Cook could serve as assistant astronomer to their appointment, Charles Green. A secondary goal of the expedition was to search for the Great Southern Continent, supposed to lie across the South Pacific below 40° S.

Cook was promoted to lieutenant for the voyage. The *Endeavour* left Plymouth on 26 August 1768 and sailed south down the Atlantic via Madeira and Rio de Janeiro. Cook stopped at Madeira to take on wine and onions, both part of his efforts to keep a healthy crew. As well as his regular crew Cook had on board a naturalist, Joseph Banks, with his retinue of naturalists and artists. Cook rounded Cape Horn and reached Tahiti in April 1769, where he prepared for the transit. The *Endeavour* anchored at Matavai Bay, which would become one of Cook's favourite locations in the Pacific and one he would return to on several occasions. He stayed at Tahiti for three months and as well as successfully observing the Transit of Venus, he made a tour of the island and surveyed and prepared descriptions of the island and people. Proponents of the concept of the 'Noble Savage' used these descriptions to enhance their argument. A Raiatean, Tupaia, was taken on board and would prove his worth as a navigator and translator.

Sailing on via Huahine and Raiatea, Cook began the search for the Southern Continent, and having found no trace of land, sailed west for land visited by Tasman in 1643. This was New Zealand and Cook made landfall at Turanganui (Cook called it Poverty Bay), near present-day Gisborne in October 1769. Cook's relationship with the Māori got off to a bad start when several men were killed and others wounded. Tupaia could understand the Māori and acted as a translator, which helped improve the later encounters. Cook was distressed that lives had been lost.

Cook left Poverty Bay and sailed south along the east coast as far as Cape Turnagain, before retracing his track north via Tolaga Bay, round East Cape and across the Bay of Plenty to the Coromandel Peninsula. Putting into Mercury Bay, he observed the Transit of Mercury. The *Endeavour* rounded Cape Colville to enter the Firth of Thames before heading north up the coast to the Bay of Islands. Cook spent a week in this bay, which was to become the first site of permanent European settlement in New Zealand. In December 1769, Cook was near North Cape when he nearly met the French explorer, Surville, who was sailing in the opposite direction. Cook rounded the north of New Zealand then sailed down the west coast of Te Ika a Maui (the North Island). The *Endeavour* was in need of repair and they needed to restock so Cook took the ship into a large inlet.

The inlet was Queen Charlotte Sound and Cook anchored in Ship Cove. It became, like Matavai Bay in Tahiti, one of his bases on future voyages. It provided safe anchorage, food and fresh water, and plentiful timber for spars. Relations with local Māori were good. In February 1770, Cook continued his voyage by passing through the strait, which Banks named after Cook. Cook proved Te Ika a Maui was an island and then sailed south down the east coast of Te Wai Pounamu (South Island). He rounded the southern tip and worked his way back up the west coast to anchor in Admiralty Bay, close to Queen Charlotte Sound. Cook had shown New Zealand to comprise two large islands, unconnected to the Great Southern Continent. He also produced a magnificent chart of the islands, together with descriptions of the country and the Māori. Cook speculated on the similarities between Tahitians and Māori and wondered about their ability to sail across the Pacific.

The *Endeavour* left New Zealand, heading west towards Australia, which was sighted at Point Hicks on 19 April. Cook then proceeded to sail north up the east coast of Australia, producing a detailed chart as he went. At the end of April, Cook entered an inlet, Botany Bay, where he stayed for six days. The country was very different from anywhere they had been and the local people were also very different. Tupaia was unable to communicate with them and they in turn made no effort to promote contact.

Cook continued north to round Fraser Island and began sailing inside the Great Barrier Reef. Progress had to be careful as they encountered numerous small islands, reefs and sandbanks. Finally, on 11 June, disaster struck when the *Endeavour* hit the reef. After 24 hours, the ship was refloated and nursed into a nearby river mouth. The ship was eventually repaired and Cook continued on to pass through Torres Strait and on to Jakarta (Batavia) on Java, where he arrived on 11 October. The Dutch authorities agreed to repair the ship but were very slow about it. Gradually, the unhealthy state of Jakarta began to take its toll as men succumbed to malaria and dysentery. Many more died as the *Endeavour* crossed the Indian Ocean and some died at the Cape of Good Hope. The *Endeavour* finally arrived at the Downs off Kent on 13 July 1771 after a voyage of nearly three years.

The return of the *Endeavour* had been greatly anticipated by the public as well as the Navy. The acclaim, however, was for Banks, whose voyage it was deemed to be. Cook, meanwhile, quietly returned to his wife and family. However, his role in the success of the voyage had not escaped the authorities and the Admiralty quickly made known their thanks, Cook being promoted to commander. While Cook had returned with charts of Tahiti, New Zealand and the coast of Australia, Banks had brought botanical and zoological specimens and his artists had hundreds of drawings recording the voyage. His and Banks' journals were handed over to John Hawkesworth to be edited for publication. The Transit had been observed successfully and while the existence of the Great Southern Continent had not been resolved, Cook submitted plans for another voyage to settle the matter. The Admiralty agreed to Cook's proposal and gave orders for a second voyage with Cook again in command.

The *Endeavour* voyage had been an establishing stage in Cook's career in that it presented him with the opportunity to make his name beyond the narrow confines of the Admiralty and in this he succeeded. Cook's humble background and lack of social standing always meant that he had to do extra well in anything he attempted. He had no family to fall back upon and while he had several friends with status in the Navy, they were not admirals. Nor did Cook have the backing of any influential politicians. If the first voyage was establishment, then the second was to be consolidation. If he could bring his ships and crew home with goals achieved his future in the Navy was assured, so Cook was keen to take his second chance. The second voyage was a logical complement to his first as it provided him with the opportunity to finish what had been left unexplored.

After the near-disaster suffered by the *Endeavour* on the Great Barrier Reef, Cook asked for two ships for safety reasons and two colliers were purchased for the voyage. Cook was in charge of the *Resolution* and Tobias Furneaux commanded the smaller *Adventure*. Joseph Banks wanted to sail again but withdrew after arguments about arrangements on board. Johann Reinhold Forster and his young son, George, were appointed in place of Banks as naturalists and their writings are a rich source of information about the Pacific. The voyage was also notable in that Cook took chronometers with him, one of which was a copy of one of John Harrison's that would revolutionise navigation.

The ships sailed from Plymouth in July 1772 and made for Cape Town, which they reached at the end of October. Cook made an unsuccessful attempt to find land sighted by the French explorer, Bouvet, in 1739. The ships then sailed south-east and they became the first to cross the Antarctic Circle before ice forced them north. Fog separated the ships and Cook turned alone south-east towards the ice, sailing for two months at 55° S without sighting land. In March 1773, Cook reached Dusky Sound in New Zealand and then was reunited with the *Adventure* at Queen

Charlotte Sound. Cook made use of the southern winter to make a sweep of the central Pacific. The two vessels sailed west from New Zealand without finding land then north to the Tuamotu archipelago, and on to Tahiti and the other Society Islands. Against Cook's wishes, at Huahine, Furneaux took on board Mai, who was to create extraordinary interest after the *Adventure*'s return to England. On their passage back to New Zealand the two vessels were separated again. The *Adventure* was driven north and took refuge at Tolaga Bay so that by the time she eventually made Queen Charlotte Sound, the *Resolution* had already departed. Disaster befell the *Adventure* when members of a shore party were killed. Furneaux decided to return to Britain immediately via Cape Horn and the Cape of Good Hope and reached there in July 1774.

In the meantime Cook had headed south again and twice crossed the Antarctic Circle, reaching 71° 102′ S on 30 January 1774. Cook finally yielded and sailed north, much to the relief of everyone on board. As he sailed north he became seriously ill. However, he continued and made a sweep of many islands and groups across the Pacific, including Easter Island, the Marquesas, Tahiti, Niue, Tonga, Vanuatu (the New Hebrides), New Caledonia and Norfolk Island. By now Cook had filled in many of the remaining vacant spaces in the Pacific and had left few to locate. His charts, especially that of the New Hebrides, represented surveying and cartography of the highest order. The *Resolution* stopped briefly at Queen Charlotte Sound once more before Cook headed for via Cape Horn. Another crossing of the Pacific without sighting land finally laid to rest the myth of a Great Southern Continent. Cook made brief visits to Tierra del Fuego, South Georgia and the South Sandwich Islands on his way to Cape Town before heading up the Atlantic via Saint Helena and the Azores to reach Britain in late July 1775.

Cook's second voyage represents one of the single greatest voyages of all time. It could not find the Great Southern Continent since, as Cook himself realised, it only exists so far south and close to the pole as to be uninhabitable but the way in which he showed this was magnificent. Once again he returned with a quantity of journals and charts, which, with the writings of the Forsters and artist William Hodges's paintings, provide a tremendous resource for students of the Pacific. Cook had set out to consolidate his position through this voyage and he had succeeded. He was now a celebrity and his fame had spread beyond naval circles. He was elected a Fellow of the Royal Society and awarded its Copley Gold Medal, his portrait was painted by William Hodges and Nathaniel Dance, and he was described in the House of Lords as 'the first navigator in Europe'.

He was due a rest and the Navy appointed him to a position at Greenwich Hospital where all that was expected of him was for him to write up the narrative of the voyage. Elizabeth Cook and the family could at last expect to see something of Cook at home in East London. In their eyes and in the eyes of many Cook had done more than enough to earn and enjoy a long retirement. But the Earl of Sandwich, the First Lord of the Admiralty, had other ideas. Mai, the Raiatean brought to Britain by

Furneaux, needed to be returned to the Pacific while the existence of the Northwest Passage between the Pacific and the Atlantic, north of America needed to be proved. The Earl sought Cook's opinion on who should lead the expedition to carry out these tasks, wanting all the time Cook to nominate himself. Cook duly obliged and Sandwich appointed him, much to the dismay of Cook's family. It would prove to be a voyage too far, from which he would not return. Cook probably regarded it as his benefit voyage with the prize for finding the Northwest Passage, one that would make him and his family financially secure. What other rewards he was promised or whether it was pride that made him accept the command we will never know. Two factors would play significant roles as the voyage progressed; Cook was now 47 years old and he was not fully recovered from the second voyage.

Cook took two ships. Now promoted to captain, he commanded the *Resolution* and Charles Clerke, who had already sailed twice with Cook, commanded the *Discovery*. No naturalists were taken and John Webber sailed as artist. Cook left Plymouth on 12 July 1776 for the Cape of Good Hope, where Clerke joined him a few weeks later. The two ships then headed for New Zealand via Kerguelen and Tasmania. The ships were in Queen Charlotte Sound for two weeks in February 1777, refitting and refreshing. Cook surprised everyone by not extracting revenge for the death of *Adventure*'s crew in 1773. The ships continued on through the Cook Islands and Tonga. Cook lingered in Tonga, passing on opportunities to visit Samoa and Fiji. His usual propensity to go anywhere and investigate had deserted him. He was also beginning to behave in other uncharacteristic ways, being harder on his crew and less tolerant of the behaviour of Pacific people he met. Eventually, he moved on to Tahiti and for the first time visited nearby Moorea. The theft of a goat angered Cook, who in a complete over-reaction burned houses and canoes. Transferring to Huahine, Cook completed his first task by returning Mai to the island in late 1777.

Cook now headed north to make his first visit to the North Pacific in search of the Northwest Passage. He visited the Hawaiian islands before surveying the north-west coasts of America from Oregon to Alaska. The ships passed through the Bering Strait and crossed the Arctic Circle but ice thwarted any further progress. Numerous inlets had been investigated but no Northwest Passage had been located. Cook returned south to the warmth of the recently visited Hawai'i to recover and restock. The British reached Maui in late November 1778 and moved on to anchor in Kealakekua Bay on Hawai'i in early January 1779. They were welcomed enthusiastically and relations were still very friendly when Cook departed in early February. However, a few days later, the *Resolution*'s foremast was damaged in a storm and, when Cook returned to Kealakekua to repair it, the reception was less friendly. On 14 February, Cook over-reacted to a theft and went ashore to take the Hawaiian chief, Kalaniop'u, hostage. In a fight that ensued at the north end of the bay, Cook and others from both sides were killed.

Charles Clerke assumed command of the expedition and took the ships back to the Arctic but their progress was again blocked by ice. Returning south, Clerke died of tuberculosis off Kamchatka. John Gore took over and brought the ships back to Britain in late 1780. Despite the deaths of Cook and Clerke, the third voyage's achievements were numerous. Tonga, Hawai'i and the north-west coast of America were described in detail and, while he did not find the Northwest Passage, Cook managed to set down the main outline of the American coast. However, any assessment of the voyage must consider Cook, whose age, poor health and tiredness led to erratic behaviour, and actions on this voyage not witnessed before. He lost some of his drive and became much harder on his crew, and less amiable and tolerant toward island people he met. He even exhibited signs of anger and violence not seen before, which no doubt contributed to his death on Hawai'i, where he reacted in a way that a younger Cook would not have done.

Cook was 51 when he died. The third voyage had been a gamble and he had lost. The benefits he had hoped for were of no consolation for his family. He had spent most of the previous 30 years at sea and most of the previous 20 years away from Britain. He had achieved things that no one, least of all Cook himself, could have ever anticipated when he enlisted in the Royal Navy in 1755. He had visited, charted and described most of the island groups of the Pacific as well as defining the ocean's boundaries. The map of the Pacific Ocean is his greatest statement.

News of Cook's death preceded the return of the expedition. Governor Behm of Kamchatka had crossed Russia and forwarded the news to Britain where it caused universal sadness in January 1780. The Earl of Sandwich wrote to Joseph Banks: 'what is uppermost in our mind allways must come out first, poor captain Cooke is no more'; while George Herbert wrote: 'Poor Cooke is truly a great loss to the Universe.'

The Royal Society had a medal struck, and in 1785 Elizabeth Cook was granted a coat of arms on behalf of her husband. Kippis's biography of Cook appeared in 1788. Unfortunately, Elizabeth Cook destroyed most of Cook's letters and other personal belongings, making the job of future biographers even more difficult.

Elizabeth Cook was only 38 years old when Cook died and three of their six children were still alive. Of these remaining children, Nathaniel died in late 1780, aged 16, when HMS *Thunderer*, the ship on which he was a midshipman, sank in the Caribbean during a hurricane. Hugh, the youngest child, attended Christ's College, Cambridge, but he died from fever in December 1793, aged 17. A month later his older brother and Cook's last surviving child, James, died in strange circumstances in Poole Harbour. He was 31 and had been commander of the sloop, the *Spitfire*. Elizabeth was granted a pension after Cook's death and used it to buy a house in Clapham. She was a widow for 56 years until she died in 1835 aged 94. She was buried with two of her sons in St Andrew the Great Church in Cambridge.

List of Abbreviations

AB	Able Seaman
DNB	*Dictionary of National Biography*
EIC	East India Company
FRC	Family Records Centre (National Archives)
FRS	Fellow of the Royal Society
HMS	His Majesty's Ship
JP	Justice of the Peace
MoD	Minstry of Defence
MP	Member of Parliament
NHM	Natural History Museum
NMM	National Maritime Museum
NPG	National Portrait Gallery
NSW	New South Wales
NZ	New Zealand
PRO	Public Record Office
RA	Royal Academy
RN	Royal Navy
UNESCO	United Nations Educational, Scientific, and Cultural Organization
VOC	Verenigde Oostindische Compagnie (Dutch East India Company)

The
Encyclopaedia

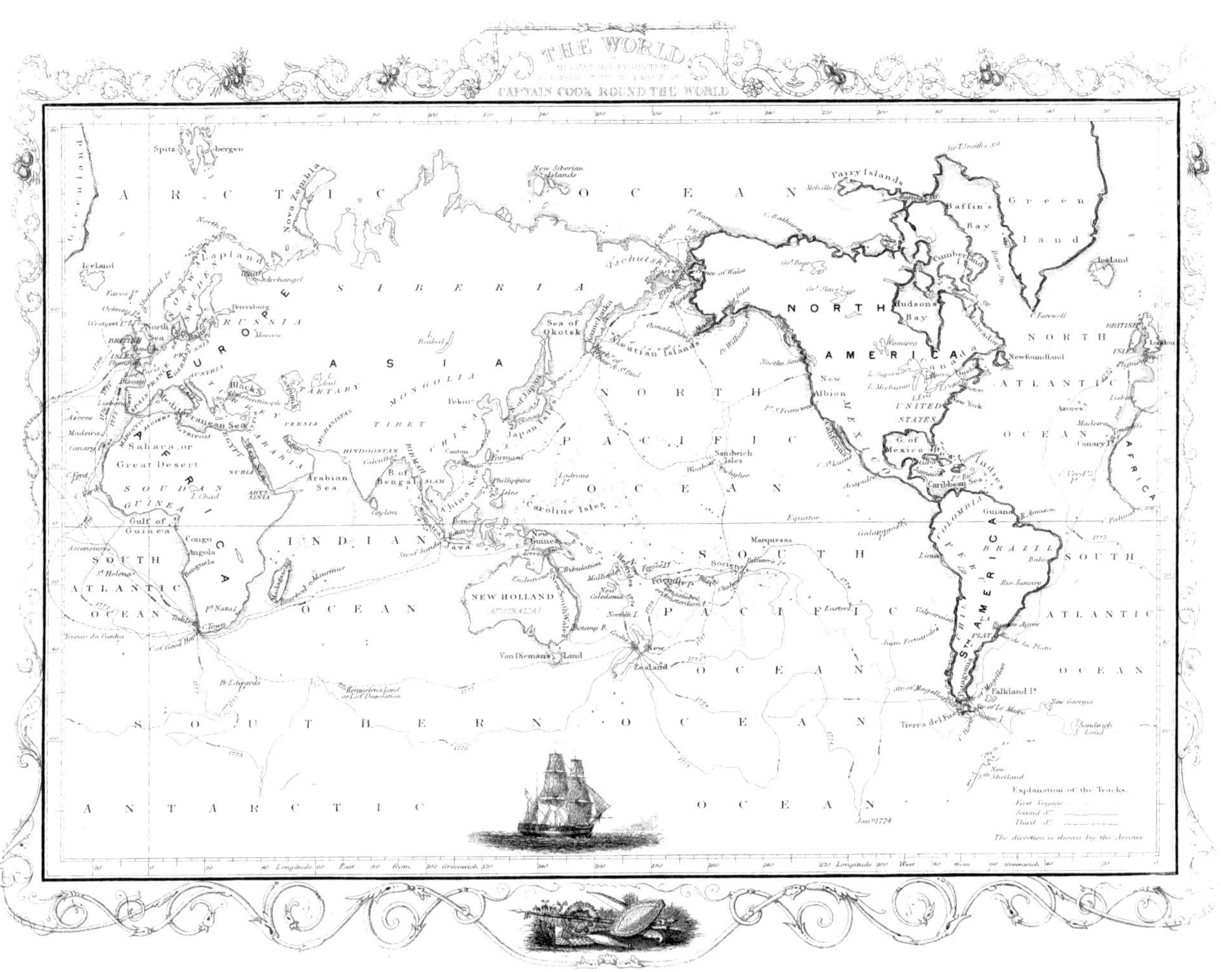

Aborigines, Australian

Recent archaeological evidence suggests the original inhabitants of Australia moved there up to 100,000 years ago. These people moved south from Southeast Asia at a time when the sea level was lower and Australia was part of a larger landmass, Sahul. Gradually they spread to occupy all parts of the continent and adapted to live in the wide variety of environments found there.

After the sea level rose again cutting the continent off, the remote location led to isolation, allowing unique cultures to develop largely without outside interruption, although limited contact occurred along the north-west coast with seafaring Malays. When Europeans arrived most Aboriginal people (as they were termed; they appear to have had no need for a communal word describing themselves) were hunter-gatherers with a complex oral culture and spiritual values based upon reverence for the land and a belief in the Dreamtime. The Dreamtime is, at once, the ancient time of creation and the present day reality of dreaming. At the time of contact, there were about 600 different Aboriginal groups, each with their own individual culture and belief structures, and speaking up to 200 languages.

People belonged to tribes led by religious leaders. They had no political chief or formal government, and the tribe was broken down into bands (hunting groups) and family units. These family units were important, as all members of a tribe were related. Careful systems governing kinship relations and regulating marriage developed. A tribe lived close to the place where its ancestors had originally settled, and close to a watering place. The size of the tribe depended on their ability to hunt and gather, and the proximity of fresh water, sometimes necessitating a semi-nomadic lifestyle. As the numbers of the tribe swelled, people set out to discover new waters and set up new territories.

Spirituality and religion played a major role in Aboriginal peoples' culture. There were many myths and rituals connected to both the tribe's ancestors and the creators of the world, none of whom ever died but merged with the natural world and thus remained a part of the present. These myths and rituals were also a source of inspiration for much Aboriginal art, including paintings, carved objects, symbolic weapons and poetic chants. While most people never left the area directly near their birthplace, a few acted as traders, walking across the continent. This travel was directed by a system of remarkable songs describing the terrain and of sources of food and water a person would need to recognise to progress safely. These 'songlines' were often very long and complex like the journeys they described.

A pen and ink drawing by John Webber depicting Cook and the crew of Resolution *meeting a group of aborigines at Adventure Bay, Tasmania, 29 January 1777. Communication was impossible. It is not known whether the sketch was done at the time or worked up following the artist's return to England in 1780. (The Royal Naval Museum, Portsmouth)*

It was then as a mysterious alien that Cook encountered Aboriginal peoples at Botany Bay and Endeavour River in 1770. Contact was limited as the local people tried to reconcile the newcomers with their beliefs. At Botany Bay, the Gweagal people observed the British from a distance with suspicion. Contact was established at Endeavour River with Guugu-Yimithir people and a small vocabulary determined. Cook wrote 'From what I have said of the Natives of New Holland they may appear to some to be the most wretched people upon Earth, but in reality they are far more happier than we Europeans; being wholly unacquainted not only with the superfluous but the necessary Conveniences so much sought after in Europe, they are happy in not knowing the use of them. They live in a tranquility which is not disturb'd by the Inequality of Condition'.

Cook does not, however, currently enjoy a good reputation with some Aboriginal peoples having been equated by them with all the wrongs perpetrated by Europeans since his arrival in their country. Those wrongs being total disruption to their lives and the drastic reduction in numbers (estimated at 90 per cent) by a combination of disease, loss of land (and thus food resources) and murder.

SEE ALSO: Australia, Indigenous peoples and Cook

Admiralty

The Admiralty was responsible for running the British navy, which had become the Royal Navy after the restoration of the monarchy under Charles II in 1660. In 1661, Sir William Penn and Samuel Pepys established the Naval Discipline Act, which included the articles of war and founded the Royal Navy by statute.

The Royal Navy was run by a series of Boards with the Admiralty Board, the most senior, being responsible for the policy direction, operational control and maritime jurisdiction of the Navy. From 1628 onwards, this was carried out by the Lords Commissioners of the Admiralty, otherwise known as the Admiralty Board. The First Lord of the Admiralty was in charge of the Admiralty Board and he had up to six Lords Commissioners to assist him. The First Lord was also a member of the Government and therefore the Minister responsible for the Navy. In Cook's time the Admiralty was situated at the north end of Whitehall in London. It is still called the Old Admiralty and a statue of Cook stands outside in the Mall.

All Commissioners were political appointments and membership of the Board changed as governments changed. Only a few Commissioners were or had been serving naval officers, though in Cook's time Anson, Hawke and Saunders served as First Lords. All other Boards, including the Navy Board and the Victualling Board, which carried out administrative duties, were answerable to the Admiralty.

Serving alongside the Admiralty Board were the Secretaries to the Admiralty, who exercised much power in their own right, often making decisions themselves without reference to the Board. Philip Stephens was the Secretary from 1763 until 1795 and he regularly dealt and corresponded with Cook, as did his deputy George Jackson.

The Admiralty dealt primarily with the fleet and especially its personnel. Everything, from orders for combat to officer appointments, emanated from Whitehall. All naval officers at the rank of lieutenant and

The Admiralty office in Whitehall, behind the colonnaded screen, from where the Royal Navy was administered. (Etching published by F West)

above were commissioned officers and this term recognised that their appointments had been sanctioned by the Admiralty Commissioners.
SEE ALSO: Navy Board, Royal Navy

Adventure, HMS

HMS *Adventure* was the companion vessel for Cook's second voyage. In 1771, the Navy Board purchased the collier, previously known as the *Marquis of Rockingham*. She was of 336 tons, 97ft 1in (29.6m) long, 27ft 11in (8.5m) wide and had been recently built by the Fishburn yard in Whitby. The ship was renamed the *Raleigh* but subsequently became HMS *Adventure* after it was realised that the name would offend the Spanish.

The *Adventure*, which cost the Navy £2103, was captained by Commander Tobias Furneaux, who had sailed as lieutenant under Wallis on the *Dolphin*. After refitting, the *Adventure* sailed on 13 July 1772 with the *Resolution*. However, the two ships separated in early November 1773 and the *Adventure* returned to Britain alone, arriving on 14 July 1774.

The *Adventure* was subsequently taken over by the Navy for use as a storeship in North America until 1783, when she was broken up. HMS *Adventure* had the distinction of being the first ship to circumnavigate the globe from west to east. Adventure Bay in Tasmania is named after the ship, as are the Adventure rupes on Mercury.
SEE ALSO: Cook's ships, Second voyage

Alaska

Alaska occupies the extreme north-west corner of North America and the neighbouring Aleutian Islands, which thread across the North Pacific towards Asia. To the south-east, another archipelago of islands fringes the continent south towards British Columbia. Alaska itself faces Siberia across the Bering Strait and is bounded to the east by Canada. The Arctic Ocean lies to the north while the Gulf of Alaska, a bight of the Pacific, forms the southern boundary. Much of Alaska lies north of the Arctic Circle so its climate is cold with much snow, ice and fog, making sailing in its waters a difficult operation. Now a state of the United States, the land was purchased in 1867 from the Russians, who had moved into the region to exploit the sea otter fur trade in the eighteenth century. The name Alaska is derived from the Unangan word 'Alyeska', meaning great land.

Native Americans crossed into Alaska from Siberia about 40,000 years ago. Successive waves of people then moved on down the continent, the extreme cold climate of Alaska not encouraging many to remain in the north. Among those remaining to eke out their existence in the northern wilderness were the Athabascans and the Eskimo-Aleuts.

Vitus Bering, sailing on behalf of Russia, found the strait separating Alaska from Asia in 1728. In 1741, he returned to Alaska, accompanied by Alexei Chirikov. Their two ships were separated but both reached the south-eastern Alaskan coast. The Russians took notice of the large local seal and otter populations and the potential for fur trading. Bases for the fur trade were established in Unalaska, Kodiak Island, and in Cook Inlet. The Spanish, concerned about Russian expansion into an area they deemed their own, sent a few expeditions north to investigate but with little reward.

The Northwest Passage was believed to exist in this region and it was the search for it that brought James Cook north in 1778. He had sailed from Nootka Sound on Vancouver Island in late April. Cook carried charts but the information shown was imprecise and in some cases pure fiction. A volcano was sighted on 3 May, which Cook called Mount Edgecumbe. It is on Kruzof Island, to the east of Baranof Island. Cook had reached Alaska. The next islands to the north were Chichagof and Yakobi where Chirikov may have landed.

Cook was now approaching the region explored by Bering and he saw a snow-covered mountain that he equated with Bering's Mount St Elias. The coast began to trend east-west, which concerned Cook. On the 12th, he rounded Cape Hinchingbrook to investigate a large inlet. A map on board, by the Russian Stählin, showed northward running channels linking to a northern ocean and this inlet could be such a channel. Cook remained for five days without finding a passage to the north. Cook called the inlet Sandwich Sound but the Earl of Sandwich later changed it to Prince William Sound.

Cook sailed out through the Montagu Strait and continued along the Alaskan coast. Another large inlet, Cook Inlet, presented itself on 25 May. Cook investigated but again without success and he left on 6 June. Cook was concerned that the trend of the coast was now to the south-west and, instead of being in latitude 65° N, he was now at 58° N sailing south. Valuable time for exploring higher latitudes appeared to be disappearing quickly. He continued, sailing to the south-east of Kodiak Island and the Alaskan Peninsula. On 26 June, Cook was lucky to anchor near Unalaska Island having narrowly avoided large rocks in thick fog.

He had reached the end of the Alaskan Peninsula and was able to sail north into the Bering Sea on 2 July.

Cook could finally sail north-east and followed the coast, tracing the north side of the Alaska Peninsula but the ships only found a river mouth and shallows and had to turn west. Cook followed the coast now to the north-west. On 29 July, the *Resolution* and the *Discovery* neared St Matthew Island in the Bering Sea. There was sadness on 3 August when the surgeon, William Anderson, died. Shortly after, they passed St Lawrence Island and then returned to the Alaskan shore.

Following the coast northwards past Cape Rodney and King Island the ships came to the Bering Strait on 8 August. Cook called the westernmost point of America (unseen by Bering), Cape Prince of Wales, before passing the Diomede Islands to reach the Asian coast. Cook sailed back through the Bering Strait past the East Cape (Cape Dezhneva) of Asia into the Chukchi Sea and the Arctic Ocean. He headed north-east to Alaska and came to the coast again near the Mulgrave Hills. In increasingly cold conditions they sailed north and round Cape Lisburne hoping to find the Northwest Passage but on 18 August near Icy Cape and at 70° 44' N ice fields stopped their progress.

Cook returned through the Bering Strait having decided that the summer was nearly over and conditions would only worsen and not allow any more exploration. He passed St Lawrence Island once more and headed east to have a final search for the Northwest Passage in that part of the Alaskan coast he had not already investigated. On 8 September the ships passed to the south of Cape Darby and entered a large bay. This was Norton Bay, the inner part of Norton Sound. Cook anchored in two places, near Capes Darby and Denbigh, and went ashore. They met local Eskimo at Shaktoolik.

By now Cook despaired of the Russian maps he was using and decided to sail south to winter in the Sandwich (Hawaiian) Islands. He sailed south out of Norton Sound and past the shallows off the Yukon Delta to be off St Lawrence Island yet again. Three days later they were back at St Matthew Island. Cook pressed on and after four gruelling months in Arctic waters Cook arrived back at Unalaska on 2 October. He put in at Samgoonoodha at the eastern end of the island and work began refitting both ships. Cook met three Russians and later the Factor, Ismailov. On 30 October 1778, Cook left Alaska for Hawai'i.

Cook had produced the first accurate charts of Alaska and shown its relationship to the rest of the American continent and to Asia. The first detailed descriptions of the country and its people had been written, together with Webber's paintings. The question of the Northwest Passage had not been resolved but Cook had shown where it did not exist.

See Also: Arctic, Third voyage

Anderson, Robert (1742–?)

Robert Anderson sailed on all three voyages with Cook. He sailed on the *Endeavour* as quartermaster and was punished on two occasions. The first time, on 30 November 1768, was for attempted desertion and the second took place on 21 June 1769 for disobedience. Anderson was obviously a popular member of the crew as the wills of several members refer to him. Robert Taylor, the armourer, refers to him as 'my true and beloved friend and brother'. In a letter to Stephens, written in December 1771, Cook recommends Anderson to be gunner of the *Resolution* on the second voyage 'provide he quallifies himself for that station'. Anderson sailed as gunner and also on the third voyage on the *Resolution* in the same capacity. He was suspected of being the author of an anonymous account of the second voyage, published in 1775. Cook charged him to find out who the real author was, which he did when he persuaded John Marra to own up.

Anderson was born in Inverness in 1742. Nothing is known about Anderson after Cook's voyages.

See Also: First, Second and Third voyages

Anderson, William (1750–1778)

William Anderson sailed on the second voyage on the *Resolution* as surgeon's mate. He rejoined Cook to sail on the third voyage on the *Resolution* as surgeon and he also doubled as naturalist on that voyage. Though not formally educated for the task, Anderson proved a more than adequate naturalist, perhaps due to his need as a doctor to understand herbs and plants. He described and assembled a valuable collection of specimens for Joseph Banks. The botanical genus 'Andersonia' is named for him. Anderson made a huge contribution to the knowledge of Pacific languages by assembling several vocabularies. Two papers were presented to the Royal Society, based on Anderson's work.

Anderson was born in 1750 near Edinburgh and died in the Bering Sea on 3 August 1778. He left a will (FRC 11/1070) and there is a short biography in the *DNB*, v1, p393. Cook was moved by Anderson's death. He wrote 'He was a sensible young man, an agreeable companion, well skilled in his profession...and to perpetuate the memory of the deceased for whom I had a very great regard, I named [it] Andersons Island.' Cook, in a rare period of disorientation on his part, had not realised that it was St Lawrence Island, already named by Bering. However, Anderson Point in Nootka Sound still honours William Anderson.

SEE ALSO: Medical aspects of Cook's voyages, Third voyage

Antarctica and Antarctic Circle

Antarctica is the continent surrounding the South Pole. It is the coldest, windiest, and driest place on earth and is almost entirely covered by ice. As a result it is virtually uninhabitable and has no indigenous inhabitants. It covers 5.39 million square miles (14 million sq km) of which about 98 per cent is thick continental ice sheet and 2 per cent barren rock. The Antarctic Circle is the parallel of latitude of 66° 32' S marking the northern boundary of the southern polar region. The Greeks chose the name 'Antarktikos' for the southern region, opposite the northern part of the world, which lay under the constellation Arktos, the Bear. From the fifteenth century on, many map-makers included the mythical continent of 'Terra australis incognita', situated where Antarctica is located.

In 1699, Edmond Halley led the first systematic search for a southern continent. He reached 52° 24' S, where he made the first recorded sighting of tabular icebergs. However, the cold, stormy weather drove him north again. During the 1700s, the French became active in exploring for new land to the south. Bouvet de Lozier was searching for the fabled 'Gonneville's Land' when he sighted land on 1 January 1739 at about 54° S latitude. He called it 'Cape Circumcision,' but it was actually an island (now called Bouvet Island). His estimate of longitude was so far off, that Cook was unable to find it in 1773.

Another Frenchman, Kerguelen-Trémarec, set sail with two ships in 1771, with specific instructions to find the southern continent. On 12 February 1772, in the south Indian Ocean, he sighted fog-shrouded land at 49° 40' S but was unable to land because of high seas and foul weather. A boat from his companion ship did land and claimed the island, Kerguelen Island, for France. Cook visited Kerguelen in 1776.

In 1767, Alexander Dalrymple published *An Account of the Discoveries made in the South Pacific Ocean Previous to 1764*, in which he made a strong case for a

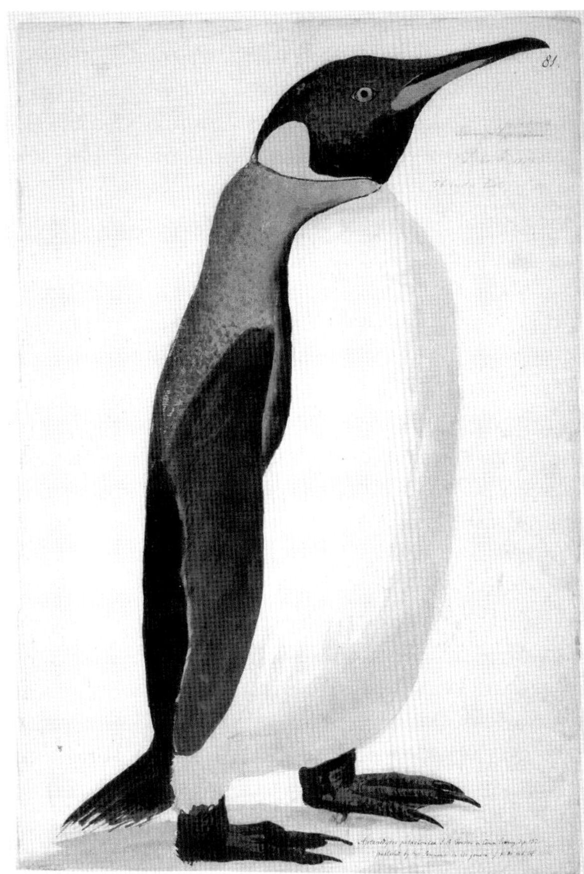

*A King Penguin (*Aptenodytes patagonicus*) from Antarctic waters, drawn by George Forster on the second voyage. (Natural History Museum)*

giant, unknown southern continent. The British government issued instructions to James Cook that, after he had observed the Transit of Venus on his *Endeavour* voyage in 1769, he was to proceed south in a search for this continent. When he returned to Britain in 1771 he had not located a southern continent but he had ideas for a second voyage to prove or disprove its existence once and for all.

In July 1772, Cook sailed from Britain with the search for the southern continent as his primary mission. On 17 January 1773, at about 40° E, Cook made the first crossing of the Antarctic Circle in history but at 67° 15' S, the ice pack forced him north again, a mere 80 miles (128.9km) from the Antarctic coastline. A year later, on 26 January 1774, Cook's ship, the *Resolution*, reached 71° 10' S at 106° 54' W in the Amundsen Sea. This was further south than anyone had ever gone before. Near the end of February 1775, Cook crossed his track of 1772, completing the first circumnavigation of Antarctica and proving that the southern continent, if one existed, was neither as large nor as habitable as once thought.

Bellingshausen, a Russian explorer, crossed the Antarctic Circle on 15 January 1820 and the next day the Russians made the first recorded sighting of the continent of Antarctica. A year later, the first recorded landing on the Antarctic continent took place on 7 February 1821, when men from the American sealer *Cecilia*, under Captain John Davis, landed at Hughes Bay. Only in 1840 was it established that Antarctica was indeed a continent and not just a group of islands. The Norwegian explorer, Roald Amundsen, was the first to reach the South Pole, which he did in December 1911. SEE ALSO: Great Southern Continent, Second voyage, Colour plate 6

Antelope, HMS, HMS *Tweed* and HMS *Lark*

These three ships are associated with James Cook's time in Newfoundland. Cook returned to Newfoundland early in 1763 as a passenger on HMS *Antelope*. The Fourth Rate ship was under the command of Thomas Graves, the Governor of Newfoundland. The ship, rebuilt in 1742 at Woolwich Dockyard, was of 853 tons, 133ft 10in (40.8m) long and 38ft (11.6m) wide and carried 54 guns. The *Antelope* was sold in 1783.

On arrival, Cook transferred to HMS *Tweed* under Captain Charles Douglas. The *Tweed* was a Fifth Rate, built by Blaydes in Hull in 1759. She was of 661 tons, 127ft 11in (39m) long and 34ft 1in (10.4m) wide and carried 32 guns. The *Tweed* took Cook to the islands of St Pierre and Miquelon, off the south coast of Newfoundland, which Cook was under instructions to survey before they were handed over to the French. Cook completed his task and the *Tweed* took him to St John's in July 1763. Cook then transferred to the schooner *Grenville*. The Navy sold the ship in 1776.

Hugh Palliser took over as Governor of Newfoundland in 1764. He and Cook travelled together on HMS *Lark*, under Captain Thompson, from Britain in May. The *Lark* was a new ship, having been built in 1762 in Rotherhithe by Bird. She was a Fifth Rate, 646 tons, 127 ft (38.7m) long and 3ft 1in (10.4m) wide, and carried 32 guns. The *Lark* was scuttled at Newport, Rhode Island in 1778 at the same time as the *Endeavour*.
SEE ALSO: Cook's ships, Newfoundland

Arctic and Arctic Circle

The Arctic is the region around the North Pole. The name Arctic comes from the ancient Greek 'arktikos' meaning bear, and is a reference to the constellation of the Bear visible in the northern sky. Much of the region is taken up by the Arctic Ocean, a body of water north of Europe, Asia and North America, and mostly north of the Arctic Circle covering 5.41 million square miles (14.056 million sq km). The Arctic Circle is the parallel of latitude of 66° 32' N, marking the southern boundary of the northern polar region. The arctic climate is characterised by persistent cold with winters of continuous darkness and summers of continuous daylight but damp and foggy weather.

James Cook entered the Arctic in 1778 looking for the Northwest Passage from the Pacific through to the Atlantic. He had sailed up the north-west coast of America without finding the passage and, on 2 July he entered the Bering Sea. He was able to sail north and passed through the Bering Strait to cross the Arctic Circle, becoming the first person to cross both polar circles, having crossed the Antarctic Circle on his second voyage. Cook sailed north in the Chukchi Sea before heading northeast in the Arctic Ocean only to be thwarted by pack ice at 70° 41' N near Icy Cape in northern Alaska. Cook was forced to retreat but believed the Northwest Passage, if it existed, was situated here. He took the ships back through the Bering Strait and eventually to Hawai'i where he was killed.

Charles Clerke took over in command of the expedition and brought the ships back though the Bering Strait in July 1779. On 18 July, he reached 70° 33' N in almost an identical position to Cook near Icy Cape but ice again stopped any further progress. The ships retreated back to Petropavlovsk in Kamchatka, having given up on finding the Northwest Passage.

The British met some isolated groups of Eskimo on the Alaskan shores of the Bering Sea and some Chukchi people in St Lawrence Bay on the Asian shore when they briefly stopped there. John Webber produced some wonderful paintings of events on this part of the voyage. SEE ALSO: Alaska, Third voyage, Colour plate 7

Art of Cook's voyages

The first general 'artist of record' on a colonial voyage was probably John White, sent out under Sir Richard Grenville on Raleigh's Virginia expedition of 1585–86. Cook's expeditions, however, were the first in which artists were included as part of a scientific initiative to study the natural history of places visited and the new societies and material cultures encountered. They were also the first to return with images systematically compiled in hundreds rather than handfuls. The credit primarily goes to Joseph Banks, whose Admiralty-approved self-appointment to the *Endeavour* with a retinue including botanical and topographical artists, set a pattern – including in their illustrations to the voyage's publication – that was officially consolidated on the two later expeditions and thereafter. The main difference in terms of medium between Cook's first and later voyages is that only the last two carried fully-trained artists (Hodges and Webber) qualified to produce a substantial body of oil paintings, most done after their return, as well as the drawings which were the greatest output of all three ventures. These ranged from on-the-spot pencil and wash sketches to fully worked-up watercolour versions, of which many were published as engravings. Most of these, but again not all, were originally linked to the printed first-hand voyage accounts but were replicated with varying accuracy in subsequent editions or works based on them.

A further distinction in the original work produced under Cook is that on the first voyage Parkinson was engaged primarily as a botanical artist and George Forster on the second as a botanist-artist assisting his father, though his graphic skills in this line were less than Parkinson's. Both treated fauna as well as flora but there is only one other drawing by Forster, of Cook's ships among Antarctic icebergs, clearly done under Hodges's tutelage. The familiarity of Parkinson's landscape and 'ethnographic' images (though that is a later term), first known through his posthumously printed *Journal* and Hawkesworth's edited official account of the *Endeavour* voyage, also makes it easy to forget that most of over 1200 drawings he did for Banks were single plant and animal studies – 955 both preliminary and finished in the former case and 377 in the latter. Banks also purchased 568 of George Forster's drawings (Hoare's figure, 301 botanical and 267 animal: Joppien and Smith give 629, 361 botanical and 268 animal), though the Forsters also took many back to Germany. Banks eventually had 753 botanical plates engraved, by 18 hands, for his proposed *Florilegium* (of which the material from the first voyage was only published in 1988). Many artefacts brought back were also only drawn and engraved by home-based professionals on return to England.

By contrast, of the natural-history productions of the third voyage, by Webber and the surgeons Anderson and William Ellis, only the relatively few plant and animal studies that Webber chose to make under his rather general orders were 'official', most of his work being topographical or ethnographic. The others' were products of their private interests. Only Ellis, who also did general views, survived to publish his own account of the voyage (1782), with illustrations which show his abilities to lie somewhere between Parkinson and Webber. He and Anderson probably steered the latter in choice of wildlife subjects and Webber certainly influenced Ellis's treatment of landscape. Alongside this broadly scientific and topographical output Cook and his men were also converting survey work to cartography. This required specific coastal views or profiles which – with Banks's support on the first voyage – were also part of the work of the artists on all three. Midshipman Elliott on the second attested to Cook's encouragement of drawing practice by himself and other warrant officers 'either Copying drawings for him [Cook], or Drawings for ourselves, under the Eye of Mr Hodges' – suggesting a tutorial role for the latter. What was being copied remains ill-defined but survey-related material probably played a large part.

Four other artists worked on the *Endeavour* besides Parkinson. Alexander Buchan, Banks's topographer and figure painter, embarked in poor health and died on arrival at Tahiti in April 1769. By then he had produced only a few drawings of the Cape Verde Islands (now lost), of crabs, fish and molluscs off Brazil, over 30 coastal views for Cook, and some fine gouache studies of the Ona people of Tierra del Fuego and their artefacts. Only one of the last was engraved in a classicised version by G B Cipriani (who had earlier taught Hodges and later provided him with similar slight help). Buchan's quality shows that his loss was serious, although nothing else is known of him and no other pre-voyage work. The topographical and ethnographic gap was thereafter filled by Parkinson and Dr Herman Spöring. Spöring, like Bank's botanist, Daniel Solander, was a Swede. He had originally trained as a doctor, then worked in England for eleven years as a watchmaker before becoming Solander's clerk. Banks engaged Spöring as his secretary for the voyage and his graphic style is careful and technical rather than inspiring. He drew a large number of coastal profiles, some landscape subjects that Parkinson did not see, and a series of almost archaeological studies of Māori canoes, especially their carved decorations. Both copied some of each other's general drawings, which after their deaths from fever contracted at Batavia were mixed up in Banks's collection. Their graphic similarities were sufficient to perpetuate the confusion until Spöring's hand was re-identified in 1954. Another consequence of the fatal stay at Batavia was the brief appearance of Charles Praval, who joined there as part of the replacement crew and who, being found to have copying ability, replicated some drawings by Spöring and Parkinson on the way home. The most recently identified of the floating studio is the extraordinary watercolour 'Artist of the Chief Mourner', so-named by Joppien and Smith in 1985. A Banks letter of 1812, found by the latter's biographer, Harold Carter, has since identified him as Tupaia, the aristocratic young Tahitian whom Cook agreed to take to England but who died from fever at Batavia. At the time Tupaia's few experiments with English watercolour were probably charming curiosities: in the wake of twentieth-century reassessments of 'primitive art', their alien immediacy collapses our temporal and cultural separation from the eighteenth-century Pacific to startling effect.

The three major interpreters of Cook's voyages – Sidney Parkinson, William Hodges and John Webber – were all of similar artisanal background, though very different talents and training, and all apparently social both as shipmates and in their ability to engage the co-operation of Pacific peoples. Parkinson, a peaceable Quaker and son of an Edinburgh brewer, was a self-taught botanical artist, with no previous known landscape or figure experience: Hodges, the son of a London retail blacksmith and *inter alia* a pupil and assistant of Richard Wilson RA, had the greatest imaginative talent and the most original aesthetic response to Pacific conditions. Webber, London-born son of a Swiss sculptor and an English mother, was raised and educated by an aunt in Switzerland (Bern) from the age of six. He did not return to England until he was 24, four months before he joined Cook, after a period of formal French 'finishing' at the Academie Royale in Paris. This to some degree aligned him with Hodges, who was also influenced by the French seventeenth-century classical school, primarily through Wilson. Webber lies between Parkinson and Hodges in an number of ways. He was more highly trained and accomplished as a topographer and figure draughtsman than the former, with whom and to a greater degree he shared a methodical approach to his work that is less evident for the more intellectually ambitious Hodges. As an oil painter (a medium untouched by Parkinson) the last was well ahead of Webber in interpreting Pacific light, weather and situation, although his means of doing so are more appreciated today than by the contemporary audience for his exhibited oils – some of which drew comments for being too raw in colour or otherwise unfinished. Hodges also had difficulties as a figure painter, especially of complex groups – at which Webber had a practised competence – and from an eighteenth-century viewpoint rather than a modern one, it is the latter who was probably closest to the ideal as an official visual chronicler. For general subjects he was also the most comprehensive and prolific and the only artist who, as far as we know, systematically listed the work he did for the Admiralty.

Hodges and Webber exhibited many oil subjects from their two voyages at the Royal Academy, of which both became members. The majority of Webber's are now unlocated, since the Admiralty – which retained both men to work up paintings and illustrations for the voyage accounts – only seems to have had four from him compared to at least 25 from Hodges. Cook himself appears in many of Webber's drawings and was the subject of at least four oil portraits by him, possibly five. That given to the Tahitian chief Tu is lost but the rest (Australian NPG, Canberra; Alexander Turnbull Library, Wellington, NZ, and an attributed one in a private US collection) seem to be versions from the original bust-length painted at Cape Town in 1776 and later engraved (NPG, London). Webber also painted other officers, portraiture being part of his general practice. Hodges's oil study of Cook, painted in London (1775–76), from which Basire's frontispiece for the official third voyage account is derived is at Greenwich, as is Nathaniel Dance's portrait, painted for Banks in 1776. Widespread engraving of the last, and its exhibition in the Naval Gallery at Greenwich Hospital from 1829, have always ensured its being the best known. Only one other formal oil portrait by Hodges is known, of Mai, probably painted for the anatomist John Hunter (Royal College of Surgeons). A number of Hodges's other portrait drawings of Pacific islanders are characterful, especially those in red chalk, a medium he favoured, but of uneven draughtsmanship. Like many of Webber's – which from the nature of the voyage have the widest ethnic range – the majority are types rather than personally identified. Webber's have greater documentary consistency and his freely drawn portrait sketches in pencil, especially from late in the voyage, match precision with a vivacity often lost in more finished versions and the engravings after them. The best of Webber's few Pacific oil portraits is that of the Raiatean 'princess' Poetua. The three large versions known are all likely to have been painted in London from a smaller oil study. This was among the 20 canvases that he listed as doing on the voyage, but which are now largely lost. The version shown at the Academy in 1784 is probably the Admiralty's, now at Greenwich (MoD Art Collection).

Looking briefly at media and style, all three of the main artists' work on paper is predominantly in monochrome – above all pencil, ink and wash, with occasional colour tinting in all three cases. Only Webber developed more highly-coloured finished versions and Parkinson only used full watercolour for his scientific drawings. The latter always worked on a relatively small scale but some of the others' panoramic landscape drawings are four or five feet across. Parkinson fulfilled his unlooked-for role as a chronicler of places and people with great credit and almost entirely without the classical conventional gloss that formal training would have given his figure work in particular, with his groups becoming increasingly lively as his confidence and the voyage progressed. He was as faithful a recorder of costume, accoutrements, tattoos and dress as he was of plants (those in his landscapes often also being specific). He made close studies of both Tahitian and Māori physiognomy, and was a better draughtsman of heads and small-scale groups than of single full-figure studies. His 'heads' above all suggest his ability to engage the willing, even humorous, co-operation of the subjects of his precise if somewhat mechanical likenesses. The fact that he also compiled the first Tahitian, Māori and Aboriginal wordlists was probably a by-product of the same engaging quality. (Both he and Webber also made ethnographic collections, the latter's now in the Bern Historical Museum.) As a view artist he seems to have preferred the quieter aspects of the Pacific landscape, and while always fairly literal in his treatment of it he also worked hard to suggest its moods through effects of light, shade and atmosphere.

Webber had the same subject preference, but less interest in weather and sky conditions except as conventional accompaniment to appropriate forms of landscape, or in setting overall tone. His key skill, seen increasingly as the voyage progressed, was as a rapid and precise draughtsman who could then combine many sketched details into informative landscape and figure compositions in wash and watercolour, be the subject the interior of a crowded hut or a sweeping exterior panorama. Despite an idiosyncratic tendency to elongate figures, his use of them probably owed much to his studies of peasant life round Paris under the engraver Jean-George Wille. He had a particular ability to compose views from an imagined aerial perspective, presumably learnt from his earlier Swiss master, the topographer Johann Ludwig Aberli. That the results well suited Cook, who worked closely with him, is shown by the latter's occasional comments that Webber's drawings describe an animated scene better than he can. His known Pacific landscape oils have similar qualities, being clear in detail and generally minimising drama in a low tonal key of greys, greens and browns – the colours of the Pacific north-west in poor weather and the tropical East Indies rather than of Polynesia.

By contrast, the work of Hodges is more expressive and often dramatic, both in his freely drawn wash studies of the south Pacific and the Antarctic and in his oils, which define both the form and colour of Polynesia as first seen by eighteenth-century Europeans. Technically, Hodges was fascinated by the brilliance of Pacific light, the transient effects of atmosphere and weather, and the sheer unfamiliarity of the subject. His greatest challenge was to interpret all three in ways that a London audience, steeped in the hierarchy that put idealised history painting above landscape, would accept. Criticism of his figure groups, raw colour and lack of finish in his exhibited oils were a result of his attempts to square this circle, though the Admiralty proved a keen client for his post-voyage labours in oil as well as retaining most of the few oils he did on the voyage. Among important paintings for them which were not exhibited were the large view of *Resolution* and *Adventure* in Matavai Bay, and the 'View of Cape Stephens...with waterspout' – both of which follow the model of 'historical landscape' that Hodges had inherited from Wilson and through him from the French seventeenth-century school. The latter in particular is a theatrical exercise in the Wilsonian sublime, derived ultimately from Gaspar Dughet's 'Jonah and the Whale'. Others, such as two versions of a view in Vaitepiha Bay or the lowering 'Monuments of Easter Island' are both original evocations of light and landscape, also alluding to the classical thematic model of mortality in paradise (*Et in Arcadia Ego*). Others, from the huge 'War Canoes of Otaheite' to small oil views of Cook's arrival on various Melanesian islands, are consciously elevated 'modern history' paintings. While all incorporate documentary detail, they are rather more complex and subordinated to the artistic theory of their time than is often recognised in their frequent modern reproduction as 'historical records'. Hodges only later (1795) wrote of his moral purpose, 'To give dignity to landscape [and]... amend the heart while the eye is gratified', and while often seen as a proto-Romantic for his technique and aspects of his composition, his aims and intellectual approach were well within conventional bounds. He was to develop them further in his later and more extensive work as the most important early British painter of India.

The later history of the output of Cook's artists is complex and the whole now widely dispersed. The Ministry of Defence still owns most of the Admiralty's paintings by Hodges and Webber (all on loan to the National Maritime Museum, Greenwich), and some drawings although many were later dispersed either by sale or other official devolution. The British Museum directly or indirectly inherited much from Banks's holdings, held there or more recently devolved to the British Library and Natural History Museum. A large amount from Banks and other sources has also found its way by sale to museums and libraries in Australia, New Zealand, the USA and Canada. All known non-botanical material, was fully catalogued by Joppien and Smith (1985–88), though a few items have subsequently changed hands and others come to light, including Hodges' oil portrait of Cook.

By Pieter van der Merwe

See Also: Artists on Cook's voyages, Portraits of Cook, Colour plates 4 & 5

'Artificial Curiosities'

The scientists who travelled on Cook's voyages were primarily botanists and zoologists, collecting plants, insects, fish and the like. However, they and other people on board traded for and acquired art and artefacts such as cloaks and other articles of clothing, weapons, carvings, and tools. These items received the generic term 'artificial curiosities'. They were taken back to Europe and distributed through museums and private collections to form the basis of what would later be called ethnographic collections.

The 'artificial curiosities' collected on Cook's expeditions represent the first collection of Pacific, Australian and north-west coast of America material brought back to the Europe. However, unlike the 'natural curiosities' such as plants and birds, there was no systematic method of organising and classifying them

A wooden headrest collected in Tahiti on the second voyage. (Forster Collection, Pitt Rivers Museum, Oxford)

and they were not treated seriously in many quarters. Many of the specimens could not be sold and were given away by Cook's people to museums and collectors.

Following this largely unorganised dissemination, confusion arose with regards the material held in museums and attributed to Cook's voyages. Many of the items listed as coming from Cook's voyages may not have done so while genuine Cook material has been lost or incorrectly described. A great deal of detective work has been carried out but more needs to be done to establish the whereabouts of Cook's artificial curiosities.

Eventually the curiosities did become a source of money for crews of European vessels as they acquired material on behalf of collectors and scientists in Europe to supplement their meagre incomes. By the mid-nineteenth century, the British Museum held more Polynesian pieces in its Ethnographical Room than it did for China and India combined.

See Also: Ethnographic results of Cook's voyages

Artists on Cook's voyages

Cook's voyages were among the first that had official artists on board, thus ensuring that they returned to Britain with a wonderful pictorial record of where they had been and what they had seen. Sailors had developed a tradition of drawing coastal views as part of carrying out surveys but these were usually amateurish at best. To carry trained artists on board was a new departure.

That it happened on Cook's voyages was fortuitous. It was only when Joseph Banks arranged for himself and his entourage to travel on the *Endeavour* that artists were included in the ship's company. Alexander Buchan, Sydney Parkinson and Herman Spöring were members of Banks' party though only the first two were designated as artists. Banks' primary interest was natural history. Buchan was taken on as the expedition's second artist to record the scenery and make a general pictorial account of the expedition, thus freeing Parkinson to concentrate on drawing the botanical and zoological specimens collected.

However, Buchan died early in the voyage and Spöring, who had travelled as Banks's secretary, was deputed to work as an artist. His coastal views are among the best visual records of the voyages while he was meticulous in depicting the detail of Māori canoe prows. Parkinson, meanwhile, was able to maintain a prolific output and his 700-plus botanical illustrations are a magnificent body of work and form the basis of Bank's *Florilegium*. His portraits of Pacific islanders are among the strongest images brought back and represent a most important early, ethnological record.

Sadly Parkinson and Spöring died before the *Endeavour* returned home to Britain so the artists were not able to turn early sketches and drawings into more sophisticated paintings. Other artists and engravers were used to prepare the work of Buchan, Parkinson and Spöring for display and inclusion in the published accounts of the voyage. Unfortunately, in the absence of their creators, some were distorted and over-elaborated to bear little relation to the originals or real life. Tupaia, the Raiatean priest who travelled with Cook from Tahiti, is now credited with the small set of paintings previously of unknown authorship but credited as the 'Artist of the Chief Mourner'.

The authorities appreciated the value of taking a trained artist when Cook and Banks returned to Britain. Banks was set to accompany Cook on the second voyage and intended to take the famous artist, Johann Zoffany, with him. However, Banks withdrew and the Admiralty appointed William Hodges, who was taken instead as the artist to paint landscapes, portraits, and draw coastal views. He was not well known but had exhibited several views at the Society of Artists earlier that year. George Forster who sailed as assistant to his father, Johann Forster the naturalist, was given the task of drawing the natural history specimens and fulfilled his duties admirably.

Hodges survived the voyage and was able to work his sketches into a series of wonderful paintings now on display in the National Maritime Museum in Greenwich. The paintings show huge evidence of his classical and European artistic background and training but still provide a most recognisable set of views of islands in the Pacific such as Huahine, Tahiti, and New Zealand. Hodges also produced many portraits of Pacific people in red chalk. Hodges painted one of the surviving portraits of James Cook.

John Webber was employed as the official artist on Cook's third and last voyage. He produced a remarkable set of images of early Alaska, British Columbia and Hawai'i, which serve as works of art and as ethnological records. During the voyage, he painted landscapes, portraits, coastal views and some natural history works. Like Hodges before him, Webber painted Cook's portrait. Cook travelled on the third voyage without a naturalist. William Anderson, the surgeon, covered this role as well as his normal duties. Nobody, either, had been taken to draw natural history specimens. Webber filled this role to a small extent but William Webb Ellis, who sailed on the third voyage on the *Discovery* as surgeon's mate proved his worth by painting landscapes, natural history specimens, and drew coastal views. Henry Roberts, who sailed on the second and third voyages, was a proven cartographer but showed he was an artist as well by painting of the most memorable views of the *Resolution*.

Rüdiger Joppien and Bernard Smith have produced a wonderful testament to the artists. The four volumes of the set of *The Art of Captain Cook's Voyages* contain reproductions of all the images together with descriptive catalogues and discussions of their artistic merits and influences.

SEE ALSO: Art of Cook's voyages, Portraits of Cook

Astronomical results of Cook's voyages

Astronomy held a privileged place in eighteenth-century voyages of exploration, and without it many voyages may have ended in disaster. Observations of the Sun, the Moon, lunar occultations of stars, Jovian satellite phenomena, solar and lunar eclipses, and selected stars were critical for determining latitude and longitude, the handmaidens of navigation and coastal mapping. This type of astronomy is now known as nautical or maritime astronomy, and all naval officers were expected to be versed in its principles and its practice. James Cook was no exception, honing his astronomical skills during the years he spent plotting the coasts of North America. At this time he also observed a total eclipse of the Sun, an account of which was published in the prestigious *Philosophical Transactions of the Royal Society* (of London).

Nautical astronomy was to play a vital role in the

success of all three Cook voyages to the South Seas, but the first voyage also involved a very different kind of astronomy, one that had nothing whatsoever to do with latitude and longitude. The 'official' reason for the voyage was the observation of a Transit of Venus, and it was hoped that this rare and spectacular event would help refine one of the fundamental yardsticks of astronomy, the mean distance from the Earth to the Sun (known as the 'astronomical unit'). Observations of the Transit from different points on the Earth's surface would produce a figure for the solar parallax, which fed into a simple equation that gave a value for the astronomical unit. Because of its ideal location, Tahiti would serve as one of these critical observing points.

The official astronomers on the first voyage were Cook and Green, but a coterie of officers, seamen, and even supernumeraries were involved in astronomical observations during the voyage, effectively serving as *de facto* assistant astronomers. These included Clerke, Harvey, Hicks, Hood, Molyneux, both Munkhouses, Pickersgill, Saunders, Smith, Solander and Spöring. Some of these acquired their observational skills from Green during the voyage, and even those with prior training honed their expertise between England and Tahiti – in anticipation of the Transit.

Astronomical instruments assigned to the *Endeavour* included two reflecting telescopes, a sextant, a quadrant, and astronomical, journeyman and alarum clocks. Cook and Solander also brought along their own telescopes. All four telescopes were Gregorian-type reflectors, with speculum metal mirrors. The sextants, quadrants and telescopes were used for various shore-based or shipboard astronomical observations, while the clocks were there to provide a reliable local time service and hence a means of determining longitude.

The Transit of Venus was the primary purpose and 'public' face of the voyage, and arose because of the unsatisfactory outcome of the many observations made during the preceding Transit. The Royal Society took on what was to prove a major maritime and scientific venture, and successfully lobbied King George III for the necessary resources and funding. As well as the anticipated scientific outcome of the voyage, there was also an element of international competition here, for other nations, and particularly the French, were planning Transit expeditions. British pride and scientific supremacy were at stake! So apart from the Cook expedition, British Transit parties were also dispatched to North Cape (in Norway), the Prince of

A portable tent observatory of the type used on Cook's second and third voyages. The design was perfected by Bayly and developed from Smeaton's first voyage prototype. (After Wales and Bayly 1777: Plate II)

Wales Fort (in Hudson Bay, Canada), Northern Ireland, and the Lizard, in Cornwall.

The Transit was scheduled for 3 June 1769, and the *Endeavour* reached Tahiti with plenty of time to spare. An observing site was selected at nearby Point Venus (as it became known), and a small fort was erected there so that the astronomers would not be interrupted during the Transit, when precise observations and measurements called for total concentration. The fort housed the astronomical instruments; some of these are described by Green and Cook: 'The astronomical clock, made by Sheldon and furnished with a gridiron pendulum, was set up in the middle of one end of a large tent, in a frame made for the purpose at Greenwich, fixed firm and as low in the ground as the door of the clock-case would admit, and to prevent its being disturbed by any accident, another framing of wood was made around this, at the distance of one foot from it...Without the end of the tent facing the clock, and 12 feet from it, stood the observatory, in which were set up the journeyman clock and astronomical quadrant: this last, made by Mr Bird...stood upon the head of a large cask fixed firm in the ground, and well filled with wett heavy sand.' Telescopes were used to observe the Transit, and these also were set up on top of casks sunk into the ground.

A few days before the Transit Cook noted that the Point Venus region had experienced some cloudy days, and, as a safeguard against inclement weather, on 3 June he decided to establish two additional observing stations. One of these was on the small island of Taaupiri off the east coast of Tahiti, and the other on the islet of Irioa just off the north-western tip of nearby Moorea. Cook, Green, Solander and Molyneux were stationed at Point Venus; Gore and the Munkhouse brothers at Moorea; and Hicks, Clerke, Pickersgill and Saunders on Taaupiri. All three stations were supplied with the instruments necessary for accurate time-keeping and required for the astronomical observations, and Green made sure that all of the observers had received appropriate instruction in their use.

The day itself was fine – if somewhat warmer than expected – and Cook reported on the Point Venus observations in his journal: 'This day prov'd as favourable to our purpose as we could wish, not a Cloud was to be seen the whole day and the Air was perfectly clear, so that we had every advantage we could desire in Observing the whole of the passage of the Planet Venus over the Sun's disk ...' The Transit, which lasted about six hours, also was successfully observed at the other two stations.

The main aim of the astronomers was to accurately time the four different 'contacts', precise moments when Venus appeared to be in contact with the limb of the Sun. The first and second contacts occurred during the ingress phase, when Venus was entering the solar disk, whilst third and fourth contacts were associated with ingress, as the Transit ended. From the viewpoint of determining the solar parallax, precise timings of the second and third contacts were crucial, but Venus was surrounded by a dusky ring and so it was very hard to decide exactly when these contacts occurred. Thus, Cook and Green recorded exactly the same time for the second contact, but in his larger and more powerful telescope Solander saw it as 13 seconds later. In contrast, Cook and Green's observations of the third contact differed by exactly 10 seconds, while Solander did not post a time. Similar discrepancies occurred with the three observers' timings of the first and fourth contacts (with variations of 26 seconds and 12 seconds, respectively).

Despite these inconsistencies, Green and Cook published their observations and those of Solander in a 1771 issue of the *Philosophical Transactions of the Royal Society*, but for some unknown reason they did not include the results obtained at the other two Transit stations. Professor Thomas Hornsby from Oxford University then used the Tahitian timings, along with observations made at four other British and non-British sites to calculate the solar parallax, coming up with a figure of 8.78″, remarkably similar to Pingré's value of 8.80″ derived from French and other observations. Beaglehole has erroneously claimed that the Tahitian observations were a failure, but in fact the parallaxes obtained by Hornsby and Pingré compare very favourably with the value of 8.794148″, which was officially adopted by the International Astronomical Union in 1976. This equates to an astronomical unit of 92,958,348 miles (149,597,870km). Tahiti therefore played a key role in unravelling one of the prime mysteries of eighteenth-century astronomy, and it is fitting that a monument should now mark the site of these all-important observations. But unfortunately it is in the wrong position. Beaglehole has pointed out that it is situated some distance from the actual site of Fort Venus!

After the Transit, the *Endeavour* sailed south-west in search of *Terra Australis Incognita*, and nautical astronomy again became the norm and provided the co-ordinates to chart the two main islands of New Zealand and the east coast of Australia. One astronomical event that offered special navigational opportunities was the 9 November 1769 Transit of Mercury. These Transits could not be used to investigate the solar parallax, but they offered a means of precisely determining longitude. The November 1769 Transit was observed from Mercury Bay in New Zealand, and was the first shore-based scientific astronomical observation made from that country. One other astronomical object worth mentioning is Comet C/1769 P1 Messier, even though it held no navigational importance. Between 27 August and 4 September 1769 this was an impressive naked-eye object with a 42° tail, and it captivated the entire crew.

After the voyage the task of writing up the astronomical observations fell to Wales, given Green's untimely death while the *Endeavour* was *en route* from Batavia to Cape Town. Unfortunately Green's notes left much to be desired, and this fact, coupled with a requirement to include astronomical observations made during the earlier voyages of Wallis and Byron, meant that the volume was a long time in coming. *Astronomical Observations Made in the Voyages Which Were Undertaken By Order of His Present Majesty* ... only appeared in 1788, and the full title goes on for several more lines and is truly astronomical in length!

When Cook's second voyage was planned there was no Transit of Venus to justify the presence of astronomers, yet Maskelyne convinced the Board of Longitude that the expedition '... may be rendered more serviceable to the improvement of geography and navigation than it can otherwise be if the ship be furnished with ... astronomical instruments ... and above all if a proper person could be sent out to make use of these instruments and teach the officers on board the ship the method of finding the longitudes ...'. Since all of the officers on the *Resolution* and *Adventure* were capable of making the required astronomical observations this statement at first sight makes little sense, until we examine the scientific instruments assigned to the vessels. In addition to the mandatory telescopes, sextants, quadrants, and clocks typical of the first voyage, there were a number of new instruments, namely two refracting telescopes, a transit telescope, and most important of all, four chronometers (one by Kendall and three by Arnold). The chronometers would provide an alternative means of determining longitude, and the crew – already familiar with 'lunars' – had to be trained in their use so that they could determine for themselves the relative merits of these two disparate approaches to what was undoubtedly navigation's greatest challenge. This educational role lay in the capable hands of Wales and Bayly, who respectively joined the *Resolution* and *Adventure* as astronomers.

Discovery and coastal mapping of the postulated Great Southern Continent was the primary target of the second voyage, but this never was to be, and instead the astronomers had to content themselves with making shipboard or shore-based observations for latitude and longitude at various Pacific ports of call. Arguably the most important of these was Queen Charlotte Sound in New Zealand, Cook's favourite revictualling centre, and during the five different *Resolution* and *Adventure* stop-overs determination of its precise location became a virtual obsession. At the end of the final sojourn Cook was moved to write: '... from the multitude of observations which Mr Wales took the situation of few parts of the world are better ascertained than that of Queen Charlotte Sound.'

In 1775 the second voyage came to an end, and once again nautical astronomy had served a vital role, particularly in successfully navigating the freezing southern ocean fringing Antarctica, positioning for the first time Dusky Sound in New Zealand and uninhabited Norfolk Island and South Georgia, confirming the positions of many Pacific islands visited previously by the *Endeavour* or Europeans on other vessels, and mapping the east coast of Staten Island near Cape Horn. But more than this, the potential of the chronometer had been proved, and this was to have a profound long-term impact on navigation, naval thinking and Maskelyne's quest for the Longitude prize. After the voyage it was left to Wales and Bayly to write up the official astronomical account, and their book was published in 1777.

Cook's third and final voyage was in search of the fabled Northwest Passage, and it demanded the presence of astronomers. Three were appointed: Bayly returned for a second South Seas stint, this time on the *Discovery*, while Cook and King shared the honours on the *Resolution*. Once again Cook was in the onerous position of commanding the expedition and at the same time fulfilling his astronomical responsibilities. Instruments assigned to the three astronomers were virtually identical to those taken on the second voyage, except that on this occasion there were no alarum clocks, and only two chronometers (both by Kendall). Once again, portable tent observatories were provided to protect the instruments. The framework comprised eight long wooden vertical poles, each with a spike in one end which was stuck in the ground. These poles supported a circular wooden ring, and attached to this were the canvas wall coverings. Attached to a second wooden ring was a conical canvas roof, which was supported by a solid wooden tripod. When required, a section of the roof could be removed to expose a triangle of sky. Generally the observatories were set up on shore whenever there were prolonged stop-overs.

As on previous voyages, regular astronomical observations proved crucial for navigation, especially during exploration of the north-west American coast and Bering Strait, but two events of special significance were the partial solar eclipses of 5 July and 30 December 1777. These were observed from the Tongan archipelago and uninhabited Christmas Island respectively, and accurate longitudes for the two observing sites were obtained by comparing the local occurrence times with those listed for Greenwich. The July eclipse was also an attraction because sunspots were prevalent on the days leading up to the event. Finally, it should be noted that the interest of the astronomers went far beyond maritime astronomy, for they also took tidal readings and studied terrestrial magnetism, following a pattern that was conspicuous during the second voyage. These men were more than mere 'astronomers'!

After the third voyage King and Bayly began work on the official astronomical volume, and the resulting volume was published in 1782. It is proper that they included Cook as an author, but how so well-known a surname could end up as 'Cooke' on the title page is a complete mystery.

When the *Resolution* and *Discovery* reached England they brought just over ten years of Cook voyage astronomy to a successful close. Maritime astronomy had performed its task admirably: there were no shipwrecks, hundreds of islands had been placed on the world map, and thousands of miles of coastline had been charted. Three weighty astronomical tomes were published, and the future of the chronometer was assured. Matavai Bay cemented its place in Transit of Venus history, and Queen Charlotte Sound could boast the best-established latitude and longitude in the world after Greenwich. In the process, Cook, Bayly, Green, King and Wales all built on their already-respectable reputations, although two of these paid the ultimate price, losing their lives in the service of astronomy, King and country. For the British public, the terminal transit of a star like Cook was a particularly bitter pill to swallow.

By Wayne Orchiston

A kanguroo [Kangaroo]. Engraving after a painting by George Stubbs. Stubbs used a skin brought to Britain by Banks and sketches by Parkinson. (Hawkesworth III fp 561)

Australia

James Cook has, in the past, been credited with discovering Australia. He never claimed this achievement for himself, knowing from charts in his possession that other Europeans had been there before him and, of course, Aboriginal people had been there for tens of thousands of years. When Cook approached the east coast of Australia in April 1770 it was, however, largely unknown to the outside world.

Aborigines settled in Australia about 70,000 years ago, spreading to inhabit all corners of the continent. The history of re-discovery by other peoples is uncertain. Malay, Chinese and even Arab ships most probably visited the north and west coasts. There are theories that the Spanish and Portuguese visited the east coast. The Lisbon earthquake of 1755 destroyed most of Portugal's historical records but a set of maps drawn in France from Portuguese originals and known as the Dieppe Maps show, it is claimed, proof of prior European visits. Before Cook, the Dutch had certainly visited the other three coasts and named the landmass New Holland but there is no evidence of them having been on the east coast. It is also claimed that Cook even used place names from these earlier maps but it is not known for certain which, if any, of these maps Cook carried on the *Endeavour*.

Cook left New Zealand on 31 March 1770 to return to Britain, having chosen to do so via Australia (New Holland), and Jakarta (Batavia) in the Dutch East Indies. He was steering for Tasmania (Van Diemen's Land) as he sailed west. Cook, though, was too far north and when, on 19 April, Cook's second-in-command Zachary Hicks sighted land it was part of the mainland of Australia that he saw. The exact point sighted remains in doubt but a headland in East Victoria is called Point Hicks to mark the event (on some maps it is called Cape Everard).

For the next five months, Cook sailed north up Australia's east coast. He stopped several times for water and for fresh vegetables. Banks and Solander collected hundreds of new botanical specimens, which Parkinson drew, while Cook and Banks wrote some of the first descriptions of Australian Aboriginal people, following only limited contact with them. Before Cook sailed for Jakarta in September 1770 he claimed the land for Britain and renamed it New South Wales. Furneaux visited Tasmania briefly for a week in 1773 in the *Adventure* during the second voyage. Cook also visited Tasmania for five days in January 1777 on the third voyage. He never returned to the Australian continent after 1770.

Cook was rightly proud of his feat of sailing the Endeavour up the length of the east coast, and of the charts drawn and information collected in the journey.

It had only taken about eight weeks sailing time to travel the 2175-mile (3500km) journey. Contact with local people had been minimal and what there had been had been difficult. Cook, therefore, had no local names to use and his charts are full of names he coined for features and places, many of which survive today. His crew was still very healthy even if his ship was not. Cook described New South Wales in his journal but he and Banks disagreed over the potential of the country.

Banks, possibly because of the huge amount of zoological and, especially, botanical specimens collected (virtually all new to European science), extolled the merits of the place. He also saw its potential to house a convict colony. Cook, though, was far less enthusiastic about the country and its potential. He only returned once for a very brief stopover in Tasmania on his third voyage and preferred New Zealand as a base. Cook described the Aborigines and their simple lifestyle and, while commenting about their apparent wretchedness, he felt that in reality they were far happier than Europeans. Interestingly, for many Aborigines, the words 'Captain Cook' have come to symbolise Europeans in general and all the bad things that have resulted from contact with the outside world.

In 1969 and 1970, many places in Australia marked the bicentenary of Cook's 1770 voyage by erecting monuments and plaques to record the passage along the east coast. The range of the monuments is large with parks and even a 'Singing Ship' near Rockhampton as well as statues and cairns. At other times, Cook's name has been used for bridges, suburbs of large cities (and, of course, Cooktown), public houses, universities and schools, and companies, especially those with a maritime connection. Some capes and other features now carry names commemorating other persons involved on the *Endeavour* voyage. The most important memorial, though, is the Historic Landing Site at Kurnell on the south side of Botany Bay.

Since 1970, there has been a reassessment and reinterpretation in Australia of Cook's position in Australian history. It has been argued that white Australians in the nineteenth century needed a hero to base their short history around and Cook was chosen for the role. Cook was credited with discovering the continent and recommending it for settlement. Cook's mythical status persisted into the twentieth century when Russell Grimwade was prepared to purchase Cook's father's cottage, transport it to Melbourne and rebuild it there. Eventually a reaction occurred. People began questioning if Australia and its Aboriginal peoples had benefited from the arrival of Europeans. Given that Cook had been instrumental in this 'invasion', Aboriginal people had already equated Cook with European domination and implicated him in land confiscations and wrongs they had suffered.

At the beginning of the twenty-first century, Cook no longer enjoys the hero status he once held in Australia. However, his feats of navigation and exploration are still recognised and celebrated, and a more balanced view of his role in events following his visits is emerging.

SEE ALSO: *Endeavour* (HM Bark), First voyage

Austrian Succession, War of the (1740–1748)

This was a general European war, which started in 1740 when the Austrian archduchess, Maria Theresa, succeeded as ruler of the Hapsburg Empire. The Elector of Bavaria, Charles Albert, advanced counterclaims while Frederick of Prussia claimed part of Silesia and soon most countries in Europe had entered the war. Prussia was joined by an alliance, comprising France, Spain, Bavaria, and Saxony. Austria meanwhile had obtained support from Hungary and the promise of aid from Great Britain, which had been at war with Spain since 1739.

Peace followed in 1743 but hostilities broke out again in 1744. The chief belligerents were now Austria, Britain and Holland on one side, and France and Spain on the other. Fighting took place in northern Italy, the Low Countries, in India, and in North America where it was known as the French and Indian War. The fort at Louisbourg on Cape Breton Island was captured by troops from New England in 1748.

During the war, Prince Charles Stuart, the Young Pretender, landed in Scotland, resourced by France, and invaded England with a highland army. His campaign dissolved and he retreated to Scotland where he was defeated at Culloden Moor near Inverness in 1745. Peace was finally declared and, on 18 October 1748, the Treaty of Aix-la-Chapelle was signed. Britain received Nova Scotia, while Louisbourg was restored to France. Cook would soon visit both places.

Cook began his career on the North Sea while this war was taking place. However, he was not directly affected until after peace was signed and the *Three Brothers,* on which he was sailing, was commissioned to transport horses and troops from Middelburg in the Netherlands to Dublin and Liverpool.

B

Banks, Sir Joseph (1743–1820)

Joseph Banks travelled with Cook on the first voyage on *Endeavour* as a supernumerary and gentleman naturalist. He paid for his place and for a retinue of scientists, artists and servants to accompany him, thus helping to ensure the historical significance of the voyage. Banks and Cook became close friends. Banks benefited from his association with Cook but he used his own prominent position to champion Cook for the rest of his life and did much to establish Cook's reputation.

Banks was born in London on 13 February 1743 into a wealthy family with estates at Revesby Abbey in Lincolnshire. Banks was educated at Harrow, Eton and, from 1760 to 1763, at Christ Church, Oxford, where he became interested in botany. Botany, however, was not taught and Banks hired his own personal tutor, Israel Lyons, to instruct him. While at Oxford his father died and Banks inherited a considerable fortune. Banks started visiting the British Museum where he met the Swedish botanist, Daniel Solander, who worked there, becoming his friend and mentor. He also began visiting the Chelsea Physic Garden, which had a large collection of foreign plants. After graduating, Banks travelled to Newfoundland and Labrador in 1766, aboard HMS *Niger* with his friend Constantine Phipps, collecting plant and other specimens.

On his return to Britain, Banks was elected a member of the Royal Society at the age of just 23. He also purchased a new house, 14 New Burlington Street, to give him a London base and to house his library and growing collection of natural history specimens. Banks possessed a wide-ranging interest in new inventions and industry as well as botany. He travelled around Britain extensively, studying fen drainage, coal mining and adding to his collection of flora, fauna and geological specimens.

In 1768, he went round the world on the *Endeavour* with Captain James Cook, during which time they landed at many points in South America, the South Pacific, Australia, New Zealand and Indonesia. Banks and his colleagues collected, described and drew a great number of plants, as well as many zoological and ethnological specimens. His scientific knowledge gained during the voyage and his promotion of his discoveries sparked considerable interest in Europe, encouraging European settlement near the Pacific islands.

Banks and Solander were both very ill with malaria and dysentery on their arrival at Jakarta. They rented a house in the country and were able to recover. When they eventually returned to Britain, they were feted by society and the press, and were presented to King George III, with whom Banks became friends. Cook was largely ignored by everyone except the Admiralty. Banks had made his mark, and his portrait was painted by several artists including Benjamin West.

Banks then prepared to accompany Cook on the second voyage but this fell through when he and the Navy could not agree about proposed modifications to one of the ships. Instead of joining Cook's voyage, Banks chartered the *Sir Lawrence* and mounted his own expedition to Iceland, the Hebrides and Orkney in 1772.

This was his last major voyage; thereafter he exercised his influence from home, which from 1776 was at 32 Soho Square, London, where his extensive botanical collections formed the basis of his herbarium. In 1778, Banks was elected President of the Royal Society, a position he held for the remainder of his life and, as such, he played a very prominent role in many aspects of British life, mainly scientific but also diplomatic. He was involved in the early settlement of Australia the introduction there and in Britain of Spanish merino sheep, the exploration of Africa and voyages such as Bligh in the *Bounty* and Matthew Flinders's circumnavigation of Australia. The Royal Institution of Great Britain was founded on 7 March 1799 at a meeting in Banks' house in Soho Square. During much of this time, Banks was an informal adviser to King George III on Kew Gardens, a position that was formalised in 1797. Banks dispatched explorers and botanists, such as Francis Masson, James Bowie and Archibald Menzies, to many parts of the world and

Banks introduces Omai (Mai) to Solander. William Parry. 1775. Banks looked after Mai during his stay in Britain from 1774 to 1775. (Captain Cook Memorial Museum, Whitby)

through his efforts Kew became the foremost botanical gardens in the world.

In 1779, Banks married Dorothea Hugessen. They had no children. In 1781, he was knighted and, in 1795, he received the order of Knight Commander of the Bath; two years later he was admitted to the Privy Council. Banks died in Isleworth, London on 19 June 1820, leaving a will (FRC 11/1634). He was buried at Heston. There have been several biographies, most notably Carter's, and many other works dealing with aspects of Bank's life and career. There is a short biography in the *DNB*, v1, p1049.

Some 75 botanical species bear his name. He is credited with the introduction to Europe of eucalyptus, acacia, mimosa, and the genus named for him, '*Banksia*'. Several portraits of Sir Joseph Banks can be found in collections. His name has been given to many geographical features, including the Banks Islands in Vanuatu, Banks Peninsula in New Zealand, and Banks Island in British Columbia.

Banks's herbarium is now incorporated with the General Herbarium at the British Museum (Natural History) in London and many items are still referred to by scientists today. After his death, some 1400 titles from his library eventually went to the British Museum, and these are now in the British Library. The Mitchell Library in Sydney has a large collection of Banks' papers and correspondence.

SEE ALSO: Botanical results of Cook's voyages, First voyage, Royal Society

Bay of Islands/Ipipiri

The Bay of Islands (35° 12' S, 174° 10' E) is an inlet in the north of Te Ika a Maui, the North Island of New Zealand. The bay is 6.2 miles (10km) deep and 4.3 miles (7km) wide at the mouth. Māori of the Ngare Raumati iwi lived in the bay, which they called Ipiriri. Thomas Kendall opened the first Christian mission in New Zealand in the bay in 1814, while sealers and whalers had made Russell their base, calling it the Hell Hole of the Pacific. The Treaty of Waitangi, a founding document for New Zealand was signed here in 1840 at Waitangi.

Seventy-one years earlier James Cook had sailed up the east coast of New Zealand to reach a headland on 27 November 1769. An arch (Hole-in-the-rock) in one of two offshore rocks amused Cook, causing him to name the headland Cape Brett after Admiral Piercy Brett. The headland signalled a large bay but Cook sailed on to a small island group where they traded for fish from Māori. Contrary winds prevented Cook sailing on so he returned from the Cavalli Islands to explore the large bay ignored earlier.

Cook worked the *Endeavour* into the bay and anchored south of a small island near the southern shore on 29 November. Landing on the island, Cook found it was called Motuarohia from local Māori before a skirmish ensued. Having taken on fresh water and vegetables, Cook tried to leave on the 30th but was becalmed. Three sailors were punished for stealing sweet potatoes from gardens on the island. Cook and a party rowed south across Te Rawhiti Inlet to the mainland but where they landed is uncertain; Te Hue Bay is the most likely. (A few years later the French explorer, Marion Dufresne, and members of his crew were killed in Te Hue Bay.) The next day, a trip was made to the neighbouring island of Moturua to replenish water supplies. A further visit was made ashore and Cook was shown round a village and a pa that may have been Tangitu Pa.

On 5 December, Cook set sail but currents nearly carried the *Endeavour* onto Whale Rock. They survived and Cook left the Bay of Islands to resume his journey north.

SEE ALSO: First voyage, New Zealand

Bayly, William (1737–1810)

William Bayly was an astronomer and mathematician who sailed with Cook on the second and third voyages. He sailed on *Adventure* during the second voyage and on *Discovery* during the third until the death of Cook when he transferred to *Resolution* for the remainder of the voyage.

Bayly was born in Bishop's Cannings, Wiltshire, the son of a ploughman in a family of three children and, in his words, spent his youth 'at the plough's tail'. His quick mind and exceptional aptitude for mathematics led to a patron arranging for him to attend a school at Stoke near Bath where he soon became an usher and later a teacher. He came to the attention of Dr Maskelyne, by then Astronomer Royal, who employed him as an assistant at the Royal Observatory Greenwich. Bayly lived in Hackney Wick where he met his life-long friend and executor of his estate, Col Mark Beaufoy, FRS.

In 1769 the Royal Society commissioned him to undertake an expedition to the North Cape of Norway to measure the Transit of Venus, along with Jeremiah Dixon. Bayly set up his observatory on the island of Maggeroe and Dixon set up further south on the island of Hammerfest. On the day of the transit, Bayly had clear sky but Dixon's view was obscured by clouds. Bayly's report was read before the Royal Society on 16 November 1769. During this period, Charles Lennox, Third Duke of Richmond, sponsored his work. Bayly then took part in Cook's voyages and was joint author of two works detailing astronomical observations of the voyages. He witnessed the murder of Captain Cook in Hawai'i and provided his own account of this tragedy.

When he returned from the sea for the last time at age 43, Bayly married and had seven children. He moved to Portsmouth in 1785 to be First Master of the Royal Naval Academy where he remained until retirement in 1806. Bayly amassed great wealth during these years largely from the sale of 'Artificial Curiosities' that he had brought back from the third voyage. In 1806 there was a Grant of Arms from King George III.

Great tragedy then befell William Bayly. His eldest son was killed in action as a midshipman aboard the

Amelia in 1799. Then, in rapid succession, his wife and remaining six children died from consumption. By 1808 at the age of 70 he was alone in wretched solitude. He purchased a new organ for Bishop's Cannings church (his home village) and provided an endowment which persists to this day. He died in December 1810 and was buried at St Mary, Portsea. Obituaries carried in several publications of the day stated 'He was one of the most eminent circumnavigators, astronomers, and philosophers of the age; and no man ever discharged his duty to his country with more fidelity'.

Bayly's journals and papers remained in the possession of the Beaufoy family from 1810 until 1909 when they were auctioned at Christies as part of the library of Henry B H Beaufoy and purchased by A H Turnbull. They reside today in the Turnbull Library in Wellington. Six of Bayly's original charts of the North Pacific from the third voyage are in the Vancouver Maritime Museum. London's Imperial War Museum archive has a 70-page mathematical treatise by Bayly. The only known likeness of Bayly is in a painting by John Webber showing him making observations outside his tent observatory at Queen Charlotte Sound, New Zealand in 1777. A plaque honouring Bayly was unveiled at Portsmouth Dockyard in 2001.

By Don Anderson

See Also: Astronomical results of Cook's voyages, Second and Third voyages

Beaglehole, John Cawte (1901–1971)

John Cawte Beaglehole, Cook's editor and biographer, came to this work almost by chance. He had just completed a PhD on British colonial history at the University of London (in 1929) and was, reluctantly, returning home to New Zealand when J A Williamson invited him to write a volume in the series, the 'Pioneer Histories'. While teaching for the WEA (Workers Educational Association) during the Depression years he used the resources of the Alexander Turnbull Library to write *The Exploration of the Pacific* (1933). In 1935 he was finally appointed to a lectureship at Victoria University College, Wellington, where he had been a student.

Writing the book convinced him of the need for an edition of Cook's journals as Cook had written them. The war, and Beaglehole's heavy involvement in teaching, writing, and working as a part-time public servant as historical adviser to the Department of Internal Affairs, delayed a start, until his plans, by good fortune, came together with those of the Hakluyt Society in 1948. The New Zealand Government and the College supported the work by creating a full-time research position for him.

The Journals of Captain James Cook on his Voyages of Discovery appeared in four massive volumes between 1955 and 1967. A supplement to the first was *The Endeavour Journal of Joseph Banks,* published in 1962. In these volumes Beaglehole displayed his superb gifts as historian and editor. From his early years he had read voraciously, and to a deep knowledge of the eighteenth century he added a mastery of the written records of the voyages. He had travelled to many of Cook's landfalls, had studied the complexities of Polynesian history as well as the eighteenth-century Admiralty, and sought to enable the reader to follow the voyages exactly and to understand why Cook said what he did say. He drew on the knowledge of experts in many fields, most notably, in the earlier years, of R A Skelton, superintendent of the map room at the British Museum and secretary of the Hakluyt Society. The introductory essays reflected great erudition, a wide-ranging imagination – and lurking sense of humour – and an architectural skill that shaped the whole enterprise. The *Journals* were followed by the long-planned biography of Cook. At the time of his death in 1971 Beaglehole had nearly finished revising the typescript. It was published in 1974, crowning a remarkable scholarly achievement.

Beaglehole accomplished much besides his work on Cook, increasingly winning recognition as a public scholar and critic with an abiding concern for the quality of life in New Zealand. He served for many years as President of the New Zealand Council for Civil Liberties, and on the board of the New Zealand Historic Places Trust. He had a practical passion for typography; he collected books and pewter and New Zealand paintings, and opened the minds of many of his students – and fellow New Zealanders – to the worlds of ideas and the arts. The passing years brought public recognition in New Zealand and overseas, honorary degrees and other awards, including, in 1970, the British Order of Merit.

By Tim Beaglehole

See Also: Biographies of Cook, Published accounts

Bering Sea and Strait

The Bering Sea covers 874,960 square miles (2,274,020 sq km), representing the northward extension of the Pacific Ocean. It is screened from the Pacific proper by

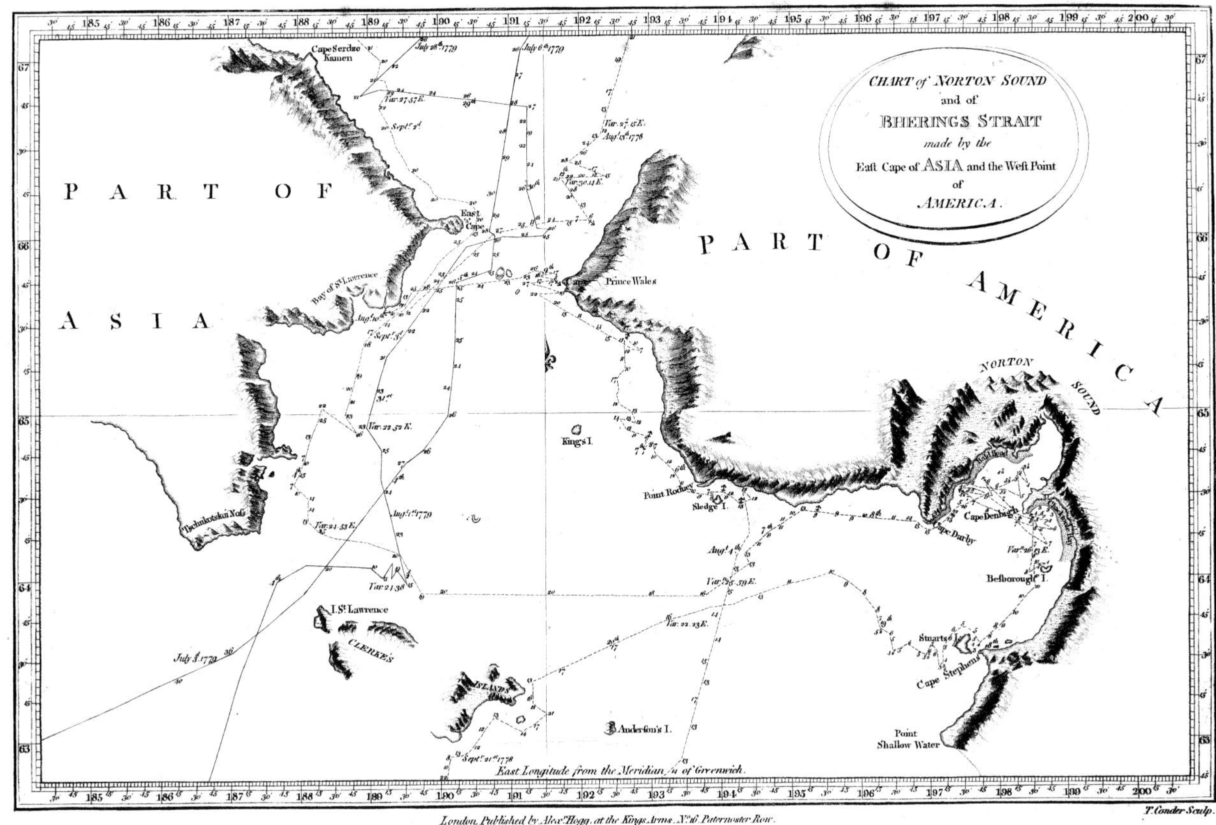

Chart of Norton Sound and of Behring's Strait made by the East Cape of Asia and the West Point of America. After Cook, 1784. (University of Waikato Map Collection)

the arc of the Aleutian Islands and the Alaskan peninsula. Its borders are defined to the east by Alaska and to the west by Siberia. The Bering Strait to the north connects it to the Chukchi Sea and the Arctic Ocean. The sea is affected by ice for many months each year, restricting navigation to the summer months from May to October. The sea has several large islands, including St Lawrence and St Matthew, and several marginal large bays, including Norton Sound and Bristol Bay.

The Russian, Dezhnev, sailed through the Bering Strait in the seventeenth century but it was the Dane, Vitus Bering, sailing for the Russians, who made the first explorations of the sea and strait, which were named after him. Russians had entered the region to exploit the sea otters and fur seals by the time Cook arrived in 1778. North of the Bering Sea, the continents of Asia and America come within 56 miles (90km) of each other, being separated by the Bering Strait. It is believed that in the past, at a time of lower sea levels, people crossed over here from Asia to populate the American continent. It is usually frozen-over from October to June.

Cook was looking for the Northwest Passage when he entered the Bering Sea on 2 July 1778. He skirted Bristol Bay and then headed north. He reached the Bering Strait on 8 August and sailed through it into the Chukchi Sea on the 11th. Pack ice forced him back through the strait on 1 September. Cook entered Norton Sound, still looking for the passage, before heading south to Unalaska, which he reached on 3 October.

Clerke brought the ships back in June 1779, this time approaching from Kamchatka and Koryakskiy. They passed through the Bering Strait in early July and spent three weeks in the Chukchi Sea with same result, thwarted by ice. Cook's expedition did not find the Northwest Passage but suspected its existence where they had been looking north of the Bering Strait. Amundsen would eventually show that the Passage did exist via this route in 1905.

SEE ALSO: Alaska, Arctic, Third voyage

Bibliographies on Cook

The life and exploits of James Cook have been covered by a vast quantity of books and journal articles, so much so that for many years there has been the need for bibliographies that provide access to that body of literature. The first attempt was prompted by the bicentenary of Cook's birth in 1928 when the Mitchell Library in Sydney compiled a bibliography in connection with an exhibition that was held in the library. Material was identified from the Library's own collections and from other people and agencies that made items available for the exhibition. The 173 pages of entries were published in 1928 under the title, *Bibliography of Captain James Cook, R.N., F.R.S., circumnavigator.* A facsimile edition was published by Burt Franklin in New York in 1968.

Over the years there have been several short bibliographical works, which have really been listings and catalogues of exhibitions. Sir Maurice Holmes made a more systematic approach and wrote two works, both published in London by Francis Edwards, the booksellers. The first was *An Introduction to the Bibliography of Captain James Cook, R.N.*, published in 1936 and the second was *Captain James Cook, R.N., F.R.S.: a bibliographical excursion,* published in 1952.

Sydney Spence wrote and published *Captain James Cook, R.N. (1728-1779): a bibliography of his voyages, to which is added other works relating to his life, conduct, & nautical achievements,* which appeared in 1960. This slight book added little to the earlier works.

It was left to the Australians to compile what at the time was the definitive bibliographic work on Cook. As part of the celebrations to mark the bicentenary of Cook's arrival in Botany Bay, the State Library of New South Wales updated and revised extensively their 1928 volume. In 1970, under the editorship of M K Beddie, *Bibliography of Captain James Cook R.N., F.R.S., Circumnavigator* appeared. This edition drew not only on its own Mitchell and Dixson collections but on all of the other major libraries and museums in Australia to produce a most comprehensive listing. It contained, as well as books and journal articles, archive material, ephemera, paintings, medals and much more. Beddie's work was published at a time of great interest in Cook. Various anniversaries to do with Cook's voyages fell during the period 1968 to 1980, prompting a huge increase in the number of books, conference papers and journal articles published and quickly rendering Beddie out of date. It remains the definitive work for earlier material but sadly the Library has no plans to ever update it.

John Robson has compiled bibliographies that aim to update Beddie. The first is a list of books from 1965 onwards. The second is a list of journal articles. Both lists are available online at http://www.CaptainCookEncyclopaedia.com

Billings, Joseph (1758–1806?)

Joseph Billings sailed on the third voyage on the *Discovery* as an AB and had an uneventful voyage. Afterwards, he traded on his Cook connection and went to St Petersburg, where he persuaded the authorities to employ him. He joined the Russian Navy as a lieutenant and, in 1785, was given command of a Russian expedition that would visit the mouth of the Kolmya River and the Chukotskiy Peninsula, before crossing to Alaska. The expedition assembled at Irkutsk in 1786 and, over the next few years, achieved most of its instructions. They reached the Aleutian Islands in 1790. It is believed that most credit for the success of the expeditions was due to his deputy, Gavriil Sarychev and not to Billings himself. After the expedition, Billings disappeared and nothing is known about the end of his life though he may have died in 1806. He was born in Turnham Green, West London, in 1758. There is a short biography in the *DNB*, v2, p494.

SEE ALSO: Russians, Third voyage

Biographies of Cook

There have been two important biographies written about James Cook. That by Reverend Andrew Kippis was the first one and became the source of much that was written by other people over the next 200 years. *The Life of Captain James Cook* by Kippis was published in 1788, just 10 years after Cook's death. Little information about Cook the person is provided as the bulk of the book covers the events of the three Pacific voyages and is drawn from the published accounts. It appears that Kippis carried out little or no research and there is little indication that he interviewed any people who had known Cook. Thus Kippis missed the opportunity to speak to people who could have provided insights into Cook's character and provided explanations for some of Cook's actions that puzzle us to this day. Cook's childhood and his life until Newfoundland are glossed over. There are mistakes that would be perpetuated in subsequent biographies that blindly followed Kippis. Kippis is important for being first but not a good biography. The next biography to appear was written by George Young, another cleric, in 1836. Young, a Scot, had moved to Whitby and his biography added some northeastern information to the Cook canon.

From then on, other biographies were published at intervals, including Kingston (1871), Besant (1890), and Kitson (1907). They are somewhat pedestrian reworkings of existing information and add nothing to our knowledge of Cook. In 1929, a translation of a French biography by Maurice Thiéry appeared. The 1930s were marked by two biographies written by naval officers: Rupert Gould (1935), and Gordon Campbell (1936); and two by Pacific authors: Joseph Carruthers (1930), and Hugh Carrington (1939). All of the biographies mentioned so far tend to show unquestioning approval of Cook and promote his position as a hero of the British Empire. Lesser biographies, often aimed at younger readers, continued to be published over the next 30 years.

In the 1950s, J C Beaglehole, the New Zealand historian, began editing Cook's *Journals* and over 20 years built up a vast knowledge of Cook's life, which was turned into a biography that was published posthumously in 1974. This book is magisterial in its scope and content, and will most probably stand as the definitive biography. Beaglehole was not able to fill all the gaps but he was able to add much new information. In recent times, Beaglehole has been criticised for not being sufficiently critical of Cook, especially in light of post-colonialist and indigenous views of history that have been written. Supporters of people like Dalrymple and Johann Forster have also maintained that Beaglehole has portrayed these men too negatively and undervalued their roles.

The only biography since Beaglehole has been Hough's *Captain James Cook* published in 1994. It draws heavily on Beaglehole and, despite the debates and reassessments that had taken place since that book's publication, still portrays Cook as unblemished hero.

SEE ALSO: Beaglehole (J C), Kippis (Andrew), Young (George)

Bligh, William (1754–1817)

William Bligh sailed on the third voyage on the *Resolution* as master. During the voyage, Bligh made many surveys and drew charts. After the voyage, he was unhappy that Henry Roberts was asked to prepare the charts for publication and that he was not given credit for having drawn the originals.

Bligh was born at Tinten Manor, St Tudy in Cornwall on 9 September 1754, the only son of Francis and Jane Bligh. Bligh first went to sea in 1762 as a Captain's personal servant on board HMS *Monmouth*. He entered the Royal Navy at the age of 16 as an able seaman, studying navigation and hydrography to become an accomplished seaman. From July 1770 until August 1774, Bligh served on HMS *Hunter* and HMS *Crescent*. He next joined HMS *Ranger* as a midshipman before becoming master on the *Resolution* for Cook's third voyage in 1776. His skill as a cartographer had brought him to Cook's attention.

After the voyage, Bligh married Elizabeth Betham on the Isle of Man in February 1781. He was then posted as master of HMS *Belle Poule*. Bligh was promoted to lieutenant in 1781 and served on HMS *Cambridge* from 1782 to 1783. Duncan Campbell, an uncle of Elizabeth Bligh, was a wealthy shipowner who traded with the West Indies where he owned several plantations. Bligh left the Navy in 1783 to work on Campbell's ships until 1787. He commanded the *Lynx*, the *Britannia* and the *Cambrian* on voyages to the West Indies.

Breadfruit was seen as a potential food for slaves on the plantations in the West Indies and it was decided to transport some plants there from the South Pacific where it had been found. Campbell owned the *Bethia*, which was purchased by the Navy Board for the breadfruit expedition and renamed HMS *Bounty*. He knew Joseph Banks well and probably recommended Bligh for the voyage. Bligh was given command of the *Bounty*, which sailed on 23 December 1787. When the *Bounty* arrived in Tahiti in 1788, the breadfruit trees had to be seeded and grown into saplings large enough for transport, a process that would take at least six months. Bligh opted to remain at the island and use the time for exploring. This allowed his men time to form strong relationships with the islanders so they were most reluctant to leave when the time came. In April 1789, a mutiny took place off Tofua in Tonga, led by Fletcher Christian.

Bligh and 18 other crew members loyal to him were set adrift on 28 April in an open longboat. Bligh's navigational skills enabled them to reach Timor in Indonesia in June after a journey of 3728 miles (6000km) over 47 days. Bligh bought a schooner, renamed HMS *Resource* in Timor and sailed it to Jakarta. He then took passage in the *Vlydte*, a Dutch East Indiaman, which took him back to Britain. A court-martial took place at Spithead, on 22 October 1790, which cleared Bligh and he resumed his naval career. In December 1790, he was promoted to captain and given command of the sloop HMS *Falcon*, followed by service on HMS *Medea*.

A second breadfruit voyage was commissioned and Bligh was given command. HMS *Providence* left Spithead on 3 August 1791 for Tahiti and successfully transported a cargo of breadfruit plants to Jamaica. In 1794, Bligh was given the Society of Arts medal for his remarkable feat of navigation during the longboat voyage. In 1801, he was made a fellow of the Royal Society for services to navigation and botany.

Bligh had command of HMS *Calcutta* in 1795 before taking over HMS *Director* in January 1796. He remained captain of the *Director* until 1801, taking part in 1797 in the Battle of Camperdown. In 1801, he was captain of HMS *Glatton*, which was damaged at the Battle of Copenhagen. Bligh was commended by Nelson for his action in the battle. After the battle, Bligh was made captain of HMS *Irresistable*, 74 guns, which he commanded until May 1802. From May 1804 until April 1805, Bligh captained HMS *Warrior*.

In February 1806, Bligh set off for the new colony of New South Wales as Governor. He had been given special instructions to sort out corruption including curbing traffic in spirits, but his actions and methods alienated many and Bligh was forcibly deposed in January 1808 by Major George Johnston of the NSW Corps. Under arrest, Bligh remained in the colony refusing to give up power until the arrival of his replacement, Macquarie, who finally arrived in December 1809. In May 1810, Bligh returned to England where he was cleared of all blame.

Bligh was promoted Rear-Admiral of the Blue in 1810 and in 1814 he became a Vice-Admiral of the Blue. In the latter years of his life, he lived at the Manor House, Farningham, Kent and died on 7 December 1817, aged 64, in Bond Street, London. He is buried in Lambeth churchyard. He left a will (FRC 11/1603) and there is a short biography in the *DNB*, v2, p680.

Bligh had a high opinion of himself and his abilities, and he expected very high standards in men under his command. However, he often felt he was let down and his reactions, which could be very erratic, and his use of bad language, led to him being an unpopular seaman and governor.

The Genus 'Blighia', which consists of some four species of evergreen tropical shrubs and trees, is named in his honour. Bligh Island (in Nootka Sound), Bligh's Island (in Prince William Sound) and Bligh Channel (the northernmost passage of Endeavour Strait, Torres Strait) are named for him.

SEE ALSO: Third voyage

Botanical results of Cook's voyages

A Swede, Carolus Linnaeus (he wrote in Latin using the Latin form of his name, Carl von Linné), looms over the botanical side of Cook's voyages. From 1742, he was Professor of Botany at Uppsala University until his death in 1778. His huge contribution to science as a whole was his method of describing natural objects and classifying them using a binomial system. He defined genera and species and developed his system so that all plants and animals would have first a generic name and then a specific one. For example, a common oak tree is *Quercus robur*, where *Quercus* is the genus and *robur*, the particular species.

The students of Linnaeus at Uppsala became his apostles, spreading his ideas around Europe. Among those students were Daniel Solander, and Anders Sparrman, who sailed on Cook's ships (the father of Hermann Spöring, who also sailed with Cook, corresponded with Linnaeus). Before the *Endeavour* voyage, Solander worked in London and introduced many British botanists to the Linnean system. Among them was Joseph Banks, who paid for Solander to travel with him on the *Endeavour*. So it was that a group of scientists, fired with new ideas about the botanical world set off to visit worlds where virtually all the plants were new to science and never previously described.

Joseph Banks was a rich young man who had attended Oxford University where his interest in science and especially botany had developed. Through the 1760s Banks corresponded with other naturalists and made collecting tours in Britain and Newfoundland. In 1764, Banks met Solander, who became his mentor. Banks was a member of the Royal Society and knew of plans to observe the Transit of Venus in 1769. In early 1768, he saw an opportunity for himself and a party of eight to join the expedition to the Pacific and made arrangements with the Admiralty.

This chance decision would prove crucial in the history of the voyage. In taking a party of naturalists, the voyage became one of the first scientific expeditions. In addition, Banks had included in his party two artists, Sydney Parkinson and Alexander Buchan, whose role was to record the voyage visually. John Ellis, a friend of Banks and Solander wrote to Linnaeus: 'No people ever went to sea better fitted out for the purpose of Natural History. They have got a fine library of Natural History... They have two painters and draughtsmen... in short Solander assured me this expedition would cost Mr. Banks £10,000. All this is owing to you and your writing'. The botanical illustrations by Parkinson, later grouped together as Banks's *Florilegium*, are among the treasures of Cook's voyages.

Banks and his party were uncomfortable at sea but from the first landfall at Madeira, they were in their element. Most things they saw were new. Plants were collected and preserved though not before Parkinson had drawn them while fresh to catch their colour and shape. Parkinson found it hard to keep up and many specimens were sketched briefly in the hope of returning to them later to finish. Unfortunately, Parkinson died crossing the Indian Ocean leaving many drawings unfinished. He did make 674 outline drawings on the voyage and 269 finished paintings.

At all the landfalls, Banks and Solander were among the first ashore, though Banks could be frustrated as off south-west New Zealand when Cook refused to enter inlets for fear of not being to get out again. Where they did go ashore they collected comprehensively and the *Endeavour* began to fill with specimens. Solander carefully described them and then placed them in his Solander cases so that most were still in good condition when the ship returned to Britain with about 30,000 botanical specimens. They had identified 110 new genera and 1300 new species (Linnaeus in his *Species Plantarum* published in 1753 had only listed 1098 genera and 5900 species for the whole world at that time). Fortunately, they had not been damaged or among the material jettisoned when the ship struck the Great Barrier Reef.

The majority of the botanical specimens collected on the *Endeavour* voyage are now lodged in the Natural History Museum in London. Small parts of the collection have been returned to museums in countries whence they first came. The National Museum in Wellington, New Zealand, received 328 specimens, the Auckland Institute and Museum received 249 specimens, and the Royal Botanic Gardens in Sydney were sent 586 specimens of Australian plants. The collection, as with those of the later voyages, is important as it depicts the natural flora of the islands before Europeans and others began exchanging plants around the world and introducing exotics to these locations.

*A print of a watercolour by Sydney Parkinson of a breadfruit plant (*Artocarpus altilis*) made at Tahiti during Cook's first voyage. It was breadfruit that Bligh was supposed to transport to the West Indies in the* Bounty*. (National Maritime Museum, Greenwich)*

While the planning for and execution of the voyage had been well carried out, the events afterwards were strangely handled. Banks had plans to publish the botanical illustrations in 14 folio volumes but Parkinson had died, leaving many items unfinished. Five artists and 18 engravers were employed to finish the work. Rather than publish in parts, Banks chose to wait to publish one large work but he then seems to have then lost interest. The scheme was shelved and not completed properly until 200 years later when Editions Alecto finally published Banks's *Florilegium*. The thousands of specimens brought back to Britain were carefully described and displayed by Solander, using the guidelines of Linnaeus. However, nothing was published thus allowing later botanists to describe and name the same specimens differently. Solander died in

1782 while Banks had become President of the Royal Society and involved in other matters.

In 1772, Banks intended to sail with Cook on the second voyage. However, disagreements over accommodation on board caused him to withdraw and another naturalist was sought. Johann Reinhold Forster, a Prussian naturalist who had been living in Britain for several years, was taken on, together with his son George. Both were extremely capable scientists though neither was primarily a botanist. However, by a good piece of luck, the Swedish botanist Anders Sparrman was at Cape Town when the *Resolution* arrived there. Sparrman, another of the apostles of Linnaeus, jumped at the opportunity to join the expedition and was employed as Forster's assistant. The botanical success of Cook's second voyage owed much to Sparrman, both from his ability and from his instruction of the Forsters, especially George, through the voyage.

The second voyage visited some of the same places visited by the *Endeavour* voyage, which reduced the possibilities for finding new species but many other islands were visited for the first time. The fact that Banks and Solander had not published their findings also helped create some confusion as to whether specimens were being described for the first time or not. Sparrman did not return to Britain so it was the Forsters who brought home 76 new genera and about 260 new species among several thousand botanical specimens. George Forster, who worked closely with Sparrman on plants, also made over 300 botanical drawings.

Shortly after their return, the Forsters published a limited edition of a work *Characteres Generum Plantarum* containing descriptions and drawings of the new genera they had discovered. George Forster, after he moved to Germany to live, published several other pieces about the botany of the Pacific Islands. His manuscripts on the botany of the voyage are now in the Musée National d'Histoire Naturelle in Paris. Over the years, the Forsters suffered several financial crises and in August 1776, George was forced to sell his main set of botanical drawings. Joseph Banks purchased them and they now reside in the Natural History Museum (NHM) in London. The actual botanical specimens, the Forster Herbarium, were dispersed to many places, having been gifted or sold by the Forsters. The NHM in London, Kew, Göttingen, Paris, Kiel, Moscow and Berlin all hold some specimens.

George Forster recounted an incident in New Caledonia in September 1774 when a small party visited the island of Balabio. He wrote: 'One of the surgeon's mates [William Anderson], who went on this excursion...likewise met with many new species of plants, of which we did not see a single specimen in the districts we had visited; but the meanest and the most unreasonable envy taught him to conceal these discoveries from us, though he was utterly incapable of making use of them for the benefit of science'.

While this piece highlights the strained relationship between the Forsters and the remainder of people on board, it introduces William Anderson. Anderson was promoted to Surgeon on the *Resolution* for Cook's third voyage and was deputed to also carry out the role of scientist aboard. It is often reported that because of the strained relationship between Reinhold Forster and James Cook on the second voyage, Cook was determined not to carry scientists with him again. Neither Anderson's journal nor any botanical collection survive from the second voyage so we are unable to refute or agree with Forster about Anderson. It is possible some of his notes went to John Pringle for Pringle's paper to The Royal Society on scurvy. While not formally educated, Anderson would have had a basic introduction to plants as part of his training to be a surgeon and there is evidence that he knew Latin. His other duties often clashed with botanising but with the assistance of David Nelson, together they made a collection. It was by no means as large as those from the first two voyages. Nelson was one of the first gardener-collectors dispatched by Joseph Banks to collect material for the developing botanic gardens at Kew and on this voyage he sailed as servant to William Bayly on the *Discovery*. Being on separate ships would not have made working together easy.

Anderson wrote to Banks from Cape Town in late 1776 about the arrival of the *Discovery*: 'a person [David Nelson] in her who understands Botany...will be able to procure you every new article in that branch, a task which I have not vanity enough to suppose myself equal to; but shall nevertheless continue to collect whatever presents itself'. Anderson was being unduly modest as he acquitted himself well through the voyage in various aspects of science, including botany but, unfortunately, he died in August 1778 in the Bering Sea. His will states: 'I leave to Joseph Banks Esquire the Natural Curiosities I have collected during this voyage with some Manuscript Note relating to them'. Nothing was ever published about the collection, though Anderson's manuscript notes and specimens are with the Natural History Museum. Nelson continued after Anderson's death and made a significant collection on Hawai'i. Some of his specimens are now extinct.

Botany was not only important from a collection and identification perspective. It also was crucial for several other reasons, including health and economic. Botany was still very closely related to medicine and doctors were expected to be acquainted with herbs and plants that could be used for medicinal purposes. It was also imperative that they recognised potentially poisonous plants before damage was done. One crucial factor on long sea voyages was scurvy and Cook and his colleagues were always looking for fresh edible greens to offset the disease. A term 'scurvy grass' has been applied to several plants that were used. Cook's scurvy grass is a term now used in New Zealand for *Lepidium oleraceum*. Both it and a native wild celery (*Apium prostatum*) were used in soups. Other plants used against scurvy included the Kerguelen cabbage (*Pringlea antiscorbutica* – named by Anderson for Sir John Pringle).

Another regular activity encouraged by Cook was the brewing of spruce beer. Cook began using beer in Newfoundland and continued the practice on all his Pacific voyages. As soon as landfall was made, local tree leaves would be collected and mixed with molasses and malt extract to produce 'spruce beer'. In New Zealand, rimu (*Dacrydium cupressinum*) and manuka (*Leptospermum scoparium*) were used while at Nootka, Sitka spruce (*Picea sitchensis*) provided the leaves. Manuka is also called the tea tree, a name bestowed by Cook.

Cook's wooden sailing ships received batterings in the course of the voyages so replacement timber for masts and spars was another resource dutifully noted, both for immediate and possible future need. The tall, straight trunks of kahikatea (*Podocarpus dacrydioides*) along the banks of the Waihou (Thames) River in New Zealand, noted on the *Endeavour* voyage, were later exploited extensively for ships' masts. In New Caledonia, the local Cook pine (*Araucaria columnaris* or *cookii*) was similarly noted.

Another of Cook's directives was to identify plants with commercial possibilities. One such was the breadfruit (*Artocarpis altilis*) first described in Tahiti. The breadfruit represents an example of the confusion caused by Banks and Solander not releasing details of plants described by them on the *Endeavour* voyage. They had named it *Sitodium altile* but the Forsters, unaware of this, renamed it *Artocarpis communis*. Banks noted its potential as a food for African slaves in the West Indies and, in 1787, Captain Bligh took the *Bounty* to Tahiti to gather over 1000 young plants for transportation to the Caribbean. David Nelson, from Cook's third voyage, sailed with Bligh as gardener, looking after the plants.

While botany was not a primary reason for any of Cook's voyages, the presence of Banks and Solander on the first gave the subject a high profile, which was echoed on the later voyages. The extensive collections of botanical specimens, together with the botanical illustrations, represent a major success and justification for the expeditions. They have provided a marvellous resource for scholars, past and future. The people concerned have been honoured by having genera and species named after them so we now have genera *Andersonia*, *Banksia*, *Forstera* and *Solandra*, and species *cookii* and *nelsonii*.

SEE ALSO: Banks (Joseph), Solander (Daniel), Forster family, Colour plates 10 & 11

Botany Bay (Kamay) and Kurnell

Botany Bay (33° 59' S, 151° 12' E) is a large inlet on the southern outskirts of present-day Sydney in Australia. The original inhabitants of the southern shore of the bay were the Gweagal clan of the Dharawal tribe. They called the point Cunnel (modern Kurnell). The small Gweagal clan were self-sufficient, hunting, gathering and fishing around the bay.

In April 1770, Cook sailed up the east coast of Australia. No landings were attempted until 28 April when, just north of Red Point and present-day Wollongong, Cook tried to land at Bulli but the surf swamped the boats and prevented him getting ashore. The next day, 29 April 1770, the *Endeavour* sailed into a large bay and anchored just off the inner shore of the bay's southern point. Local Gweagal people watched them arrive. The British rowed towards the shoreline in longboats and, as they landed (led by Isaac Smith, a cousin of Cook's wife), all but two Gweagal men ran away. The two remaining men faced the boats, waving spears over their heads and shouting to the strangers. The British tried to converse with the two who remained but no one, including Tupaia, could understand or be understood. The situation worsened and the British fired their guns and the Gweagal men threw their spears. For the rest of the stay no further direct contact took place. The Gweagal watched and followed at a distance. This happened when Gore made a journey up the bay to collect oysters.

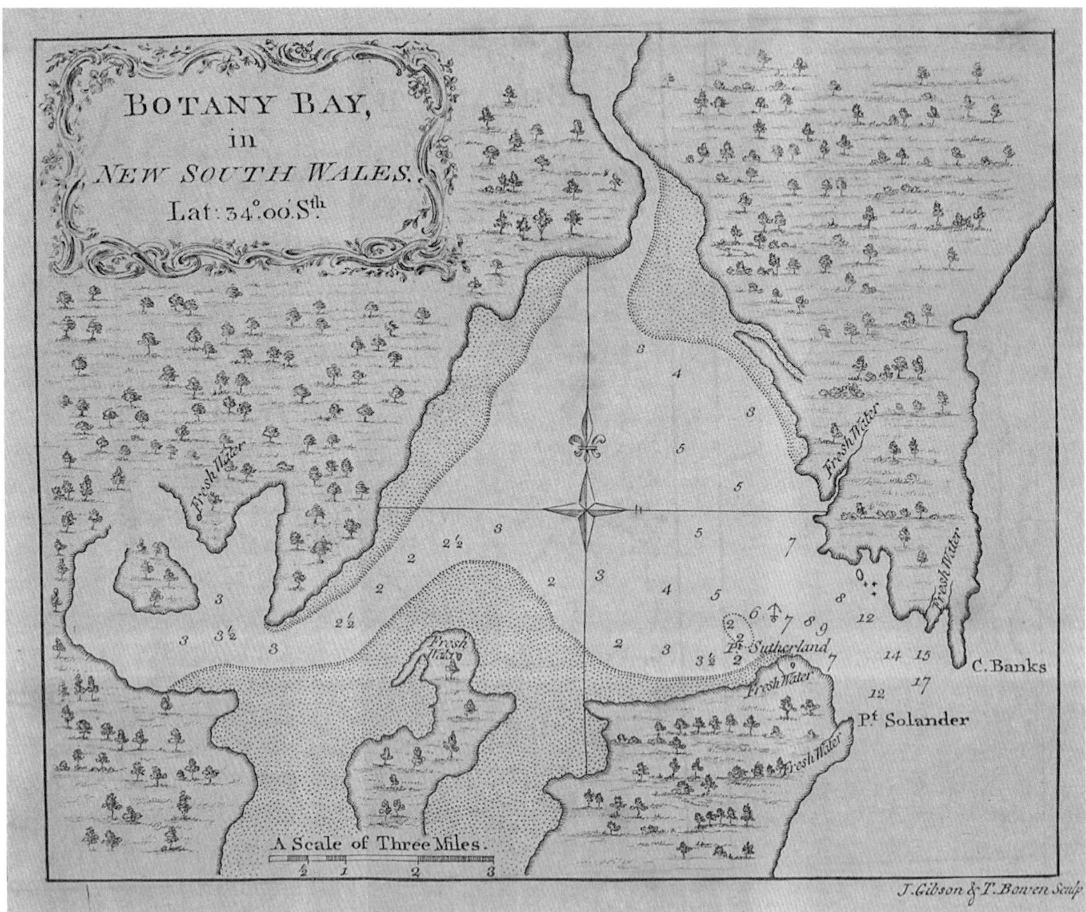

Botany Bay in New South Wales. Lat: 34° 00′ S. Engraved by J Gibson and T Bowen after Cook and Smith. (Hawkesworth fp 481)

The *Endeavour*, remained anchored in Botany Bay for eight days and Cook and his team of scientists explored and mapped the area. The British made several excursions around the bay including one up a river on the north side where they explored inland and commented on soils and vegetation (this river, near Sydney Airport, is now called Cook River). A crewman, Forby Sutherland, died on 1 May and was buried near the landing point (the inner point was named for him). Spoor and tracks of animals were seen but actual sightings were unsure (a small rat-like animal may have been a wombat). Banks and Solander collected many botanical specimens, occasioning the bay's eventual name. At first it had been called Sting-ray Bay after the many fish that had been caught.

On 6 May, Cook took the *Endeavour* out of Botany Bay and headed north, soon passing an inlet he named Port Jackson. The inlet would become the site of Australia's first European settlement and eventually became Sydney. The landing area at Kurnell, now within Botany Bay National Park, is commemorated as an important historic site.

See Also: Australia, First voyage

Bougainville, Louis-Antoine de (1729–1811)

Louis-Antoine de Bougainville was born in Paris on 11 November 1729, the son of a notary at the Chatalet. Bougainville showed an aptitude for mathematics and received special teaching from the Encylopaedist, d'Alembert. He wrote *Traité du calcul-intégral* in 1754. He studied law but abandoned that profession in 1753 to enter the army in the Corps of Musketeers. In 1755, he was sent to London as secretary to the French embassy, and became a member of the Royal Society. In 1756, he went to Canada as aide-de-camp to the Marquis de Montcalm; and having distinguished himself in the war against Britain, was rewarded with the rank of colonel and the cross of St Louis.

After the peace in 1763, Bougainville conceived the project of colonising the Isles Malouines (Falkland Islands) and made two voyages to initiate a French settlement. The Spanish objected to the settlement and, after pressure, the French government gave in to them. As compensation, Bougainville was offered the opportunity to lead an expedition to the Pacific.

Bougainville left Nantes in late 1766 and formally handed over the Malouines to Spain in 1767. He then headed into the Pacific. Accompanied by naturalists and astronomers, Bougainville visited Tahiti, the Samoan group, Espiritu Santo in Vanuatu and rediscovered the Solomon Islands, one of which, Bougainville, was named for him. He completed his circumnavigation of the world and returned to France in March 1769. Apart from interesting descriptions of Tahiti, which contributed to the debate on the idea of the 'Noble Savage', Bougainville's voyage added little to European knowledge of the Pacific.

Bougainville wrote an account of the voyage, *Voyage autour du monde*, which appeared in 1771. However, it lacked scientific contributions from his naturalist, Commerson, who had not returned to France and this diminished its impact. While it sold well, the work was not acknowledged in French society and no further voyages resulted. Bougainville, who had led the first scientific voyage to the Pacific, had missed his chance for immortality, which then passed to Cook. Instead, Bougainville joined the French navy and saw action off North America and in the West Indies during the War of American Independence. He was applauded for his actions in the Battle of Chesapeake Bay but censured for his lack of action at the Battle of the Saintes in April 1782. He married in 1780 and had four children.

Bougainville survived the French Revolution and became a favourite of Napoleon, who made him a senator, a comte, and a member of the Legion d'Honneur. Bougainville obtained the rank of vice-admiral in 1791. He was elected a member of the Institut at its formation, and became a member of the Board of Longitude. He died at Paris on 31 August 1811 and is interred in the Pantheon. While not being a great explorer, Bougainville was a most interesting man of many parts, a true renaissance man. As well as an island in the Solomons, his name was given to the *bougainvillaea* vine.

SEE ALSO: France and French reaction to Cook

Bouvet Island (Bouvetøya)

This uninhabited volcanic island, which lies on the Mid-Atlantic ridge (54° S, 3° 30' E), is one of the most isolated places on earth, being 994 miles (1600km) south-west of the Cape of Good Hope. It is only 22.5 square miles (58.5 sq km) in area and 93 per cent covered in ice. Norway runs an automated meteorological station on the island. Other islands are reputed to have been sighted in the vicinity, such as Lindsay and Thompson. The latter is now believed to have been destroyed by a volcanic explosion in 1895.

Bouvet Island was discovered on 1 January 1739 by Jean-Baptiste Lozier Bouvet sailing in the *Aigle*. He was unable to land, and failed to accurately fix the island's location. He was unsure, therefore, if the land he had seen was an island or part of the fabled Southern Continent. He named the headland Cape Circumcision.

Cook attempted to find Cape Circumcision in December 1772, but he was looking too far south owing to Bouvet's incorrect co-ordinates. Cook thought Bouvet had probably seen an iceberg. Near the end of his second voyage, Cook made a second attempt to find the cape. This time, *en route* from South Sandwich to the Cape, he was again far to the south of its actual position. Cook was able to state that, if it existed, it was not a part of Antarctica. Captain Lindsay, in the *Swan*, sighted Bouvet Island on 6 October 1808 and fixed its position.

SEE ALSO: Second voyage

Buchan, Alexander (?–1769)

Alexander Buchan sailed on the *Endeavour* as an artist. Nothing certain is known about Buchan before he joined the *Endeavour* voyage as one of the artists employed by Joseph Banks, though he was probably Scottish, possibly from North Berwick in East Lothian. He was taken on as the expedition's second artist to record the scenery and make a general pictorial account of the expedition, thus freeing Parkinson to concentrate on drawing the botanical and zoological specimens collected.

Buchan proved to be an epileptic and suffered a fit while accompanying the shore party on Tierra del Fuego on 16 January 1769. He recovered from this and no more attacks are mentioned over the next three months, during which he completed a number of drawings and paintings. His drawings of the Haush people of Tierra del Fuego at the Bay of Good Success are his best known. However, he suffered a fatal attack on 17 April 1769 at Matavai Bay in Tahiti. Buchan's body was buried at sea so as not to alert the Tahitians and in case a shore burial might offend native customs.

After Buchan's death, his drawings came into Banks' possession. With the exception of several drawings of Atlantic marine life now preserved with the drawings of Sydney Parkinson in the Natural History Museum, all of Buchan's known drawings are preserved in the British Library.

SEE ALSO: Artists on Cook's voyages, First voyage

Burney, James (1750–1821)

James Burney was born in London on 13 June 1750, the son of Charles Burney the musicologist. The family soon moved to King's Lynn where a daughter, Fanny, later to be a famous novelist and diarist, was born. The family was acquainted with the Vancouvers. In 1760, the Burneys moved back to London but James was dispatched into the Navy.

Burney became captain's servant on the *Princess Amelia,* serving in the Bay of Biscay. This was followed by service as a midshipman in the Mediterranean. In 1770, James sailed to Bombay with the East India Company. On his return, plans were being made for Cook's second voyage and Charles Burney used his friendship with the Earl of Sandwich, First Lord of the Admiralty, to secure James a position on board.

Burney sailed as an AB on the *Resolution* but after an illness forced the first lieutenant on the *Adventure* to return home from the Cape, he was promoted on 18 November 1772 to be second lieutenant on that ship under Tobias Furneaux. His most dramatic action on the voyage came when he was detailed to lead a party to Grass Cove, in Queen Charlotte Sound, New Zealand, which discovered that 11 of their colleagues had been killed the day before by Māori. Burney kept a log and a journal during the voyage, recording the music of various islanders, and he made surveys and drew charts.

The *Adventure* reached Britain in 1774 and Burney was involved with introducing Mai, the Raiatean, to London society. However, he was soon appointed second lieutenant on HMS *Cerburus* and sailed to Boston in Massachusetts. His father once again pulled strings and James was summoned back to Britain to sail on Cook's third voyage.

He was appointed first lieutenant on HMS *Discovery* under Charles Clerke. Clerke was delayed and so it fell to Burney to take the ship from the River Thames to Plymouth where its commander finally joined them. After Clerke's death in August 1779, Burney transferred to the *Resolution.* When the ships arrived at Orkney, Scotland, James King, who had taken over command of the *Discovery* was sent ahead to London by land, so by a strange twist of fate Burney commanded the ship on its last leg to the Thames. Burney kept a journal on the third voyage.

In November 1781, Burney was given charge of HMS *Latona,* which patrolled in the North Sea for several months. He was promoted post-captain in June 1782 and given command of HMS *Bristol,* which he sailed to India. Unfortunately, he became seriously ill and had to return home to Britain, ending his active naval career.

Burney married Sally Payne in 1785 and they had three children, though one died in infancy. In 1798, Burney eloped with his half-sister, Sarah Harriet, and they lived together for five years before James returned to his wife and children. He had begun a new career as a writer and from 1803 until 1817 the 5 volumes of his major work, *A Chronological History of the Discoveries in the South Seas or Pacific Ocean,* were published. They were followed in 1819 by *A Chronological History of the North-Eastern Voyages of Discovery; and of the early Eastern navigations of the Russians.* He was elected a Fellow of the Royal Society in 1809 and after a very long wait and much fruitless lobbying (he was probably tarnished through acquaintance with the Earl of Sandwich, who was now out of favour) he was promoted to rear-admiral on the retired list in 1821. A few months later he died on 17 November 1821, leaving a will (FRC 11/1653) and was buried in St Margaret's, Westminster.

There is a brief biography in the *DNB*, v3, p418. James Trevenen described him as 'not only a good man, but a good seaman, [and] a good officer'. Burney's Beach in Queen Charlotte Sound, New Zealand is named for him while Burney Island in the Arctic Ocean has reverted to being called Kolyuchin Island. Part of his journal for the second voyage has been published.

SEE ALSO: Second and Third voyages

Canada

When James Cook arrived at Halifax in the spring of 1758, he was a capable but undistinguished Sailing Master in the Royal Navy, serving in HMS *Pembroke*, 64 guns. Over the next nine years, as his active professional life developed in the waters of coastal Canada and Newfoundland, he was transformed from a simple warrant officer into a competent navigator, innovative chartmaker and surveyor whose superior skills led him to be selected to command the first of three epic voyages of oceanic exploration, and a role in the forefront of European scientific and philosophical investigation of the Pacific. Cook's experiences on the coasts of Nova Scotia, the Gulf and River Saint Lawrence, and on the coast of Newfoundland were, it can be argued, the anvil on which the steel of Cook's abilities were shaped. Those abilities would lead him to be later recognised as one of the most competent participants in the eighteenth century's European burst of seaborne exploration and scientific inquiry into the Pacific after the close of the Seven Years' War.

Cook's emergence as a surveyor and chartmaker began with his chance encounter with the Dutch-born military surveyor, Samuel Holland, at Louisbourg in the summer of 1758. Cook learned from Holland the techniques of land surveying, and combined that science with existing naval chartmaking techniques to produce chartwork and marine surveys of a wholly new level of accuracy. His participation in the ascent to Quebec in 1759 of the Royal Navy fleet carrying James Wolfe's troops, his key role in the success of that ascent, and his preparation of charts resulting from that voyage and other survey work on the Nova Scotian and Newfoundland coasts as the Seven Years War ended led to his selection to undertake a major survey of the west and south coasts of Newfoundland. The extraordinary quality of this work, coupled with concurrent demonstrations of his astronomical observation skills, led to his selection in 1768 to command HM Bark *Endeavour* on her Pacific voyage, on behalf of the Royal Society and the Royal Navy, when both parties could not agree on another suggested commander.

The examination of James Cook's period of North

Ships in the harbour at Halifax, Nova Scotia, in the 1760s. (Engraving published by R Short, 1766)

American service arguably reveals that the development of Cook's innovative chartmaking and surveying skills and other qualities which led to the selection for the Pacific voyages, came as a direct consequence of his experiences in North American waters, and that the period 1758–67 was not only the most formative for his life, but arguably for British and European exploration of the Pacific in the remainder of the eighteenth century.

Cook had entered the Navy in 1755, for reasons of his own and much to the astonishment of both the Walker brothers whose employ he left, and the Royal Navy, who were only too pleased to receive him into their pay. At the time of his entry into the Navy he was a highly competent coastal mariner who had learned his trade in the Walkers' colliers along the treacherous North Sea coast and on a few passages to Ireland and Norway. His practical seamanship was unmatched, and combined with his physical and personal qualities to produce promotion out of the ranks of the common seamen within a month of his joining the Navy. His scholarly self-instruction in mathematics and the scientific bases of navigation were not yet developed to a similar degree, however, and it would only achieve a equal level of competence with his physical seamanship when he had had the benefit of additional encouragement from perceptive commanders such as Hugh Palliser of *Eagle*, and, in particular, John Simcoe of *Pembroke*, under whom Cook first came to North American waters.

The arrival of *Pembroke* at Halifax in the spring of 1758, with over 20 of the ship's complement ill with scurvy, brought Cook to a harbour that arguably he was to know better than any in his career save his collier home port of Whitby, as from 1758 until 1762 Cook was based at Halifax, first as Sailing Master of *Pembroke*, and then of *Northumberland*, 64 guns. The latter vessel remained on station at Halifax with a small squadron when the armada that had carried James Wolfe to Quebec returned to Britain. The transatlantic passage had been Cook's longest, and *Pembroke*'s ships' company had been so incapacitated by scurvy that the ship had remained at anchor in Halifax as the remainder of the squadron with which she had crossed sailed northward for the assault on the fortress of Louisbourg. The genesis of Cook's almost obsessive concern for the health and cleanliness of his crews has not been fully documented, but it may have arisen from his experiences in the tidy, well-kept ships of the Quaker Walkers compounded by the dismay at first seeing how a transoceanic vessel like *Pembroke* could be rendered incapable of service by scurvy, which usually did not hold on coastal vessels.

Pembroke finally embarked her convalescent seamen from the hospital at Halifax and sailed north along the iron, evergreen-clad coastline of Nova Scotia to join the fleet under Vice-Admiral Richard Boscawen, which had carried the assault troops of General Jeffrey Amherst to Louisbourg. *Pembroke* arrived at the fleet's anchorage in Gabarus Bay, south of the fortress, on 12 June 1758, to learn that a successful landing had been made on 8 June, and a slow but steady investment of the fortress was underway. The task of the fleet was largely to provide support to the troops ashore, which proved a challenging task in the abnormally squally and tumultuous weather that swept over the anchorage. Over 100 boats from the various warships and transports were lost in the powerful surf that swept the single landing beach, at what later came to be known as Kennington Cove.

It was just off this beach that the most significant event in James Cook's transformation from an undistinguished sailing master into something far more took place. On 27 July 1758, one day after the French garrison had surrendered, Cook came in to Kennington Cove beach with *Pembroke*'s longboat, on unrecorded business ashore. As Cook arrived, his attention was drawn to the figure of an engineer officer in the grasslands just off the beach, employing a strange device and apparently making some kind of observations of the cove. Intrigued, Cook approached him, and asked what he was about. He soon found himself in conversation with a pleasant man of about his own age, Samuel Holland – more properly Van Hollandt, as he was Dutch in origin – who explained that he was carrying out a survey of the cove using a plane table. A plane table had a small, square flat surface supported on a tripod; Holland would sight over the top of the table at distinguishing marks using a rotating telescope fixed to the table's centre, and make notes of those observations. Cook learned that the process allowed the creation of an accurate diagram in which all physical features could be placed in correct relation to one another, and to a base line with a known magnetic heading, obtained from a box compass affixed to the table. It was a concept that grasped Cook's imagination immediately, and he extracted from the agreeable Holland a promise to instruct Cook in the technique the next day. On returning aboard *Pembroke*, Cook reported his encounter to Captain John Simcoe, who not only approved of Cook's initiative but requested that Holland be brought on board the vessel to impart the instruction to Simcoe as well as Cook. Although Cook would later benefit from association with other highly competent surveyors during his stay in Canada, such as J F W DesBarres, author of the *American Neptune*, it was this contact and period of learning with Holland that was instrumental in launching Cook toward his own apogee of achievement as an innovative maritime surveyor and cartographer. Through instructions that all Masters and Master's Mates had to observe in 1758, Cook was required as a matter of duty to produce charts and sailing directions for any harbour his ship visited. The quality of these drawings and writings varied as greatly as the capacities of the men who undertook them. For Cook, the electrifying realisation which emerged out of the instructional sessions with Holland was that a combination of land surveying methods and accuracy with these established methods of marine sounding, surveying and chartmaking would offer the prospect of new exactitude in the heretofore very inexact science of marine charting. Cook's signal contribution to the state and competency of marine hydrography was in this innovative exercise of two traditions of observation as a single art with a uniform standard of precision, which raised chartmaking and the recorded basis of navigation to a whole new level. The importance to Cook's career, and to the history of western exploratory hydrography and chartmaking, of that chance meeting on the windy beach of Kennington Cove near Louisbourg, Cape Breton Island, cannot be overstated.

As *Pembroke* rode at anchor within the harbour of Louisbourg in the waning summer of 1758, Cook continued to develop his surveying skills under Holland's tutelage until the demands of war called him to put them unexpectedly to use. *Pembroke* was dispatched with a small squadron to carry troops into the Gulf of Saint Lawrence, where the army was to carry out the inglorious work of burning and destroying French settlements that might send supplies to the colonial capital at Quebec. One of these was the town and harbour of Gaspé, on the mainland. Cook's reaction to the business of carrying war to a defenceless civilian population is unknown, but he busied himself on the Gaspé expedition with observing, sketching and sounding, doing the latter from *Pembroke*'s boats and possibly exercising his new land survey skills as well. On the return of the squadron to Louisbourg, Cook appears to have secured from Simcoe permission to spend time penning a chart and survey of the harbour of Gaspé. The result was a carefully-drawn two-sheet effort in a scale of two inches to the mile, and Cook was successful in obtaining its publication in London by Mount & Page in 1759. The publication of this chart of a small, beleaguered Canadian port marked Cook's emergence into the serious realm of surveying and charting beyond the ordinary duty of a Sailing Master.

The bleak days of late autumn fell over the captured fortress, and the Royal Navy vessels were ordered back to Halifax, to secure themselves for the long northern winter. *Pembroke* came to anchor in Halifax harbour on 19 November 1758, below the muddy, rough-sawn town and its palisaded hilltop citadel. The campaign of the following summer would, according to a grand strategy ordered by Prime Minister William Pitt, be an ascent of the Saint Lawrence with an army like that which had taken Louisbourg, but with orders to capture Quebec itself. Cook's production of the Gaspé chart and his increasing competence in charting and survey work, led to his being ordered, along with Holland, to busy themselves in *Pembroke*'s great cabin under Simcoe's encouraging eye in the compilation of all known French and other charts of the Saint Lawrence into a folio that could be used to guide the great fleet up the treacherous passages of the river.

The coming of spring led to the arrival of troop transports from Britain and a sizeable escort of warships, all under the command of Vice-Admiral Charles Saunders, who had replaced Boscawen. Cook's *Pembroke* was assigned to an advance squadron under Rear-Admiral Durrell that sailed from Halifax on 5 May 1759 and attempted to work its way into the Gulf and River Saint Lawrence, which was choked by an unusually heavy ice pack. With the main force halting at Louisbourg to pick up additional troops for the attack on Quebec, Durrell's force busied itself penetrating the river and allowing for the discovery of the safe channel – the French had taken up what buoyage there was – and the completion of a workable chart of the river. In *Pembroke*, Cook soon found that the compilation of French charts was insufficiently accurate to be relied upon, and took the initiative in forming a sounding flotilla of ship's boats from the squadron, each carrying that ship's Sailing Master or Master's Mate, which sounded ahead of the fleet as it advanced up the several hundred miles of the river in stages, depending upon whether the winds were fair or foul. The greatest challenge to this technique came just below Quebec, at the eastern end of the Île d'Orleans, where the safe navigation channel was known to cross from the northern side of the river to the southern for entry into the wide Basin below Quebec, in a swooping track known as the Traverse. Cook's boats sounded diligently while the squadron waited at anchor downstream, and discovered that the Traverse was a narrow channel no wider in some places than the extreme beam of some of Saunders' largest ships. Cook devised a method of marking the channel whereby the flotilla of boats moored themselves as buoys on either side of the channel, marking a clear if constricted passage into the wider anchorage of the Basin. With a favourable east wind, all 140-odd vessels of the fleet sailed one by one in slow majesty through this remarkable assemblage. By 27 June 1759, all of Saunders' fleet, including his flagship *Neptune*, 90 guns, had come to anchor in the Basin below Quebec, and the assault could begin.

The siege, however, would last all summer, as the army's commander, Major-General James Wolfe, could not decide on a method of attacking the very formidable French defences, and the towering rocky citadel of the heights of Quebec themselves. Cook was kept busy in sounding those waters that were safe to operate boats in – Indian warriors and Canadian militia would frequently race out in swift birchbark canoes to attack naval longboats engaged in sounding – and had some controversy attached to his name when an abortive assault landing on the Beauport shore below Quebec went awry, at least in part because the assault transports and boats had gone aground on a ledge Cook's surveys had not reported. Cook's energy in continuing with the sounding and chartwork, when his other duties would allow, nonetheless had brought him by this point, scarcely a year after first asking Samuel Holland what his strange instrument was called, to be referred to as the 'Surveyor of the Fleet'. Cook played no direct role, as far as is known, in the night assault of 12 September by troops under Wolfe that scaled the heights to the Plains of Abraham by means of the pathway at the Anse au Foulon. At the successful conclusion of the siege, when Saunders' main force was preparing to return to Britain bearing with it the body of James Wolfe, Cook was transferred into *Northumberland*, 64, which would remain at Halifax over the coming winter and return to Quebec in 1760 to support the garrison the British were leaving behind. Cook used the descent of the river to complete observations made on the way up by both himself and Holland, and on arrival at Halifax was able to complete 'A New Chart Of The River St Lawrence', which was a huge work of some twelve sheets, in dimensions each 35in by 90in, with a main scale of one inch to two leagues [six miles] and an inset scale of one inch to one league. In April of 1760, Vice-Admiral Saunders recommended to the Admiralty that Cook's application to publish this enormous chart folio be granted. Cook's charts brought a new level of reliable navigation to the great river just as its new custodians needed such reference; but it had been Cook's leadership in the trying work of finding the passage up for the huge fleet that had provided James Wolfe and his troops the opportunity Pitt wished them to have: the capture and retention of the heart of Canada.

Northumberland lay at Halifax over the winter of 1759–60, cocooned against the ice and snow, and Cook continued his personal studies of mathematics, navigation and astronomy, 'bringing in his hand' as he completed the great work of the Saint Lawrence chart. Cook would return again to Quebec the following summer, albeit briefly, but now entered into a period where his life and activities were centered on Halifax and the routine of the squadron. He nonetheless produced no less than four superb charts of Halifax harbour, and worked with the accomplished military surveyor J F W DesBarres, who like Cook had made land surveying and marine charting into a composite science, and would produce the masterful charting of the Nova Scotian and adjacent coasts entitled *The Atlantic Neptune.*

In 1762, a last French attempt to secure bargaining power in the peace treaty which was to end the Seven Years War led to their attack and capture of the port of St John's on the rocky eastern shore of Newfoundland. *Northumberland* took part in the combined force that successfully forced the French out of Newfoundland, and during this service Cook produced charts of Placentia, on the west side of the Avalon Peninsula, of St John's harbour, and of two fishing ports, Harbour Grace and Carbonear. In addition, he now produced a compendium 'Description of the Sea Coast of Novascotia [*sic*], Cape Breton Island, and Newfoundland', along with detailed Sailing Directions which would be published in several editions of the *Newfoundland Pilot*, produced by Thomas Jeffreys in London. So extraordinary was the quality of this work that, at the end of the war when *Northumberland* was paid off and Cook might have expected to re-enter the struggle for survival in the civilian world, he was retained as a result of requests made by Thomas Graves, governor of Newfoundland, to do further survey and charting work of that island. His first task was to complete, in the summer of 1763, a speedy but reliable survey of the islands of St Pierre and Miquelon which were being turned over to the French. Cook completed the work, to what was now his customary standard of excellence, while the newly-appointed French governor paced fuming on the quarterdeck of his ship.

Thomas Graves was replaced as governor of Newfoundland by Hugh Palliser, who had commanded Cook in HMS *Eagle* before Cook had come to Canada. Palliser now continued Cook's work as a surveyor and chartmaker by having him undertake a detailed survey of major portions of the coast of Newfoundland, in a pattern that would see Cook spend the summer on the island's coast working from his small command, the schooner (later brig) *Grenville*, and returning to Britain for the winter to work up fair copies of his charts and Sailing Directions. From 1764 to the end of the summer of 1767 Cook managed a survey of the west and south coasts of Newfoundland to such exacting detail that his charts remained in use within living memory. He demonstrated an additional and important skill during this period, one that would bear heavily on his career. On 5 August 1766, aware that an eclipse of the sun was predicted, Cook observed it carefully from the Burgeo Islands off the south coast of Newfoundland, and wrote up his observations. These he presented in the autumn to Dr John Nevis of the Royal Society, who in turn read them to a meeting of the Society. Bevis went on to report that Cook's observations allowed another astronomer to compare them successfully with a set taken at Oxford, and to deduce accurately the longitude of both places of observation. Cook's expertise was duly noted by the gentlemen of the Society.

In April of 1768, as Cook was preparing for another summer on the Newfoundland coast, he was informed that the Admiralty had decided to send another individual in his place, the highly competent Michael Lane, and to employ Cook elsewhere. Cook had therefore completed a remarkable four years of surveying and navigating on one of the most varied and challenging coastlines in the world, and the products of all this work were four extraordinarily detailed, accurate, and carefully penned charts of Newfoundland, with accompanying sailing directions. They joined the enormous chart of the Gulf and River Saint Lawrence as a striking advancement in the professional standards of marine surveying and charting in waters of North America which were vital to Britain's interests. It had not been lost on both the Admiralty and the Royal Society that Cook, though technically still at the warrant rank of Sailing Master, had effectively commanded a minor war vessel in a lengthy and distant commission, had produced superlative chartwork and surveying, and had also demonstrated a professional capability as an astronomical observer and mathematician. When the Royal Society and the Admiralty could not agree on the appointment of Alexander Dalrymple to command a small vessel which was to set off for the South Pacific to carry out astronomical observations and survey new coastlines should they be found, it was not long before the name of Cook came to the fore. Before 1768 closed he had become Lieutenant Cook, in command of HM Bark *Endeavour*, and bound on a world-girdling voyage of scientific observation, exploration, and discovery.

The shaping of Cook's fine metal into the instrument selected for this task had taken place in the waters now known as Canada, in the River and Gulf of Saint Lawrence, the Nova Scotian coast, and on the rocky shores of Newfoundland. As much as his growth and development in the world of the North Sea colliers, it was Canada that turned a competent but undistinguished warrant officer into the seaman and surveyor capable of the Pacific voyages, and the greater destiny they would hold for him.

By Victor Suthren

See Also: Newfoundland, Quebec

Cape Town and the Cape

For many centuries, Cape Town (33° 56' S, 18° 28' E) on Table Bay next to the Cape of Good Hope, has occupied a very important position in controlling sea traffic to the Indian Ocean and beyond. The port acted as a recovery and restocking point for countless ships. The Cape Peninsula has a long and eventful history with evidence of prehistoric people from 600,000 years ago. Khoikhoi (Hottentot) and San (Bushmen) people occupied the region prior to the arrival of Europeans. Bartolomeu Dias, the Portuguese sailor, who was attempting to find a sea route to the riches of the East, rounded the Cape in early 1488.

On 6 April 1652, the Dutchman, Jan van Riebeeck, stepped ashore at Table Bay to establish a post for the Dutch East India Company, where their ships,

The Dutch settlement at the foot of Table Mountain and the anchorage with ships of the Dutch East India Company. (Etching published by Robert Sayer, 1754)

sailing to the Dutch East Indies, could restock. A fort was established at the foot of Table Mountain and it soon grew into the settlement of Kaapstad or Cape Town. The local Khoi-San people were driven away.

Cook first visited the Cape in 1771 on his return to Britain. He made further visits on the second and third voyages. Gore was unable to make Table Bay at the end of the third voyage and anchored instead in False Bay to the south. When Cook called in to the Cape, it was still a Dutch settlement and he was required to observe formalities in order to obtain supplies and make repairs. The British annexed the Cape in 1806.

Captain Cook country

Captain Cook Country is a term formed by the Captain Cook Tourism Association to describe part of Cleveland, a region of north-east England associated with James Cook. It stretches from the historic port of Whitby, with its ancient cliff-top abbey, west along the rugged coastline to the mouth of the River Tees and Cook's birthplace at Marton in Middlesbrough. Inland, the dramatic North York Moors form a beautiful back-drop to quiet market towns and peaceful villages. Marton has been swallowed by the industrial conurbation of Teesside but much of the scenery along the way is little changed from the days Cook lived there.

A Captain Cook Country Tour has been developed that links places associated with the early life of the explorer. Various museums have been created in the region celebrating different aspects of Cook's childhood and the tour visits them all. The circular tour, 70 miles (113km) long begins at Marton, Cook's birthplace and leads via Great Ayton and Roseberry Topping to the spectacular coast at Staithes. Further east, Whitby offers two museums with Cook material and many other features redolent of Cook. The route then leads back across the beautiful North York Moors via Guisborough to Marton. Nearby Middlesbrough and Stockton also have sites with relevance to Cook such as the Bottle of Notes and an *Endeavour* replica.

SEE ALSO: Cleveland

Captain Cook Society (CCS)

An international society for people interested in James Cook; its main activities are a quarterly journal, *Cook's Log*, a web site (www.CaptainCookSociety.com) and occasional meetings.

The CCS was started by some philatelists interested in collecting stamps portraying Captain Cook, his ships, etc. It quickly grew to encompass people with specialist interests in coins, books, engravings, etc, and other people with a more general interest in James Cook and the results of his voyages – scientific and artistic. The CCS now has over 350 members living in over 20 countries, many of whom have contacted each other to enhance their knowledge of a shared interest.

Formed in 1975 as the Captain Cook Study Unit, the society changed its name to the Captain Cook Society in 2001. Membership is open to all with one rate for everyone throughout the world. A branch was formed in Australia in 1984, with its own newsletter, *Endeavour Lines*, and occasional meetings.

Cook's Log, the paper-based journal, is produced four times a year with a mix of research articles, descriptions of individuals' visits to Cook sites, book reviews, news of Cook-related developments around the world, information about stamp issues, items for sale and auction, and details of members' own particular interests in Cook. Back issues are always available. A CD-ROM has been produced of all issues, with many illustrations appearing in colour, electronic links between related articles, a list of all articles on the CD-ROM, and a searchable index of all words making it easier to find information.

The Society's web site was created in 1997. It reflects the society's activities, reproduces many articles published in its journal (including an invaluable chronology of Cook's life) and takes advantage of the features of the web to include many items for which there is insufficient room in the journal. There is an extensive set of links to other places on the web featuring Cook.

By Ian Boreham

See Also: Philately, Websites and CD-ROMs

Cartographic results of Cook's voyages

Cook's surveying career began on 27 July 1758, the day after the French surrendered Louisburg to the British. That afternoon Cook, then master of the 64-gun *Pembroke,* Captain John Simcoe, landed at Kennington Cove to stretch his legs. Here his curiosity was aroused by an army officer carrying a small square table, supported by a tripod, who set the table down in several places and then squinted along the top in various directions, after which he would make notes in a pocket-book. The officer turned out to be Samuel Holland, a military surveyor, and his instrument a plane table, an essential instrument in topographical surveying. Cook invited Holland on board the *Pembroke* to meet Simcoe, a man of scientific leanings, to enable them both to learn more about this instrument. This meeting with Holland had almost immediate results. A short time later when the *Pembroke* was part of a squadron sent to raid and destroy French settlements in the Bay of Gaspé, Cook took the opportunity to survey the bay, the results of which were published the following year by the well-known firm of Mount and Page. That winter, which was spent in Halifax Harbour, enabled Cook to renew his acquaintance with Holland, during which they worked together in compiling a chart of the St Lawrence River from 'plans in Admiral Durell's possession', which was used as a basis for the so-called 'Exact Chart of the River St Lawrence' published by Jefferys in 1757. That same winter, ably tutored by Captain Simcoe, Cook studied mathematics and astronomy, both fundamental to the latest techniques in finding longitude.

During the following year's campaign, Cook, with other masters of the fleet, took part in the important survey of The Traverse in the approaches to Quebec, which enabled the British fleet to negotiate this dangerous stretch of water and invest the city, thus ensuring its eventual capitulation. Shortly afterwards Cook was appointed master of the 70-gun *Northumberland*, Captain Alexander, Lord Colvill. Over the next few years Cook appears to have devoted his time mainly to the routine tasks of a master, during which he compiled some useful sailing directions for the St Lawrence River and its approaches, a number of copies of which have survived in various collections. He also routinely surveyed Halifax Harbour, which has survived in manuscript form. However, 'A Draught of the Harbour of Halifax Surveyed...by James Cook, when Master of his Majesty's Ship the *Mars*' which was engraved by E Bowen and published by the author, Dec. 1766' has caused considerably confusion, since it was not the work of the future Pacific explorer, but the work of a different James Cook.

The next milestone in Cook's surveying career occurred in 1762, when an expedition was mounted to recapture St John's, Newfoundland, which had been captured by the French as a final fling in the Seven Years War. The expedition was commanded by Commodore Colvill, flying his broad pennant in the *Northumberland.* This enabled Cook to draw two coastal profiles in the approaches to the island, to survey Placentia Harbour and the Bay of Bulls and carry out a running survey of the approaches to St John's. After the capture of St John's, Cook surveyed the harbour itself and then, in conjunction with J F W DesBarres, later well known for his *Atlantic Neptune*, Grace and Carbonear Harbour. In his report to the Admiralty, Colvill wrote, 'that from my Experience of Mr Cook's Genius and Capacity, I think him well qualified for the Work he has performed, and for greater Undertakings of the same kind.' Although the Admiralty's sole response to Colvill's letter was the routine endorsement 'Rec^{d}' with the date, its effect was far reaching. When Thomas Graves, the Governor of Newfoundland, asked for a marine surveyor to chart the west coast of Newfoundland, it appears that he specifically asked for Cook, having been himself present at the recapture of St John's. Thus these 172 surveys led directly to Cook being appointed first as marine surveyor of Newfoundland and subsequently to the *Endeavour* and his three Pacific voyages.

Cook was employed on the survey of Newfoundland from 1763 to 1767 in the 68-ton Massachusetts-built schooner *Grenville*, with a crew of ten including himself, during which he surveyed, to a high standard of accuracy, the whole of the west coast and most of the south coast of Newfoundland and part of Labrador. In his surviving journal and log Cook gives very little information of the survey methods he used, but it is clear that in sheltered bays and anchorages he measured a base on shore and erected flags as survey marks. On long stretches of coast he landed to observe a rudimentary system of triangulation, which he tied in where possible to a series of observation spots whose latitude he observed with considerable accuracy. Cook was, however, unable to take observations to obtain his longitude with the result that both his manuscript and the resulting engraved charts were not graduated for longitude. However, in August 1766 Cook observed an eclipse of the sun from which a John Bevis was able to compute the longitude of Cook's observation spot, which the surveyor was able to incorporate in his sailing directions and to compute the longitude of various other places on the south coast of the island. Cook employed Thomas Jefferys to publish his surveys in 1769–70 in *A Collection of Charts of the Coasts of Newfoundland and Labradore &c... Drawn from Original Surveys taken by James Cook and Michael Lane, Surveyors, Joseph Gilbert and other Officers in the King's Service*. They were later incorporated in the famous volume *The North America Pilot*. Cook's sailing directions were consolidated into *The Newfoundland Pilot*, also published by Jefferys in 1769. The quality of Cook's surveys were such that they were not superseded in part until the 1830s by the surveys of Captain Henry Wolsey Bayfield, who was a great admirer of Cook's work, commenting on 26 August 1833, when off Cape Rich, 'Cook's Survey appears excellent as far as I have been able to judge and the Soundings are also correct'.

In 1768, Cook was promoted lieutenant and appointed by the Admiralty in command of the *Endeavour* Bark on the first of his three Pacific voyages. For almost 200 years knowledge of the cartographic results of Cook's Pacific voyages was confined to the engraved charts in the official accounts of these voyages and the numerous unofficial accounts published in the British Isles and in various European countries, based on these accounts. Navigators working in the Pacific carried Cook's *Voyages*, not only for the charts and navigational views they contained, but also for descriptions of the coasts and the native peoples they might encounter. While these accounts were still readily available, private chart publishers in the British Isles saw little need to publish single-sheet charts. There were, however, a few exceptions, such as three charts by Alexander Dalrymple of the east coast of Australia and various small-scale charts covering the Pacific as a whole. Thus many of the surveys carried out by junior officers on board Cook's ships remained in relative obscurity in various logs and journals in the Admiralty archives until their transfer to the Public Record Office (now the National Archives) in about 1870 and in other institutions.

Cook's personal copies of his Pacific and some of his Newfoundland surveys were kept by his widow until she passed them some time before her death to her cousin Admiral Isaac Smith. Eventually some of these were acquired by the British Museum until their transfer to the newly constituted British Library in 1972. Others were acquired by the Australian collectors William Dixson and J A Ferguson, which they eventually bequeathed to the State Library of New South Wales and the National Library of Australia. These became more widely known by the publication by the Trustees of the State Library of New South Wales in 1928 of *The Bibliography of Captain James Cook*, with a much fuller second edition in 1970 under the editorship of M K Beddie. Several charts were also acquired by the Alexander Turnbull Library, the National Library of New Zealand.

It was only when the Hakluyt Society published Cook's Pacific journals between 1955 and 1967, under the editorship of J C Beaglehole, that the extent of Cook's cartographic achievements became known, since the Society included in the preliminary pages of the these volumes details of the graphic records of each voyage and their locations, compiled by R A Skelton, the Map Curator of the British Museum, together with a selection of the surviving manuscript charts in an accompanying atlas. Finally, it was not until the Hakluyt Society published between 1988 and 1997 *The Charts and Coastal Views of Captain Cook's Voyages*, under the chief editorship of Andrew David, that the full extent of the cartographic record of Cook's three voyages became known.

The principal collection of manuscript charts by Cook relating to his first voyage to the Pacific is contained in Additional Manuscript 7085 in the British Library, with an elaborate title page 'Charts, Plans, Views and Drawings, taken on board His Majestys Bark *Endeavour* in the Years 1768, 1769 and 1770, by Lieut[t] Jam[s] Cook Commander', together with a contents list comprising 42 numbered folios. Of these, 26 folios comprised manuscript charts and plans by Cook, drawn by Isaac Smith, master's mate, who had also served with Cook in the *Grenville*. The remaining folios consist of drawings of artefacts, landscapes and coastal views drawn by Charles Praval, who joined the *Endeavour* as a supernumerary, a week before her departure from Batavia. Other surveys were carried out by Robert Molyneaux, the *Endeavour*'s master and Richard Pickersgill, master's mate. All the engraved charts in the published account of this voyage are based on Cook's surveys.

There is no principal collection of manuscript charts by Cook relating to his second voyage to the Pacific. However, an important collection of fourteen charts by Cook were originally contained in the journal he forwarded to the Admiralty from the Cape of Good Hope, now held in the National Archives at Adm 55/108. Eleven of these charts have, however, been extracted for protection are now held individually at MFQ 533 and MPI 85 to 94. Once again the majority of these charts were drawn by Isaac Smith, but some of them were drawn by Able Seaman Henry Roberts, a talented artist and draughtsman. Individual charts by Cook are also held in the British Library in Additional Manuscripts 15500, 15743, 27887 and 31360. These are drawn by Isaac Smith, Henry Roberts and an unidentified artist. Many of the other second voyage officers also carried out surveys. Most notable of these are those carried out by Joseph Gilbert, master of the *Resolution*, whose log, now held in the National Archives at Adm 55/107, contains 30 charts and coastal views. An important chart by Gilbert, titled 'Part of the Southern Hemisphere shewing the *Resolution*'s track through the Pacific and Southern Ocean' on loan from the United Kingdom Hydrographic Office, is held in the National Maritime Museum at G201:3/4. The astronomer, William Wales, also carried out a number of surveys, which are held in Cambridge University Library at RGO 14/58. All the engraved charts in the published account of this voyage, except one, are based on Cook's surveys. The exception is 'A Sketch of Van Diemen Land, Explored by Capt[n] Furneaux, in March 1773'.

Once again there is no principal collection of manuscript charts by Cook relating to his third voyage to the Pacific. During this voyage Cook delegated much of the survey work to his junior officers, principally to William Bligh, master of the *Resolution*, although only three manuscript surveys by Bligh have survived. This is probably because he took many of them with him in the fateful voyage of the *Bounty*, recording in his account of that voyage that he was unable to save 'a box with my surveys, drawings, and remarks for fifteen years past, which were numerous'. Bligh's role as Cook's principal surveyor is supported by the fact that he was allocated one-eighth of the profits from the sale of the official account of the voyage, less one hundred guineas. His massive 'Chart of the Discoveries of His Majesty's Ships *Resolution* and *Discovery* on the Coast of Asia and America in search of a communication between the Pacific and Western Ocean' held in the United Kingdom Hydrographic Office, at A317 Press 88, is perhaps the most impressive cartographic record of all three of Cook's Pacific voyages. During this voyage, Henry Roberts, now master's mate on board the *Resolution*, carried out a number of surveys as did Edward Riou from the same ship. On board the *Discovery* Thomas Edgar, her master, Lieutenant James Burney and Midshipman George Vancouver all carried out surveys as did the astronomer William Bayly. All the engraved charts in the published account of this voyage have now been attributed to Cook or to missing surveys by Cook and Bligh, except the eastern harbour on the north side of Eimeo (Moorea) which has been attributed to Edgar.

The cartographic results of Cook's voyages illustrate his genius as a hydrographic surveyor. The surveys he carried out when he was master of the *Pembroke* and the *Northumberland* were what one would expect of any capable master, whose responsibility included navigation and carrying out minor surveys. Cook's survey of Newfoundland superseded earlier surveys, which depicted inaccurately the general run of the west and south coasts of the island. His task therefore was to improve on the existing charts by as an accurate survey as possible. However, in the Pacific, Cook was a more a discoverer than a surveyor, forcing him to adapt his survey methods accordingly. For instance, during his first Pacific voyage, had he adopted the same standard of accuracy that he had achieved in Newfoundland, he would only have had sufficient time to survey part of

New Zealand's North Island and would have had to abandon any attempt to survey the east coast of Australia. Nevertheless, his resulting surveys were remarkably accurate, due in no small measure to his ability, during his first Pacific voyage, with the help of Charles Green, the astronomer appointed to the expedition, to obtain his longitude by the newly developed method of lunar distances. This method of finding longitude was further refined during his second and third voyages by the use of Larcum Kendall's chronometer K2, with the help of the astronomer William Wales, during the second voyage and by James King during his third voyage.

Cook's cartographic achievements are best illustrated by the world chart he instructed Henry Roberts to compile during the third voyage. This chart was completed at the end of the voyage, using all known sources, and was included in the atlas accompanying the published account of the voyage as 'A General Chart Exhibiting the Discoveries made by Captn James Cook in this and his two preceeding Voyages'. It gives an excellent overall picture of Cook's cartographic achievements during his three Pacific voyages, including all the major land masses in this vast ocean, showing that only a few minor islands were left for Cook's successors to discover and survey.

By Andrew David

See Also: David (Andrew), Surveys and running surveys

Cats (Barks)

Cat was the name given to a type of vessel used in the North Sea in the eighteenth century. The name Bark was sometimes used for the same type of vessel. They were employed to move coal from the Tyne to London and were strongly built so they could carry about 600 tons of coal. Cats were based on a Norwegian model with a narrow canoe stern, projecting quarters and a deep waist. They were noticeable for not carrying a figurehead on the bow. They had a shallow draught, which helped when inshore and near the sandbanks around the mouth of the Thames.

When James Cook was appointed to lead the 1768 voyage to the Pacific, he found that the Navy Board had already selected a ship of this type, the *Earl of Pembroke*. Cook was experienced with cats, having spent his apprenticeship on them from 1747 to 1755. The *Earl of Pembroke* was renamed HM Bark *Endeavour*. The word bark was used in the name to differentiate the vessel from an existing HMS *Endeavour*.

A watercolour painting of a cat, or collier bark, leaving Whitby harbour around 1790, by John Bird. (Captain Cook Memorial Museum, Whitby)

See Also: Cook's ships, North Sea and the coal trade

Charlton, William (1758–1810)

William Charlton sailed on the third voyage on the *Resolution* as an AB. He kept a journal. Charlton attended the Naval Academy at Portsmouth from 1772 until 1775 in company with Ward and Trevenen. He became a lieutenant in May 1782 and was in command of *Helena*, 14 guns, in Jamaica from 1793 until 1795. From 1799, he commanded the gun brig *Hasty* and is listed as still being in charge when he died. He was made a commander in January 1806 and a captain in June 1810. He was born in London in 1758 and died on 7 August 1810, leaving a will (FRC 11/1518).

See Also: Third voyage

Chronometers

No easy, precise method of calculating a ship's longitude on the open seas had been invented by the middle of the eighteenth century. Instruments had been developed to measure latitude but calculating how far a ship travelled east or west remained a problem, often with tragic results. In 1714, the British Parliament had offered a prize of £20,000 to anyone who could discover a method of finding the longitude within 30 miles during a sea voyage. The Board of Longitude was set up to administer the prize. John Harrison, a British carpenter turned watchmaker, believed that a chronometer would provide the answer. If a chronometer could be made that accurately kept the time of the prime meridian at Greenwich, then the difference between it and local time would give the longitude of the place of observation.

Harrison made it his life's work to develop a

John Harrison created a series of chronometers to help determine longitude. This, his second machine (H2.) was finished in 1737 but did not do well in tests. (National Maritime Museum, Greenwich)

chronometer that would meet the requirements set down in order to win the prize. In 1730, he took his plans to London to show Edmond Halley, the Astronomer Royal, who referred him to George Graham, the foremost clockmaker of the time. Graham was impressed and agreed to fund Harrison's work. Over the next 43 years, Harrison produced a series of marine chronometers but had to fight the Board of Longitude, which refused to accept that his instruments had satisfied the requirements to win the prize. The Board was influenced by astronomers, who believed that an alternative method using lunar tables was the correct solution and would accept no alternatives.

In the late 1760s Harrison had produced his fourth in his series of timekeepers, H4. Larcum Kendal, a watchmaker, then made a copy of this instrument and Cook was asked to test it on his voyage. John Arnold, another watchmaker, made three other watches based on Harrison's originals and these were to be tested also. This work would be entrusted to the astronomers on board. Cook was not convinced by chronometers at first but gradually realised their worth and, by the third voyage, was convinced. His comments on the second voyage progressed from: 'what is in some measure necessary in order to come at the utmost accuracy, is a good watch; but for common use...one may do without' to 'Mr Kendals Watch has exceeded the expectations of its most Zealous advocate and by being now and then corrected by the lunar observations has been our faithful guide through all the vicissitudes of climates'.

After Harrison's death in 1776, Arnold and others continued to develop the instrument. By the mid-nineteenth century, chronometers had become accurate and cheap to produce. Sadly, Harrison's originals were left at Greenwich unattended and began to decay. From the 1920s, Rupert Gould spent years restoring them. They are now on show at the Royal Observatory, Greenwich.

SEE ALSO: Harrison (John)

Clerke, Charles (1743–1779)

Charles Clerke, who sailed on all three voyages with Cook, was born at Brooke Farm, Wethersfield, Essex in 1741, but not baptised until 22 July 1743. He entered the Navy about fourteen years later and saw continuous service during the Seven Years War, 1756 to 1763, aboard HMS *Dorsetshire* and HMS *Bellona*. He was in the mizzen-top of the *Bellona* in 1761 when the mast was shot away, he being the only survivor from those who fell overboard as a result. He sailed around the world with Byron in the *Dolphin*, from June 1764 to May 1766. His description of the Patagonians was published by the Royal Society.

On the first voyage on the *Endeavour*, he was a master's mate until 26 May 1771. After the death of Hicks (second lieutenant), Cook promoted John Gore (third lieutenant) in his place, and 'gave Mr Charles Clerk an order to Act as Lieutenant in the Room of Mr Hicks deceased, he being a young Man extremely well quallified for that station'. Thus Charles Clerke became third lieutenant in place of Gore. Unfortunately, some authors misunderstand Cook's words and say he was promoted Lieutenant in place of Hicks. The Admiralty later confirmed the appointment, commissioning him on 31 July 1771. He kept a journal during the voyage.

In November 1771 Clerke was appointed second lieutenant of HMS *Drake*, which was renamed *Resolution*. Having committed himself to sail again with Cook, Clerke turned down an offer from Banks to sail with him on a trip to Iceland. He again kept a journal and a log.

Captain Charles Clerke, by Nathaniel Dance. Clerke sailed on all three of Cook's voyages. This portrait was painted in 1775 before Clerke joined the third voyage as captain of HMS Discovery. *He died at sea in August 1779. (Government House, Wellington NZ)*

In August 1775 Clerke was given command of the *Favourite*, a sloop. But in February 1776 he was once again with Cook for the third voyage as commander of the *Discovery*. He was unable to leave England with Cook in July, as he was in prison having stood guarantor for the debts of his eldest brother, Sir John Clerke, who had gone off to the East Indies in 1772 owing the then huge sum of £4000. He set sail in August and the *Discovery* joined the *Resolution* at the Cape of Good Hope on 10 November.

After Cook's death on 14 February 1779 he transferred to the *Resolution* and took command of the whole expedition. He demanded and obtained Cook's remains from the natives, but refused to exact revenge upon them, though pressed to do so by his men. He carried out Cook's intended second attempt to find the Northwest Passage, but it also failed, and the ships sailed to Petropavlovsk where, just offshore on 22 August 1779, Clerke died of tuberculosis which he had picked up in the debtors' prison. He kept a log and proceedings until a month before his death. On 29 August Clerke was buried ashore, in accordance with his wishes, in the cemetery at Petropavlovsk. He was 38 years old.

Clerke left two wills (FRC 11/1067 and 11/1070). There is a short biography of him in the *DNB*, v4, p502. Port Clerke (Tierra del Fuego), Clerke's Rocks (South Georgia) and Clerke Peninsula on Bligh Island (in Nootka Sound) are named for him. A small obelisk, at Petropavlovsk, Russia, erected by the British Admiralty in 1913 commemorates Captain Charles Clerke, with an inscription in English.

By Ian Boreham

See Also: *Discovery* (HMS), First, Second and Third voyages

Cleveland

Cleveland is the region of north-east England where James Cook was born in 1728. It was part of what used to be called the North Riding of Yorkshire. It is bounded to the north by the River Tees, to the south by the North Yorkshire Moors and to the east by the North Sea. A low-lying area, it was rich agricultural land supporting many farms but to the south the land rose and gave way to the Cleveland Hills, which stretch eastwards to the coast where they form some of England's highest cliffs (hence the name Cleve-land).

Cook's father came south from Scotland to find work in the area in sometime about 1715 to 1720. He attended hirings in the local market towns of Yarm, Stockton and Guisborough. Major towns such as York and Newcastle were a day's journey away, while London was many days and 248 miles (400km) to the south. The whole area from Yorkshire north to Edinburgh had once been the ancient Kingdom of Northumbria.

In the early eighteenth century, when Cook was born, the area was still largely untouched by the Industrial Revolution. Alum was extracted from quarries along the coast but mostly the area was rural. Not long after Cook, the nearby Durham coalfield was developed and the Stockton and Darlington Railway was extended to transport the coal to a newly-created port on the south bank of the River Tees. This eventually became Middlesbrough, which now dominates the area and has grown to swallow Cook's birthplace at Marton.

For a period in the late twentieth century, Cleveland was constituted as an English county but in 1996 it was broken up into its constituent parts. The name is still used for the region, which is synonymous with Cook. The local tourist board has created the concept of

'Captain Cook Country', but Cook's contribution to the region was being realised as early as the late eighteenth century.

The first visual record of those Cleveland locations connected with James Cook was made by the Yorkshire artist George Cuit in the 1780s. Cuit's drawings of Marton, Ayton, Whitby etc had been commissioned by Constantine Phipps – then Lord Mulgrave, the close friend of Joseph Banks, who had entertained Mai in Yorkshire in 1775 and who had been a sponsor of Cook for his membership of the Royal Society. Cuit produced a suite of nine watercolour drawings, each approximately 12in x 16in (300mm x 404mm). These historically-important topographical views are now part of the Gott Collection held by the municipal art gallery in Wakefield, Yorkshire.

Even in recent years, Cook's name has continued to be used for developments, including the Captain Cook Shopping Centre in Middlesbrough while the main hospital is now called the James Cook University Hospital.

SEE ALSO: Cook's early years

Coastal views

Before the days of photography, coastal views showing the coastline as seen from a ship offshore were a very important part of the record produced by seamen and navigators when charting new coasts. Used in conjunction with charts, the views assisted sailors on ships visiting the location for the first time to identify features on a coast they would not be familiar with and establish their position.

The master or another junior officer would make sketches showing headlands, islands, rocks, inlets and other prominent features. Sometimes these sketches would be drawn directly into the log book. The vertical scale was often exaggerated. The standard varied immensely, reflecting the different abilities of the men, though artistic renderings were not essential. Cook was lucky to have skilled artists on his voyages. Hermann Spöring, who sailed on the *Endeavour* voyage, produced some excellent coastal views, his representations of the coast of New Zealand being very true to life and beautifully drawn. In contrast, Joseph Gilbert's efforts on the second voyage have a cartoon-like quality to them. Hodges' views of Dusky Sound, though, are among the loveliest of the art produced on Cook's voyages.

Cook himself drew coastal views early in his career

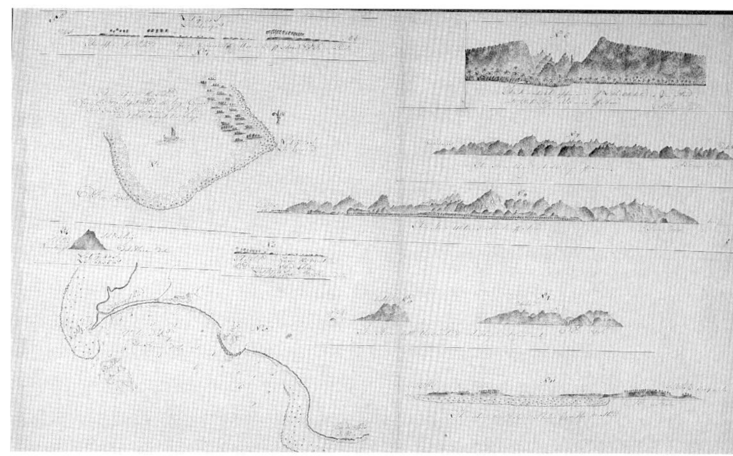

'Island at Lat. 17 00′ S and Long. 142 30′ W Matavai' by Peter Fannin, master of the Adventure. *The duties of a master included drawing sketches and charts of harbours such as Matavai Bay in Tahiti. (Royal Naval Museum, Admiralty Library Manuscript Vz11/55)*

but not particularly well. One of his first efforts depicts Cape Chapeau Rouge on the Burin Peninsula in southern Newfoundland, drawn *en route* from Halifax to Placentia in 1762.

SEE ALSO: Art of Cook's voyages

Coat of Arms, Cook's

A Coat of Arms was granted to James Cook's widow, Elizabeth, for her and her descendants to use. After Cook's death, Elizabeth Cook had conveyed to the Earl of Surrey, deputy with the Royal Approbation to his father the Duke of Norfolk, Earl Marshal and hereditary Marshal of England, her desire to preserve the memory of her husband through the issue of a coat of arms. By warrant under the Earl Marshal's hand, on 28 October 1784, the Kings of Arms were authorised to devise, grant and assign armorial ensigns worthy of the character of Captain James Cook.

The grant was made on 3 September 1785 under the seals of Isaac Heard, Esquire, Garter Principal King of Arms, and Thomas Lock, Esquire, Clarenceux King of Arms. The blazon of the arms is as follows: 'Azure, between two Polar Stars Or, a Sphere on the plane of the Meridian, North Pole elevated, Circles of Latitude for every ten degrees and of Longitude for fifteen, shewing the Pacific Ocean between sixty and two hundred and forty West, bounded on one side by America and on the other by Asia and New Holland; in memory of having explored and made Discoveries in that Ocean, so very far beyond all former Navigators: His Track thereon marked with red Lines'.

The crest: 'On a Wreath of the Colours an Arm embowed, vested in the Uniform of a Captain of the Royal Navy, in the Hand the Union Jack on a Staff proper, the Arms encircled by a Wreath of Palm and Laurel. The crest motto is "Circa Orbem"'.

The main motto: 'Nil Intentatum Reliquit'.

The crest motto translates as 'Around the world' reflecting Cook's circumnavigations. The main motto translates as 'He left nothing unattempted' or by extension 'He left nothing unexplored', a testimony to Cook's thoroughness. As all of the Cook's children died without issue the arms cannot be used today and remain solely a memorial to James Cook.

SEE ALSO: Colour plate 3

Coleridge, Samuel Taylor, and *the Rime of the Ancient Mariner*

Samuel Taylor Coleridge's famous poem, *The Rime of the Ancient Mariner* was published in 1798 in the book *Lyrical Ballads,* jointly authored with Wordsworth. The book marked the beginning of the Romantic Movement in Britain. Coleridge, born 1772, was the youngest son of the vicar of Ottery St Mary, Devonshire. His father died in 1782 and Coleridge was sent away to Christ's Hospital School in London. Coleridge spent nine years at the school before winning a scholarship to Jesus College, Cambridge.

There has been much speculation about where Coleridge drew inspiration from for his most famous poem about the Ancient Mariner. Coleridge was known to be an avid reader and his reading matter would have included the narratives of explorers, especially as his older brother Frank had joined the Navy. Shelvocke is one seaman usually cited, given that one of his crew shot an albatross which had followed the ship in bad weather.

Until Bernard Smith, the Australian art historian, put forward the idea in the 1950s, nobody seriously mentioned Cook in connection with Coleridge. Smith, though, introduced a most plausible link between the two men in William Wales. Wales sailed as astronomer aboard the *Resolution* on Cook's second voyage before becoming the mathematics master at Christ's Hospital during Coleridge's time at the school. The young Coleridge would have listened to stories about the voyage from Wales and have read the journals of the voyage.

Analysis of the poem's text shows close comparisons with the events and descriptions from Cook's voyages and strengthens the likelihood that Cook and Wales, while not the only source, were very influential on Coleridge and represent a major source.

SEE ALSO: Literature of Cook's voyages, Poetry, Wales (William)

Collett family

The Collett family of High Wycombe in Buckinghamshire provided three brothers who sailed with Cook to the Pacific. William Collett sailed on all three voyages, Richard sailed on two, while Joseph only sailed on one, the third. They obviously impressed Cook as, on the third voyage, two of them were employed as masters-at-arms, the naval policemen on board the ships.

William sailed on the *Endeavour* voyage and the second voyage on the *Resolution,* both times as an AB. However, on the third voyage on the *Resolution*, he became the master-at-arms. During this voyage he was assaulted on the island of 'Eua in Tonga on 16 July 1777. William was born in 1749 and may have died in 1815, leaving a will (FRC 11/1575).

The youngest of the brothers, Richard, sailed on the second voyage on the *Resolution* as an AB but, like his brother, became a master-at-arms on the *Discovery* for the third voyage. He was born in 1753. Joseph, the oldest Collett, only sailed on the third voyage on *Resolution* as the gunroom servant. He was born in High Wycombe in 1748 and may have died in 1811, leaving a will (FRC 11/1525).

SEE ALSO: First, Second and Third voyages

Colnett, James (1753–1806)

James Colnett, who sailed on the second voyage on the *Resolution* as a midshipman, was born in Stoke Damerel outside Plymouth in 1753. Colnett began his naval career on HMS *Hazard* as an AB in 1770. After his voyage with Cook, he was gunner on the *Juno* and master on the storeship *Adventure.* He was made a lieutenant in 1779 and served on HMS *Bienfaisant* and HMS *Pégase.* Afterwards he commanded the *Prince of Wales* on a fur trading voyage to the North Pacific in 1786. Moving to the *Argonaut,* he was a principal player in the events that led to the Nootka Incident in 1789, which nearly led to war between Britain and Spain. Colnett was arrested and imprisoned in Mexico for several months.

He led a surveying expedition to the south-east Pacific for the Navy in the *Rattler* from 1793 to 1794. Colnett rejoined the Navy and became a commander in 1794 and a captain in 1796. He was in command of

1

[1] Captain James Cook, by Nathaniel Dance. Commissioned by Joseph Banks and painted in 1776, Cook may have never seen the completed portrait. (National Maritime Museum, London) *SEE: Portraits of Cook*

2

3

[2] The bark Earl of Pembroke, *later* Endeavour, *leaving Whitby Harbour in 1768, by Thomas Luny (1759–1837), painted about 1790. (National Library of Australia) See: Endeavour, HM Bark; Whitby*

[3] Cook's coat of arms. This was granted to Elizabeth Cook, Cook's widow, in 1785. The main motto Nil Intentatum Reliquit *translates as 'He left nothing unattempted', or by extension 'He left nothing unexplored'. (The College of Arms) See: Coat of Arms, Cook's*

[4] HMS *Resolution* off Cape Stephens with waterspout, May 1773, *by William Hodges. It shows the influence of Hodges' teacher, Richard Wilson, in its composition and style. (National Maritime Museum, London, MOD Art Collection) See: Art of Cook's Voyages*

[5] HMS *Resolution* and *Adventure* with fishing craft in Matavai Bay, *painted by William Hodges, c1773. Matavai Bay in Tahiti was one of Cook's favourite places in the Pacific and one he returned to on several occasions. (National Maritime Museum, London) See: Art of Cook's Voyages*

4

5

6

7

[6] Adventure *and* Resolution *with icebergs, by Peter Fannin. Fannin was master on the* Adventure. *Early on the second voyage in Antarctic waters, men are depicted collecting ice from the icebergs for drinking water. (Royal Naval Museum, Admiralty Library Manuscript, Vz11/55)* SEE: *Antarctica; Fannin, Peter; Second Voyage*

[7] A party from HMS Resolution *shooting sea horses, by John Webber. On the third voyage in the Arctic Ocean, walruses were easy targets and were killed for fresh meat and as a source of oil. (National Maritime Museum, London, MOD Art Collection)* SEE: *Arctic*

*[8] An Alaska Longspur (*Calcarius lapponicus alascensis*) sketched by William Ellis on the third voyage. (Natural History Museum 6180)* SEE: *Alaska; Ellis, William Webb*

[9] 'Ahu 'ula, A Hawaiian feathered cloak. This cloak was presented on 26 January 1779 to Captain Cook by Kalaniop'u. (Museum of New Zealand Te Papa Tongarewa) SEE: *Hawai'i*

9

*[10] Old Man Banksia or Wattung-urree (*Banksia serrata *L.), a member of the Proteaceae (Protea Family) found in South-eastern Australia, and very different to what the British were used to. Joseph Banks and his party saw this species at Botany Bay in March 1770. Line engraving by Gabriel Smith after Sydney Parkinson and John Frederick Miller. (Natural History Museum, London, Banks Florilegium part 13, pl 285) SEE: Botanical results*

*[11] Pohutukawa (*Metrosideros excelsa *Banks), a member of the Myrtaceae (Myrtle Family), and known as the New Zealand christmas tree. Joseph Banks and his party came across this species at Mercury Bay in November 1769. Line engraving by Gabriel Smith after Sydney Parkinson. (Natural History Museum, London, Banks Florilegium part 21, pl 445) SEE: Botanical results*

[12] A Tahitian mourning dress, collected in Tahiti on the second voyage. (Forster Collection, Pitt Rivers Museum, Oxford) SEE: Tahiti

[13] Playing on Lono's Island, *by Raymond A Massey. The arrival of HMS* Resolution *and* Discovery *in Kealakekua Bay on 17 January 1779 is shown from the shore at Ka'awaloa. (The artist) SEE: Kealakekua Bay*

[14] Fetched Captain Furneaux for Breakfast, *by Robin Brooks. The title refers to a meeting onboard* Resolution *on 14 December 1772 when Cook discussed with Furneaux options should the two ships become separated, which happened a few days later. (The artist) SEE: Second Voyage*

[15] A Kind of Second Paradise (Tolaga Bay), *1992, by Nigel Brown. This painting is one of a series of paintings and drawings by Brown using Cook as a symbol for British actions in the Pacific. (University of Waikato; The artist)* *See: Lono and Makahiki*

16

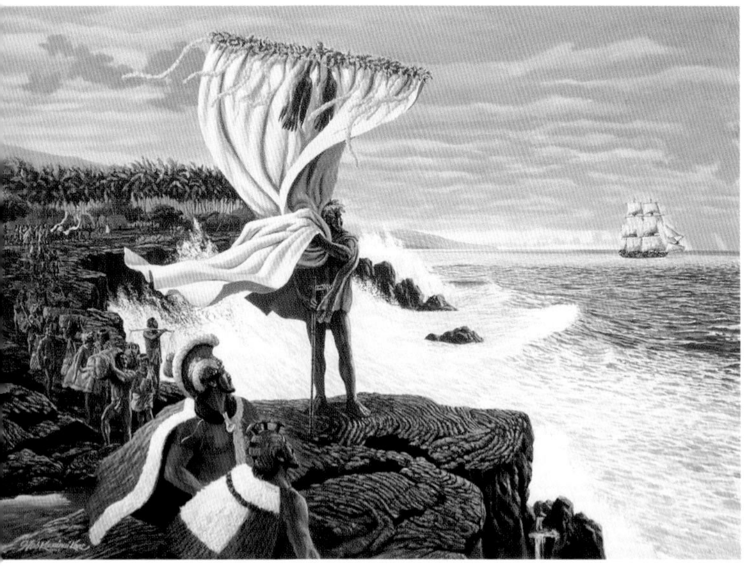

[16] Visitors from Another World, *by Herb Kawainui Kāne. The Makahiki procession round Hawai'i pauses to watch Cook's* Resolution. *The bearer holds the akua loa, the standard of Lono. (The artist)* *See: Lono and Makahiki*

[17] The Death of Cook, February 14 1779, *by Herb Kawainui Kāne. A reconstruction of the scene but a more correct depiction of the terrain, the Hawaiian clothing and implements, and based on the first-hand accounts. (The artist)* *See: Cook as god and Cook's death*

Hussar, 14 guns, when it was wrecked near Île Bas in December 1796. He then commanded HMS *Glatton,* 56 guns, a convict transport, which left Portsmouth in September 1802 and arrived in Sydney in March 1803. It returned to Portsmouth in September 1803 with a cargo of timber. With Catherine Aulce, he had a daughter, Elizabeth. He died in 1806, leaving a will (FRC 11/1451). Several geographical features bear his name: Cabo Colnett on Staten Island, Argentina; Cape Colnett and Mount Colnett in New Caledonia.

SEE ALSO: Sea otter fur trade, Second voyage

Colvill, Alexander, 7th Baron Colvill (1717–1770)

Alexander Colvill was the son of John Colvill, 6th Baron Colvill and his wife Elizabeth. He was born on 28 February 1717 in Dundee and joined the Royal Navy in 1733 on board HMS *Line*. By 1739 he was a lieutenant and in the West Indies on the *Alderney.* In 1742, he transferred to the Mediterranean fleet before he took charge of HMS *Leopard* in 1744. He distinguished himself over the next few years and returned to Britain in 1748 with £5000 prize money.

From 1749 to 1752, Colvill commanded HMS *Success* in New England. In 1753, he was given command of the 70-gun HMS *Northumberland,* on which he sailed for the next nine years. Colvill took part in the capture of Louisbourg in 1758 and was present at the siege of Quebec in 1759. After the French surrender, Saunders appointed Colvill as commander-in-chief of the North America Station and transferred a new master, James Cook, to the *Northumberland* from the *Pembroke.*

Colvill took his ships back to Halifax in Nova Scotia but returned to Quebec in 1760. 1761 and most of 1762 were spent at Halifax, where he worked on improving the dockyard facilities. News reached Colvill in July 1762 of the French capture of St John's in Newfoundland so he sailed to Newfoundland to take part in the recapture. Colvill took the *Northumberland* back to Britain in late 1762 and his connection with Cook ended then when both left the ship.

Colvill was appointed port admiral at Plymouth in 1763 but later that year was persuaded reluctantly to take on again the North American command where he remained until 1766. He was never employed again after his return to Britain. He died on 21 May 1770 at Drumsheugh, near Edinburgh. He married Lady Elizabeth Erskine in 1768 but they had no children. However, he did have children with several women in North America.

He had given Cook the opportunity to prepare charts in Canada and Newfoundland and his commendations brought Cook to the attention of Thomas Graves, Governor of Newfoundland. Cook named a cape in New Zealand after Colvill. There is a short biography of him in the *Dictionary of Canadian Biography*, v3, pp131–3.

SEE ALSO: Canada, *Northumberland* (HMS)

Cook, Elizabeth (1741–1835)

Elizabeth Cook was born Elizabeth Batts in January 1741 and was baptised at St John's Church in Wapping, East London. Her parents were Samuel and Mary Batts, who ran the Bell alehouse in Execution Dock, near the corner of Brewhouse Lane and Wapping High Street. Samuel was much older than Mary, having been married before and already had a daughter, Sarah. He died in 1742 and Elizabeth was sent to live with Quaker friends, the Sheppards, at Crouches Yard in Barking. James Sheppard was the London agent for John Walker, Cook's employer.

In July 1745, Mary Batts married John Blackburn and they continued to run the Bell until 1750. Cook probably lodged at the alehouse during this time while the colliers were discharging their cargo nearby. By 1755, the Blackburns had moved to live in Upper Shadwell and Elizabeth appears to have lived there, as well as continuing to stay in Barking.

When Cook returned to Britain in late 1762, he quickly courted and married Elizabeth. He is recorded as living in Shadwell and she in Barking. They were married by Rev. George Downing at St Margaret's Church, Barking on 21 December 1762. The couple made their first home at 126 Upper Shadwell and their first child, James, born on 13 October 1763 was baptised in St Paul's Church, Shadwell. When James Cook returned from Newfoundland in late 1763, the family moved to a new home in Assembly Row in Mile End.

The Cooks had five more children. Nathaniel was born in 1764, Elizabeth in 1767, Joseph in 1768, George in 1772, and Hugh, who was born in 1776. Elizabeth, Joseph and George had all died in infancy before James Cook left on his final voyage in 1776. James Boswell visited the Cooks in Mile End before Cook's departure and described Elizabeth as 'a decent plump Englishwoman'.

After Cook's death, King George III granted

Elizabeth Cook an annuity of £200. She also benefited financially from sales of the published accounts of the voyages. Her second son, Nathaniel, died in 1780. Some time in the 1780s, Elizabeth moved to a house on Clapham High Street in South London. Her cousin, Isaac Smith, who had sailed with Cook, lived with her there for many years. He was now a retired rear-admiral with property nearby in Merton. The two cousins lived together until Isaac died in 1831. Elizabeth herself died on 13 May 1835, aged 94. She had been a widow for 56 years. She was buried in Great St Andrew Church in Cambridge.

Unfortunately, Elizabeth Cook appears to have destroyed most of the material in her possession relating to Cook. No correspondence between them has survived.

SEE ALSO: Cook family

Cook and the geographers

By the middle of the eighteenth century considerations of geographical science, government strategy, and mercantile acquisitiveness pointed to the exploration of the Pacific as one of the most important global objectives left to Europe. By now there were published accounts of the main Pacific voyages from Magellan to Anson, although they produced as much confusion as enlightenment. Islands had been sighted and resighted, identified and then lost again, but if the map of the Pacific was dotted with island groups whose position and names changed with cartographical fashion, it was also marked with squiggles of coastline which hinted at lands of continental dimensions. A world map published by the leading French geographer Philippe Buache in 1755 summarised the possibilities in the South Pacific. It showed New Holland joined to New Guinea and Van Diemen's Land, and incorporated Espiritu Santo (Vanuatu) to the north-east into a vastly extended Australian continent. To the south-east New Zealand was shown as the outlying fringe of a great continental landmass stretching away towards Cape Horn. Shadowy outlines represented reported sightings of the supposed continent from the sixteenth century onwards. Its looming presence dominated the instructions of the British and French discovery expeditions of the mid-1760s commanded by Byron, Wallis and Bougainville, but their voyages did little to settle the issue of *Terra Australis Incognita*. Yet within a few years there was no longer any doubt, for Cook's voyages revealed the Pacific in a way no previous expeditions had done, and in doing so brought to the forefront the question of the relationship between explorers and geographers.

Among the voyages of Cook's contemporaries the narrative published in 1771 of Bougainville's voyage had contained little in the way of precise navigational information. The British navigator Philip Carteret thought the book 'more amusing to the landman than usefull to the Seaman', while the astronomer William Wales noted the difficulty of finding locations in the French account. On Tahiti, for example, 'I looked in vain for its situation in M. Bougainville's Voyage, although the Article *Geographical* stands in the Margin. He seems industriously to have concealed his Latitudes and Longitudes during his whole run across this vast Ocean.' A few years earlier, John Callander in his collection of Pacific voyages published in 1766–68 had omitted latitudes and longitudes from his account of Commodore Byron's track across the Pacific, so that 'enemies of our country may not avail themselves of our discoveries'. On hearing of Bougainville's forthcoming voyage, Alexander Dalrymple had suspended his correspondence on geographical matters with the French scholar Charles de Brosses, in case it might 'facilitate the enterprises of a rival State'. Whatever its merits and demerits as a detailed record of a discovery voyage, Bougainville's account was notable for a thunderous, and much-quoted, denunciation of speculative geography and its practitioners – 'Geography is a science of facts', he insisted. This leads us straight to Cook, and in particular to his relationship with Dalrymple. In the view of the eminent Cook scholar, J C Beaglehole, this was one of antagonism between, on the one hand, the precise, practical navigator, and on the other a geographer whose 'leading characteristics were intellectual indiscipline and self-conceit, a perfect inability to discriminate', and whose concept of *Terra Australis* 'was an illusion raised by abstract thought'. Dalrymple's biographer, Howard Fry, saw the matter rather differently, and stated the case not only for Dalrymple but for speculative geography generally. 'The important point was that his theories should be sufficiently in accord with the knowledge of his time to be plausible, and sufficiently enticing and challenging to inspire further exploration.' On his first two voyages Cook demonstrated that there was no great southern continent as argued by Dalrymple in his *Account of the Discoveries made in the South Pacifick Ocean Previous to 1764* (1769), and his *Collection of the Several Voyages and Discoveries in the South Pacific*

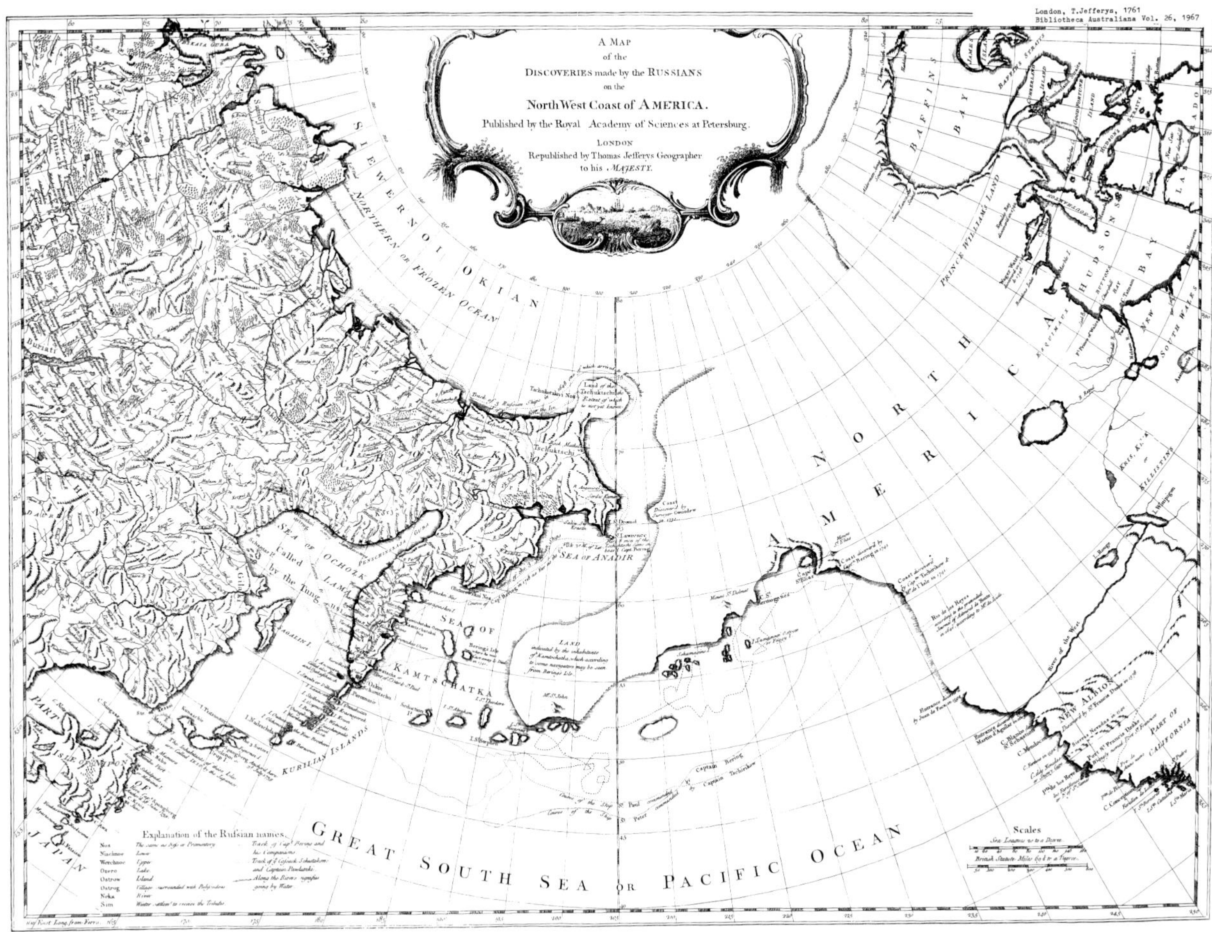

Ocean (1770–1). Cook had a copy of the first and its accompanying 'Chart of the South Pacifick Ocean' on the *Endeavour*, for Dalrymple had presented Joseph Banks with the book in pre-publication form before the vessel sailed in 1768. Cook had copies of all three volumes on his second voyage.

A Map of the Discoveries made by the Russians on the Northwest coast of America, by S Müller, 1761. (University of Waikato Map Collection)

Cook's avowed antagonism towards theoretical geography sprang from his passion for accuracy, based on first-hand observation. Early on the first voyage he set out his approach as he charted the Cape Horn region: 'In this Chart I have laid down no land nor figur'd out any shore but what I saw my self, and thus far the Chart may be depented upon.' The same emphasis is there in a later journal entry, where Cook dismissed Dalrymple's speculation that the Spanish navigator Quiros may have sighted a continent with the words 'hanging Clowds and a thick horizon are certainly no known Signs of a Continent'. Among the matters cleared up by Cook on his first voyage was the existence of Torres Strait. On board he had the latest word on the subject in the form of Dalrymple's 'Chart of the Southern Pacifick Ocean', where on the basis of Spanish documents of the early seventeenth century Dalrymple showed Torres' track of 1606 running between New Holland and New Guinea. Cook saw the significance of his own passage through Torres Strait in modest terms: 'as I believe it was known before tho' not publicly I clame no other merit than the clearing up of a doubtfull point'; but he failed to acknowledge any debt to Dalrymple's chart. A few days later he entered in his journal a long complaint about the accuracy of existing charts, blaming navigators, geographers and publishers alike – 'so that between the one and the other we can hardly tell when we are possessed of a good sea Chart until we our selves have proved it'.

On his second circumnavigation Cook had

Dalrymple's 1769 chart of the South Atlantic to add to the earlier one of the South Pacific. Unlike on his first voyage, Cook's journal on the second contains more than a dozen references to Dalrymple's maps or texts. They were guides, to be confirmed or corrected by observation. So Dalrymple's 1769 chart showed a mixture of genuine if imprecise South Atlantic sightings, probably of South Georgia, made by French vessels and an imaginary 'Golfo de St Sebastiano' taken from an Ortelius map of 1587. Even before sailing Cook was doubtful about this feature, but he acknowledged that had not Dalrymple and French cartographers marked the sightings of South Georgia on their maps he would probably have passed to the south of it. Academic geography had its uses, and when in 1775 Cook exchanged information with the French explorer Crozet his comments could have come straight from the pen of Dalrymple: 'It will hardly be necessary to resume the Subject unless all the discoveries, both Ancient and Modern, are laid down in a Chart and then an explanatory Memoir will be necessary and such a Chart I intend to construct when I have time and the necessary materials.'

In his first two Pacific voyages Cook demolished the thesis that a large temperate continent existed in the southern hemisphere. His scepticism about speculative geography makes the events of his third voyage to the northwest coast of America the more puzzling. He was searching for a Northwest Passage in a region reached by the Russian expeditions of Bering and his successors sailing from Kamchatka, but their explorations were patchy and poorly mapped. In the gaps left by their surveys the French scholars Philippe Buache and J N Delisle had inserted an intricate network of straits allegedly discovered by Juan de Fuca in 1592 and Admiral de Fonte in 1640. The existence of these waterways Cook rejected out of hand, but he relied on an equally fallible account written by Jacob von Stählin, Secretary of the St Petersburg Academy of Sciences, *An Account of the New Northern Archipelago, Lately Discovered by the Russians*. This claimed to show that a Russian naval officer, Ivan Synd, had found that Alaska was not a peninsula but a large island, and that there was a wide strait in latitude 65° N between it and the American continent which led into the polar sea. If current theories that the northern seas were ice-free were correct, Synd's discovery opened the way for a Northwest Passage around the top of the American continent; and Cook's instructions for his final voyage were drawn up on this assumption. By relying on this example of speculative geography Cook was behaving out of character, and led his final expedition in search of a will-o'-the-wisp.

The season of 1778 on the north-west coast of America was one of frustration for Cook and his crews. The ships sailed past those regions where the French geographers had showed the openings of Fuca and Fonte, and headed steadily north towards latitude 65° N. The ships entered Prince William Sound and Cook Inlet in a vain attempt to find the strait shown on Stählin's map, but the only way through to the north was the strait far to the west discovered by Bering fifty years earlier, and by the end of the summer this was closed by ice. Russian traders encountered at Unalaska knew nothing of a great strait between Alaska and America, and once he understood how he had been misled by Stählin Cook entered a furious outburst in his journal: 'What could induce him to publish so erroneous a Map? … A map that the most illiterate of his illiterate Sea-faring men would have been ashamed to put his name to.' Cook discovered much in his last survey. He traced many miles of intricate coastline from Vancouver Island to Bering Strait, but he lacked the professional detachment which had always been one of his strengths. His ships were not reinforced to meet ice, he took no Russian-speaking crew members with him, and he relied on accounts and maps that lacked all credibility. That he recognised his predicament was shown in his last letter to the Admiralty, in October 1778: 'We were upon a Coast…where no information could be had from Maps, either modern or ancient: confiding too much in the former we were frequently misled to our no small hinderence.'

After Cook's third voyage one of his officers, James King, claimed that 'The Grand Bounds of the four Quarters of the Globe are known', and he had little doubt that the major advance to this knowledge came from Britain. There was a dominance, though by no means a monopoly, of British accounts and charts of the Pacific in this period, for by the time of Cook's voyages the Admiralty had agreed that full versions of his journals and charts should be published as soon as possible after his return. This was not simply a matter of science or philanthropy; it was also a sign of burgeoning confidence and ambition. As Dr Douglas, the editor of Cook's journals of his last two voyages put it, 'Every nation that sends a ship to sea will partake of benefit [of the published accounts]; but Great Britain herself, whose commerce is boundless, must take the lead in reaping the full advantage of her own discoveries.' The eighteenth-century process of enquiry about the world was European rather than narrowly British in scope, but its best-known manifestation came in the person and work of Captain Cook. Boswell hinted at one reason for this when he wrote of the explorer that he had 'a ballance in his mind for truth as nice as scales for weighing a guinea'. Cook and his officers were consciously setting new standards in their surveys. As Cook wrote of his chart of the North Island of New Zealand on his first voyage, 'I believe that this Island will never be found to differ materially from the figure I have given it.' There was an unrelenting determination to show things as they were, to replace myth and fantasy by empirical observation and prompt publication. In this process the speculative geographers found little place. Their role in stimulating interest in distant regions was ignored in the face of complaints about their uncritical approach, their lack of seagoing experience, their casual misdirection of explorers. There is a sharp edge to the satisfaction with which the explorers of the eighteenth century contraverted the geographers of their day – the 'closet navigators', the 'speculative fabricators of geography', the 'purveyors of vague and improbable stories'. Dr Douglas was one of those who saw explorers and geographers as natural adversaries. 'The fictions of speculative geographers in the Southern hemisphere, have been continents; in the Northern hemisphere, they have been seas. It may be observed, therefore, that if Captain Cook in his first voyages annihilated imaginary southern lands, he had made amends for the havock, in his third voyage, by annihilating imaginary Northern Seas.'

Such strictures underestimated the importance of promotional geography in securing support for discovery ventures, and the difficulties under which cartographers laboured as they tried to make sense of the journals and maps in front of them. If the navigators complained that they were the victims of armchair scholars and their speculative theories and maps, so might geographers retort that they were at the mercy of navigators and their muddled, inaccurate observations. Cook himself wrote of fellow seamen who 'lay down the line of a Coast they have never seen and put down soundings where they have never sounded, and after all are so fond of their performances as to pass'd the whole off as sterling under the Title of a Survey Plan &c.' Emphasis on conflict between explorers and geographers can obscure the relationship of dependence and collaboration which existed between them. The link between navigators and scholars – whether one of collaboration or antagonism – was always important, and sometimes crucial, in explaining the spread of geographical knowledge.

By Glyndwr Williams

See Also: De Brosses (Charles), Pacific exploration before Cook, Dalrymple (Alexander)

Cook as god and Cook's death

A first encounter

When on 18 January 1778 he sighted the leeward end of the group he later named the Sandwich Islands, James Cook and his subordinates became the first Europeans known to have encountered this archipelago. Two weeks of contact with the inhabitants of Kaua'i and Ni'ihau indicated linguistic, cultural, and physical similarities to many South Pacific peoples. From the start enthusiastic trading of goods took place, though in the chaos of the first landing at Kaua'i a man was shot dead. Cook tried to prevent the spread of venereal disease to these populations, but the combined artifices of his men and local women negated that effort. During his several excursions on shore he was amazed to see people prostrating themselves before him and much ceremony attending his movements. Nowhere else had Cook experienced such veneration.

On 26 November 1778 *Resolution* and *Discovery* returned to the Sandwich Islands from ten months in north-west American waters, coming-to off Maui. As they moved from this island's northern to its eastern side, foodstuffs were exchanged for ironware while women were kept at bay. Many men came aboard, however, including an elderly chief, who gave Cook his red and yellow feather cap and cloak. But rather than land on 'Mowee', the Captain aimed for a larger island visible to the south, which the natives called 'Owhyhe'. The next morning, 1 December, they were standing off Hawai'i, its snow-capped mountains high above and white flags fluttering along the shore and on canoes.

For the next four weeks Cook moved his vessels slowly along the east coast, battling huge seas, tacking in and out, bartering urgent supplies with canoes, and controlling a belligerent crew. Early in the new year, around the southern end of the island, both his tactics and the context changed: crowds were now visible ashore, canoes surrounded the ships, trade flourished, and women were allowed on board. Finally, on 17 January 1779, the ships anchored in Kealakekua, a large west coast bay, where they were welcomed by an estimated 1500 canoes and 10,000 joyful people. Nowhere else in the South Seas had Cook and his men seen such a vast and peaceful gathering.

At the north-west end of this bay lay the settlement of Ka'awaloa, home of the island's royal family, while near the south-east end was the religious centre of Hikiau. From the former came a young chief, Palea, who cleared the crowds from the decks; from the latter came an old priest, Ko'a'a, who with much ceremony and prayer presented Cook with a small pig and two coconuts and wrapped him in a red cloth. This pair then took the Captain and several officers ashore to Hikiau, past villagers prostrate on the ground, to be met by priests with dog hair-tipped wands who led them to a large stone ritual platform, or *heiau*, all the while repeating a chant ending 'Erono'.

Roughly 20 by 40 yards in area, the *heiau* was surrounded by a wooden fence adorned with human skulls, while inside was featured a wooden 'oracle tower', a semicircle of grinning wooden images, and an altar topped with a decaying hog. There, amidst much chanting, Ko'a'a and a younger priest called Keli'ikea took Cook through a complex ceremony that featured him being wrapped in a red garment, having to bow before and kiss a cloth-enveloped image, being sat down between two other carvings, and being presented with a cooked hog. Food was then eaten, kava drunk, and the Captain and his officers anointed with coconut oil. After this Cook responded with a gift of iron pieces and the wand-bearers led the procession back to the boat, where commoners again fell on their faces.

A field next to the *heiau* was given to Cook by the priests for his observatories. Because the priests made it *tapu*, no ordinary Hawaiians would go near it. Each morning the chief Palea cleared the overnight women off the ships to allow work to begin. While some petty thieving occurred, relations between the two peoples remained exceptionally good. Each time Cook came ashore the priest Keli'ikea preceded him with wand and 'Erono' incantations. People in canoes would squat while those on land would prostrate themselves; only chiefs and priests could approach the Captain. While visiting a house he again was placed before a carved image, dressed in red cloth, presented with a pig, and fed pork and kava. Meanwhile, the men at the observatory received large gifts of food daily, always in the name of Ka'ō'ō, the senior priest and Keli'ikea's grandfather, who was at Maui with the 'king'.

The return of the king

On 24 January the imminent return of the king, or *ali'i 'ai aupuni,* caused the whole bay to be closed by a *tapu*. Two days later Kalaniopu'u arrived in a long convoy of canoes, several of which stopped at the *Resolution*. Cook was surprised to see that he was the same chief who had visited the ship at Maui two months earlier. After receiving gifts from the Captain, and formally exchanging names, Kalaniopu'u went on to Ka'awaloa.

Next day three large double canoes brought the bay to a halt. Kalaniopu'u and his chiefly retainers, resplendent in red-and-yellow feather cloaks and helmets, were in the first. Chanting priests, led by Ka'ō'ō, and four god images, filled the second. Pigs, coconuts and vegetables occupied the third. Cook followed behind. They went to the observatory, where Kalaniopu'u put his own cloak on his namesake's shoulders, a helmet on his head, a regal feathered fan in his hand, and a half dozen more cloaks at his feet. Ka'ō'ō then wrapped Cook in a ritual cloth and offered him a sacrificial pig, while Keli'ikea and company recited the usual chants. Finally the king went to the ship where he was fed and given iron and similar treasures.

More gifts were exchanged over the following days, and relations between visitors and hosts were judged better than the British had experienced anywhere in the Pacific. Just one Hawaiian was flogged for theft – by Captain Clerke on *Discovery*. Because of the abundance of provisions, Cook now allowed open trade. Ka'ō'ō even gave permission for the decaying fence around the *heiau*, and some of its carvings, to be taken to the ships for firewood. The same day, 1 February, when the old seaman William Watman died and the Hawaiians asked that he be buried in the *heiau*, Cook agreed and personally led the service. As the grave at the foot of one of the remaining images was being filled, Ka'ō'ō threw in a dead pig, coconuts and bananas, and for the next three nights he and other priests maintained a respectful vigil over the site.

By this time Kalaniopu'u, and many other Hawaiians, had begun to enquire as to when the visitors planned to leave, and – unlike Tahitians and Tongans in similar circumstances – seemed happy when told that it would be soon. Nevertheless, he and Ka'ō'ō tried to encourage Lieutenant King, who they thought was Cook's son, to remain with them. The *ali'i 'ai aupuni* and his priest also ordered a final collection from their subjects. Accordingly, the day before departure, a vast quantity of food produce was laid out, along with bundles of tapa and red and yellow feathers, and ironware from the ships. Ka'ō'ō presented the iron and feathers to Kalaniopu'u, who passed the bark cloth and some of the feathers to Cook and the foodstuffs to both Cook and King. The Captain in his turn gave much of the food back to the people. Sad farewells and lamentations followed, and the visitors returned to their ships.

On the morning of 4 February *Resolution* and *Discovery* departed Kealakekua Bay. Two days later they were standing off north-west Hawai'i, while one of their passengers, the priest Ko'a'a, was taken ashore. A severe storm came up, and afterwards the foremast of the *Resolution* was found to be badly damaged. Because the only protected anchorage Cook knew in this archipelago was Kealakekua, he reluctantly decided to return. A notable visitor to *Discovery* was the young chief, Kamehameha, a kinsman of Kalaniopu'u and later the first ruler of the Kingdom of Hawai'i; at Clerke's insistence he exchanged his beautiful feather cloak for nine iron daggers.

An event on a beach

Just one week after leaving, the ships arrived back at Kealakekua. This time there was no welcome, as Kalaniopu'u ordered a *tapu* until after he visited the ships. He asked why they had returned, and was clearly unhappy with the answer. Nor was he pleased when the priests gave Cook land and huts near the *heiau* for the repair operations, and imposed a *tapu* to keep locals away. Over the following days canoes plied the ships with produce, and many locals came on board.

Then on 13 February a man who had stolen the armourer's tongs on the *Discovery* was given 40 lashes. Believing that theft was becoming much worse than during the first visit, Clerke ordered all Hawaiians except chiefs off the ship. That afternoon, Kalaniopu'u visited and presented him with a cloak and a hog. Around the same time near the *heiau* a group of locals employed to help fill water casks for the *Discovery* was being hindered by a chief and his followers. When a lightly-armed marine was posted to protect them, the crowd threw stones at him. On being told of this incident, Cook ordered sentries on shore to load their muskets with ball rather than small-shot and to respond with gunfire to any similar incidents.

Even later the same day, as Clerke was entertaining the chief Palea in his cabin, the armourer's tongs were once more stolen. Muskets were fired at the fleeing miscreant, and Palea left promising to return the property. At that time, however, Cook was ashore and set out with a marine to catch the thief. But an unfriendly crowd sent them in the wrong direction, and then laughed when threatened with a musket. Humiliated and angry, Cook returned to the base. There he learned how, in the chaos of the chase, a sailor had struck Palea on the head with an oar, which in turn had resulted in an assault on an officer, stones being thrown at a boat, and the boat's fixtures being stolen. Only the intervention of Palea restored order and property.

Returning to *Resolution*, Cook expressed his regret that the behaviour of 'the Indians' would probably oblige him to retaliate with force. Before retiring he ordered all women and other natives off the ship. During the night a sentry at the observatory fired a shot at a marauder. Around dawn the *Discovery*'s large cutter was found to be missing. Never before had Cook had a boat stolen. He ordered a blockade of the bay, and the firing of the ship's guns to force several large canoes back to shore.

Around 6am Cook left for Ka'awaloa in three boats with Lieutenant Phillips and nine well-armed marines. His intention was to take Kalaniopu'u hostage until the cutter was returned. Lieutenant King, meanwhile, was approaching Ka'ō'ō and the priests, and found them keen to maintain peace in their part of the bay. Cook and his soldiers landed in a rocky cove near the royal village. The cutter went further out in the bay to stop canoes from leaving, while the pinnace and launch remained some yards off shore, to avoid the lava. Marching into the village, the Captain found Kalaniopu'u's two young sons; they knew him well and took him to their father's hut.

It soon became clear that Kalaniopu'u knew nothing about the stolen cutter, and he accepted the request to accompany Cook to the ship. Then his wife appeared, and two lesser chiefs, who all pleaded with him, saying he would be killed. Kalaniopu'u sat down, frightened and dejected. A noisy crowd gathered around, many with stones, spears, and even iron daggers. When the marines were forced to pull back to the water's edge, Cook told Phillips he was abandoning his plan: 'We can never think of compelling him to go on board without killing a number of these people', he said.

As the Captain began to walk slowly back towards

the boats, two things appear to have happened. First, at the other end of the bay, musket-fire had killed a high ranking chief who was trying to leave in a canoe. When another chief hastened to the ships to complain to Cook about this incident, he was ignored; thus he came to Ka'awaloa, where it was the crowd that heard his news – which only increased their anger. Second, while he was moving slowly towards the boats Cook thought himself to be threatened by a man with a dagger and a stone, and so responded by firing the small-shot barrel of his musket. Protected by his heavy war mat, the man was uninjured.

Now a chief attempted to stab Phillips, stones were thrown, and a marine was knocked down. Cook fired his other barrel, with ball, and killed a man. Philips too fired, and the Captain ordered the marines to do likewise, but they were already overwhelmed. As those in the boats joined the shooting, Cook shouted 'Take to the boats!', which some marines were already doing, and he signalled the boats in closer. The pinnace did so, but the launch – mistaking his signal – moved even further out. Cook was clubbed from behind, then stabbed in the neck or shoulder with an iron dagger, and on falling face down in the water was held under and finished with more clubs and daggers. Four marines also were killed. Heavy fire from the *Resolution* seems finally to have dispersed the crowd. But, for reasons unknown, the men in the boats failed to reclaim the bodies of their commander and comrades.

On the Hawaiian side, four chiefs and thirteen commoners were said to have been killed. Perhaps that is why Clerke chose not to wreak vengeance – though some subordinates did engage in a brutal action against innocent people near the *heiau*. It was the priests Ko'a'a and Keli'ikea who arranged for the return of those parts of the Captain's body that had survived the ritual dismemberment and burning usually associated with the death of a great chief. Some locals asked the visitors if 'Erono' would return, and what would he do to them when he did. When Kalaniopu'u's young son Keoua came on board *Resolution*, where he had spent much time with Cook, he wept aloud for 'the Orono'. On 21 February 1779, the day before his ships finally departed from Kealakekua, the remains of James Cook were buried at sea with full naval honours.

The catastrophe to come

On 10 January 1780 the news of Cook's death reached London, having been dispatched overland from Kamchatka when *Resolution* and *Discovery* called there after leaving the Sandwich Islands. Already a national and international hero of rare proportion, the unique circumstances of his passing 'propelled his memory far beyond the level of mere fame into those exalted realms of the human imagination where only gods, saints, heroes and martyrs dwell' (Smith 1979). Many imaginative literary accounts and artistic representations of the drama of his last moments were produced. But because the facts of Cook's death could only remain cloudy, and were always refracted through a Eurocentric lens, reality and mythology were invariably entangled in the many retellings of this particular Enlightenment paradigm.

British ships visiting Hawai'i, meanwhile, would be greeted with the cry 'Britanee! Britanee!', and the same questions about Cook were still being asked by the locals – whether he would forgive them and when he might return. It was said that several *heiau* were dedicated to his memory, that his bones were still venerated as sacred relics, and that sacrifices were offered to him as to other gods. In 1793, Edward Bell reported: 'The Natives seem to consider [Cook's death] as one of the most remarkable events in their History, almost every child able to prattle can give you an account of it – at that time they look'd up to him as to a supernatural being, indeed they call him the "Orono" or great God, nor has he to this day lost any of his character or consequence with the Natives they still in speaking of him style him the Orono and they are to be believ'd, most sincerely regret his fate.' (cited in Salmond 2003).

At that time, however, Hawaiian society and culture were dramatically and painfully changing, through depopulation caused by introduced disease and civil conflict. In the early 1800s Calvinist missionaries from the United States stepped into the vacuum. No friends of Britain, they accused Cook of participating in 'savage' rites, of allowing himself to be worshipped, of introducing venereal disease, of unwarranted violence, and of exploiting the common people. Such views were then taken up by young islanders educated in church schools, including Samuel Kamakau, the first indigenous historian. Ultimately they became the standard Hawaiian view of Cook.

It was to be another century before greater clarity on these issues began to emerge, primarily through the endeavours of the New Zealand historian, J C Beaglehole. His 1964 essay 'The Death of Captain Cook' effectively begins with a declaration of war on the missionaries' position above. Beaglehole's alternative is best summarised by his view that 'on this voyage Cook was a tired man... Cook should have been forbidden to go on the voyage, or else the voyage should have been postponed... the hands that signed his commission signed his death-warrant' (p.293). By his third Pacific voyage, Beaglehole argues, Cook had lost his navigational spirit, was no longer in touch with 'the genus *Seaman*', had become brutal in his dealings with natives, and was increasingly irrational.

Two of Beaglehole's books also deal, in part, with the circumstances of Cook's death: notably, the third volume of his edition of the Cook journals, and his pioneering biography of Cook. A feature of the latter are its reflections on traditional Hawaiian culture, starting with his question as to 'why Cook should have received such extraordinary notice at this particular island'. Beaglehole comments usefully on the practice of *kapu moe*, 'sacred obeiance', and the semi-divine status of *ali'i kapu*, 'high chiefs'; and on Ku, god of war and human sacrifice, and his opposite, Lono [Rono], god of light, peace, and fertility.

Most detailed, however, is his account of the season called *makahiki*, which ran for four months, from October or November to January or February. During this time warfare was forbidden, hard work was in abeyance, games and sport were the norm, and food was abundant. It was also when tribute was gathered, in a procession that moved clockwise around the island. God of this season was *Lono makua*, 'Father Lono', and his presence was 'symbolised by a long staff bearing a banner of *tapa*, attached to a cross-piece somewhat like the yard of a ship's mast, and in form much like a ship's sail'. By sheer circumstance, Cook's visit to Hawai'i became overlaid in time and space with this cultural event: 'And now, proceeding slowly round the island in the festival direction, bearing the banners of Lono, bearing articles which were as good as gifts, though dispensed in trade, came vessels from afar captained by a chief of goodwill. Possibly the white cloth flying on the shore and on the canoes were emblems of Lono, and Cook's ensign seemed a divine acknowledgement of them. We seem to be right in saying, without too much discrimination between aspects of the divine, that Lono had returned incarnate in Cook.' (Beaglehole 1974, p659)

Similarly, when Cook was welcomed ceremonially on to the *heiau* at Kealakekua, it was as Lono, and the small clothed image he was obliged to kiss was *Ku-nui-akea*, 'Great Widespread Ku': 'all this was bringing together of god and god'. Likewise the ritual that surrounded Cook generally during his first visit to Hawai'i – the red cloth and sacrificial offerings, the attention and prayers of the priests, the prostrations of ordinary folk: 'all this was appropriate to a god, not to a sea-captain'.

How then does Beaglehole account for the killing of Cook? Consistent with his earlier essay, he contrasts the navigator's essential humaneness with the tired and irrational figure of February 1779, whose tactical miscalculations and violent overreactions significantly contributed to his own demise. But, also, at least implicit in his analysis, is the theme that the return of Kalaniopu'u in late January signified the end of the *makahiki*, thus explaining the king's desire to see 'Orono' depart, and his distinct unhappiness when Cook came back. The growing disrespect shown by Hawaiians to an increasingly threatening Cook – not the peaceful 'Orono' they had known and would properly expect – also fits this scenario.

The anthropologist Marshall Sahlins, in a series of celebrated essays and books, significantly developed this basic argument, and extended its logic into other dimensions of Hawaiian and Polynesian culture history. His analysis of Cook's death was in turn famously challenged by the Sri Lankan anthropologist, Gananath Obeyesekere, who insisted that Sahlins perpetuates the myth 'that the Western civilizer is a god to savages'; in his counter-view, it was Cook who was the irrational savage and the Hawaiians who were rational and humane. While many early reviewers were seduced by the eloquence of Obeyesekere's argument, academic commentators now generally recognise Sahlins' work as more scholarly and authoritative (cf Borofsky).

Although they accept many of the findings of this recent research, indigenous Hawaiian intellectuals remain suspicious of the ongoing *haole* (white) fascination with Captain Cook and, especially, with his death. The activist Haunani-Kay Trask, for example, describes him as 'a rude and arrogant racist' who natives of the Pacific still regard as a 'Great White Evil'. Likewise, the historian Lilikala Kame'eleihiwa tauntingly claims that 'from the Hawaiian perspective... the best part about Cook's visit is that we killed him, as the *mana* [spiritual power] of his death accrues to us'. Such rhetoric may offend Western sensitivities, but it serves as a reminder that the death of James Cook in Hawai'i, as tragic and unnecessary as it was, also effectively sounded the death knell for many Pacific individuals, communities and lifeways in the catastrophe of colonialism that followed in his wake.

BY TOM RYAN

SEE ALSO: Hawai'i, Lono and Makahiki, Religion and Cook, Colour plates 16 & 17

Cook family

The explorer James Cook was born in Cleveland, north-east England, the son of James (senior) and Grace Cook. James senior was born on 4 March 1694 in Ednam in Roxburghshire, Scotland. He was the son of John and Jane Cooke, who had married on 19 January 1693 in Smailholm, also in Roxburghshire. James Cook senior is believed to have moved south from Scotland to the Cleveland region of north-east England sometime between 1715 and 1724, though the reasons for the move have never been established.

In Cleveland, he became an agricultural worker. Work was seasonal and he would be hired at markets, moving when and wherever work was available. He met Grace Pace and they were married on 10 October 1725 at St Peter & St Paul Church, Stainton-in-Cleveland. Grace, who was born in 1702, came from nearby Thornaby-on-Tees and was the daughter of John and Deborah Pace.

The Cooks continued an itinerant life for some years and had the first of their eight children (they would have three sons and five daughters) in 1727 when they were living in Morton, Cleveland. This was James Cook's elder brother, John. James Cook, the explorer, was the next child and he was born on 27 October 1728. The family had moved to Marton in Cleveland. They moved again before their next child, the first daughter, was born. This was Christiana, who was born on 31 January 1730 at Ormsby, just to the east of Marton. Christiana survived to adulthood and married a man called Cocker. Very little is known about them and it is uncertain whether they had any children.

Another daughter, Mary, was born in 1732 but she died on 30 June 1737. The Cooks had moved to Great Ayton in 1736 so Mary was buried at All Saints Church in that village. Cook senior had secured a position of hind or foreman at Aireyholme Farm, just outside the village. The move guaranteed the family a permanent home and marked the end of their wanderings. A third daughter, Jane, was born in 1737 in Great Ayton but she died on 12 May 1742 and was also buried at All Saints Church. When another girl was born on 1 August 1740, the name Mary was used again. However, Mary II died on 17 June 1741 and was buried like her elder namesake in the same church.

Cook's next sister, Margaret, was born in July 1742 at Great Ayton. She was one of only two of his sisters who survived to adulthood and is the only other member of the family known to have had children. She married James Fleck, a fisherman from Redcar, on 4 September 1764 in Great Ayton before moving to live in Redcar. The Flecks had eight children (James, Margaret, Grace, Mary, Thomas, William, John and Christiana) and it is through them that anyone claiming to be related to James Cook must trace their connection.

The last of James Cook's brothers was William, who was born on 12 January 1745 in Great Ayton. Not long after William's birth, James Cook left home to work in Staithes. Cook moved next to Whitby and not long after he began sailing on the *Freelove*, young William died on 29 January 1748 in Great Ayton.

James and Grace had no more children and sadly lost their eldest son, John, in 1750. John was single. James was between ships at Whitby at the time. The coal ships on which Cook sailed to London unloaded their coal at the wharves around Wapping. It is believed that Cook became acquainted with the Batts family in Wapping at this time and maintained the friendship after he joined the Navy in 1755. He probably stayed with the family at their alehouse, The Bell, when he was in London.

In late 1762, Cook returned to London after spending four years in North America. He quickly courted and married Elizabeth Batts. The couple were married on 21 December 1762 in Barking Parish Church, East London. Her mother, Mary Batts (*née* Smith) had married again after the death of Elizabeth's father and her new husband was John Blackburn. Elizabeth was 13 years younger than Cook, having been born in 1741 at Barking and baptised in St John's Church, Wapping. The Cooks moved to live at 126 Upper Shadwell but James sailed back to Newfoundland in early 1763. When he returned their first son, James, had been born on 13 October 1763. The family then moved to live in Assembly Row in Mile End where Nathaniel, the second son, was born on 14 December 1764.

Cook's parents had left Aireyholme Farm in about 1755 and had built a house in Great Ayton. His mother, Grace, died on 18 February 1765 and was buried with five of her children at All Saints Church. James Cook senior remained in Ayton until 1771 when he moved to live with his married daughter, Margaret Fleck, in

Redcar. He died on 1 April 1779 and was buried at St Germain's in nearby Marske. Margaret died on 16 October 1804 and was buried at Marske with her father.

The Cook's first daughter, Elizabeth, was born in 1766 and a third son, Joseph, was born on 26 August 1768, just as Cook was leaving Plymouth on his first Pacific voyage, aboard the *Endeavour.* Sadly, Joseph only lived for a few weeks, dying on 13 September 1768. Before Cook returned to Britain, his daughter Elizabeth had also died on 9 April 1771. Both the dead children were buried at St Dunstan's Church in Stepney.

Cook was home with Elizabeth and their two sons, James and Nathaniel, for several months in 1771 and 1772. Both boys were set for careers in the Navy. Another son, George was born on 8 July 1772 just before Cook sailed on his second voyage but George only survived until 1 October 1772. Cook's second voyage ended in 1775 and he resumed family life at Mile End. The Cook's last child, Hugh, was born on 23 May 1776. Cook had been persuaded to sail to the Pacific for a third time and he left his family for the last time in July 1776.

Cook was killed in Hawai'i in February 1779, only a few weeks before his father died. Elizabeth Cook learned of her husband's death at the beginning of 1780 and later that year she also learned of the death of her second son, Nathaniel, who had died on 5 October 1780 when his ship HMS *Thunderer* sank during a hurricane in the West Indies.

Elizabeth took comfort in her remaining two sons, James and Hugh, but tragedy struck again in 1793. Hugh had gone to Christ's College, Cambridge, to study to become a priest but he died on 21 December 1793 from scarlet fever. He was buried at nearby Great St Andrew's Church, Cambridge. Within weeks, James, the eldest son, had drowned on 24 January 1794 in Poole Harbour on his way back to his ship *Spitfire*. He too was buried at Great St Andrew's Church, Cambridge.

By now, Elizabeth Cook was a widow and all her six children had predeceased her. She had, by now, moved from Mile End to Clapham in south London, where she lived with her cousin, Isaac Smith, who had sailed with Cook. Elizabeth Cook was 94 when she died on 13 May 1835. She was buried with her children at Great St Andrew's Church, Cambridge.

See Also: Cook (Elizabeth)

Cook Inlet

Cook Inlet (60° N, 152° W) on the central south coast of Alaska extends north and then east from the Gulf of Alaska. It divides into two arms: Knik Arm to the north and Turnagain Arm to the south, with Anchorage on the peninsula between the two. The inlet is about 186 miles (300km) deep and in places is 31 miles (50km) wide. By the time of first contact with Europeans in 1756, the Eskimo people who had originally settled the area had been displaced by the Athabaskan Dena'ina people.

On 25 May 1778, James Cook, who had been sailing along the Alaskan coast looking for an opening that could be the Northwest Passage, worked his ships past the Barren Islands into the entrance of a large inlet. The inlet stretched north and Cook sailed close to its eastern shore at Cape Bede and crossed Kachemak Bay to an anchorage. The ships proceeded with high hopes up the inlet past Kalgin Island and anchored off Fire Island on 1 June. These hopes were not realised as Cook became aware that the water of the inlet was fresh and not salty.

The head of the inlet divided into two and Bligh was sent north up Knik Arm to check while Cook himself tried the other arm, soon finding its end. Cook called it Turnagain Arm and, on Bligh's return, decided to leave the inlet. James King landed at Possession Point, near Fire Island and buried a bottle. On 6 June Cook left the inlet that the Earl of Sandwich later directed should be called Cook's River. George Vancouver changed it to Cook Inlet. Cook had still not found the Northwest Passage and now found himself heading south-west outside Kodiak Island. Anchorage, at the head of Cook Inlet, has a statue of Cook in Resolution Park.

See Also: Alaska

Cook Islands

The Cook Islands (21° S, 158° W) comprise 15 islands covering 92.3 square miles (240 sq km) spread over 692,574 square miles (1.8 million sq km) of ocean in the central South Pacific between Tonga to the west and the Society Islands to the east. They consist of two scattered groups; a southern group of nine 'high' islands mainly of volcanic origin although some are virtually atolls, where the majority of the population lives; and a northern group comprising six true atolls. The people are Polynesians and it is believed they arrived from French Polynesia about AD 500. The written history of the Cooks began with the sighting of Pukapuka by the Spanish explorer, Mendaña, in 1595 followed by a landing on Rakahanga in 1606 by another Spanish explorer, Quiros.

Between 1773 and 1779 Captain James Cook sighted

and landed on many of the southern group. The name 'Cook Islands' was given to the group by the Russian explorer, Krusenstern, in honour of the British navigator when it appeared for the first time on a Russian naval chart in the early 1800s. On 23 September 1773, Cook reached an atoll with two small uninhabited islands that he named the Hervey Islands. They were Manuae and Te Au O Tu, later included in the Cook Islands. Cook was again in the region in June 1774 when he arrived at another atoll. He took the ship in close while Gilbert went ashore to examine the string of uninhabited, small islets dotting the fringe of the atoll. There was no passage that allowed the *Resolution* into the lagoon. The atoll was called Palmerston Atoll and is part of the Cook Islands. They departed on 22 June.

On his third voyage, Cook sailed east from New Zealand to about 160° W when he turned north. He arrived at the island of Mangaia on 29 March 1777. The ships approached from the south but heavy surf and a reef prevented them getting ashore. From the ship they could see people walking about. Cook sailed up the island's west coast while Gore was sent to find a way of landing. He was unsuccessful but he did make contact with islanders in canoes who told him the island's name. One local, Mourua, came out and boarded the *Resolution*.

Sailing northwards, they came to Atiu but lack of wind delayed their arrival there. Cook again sent Gore off to attempt to land but the reef stopped him getting ashore. A double canoe brought a chief out to the ships. He presented Cook with a pig and made a speech asking for a dog. Mai gave the Chief one of his dogs. On 3 April, canoes took Gore, Anderson, Mai and Burney ashore where they were presented to three chiefs. They stayed all day on the beach while an umukai (a feast to welcome strangers) was prepared for them. Mai feared they were about to be eaten but eventually they were returned unharmed to the ships.

Cook left the next day for a smaller uninhabited, sandy isle, Takutea, to the north-west. The animals needed feed and Gore obtained scurvy grass and coconuts. Cook next headed for Manuae (his Hervey Island, visited four years earlier), which he found inhabited, much to his surprise, as there had been no signs of life in 1773. The ships left for Tonga via Palmerston Atoll.

Cook never visited Rarotonga, the largest of the Cook Islands, nor any of the Northern Cooks. The country voted in a referendum in 1994 to keep the name Cook Islands and not change to a Polynesian name.

SEE ALSO: Polynesia, Second voyage

Cook's early years

James Cook was born in a cottage in the village of Marton, North Yorkshire in 1728. Most people who are interested in Cook know these facts, but few can recall any more details about Cook's early life. For somebody whose later life and whereabouts is known in so much detail thanks to his journals, the logs of naval vessels and the muster roles of colliers, Cook's early years remain relatively unknown. This is not unusual for somebody from such a humble background. Whilst it was some years before the young James Cook made his mark on the world, a range of contemporary records have enabled parts his early life to be reconstructed.

The Cook family at Marton

James Cook was the second of eight children born to James Cook (Senior) and Grace Pace. Grace was a local girl from the village of Thornaby and James had made his way south (from his native Ednam, in Roxbroughshire, Scotland), in search of work. They had been married in Grace's parish church at Stainton on 10 October 1725.

James Cook (Senior) was a labourer working on farms in the area. Some early biographers of Captain Cook state that his parents lived at Morton after their marriage. This is not a misspelling of Marton, as Morton is an area of rich farmland situated between the villages of Ormesby and Great Ayton. Evidence that the parents lived in that area can be taken from the baptism in January 1728 of their first child, a son named John after both of his grandfathers. By the time of their second child, the family had moved to Marton and were living in a simple cottage with daub and wattle walls and a thatched roof. The cottage has been variously described as a 'mud house' and '...a low cottage, of two rooms, one within the other the walls of mud and covered with thatch'. This description is typical of a farm labourer's cottage, a home that was often damp and unhealthy for those residing there.

The Cook family's second child was called James, after his father, and was born on Sunday 27 October 1728. Exactly a week after his birth he was baptised at Marton parish church. It is said that James Cook (Senior) was employed by a Mr Mewburn a local farmer. A plan of the Marton Estate from 1764 shows that George Mewburn had a farm in West Marton. Moreover, the alleged site of Cook's birthplace lies just across the road from Mr Mewburn's farm. As a labourer, James Cook (Senior) had to take work where and when it was available and this resulted in the family moving to different cottages within the area. In 1731, the baptism of their third child, Christiana, was performed in Ormesby parish church, whereas Mary, their fourth child was baptised at Marton. The location of the family's second cottage in Marton is not known, although it is believed to have been in the south-west of the village, and in the early 1900s a field was known locally as 'Cook's Close'.

Marton is not just the starting point for Cook's life, it is also the location of the first of several local legends relating to his early years. It is said that Cook received his first education at Marton from a Dame Walker. He is said to have 'tending the stock, took the horses for water and ran errands for the [Walker] family' and in return was taught his alphabet and how to read. Graves, in the earliest published history of the Cleveland area recorded that James, 'as well as the rest of the younger part of his family was taught to read by the school mistress of the village at an expense which we...can easily suppose did not exceed one shilling per quarter'. Whilst local legends are perpetuated by word of mouth, there is one contemporary record that appears to substantiate the story. In 1743, Thomas Herring, the recently installed Archbishop of York, undertook a detailed survey of his diocese. All parishes were sent a questionnaire in which the incumbent was asked to record the physical condition of their church as well as various other facilities in the parish. One of these questions asked if there was a school in the parish, and if so, how many children attended. In his response to this question, Philip Kitcheon, the Vicar of Marton wrote: 'There is no school house, a widdow Woman teaches a few small children to read in her own house.' Was this 'widow Woman' the legendary Dame Walker? Certainly the name Walker was common in the village of Marton in the 1700s. The name can be found on headstones in the parish churchyard and in the parish register. Indeed the church registers record that there were four marriages in the first quarter of the eighteenth century, each one coincidentally resulting in a new Mary Walker for the parish. Is it too much coincidence that one of these brides was even described as a school mistress at the time of her marriage? So it appears that contemporary records are able to substantiate the legend about Cook's early education in the village. All early biographers agree that the Cook family left the village of Marton in 1736, when the young Cook would have been eight years old.

South-east view of Marton showing the remains of the clay-built cottage where Cook was born. (Gott Collection, Wakefield Art Gallery)

The Cook family moves to Great Ayton

One of the most important times of the year for farm labourers was Martinmas – that period leading up to St Martin's day on 11 November. This marked the end of the farming year with the harvest long since gathered in and winter sowing yet to begin. Before the new farming year started there was an opportunity for change for both labourers and farmers alike. In Cleveland, as in many other villages throughout the North Riding of Yorkshire, labourers and servants attended their local Martinmas Hirings in the hope of advancing their position in life.

The nearest Hiring to Marton was at the market town of Stokesley, some six miles to the south. There, farmers and farm labourers would gather and discuss the terms of employment for the forthcoming year. James Cook (Senior) would have attended this hiring, probably taking his two eldest sons to show any prospective employer that although he had reached middle age he had two extra pairs of hands to assist him in his duties. Who knows what offers of employment James Cook (Senior) received on that day at Stokesley; history only records that he was successful in gaining a new position at Aireyholme Farm, Great Ayton. Employment was not just measured in monetary terms, and labourers could ask for various payments in kind, such as accommodation, clothing allowances etc. Once the terms of employment had been agreed the unwritten contract was sealed by the farmer who handed over the customary 'godspenny' to his new employee as a gesture of good faith. Over centuries the godspenny had grown

South-east view of Airy Holme Farm near Great Ayton. (Gott Collection, Wakefield Art Gallery)

in value and in Cook's day would have been one or two shillings.

A change of employment also provided labourers with a short break from their daily chores, and the Martinmas hirings were often accompanied by local festivities and other opportunities for people to drink or gamble away their godspenny. Being a canny Scot and probably teetotal, it is unlikely that James Cook (Senior) would have frittered his away when he had a growing family to feed and clothe.

The Skottowe connection

The cluster of sandstone barns and byres that form Aireyholme Farm still huddle together on the southern shoulder of the promontory known as Roseberry Topping, though in Cook's day it was called Ounesbury Topping. It is a mixed farm with cattle grazing on the upper pastures and other lands being used for growing crops. Cook's father has been variously described as 'hind', 'head servant' or 'bailiff', although all biographers agree that he would have had some responsibility for running the farm.

The name of the farmer who hired James Cook (Senior) has long since vanished into the mists of time, but the owner of the farm, Mr Thomas Skottowe, is another Cleveland character associated with the young James Cook. Compared with the mythical 'Dame Walker,' Skottowe is known to have existed. He was the Lord of the Manor of Ayton, a landowner with status in the local society, and a Justice of the Peace (JP). In common with many of his fellow gentry, Skottowe was not averse to paying for the education of promising youngsters. The young James Cook received the benefit of such 'noblesse oblige' and attended the school that stood in the centre of the village.

In 1743 the vicar of Ayton Parish Church responded to Archbishop Herring's questionnaire with the following: 'There is one Public School in our Parish: and generally twenty or thirty children are taught in it. Due care is taken to instruct them in the Principles of ye Christian religion according to ye doctrines of ye Church of England…'

Biographers differ in their accounts of Cook's scholastic ability. Heaviside reported that Cook was so accomplished at mathematics that he never made a mistake. In contrast Graves recorded that there was nothing to distinguish Cook from the other boys academically, although his behaviour set him apart from the others: 'It has been asserted by those who knew him at this early period of his life, that he had such an obstinate and sturdy way of his own, as made him sometimes appear in an unpleasant light; notwithstanding which, there was a something in his manners and deportment, which attracted the reverence and respect of his companions'.

Biographers agree that Cook attended the village school for about four years until he was 12 years old. It is assumed that he continued in the village for a further four years helping his father with the running of Aireyholme Farm. Where a local worthy had sponsored the education of a child, it was not uncommon for them to assist in obtaining the youth his first employment as well, thereby ensuring that their education was put to good use. This seems to have applied in the case of James Cook as there are several links between Thomas Skottowe and William Sanderson of Staithes for whom Cook started work in 1744.

Cook moves to Staithes

It was at the small fishing village of Staithes that James Cook encountered the third Cleveland character that is associated with his early years – William Sanderson. Like Mr Skottowe, William Sanderson was flesh and blood and not the product of legend. Sanderson was a merchant with a shop that stood on the sea front, overlooking the small harbour. It may be no coincidence that Cook came to work as an assistant in the shop at the time that Mrs Sanderson was expecting her second child. The move to Staithes could not have provided a greater contrast in Cook's life. The peace and tranquillity of rural Great Ayton was replaced by the incessant cry of the seagulls, and the crash of the waves against the quay outside the shop every high-tide. Legend has a way of elaborating history, and Cook's brief stay at Sanderson's shop has given rise to various stories which all involve a disagreement between the two over a shilling that disappeared from the shop till.

Cook only stayed at Sanderson's shop for about 18 months. His period at Staithes seems to have awoken in the young man a spirit of adventure that would stay with Cook for the next 30 years or so. Young (1817) recorded that Sanderson recognised the youth's attraction to the sea and used his business connections to find a suitable position for Cook at the nearby port of Whitby. Cook had been placed with Sanderson by Thomas Skottowe, and the merchant knew that he would have to account to the JP for his actions. He would have to find him a position with somebody who would look after the young man and provide him with suitable training, ideally an apprenticeship. In 1746, therefore, Cook moved to Whitby to work for John Walker and live in his house in Grape Lane.

By Clifford E Thornton

See Also: Cleveland, Great Ayton, Marton

Cook's ships

While the Royal Navy was well placed to mount expeditions such as those undertaken by James Cook to the Pacific, the vast majority of the vessels it owned were built to fight, possessing a combination of speed and firepower, which would make them more effective than their opponents. These were not the characteristics of vessels which could sail for thousands of miles, carrying a naval crew as well as civilian scientists and all the necessary equipment. Most of the small craft, which might have been suitable, were already required for duties in home waters. This was especially so in the peacetime of 1768 when few small vessels were kept in service and those that were, were fully employed in anti-smuggling duties, amongst other things. Another reason why purpose-built vessels were not available was that the Navy did not have a surveying department, under a hydrographer, until the early 1790s. Such a department would have required the kind of specialist vessels that were needed for exploration and charting work.

When, in 1740, there was to be an expedition to the Arctic commanded by Captain Middleton, the Navy chose a type of craft purpose-built for the Navy and possessing some of the qualities required for a voyage of exploration. This was a bomb vessel, the *Furnace*. Bomb vessels were built to carry heavy mortars and had a low length to beam ratio, as well as a flat bottom and square stern. This allowed the vessels to ground without capsizing, and the low length to beam ratio meant they had more internal space for extra crew and stores. They also had strong internal framing, and the mortar beds, on which the mortars sat, could be removed, creating more internal space. Even so, the *Furnace* had to undergo extensive and expensive refitting before she was ready to undertake her Arctic voyage. Two further bomb vessels would be used on Arctic exploration in the eighteenth century. They were the *Racehorse* and *Carcass* in the expedition commanded by Captain Phipps, who as a close friend of Joseph Banks hosted Mai on his trip to Yorkshire. However, one of Phipps's midshipmen on that voyage, Horatio Nelson, would go on to have a more distinguished career. Bomb vessels displayed the type of characteristics which were needed for a vessel that was to undertake long voyages. Large internal space combined with strength and the ability to take the ground without capsizing were essential. However, all the bomb vessels that were in service when Cook's expedition was under discussion were in use as patrol vessels and none would have been available for the first voyage.

As no other suitable vessels were available, the Navy decided to buy one and convert it for the voyage, which was to be undertaken at the behest of the Royal Society of London. It was in this way that, perhaps Cook's most famous vessel, the *Endeavour*, came into Royal Naval service. Built by Fishburn in Whitby, she had been named the *Earl of Pembroke* and was three and half years old when bought into the service by the Navy Board in March 1768. She was a collier brig, a type of vessel with much the same characteristics as the bomb vessel and normally used to ship coal from north-east ports to London. The Navy classed the *Endeavour* as a bark. She had a broad floor to her hold, which gave her a flat bottom, ideal for sitting on the mud if she need to be beached to carry out repairs whilst in the Pacific. Added to this, her squared-off stern and bluff bows meant she had a large internal capacity, which could be used for both cabin space and for the stowage of provisions for the 95 people who sailed on her. With a marked tumblehome, she was the complete antithesis of what might be expected of a Royal Naval vessel.

After the *Endeavour* was purchased from her owner, Thomas Milner, for the sum of £2840 10s 11d, the Navy spent almost twice that amount, £5394 15s 4d, on refitting her for the expedition. Much of this was to do with sheathing the hull, against ship worm, and the division of her 'tween deck for extra cabin space for Joseph Banks and all those who were to observe the Transit of Venus and collect botanical specimens. It is worthy of note that, for the £8000 spent on her purchase and refit, they could have built and equipped a 36-gun frigate.

The strength of the *Endeavour* is attested by the ship surviving striking the reef off Cape Tribulation in north-east Australia, when she was badly holed and it took two days to get her off. Cook and his crew had to stop the leak with a fother (or patch) of sail cloth, heaved under the ships and sealed with tar and oakum. *Endeavour* had to be beached and the repairs took six weeks to complete. It showed, also, both the self-reliance of a small crew with carpenters and sail-makers aboard, and the stout construction, and grounding capabilities of colliers. Further repairs had to be carried out at Batavia (Jakarta) and it was 2 years and 11 months after leaving Plymouth in 1768 that the *Endeavour* returned to Britain. She was refitted after her return and, at the cost of £3563 10s 10d was used as a store ship, making three voyages to the Falkland Islands. She was sold out of government service for £645 in 1775.

There is some scholarly debate as to what happened to *Endeavour* after she left government service. One theory is that she was sold and used again as a collier until 1790, when she was bought by an American and put on the French registry as a whaler, renamed *La Liberté*. She was supposed to have been lost in 1793 off Newport, USA, and broken up. The other version, at the time of writing, is that she was renamed the *Lord Sandwich* and used as a transport in the War of American Independence. She was supposedly scuttled in 1778.

On Cook's second voyage, two vessels were required after Cook himself requested two similar ships to the *Endeavour*. He wrote at the time: 'The ship must not be of great draught, but of sufficient capacity to carry a proper quantity of provisions and stores for the crew and of such construction that she will bear to take the ground and of such a size that she can be conveniently laid on shore if necessary for repairing any damages or defects.'

Cook was happy with the type of vessel but wanted a companion ship for safety reasons. The Admiralty bought in two more collier brigs. They were the *Marquis of Granby* and the *Marquis of Rockingham*, which once again had been built at Whitby by the same builder, Fishburn, and in the same year, 1770. Originally to be renamed *Drake* and *Raleigh*, their names were changed to *Resolution* and *Adventure* so as not to offend the Spanish. The vessels were classed as sloops.

The *Resolution* was slightly larger than the *Endeavour* and had greater room below deck. She cost the Admiralty £4151 and then underwent extensive conversions at Deptford. The conversions included heightening the waist of the vessel, the addition of an upper deck, and raising the level of the poop, which would give greater room below for cabins, particularly for Joseph Banks, who had asked for most of the alterations to be carried out. When the *Resolution* was trialled at sea she was found to be top-heavy and most of the alterations were removed at Cook's insistence for the safety of the ship. This lead to Banks leaving the expedition and the further refit cost the Admiralty £6565. The ship was also fitted with anchors to deal with ice and apparatus to distil fresh water from salt water. Cook would take *Resolution* with him on what turned out to be his third and last voyage as well as the second. She returned from the third voyage in 1780 and was subsequently converted to an armed transport. She sailed for the East Indies only to be captured by the French East Indies squadron under Suffren. Sailing in 1782 under French colours, she was reported captured, although once again there is some debate and confusion as to her final fate. The *Adventure*, bought at the same time as the *Resolution*, cost the Admiralty £2103. She was slightly smaller than either *Endeavour* or *Resolution*. She survived her voyage with Cook and in 1780 was converted into a storeship. She was sold out of the Navy in 1783. Another possibility suggested was that she returned to trade and was wrecked in the St Lawrence river in 1811.

The smallest of Cook's ships was the *Discovery*. At £2415, the cost of her purchase by the Admiralty and subsequent conversion was considerably less than for any other of Cook's ships. The crew numbered 70 officers and men. *Discovery* survived her voyage with Cook and was eventually broken up at Chatham in Kent in 1797.

Given that Cook's first voyage only carried a semi-official status, it is not surprising that the Navy did not use one of its own vessels to mount the expedition and especially so, when linked to the perennial shortage of small vessels from which the Navy suffered. This was even more so in times of peace so that buying-in made perfect sense. In fact, the Navy sometimes even purchased larger vessels in time of war. All of Cook's ships were small and carried a minimum of guns so none were rated (a First Rate carried 100 or more guns, whilst a Fifth Rate carried at least 32 guns).

The Navy Board was used to fitting out transports and victualling them for service in wartime so one Whitby collier, such as *Endeavour*, posed little challenge, even allowing for the nature of the voyage to be undertaken. It is not possible to provide a comparison that shows how much such vessels as *Endeavour*, *Resolution*, *Adventure* and *Discovery* would have cost had they been converted in a private yard. The Royal Dockyards were always more expensive but they were highly proficient in what they did and there were few complaints about their workmanship. The state of the *Resolution* during the third voyage was an exception.

Colliers were not fast ships, indeed they were particularly slow, and nor did they ride well in the water. Though the colliers were not always the best sailors, their combination of capacity and strength made them a good choice for long journeys and able to stand up to the pounding of the oceans and variety of conditions they would encounter. Whitby colliers, such as the *Endeavour, Resolution, Adventure* and *Discovery*, proved to be as near perfect a type of vessel as could be found at the time for Cook's needs. They were ideal as ships for the voyages of exploration undertaken by James Cook during the latter part of the eighteenth century. As Cook himself wrote: 'From the knowledge and experience that I have had of these sort of vessels I shall always be of the opinion that only such are proper to be sent on discoveries to distant parts.'

By Christopher Ware

See Also: Royal Navy, *Adventure*, *Discovery*, *Earl of Pembroke*, *Endeavour*, *Resolution*

Cooktown, and Endeavour Reef and River

At 10.30pm on 11 June 1770 disaster struck the *Endeavour*, which had navigated its way safely through hundreds of coral reefs, cays or sandbanks and small islands on the east coast of Australia. The ship ran aground on a reef (later called Endeavour Reef). Everything was done to free the ship including throwing cannons, stone ballast and stores overboard to lighten the load and allow her to float off. High water came but still the ship was stuck fast and the three pumps that worked were losing the battle against the leaks. However, Midshipman Munkhouse prepared a fothering to cover the hole and, after being on the reef for 23 hours, the ship was finally freed and made for shore.

James Cook nursed the *Endeavour* into a river mouth on 18 June 1770, and the ship was careened on the beach for repairs to begin. The extent of the damage was soon realised. The fothering had been successful, while large pieces of coral had broken off and plugged the holes to a large extent. It would take some time but it was repairable and the carpenters set to work.

During the time taken for repairs, Cook and his men explored the hinterland, went hunting and collected botanical and zoological specimens. The local aboriginal people, members of the Guugu Yimithirr (Gogo Yimidir) tribe were indifferent to the visitors at first and went about their normal activities such as fishing. Gradually though, contact was established and by 19 July some of them went on board the *Endeavour*. Communication was difficult but they let it be known that they did not approve of the large number of turtles that were caught. Their language, Guugu (meaning speech) Yimithirr (meaning this way) was spoken along the coastline from the Annan River in the south to the Jennie River in the north. A clan group, the Gamay Warra, part of the Guugu Yimithirr were based near Waymbuurr, as they called Cooktown. Cook's party collected a wordlist of Guugu Yimithirr language in 1770, including:

English	Cook's name	Present day
Hair	morye	muuri
Eyes	meul	miil
Lips	yembe	yimbi
Nose	bonjoo	bunhu
Kangaroo	kanguru	

It was here that the kangaroo was first collected and described. The Guugu Yimithirr live now in Hopevale, north of Cooktown and only about 100 people who can speak the language remain.

After seven weeks the repairs had been completed, and Cook sailed on 4 August. He realised the *Endeavour* was still in a delicate condition and needed to reach Jakarta for proper repairs. He decided it would be safer to sail in the open sea than staying inside the reef. Cook sailed the *Endeavour* past Lizard Island and, after the crew had located a gap, he took the ship through the reef on 14 August into deep water.

Cook named the river Endeavour River after his ship. One hundred years later, a settlement began in October 1873 to service the new gold field inland at Palmer River.

A view of the Endeavour River, on the coast of New Holland, where Endeavour *was careened on the shore, in order to repair the damage which she received on the reef. An engraving by Will Byrne after Parkinson. (Hawkesworth III fp 557)*

The population of Cooks-town, quickly rose to 4000 and the town's name changed to Cooktown (15° 29' S, 145° 15' E) in June 1874.

Various memorials commemorate Cook's visit to Cooktown. The James Cook Historical Museum, which was refurbished in 1999, houses the anchor and cannon of the HM Bark *Endeavour*. A monument (built 1887) and a statue are located by the Endeavour River, close to where the ship was careened. A cairn on Grassy Hill marks the visit.

SEE ALSO: Australia, First voyage

Cooper, Robert Palliser (1743–1805)

Robert Palliser Cooper sailed on the second voyage on the *Resolution* as first lieutenant. He kept a journal. Cooper became a lieutenant in December 1766 and served aboard HMS *Niger* on the Newfoundland and West Indies stations. His cousin, Hugh Palliser, who was Governor of Newfoundland, made him a customs officer for the island. After his voyage with Cook, Cooper became a commander in August 1775 and was put in command of HMS *Hawke*. He became a captain in January 1778 and made rear-admiral in 1795.

Cooper was baptised in St Mary Magdalene Church, Lincoln in 1743. He married Harriet Harden in St Mary's Church, Portsea on 27 July 1805 and died a few months later on 27 October 1805. He left a will (FRC 11/1433). Islands in South Georgia and New Zealand were named after Cooper.

SEE ALSO: Second voyage

Copley Medal

The Copley Medal is the premier award of the Royal Society, given annually for outstanding achievements in research in any branch of science. Its origin lies with Sir Godfrey Copley, a wealthy landowner from Sprotbrough, near Doncaster, South Yorkshire, who made a £100 bequest to the Royal Society in 1709. It was later decided to mark the bequest by awarding a medal each year, beginning in 1731. Five years later, it was agreed that the medal, to the value of £5, be awarded for either for the most important scientific discovery or for the greatest contribution made by experiment.

James Cook was awarded the Copley Medal in 1776 for his Paper, 'giving an account of the method he had taken to preserve the health of the crew of H.M. Ship the *Resolution*, during her late voyage round the world. Whose communication to the Society was of such importance to the public'. Cook read the paper to the Society on 7 March 1776 and only learned of his prize at the Cape in a letter from Sir John Pringle. Other winners include Charles Darwin, Albert Einstein, Benjamin Franklin and Ernest Rutherford.

SEE ALSO: Royal Society

D

Dalrymple, Alexander (1737–1808)

Alexander Dalrymple, the hydrographer, was born on 24 July 1737, the seventh son of Sir James and Christian Dalrymple, at New Hailes (east of Edinburgh). He received a basic education at the school in nearby Haddington and at home from his eldest brother. In 1752, he obtained an appointment as writer in the East India Company's (EIC) service. He went south to London, and attended Fort Hills, where he received instruction in arithmetic and bookkeeping in readiness to work for the company. Dalrymple sailed for India in December 1752, and reached Madras in May 1753. Owing to deficiencies in his education, he was placed, on his arrival in India, under the storekeeper. However, he came to the attention of the Governor, Lord Pigot, and of Robert Orme, the historian, then one of the members of Council, and he was removed to the secretary's office.

Lord Pigot himself gave him lessons in writing, while Orme gave him some instructions in accounts. Dalrymple, who had been promoted to deputy-secretary, read avidly about trading possibilities in the East Indies and became obsessed with the subject at the expense of his own career in the EIC. He went so far as to decline an appointment as secretary in order that he might give his undivided attention to his project. In doing so, he lost the certainty of acquiring a large fortune. He also placed himself in dispute with the company, which plagued his later life.

To pursue his scheme, Dalrymple made a voyage to the East Indies in 1759 in the *Winchelsea* and *Cuddalore*. He made a commercial treaty with the Sultan at Sulu, off north-eastern Borneo. Dalrymple returned to Madras and, in May 1762, was given command of a small vessel, the *London*. However, its cargo of goods was too small to trade. He was obliged to negotiate new terms, which were far less advantageous to Dalrymple. He did secure EIC rights to the island of Balambangan, off Borneo, but even this fell through. Dalrymple spent time in Manila before reaching Canton in November 1764. He returned to Britain in 1765.

As the authorities in Britain were not convinced by Dalrymple's arguments for more trade in the East Indies, he turned his attentions to the South Pacific instead, in which he was influenced by writers such as Charles de Brosses. The idea of 'Terra australis', a Great Southern Continent, began to develop. He published his *An Account of Discoveries in the South Pacifick Ocean previous to 1764* in 1767, which led him to be considered by the Royal Society (of which he was a member) for commander of an expedition to observe the Transit of Venus in 1769. Sir Edward Hawke, First Lord of the Admiralty, insisted that only a Royal Navy officer could command one of their ships and Dalrymple was excluded from the expedition. Some authors have written that Dalrymple maintained an animosity towards Cook after Cook displaced him on the *Endeavour* voyage but there is no real evidence to support this.

Dalrymple maintained contact with the EIC and, on the appointment of his friend, Lord Pigot, as Governor of Madras (Fort St George) in 1775, he made application to be reinstated in the service. This was granted and he went out to Madras as a member of Council. However, he was required to return home in 1777, under an order of the general court, so that his conduct could be investigated. In 1779, he was appointed a hydrographer of the East India Company. The Court of Directors resolved in 1780 that, as there were no charges against him, he could be again employed in their service but he never received an appointment, even though he obtained a pension from the company.

The Admiralty established the Hydrographic Office in 1795 and appointed Dalrymple as its first hydrographer. In 1808, however, it insisted that Dalrymple resign. He died shortly after at his house in Marylebone on 19 June 1808. He left a will (FRC 11/1482). There is a short biography in the *DNB*, v5, pp402–3.

SEE ALSO: Pacific exploration before Cook, Royal Society

David, Andrew

Andrew David joined the Royal Navy in 1943, and during a career of more than forty years served in Western Australia, the Persian Gulf, Africa, the Mediterranean, the West Indies and around the British Isles. In 1961 he commanded HMS *Medusa*, conducting surveys of the west coast of England and Wales. From 1961 to 1985 he worked in the Hydrographic Office of the Ministry of Defence, where he took a particular interest in its collection of manuscripts relating to voyages of discover in the eighteenth and nineteenth centuries. For several years after his retirement in 1985 he continued to write Admiralty sailing directions for the Hydrographic Office.

Lieutenant-Commander David has given papers on cartography and voyages of discovery at international conferences in many parts of the world. He has served on the councils of the Hakluyt Society and the Society for Nautical Research and is a Fellow of the Royal Geographic Society. He was the chief editor of *The Charts and Coastal Views of Captain Cook's Voyages*, published by the Hakluyt Society and has written extensively on matters to do with Cook's voyages, especially on the charts.

SEE ALSO: Cartographic results of Cook's voyages

De Brosses, Charles (1709–1777)

Charles de Brosses was born at Dijon in 1709. He studied law, becoming a magistrate and later the first president of the Parliament of Burgundy. De Brosses was also a classical scholar and visited Italy, later writing extensively about ancient Italy and the Roman Empire.

He was a friend and correspondent of many scholars of the time, including the naturalist Buffon. He also read the writings of the mathematician Maupertuis, which stimulated his interest in the history of the Pacific and what remained to be discovered in that region. This led de Brosses to write *Histoire des navigations aux terres australes*, which was published in 1756. In this work, he first laid down the geographical divisions of Australasia and Polynesia. The work, illustrated with maps by Robert de Vaugondy, was taken on the *Endeavour* voyage. It was very influential on Dalrymple and others interested in the Pacific, such as Bougainville. A pirated translation was published in Britain by John Callender without acknowledging de Brosses.

In 1765, his work on the origin of language, *Trait de la formation mecanique des langues* appeared. He also contributed the articles on Languages, Music, and Etymology to the *Encyclopédie*. De Brosses succeeded the Marquis de Caumont in 1758 in the Academie des Belles-lettres but when in 1770 he presented himself at the Academie Français, his candidature was rejected owing to Voltaire's opposition on personal grounds. De Brosses died in 1777.

SEE ALSO: Pacific exploration before Cook

Deptford and Woolwich

In 1512 Henry VIII decided to build two Royal Dockyards on the Thames. He chose Woolwich and Deptford as his sites as they were also conveniently near his Palace at Greenwich, which meant that he could watch the shipbuilding in progress. The Navy Board assumed responsibility for running the dockyards and for the repair and building of all naval warships. The dockyards contained dry and wet docks; workshops; mast ponds and houses; timber sheds and storehouses. There was also a ropeworks to supply rope for rigging. Several of Cook's ships were repaired and refitted at these yards.

One dockyard was established at Deptford (51° 29' N, 0° 03' W), 3 miles (5km) downstream from the Tower of London. Deptford, on the south bank of the Thames in Kent, had only been fishing village up to that time. The Admiralty Victualling Yard was moved to Deptford in 1742. Cook brought the *Grenville* to Deptford for it to be changed from a schooner to a brig in 1764. It was here that the *Grenville* was run into by a collier in 1766. The *Endeavour* was fitted out here and all the modifications demanded by Banks for the *Resolution* prior to the second voyage were carried out here as well. Deptford Dockyard later proved to be too far up the Thames and closed in 1869.

Woolwich (51° 29' N, 0° 04' E), is situated on the south bank of the River Thames, 4.3 miles (7km) east of Greenwich. It was the location of the second dockyard from 1512. Ordnance storehouses were developed on the present site of Royal Arsenal West, then known as Woolwich Warren, from 1671. It was converted from a storage depot to a munitions factory in 1696 when the Royal Laboratory was constructed for the purpose of manufacturing ammunition, fuses and gunpowder. From 1717, Woolwich Warren was the location of the Royal Brass Foundry, which cast all the guns for government service. Even surveying ships such as used by Cook carried a small amount of munitions and it was customary for ships to call at Woolwich when

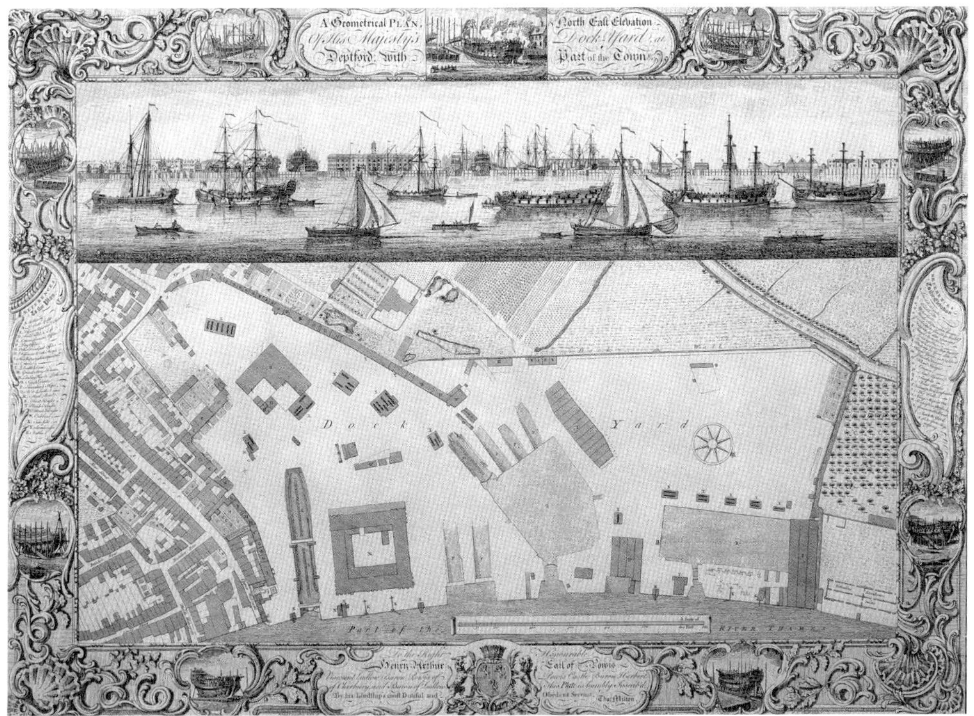

This print, showing Deptford and Woolwich dockyards, is one of a series of naval dockyards executed by Thomas Milton. Published c*1753, it was dedicated to Henry Arthur Earl Powis Viscount Ludlow. (Royal Naval Museum, Portsmouth, Art collection 1955/3)*

heading downstream to take on their supplies needed on their voyage.

SEE ALSO: Dockyards

Discipline and punishment

Discipline on eighteenth-century Royal Navy ships was strict and directed by the Articles of War, which served as the law on board. It was read at least once a month, usually if church service was held on Sunday, or when punishment was inflicted. The Articles were originally established in the 1650s and were amended in 1749 and again in 1757.

For James Cook discipline was most important as it lay at the heart of an efficiently-run ship. Cook was most diligent in carrying orders given to him and expected others to do the same. In his upbringing, he would have soon learned that you did not question orders and you always did as you were told. Cook had risen through the ranks from being an able seaman to be captain of his own ship, which allowed him an understanding of how the most lowly member of his crew felt and an appreciation of how hard and tedious the work could be. By the same token, Cook felt it had earned him the respect of his men and that they should carry out his orders without question and to the letter.

Men on board all had particular tasks and Cook expected everyone to perform them to their best ability. He had high expectations of himself and expected the same of all his crew from his lieutenants down. Cook felt vulnerable on the *Endeavour* voyage and knew that the slightest failure would count against him on his return to Britain, where he had no patrons to protect him.

Cook saw it as a two-way matter. If he ensured a capable, efficient and healthy crew, they, in their turn, would help in achieving what he hoped to do. To this end he introduced regimens of cleaning of the men's clothes and ship on a regular part of the process of keeping the crew healthy. He also insisted on a diet including unpopular foods such as sauerkraut, which in order to get the ordinary sailors to eat, he made great play of getting the officers to partake. When some men refused, Cook was not slow to punish them openly, thus setting an example to the others.

Cook kept his station and generally did not mix freely with the ordinary seamen or even his junior officers.

Summary of punishments:

	Men punished	**No. of punishments**
Grenville	6	6
First voyage	22	28
Second voyage	19	33
Third voyage	43	66
Ordinary seamen	63	91
Marines	23	35
Midshipmen, etc	4	7
Total	**90**	**133**
Offence		
Neglect of duty	26	
Theft	26	
Disobedience	16	
Drunkenness	12	
Insolence	11	
AWOL	8	
Desertion	7	
Other	27	
Total	**133**	

However, there is always the sense from the journals that he knew them all, together with their traits and problems. In their turn, the men may not have known him well but he earned their respect and most of them were prepared to do anything for him. Someone like Samuel Gibson, the marine, who was punished for attempted desertion on the first voyage, became his champion and sailed on all three voyages. Cook recognised that the crew also needed to enjoy themselves and encouraged music and dancing on board. On occasions he even relaxed the rules, for example, allowing men to overindulge when Crossing the Line (Equator), for which he was criticised by Forster for slackness.

Punishment by flogging was common on eighteenth-century Royal Navy ships and Cook was not much different from other captains in ordering it to be carried out. It was a deterrent to show that he was serious and expected his orders to be followed. Cook was generally ready to punish what he saw as misdemeanours. However, he was consistent in applying punishment and the men would know that certain actions would be punished. Bligh, the master on the third voyage, punished less than Cook on his *Bounty* voyage but he was erratic and lost the trust of many of his men.

Midshipmen and other petty officers would not normally be sentenced to flogging. Instead, they would be demoted or 'sent before the mast', meaning they no longer had access to the quarterdeck. Several midshipman were reprimanded in this way.

It is difficult to calculate exactly the number of men punished. Several names that appear on punishment lists do not appear on the muster rolls and are not mentioned in any other context, *eg* Garratty and Keplin.

Other offences included loss of French horn, counterfeiting money and tampering with food.

SEE ALSO: Royal Navy

Discovery, HMS

The support vessel on Cook's third voyage was HMS Discovery. She was built in 1774 by the Langborn yard in Whitby for William Herbert, from whom she was purchased, by the Navy Board, in January 1776. She was of 299 tons and the smallest of Cook's ships, being 91ft 6in (27.9m) long, and 27ft 6in (8.4m) wide. Originally a brig-rigged collier named the *Diligence*, the vessel was re-rigged as a ship.

The *Discovery* cost £2415 including alterations. She sailed on Cook's third voyage on 1 August 1776, twenty days after Cook on the *Resolution* but caught up at the Cape. The two ships remained together until the end of the voyage on 7 October 1780. Commander Charles Clerke captained the *Discovery* until Cook's death at Hawai'i, when he transferred to the *Resolution*.

After the voyage in May 1781, the *Discovery* was converted to a navy transport vessel. She was eventually broken up at Chatham in October 1797. Her name has been used for various ships, including those of Vancouver and Malaspina (*Descubierta*), as well as one of the American Space Shuttles.

SEE ALSO: Cook's ships, Third voyage

Dixon, George (?–1800?)

George Dixon sailed on the third voyage on the *Discovery* as the armourer. In 1785, the King George Sound Company was formed to exploit the sea otter fur trade identified by Cook's third voyage. Two ships were purchased and Dixon and Nathaniel Portlock were appointed captains. Dixon commanded the smaller *Queen Charlotte,* which sold its furs in Macao in late 1787. The ship arrived back in Britain in September 1788. He named the Queen Charlotte Islands after his ship, while the strait that divides those islands from Prince of Wales Island was named Dixon Entrance after him.

An account of Dixon's voyage by William Beresford, the ship's supercargo, was published. Dixon also became involved in a dispute with John Meares over Meares' false claims of his achievements in the North Pacific. Dixon may have moved to Gosport, near Portsmouth, to become a teacher of navigation. A book, *The Navigator's Assistant,* published in 1791 may have been written by him. He is thought to have died in 1800. There is a short biography in the *DNB*, v5, p1028.

SEE ALSO: Third voyage

Dockyards

Cook had experience of dockyards at Deptford, Woolwich, Sheerness, Portsmouth and Plymouth though mostly at Deptford where the *Grenville* and his Pacific ships were prepared for action. The dockyards were usually run by civilian employees of the Navy Board, who were not necessarily sea officers. The senior official of each yard was the Commissioner, appointed by, and nominally a member of, the Navy Board. Under him were the Clerk of the Cheque and the Storekeeper, who with their clerks were responsible for the financial and administrative business of the yard; the Master Shipwright, who with his colleagues, the Master Sailmaker, Anchorsmith, Rigger, Boatbuilder etc, was in charge of the building and repair work of the yard; and finally the Master Ropemaker who ran the Ropeyard.

The Commissioners were usually retired sea officers; dockyard shipwrights, having served their apprenticeship, often became carpenters in the Navy, and might return to be Master Shipwrights. Joseph Gilbert, the *Resolution*'s master, became master attendant at Portsmouth and Deptford dockyards after the voyage.

SEE ALSO: Navy Board, Royal Navy

Douglas, John (1721–1807)

John Douglas, a Scottish man of letters and Anglican bishop, was born at Pittenweem, Fife, the son of a shopkeeper, on 14 July 1721. He was educated at Dunbar and, from 1738, at Balliol College, Oxford, where he took his M.A. degree in 1743. He joined the Foot Guards in Flanders as chaplain but returned to England when the 1745 Jacobite rebellion occurred.

In 1747, he was ordained priest, and became curate of Tilehurst, near Reading. The following year, he published his first literary work, *The Vindication of Milton*. The Earl of Bath then installed him as vicar of High Ercall, Shropshire in 1750. Douglas only resided occasionally in his parishes and preferred to live in London. In 1752, he married Dorothy Pershouse, who died three months after the wedding.

For many years, Douglas engaged in writing political pamphlets. In 1761, he was appointed one of his Majesty's chaplains, and in 1762, through the interest of the Earl of Bath, he was made Canon of Windsor. In 1764, he exchanged his livings in Shropshire for that of St Austin and St Faith in Watling Street, London and, in 1765, married again to Miss Elizabeth Rooke. Douglas moved from the chapter of Windsor to that of St Paul's in London in 1776. At the request of the Earl of Sandwich, First Lord of the Admiralty, he prepared for publication the journal of Captain Cook's second voyage. In 1781, again at the request of Sandwich, he prepared for publication the journal of Captain Cook's third and last voyage and for which he supplied the introduction and notes.

In 1787, Douglas was made Bishop of Carlisle and, in 1788, he succeeded to the Deanery of Windsor, for which he vacated his position with St Paul's. He became Bishop of Salisbury in 1791. However, Douglas was not an outstanding churchman and he preferred to stay in London. He was a FRS. Bishop Douglas died on the 18 May 1807 and was buried in one of the vaults of St George's chapel in Windsor Castle. There is a short biography in the *DNB*, v5, pp1242–3.

SEE ALSO: Published accounts

Dusky Sound/Tamatea

Dusky Sound (45° 45' S, 166° 35' E) is a large inlet in Fiordland on the south-west coast of Te Wai Pounamu, the South Island of New Zealand. The inlet is 15.5 miles (25km) deep and 4.9 miles (8km) wide at the mouth. The terrain, which is mountainous and covered in thick vegetation makes access by land extremely difficult. Māori had begun to explore Fiordland from about 800 years ago and a few from the Ngāti Mamoe iwi were inhabiting the sound when Cook arrived in 1773.

Cook had sailed past the entrance to the sound in 1770 but had been reluctant to enter because of prevailing winds and currents, much to the disgust of Joseph Banks. In 1773, Cook had just spent several months in Antarctic waters and needed to repair the *Resolution* and to rest his crew. On 25 March, land was sighted and the next day Cook brought the *Resolution* into Dusky Sound. While the *Resolution* waited by Anchor Island, boats were dispatched to find a suitable anchorage. Pickersgill found one on the south side of

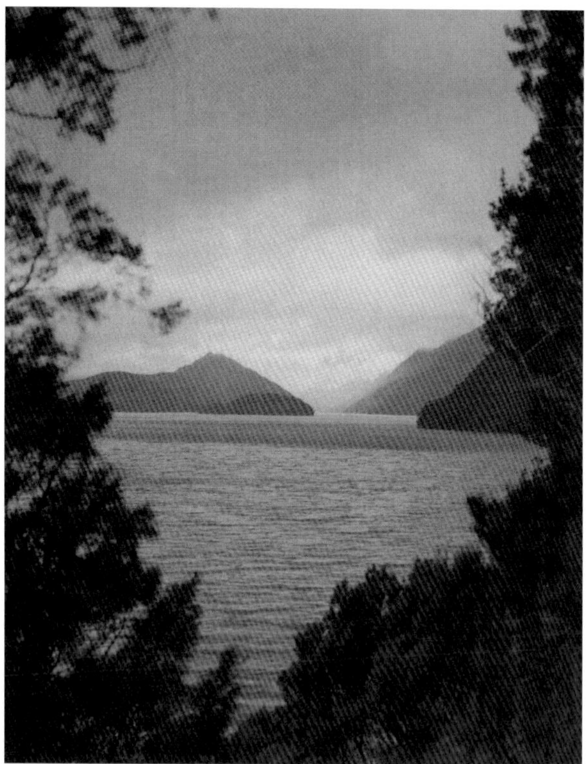

Dusky Sound, looking east from Astronomer's Point up Cook Channel. (Mark Adams)

the inlet. It was later called Pickersgill Harbour. A clearing was made ashore for the astronomers to work, earning the spot the name Astronomer's Point, while a brewery was set up using rimu and manuka trees. Officers began to explore the sound and, at Cascade Point in Cascade Cove, Māori were seen in the distance. These people followed them back to the ship, but no contact resulted. Cook found the Māoris' camp but it was deserted.

More exploration took place in order to shoot wildfowl and seals for food. Many local features were named for the animals shot there and the detailed charts compiled show Woodhen Cove, Duck Cove and Seal Rocks. Luncheon Cove and Supper Cove denote the meals enjoyed. Gradually contact was established with local Māori. Gifts were exchanged with a small family on Indian Island and others visited the ship.

Cook explored the Acheron Passage and realised that it gave egress to the sea. He therefore sailed by that route when he left Pickersgill Harbour on 30 April. Progress was very slow and it took until 5 May to reach Passage Point. Pickersgill and the Forsters spent two days up Wet Jacket Arm while Cook investigated Breaksea Sound. Gilbert, the master, charted the passage to the sea. On 11 May, the *Resolution* sailed back out into the open sea and north up the coast to find Furneaux and the *Adventure.*

Most of the features in Dusky Sound carry names either given by Cook or named at a later date after Cook's crew and ship. At Astronomer's Point, it is still possible to see the stumps of the trees cut down by Cook's men.

SEE ALSO: New Zealand, Second voyage

Dutch explorers

The Dutch gained a foothold in the Pacific through the actions of the Dutch East India Company (Verenigde Oostindische Compagnie or VOC), which established itself at Batavia (Jakarta) at the beginning of the sixteenth century. They concerned themselves primarily with the spice trade and created trading posts throughout the Dutch East Indies (Indonesia). The Moluccas and Ceram were especially important.

Other Dutch companies resented the monopoly of the VOC and looked for ways of circumventing them. Willem Schouten and Jacob Le Maire led an expedition in 1615, which looked for a different way of entering the Pacific not involving the Straits of Magellan. In January 1616, they discovered the Strait of Le Maire between Staten Island and Tierra del Fuego. A few days later, they rounded Cape Horn, which they named after one of their ships, recently lost, the *Hoorn.* They continued across the Pacific, seeing few islands, only to be arrested by the VOC when they reached the East Indies.

The VOC began to expand its horizons and explored north as far as Japan. In 1642, an expedition was sent south to explore the south-west Pacific. Abel Tasman visited Tasmania, which he named Van Dieman's Land. He also visited New Zealand and parts of Tonga, Fiji, New Ireland, and New Britain. He proved that Australia was not part of a great Antarctic continent.

Jacob Roggeveen led an expedition to the Pacific on the understanding he did not infringe on VOC-controlled territory. On Easter Day, 5 April 1722, he arrived at an isolated island in the south-east Pacific. This was Rapa Nui, which the Dutch called Easter Island. He continued west via several of the Tuamotus, Bora Bora and Samoa to Batavia, where he was also arrested.

This marked the peak of Dutch interest in the Pacific and there were no further expeditions of note.

SEE ALSO: Pacific exploration before Cook, Tasman (Abel)

E

Eagle, HMS

The first ship that Cook was assigned to in the Royal Navy was HMS *Eagle*. One of many Navy ships to carry this name, this *Eagle* was built by Barnard at Harwich in 1745. She was a Fourth Rate of 1124 tons, 147ft by 42ft (44.8m by 12.8m), and carried 58 guns.

On 25 June 1755, Cook joined the ship at Spithead, where she had just come out of Portsmouth Dockyard after repairs. The captain was Joseph Hamar. Cook had been promoted to master's mate by the time the *Eagle* sailed on 4 August. The *Eagle* patrolled off Southern Ireland before putting into Plymouth where Hamar was replaced by Hugh Palliser. Palliser resumed the patrols in the Bay of Biscay and the English Channel.

Cook and the *Eagle* took part in several actions against French shipping, including the capture of the *Triton* and the *Duc d'Aquitaine*. After repairs, Palliser took the *Eagle* across to Canada but without Cook, who successfully took his master's examination in June 1757. Cook was then transferred to HMS *Solebay*. Palliser bought the storm-ravaged *Eagle* back to Britain but left the ship in February 1758. The Navy sold the *Eagle* in 1767.

SEE ALSO: Cook's ships, Seven Years War

Easter Island/Rapa Nui

Easter Island (Rapa Nui) (27° 08' S, 109° 22' W), in the south-east Pacific, is over 1988 miles (3200km) from Tahiti and Chile, making it one of the most isolated places on Earth. A small triangular island, it is best known for the giant stone statues, known as 'Moai', that dot the coastline. The island, which has an area of 63.8 square miles (166 sq km), is now a province of Chile. The main settlement is at Hanga Roa near the south-western corner of the island.

The first inhabitants of the island were Polynesians and radio-carbon dates suggest that it was settled sometime before the fourth century AD, probably from Eastern Polynesia, most probably the Marquesas. The early settlers called the island Te Pito O Te Henua (Navel of The World). The Dutch explorer, Jacob Roggeveen, arrived at the island on Easter Day in 1722 and named it Easter Island. Today, the land, people and language are all referred to locally as Rapa Nui.

Woman of Easter Island. Engraved by J Caldwell after Hodges. (Cook I fp 291)

Cook visited the island for three days in the course of the large sweep of the ocean he undertook in 1774 during the second voyage. He himself was still sick when the *Resolution* arrived on 14 March and he remained on the ship while a small party led by Wales, the Forsters, and Pickersgill went ashore for a tour of the island. The Forsters provided a description of what they observed while William Hodges, the artist, produced of a painting of the moai at Orito.

SEE ALSO: Polynesia, Second voyage

Edgar, Thomas (1745–1801)

Thomas Edgar sailed on the third voyage on the *Discovery* as master. He kept a log and a journal, and he made surveys and drew charts. After the voyage, Edgar was promoted to lieutenant in 1781. He visited the Falkland Islands from 1786 to 1787 on board the whaler, *Hope*. He surveyed part of the coast and is commemorated by Port Edgar on West Falkland, while Hope Reef honours the ship. Arrowsmith published

Edgar's chart of the Falklands in 1797. In 1795, he became keeper of Dungeness Signal Tower in Kent until his death in 1801.

Edgar was born in Woolwich in 1745 and died in Lydd, Kent on 17 October 1801, where he was buried in All Saints Church. He left a will (FRC 11/1365). His gravestone records that he joined the Navy when he was ten and served with Hawke in 'that memorable Engagement', presumably the Battle of Quiberon Bay in 1759.

SEE ALSO: Third voyage

Education, Cook's

James Cook, to use twenty-first century terminology, was an example of lifelong or continuing education. Cook had little in the way of formal education but through application and a drive for self-improvement, he was still learning at his death.

Cook was born in very poor circumstances in Marton, which had no school at the time. It is believed that the young boy was taught the alphabet and how to read by a local woman in return for running errands. The Cooks moved to Great Ayton when James was eight and his father's new employer, Thomas Skottowe, arranged for him to attend the local village school. Michael Postgate had founded the school in Ayton in 1704 and, by Cook's time, the teacher was William Rowland, a local man born in Stokesley in 1714. Rowland taught Cook arithmetic and how to write. Cook remained at the school for four years and then spent some time working on the farm but when he went to Staithes in 1745, he was educated sufficiently to work in a shop.

Cook soon moved to Whitby to become a seaman working for John Walker. He lived in the Walkers' attic and it is recorded that Cook read books on seamanship and mathematics to help him progress. Life aboard the colliers proved a practical education paralleling the theory of the books. When Cook entered the Royal Navy he was soon able to easily pass the masters' examination, which indicates his proficiency.

The next major event occurred following the siege of Louisbourg in 1758 when Cook met Samuel Holland. Holland taught Cook the rudiments of land surveying, which Cook adapted to marine surveying and charting over the next few years in Canada and Newfoundland. He had also learned sufficient astronomy to be able to observe a solar eclipse in 1766 and prepare the results for presentation to the Royal Society.

Cook was, therefore, a more than competent sailor at the beginning of the *Endeavour* voyage, versed in mathematics, astronomy, surveying, navigation and seamanship. The first voyage shows him developing further and learning from Joseph Banks. At the beginning of the voyage, Cook's journal is a traditional seaman's list of matters to do with sailing the ship but as the voyage progresses, Cook begins to include ethnographic and scientific detail. By the second and third voyages, Cook's journals have become valuable sources of information on many subjects, not least descriptions of Pacific peoples at the time of contact.

Elliott, John (1757–1834)

John Elliott sailed on the second voyage on the *Resolution* as an AB. He was related to the Wilkinson ship-owning family, which had dealings with the Royal Navy, and through them secured his place on the ship. Elliott kept a log, made surveys, and drew coastal views and charts. After sailing with Cook, he sailed on East India Company vessels from 1775 to 1778, and was on board the *Colebrooke* when it was wrecked at the Cape in August 1778. He rejoined the Royal Navy and was made fourth lieutenant on HMS *Ajax* in 1779 in the West Indies. In 1780 he was promoted to first lieutenant but was badly wounded at the Battle of the Saintes, off Guadeloupe in the West Indies in 1782. After this, he never returned to full active service. He was made a superannuated commander in March 1814. He wrote his *Memoirs* in 1813, which included a description of Cook's second voyage. It is useful for the brief comments he makes about some of his colleagues.

Elliott was born in Helmsley, North Yorkshire on 11 January 1757. He married in 1784 and had 14 children before dying in Ripon, North Yorkshire on 13 September 1834. There is a memorial to him in Ripon Cathedral.

SEE ALSO: Second voyage

Ellis, William Webb (1756?–1785)

William Ellis sailed on the third voyage on the *Discovery* as surgeon's mate. He also painted landscapes and natural history specimens, and drew coastal views. Samwell described him as 'a genteel young fellow and of good education'. It is thought that he was educated at Cambridge and then at St Bartholomew's Hospital, London. Before Charles Clerke died, he commended Ellis to Banks in a letter 'I must beg leave to recommend to your notice Mr Will. Ellis one of the Surgeon's mates who will furnish you with some drawings & accounts of the various birds which will come to your possession, he has been very useful to me in your service in that particular.'

After the voyage, Ellis saw Banks and presented his drawings to him. However, Ellis was in financial difficulties and succumbed to an offer of 50 guineas to write an account of the third voyage, which was published in 1782. Banks also gave him some money but Ellis had ruined his prospects in the Navy through publishing without permission.

Ellis was born in 1756(?), and died in June 1785 when he fell from a mast at Ostend in Belgium, where he was joining the scientific team of an Austrian expedition about to sail to the Pacific.

SEE ALSO: Artists on Cook's voyages, Third voyage

Endeavour, HM Bark

In March 1768, the Admiralty instructed the Navy Board to purchase a vessel for an expedition promoted by the Royal Society of London to observe the Transit of Venus in 1769. The ship chosen was the *Earl of Pembroke*, 3½ years old, built by the Fishburn yard at Whitby and owned by Thomas Milner. She had been used as a collier in the North Sea. Cook did not take part in the selection process but would have approved of the choice, being familiar with colliers from his time in the North Sea.

The *Earl of Pembroke* was renamed HM Bark *Endeavour*, and fitted out at Deptford with square-rigging on all masts. She was termed a bark on account of the shape of the hull. She was of 368 tons, 97ft 1in (29.6m) long with a breadth of 29ft 2in (8.9m). The original purchase cost was £2840 10s 11d; alterations for the first voyage cost £5394 15s 4d and subsequent refits £3563 10s 10d, a total of £11,798 17s 1d. The *Endeavour* voyage began on 25 August 1768 and finished on 13 July 1771 during which she survived

Profile and sail plan of Endeavour. *She was taken into the Navy in 1768 and this sail plan was reconstructed from a list of spar dimensions dated 1771. (David MacGregor)*

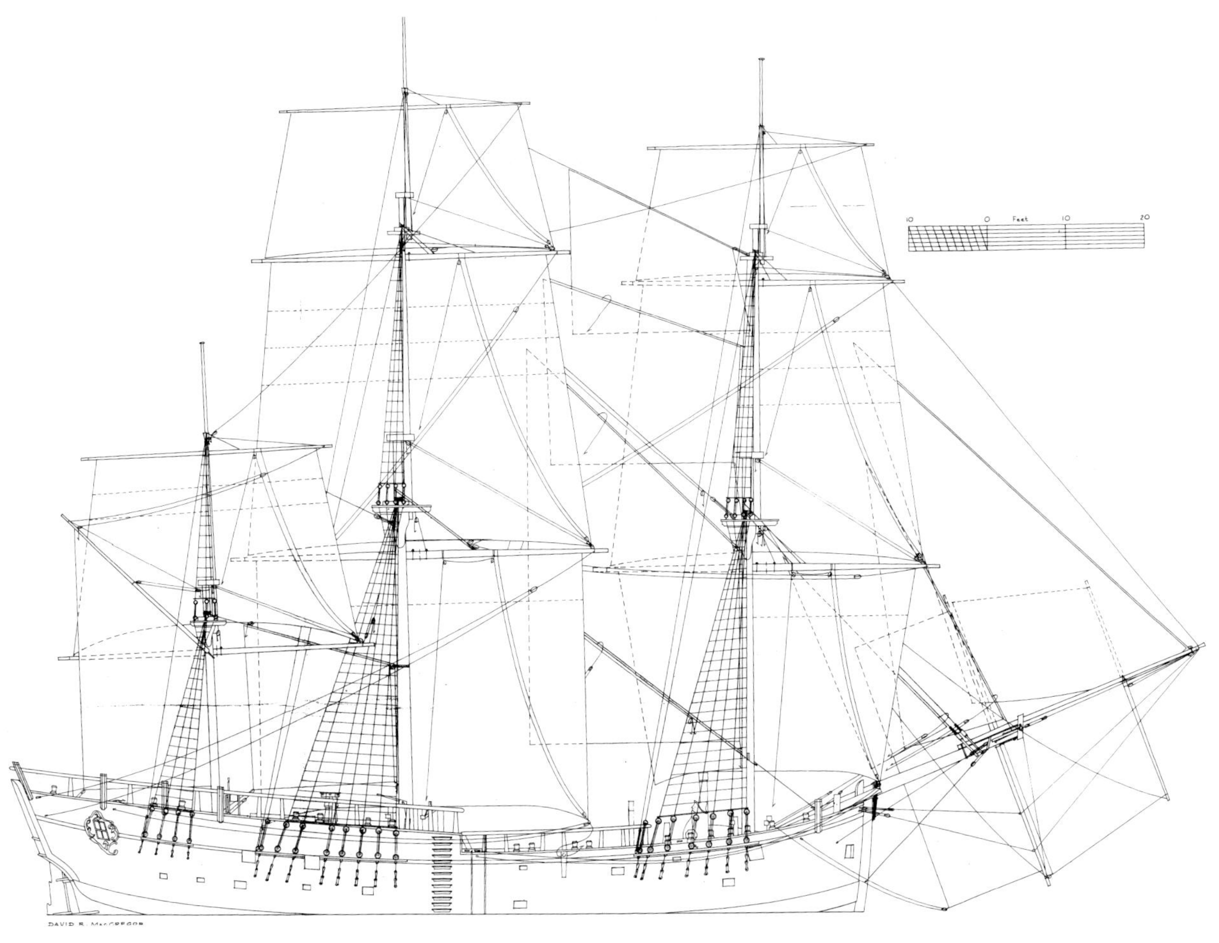

running onto the Great Barrier Reef. This prompted Cook to advise using two ships for future expeditions. Cook captained the voyage with a rank of lieutenant.

Endeavour's history after Cook's voyage has been uncertain for many years but in the 1990s a clearer picture emerged. The ship made three visits to the Falkland Islands between 1771 and 1775 as a supply ship but fell into 'wretched disrepair' and in 1775 was sold off for £645. After being repaired in 1776, the ship was renamed the *Lord Sandwich* and put into government service as a troop transport during the War of American Independence. She may also have served as a prison ship in Newport Harbor before she was sunk there, along with several other British vessels, in early August 1778, in an attempt to blockade the port from attacking American and French forces. Divers have attempted, so far without success, to find the wreck. Not all of this later history has been confirmed and may never be.

A replica of the *Endeavour* was launched in 1993. Her name has been used for several geographical features, especially in Australia, and for one of the American Space Shuttles. Two recent books, one by Ray Parkin (*H.M.Bark Endeavour: her place in Australian history*) and the other by Karl Heinz Marquardt (*Captain Cook's Endeavour*) contain detailed drawings and information about the ship.

SEE ALSO: Cook's ships, First voyage, Colour plate 2

Endeavour replica

The *Endeavour* replica is a near exact copy of the ship, HM Bark *Endeavour*, which Cook used for his first voyage and in which he visited Australia. The original, therefore, occupies a special place in the history of Australia and it was decided to build a replica of Cook's ship, in anticipation of the Australian bicentennial in 1788. The vessel would become part of the Australian National Maritime Museum's floating collection.

It was arranged for a shipyard in Fremantle, Western Australia, to build the ship and the keel was laid in October 1988. The project was plagued with financial problems as sponsors pulled out but eventually a charitable trust, the HM Bark *Endeavour* Foundation, was formed. This oversaw the construction and commissioning of the vessel. Historical authenticity was the primary concern. The original ship had been surveyed and detailed information was obtained from records surviving in the National Maritime Museum at Greenwich. Certain alterations were made to meet modern safety standards. Different timbers were used, with jarrah instead of oak for the hull and douglas fir for the masts and decks.

A 4pdr gun on the Endeavour *replica. Guns from the original ship were jettisoned with ballast in 1770 when the ship hit the Barrier Reef, to help her refloat. Six coral encrusted guns were recovered by divers in 1969 and cleaned. (Julian Mannering)*

Conditions below decks are as close to the original as possible. Crew sleep in hammocks slung from the deck head of the lower deck sleeping flat, as Cook's crew did. Some concessions to the twenty-first century have been necessary, such as auxiliary engines, generators, a desalination unit, modern bilge pumps, heads, showers and an electric galley. The replica also has a complete range of modern communications and navigation equipment, including a Global Positioning System (GPS).

The replica was launched on 9 December 1993. She was then rigged and underwent sea trials before being commissioned on 16 April 1994. The ship sailed for Sydney on 2 October 1994, arriving on 18 December where she was displayed at the Australian National Maritime Museum until April 1995. Since then the ship has toured the world. Extended stopovers in ports allow people to inspect the vessel and, to date, thousands have taken the opportunity. Volunteers are then able to join the ship to help sail it to the next port on the schedule. The *Endeavour* replica sails under the command of Captain Chris Blake with an experienced, professional crew of 14 looking after the volunteer crew.

English Channel and Bay of Biscay

Britain's early history is marked by many invasions by peoples from the south, crossing the stretch of water now known as the English Channel. As Britain became more powerful and able to defend itself against further invasions, control of the sea became most important and much effort was spent in building up its navy. Ships regularly patrolled the English Channel and adjacent stretches of water such as the Bay of Biscay and the North Sea.

The English Channel, commonly called the Channel (and in French 'La Manche'), is the narrow sea separating Britain from France. At its entrance in the west between Brittany and Cornwall its breadth is 124.2 miles (200km). This gradually narrows and at the Strait of Dover 335.5 miles (540km) to the east its breadth has decreased to 21.7 miles (35km). The Bay of Biscay (in French, 'Golfe de Gascogne') is an inlet of the Atlantic Ocean bounded to the east by France, as far north as Ushant ('Ouessant'), and to the south by Spain as far west as Cape Ortegal. The bay is noted for its sudden, severe storms and its strong currents.

During the eighteenth century, France represented the greatest threat to Britain and the two countries fought several wars during this time. On each occasion, a major part of British policy involved sending its ships out to patrol off the French coast and blockade ports, especially Brest, Le Havre, Cherbourg, St Malo and La Rochelle. This prevented France assembling and dispatching invasion forces and also stopped France sending assistance to other theatres of war such as Canada and India.

Cook joined the Navy in 1755 and was immediately dispatched to serve on HMS *Eagle* in the western approaches to the Channel. Over the next three years, especially after war had been formally declared in 1756, Cook took part in patrols on ships, including the *Eagle* and the *Pembroke.* He even spent time on a cutter close in shore on the Brittany coast. At other times, he was involved in naval actions helping capture the *Triton* and a French East Indiaman, the *Duc d'Aquitaine.*

SEE ALSO: *Eagle* (HMS), Seven Years War

Enlightenment

The Enlightenment was an intellectual movement, which took place during the eighteenth century, driven by the *philosophes*, the French rationalist philosophers who fully articulated the values and consequences of Enlightenment thought. It was primarily French because French culture dominated Europe at the time and its principal figures thrived in the salons of Paris. These figures included Descartes, Pascal, Montesquieu, Voltaire, Diderot, and Rousseau.

The movement named itself as its members believed that they were more enlightened than their compatriots and had a duty to enlighten them. They believed that human reason could be used to combat ignorance, superstition, and tyranny and to build a better world. Their principal targets were religion (embodied in France by the Catholic Church) and the domination of society by a hereditary aristocracy and royalty.

The movement found support in the French middle-class or bourgeosie, which was expanding and seeking a more prominent role in government and other affairs. By 1750, literacy levels had increased and more people were able to follow and contribute in debate. A parallel concept, and involving many of the same people, was the *Encyclopedie*. This work was planned by Denis Diderot, and was announced as a *Dictionnaire raisonne des sciences, des arts, et des metiers*, providing a complete alphabetical treatment of the whole field of human knowledge from the standpoint of the Enlightenment. Other *Encyclopedistes*, as the authors were known, included d'Alembert and the Chevalier de Jaucourt. It was published from 1751 to 1772 in 28 volumes.

Britain had developed its own Enlightenment, mostly based in Edinburgh. The principal thinkers in Britain were the Scot David Hume and the Englishman John Locke.

The Enlightenment affected how the narratives of voyages such as Cook's were received but it, in turn, was influenced by the content and ideas expressed in those narratives. The voyages added considerably to human knowledge and endorsed the positivist way of thinking of the time. The later part of the eighteenth century saw the realisation of some of the ideals of the Enlightenment with the independence of the United States and the French Revolution.

Ethnographic results of Cook's voyages

The three Pacific voyages of James Cook opened entirely new vistas of geographic and scientific knowledge to the Western world, but at the time of these historic voyages ethnography as a scientific discipline did not exist. In the eighteenth century the study of human society and culture was largely an amalgam of observations made by navigators, missionaries and other travellers that was interpreted by philosophers, historians and adventure writers, all of whom had distinct preconceptions about non-Western peoples that affected the selection and presentation of information about them. From the point of view of cultural history, the results and collections from Cook's three Pacific voyages are of seminal importance for the ethnographic study of certain Pacific peoples and for the development of method and theory in ethnohistory. During Cook's voyages the first extensive contact with Pacific people was made and the interaction was long and friendly enough to reach at least a minimal level of understanding. Hundreds of objects were collected during Cook's voyages and hundreds of pages were filled with accounts of native customs. The written accounts and collections made by Joseph Banks on the first voyage, Reinhold and George Forster on the second, and William Anderson and David Samwell on the third mark these individuals as the first Pacific ethnographers.

At the time of Cook's voyages the study of indigenous peoples was primarily a natural history approach concerned with cataloguing the varieties of mankind. Variations of physical traits and social and cultural conditions were recorded in much the same way as were plants and animals. Houses, canoes, clothing, portable objects and the people themselves were described, illustrated, and collected if possible. Rituals, entertainments and daily life were observed, experienced, illustrated and recorded. Comparative vocabularies and language acquisition were attempted while artists depicted people, ceremonies, and objects that could not be acquired. Recording and collecting was part of the brief to ships' companies and they did these jobs well. Cook's voyages became a model emulated by French, Spanish, Russian and American expeditions.

The 2000 artefacts collected during Cook's voyages form the earliest corpus of Pacific objects that can be identified today and the illustrations that derive from these voyages form an impressive visual archive. Now considered works of art, each object is treasured by the museum or private collector who holds it, as well as being an important cultural identity marker to Pacific islanders. The collections were received into eighteenth century enlightened Europe as 'artificial curiosities' and described in glowing terms. The carving was 'singular', the cloth made of bark 'curious, and the incising 'ingenious'.

Once ships had returned to their home countries, however, scientists and sailors alike easily lost interest. After an initial flurry to publish the results of the voyages, journals were dispersed and lost, illustrations filed away and forgotten, objects removed to the attic and their precise histories thought to be unimportant. Instead of specific locality identification, 'Otaheite' became a general label for objects and illustrations from all over Polynesia and even the north-west coast of America. Soon clubs from Guyana were mixed with those from Tonga and even bows and arrows from America and Asia became 'Tahitian' and 'Hawaiian'. Objects and paintings eventually became aspects of interior decoration and part of European flights of fancy. Weapons were extracted from the collections to become examples of exotica in armouries and country houses. Finally, objects and illustrations, no longer loved, were to find their separate ways to museums, archives and auction houses. In addition to the importance of the voyages to Pacific ethnology, the history of taste in eighteenth-century European society can be explored through Cook's voyages.

Officers, crew, and supernumeraries wrote comments and collected objects from newly-discovered lands. What were 'new discoveries' to the Europeans, however, had been known to Pacific peoples for hundreds of years. Discovery and integration of knowledge operated in both directions; Cook and his companions had as much difficulty fitting their new knowledge into eighteenth-century European views of the world as Pacific people had in fitting these strange white men and their curious ships into Pacific world views.

Language was viewed as a means of discovering relationships between peoples and was studied and advanced by Reinhold Forster during the second voyage. Steeped in eighteenth-century philosophy and the comparative tradition, he compared Pacific peoples to one another and how they related to Greeks and other classical and Western cultures. Trained in the new Linnean methods of classification, he treated objects much as he treated plants and animals, rather than products of distinctive cultures. Catalogues were simply lists of objects by artefact type, similar to systematic organisations of plants and animals and could be prepared by a knowledgeable taxonomist.

Ethnographic objects were acquired through gift or trade. Trade for provisions was the main concern of the ships' officers. Official gifts from a ship's captain to those possessing prestige and power were often reciprocated with food and appropriate ceremonial gifts, while items of everyday use usually came through trade between islanders and the ship's companies. Trading and gift exchange were selective on both sides. During the first voyage Tahitian mourners' dresses were depicted and descriptions were made, but it was not possible to acquire one. However, during the second voyage several were acquired through trade involving red feathers procured previously in Tonga. We do not know why. Was it simply because of the difficulty Tahitians had in obtaining red feathers for themselves? Was it because only sacred things could be traded for sacred things? Or, perhaps, was it because at first contact the Tahitians thought that a mourning dress would bestow too much prestige and power on the visitors and bring these strangers without prestigious genealogies into Tahitian categories? Whatever the problem was during the first voyage, it was resolved by the second, when six complete mourning dresses and several parts were acquired.

A Night Dance by Women at Hapaee. The dance was part of the entertainment put on on Lifuka in the Hap'apai Group, Tonga in late May 1777. Engraved by W Sharp after Webber. (Cook 7 King, Atlas)

Another important aspect was occasion. Appropriate occasions brought out appropriate goods. Tahitians often gave large pieces of barkcloth on first meeting, which was interpreted as a peace offering or a show of goodwill. Webber's illustration of 'A young woman of Tahiti bringing a present' shows that the base of the present, a large piece of barkcloth, was topped with two feathered gorgets. The usual use of these gorgets was in warfare; but a trading transaction involving them was probably not appropriate while being worn. It was during a ceremonial exchange on the second voyage, in which the Māori Chief Teiratu gave an oration before boarding Cook's ship and Cook in his turn, visiting the Māori group ashore distributed gifts and medals, that the most elegant and valuable Māori objects of all three voyages were acquired. These include the *pu tatara* (shell trumpet) now in Cambridge and the *toki poutangata* (ceremonial adze) now in Oxford. In Hawai'i it was in conjunction with the ceremonial visit of Kalaniopu'u to Cook's ships and Cook's subsequent visit on shore on 26 January 1779, which took place nearly three months after Cook's arrival, that the most important pieces of featherwork were acquired.

'At Noon Terreeoboo [Kalaniopu'u] in a large Canoe attended by two others set out from the Village, & paddled towards the Ships in great state. In the first Canoe was Terreeoboo, In the Second Kao with 4 Images, the third was fill'd with hogs & Vegetables, as they went along those in the Center Canoe kept Singing with much Solemnity; from which we concluded that this procession had some of their religious ceremonys mixt with it; but instead of going on board they came to our side, their appearance was very grand, the Chiefs standing up drest in their Cloaks and Caps, & in the Center Canoe were the busts of what we supposed their Gods made of basket work, variously covered with red, black, white, & Yellow feathers, the Eyes represent'd by a bit of Pearl Oyster Shell with a black button, & the teeth were those of dogs, the mouths of all were strangly distorted, as well as other features; we drew out our little guard to receive him, & the Captn observing that the King went on shore, followd him. After we got into the Markee, the King got up & threw in a graceful manner over the Captns Shoulders the Cloak he himself wore, & put a featherd Cap upon his head, & a very handsome fly flap in his hand; besides which he laid down at the Captains feet 5 or 6 Cloaks more, all very beautiful, & to them of the greatest Value; his attendant brought 4 large hogs, with other refreshments which were also presented.' (Cook and King 1784).

The occasion was depicted by Webber and many of these feathered pieces can be traced to their present locations. For other objects the trail is less clear.

Collecting was selective and depended not only on opportunity and occasion but also on categories of trade and gift, gender interaction and the prestige of women in certain societies, as well as on the appropriateness of recipients having specific objects. The appropriate time also had to be found. This was also true on the European side. Firearms were not usually traded or given and it was only just before leaving that Cook gave to the Hawaiian chief Kalaniopu'u 'a complete Tool chest'.

The selectivity of Hawaiian objects collected is a case in point. There are numerous pieces of featherwork, but no stone food pounders, numerous pieces of barkcloth, but only one barkcloth beater, numerous weapons, but few tools, numerous ornaments, but few baskets. Acquisition was related to where interactions took place as well as to the fact that Hawaiians were probably loath to trade objects they needed every day. Objects acquired in Hawai'i are principally those that were carried or worn and objects appropriate to Cook's status. A similar configuration of objects was collected in New Zealand – primarily clothing, ornaments, weapons, and a few tools and canoe-related objects, which reflects where interaction usually took place – at sea and near the beach – and with whom it took place – men rather than women. In Tahiti and Tonga, however, there are numerous baskets and household objects such as neckrests, bowls, food pounders and tools in addition to ceremonial clothing, ornaments and weapons, a configuration that suggests that there was more interaction at the household level in Tahiti and Tonga and that interaction with women was freer and more regular. Thus, although from the point of view of ethnographic collecting in Oceania, Cook's voyages are without doubt the most important voyages ever, even these extensive collections can give only a partial view of the eighteenth-century material culture of the peoples encountered. By themselves the objects are mute as to their history, meaning and aesthetics.

Of utmost importance to our understanding of Pacific societies and their cultures is the description and depiction of events. Of special significance are those events which have little or nothing to do with the ships, such as the *inasi* ceremony in Tonga during the third voyage, but even those events that were staged as entertainment for the ships reveal much about indigenous culture. Two illustrations of Tahitian musicians from the first and third voyage are revealing. A first voyage drawing shows that drummers struck their drums with both palms (rather than with sticks) and that two tones must have been desired – from a short squat drum and a tall thin drum. The drummers sat on the ground while the noseflute players sat on stools. The flute players closed a nostril with the thumb of one hand and covered holes farther down the flute with a finger of the other hand. 'Dance at Otaheite' by Webber illustrated the placement of the drummers at the rear of the performing space. Here again there are drums of two different sizes and another musician who claps his hands. In this formal setting both men and women were performers but their roles were gender-specific. The women perform synchronised movements in a standing position with their legs demurely parallel and covered, while the men open the legs wide in a squat position and ether mimic the women's arms movements or make contrasting motions. Only men play the drums. The women wear headdresses of fine plaited hair decorated with flowers, feather ornaments, and elaborate bark clothing while the men wear a simple wraparound. When analysed in the light of knowledge of Tahitian dance today, we find depicted the prototypes for modern dance genres and gender-differentiating movements. We also find a complete difference in musical accompaniment. The nineteenth-century introduction of slit gongs (perhaps from the Cook Islands) changed the subtle differentiation of two-toned hand-struck sharkskins to the more intense rhythmic orchestration now considered 'traditional'. These slit gong ensembles play down the more traditional importance of the poetry, which Forster noted connected the movements with 'the words spoken by the master of the ballet'. Similarly, by using Webber's Tongan dance illustrations it is possible to recognise movement motifs used in Tonga today.

The accuracy of the drawings of objects and events and their attendant descriptions, as well as the existence of actual objects depicted and described, give the possibility of associating them with traditions now long passed away. The illustrations and descriptions of funerary rituals and disposal of the dead in the Society Islands, as well as objects and information associated with the chief mourners, enhances knowledge about the importance of funerals in hierarchical Polynesian societies. Descriptions and depictions of events show how interpersonal relationships are governed by principles of rank. In Tonga who wears what and eats in the presence of whom is noted in the journals. Interaction between local women and the men of the ship's companies varied in each society according to the rank of the women and the prestige given to them.

Our fullest information and most enlightening ethnographic interpretations come from those areas with repeated visits by Cook's ships and/or the longest stays – the Society Islands, New Zealand, Tonga and Hawai'i. But even areas where the ships stayed only a short time on one visit the information, objects, and illustrations are extremely important.

Ethnographic study reveals that during the

eighteenth century there was greater variation in certain artefact types. Within this range of variation some styles persisted while others lost favour and fell out of fashion. The types that persisted can be considered prototypes from which more standardised objects evolved during the late eighteenth and early nineteenth centuries. This evolution from variation to 'classic' form is easy to see in some areas. New classic forms sometimes depended on new tools, or the extension of power by certain individuals. Power and prestige may have been enhanced by interaction with Cook and other Europeans. Immediately on contact with Europeans, Pacific Islanders realised the superiority of metal tools over stone tools. New tools and new visual images were instrumental in changing traditional workmanship into evolved forms. Metal formed into adze blades and instruments for incising and cutting not only made the work faster, but encouraged complex refinements. By the end of the eighteenth century, objects in some areas had acquired a standardised elegance that has come to be accepted in the anthropological and art historical literature as the classic forms. Usually it has been assumed that these classic forms existed at the time of first European contact, but with the identification and documentation of Cook voyage objects, it now appears that the classic forms evolved in the immediate post-contact period. The earliest documentable use of iron is the cutting tool collected by the Forsters in Tonga during Cook's second voyage. Forster notes that the nail from which it was made was brought to Tonga by Tasman in 1643 and used as gouge or borer. Other nails were said to have come from Captain Wallis in 1767. As more and more metal for carving tools became available we can trace the parallel evolution of more and more complex carving, especially on clubs and flywhisk handles, with changes even noticeable between the second and third voyages.

Some artefact types that once had a variety of forms but changed to a classic form have little to do with imported iron or tools. For example, all of the Hawaiian feather cloaks and capes documented to Cook's third voyage have straight necklines and vary in overall form from a trapezoidal shape to one with a shaped neckline and a shaped hemline. The earliest known 'classic' feathered cloak, with a shaped neckline and shaped bottom, was collected in the mid-1780s. This change in shape can be related to an evolution from the function of cloaks as sacred protection to their use for ceremonial wear. Also, worthy of note is the near absence of 'classic'

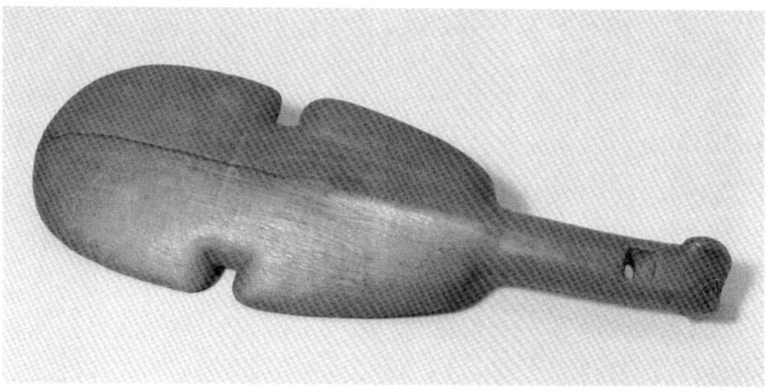

A Kotiate, a wooden Maori implement collected in New Zealand on the first voyage. (Banks Collection, Pitt Rivers Museum, Oxford)

characteristics typical of objects collected in the nineteenth century in Nootka Sound. Masks, sculptures, bowls, and rattles collected on Cook's voyage are not highly painted nor do they have stylised double-pointed oval eyes that one might expect if familiar with the later collections.

Ethnographic research concerned with Cook's voyages was relatively stagnant during the nineteenth century and the first half of the twentieth century, but resurfaced in the 1960s and 1970s leading up to the 200th anniversary of the voyages. Only then were the ethnographic collections studied systematically. These studies were concerned with (1) what objects were collected and why and (2) the subject of variation and 'classic' form. During this time the primary concern was identifying and documenting collections and individual objects and illustrations resulting in inventories and catalogues. Since the 1980s research has been concerned with analysis and interpretation and what can be learned about societies from studying the objects collected, the numerous illustrations and the descriptions of events in journals. Indigenous voices have also become more and more important, adding their views of the world and material culture and its relationships to social structure, religion, and politics. Many types of objects made in the eighteenth century are no longer made and those from Cook's voyages are treasured today as cultural heritage. Ethnographers are responsible both to science and to the indigenous people with whom they study, and research on Cook's voyages makes information available for advancing cultural and ethnic identity. Through memory and oral tradition a fuller understanding of Cook's voyages is being advanced and will continue to add to their ethnographic results.

By Adrienne L Kaeppler

See Also: 'Artificial Curiosities'

Falmouth, HMS, and HMS *St Albans*

In April and May 1756, James Cook was a passenger on two Royal Navy ships. HMS *Falmouth* took him back to Plymouth in April after Cook had spent some time commanding a cutter off the north Brittany coast. HMS *St Albans* then took him back to sea to rejoin HMS *Eagle* in May.

The *Falmouth* was a Fourth Rate built in Woolwich Dockyard in 1752. She was of 1052 tons, 144ft by 41ft (43.9m by 12.5m) and carried 50 guns. The *St Albans* had been built by West at Deptford in 1747 and was a Fourth Rate of 1191 tons, 149ft 11in by 42ft 11in (45.7m by 13.1m) and carried 60 guns. The *Falmouth* was beached in 1765 while the Navy sold *St Albans* the same year.

SEE ALSO: Cook's ships

Fannin, Peter (?–?)

Peter Fannin sailed on the second voyage on the *Adventure* as master. Fannin made surveys, and drew charts and coastal views. A chart by him of Tory Channel shows he visited that passage independently of Cook while the *Adventure* was at Queen Charlotte Sound, New Zealand.

After Cook's voyage, he retired in 1775 to Douglas, Isle of Man, where he opened a School of Navigation. He left the island again in early 1794, possibly to rejoin the Navy because of renewed fighting between the British and French. His wife, Elizabeth (née Booth), who remained on the island, died in 1808. He published his *Correct Plan of the Isle of Man* in January 1789, which was the basis of most maps of the island for the next 50 years. It gave an indication for the first time of the roads on the island as well as the first town plan of Douglas. Nothing is known of Fannin's early life or when and where he died.

SEE ALSO: Second voyage, Colour plate 6

Fiction, Cook in

The life and voyages of James Cook have, surprisingly, generated only a small number of works of fiction. Several writers have chosen a fictional style to retell events in Cook's life but very few have chosen to use Cook or his voyages as a platform from which to develop a new ideas or works. Whereas the twentieth century saw a genre develop in which writers such as C S Forester and Patrick O'Brian placed their heroes (Hornblower and Aubrey), right in the middle of naval action in the Napoleonic wars, nothing similar has happened with Cook. Most probably, Cook's reputation for sobriety (so no illicit love affairs) and the lack of warfare have caused him not to appeal to would-be authors.

Two of the great books of English literature have used narratives of journeys to exotic locations in the tropics as their source. Swift's *Gulliver's Travels* is a satire on British society using the writings of explorers such as William Dampier to convey his points, while Defoe's *Robinson Crusoe* uses the romance and intrigue of a tropical island to examine the way man behaves. Both books predate Cook's voyages but nothing of similar quality draws upon Cook.

R M Ballantyne wrote one of the most famous books in the tropical island tradition, *The Coral Island* but a much lesser-known work, *The Cannibal Islands* published in 1869, was one of the first to use a fictional style in telling Cook's story. Other writers, including Hammond Innes (*The Last Voyage*, 1978), Paul Rodgers (*To Kill a God*, 1987), and O A Bushnell (US, *The Return of Lono*, 1956; UK, *The Last Days of Captain Cook*, 1957) have written novels based on the third voyage. Godfrey Blunden (*Chaco Harbour*, 1968) used events in Australia in 1770 for his book. Marelle Day (*Mrs Cook*, 2002) and Karen Hesse (*Stowaway*, 2000) have used fiction to amplify the stories of Elizabeth Cook and Nicholas Young (Young Nick). Eric Baume attempted something more ambitious with the *Devil Lord's Daughter*, which appeared in 1948 in that he invented new characters and events.

Interestingly, Alistair Maclean, one of the most popular fiction writers of the twentieth century wrote a proper biography, *Captain Cook*, published originally in 1972. It has appeared in countless editions and

translations to be, probably, the most published book about Cook.
SEE ALSO: Literature of Cook's voyages

Film and television, Cook in

Film and television have largely ignored James Cook. Whereas Bligh and the *Bounty* mutiny have generated several movies, Cook's voyages have never been the subject of one. Interest is occasionally expressed in using them as the basis of a film but the idea always lapsed. One famous director who showed interest was David Lean, the director of *Lawrence of Arabia*. In 1977, Lean became involved in a project to film the recovery by Kelly Tarlton of Cook's anchors from the coral reef near Tautira in eastern Tahiti. A documentary, *Lost and found: the story of an anchor* was shown in 1979.

In 1975, the BBC showed a series called *The Explorers*. One episode, entitled *Captain James Cook,* 54 minutes in length and directed by John Irvin, was devoted to James Cook. Dennis Burgess portrays Cook in a production that reconstructs the events of the first voyage to the Pacific. Unfortunately, the time allotted does not allow much more than an overview. A companion book to the series was released. The release of Bank's *Florilegium* was marked in 1984 by a programme *The Flowering of the Pacific: Banks' Florilegium*. The documentary explained the process by which the botanical plates were produced and showed the beautiful prints they generated.

Captain James Cook was an eight-hour television series written by Peter Yeldham and directed by Gordon Clark in 1987. It starred Keith Michell as James Cook and concentrated largely on the *Endeavour* voyage, and describes itself as 'the epic tale of history's greatest ocean explorer'. To a large extent it succeeds, given the logistics of attempting to recreate many of the events in Cook's life. It was subsequently released on video. The screenplay was reworked by John Hooker and a book was released by Penguin. *Sea Tales: The Fatal Voyage of Captain Cook,* directed by Melissa Jo Peltier, was a video released by A&E Network in 1997 dealing with events in Hawai'i.

A different approach was taken in 2002 by the makers of *The Ship*. In the vein of 'reality television', a concept prevalent at the time, the BBC set out to reconstruct part of the *Endeavour*'s voyage using the replica of the ship and having volunteers crew the ship in conditions as close to the eighteenth century as possible. The passage from Cairns, in northern Australia, to Bali, in Indonesia (events prevented the ship going to Jakarta), was filmed and directed by Christopher Terrill. Historians, artists and members of Pacific indigenous peoples were taken along to interpret events and put things in context. Though providing lovely images of the *Endeavour* replica at sea and giving some idea of what life must have been like on board, the series was only a partial success. Editing, possibly to half its length, would have improved the programme.

Various videos have been released depicting the *Endeavour* replica. *Captain's Log,* a television series in 2001 depicting the maritime history of New Zealand, used Cook as its link and portrayed many of the places associated with Cook. Though it has never been confirmed, it has been suggested by some that the television series *Star Trek* used Captain James Cook for its hero, Captain James Kirk.

A completely different approach is taken by the documentary, *Too Many Cooks*, directed by Penny McDonald. It centres on Paddy Wainburranga of the Rembarrnga tribe from the centre of Arnhem Land in Northern Australia as he relates and paints the Rembarrnga history of Captain Cook. It bears little relationship to the conventional European version of Australian history upheld by non-Aboriginal Australians.

First voyage (1768–1771)

Lieutenant James Cook (he was not yet a captain) began his first voyage to the Pacific Ocean on 26 August 1768 when his ship left Plymouth. It was the start of a three-year voyage that would totally change his life. Astronomers had calculated that a Transit of Venus would take place in June 1769. British scientists from the Royal Society argued that Britain should play its part and send people to different parts of the world to take observations. The Pacific Ocean was expected to be the best place to watch the Transit so the Society asked the Royal Navy for a ship to transport them there. They also nominated one of their members, Alexander Dalrymple, to command the voyage. Dalrymple believed that a very large mass of land, a Great Southern Continent or *Terra australis incognita,* would be found in the South Pacific region. The Admiralty, the governing body of the Royal Navy, agreed to supply a ship but would only allow one of its own officers to command it. A search was made and a collier, *The Earl of Pembroke,* was selected as the ship. The ship, which had been used to transport coal from the River Tyne to

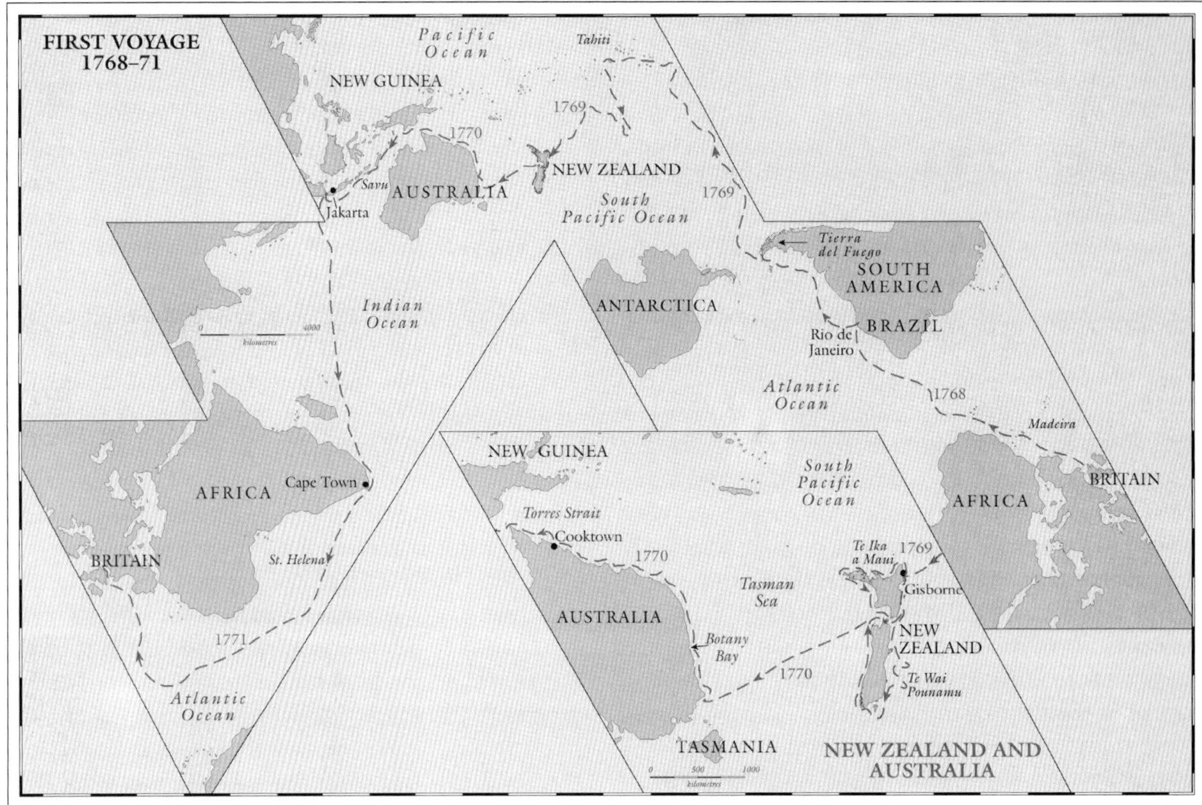

London, was cleaned up, modified and renamed HM Bark *Endeavour.*

The Admiralty next looked for someone to take charge of the ship. Their choice was James Cook, not yet an officer, but a sailor of considerable experience. He had risen to the rank of master and had spent several years surveying the island of Newfoundland. He had also worked on the North Sea coal trade so was acquainted with ships like the *Endeavour.* In 1766, Cook had observed a solar eclipse and written the details up as a paper for the Royal Society. His astronomical skills helped persuade the Royal Society of Cook's suitability. He would assist Charles Green, who had been chosen by the Astronomer Royal to lead the observations.

In early 1768, Captain Samuel Wallis returned to Britain from the Pacific where he had visited the island of Tahiti. He reported positively about the island and its people and, as it lay in an ideal place, it was chosen as the location for observing the Transit. The British Government decided that the Transit's observation would not be the only objective of the voyage. It prepared secret instructions for Cook for him to carry out after Tahiti in which he was to search the Pacific for the Great Southern Continent.

Joseph Banks was a rich amateur scientist and member of the Royal Society, who wished to go on the *Endeavour* voyage and offered the Navy money to pay for himself and a party of scientists, artists and servants to travel. The offer was accepted and the ship was modified to accommodate them. Their presence helped make the voyage a memorable one as it became one of the first where science played an important role.

The *Endeavour,* only 98ft (30m) long and with 94 men on board, sailed out into the Atlantic and made for the island of Madeira. Cook was determined to run a healthy ship. To this end he made all the crew bathe themselves and wash their clothes regularly. He also made them clean and air the ship often. Most importantly, he insisted that their diet would be as healthy as possible in an attempt to offset scurvy, the scourge of long sea journeys. At Madeira, he took on board fresh meat, fruit and vegetables (he would try to do this at every port of call), including a large load of onions for making sauerkraut.

The *Endeavour* continued down the Atlantic, calling in at Rio de Janeiro, before rounding Cape Horn to enter the Pacific. In April 1769, Cook reached Tahiti in plenty of time to prepare for the Transit. The British were

A war canoe of New Zealand, with a view of Gable End Foreland. An engraving by John James Barralet after Parkinson. (Hawkesworth III fp 463)

allowed to build an observatory at Point Venus, close by their anchorage in Matavai Bay on Tahiti's north coast. The astronomers successfully made their observation of Venus on 3 June. Cook then made a tour of the island with Banks and together they recorded the life and customs of the Tahitian people. When they left Tahiti on 13 July Banks persuaded Cook to take Tupaia, a Raiatean, with them. This was a good move as Tupaia proved an able navigator and interpreter.

The British called at several neighbouring islands before Cook sailed the *Endeavour* southward. He had opened the second part of his instructions. Over the next two months they searched the ocean without finding the southern continent. Cook was already beginning to doubt its existence and decided to make for New Zealand, sighted 130 years earlier by the Dutch sailor, Abel Tasman.

On 8 October he reached land and Cook spent the next six months sailing around New Zealand proving it was not part of a continent. He produced wonderful charts of the islands. However, his encounters with Māori, the local Polynesian people, were not always the best and on some occasions Māori were killed, much to Cook's regret. Tupaia was most useful as a translator, helping the two sides understand each other. Cook and Banks wrote the first descriptions of the Māori.

The *Endeavour* was ready to return to Britain and it was decided to go via Batavia (Jakarta) in Java where the ship could be repaired. Cook sailed west and on 19 April 1770 reached more land. This was New Holland, later to be called Australia. Sailing north up the coast, Cook found a bay, which he entered and where he stayed a week. He called it Botany Bay after Banks had collected many plant specimens. The local people, Aborigines, kept their distance and contact was minimal. Cook continued north up the coast and encountered the Great Barrier Reef. Disaster struck on 11 June when the *Endeavour* ran aground on the coral. It took a day to refloat the ship and it was nursed into the mouth of a nearby river (later named after the *Endeavour*). The British were stuck there for two months while holes in the ship's side were repaired.

A view in the Island of Otaheite; with the house or shed called tupapow, under which the dead are deposited, and a representation of the person who performs the principal part in the funeral ceremony in his peculiar dress. Engraved by William Woolett after Parkinson. (Hawkesworth II fp 184)

Finally, in August, they sailed and passed through the

Torres Strait between Australia and New Guinea. Cook was able to sail west and reached Batavia in October. The Dutch, who controlled Batavia, agreed to repair the ship but they were very slow and the British had to wait. While they waited many men became ill and eventually many died from diseases contracted in Java. Cook's good work keeping a healthy crew free from scurvy was undone as men died on the crossing of the Indian Ocean to Cape Town. After a brief stop at the Cape, Cook sailed up the Atlantic. He had largely disproved the idea of the Southern Continent but was forming a plan for another voyage sailing further south closer to the Pole. The reception in Britain was fantastic but it was mainly for Banks. Cook was still unknown to most people and he returned quietly to his wife and family in Mile End, London.

The Admiralty, however, recognised Cook's considerable role in the success of the voyage. The logs, journals and charts, together with the scientific specimens collected and described, the descriptions of people and the drawings and paintings, were a wonderful record of an exceptional voyage. Cook had carried out his instructions and bought home the ship and a healthy crew (despite Java). The Transit of Venus had been observed and Cook had made a search the Great Southern Continent. For Cook, though, it had only been a start. He had already formulated plans for another voyage to search for the continent and settle its existence once and for all.

SEE ALSO: Banks (Joseph), *Endeavour* (HM Bark)

Florilegium of Joseph Banks

Between 1980 and 1990, Alecto Historical Editions, in association with the Natural History Museum in London published a limited edition of Banks' *Florilegium*. One hundred numbered sets were made, taken from the original copper-plates and published in 35 parts. It consisted of 743 botanical line engravings, after the watercolours drawn from nature by Sydney Parkinson of specimens collected by Joseph Banks and Daniel Solander on Captain James Cook's first voyage from 1768 to 1771. The engravings were printed in colour for the first time from the original eighteenth-century copperplates. The plates, bequeathed by Banks to the British Museum depict some of the first plants from the Pacific, New Zealand and Australia to be studied by European scientists.

Parkinson always attempted to complete a watercolour before the fresh specimen had wilted and faded, but as back-up he would also make a quick outline field sketch, colouring parts to assist the final work. Unfortunately, Parkinson died on the voyage having only completed 280 of 900-plus drawings. Banks used other artists including John Cleveley, John Frederick Miller, and Frederick Polydore Nodder to finish the work.

Eighteen engravers made 743 engraved copperplates from the completed watercolour drawings over the years 1771–84 under the eye of Banks and at a cost to him of over £7000. However, no publication eventuated. Reasons such as Solander having died in 1782, Banks being a very busy man, and his finances being stretched have been suggested. The *Florilegium* contains plates depicting the botany of Australia (337 plates), Brazil (23), Java (30), Madeira (11), New Zealand (183), The Society Islands (89), and Tierra del Fuego (65).

SEE ALSO: Banks (Joseph), Botanical results of Cook's voyages, Parkinson (Sydney)

Flower, Peter (1748–1768)

Peter Flower had one of the longest naval relationships with Cook and yet little is known about him. Flower was born in Guernsey in 1748 and drowned in an accident in Rio de Janeiro harbour on 2 December 1768, early in the *Endeavour* voyage. Before that Flower had served with Cook for five years in Newfoundland. Starting in 1763, Flower had been one of Cook's two assistants who helped him survey the islands of St Pierre and Miquelon. He returned to Newfoundland with Cook every year until 1767 as an AB. He was punished for drunkenness on 20 August 1764 at Noddy Harbour. He began the *Endeavour* voyage as an AB. Flowers Cove and Flower Ledge in northern Newfoundland are named after him.

SEE ALSO: Newfoundland

Forster family

Forster, Johann Reinhold (1729–98) and Johann George Adam (1754–94) were father-and-son naturalists on the *Resolution* on Cook's second Pacific voyage. Reinhold Forster was born on 22 October 1729 in Prussia, though he was of British descent. His son, known in England (and in English) as George and in Germany (and German) as Georg, was also born in Prussia on 26 November 1754. After studying theology at the University of Halle, serving as a Lutheran pastor, and being employed by the Russian government to report on the German colonies on the Volga, Reinhold decided to seek his fortune in England.

With George he arrived in London in October

J R and G Forster at Tahiti painting a bird. By John Francis Rigaud, London, 1780. (By permission of Peter Rheinberger).

1766, the rest of the family joining them later. Reinhold set about establishing himself in scientific circles and in 1767 he was appointed to succeed Joseph Priestley as a tutor at the Dissenters' Academy in Warrington. In November 1770 he returned to London. Making his living by writing and translating, and benefiting from the support of such patrons as Daines Barrington, he continued to make a name for himself as a natural historian. He was thus in an excellent position to fill the position left vacant when Joseph Banks withdrew from Cook's second voyage. On 12 June 1772 he and George, then aged only 17, were appointed 'at the King's pleasure' naturalists to the expedition. The voyage was the making of the reputations of both men. They made detailed observations of the natural history and cultures of the islands they visited and made extensive collections of both natural history specimens and ethnographic artefacts (the major collections now being in the Pitt Rivers Museum, University of Oxford and the Institut für Ethnologie, University of Göttingen).

On their return, they published books about the voyage, both men providing detailed accounts that are still used by scholars today. Reinhold seems to have been a difficult character: self-important, quick to take offence and with a talent for turning friends into enemies. He was apparently not much liked on the *Resolution* and soon after the voyage he argued and fell out with many influential people in England, including the Earl of Sandwich and Cook himself. Contractually prevented from publishing his own account of the voyage before Cook's had appeared, Reinhold encouraged George, who was under no such restriction, to use his journals to compose his own account. George's *Voyage* appeared in March 1777, two months before Cook's account. Reinhold's *Observations* appeared the following year. Thanks to George's efforts, in November 1779 Reinhold was able to leave England when he was given a teaching position at the University of Halle, where he had been a student. Reinhold continued to teach, write, and translate natural history until his death on 9 December 1798 at the age of 69. Though outlived by his father, George achieved greater fame, though this was more for his political writings than for his science. This was especially so in Germany where the eighteen-volume critical edition of his Werke is testament to his importance to German intellectual history. George died in Paris on 10 January 1794 at the age of 39.

Cook scholars, especially Beaglehole, have not been very kind to Forster senior. His personality and arguments have unfairly overshadowed his, and George's, huge scientific contributions. There has been a rehabilitation since the 1970s, led principally by Michael Hoare, who edited the Hakluyt Society edition of Forster senior's journal and wrote his biography. Several features, especially in Dusky Sound, New Zealand, have been named after the Forsters.

BY JEREMY COOTE

SEE ALSO: Second voyage

France and French reaction to Cook

The voyages of Cook transcended the normal rivalry that existed through the eighteenth century between France and Britain. Interest in his voyages soon grew and the journals of the voyages were quickly translated into French and sold in greater quantities than those of Bougainville, France's own circumnavigator. Cook's reputation immediately gained hold in France and would-be explorers, such as Lapérouse, admired him and set out to emulate him.

The quality of his charts drew admiration. Crozet who sailed with Marion Dufresne in 1774 wrote: 'As soon as I obtained information of the voyage of the Englishman, I carefully compared the chart I had prepared of that part of the coast of New Zealand along which we had coasted with that of Captain Cook and his officers. I found it of an exactitude and of a thoroughness of detail which astonished me beyond all powers of expression, and I doubt whether the charts of our French coasts are laid down with greater precision. I think therefore that I cannot do any better than lay down our track off New Zealand on the chart prepared by this celebrated explorer.'

Benjamin Franklin, who was the representative of the new American Government in Paris, persuaded the French government to issue an edict granting Cook's ship free passage on their return from the third voyage.

Cook's journals were read by all types of people including Queen Marie Antoinette, who is reported to have had copies with her prior to her execution, and the Marquis de Sade who wrote his novel *Aline et Valcour* after he had read them in prison. Jean-Joseph Laborde, who lost two sons on Lapérouse's voyage, erected a monument, le Cénotaphe du navigateur Cook, at Méréville. It was now stands in the Parc du Château de Jeurre at Etampes, south of Paris.

SEE ALSO: Bougainville (L-A de), Lapérouse (J-F de G)

Freelove

The *Freelove* was a collier working in the North Sea coal trade. She was the first ship that James Cook sailed on after he joined the Walkers, the Whitby ship owners. The ship was built in Great Yarmouth, Norfolk in 1742 and operated by the Walkers. She was a three-masted vessel, square-rigged, of 341 tons, 105ft 11in (32.3m) in length with a beam of 26ft 11in (8.2m). She carried a complement of 19, comprising master, mate, carpenter, cook, 5 seamen and 10 servants or apprentices.

Cook began as a servant aboard the *Freelove* on the North Sea transporting coal from Newcastle to London. His first known voyage was from 29 September 1747 until 17 December 1747. However, the muster record for that voyage records Cook as already having sailed on the *Freelove*. It is possible that Cook's first spell at sea took place in late 1746 soon after he moved to

Carrying coals from Newcastle, *by Raymond A Massey. The* Freelove, *one of the ships on which Cook sailed, is shown leaving Newcastle-upon-Tyne in 1765. (The artist)*

Whitby to work for the Walkers. A second voyage took place from 26 February 1748 to 22 April 1748. John Jefferson was the master.
SEE ALSO: North Sea and the coal trade, Walker (John), Whitby

Friendship

James Cook joined the *Friendship*, a Whitby collier owned by the Walkers, on 31 July 1751. Cook was a seaman and Robert Watson, who had been the master on the *Three Brothers*, Cook's previous ship, was the master. However, in March 1752, Watson was replaced as master by Richard Ellerton and Cook was promoted to be mate. For the voyages in 1753, John Swainston replaced Ellerton but Ellerton returned for 1754 and 1755.

Cook left the *Friendship* when the ship was in the Thames on 14 June 1755. He enlisted in the Royal Navy three days later. Cook had sailed aboard the *Friendship* for nearly four and a half years, all of it involved in transporting coal to London.
SEE ALSO: North Sea and the coal trade, Walker (John), Whitby

Furneaux, Tobias (1735–1781)

Tobias Furneaux was born in Swilly, outside Plymouth on 21 August 1735. He entered the Navy in his teens and by 1755 was serving as a midshipman aboard HMS *Marlborough*. During the Seven Years War, the *Marlborough* was stationed in the West Indies as the flagship of Vice-Admiral Cotes. Furneaux returned to England as fourth lieutenant on HMS *Edinburgh*. In December 1760, he joined the *Melampe* in the English Channel and eventually was promoted to first lieutenant in July 1762. The *Melampe* sailed to Barbados in 1763 where Tobias was transferred to the *Ferret*. He returned to Britain and was paid off in July 1763. Furneaux returned to live at Swilly on half pay and prize money until commissioned as second lieutenant under Samuel Wallis on the *Dolphin*.

Wallis' *Dolphin* voyage lasted from August 1766 until May 1768. Afterwards, Furneaux was paid off in June 1768 and recuperated at Swilly. His next appointment in December 1770 was as third lieutenant of the *Trident*. However, he was soon transferred to HMS *Torbay*, where he rejoined Captain Wallis.

In November 1771, Furneaux was selected to command HMS *Adventure*, Cook's companion vessel for the second voyage, and he was promoted commander. The expedition left Britain on 13 July 1772. The ships sailed together via the Cape but in Antarctic waters, on 8 February 1773, they were separated during thick fog. Furneaux took the *Adventure* on an eastward course and arrived at Tasmania on 9 March, then called Van Diemen's Land. He anchored for a few days in Adventure Bay before sailing up and charting the island's east coast. Some islands near the opening into Bass Strait were named after Furneaux. The *Adventure* proceeded to New Zealand where she was rejoined by the *Resolution* in April.

The *Adventure* accompanied Cook for the first sweep of the Pacific, calling in at Tahiti and Huahine. At Huahine, Furneaux took on board Mai (Omai), who travelled with him to Britain. As the ships neared New Zealand, they were separated again in late October 1773. After putting in at Tolaga Bay, Furneaux eventually made it to Queen Charlotte Sound only to find Cook had already left. During their stay, 11 men were killed by Māori while ashore collecting wood and water. Furneaux decided to return immediately to Britain and left on 18 December.

Furneaux crossed the Pacific at about 50° S, rounded Cape Horn and reached Cape Town. The *Adventure* was probably the first ship to circumnavigate the world west to east. She then sailed up the Atlantic to anchor at Spithead on 12 July 1774, a year ahead of Cook. Furneaux was a capable officer but lacked the flair and drive needed for Pacific exploration.

Mai was taken to London where he became a celebrity. Furneaux though was promoted captain in August 1775 and given command of HMS *Syren*, a Sixth Rate frigate, which he took to join Rear-Admiral Parker's squadron off the American coast in January 1776. He saw action at Charlestown and at Newport, Rhode Island during 1776. 1777 was a bad year as the *Syren* was lost in the November and Furneaux and his crew were taken prisoner. They were released early in 1778. Furneaux was soon invalided back to Britain with gout and he died at Swilly on 19 September 1781. He was buried in the family vaults at Stoke Damerel Church.
SEE ALSO: *Adventure* (HMS), Second voyage

Gibson, Samuel (?–1780)

Samuel Gibson sailed as a marine on all three of Cook's voyages. On the first voyage on the *Endeavour*, Gibson was a marine private. He deserted with fellow marine, Clement Webb, on 9 July 1769 whilst at Tahiti. He was recaptured on the 12th and was punished on 14 July by being 'close confin'd' for a while. He rejoined Cook for the second voyage on the *Resolution*, now promoted to corporal of marines. He was, by now, a favourite of Cook and valued for his ability to understand and speak Pacific Island languages. By the time of the third voyage, Gibson had been promoted again to sergeant of marines on board the *Resolution* and was with Cook when the captain was killed at Hawai'i.

On the return part of the voyage to Britain, Gibson was taken ill as the ships passed through the East Indies. He never fully recovered. The ships were unable to enter the English Channel and were forced north to Orkney, where, in the month ashore, Gibson married an Orkney woman. His wife, Jean, was from Walls, Orkney. Unfortunately, Gibson had not recovered from his illness and, shortly after the ships left Orkney, he died 22 September 1780. He left a will (FRC 11/1070).

SEE ALSO: First voyage, Marines, Second and Third voyages

Gilbert family

Joseph Gilbert (1733–1821) and his son, George (1758–1786?), both sailed with Cook. Joseph sailed on the second voyage on the *Resolution* as master. He kept a log, made surveys and drew coastal views and charts. Gilbert was employed in Newfoundland as surveyor in the 1760s at the same time as Cook and worked closely with Palliser. He was responsible for charting around the Bay of Islands and the east coast of Labrador. Gilbert Inlet in Labrador is named for him.

During Cook's second voyage, Gilbert was wounded at Erromanga in Vanuatu on 4 August 1774. The Gilbert Islands at the mouth of Breaksea Sound in New Zealand and the Islas Gilbert off the southwestern coast of Tierra del Fuego, South America, are named for Gilbert. After the voyage, Gilbert became master attendant at Portsmouth Dockyard from 1776 until 1791. He then transferred to be master attendant at Deptford Dockyard from 1791 until 1802. The position of master attendant carried the rank and status of lieutenant. Joseph Gilbert was born in Boston, Lincolnshire in 1733 and died in Fareham, Hampshire in 1821, leaving a will (FRC 11/1639).

George Gilbert sailed on the third voyage on the *Resolution* as an AB until 3 April 1778, when he was promoted to midshipman. On 6 September 1779, he was transferred to the *Discovery* as midshipman. He was born in 1758 in Treston, an unidentifiable village; possibly Freiston, outside Boston, Lincolnshire. Gilbert kept a journal, in which there is a detailed description of Cook's death. He was made a lieutenant in November 1781 and joined the *Barfleur* as sixth lieutenant. He was fifth lieutenant on HMS *Magnificent* in the West Indies in 1783. He may have died in April 1786.

A third Gilbert, Richard, joined the *Resolution* on the second voyage at Cape Town as an AB and was discharged there three years later in November 1775. He was born in Boston so may have been related to the other Gilberts above.

SEE ALSO: Second and Third voyages

Gore, John (1730?–1790)

John Gore sailed on the first voyage on the *Endeavour* as third lieutenant to 26 May 1771. It was Gore's third trip to the Pacific. After Hicks' death on 26 May 1771, Gore was promoted to second lieutenant. He kept a journal. He rejoined Cook to sail on the third voyage on the *Resolution* as first lieutenant. When Cook was killed on 14 February 1779, Gore transferred to become commander of the *Discovery* and then, after Clerke's death on 23 August 1779, he returned to the *Resolution* as commander and assumed command of the whole expedition. He brought the ships back to Britain successfully but incurred the anger of some of the crew by remaining so long in Orkney. Trevenen referred to him as 'that old conceited American'. Gore kept a log

A Portrait of Captain John Gore, by John Webber painted about 1780. Gore sailed on the first and third voyages. He commanded the ships of the third voyage on their return to Britain. (National Library of Australia, NK1)

in which he independently named features. Around Cook Inlet, for example, he named things after his partner Nancy.

Gore is believed to have been born in America in 1730 though no details of his early life have been confirmed. He joined the Navy in 1755 and saw service on HMS *Windsor, Bellona* and *Aeolus.* Gore twice sailed to the Pacific on HMS *Dolphin* as master's mate, first on Byron's voyage in 1762 and secondly with Wallis from 1766 to 1768. Gore chose not to go on Cook's second voyage and went instead as a guest of Banks to Iceland aboard the *Sir Lawrence.* Perhaps he wanted a rest, having made three long Pacific voyages, or was unhappy with Cook's command. Whatever his reasons, he joined Cook for the third voyage.

Gore was promoted to captain on 3 October 1780 and posted to Cook's old position at Greenwich Hospital. He died in 1790. Various geographical features were named for Gore; Gore Bay in New Zealand, Gore Island in Nootka Sound, and Gore Point in Alaska.
SEE ALSO: First and Third voyages

Graves, Thomas, Baron Graves (1725–1802)

Thomas Graves was born in Thanckes, Cornwall, on 23 October 1725 to a naval family, his father being Rear-Admiral Thomas Graves. Young Thomas entered the navy and was serving under Captain Medley in the West Indies by 1741. He was made a lieutenant in 1743 in HMS *Romney.* By 1755, he was in command of HMS *Sheerness.*

In 1761, Graves was appointed Governor of Newfoundland and had command of HMS *Antelope.* It was during his tenure that the French captured St John's, causing James Cook to go to Newfoundland aspart of the British force that recaptured the capital. Graves was already concerned about the lack of good charts of the island by the British and had made representations to the Admiralty. He saw examples of Cook's work in 1762 and organised Cook's appointment as surveyor as well as securing the *Grenville* schooner for Cook to use in 1764.

Graves left Newfoundland in 1764 and resumed his naval career. He became a rear-admiral in 1779 and vice-admiral in 1787. He returned to active service during the War of American Independence and became commander-in-chief of the North American squadron in 1781. He was commander-in-chief at Plymouth in 1788. He was made Admiral in 1794 on the *Royal Sovereign* and took part in the Battle of the Glorious First of June. He was wounded and resigned his command but was made Baron Graves. He died on 9 February 1802. Graves had married Elizabeth Williams in 1771 and they had three daughters and ason.

There is a short biography in the *DNB*, v8, pp438–40. The Graves Light in Boston Harbor, Massachusetts is named after him.
SEE ALSO: Newfoundland

Great Ayton

Great Ayton is a village situated at the foot of the Cleveland Hills in North Yorkshire. It is located 6 miles (10km) south-east of Middlesbrough. The River Leven flows through the village linking the spacious greens of High Green and Low Green. The village was sometimes called Yatton.

James Cook and his family moved 4 miles (6km) from Marton to Great Ayton when he was seven. His father had obtained a position as hind or bailiff of Aireyholme Farm, on the outskirts of the village to the north-east under Roseberry Topping. The farm belonged to the Lord of the Manor, Thomas Skottowe, who arranged for James to attend the local school.

A Schoolroom Museum now occupies the former charity school where Cook was educated. The present building was erected in 1785 on the site of, and using materials from, the original charity school built in 1704 by local landowner Michael Postgate. Cook left Ayton in 1745 to work in Staithes and Whitby but his family remained on at Aireyholme.

In 1755, Cook's parents had a cottage built in Bridge Street in the village and retired there. His mother died in 1765 and his father was persuaded to move to Redcar in 1771 to live with his daughter, Margaret. The cottage was later shipped to Australia and reassembled in Melbourne. A granite obelisk marks the site. Cook's mother and several of his brothers and sisters are buried in the churchyard of All Saints Church, off Low Green.

A statue by Nicholas Dimbleby of Cook as a boy was unveiled on the High Green in 1997, while the Captain Cook Monument, erected in 1827 on Easby Moor, overlooks the village.

SEE ALSO: Cleveland, Cook's early years

Great Barrier Reef

The Great Barrier Reef extends for more than 1200 miles (2000km) off the east coast of Australia, from just south of the Tropic of Capricorn to the coastal waters of Papua New Guinea. The reef system comprises some 3400 individual reefs, including 760 fringing reefs, which range in size from under 1 hectare to over 10,000 hectares to produce the most spectacular marine scenery on earth. There are approximately 300 coral cays and 600 continental islands. It is an ecosystem that has evolved over millions of years. The reef is not one continuous barrier, but a broken maze of reefs and cays with gaps in between. The reef was declared a World Heritage Site by UNESCO in 1981.

In May 1770, James Cook, in the *Endeavour*, rounded Fraser Island on the east coast of Australia and headed north-west, unaware that he was approaching the southern end of the Great Barrier Reef. The *Endeavour* sailed on between the outer reef and the land, not realising the potential dangers lying just to the east. As they sailed north, however, they began to encounter the first of many small islands and reefs. Cook, now alert to the problem, began sending the ship's master ahead in one of the small boats to navigate a passage, an action that would be repeated often.

After negotiating hundreds of islands, on 10 June, Cook passed the northern end of Trinity Bay. He later called the headland Cape Tribulation, after the events of the next day had unfurled, as he deemed it was a portent for what was to follow. The *Endeavour* finally ran aground on the reef (later called Endeavour Reef) on 11 June 1770 at 10.30pm. The ship was eventually refloated and nursed into an inlet on 18 June where over eight weeks it was repaired.

Cook realised the *Endeavour* was still in a delicate condition and needed a proper overhaul at Batavia. He decided to return to the open sea and leave the perils of the reef. After the crew had located a gap, Cook thankfully took the ship out through the reef on 14 August into deep water. Cook soon realised he was also out of sight of land and was unable to continue charting the coast. The ship was leaking and Cook, needing the shortest route to Batavia for proper repairs, was on the lookout for Torres Strait between New Holland and New Guinea. Cook was uncertain whether the strait really existed but knew he should regain the coast just in case it did. After two days outside the reef, he began searching for a way back inside. Approaching the reef from the open sea was dangerous and the *Endeavour* was nearly driven onto the coral and destroyed. Small boats towed the ship, which, with the help of ebb-tides and good luck, was saved. The gap was named Providential Channel and Cook, inside the reef once more on 17 August, decided to remain close to the shore.

Sailing on, they came to the northernmost tip of the east coast on 21 August, a point Cook called York Cape (the words were later reversed). Rounding the cape Cook anchored and went ashore on a small island. From the top of a small hill Cook was convinced he had reached the north of New Holland and that a strait did exist allowing him to sail west. He then raised the flag and claimed the whole of the east coast of New Holland for Britain but, in doing so, renamed it New South Wales. Cook then sailed the *Endeavour* west into the Arafura Sea and away from the Great Barrier Reef.

SEE ALSO: Australia, Cooktown

Great Southern Continent, Terra Australis Incognita

On the *Endeavour* voyage, James Cook carried secret instructions to be read after he had observed the Transit of Venus in Tahiti. The instructions authorised Cook to search for and take possession of 'a Continent or Land of great extent' thought to exist in southern latitudes. He was further instructed 'with the Consent of the Natives to take possession of Convenient

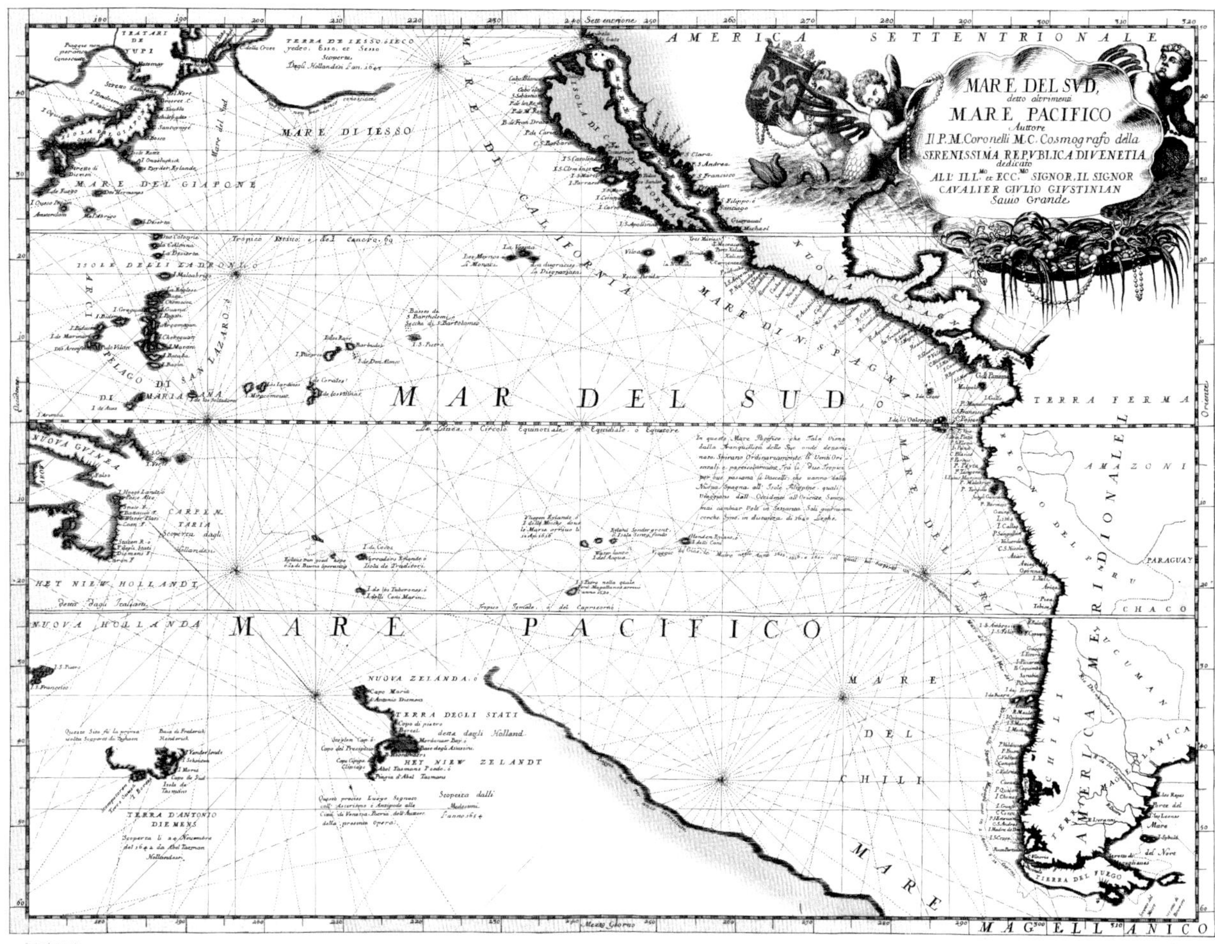

Mare del Sud ditto altimenti Mare Pacifico, by V M Coronelli. 1696. The chart shows the known Pacific at the end of the seventeenth century. The southern continent is suggested. (University of Waikato Map Collection)

Situations in the Country in the Name of the King of Great Britain'. In the event that he found such a continent, he should chart its coasts, obtain information about its people, cultivate their friendship and alliance in the King's name.

'Terra Australis Incognita', the unknown Great Southern Continent, was imaginary land that had appeared on European maps from the fifteenth to the eighteenth century. It had been first introduced by Ptolemy, a Greek cartographer, who believed that the Indian Ocean was enclosed on the south by land. When, during the Renaissance, Ptolemy became the main source of information for European cartographers, the land started to appear on their maps. Scientists argued that there should be a large landmass in the south as a counterweight against the known landmasses in the Northern Hemisphere. Usually the land was shown as a continent around the South Pole, but much larger than actual Antarctica, spreading far north in particular in the Pacific Ocean region.

Various European explorers had made tentative attempts to locate 'Terra Australis Incognita' before it was finally put to rest by Cook. After reading his instructions, Cook sailed south from the Society Islands to look for the fabled landmass. He reached 40° S without finding land and headed west for New Zealand. He circumnavigated these islands showing they could not be part of a large continent and headed for Australia. Cook felt he had not resolved the problem of a Great Southern Continent and formulated a plan for another voyage, in which he would settle the matter once and for all. He proposed to sail around the world at as high a latitude as possible.

The Admiralty agreed and, in 1772, Cook set off on his second voyage. He succeeded in circumnavigating

the globe close to 60° S latitude and in some places even crossed the Antarctic Circle. Cook showed that any possible southern continent must lie well within the cold polar region and be so cold as to be uninhabitable. That continent was later called Antarctica. Cook was unlucky in that when he was sailing the climate was much colder then than in other centuries and the ice layer around Antarctica was much thicker than usual.
SEE ALSO: Antarctica and Antarctic Circle, Pacific exploration before Cook, Second voyage

Green, Charles (1734–1771)

Charles Green sailed on the *Endeavour* as astronomer. Green was baptised in Wentworth, Yorkshire (north-west of Rotherham) on 26 December 1734. He was the youngest son of Joshua Green, a Swinton farmer, and received an education mostly from his older brother, John. John became a master at a school in Soho, London, and Charles went south as an assistant teacher. In 1760, Charles became an assistant to James Bradley, the Astronomer Royal at Greenwich. He helped Bradley observe the Transit of Venus at Greenwich in 1761.

When Nathaniel Bliss replaced Bradley in 1762, Green remained as assistant. He travelled to Barbados in 1763–64 with the astronomer, Nevil Maskelyne, to test John Harrison's chronometer. Green returned to Greenwich ahead of Maskelyne and, on the death of Bliss, took interim charge of the Royal Observatory until March 1765.

Maskelyne was appointed Astronomer Royal with Green, once again, as assistant, but they had a violent disagreement and Green joined the Navy, becoming the purser on HMS *Aurora*. However, they were reconciled sufficiently for Maskelyne to recommend Green for the *Endeavour* voyage, which he joined in early 1768. He was appointed by the Royal Society as astronomer, and was responsible for organising the viewing of the Transit of Venus. The Royal Society agreed to pay Green 100 guineas a year and a victualling allowance of 120 guineas.

Green helped train many of the *Endeavour* crew in astronomical observation. He wrote at Rio: 'I thought it a little odd when I found that no person in the ship could either make an observation of the Moon or Calculate one when made'. The observation of the Transit at Tahiti in June 1769 proved relatively successful. Sadly, Green died from dysentery in the Indian Ocean on 29 January 1771 before he had managed to put his astronomical papers in order. He was unmarried. There is a short biography in the *DNB*, Missing Persons volume, p269.
SEE ALSO: Astronomical results of Cook's voyages, First voyage

Greenwich

Greenwich, in south-east London on the south bank of the River Thames is the location of the National Maritime Museum and the original Royal Observatory, both with strong links to Cook.

On James Cook's return after his second voyage, he was presented at Court and promoted to Post Captain of HMS *Kent*. However, before Cook could take up this command, he was appointed to the Greenwich Hospital as Fourth Captain. This was something of a sinecure for Cook as he received a pension and was entitled to live at the Hospital (he chose, instead, to continue living at Mile End). It was intended that Cook use the opportunity to write up the records of the second voyage for publication.

The Hospital had been established in 1694 by King William III in memory of his wife, Queen Mary, who had wished to help seamen. Its aims were to support seamen incapable of further service and unable to maintain themselves; to support widows of seamen; and to support and educate the children of seamen. By 1714, the aims were being met. Old and wounded sailors were being cared for, as were their widows and children. A school was founded for the teaching of writing, arithmetic and navigation. Other captains of the Hospital included Hugh Palliser and John Gore. When the hospital closed, the vacated buildings became the home of the National Maritime Museum. The Museum now holds a large collection of material relating to Cook, including portraits and many of Hodges' paintings.

The Royal Observatory was established in Greenwich on 22 June 1675 by King Charles II. He appointed John Flamsteed as his first Astronomer Royal to devise ways of calculating time at sea so that longitude could be determined. Nevil Maskelyne was Astronomer Royal from 1765 until 1811. Maskelyne was involved in the appointment of Charles Green, William Wales and William Bayly as astronomers on Cook's ships. He was also very involved in the testing and acceptance of the marine chronometers developed by John Harrison. Some of those chronometers can be seen at Greenwich. The Royal Observatory, Greenwich is also the source of the Prime Meridian, longitude 0° 0' 0" which was confirmed by an international conference in 1884. The

Greenwich Hospital viewed from the north side of the Thames, painted by Robert Dodd, 1792. (National Maritime Museum, London)

Observatory proper moved south to Sussex in 1948 leaving the Greenwich site as a museum.
SEE ALSO: Astronomical results of Cook's voyages, Museums

Grenville, HM Schooner

Thomas Graves, the Governor of Newfoundland, appointed Cook as a Surveyor in early 1763. In September 1763, Graves arranged for a schooner to be made available in St John's for Cook to use in his duties. She had been built in Massachusetts in 1754 as the *Sally*, and renamed the *Grenville* after George Grenville, the First Lord of the Admiralty.

The *Grenville* was of 69 tons, 55ft 1in (16.8m) long by 17ft (5.2m) wide and carried 12 guns. Cook was designated her master and she represented his first command in the Royal Navy. Over the next few years from 1763 until 1767, the schooner enabled Cook to survey the north-western, southern and western coasts of Newfoundland.

Cook spent the summers in Newfoundland actively surveying and, from 1764 onwards, sailed the *Grenville* back to Britain each autumn, returning again in the spring. In December 1764, The schooner was changed into a brig. Cook parted with the *Grenville* in December 1767. Matthew Lane, who had been Cook's assistant in 1767, assumed command and took the brig back to Newfoundland in 1768 to complete the surveys. The *Grenville* was broken up in 1775.
SEE ALSO: Newfoundland

Grindall, Richard (1750–1820)

Richard Grindall (Grindle) sailed on the second voyage on the *Resolution* as an AB. After the voyage, he was promoted to lieutenant in 1776, commander in 1781, and captain in 1783. Grindall was in command of HMS *Thalia*, 36 guns, from 1793 to 1795. He then took charge in early 1796 of HMS *Carnatic*, a Third Rate guardship of 74 guns, at Plymouth. Grindall commanded HMS *Ramillies* from 1799 until 1800 while the ship was at Plymouth. In 1801, he took command of HMS *Formidable* (90 guns), in which he sailed in the Channel Fleet and off Ireland until 1802. He was given command of HMS *Prince* (98 guns), in 1803 and was in command at the Battle of Trafalgar in 1805. After the battle, he became a rear-admiral in 1805, and a vice-admiral in 1810.

Grindall was born in London in 1750. Grindall married in 1772, just hours before he joined the voyage though he kept it a secret from his messmates. He and his wife Katherine had one son, Rivers. Richard Grindall was knighted in 1815 and died on 23 May 1820, leaving a will (FRC 11/1631). The Grindalls are listed as living in Wickham in Hampshire. Grindle Rock in the South Sandwich Islands is probably named after him.
SEE ALSO: Second voyage

Harrison, John (1693–1776)

John Harrison was born on 24 March 1693, in Foulby, near Wakefield, Yorkshire, but the family moved to Barrow-on-Humber soon after. His father, Henry, was an estate carpenter and surveyor and, while in Barrow, John trained in his father's shop. John also learned about the tuning of bells and sang in the Barrow church choir. His interest in music was to be influential in the development of his scientific ideas. Harrison married in 1718, and a son, John, was born a few months later. By this time, he was specialising in making clocks, helped by his youngest brother, James. Two innovations date from this time. One was the grid-iron pendulum, which kept the going rate of a clock at all temperatures. The other innovation was the grasshopper escapement.

In 1714, an Act of Parliament offered a prize of £20,000 for a solution to the longitude problem, the problem being how to calculate longitude at sea. Harrison began working on a clock that could be used at sea for this purpose. His first wife, Elizabeth, died in May 1726 and in November he married again to another Elizabeth. They had two children, William, born 1728, and Elizabeth, born 1732. Harrison went to London to meet the Astronomer Royal, Edmond Halley. Halley referred him to George Graham, a leading London clockmaker, who offered him a loan. Over the next five years, the Harrisons worked on his first practical marine timekeeper (later known as H1). It was taken on trials to Lisbon in 1736. The results were good enough for further funding.

The Harrisons moved to London to be near the other scientific instrument makers and their suppliers, and John began work on the second machine (H2). This was finished in 1737 but did not do well in tests. Realising a design deficiency, Harrison started on H3 for which another £500 was awarded. Harrison continued working on H3 but it was not ready for testing at sea until 1761 but by then Harrison had made a clock watch (H4) that produced a much better performance. Trials of H3 and H4 during the period 1760 to 1762 showed they were a remarkable success. William took H4 to the West Indies and it was only 5.1 seconds slow on arrival in Jamaica, after a voyage of 62 days. However, the Board of Longitude was most reluctant to award Harrison the prize, quibbling over matters to do with wording of the prize. The new Astronomer Royal, Nevil Maskelyne, who advocated the lunar method of determining longitude, was prominent in not awarding the prize.

James Cook successfully trialed a copy of H4, known as K1, on his second and third voyages charting the Pacific. The Board of Longitude continued to drag its feet and, in 1772, Harrison appealed to King George III, whose private astronomer tested and supported the claims to accuracy of what by then was H5.

Eventually, Harrison was awarded the full prize in June 1773 and paid the money owing to him, not by the Board of Longitude but by a special Act of Parliament. He had finally gained the recognition he deserved for his achievement in providing a solution to the longitude problem. Harrison died on 24 March 1776, leaving a will (FRC 11/1018). He is buried at Hampstead Parish Church.

SEE ALSO: Chronometers, Longitude

Harvey, William (1752–1807)

William Harvey sailed on all three of Cook's Pacific voyages, beginning on the *Endeavour* as second lieutenant Hicks' servant. He was rated an AB until 7 February 1771 when he was promoted to midshipman. Harvey rejoined Cook for the second voyage on the *Resolution* as midshipman. He kept a journal and a log. On the third voyage he was on the *Resolution* as master's mate but on 31 October 1777 he was disrated to midshipman after falling asleep on watch on the island of Huahine and allowing a prisoner to escape. Cook sent him to the *Discovery*. After Cook's death on 17 February 1779, Harvey was promoted to be third lieutenant on the *Resolution*. He again kept a log.

Harvey was made a commander on 21 October 1790. In 1801, he was listed in command of HMS *Amphitrite* as guard ship off The Needles on the Isle of Wight.

Harvey was born in London in 1752 and died on 12 July 1807, leaving a will (FRC 11/1471). He was buried at St Cecilia's Church, Little Hadham, Hertfordshire (near Bishop's Stortford).
SEE ALSO: First, Second and Third voyages

Hatley, John (1760–1832)

John Hatley sailed on the third voyage on the *Resolution* as an AB. On 1 September 1777, he was made a midshipman. He was born in Ipswich in 1760. Hatley joined the voyage from the yacht *William and Mary*. After Cook's voyage, he was promoted to lieutenant in September 1782 and served on HMS *Active* and HMS *St George*. He was promoted to commander on 3 August 1797 and had charge of HMS *Winchelsea* in 1800 while it was being fitted out at Portsmouth. Hatley was made captain on 29 April 1802 and was in command of HMS *Boadicea*, 38 guns, when she sailed to the Indian Ocean in 1808 and took part in the attacks on Reunion and Mauritius. He transferred to HMS *Raisonable*, 64 guns, and returned to Britain. He died on 12 December 1832, leaving a will (FRC 11/1810).
SEE ALSO: Third voyage

Hawai'i (Owhyhee)

Hawai'i (19° 30' N, 155° 30' W), called the 'Big Island', is the largest and most easterly of the Hawaiian Islands. It is the youngest island, still being shaped by the active volcanoes that formed it. Despite its relatively young age the island was covered in tropical vegetation, though the west coast is in rain shadow from the snow-covered volcanoes. It was discovered and settled by Polynesians at some time before AD 500.

In late 1778, Cook was looking for a warm place where he could restock and repair his ships and his men could recover from the hardships of sailing in the Arctic. His ships had sailed south from Alaska and, on 26 November 1778, they reached the coast of Maui, one of the eastern Hawaiian Islands. The ships sailed along the coast of Maui. Near the eastern shore of the island, Cook was visited by an elderly chief and his retainers. He was unaware that this was Kalaniopu'u, King of Hawai'i Island. The old chief inspected *Resolution*, then departed, leaving a young chief, Kamehameha, to give

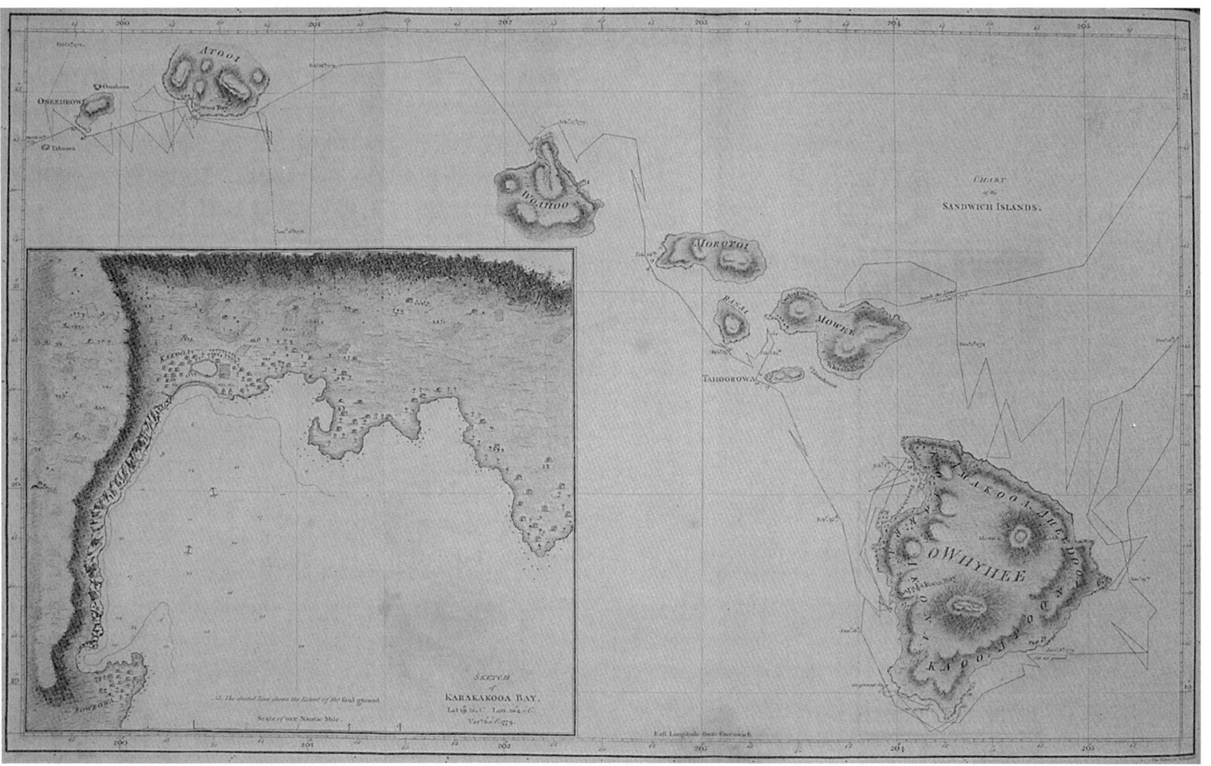

Chart of the Sandwich Islands with a sketch of Karakakooa Bay. Cook died on the promontary of Kowrowa (Ka'awaloa) at the bottom left of the inset of Kealakekua Bay, Hawai'i. Engraved by W Harrison after Bligh and Cook. (Cook & King III pl 59, fp 1)

Cook sailing directions to Hawai'i, promising that he would find hospitality and plenty of provisions.

He approached Upolu Point on 1 December and could see the snow-covered volcano of Mauna Kea. For unknown reasons, Cook now began a slow clockwise circumnavigation of the island without trying to land, even though the ships were leaking. The nature of the coast made it hard to land and strong winds made it difficult for the ships to stay together. They had reached Cape Kumukahi, the easternmost point on the island, by 19 December only to be forced back north. Working their way south they rounded the south of the island in early January 1779. Turning northward along the leeward west coast of the island, Cook sent Bligh to explore along the shore for springs of fresh water. Now, Cook's ships were surrounded by a growing escort of canoes. On 17 January, when Bligh found safe harbour and fresh water at Kealakekua Bay, the canoe flotilla was estimated at 1000 with 10,000 persons on the water.

The *Resolution* and the *Discovery* anchored in the bay. The ships' crews were all very tired and more than ready to go ashore. They had not understood why Cook had skirted the island for six weeks without landing. Cook was welcomed in a ceremony at Hikiau Heiau. They had arrived at the time of Makahiki, a part of the year associated with the god Lono, and it has been suggested that Cook was actually equated with Lono. Kalaniop'u appeared and settled at Ka'awaloa across the bay. The local people supplied food, wood and fresh water to Cook's crews but relations began to sour and Cook realised it was time to leave.

They sailed on 4 February and worked north up the coast. Before they had cleared the north of the island gales began and broke the *Resolution*'s foremast off Kaiwaihoe Bay. Cook was forced to return, reluctantly, to Kealakekua Bay where Kamehameha received him on 11 February. Their reception this time was not so warm. Kalaniopu'u made known his displeasure at the return. Relations were now strained. On the 14th, Cook went ashore at Ka'awaloa intending to take the King hostage. Before Cook could return to his ship a fight broke out on the foreshore in which he, four marines and several Hawaiians died. Clerke took the ships out of Kealakekua Bay on 22 February 1779.

SEE ALSO: Cook as god and Cook's death, Third voyage, Colour plate 9

Hawaiian Islands and Hawaiians

The Hawaiian Islands (21° N, 157° W) form a chain of

A canoe of the Sandwich Islands, the rowers masked. The background is the north side (Ka'awaloa) of Kealakekua Bay, Hawai'i. (Engraving by C Grignion after Webber)

137 islands in the north central Pacific Ocean about 2845 miles (4000km) from the west coast of North America. In the south-east, the five major islands are Kaua'i, O'ahu, Moloka'i, Maui and Hawai'i. The islands are all volcanic in origin with Hawai'i being the latest centre for volcanic activity. The islands have developed a unique fauna and flora through their remoteness.

The first people to occupy the islands and who were present when Cook arrived in 1778 were Polynesians, who settled there some time before AD 500. Linguistic and cultural evidence suggest that the first inhabitants came from the Marquesas Group, to the north-east of Tahiti. During the twelfth and thirteenth centuries, new immigrants from Tahiti of high, chiefly and priestly status arrived at the islands and assumed power over the original inhabitants.

After a time of voyaging back and forth between the Society Islands and the Hawaiian Islands, contact with southern Polynesia ceased. During the 400 years of isolation that followed, a unique Hawaiian culture developed. Hawai'i was a highly stratified society with strictly maintained castes. The ali'i (chiefs) were at the top and ruled over the land. Below them, the kahuna (priests or professionals) were experts on religious ritual or specialists in canoe-building, herbal medicine, and healing. The maka'ainana (ordinary people) carried out most of the work but were above the kauwa, who were outcasts or slaves. A system of laws known as kanawai enforced the social order. Certain people, places and things were sacred at certain times and were kapu, or forbidden. Fishing and farming were regulated in this way and non-observation could result in death.

In January 1778, on his third voyage into the Pacific in his search for the Northwest Passage, James Cook landed his ships *Resolution* and *Discovery* at Waimea on Kaua'i. He named the group of islands the Sandwich Islands in honour of the Earl of Sandwich though the local name, Hawai'i was soon in common use. They were the first Europeans to make a documented landing in Hawai'i though Spanish galleons may have made earlier visits. Cook returned in November 1778, this time making landfall at the eastern end of the chain at Maui. He circled Hawai'i Island to anchor at Kealakekua Bay. During a dispute between him and some Hawaiians, Cook was stabbed to death.

Charles Clerke assumed command and, after relations between the two sides had been restored, the ships sailed on 22 February 1779. Clerke was intent on continuing what Cook had started and took the ships north-west to investigate the smaller islands of Lana'i, Moloka'i and Kaho'olawe. The ships next anchored in Waimea Bay on the north-west coast of O'ahu but quickly moved over to Kaua'i. On 2 March, the ships anchored again at Waimea on Kaua'i. Their reception was cool though hundreds gathered on the beach to watch the crew get water. Clerke wanted more yams for the voyage ahead and felt Ni'ihau would provide a better source. The ships sailed across to anchor near Leahi Point. The *Resolution* and the *Discovery* set sail for Kamchatka on 15 March, sailing west from Ni'ihau.

The British visits were recorded by the accounts written by members of the crew. Together with the portfolio of paintings done by Webber and the specimens and artefacts taken on board, they provide an ethnological record of the Hawaiian way of life at the time of contact. The British, however, had problems transcribing what they heard of the Hawaiian language onto paper. The Hawaiian 'l' sound was heard and written as an 'r' so Kealakekua and Lono became Karakakooa and Orono respectively. Other problems existed with 'p' and 'b', and with 't' and 'k'. Hawai'i was written as Owyhee and Kaua'i as Atooi.

Kamehameha, who received Cook at Kealakekua, founded the Kingdom of Hawai'i Island and gradually extended his rule over the other islands. The Kingdom of Hawai'i was internationally recognised and the name replaced that of the Sandwich Islands, bestowed by Cook. After the monarchy's overthrow in 1893 it became briefly the Republic of Hawai'i and then, after annexation to the US, the islands became the Territory of Hawai'i. Finally, in 1958 it became the State of Hawai'i.

The effects of contact with Europeans have not always been good for native Hawaiians. Introduced diseases have taken their toll while their way of life and culture has been drastically altered. Although foreign contact was inevitable, Cook is blamed by some for starting that process.

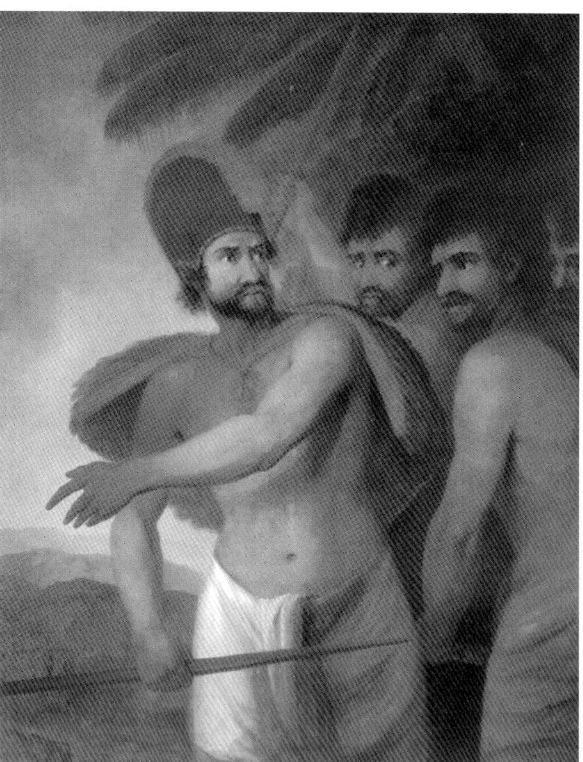

A Chief of the Sandwich Islands leading his party to battle, by John Webber. The painting shows the distinctive helmet and cloak worn by Hawaiian leaders. (National Library of Australia, NK1)

SEE ALSO: Indigenous peoples and Cook, Polynesia

Hawke of Towton, Edward Hawke, 1st Baron (1710–1781)

Edward Hawke was born on 21 February 1710 in London and joined the Navy in February 1720. He was promoted in 1734 to the rank of captain. Having broken the line of battle to attack the enemy in the engagement off Toulon on 11 February 1744, Hawke was deprived of his commission, but soon after restored. He was promoted in July 1747 to the rank of rear-admiral and inflicted a major defeat on a French squadron off La Rochelle. In 1747, he was elected MP for Portsmouth, which he continued to represent for 30 years.

During the Seven Years War in 1756, Hawke relieved Admiral John Byng as commander in the Mediterranean and was appointed an admiral in 1758. In November

1759, after blockading the French ports in the Bay of Biscay for six months, he won his greatest victory, defeating the French fleet in Quiberon Bay. His victory averted the danger of a French invasion of Great Britain.

As Sir Edward Hawke, he served from 1766 until 1771 as First Lord of the Admiralty and, as such, was instrumental in dispatching the *Endeavour* in 1768 with James Cook in command. He was raised to the peerage in 1776. During his long career Hawke did much to improve conditions in the fleet. Hawke married Catherine Brooke and they had two children. He died on 17 October 1781 and there is a memorial to him in St Nicholas's Church, North Stoneham, Hampshire. Cook named Hawke's Bay in New Zealand and Cape Hawke in New South Wales after Hawke.

SEE ALSO: Admiralty, Seven Years War

Hawkesworth, John (1720–1773)

John Hawkesworth, the English miscellaneous writer, was born in north-east London in 1720. He was self-educated, having had no formal schooling and, in 1737, became a clerk to an attorney. Hawkesworth was married in 1744 to Mary Brown, who ran a boarding school at Sydenham in Kent. The couple moved into Thornhill Mansion in Bromley, Kent where Samuel Johnson was a frequent guest in the 1740s and 1750s.

Hawkesworth made his first appearance in print in June 1741. From 1744 to 1752, his main employment was with the *Gentleman's Magazine* and when Johnson gave up his editorial duties after 1743, Hawkesworth gradually took them over. He started a new essay paper, the *Adventurer*, which ran twice weekly, from 1752 until 1754. In 1756 he received the degree of doctor of laws from Lambeth Palace, awarded by the Archbishop of Canterbury in recognition of the merit of his *Adventurer* essays and the probity of his character.

In 1754–55, Hawkesworth published a 12-volume edition of Swift and wrote the libretto of an oratorio *Zimri* in 1760. In 1771, he secured his most famous commission on a recommendation by Charles Burney, backed up by Garrick. He was authorised by the Earl of Sandwich, First Lord of the Admiralty, to compile the official account of the voyages to the South Pacific made between 1764 and 1771 by Byron, Wallis, Carteret and James Cook.

Hawkesworth sold the copyright for £6000 and his edition of the voyages was published in June 1773 by Strahan and Cadell. Hawkesworth altered the text to bring it into line with the standards of style and decorum he judged appropriate and chose to retain the first-person narrative mode, which meant that he appeared to be putting his own words into the captains' mouths. The captains protested against this interference with their text, and Hawkesworth was accused of misrepresentation and profiteering. In April 1776, Cook expressed his own unhappiness while dining with James Boswell, who replied '"Why, Sir", said I, "Hawkesworth has used your narrative as a London Tavern-keeper does wine. He has brewed it".'

However, *An Account of the Voyages* was a best-seller and was quickly translated into French and German editions. Hawkesworth, though, was deeply wounded by the hostile criticism, and it severely affected his health. He died in London a month later, on 17 November 1773. He was buried at Bromley, Kent and there is a monument in the church to his memory.

SEE ALSO: Literature of Cook's voyages, Published accounts

Hergest, Richard (1754–1791)

Richard Hergest sailed on Cook's second and third voyages. He was aboard the *Adventure* as an AB until 1 January 1773 when he was made a midshipman. He kept a journal. On the third voyage he sailed on *Resolution* as a midshipman until 1 November 1776. He was then made an AB until 24 August 1779 before becoming a midshipman again. He became a lieutenant in December 1780. In 1790, he was given command of HMS *Daedalus*, a storeship, but while *en route* to meet George Vancouver's expedition at Nootka Sound, he was killed at O'ahu, Hawai'i on 11 May 1791.

A few months earlier, he thought he discovered new islands in 1791 and Vancouver named them the Hergest Islands in his honour. However, they were the Northern Marquesas, which Ingraham had visited a year earlier.

SEE ALSO: Third voyage

Hicks, Zachary (1739?–1771)

Zachary Hicks was second lieutenant on the *Endeavour*. The muster record lists him as having been born in Stepney in 1739 but it is possible he came from Ripon in Yorkshire. Prior to the voyage, he had served on HMS *Launceston*, a Fifth Rate of 44 guns, as an AB and midshipman during 1766–67. He was transferred as acting lieutenant on board HMS *Hornet*, a sloop of 14 guns before, in May 1768, he was appointed by commission as second lieutenant on the *Endeavour* as Cook's second-in-command.

Hicks was already showing signs of tuberculosis when he sailed and this may have affected his performance. Beaglehole describes Hicks as a steady, efficient and competent officer but assesses him as unimaginative and matter-of-fact based upon the writing in his journal and log. Hicks was taken hostage by the Viceroy in Rio de Janeiro during the diplomatic impasse when the *Endeavour* reached Brazil. He later led the third Transit of Venus observation party to Motu Taaupiri in north-east Tahiti. His most famous moment came on 19 April 1770 when he was the first person on board to sight the Australian coast. His health was failing and he was sent ashore at Batavia (Jakarta) to recover. Instead it worsened and he died on 26 May 1771 as the expedition sailed north up the Atlantic, 10° N of the Equator.

Cook wrote 'he died of a Consumption which he was not free from when we saild from England so that it may be truly said that he hath been dieing ever sence'. Hicks kept a log and a journal from 27 May 1768 until 14 March 1771 when he was too ill to continue. A section of his journal is reproduced in the *Historical Records of New South Wales, vol. 1, part 1: Cook 1762-1780*. Hicks Bay in New Zealand and Point Hicks on the south-eastern coast of Australia are named for Hicks.

SEE ALSO: First voyage

Hodges, William (1744–1797)

William Hodges went on Cook's second voyage on the *Resolution* as the artist to paint landscapes, portraits, and draw coastal views. Hodges was born on 28 October 1744 in London, where his father was a blacksmith in St James's, off Piccadilly. He was educated at William Shipley's drawing school before serving as pupil and assistant to the landscape painter Richard Wilson from 1763 to 1766. He also attended the drawing and sculpture classes of G B Cipriani and Joseph Wilton at the Duke of Richmond's sculpture gallery. On leaving Wilson, he resided in London, and also for a time at Derby, where he painted some scenes for the theatre. From that year until 1772, he exhibited several views at the Society of Artists.

Not having much success in London as a painter, Hodges took the opportunity that arose in 1772 to join Cook's voyage as artist. Hodges made many studies, including some portrait drawings and a few finished oils. Upon his return in 1775, he was employed by the Admiralty to finish his drawings and superintend the engraving of them for the published account of the voyage. A set of 24 oils from the voyage have been the property of the Admiralty since they were painted and are now on display at the National Maritime Museum, Greenwich, London.

A portrait of William Hodges, by Nathaniel Dance. (National Maritime Museum, London)

His first exhibition at the Royal Academy was in 1776 when he submitted a view in Otaheite, followed over the next two years of some views of New Zealand and elsewhere. On 11 May 1776, Hodges married Martha Nesbit but unfortunately, she died within a year. In 1779, he sailed for India, where he travelled and painted extensively under the patronage of the Governor-General of Bengal, Warren Hastings.

He returned in 1783 to London and settled in Queen Street, Mayfair, where he built himself a studio. He exhibited his views in India and published a memoir of his travels there. On 16 October 1784, Hodges married his second wife, Lydia Wright. Unfortunately, she too died after only a few months of marriage, and shortly afterwards, on 1 December 1785, he married, for a third and last time, a Miss Carr.

Hodges was elected a member of the Royal Academy in 1789 and continued to exhibit there until 1794. He had got into financial difficulties and made an unsuccessful trip to seek patronage in Russia in 1792. In 1794, Hodges held a private exhibition in London of a selection of his work, which did not receive support and on its close he retired from his profession. It had contained two contrasting 'moral' landscapes, the 'Effects of Peace' and the 'Consequences of War', which Gillray used as the basis of two satirical cartoons critical of the Duke of York, who had the exhibition closed.

Hodges attempted to retrieve his fortune by moving to Devon, where he became partner in a small bank at Dartmouth, but it collapsed early in 1797. He died in Brixham on 6 March 1797, officially of 'gout of the stomach', though it was possibly suicide. His death left his wife and children in poverty and she survived him only a few months, dying at Tunbridge later that same year. There is a short biography in the *DNB*, v9, p955. Mount Hodges in New Zealand is named after him.
SEE ALSO: Art of Cook's voyages, Artists on Cook's voyages, Portraits of Cook, Second voyage

Hollamby, William (1746–1798)

William Hollamby (Hollanby) sailed on the third voyage on the *Discovery* occupying a series of positions. He began as quartermaster but, on 31 December 1777, he became master's mate. On 31 December 1778 he reverted to quartermaster. After Clerke's death Hollamby became a midshipman on 24 August 1779 but on 29 April 1780 he became a master's mate once more. After the voyage, he was made lieutenant in May 1781 and commander in December 1783. Hollamby was an agent to transport ships at his death. He was born in London in 1746 and died in 1798, leaving a will (FRC 11/1303).
SEE ALSO: Third voyage

Holland, Samuel Johannes (1728–1801)

Samuel Holland, the engineer and surveyor, was born 1717 in Murnwageen, Netherlands. He married twice; the first time in 1749 in Nijmegen, Netherlands to Gertrude Hasse. Shortly after, he left the Netherlands and his wife, and moved to Britain where he joined the British army.

In 1756, Holland was sent to America where he spent most of the remainder of his career. He was soon employed in making a map of the province of New York before attending the siege of Louisbourg in 1758, when he served under Wolfe. After the surrender of Louisbourg, while making a plan of the town and its environs, he met James Cook at Kennington Cove. Over the next few weeks, he instructed Cook in the use of the plane table and other surveying techniques.

In 1759, Holland accompanied Wolfe to Quebec and was promoted to the rank of captain. In 1761, he began surveying the settled portions of the Province of Quebec, and in the following year carried his plans to England, where he remained until 1764. He returned to Canada to map Prince Edward Island from 1764 until 1766. In 1766, he was appointed Surveyor General of the Province of Quebec and also of the Northern District of America. It was in his capacity of Surveyor General of the Northern District of America that he surveyed and wrote his description of Cape Breton Island.

Holland completed surveys in the Gulf and the Lower St Lawrence and then in New Hampshire, New Jersey, New York and Massachusetts. In 1778, he was transferred to Quebec and, in 1791, he drew the boundaries between Upper and Lower Canada. Holland married a second time on 3 September 1787 in Perth Amboy, New Jersey to Marie-Josephate (Josette) Rolette. They would have ten children together. Holland died at Quebec on 28 December 1801. A red rose and a river in Ontario are named after him.
SEE ALSO: Canada, Louisbourg, Surveys and running surveys

Home, Alexander (1751–1823)

Alexander Home sailed on the third voyage on the *Discovery* as a master's mate until 31 December 1777. He was next a quartermaster until 31 December 1778 when he became a master's mate again. On his return to Britain, Home was promoted to lieutenant in 1780 and served in American waters where his sight was injured. He retired from active service and was made a superannuated commander in December 1815. He was born in Berwick in 1751 and died on 21 February 1823 in Buskenburn, Berwickshire.
SEE ALSO: Third voyage

Hood, Alexander (1758–1798)

Alexander Hood sailed on the second voyage on the *Resolution* as an AB. He kept a journal. He was the first on board to sight the Marquesas Islands in 1774. Fatuhuku in the Marquesas was called Hood's Island by Cook but the island later reverted to its Marquesan name. After the voyage, Hood served on HMS *Marlborough*. He was promoted to lieutenant in July 1777, commander and captain in 1781. In 1794, Hood captained HMS *Hebe,* 38 guns. He was given command of HMS *Mars,* 74 guns, in 1797 and died in action off Brest in 1798 as his ship captured the French ship

Hercule. Hood was born in London in 1758 and died on 21 April 1798, leaving a will (FRC 11/1316). He was buried at All Saints Church, Wootton Courtney, Somerset (near Minehead).
SEE ALSO: Second voyage

Huahine

Huahine (16° 45' S, 151° W) is the easternmost of the Leeward Society Islands in the South Pacific. It is 105 miles (170km) WNW of Tahiti and now forms part of the territory of French Polynesia. Huahine comprises two islands, Huahine Nui (to the north) and Huahine Iti, separated by a narrow and shallow lagoon. Fare is the main settlement, on the north-west coast of Huahine Nui.

The islands were one of the first in the region to be inhabited by Polynesians and remains of extensive marae (religious sites) exist. Cook visited the islands on each of his voyages, anchoring off Fare. On the *Endeavour* voyage Cook arrived on 17 July 1769 and stayed three days. He was received by Ori, a chief, who welcomed Cook again on his second voyage in September 1773. Cook sailed through Passe Avapeihi to anchor near Fare. Provisions were in good supply and trade was brisk. Sparrman went inland where he was robbed and stripped, which led to a tense situation. Ori offered himself as hostage but the matter was quickly resolved. Cook decided to leave and on 7 September they sailed with an extra passenger on the *Adventure*. This was Mai (Omai) who would gain fame in London.

Six months later in May 1774, Ori gave the British a more lukewarm reception and Cook left after eight days. Their stay was marked by several incidents, including Forster's servant Scholient being attacked and robbed. The purpose of the visit on the third voyage was to return Mai (Omai). Cook arrived on 12 October 1777 at Fare to find that his friend Ori was no longer the chief. Land was purchased near Fare and a house was built. All the gifts that Mai had brought from Europe were put ashore, together with horses and other animals. A tearful Mai remained on the island when the British left on 2 November.
SEE ALSO: Society Islands

A View of the Harbour of Huaheine (Fare), *by John Webber. 1777. Cook visited Huahine to return Mai to the island. (British Library)*

I

Indigenous peoples and Cook

The secret instructions that James Cook received from the Admiralty in July 1778 specified that the astronomical observation of the Transit of Venus from King George's Island, or Tahiti, was the main object of his expedition. His second purpose was to search for the Great Southern Continent, in the area to the south of Tahiti and to the east of New Zealand. A third instruction required that, on discovering Terra Australis or, failing that, reaching New Zealand, Cook was to describe the soil, minerals, flora, animals, birds, and fish, and to cultivate a friendship with the inhabitants, and observe their 'Genius, Temper, Disposition and Number'. In addition, he was to gain the consent of the natives before taking possession of the country in the name of George III.

Just before embarking, Cook also was given written instructions by the Earl of Morton, president of the Royal Society, which included 'Hints' about how to handle indigenous peoples. Importantly, 'the utmost patience and forbearance with respect to the Natives' was advised, as were checks on 'the petulance of the Sailors' and 'the wanton use of Fire Arms', because 'shedding the blood of those people is a crime of the highest nature'. Regarding the rights of the locals, the president continued: 'They are the natural, and in the strictest sense of the word, the legal possessors of the several Regions they inhabit. No European Nation has a right to occupy any part of their country, or settle among them without their voluntary consent. Conquest over such people can give no just title; because they could never be the Agressors. They may naturally and justly attempt to repell intruders, whom they may apprehend are come to disturb them in the quiet possession of their country, whether that apprehension be well or ill founded. Therefore should they in a hostile manner oppose a landing, and kill some men in the attempt, even this would hardly justify firing among them, 'till every other gentle method has been tried.'

Morton recommended several non-violent ways of convincing natives 'of the Superiority of Europeans'. For instance, shooting guns at birds or objects to 'strike them with amazement and awe', or playing drums or trumpets to impress them. Alternatively, during a landing 'trinkets' could be left on the shore while the visitors retreat in the ship's boats, from where 'the behaviour of the natives might be distinctly observed, before a second landing [is] attempted'.

The first contact with indigenous people during any of Cook's voyages into the Pacific occurred in January 1769 when a group of 50 to 60 'Patagonians' was observed on a cliff top near the tip of Tierra del Fuego. In reality, members of the Haush tribe did not appear to have had previous direct contact with Europeans, and were reluctant to accept their trinkets and friendship. Once relations were established, however, the Europeans unanimously denigrated the material paucity of these hunter-gathers' daily existence. Cook himself described these natives as 'the miserablest people on earth', and during a similarly brief visit to the same area in late 1774, he caricatured their neighbours, the Yamanas, as malodorous and 'a little ugly half starved beardless Race'.

A significant aspect of these contacts with the inhabitants of Tierra del Fuego was that the 'scientific gentlemen' on *Endeavour* measured the height of some of this population, to show that they were in the same height range as most other human groups. Thus, the claim that these people were a 'race of giants' was finally consigned to the dustbin of history – a full 250 years after it had been invented by Magellan, who also gave them the name 'Patagonians' meaning 'Big Feet'.

But if Cook and his men undermined one European myth by exposing it to the harsh light of empirical scrutiny, their accounts of their experiences at their next stop were to reinforce another powerful Western fantasy. Tahiti had been visited in 1767 by Wallis, who subdued the locals with a barrage of cannon and gunshot, and in 1768 by Bougainville, who popularised the notion of an arcadian island paradise, and who the British now credited with introducing 'the venereal', or 'French disease'. Cook was to call four times at this group, which he named 'Society Islands' after his scientific sponsors, staying a total of six months. These visits were characterised mainly by reciprocity between the two groups, with intermittent thefts by the locals and violent overreactions by the English.

Cook and his men likewise portrayed these islands and their inhabitants in romanticised, primitivist terms. It was in Tahiti that the visitors, and Europeans generally, were first introduced to the practices of and words for *tatau* (tattoo) and *tapu* (taboo). Here too the captain established special name-exchange friendships with several important chiefs, and witnessed important customary practices, including war expeditions and a human sacrifice. However, this society was already undergoing major sociopolitical changes, which were accelerated by the arrival of Westerners and the introduction of their commodities, animals and diseases.

The one prior European visitor to New Zealand, Abel Tasman in 1642, had only brief and bloody contacts with its indigenous inhabitants. During their five forays into these waters, Cook and his men had extensive interactions with the natives (the term 'Māori' not having yet attained its modern meaning), though in their first landing, at Turanga-nui (Poverty Bay) on the east coast in October 1769, four warriors were shot dead, five wounded, and three kidnapped. Afterwards, Cook wrote: 'Thus ended the most disagreeable day My life has ever seen, black be the mark for it and heaven send that such may never return to embitter future reflection'. Bodily tattooing and elaborate wood and stone carving – plus a general accessibility to women – were what most impressed about these islands. Their inhabitants' seemingly limitless capacity for warfare, meanwhile, and especially their attachment to cannibalism, including their infamous feasting on some of the *Adventure*'s crew, served to encourage a dark notoriety about New Zealand in European minds.

While surveying the east coast of Australia in mid-1770, Cook and his associates became the first Europeans known to have encountered the native 'New Hollanders' of that side of the continent. Most often these indigenees remained on land and in the distance, avoiding close contact with the outsiders; at other times, when the ship or its personnel intruded into a group's coastal waters, the natives simply ignored them. In one place local men (Gweagal) defiantly threw spears at a landing party – and suffered smallshot in reply; at another, after local men (Guugu Yimithirr) visited the *Endeavour* to reclaim turtles caught by the visitors, one of them suffered smallshot wounds. Trinkets offered to or left for the natives usually went untouched: they were not interested in either the strangers' goods or any form of exchange. Cook described these people as having 'lank' rather than 'woolly' hair, and being 'of a dark brown colour, but not black', thus contradicting Dampier's claim that they were 'negroes'. Of their general conditions of life, Cook wrote admiringly: 'From What I have said of the Natives of New-Holland they may appear to some to be the most wretched people upon Earth, but in realty they are far more happy than we Europeans; being wholly unacquainted not only with the superfluous but the necessary Conveniences so much sought after in Europe, they are happy in not knowing the use of them. They live in a Tranquillity which is not disturb'd by the Inequality of Condition: The Earth and sea of their own accord furnishes them with all things necessary for life…'.

Six years later Cook returned to Van Dieman's Land, or Tasmania. Local people soon arrived at his camp – 'Eight men and a boy: they came out of the Woods to us without shewing the least mark of fear and the greatest confidence imaginable, for none of them had any weapons'. Gifts of beads, trifles, and ironware were accepted, though without obvious interest or gratitude. When some tried to help the seafarers with their work, a jittery crewman fired in the air, sending natives scattering. But they returned next day, with women and children. When some seamen sought sexual favours from the former, a male elder ordered the women and children to leave. Some of the Europeans wrote glowingly of these people, as the captain had done earlier for their kinsfolk to the north, while others were disparaging, comparing them with the Patagonians. Cook, by now a seasoned observer of tribal peoples, in this instance avoided both primitivisation and bestialisation, opting for straightforward description.

Racist notions came to the fore in the interactions between Cook's party and the peoples of the archipelago he called New Hebrides, now known as Vanuatu. In July 1774, at the island of Malekula, after an altercation on the ship, the captain was confronted on the beach by up to 500 armed men; a chief came to his rescue, by offering him a green branch and presenting him with a small pig. Cook hoped that this would signal the start of trade, but such was not to be: the local people seem to have regarded him as a *tamar*, or returning spirit, and were keen for him to leave. Well used to Polynesian languages, Cook noted that theirs was not of that family, and reported their attributes as 'almost black or rather a dark Chocolate Colour, Slenderly made, not tall, [with] Monkey faces and Woolly hair'.

At the nearby island of Erromango, where the inhabitants tried to capture his boat because they feared he was a ghost, Cook ordered his crew to fire. One of his men was injured by a spear, while one or two natives died. Then at the island of Tanna, when natives boarded the ships and pilfering began, he ordered muskets and cannon fired as a warning. Relations improved, but locals displayed no desire for the visitors' trade goods, and threatening behaviour continued. Eventually better communication opened, and food was given to the strangers, but then a marine unjustifiably shot and killed a man. Later the captain reflected in his journal on Earl Morton's 'Hints', reminding himself that Pacific peoples were justified in opposing unsanctioned landings on their shores, and that his party has no legal basis for responding with uncontrolled firepower.

Following a brief call at Espiritu Santo, they next came to a high island, which the captain named 'New Caledonia'. Though welcomed by a large and unarmed crowd, their visit here was relatively brief; but long enough for the visitors to realise there was not much food to be traded, only weapons and the like. In another written reflection, Cook here pondered his impression that the women in the western islands are 'far more Chaste than those of the Eastern Islands'.

Easter Island, visited by Roggeveen in 1722, was one of these 'Eastern Islands'. Cook and *Resolution* called there in March 1774. Though it is geographically closer to Chile, he and his men observed that the people spoke a language related to Tahitian and Māori, and shared with them many other cultural and physical features. Crowds welcomed the English ashore, plant foods were traded for nails, and women came off to the ship by boats. The unique stone statues were examined, and Cook speculated on the technology and organisation necessary to carve and construct them. But because Easter Island's natural resources obviously had become degraded, so that the potential for supplies would always be limited, the ships headed back out to sea.

Geographically speaking the islands of the Marquesas group also belong to Cook's 'eastern' category. In 1595 Mendaña had violently touched here; in April 1774 Cook was the second European to make contact. The intricate tattoos worn by the men of this island particularly impressed those on the ship. Initially, tradable food appeared to be scarce, and some of those who did trade were dishonest. Cook fired a musket ball over one offender, and when an iron stanchion was stolen and he called for a similar shot over the new thief's head, an officer misheard and shot the man dead. Fortunately a bough-waving chief paddled out to re-establish peace. Just when trade was beginning to pick up, crewmen undermined it by exchanging red feathers brought from Tonga – such treasures being very rare and desired in Marquesas – for pigs and similar. Only near the end of the stay were native women encountered, and several of them subsequently slept with the visitors.

Westwards beyond the Society group, in the double-archipelago that is today named after Cook, he and his ships in March 1777 came into contact with two unexpected islands. One of them was the raised atoll of Mangaia, which the captain rightly judged to be a potentially rich source for supplies, but which had no safe access. Numerous people here swam out to the boats, creating havoc aboard. Just one man, a warrior-chief was taken out to the ship, where he was presented with a knife and drawn by the ship's artist. He was keen for the visitors to come ashore – though present-day traditions say strangers were usually treated as invaders and killed. A couple of days later the ships sighted Atiu, a smaller member of this scattered group, but again with no good access for ships' boats. Here several members of Cook's party were canoed ashore, where they were fed and entertained over most of a day.

Further west again, isolated but also a raised atoll, as large in area as all the Cook Islands combined, stands Niue. In June 1774 *Resolution* hoved to off its northern end, allowing the captain in the ship's boats to search for landing places along its north-west quarter. On two occasions they landed on its jagged coral coasts, only to be attacked with spears and stones by charcoaled warriors. Cook and his men fired back, causing an unknown number of injuries. Unwilling to force the issue over a place lacking access and with no visible supplies, he departed, in the process re-naming it Savage Island.

A few days later, still moving westwards, Cook's ship hit the northern part of that long archipelago then and now called Tonga, but which he chose to call the Friendly Islands. A year previously he had visited the southern part of this group, and in 1777 he would return to survey the totality. In the early 1600s, Tasman and other Dutch navigators had mapped several of these islands. Like them, Cook was intrigued by this kingdom's elaborate political system, centred on the sacred-chief called the Tu'i Tonga, whose *mana* spread over the whole archipelago and who drew tribute from several neighbouring societies. Cook established close relations with several leading chiefs, and participated in many ceremonial activities. While theft was a regular problem, and the captain and his men several times resorted to extreme violence, the plenitude of supplies and the affections of the women ensured that Tonga, with Tahiti, was a preferred Pacific Island stopover for his ships.

Far to the north lies the archipelago Cook called the Sandwich Islands, but which is now generally known as Hawai'i. In January 1778, when they rested for two weeks in the leeward part of this group, *Resolution* and *Discovery* became the first European ships known to have directly encountered this isolated but elaborate Polynesian society. Ten months later they returned, to remain for the next quarter of a year, in and around the actual island of Hawai'i. The details of this sojourn are well known. Very briefly, the local people honoured Cook as a returned god-chief called Lono; the people provided his men with every service and luxury; Cook became increasingly violent and irrational; locals killed him when he tried to kidnap the king. At least fourteen Hawaiians also were killed that day, and many were wounded, and others likewise in a British revenge attack.

While absent from Hawai'i, Cook was surveying the American north-west coast. There the main indigenous groups that he had contact with were the Mowachaht bands of the Nuu-chah-nulth nation, who lived in Nootka Sound where the ships were rested and repaired before heading north to Arctic waters. These people were unlike any of the 'Indians' encountered in the Pacific Islands or Australia. While they already possessed some metals, they wanted more iron, axes, and cloth. They were found to be totally honest in trade, exchanging mainly furs and artefacts; some women also traded sex. Peace prevailed for the month the ships were in port, and some of Cook's group visited the main ceremonial centre.

In the course of his explorations Cook had significant interactions with the indigenous inhabitants of fifteen different Pacific nations or states (as currently defined), and for six of these populations he was their first direct contact with the European world. At least twenty-five indigenous Pacific individuals were killed by Cook or his subordinates during his three voyages. Probably a similar number suffered significant wounds, usually inflicted by musket or cannon fire, but also through whippings or other punishments. A lesser number appear to have endured kidnapping or similar deprivation of freedom, and then usually for only a matter of hours. Though the captain himself probably never had sexual relations with any Pacific person, his men introduced venereal disease into at least three major indigenous populations, and they spread it in many others.

Unsurprisingly, the phrase 'Captain Cook' represents pain and trauma for many present-day native Pacific communities. That is why public celebrations of his achievements were not welcomed, and sometimes were directly challenged, by some indigenous organisations during the 1960s–70s bicentenary period. At a time when many other colonised peoples and nations around the world are celebrating their re-found independence, these objectors were saying, why should we celebrate an event that undermined our sovereignty and initiated our greatest tragedy? Similar feelings were stirred recently by the sailing of the replica *Endeavour* in Pacific waters. For instance, in 1995 at Gisborne, New Zealand, local Māori tribes successfully demanded that a visit by the ship entail public acknowledgement of the deaths and injuries associated with Cook's 1769 visit.

Elsewhere in the region there are indigenous communities which – according to the British records from Cook's voyages – had no direct contact with Cook, but which now have incorporated him into their mythology and ritual. Most spectacularly, in recent decades across northern Australia, 'Captain Cook' and 'Captain Cook Law' have come to play a major part in oral tradition and ceremonial life. Likewise, he is a central figure in the work of many contemporary Aboriginal artists and story tellers, most notably Paddy Forham Wainburranga, whose 'Too Many Captain Cooks' series of bark paintings and narrative performances has attracted a wide audience.

In other parts of the Pacific, Cook has been woven into the very fabric of official history and identity. Though they have been a self-governing nation for the past three decades, successive governments of the Cook Islands have chosen to keep the name which some of their people consider to be a legacy of their colonial past. On the nearby island of Niue, Cook's 'Savage Island', *Kapene Kuki* is variously celebrated and denigrated in song and dance, and the man himself has come to stand for all Europeans who had contact with their ancestors in pre-Christian times. Even the state of Hawai'i, in a tradition that links back to its pre-colonial indigenous monarchy, still incorporates Cook's Union Jack in its own official flag.

BY TOM RYAN

J

Jackson (Duckett), Sir George (1725–1822)

George Jackson was born on 24 October 1725 in north Yorkshire. Jackson joined the Navy Office about 1743 and became secretary to the Navy Board in 1758. He moved to the Admiralty in 1766 where he became assistant secretary to the Lords Commissioners of the Admiralty, under Philip Stephens. At the same time, he became judge-advocate of the fleet. He resigned as assistant secretary in 1782 but remained judge-advocate. Jackson served as an MP and was knighted in 1791. There is a short biography in the *DNB*, v10, pp527–8. Cape Jackson in New Zealand and Port Jackson (the future site of Sydney) were named after him.

SEE ALSO: Admiralty

Jakarta (Batavia)

The islands of Indonesia occupy a strategic position between the Indian and Pacific Oceans and Jakarta, on the north-west coast of Java, has for several hundred years been a prominent port of call for shipping. The city (6° 8' S, 106° 45' E) had its origins as a small harbour town called Sunda Kelapa, but its founding dates back to 1527 when it was named Jayakarta (meaning city of great victory) by the neighbouring Sultanate of Banten.

The Dutch Vereenigde Oost-Indische Compagnie (VOC or Dutch East India Company) wanted a base in the region for its activities. It captured and destroyed the Javanese village in 1619. In its place, they built a new city of canals, roads and small houses, a Little Holland in the Tropics. The name was changed to Batavia, in honor of a medieval Netherlands Kingdom, Batavia. The climate and the canals, breeding places for diseases, soon gave Batavia a reputation for being unhealthy and it was known as the Graveyard of the Orient.

During his first voyage, Cook had problems with the *Endeavour,* which badly needed repairs. He knew of Batavia so nursed the ship all the way from New Zealand to the Dutch port. The Dutch authorities insisted on carrying out the repairs, which then took several months. Cook, who had prided himself on maintaining a healthy crew up to that time was devastated as men became ill and six died, including the surgeon, Munkhouse, and Tupaia. Cook could not leave soon enough but dysentery and other diseases went with the ship and 24 men died on the passage to Cape Town.

SEE ALSO: Medical aspects of Cook's voyages, First voyage

Jefferys, Thomas (1719?–1771)

Thomas Jefferys, engraver, cartographer and publisher, was born about 1719, and apprenticed to the London mapmaker Emanuel Bowen in 1735. His independent career began about 1744 in Clerkenwell, but by 1750 he acquired more central premises at Charing Cross. He was appointed Geographer to George III in 1760, having previously held the warrant of Geographer to the Prince of Wales.

Jefferys became the leading London mapseller of his time, his output including his own large-scale surveys of six English counties, as well as many significant atlases and geographical texts. He also produced numerous maps for the books and magazines of the period. He is remembered particularly for some of the finest eighteenth-century maps of the Americas, culminating in the atlas published in association with Robert Sayer as *A General Topography of North America* in 1768, which included many of Cook's early charts. Jefferys also engraved Cook's 12-sheet *A New Chart of the River St Laurence* (1760), published his *Directions for Navigating the Gulf and River of St Laurence* (1760), and published *The Newfoundland Pilot*, based primarily on Cook's work, in 1769.

Despite a bankruptcy in 1766 – a business failure almost certainly related to the expense of the county surveys – Jefferys played a major part in the emergence of London as a centre of cartographic publishing. His business survived with the help of friends and continued after his death in 1771 in the form of a partnership between his eldest son, also Thomas, and the well-known William Faden. Jefferys left a will (FRC 11/972) and there is a short biography in the *DNB*, v10, p706.

BY LAURENCE WORMS

SEE ALSO: Newfoundland

Kalaniopu'u (?–1782)

Kalaniopu'u was the paramount chief (ali'i nui, or king) of Hawai'i at the time of Cook's arrival in 1778. About 1775, Kalaniopu'u had replaced Alapa'inui, who had died. His life was one of constant strife, conducting continual sorties against the island of Maui, where he claimed lands, partly in his own right and partly through his marriage with Kalola, a sister of the ruling chief of Maui.

Cook arrived off the coast of Maui in November 1778 and his ships stood off Kahului from where many canoes came to visit the ships. Beating to windward, the expedition reached the northeast point of Maui, where Cook was visited by Kalaniopu'u and his nephew Kamehameha, who would later rule all the Hawaiian islands, visited the ships. Cook circled Hawai'i and anchored in Kealakekua Bay. On 25 January Kalaniopu'u appeared and settled at Ka'awaloa on the northern shore of the bay. Relations were friendly and gifts were exchanged the next day near the heiau at Napo'opo'o.

Cook left the bay on 4 February but storm damage forced him to return on the 11th. The reception this time was not so warm. The British had already overstayed their welcome and the King made known his displeasure at the return. Relations were not as good and thefts by Hawaiians caused Cook to react. He led an armed party ashore to seize Kalaniopu'u as a hostage but Cook and his men were surrounded on the shore before he could return to his ships. Cook died in the ensuing conflict. Kalaniopu'u himself died in 1782 in Waio'ahukini.

SEE ALSO: Cook as god and Cook's death, Hawaiian Islands and Hawaiians

Kamehameha I (1758–1819)

Kamehameha was the first ruler of the entire group of Hawaiian Islands when he unified them in 1810. He is believed to have been born in Kohala, Hawai'i, about 1758 but it may have been earlier. A comet appeared in the sky and this was interpreted by the kahunas (priests) to mean that a mighty ruler of Hawai'i was about to be born. Keku'iapoiwa was his mother but there is doubt about who was his father.

Tereoboo, King of Owhyee, bringing presents to Cook. The engraving depicts the arrival of Kalani'opu'u at Kealakekua Bay and his visit to the Resolution *on 26 January 1779. Engraved by B T Pouncy after Webber. (Cook & King (Atlas) pl 61)*

Ali'i (chief) Alapa'inui, fearing the child as a threat to his power, ordered that he be killed at birth and, for this reason, he was entrusted to chief Nae'ole, who looked after him until he was five. He was then allowed back at court. Kalaniopu'u was a chief of Hawai'i and an uncle of the boy, who grew up under his uncle's care. He was given the appellation Pai'ea (hard shelled crab) respectfully by Maui warriors when they saw him, as a youth, fighting in battle against them, moving like a crab moves with claws outstretched from side to side in a fight. He was then in his youth and no longer a boy. Later, Pai'ea was then renamed Kamehameha, meaning lonely one. When Kalaniopu'u died in 1782, his power was divided between Kamehameha and Kalaniopu'u's natural son Kiwala'o, who inherited the kingship.

The relationship between Kamehameha and Kiwala'o was cold. After Kalaniopu'u's death, a series of civil wars broke out, first on the island of Hawai'i and then throughout the island chain. Kamehameha rose to power through these wars. He defeated Kiwala'o taking control of Kohala, Kona, and Hamakua. Kiwala'o's brother, Keoua, who remained an opponent, still controlled half of the island of Hawai'i. When his army, passing the region of volcanoes, was devastated by a volcanic explosion, Keoua feared that Pele, spirit of the volcanoes, was against him, and he lost heart.

Kamehameha invited Keoua to visit in 1791 and, during the visit, he was killed. Having gained control of his home island, Kamehameha turned to the other islands. He planned another invasion of Maui to subdue Kahekili, who also controlled the islands of Moloka'i, Lana'i, O'ahu, and Kaua'i. In preparation for the invasion, Kamehameha purchased weapons from American and European ships trading with Hawai'i. Several sailors from these ships also assisted him.

In 1794, Kahekili died and his son, Kalanikupule, defeated Kaeo Kaeokulani in the civil war that followed. Kamehameha immediately attacked and conquered Maui and Moloka'i before heading for O'ahu. His canoes landed at Waikiki, and his warriors pursued Kalanikupule's army up the Nu'uanu Valley. The valley rises to a high precipice, over which hundreds of the last O'ahu warriors, trapped, plunged to their deaths.

Only Kaumuali'i, the king of Kaua'i, remained independent so Kamehameha planned to invade Kaua'i. Kaumuali'i, realising he faced certain defeat, came to Honolulu in 1810 to pledge his loyalty. 1810 marked the end of civil wars in Hawai'i and the establishment of Kamehameha as king of the whole island group. Kamehameha based himself at Kailua in Kona on Hawai'i.

Kamehameha accompanied his uncle Kalaniopu'u aboard Cook's ships in 1778 and received Cook at Kealakekua Bay in 1779. He formed a close friendship with George Vancouver, who had sailed with Cook and who visited Hawai'i three times in the 1790s. Vancouver gave Kamehameha assistance and in return Kamehameha signed a treaty of free association with Britain. Kamehameha was a proven warrior and became an effective ruler. He died in 1819.

See Also: Hawaiian Islands and Hawaiians

Kaua'i and Ni'ihau

Kaua'i (22° N, 159° 30' W) and Ni'ihau (22° 20' N, 160° 10' W) are the westernmost and oldest of the main Hawaiian Islands. The volcanic shield of Kaua'i is 5 million years old. Parts of the island remain mountainous with high rugged cliffs (pali) around much of the coast. Ni'ihau is slightly younger than Kaua'i and less mountainous. Kaua'i is larger (550 square miles/ 1430 sq km) than Ni'ihau (69 square miles/180 sq km). It is believed the Hawaiian islands have been inhabited since before AD 500 but the westernmost islands were probably settled some time later. Before European contact, Kaua'i had become one of the four great chiefdoms of the islands.

As James Cook approached the Hawaiian Islands on 18 January 1778, James Ward sighted the island of O'ahu. Cook steered though for another island to the north-west and was soon surrounded canoes full of people off high cliffs at the south-east corner of Kaua'i Island. He sailed along the south coast past Poipu, watched by people on shore, until he found an anchorage at the mouth of the Waimea River. Cook was amazed to find he could communicate with the people, who were another example of the Polynesian diaspora. He speculated about the sailing and navigation ability of the Polynesians that had enabled them to spread all round the Pacific.

Cook crossed to the neighbouring island of Ni'ihau, reaching it on the 29th. He took the ships round to the west coast and anchored between Pahau and Le'ahi Points near Ke'elinawai. Cook went ashore and went for a walk, climbing Mau'uloa, a small hill. On 2 February, the ships sailed north having, at first, been forced south towards Ka'ula.

After Cook's death in February 1779, Charles Clerke, now in command, sailed back to Kaua'i. On 2 March, the ships anchored again at Waimea. The reception was cool and the British wondered if the news of Cook's death had preceded them. Contact gradually improved and many pigs were obtained. Queen Tu'mutta'ha'no, recently restored to power, visited the ships and gifts were exchanged.

Clerke wanted more yams for the voyage ahead and felt Ni'ihau would provide a better source so the ships sailed across to anchor near Le'ahi Point. Yams, though, were in short supply. Clerke was ready to leave when canoes arrived from Queen Tu'mutta'ha'no laden with yams and pigs. The *Resolution* and the *Discovery* set sail for Kamchatka on 15 March 1779. Waimea now has a statue of Cook in the middle of town, and a cairn in Lucy Wright Beach Park marks the spot where Cook landed.

See Also: Hawai'i, Third voyage

Kealakekua Bay

Kealakekua Bay (19° 28' N, 155° 55' W), the pathway of the gods, is a bay on the western coast of Hawai'i, the

'Big Island'. The bay is framed by Cook Point, at the north-west, and Palemano Point, to the south-east. The high cliffs of Pali Kapu o Keoua separate the two ends of the bay. The settlement of Ka'awaloa and Puhina o Lono Heiau were situated in the northern part while Napo'opo'o and Hikiau Heiau were in the south. The British transcribed the name of the bay as Karakakooa.

James Cook reached the west coast of Hawai'i in January 1779. Sailing north, he asked Bligh to sound a large bay that might prove an anchorage and find a source of fresh water. (Interestingly, Bligh had stopped earlier along that coast but not found good water. However, it does make him the first recorded European to set foot on Hawai'i Island.) Bligh reported favourably, and, on 17 January, the *Resolution* and the *Discovery* anchored in Kealakekua Bay. The British were welcomed by a flotilla of over 1000 canoes and Cook was welcomed ashore by ali'i (chiefs) Palea and Kanina and kahuna (priests) Koaa and Keli'ikea in a ceremony at Hikiau Heiau. Cook had arrived at the time of Makahiki, a part of the year associated with the god Lono. People accorded Cook a high status and bestowed on him the title Lono, but debate continues as to whether Cook was actually equated by the Hawaiians with the God Lono.

Land near the heiau was acquired for an observatory and as a work area for repairs. Relations were most cordial and trade was brisk. On 25 January, Kalaniopu'u, the ali'i or king appeared and settled at Ka'awaloa across the bay. Gifts were exchanged the next day near the heiau at Napo'opo'o. However, things began to deteriorate on 1 February. The ships' crew did not respect local religious sensibilities when, collecting firewood, they took fence posts and wooden carvings from the heiau. Then William Watman, a sailor, died and was buried near the heiau, demonstrating the mortality of the Europeans.

Cook realised it was time to leave and did so on 4 February. However, gales began, which shattered his foremast, forcing Cook to return, to Kealakekua Bay where Kamehameha received him on the 11th. The reception this time was not so warm. The British had already overstayed their welcome and Kalaniopu'u made known his displeasure at their return. Cook's visit had placed great economic hardship upon the local people, who had provided food, water, and fuel for the crews. In addition, Kalaniopu'u had recently collected the yearly tribute from the people in the area as part of Makihiki. Relations were now strained. After one incident Cook went ashore at Ka'awaloa early in the morning of 14 February, intending to take Kalaniopu'u hostage. Before Cook could return to his ship a fight broke out on the foreshore in which he, four marines and several Hawaiians died.

View of Karakakooa, in Owhyhee. The engraving shows Resolution *and* Discovery *in Kealakekua Bay, Hawai'i, with the heiau at Hikiau to the right. Engraved by W Byrne after Webber. (Cook & King (Atlas) pl 68)*

Charles Clerke assumed command of the *Resolution* with Gore switching to take charge of the *Discovery*. Everyone was in a state of shock but Clerke quickly decided to take no reprisals, instead concentrating on recovering the remains of Cook and the marines. Cook's body had been given the mortuary treatment of a chief. The large bones, believed to contain the man's psychic power, were kept as sacred relics, the flesh put into the sea. As bones had been distributed to various people their retrieval took time. Koaa acted as an intermediary and, on the 20th, some of Cook's body parts were handed over. These remains were buried in the waters of Kealakekua Bay on 21 February and the ships sailed the next day. Relations between the two sides were largely restored.

A monument was erected in 1874 on the north shore of the bay near where Cook met his death. A plaque marks the spot where he died. The settlement of Captain Cook is located high above the cliffs of Kealakekua Bay.

SEE ALSO: Cook as god and Cook's death, Hawai'i, Colour plate 13

Kempe family

Arthur Kempe (1743–1823) was born in 1743 at Veryan in Cornwall, the seventh of eight children. He joined the Royal Navy and sailed to the Pacific as a midshipman aboard the *Dolphin* under Captain John Byron. In 1772, he was appointed second lieutenant on HMS *Adventure*,

52 guns, Cook's companion vessel on the second voyage. When Joseph Shank was sent home ill from the Cape in November 1772, Kempe was promoted to first lieutenant; during the voyage he kept a log and a journal.

In 1780 Kempe was promoted to post captain. He was made rear-admiral in 1799, vice-admiral of the blue in 1804, and admiral in 1810. Eventually, he became admiral of the red in 1821. He married Anne Coryton and they had four children. Kempe died in Veryan in 1823, leaving a will (FRC 11/1668).

His second cousin Samuel Kempe sailed with him as a midshipman on the *Adventure* but died from sunstroke in the South Atlantic near the beginning of the voyage.
SEE ALSO: Second voyage

A view of Christmas Harbour. A sailor can be seen killing penguins. Engraved by J Newton after Webber. (Cook & King (Atlas) pl 4)

Kerguelen Island

Kerguelen Island (49° S, 70° E) is situated in the Southern Indian Ocean, midway between Africa, Antarctica and Australia. The main island, roughly 74 miles by 87 miles (120km by 140km), occupies 2568 square miles (6675 sq km) and is surrounded by 300 other smaller islands. The coast of Kerguelen is deeply indented, whilst the interior is heavily glaciated. It remains uninhabited except for scientists.

The island was discovered on 12 February 1772 by the French explorer, Yves de Kergulen-Trémarec, who was searching for the southern continent. Kerguelen never landed on the islands bearing his name as he was unable to anchor so he returned to Mauritius. De Boiguehenneuc, captain of Kerguelen's second ship, landed at Gros-Ventre Cove and annexed the island for France. Kerguelen gave a much-exaggerated account of the island's potential, calling it La France Australe. Kerguelen made another expedition to the island in late 1772, again without landing.

Cook called at Kerguelen on his third voyage in late 1776. On 25 December, Cook anchored in Oiseau Bay, which he named Christmas Harbour. Cook's men discovered a bottle containing a message in Latin left by Kerguelen's men. Cook wanted to call it Desolation Island on account of the cold and inhospitability, but retained the name Kerguelen Land.

Cook's crew was able to replenish stocks of water and fresh meat by taking penguins and other birds. Green vegetables were less abundant, but the sailors discovered the Kerguelen cabbage (*Pringlea antiscorbutica*), which helped ward off scurvy. Cook moved to another harbour, Port Palliser, before he left the island on 30 December. Several features still bear names given by Cook (Île Howe, Cap Sandwich, Mont Campbell) while Cook Calotte (glacier) is named for Cook himself.
SEE ALSO: Third voyage

King, James (1750–1784)

James King, who sailed on Cook's third voyage, was born in July 1750 in Clitheroe, Lancashire, where his father was the local curate. His father later became Chaplain to the House of Commons in London and, from 1772 until 1776 was a Canon of Westminster, before moving to become Dean of Raphoe in northern Ireland. The Kings had connections and, when he was 12, James went to sea under the patronage of a cousin, Captain William Norton, on the *Assistance,* a Fourth Rate of 50 guns on a voyage to Virginia. King served as a midshipman on various ships before spending time from March 1768 on HMS *Guernsey* on the Newfoundland station.

In January 1771, King was appointed lieutenant and served on four vessels. However, in 1773, he took leave on half-pay to study sciences in Paris and later at Oxford University with his brother Walker, a fellow of Corpus Christi College. At Oxford, he met Dr Thomas Hornsby, the Savilian Professor of Astronomy, who, when Cook's third voyage was being planned, recommended King. King and his brothers, Thomas and Walker had all become close friends of the politician, Edmund Burke, and his family through Burke's son Richard.

King, who combined naval experience with his scientific background, joined the *Resolution* as second lieutenant and as the 'Nautical & Astronomical Observer' as was Mr Bayly aboard *Discovery*. He shared the astronomical duties with Cook and Bayly and these three had sole charge of the chronometers. He proved

A Portrait of Captain James King, by John Webber painted about 1782. King was a popular officer, who captained the Discovery *back to Britain and edited the journals for publication. (National Library of Australia, R3631)*

to be a very good and popular officer. James Trevenen would later write 'in short, as one of the best, he is one of the politest, genteelest, & best-bred men in the world'.

After Cook's death, readjustments took place among the crews with Charles Clerke changing ships to become overall commander and King being promoted to first lieutenant. When Clerke himself died in August 1779, King transferred to the *Discovery* as its commander and brought the ship home to Orkney. At Orkney, John Gore, who was now commanding the expedition, sent King ahead with copies of the journals, which, on 4 November, he presented to the Board of Longitude. He was later given the task of editing the documents from Cook's voyage for the official account that was published in 1784. Artefacts collected by King were donated to Trinity College, Dublin, and King received a LLD in return.

King was made post-captain on his return and was appointed to the *Crocodile,* a Sixth Rate of 24 guns operating in the English Channel. In 1781, King commanded the *Resistance,* which escorted a fleet of merchant ships to the West Indies. His health, which had long been poor, was now very poor. In June 1784, he was nursed by Jane Burke, the wife of Edmund Burke, at their house in Beaconsfield. Later that year, he left for Nice in the south of France to recuperate. Friends including Trevenen accompanied him. John Law, the *Discovery*'s surgeon attended him but King did not recover and died of tuberculosis on 16 November 1784.

King was elected a Fellow of the Royal Society in 1782 and was given an honorary LLD Oxon. There is a memorial to King in Woodstock, outside Oxford. King Island in the Bering Sea and King Passage in Nootka Sound are named for him. Norton Sound in Alaska was named after King's relation, Sir Fletcher Norton, Speaker of the House of Commons, and brother of William with whom King sailed on the *Assistance.* Edmund Burke wrote an affectionate piece about King beginning 'some particulars of him which may illustrate this material point of courageous and manly prudence'.
SEE ALSO: Published accounts, Third voyage

Kippis, Andrew (1725–1795)

Andrew Kippis, the nonconformist divine and biographer, was born at Nottingham on 28 March 1725, the son of Robert Kippis, a silk-hosier. He was educated at Sleaford, Lincolnshire, until 1741 when he went to the nonconformist academy at Northampton. In 1746, Kippis became minister of a church at Boston before moving in 1750 to Dorking in Surrey. He next moved in 1753, this time to become pastor of a Presbyterian congregation at Westminster, where he remained until his death on 8 October 1795. He married Elizabeth Bott in 1753, and was elected a fellow of the Antiquarian Society in 1778 and a fellow of the Royal Society in 1779.

Kippis was a very voluminous writer. He contributed extensively to *The Gentleman's Magazine*, *The Monthly Review* and *The Library*, and he had a good deal to do with the establishment and conduct of the new Annual Register. He also published a number of sermons, some religious pamphlets and some biographies of prominent theologians. His chief work was as editor of a second edition of the *Biographia Britannica*, though only five volumes were published between 1778 and 1793.

Kippis wrote *The Life of Captain James Cook,* the first biography of the explorer, published in 1788. Unfortunately, he appears to have only carried out a minimum of research. The volume dwells almost exclusively on the voyages. Cook's life before the *Endeavour* voyage is dealt with very briefly and, given that many people who had known Cook were still alive and available for interview, a huge opportunity was missed.
SEE ALSO: Biographies of Cook

Lane, Michael (1740–1794)

Michael Lane was master's mate and assistant surveyor to Cook on the Newfoundland survey in 1767. He took over command of the *Grenville* in 1768 when Cook left to join the *Endeavour*. The results of the survey were published jointly in their names and many of the charts later appeared in the *North American Pilot*. Before joining Cook, Lane spent time on HMS *Guernsey* as the schoolmaster. Lane took part in Richard Pickersgill's unsuccessful expedition in HMS *Lyon* to find the Northwest Passage from the east in 1776. He became a lieutenant in October 1777. Lane was born in London in 1740 and died in 1794.

SEE ALSO: Newfoundland

Lapérouse, Jean-François de Galaup de (1741–1788?)

Jean-François de Galaup de Lapérouse was born on 23 August 1741 near Albi, France. He entered the French Navy when he was 15 and spent nearly 30 years serving in the Indian Ocean, the West Indies, Canada and home waters off France. During his time on the Île de France (Mauritius) he met and courted Eléonore Broudou but it was only in 1783 that they married. He was appointed in 1785 to lead an expedition to the Pacific to emulate the exploits of Cook. His ships were the *Astrolabe* and the *Boussole*, both 500 tons. They were storeships, reclassified as frigates for the occasion. Lapérouse was a great admirer of James Cook and tried to match his achievements. He recognised the value of good relations with Pacific islanders and he was well-liked by his men. Among his 114-man crew there was a large staff of scientists: an astronomer, a physicist, three naturalists, a mathematician, three draftsmen, and even both chaplains were scientifically schooled.

The expedition left Brest on August 1785, rounded Cape Horn, and visited Concepción in Chile. Lapérouse then sailed by way of Easter Island and Hawai'i to Alaska, where he entered an inlet in July 1786. The French explored the inlet and met the local Tlinget people. Tragedy struck when two longboats, carrying 21 men, were lost near the mouth of the bay, called Port des Français by Lapérouse, but now known as Lituya Bay. The French headed for Monterey in California, where they recovered.

Lapérouse crossed the Pacific to Macao, where he sold the furs acquired in Alaska, dividing the profits among his men. The next year, after a visit to Manila, he set out for the north-east Asian coasts. He visited the mainland coast of Tartary, then crossed over to Sakhalin. Lapérouse was enthusiastic about the people of Sakhalin. Lapérouse wanted to sail through the channel between Sakhalin and Asia, but failed, so he turned south, and sailed through La Pérouse Strait between Sakhalin and Hokkaido to reach Petropavlovsk in Kamchatka in September 1787. The French restored the memorial to Charles Clerke for Cook's last voyage, who had died near there in 1779. Letters were received from Paris ordering him to investigate the settlement the British were to erect at Botany Bay in New South Wales.

The French sailed south via Samoa (the Navigator Islands). Tragedy struck again on Tutuila when a fight broke out leaving 39 Samoans and 12 French dead, among them de Langle, commander of the *Astrolabe*. Lapérouse continued to Botany Bay, arriving on 26 January 1788, just as Captain Arthur Phillip moved the colony from Botany Bay to Port Jackson. The British received him courteously, but were unable to help him with food as they had none to spare. Lapérouse sent his journals and letters to Europe with a British ship, obtained wood and fresh water, and left.

Neither Lapérouse nor any of his men were ever seen again. In 1826, Peter Dillon found evidence of that the ships had foundered on the island of Vanikoro in the Santa Cruz Islands, the final tragedy of the voyage. Both ships had been wrecked on the reefs, probably during a hurricane. No Frenchmen survived to tell the final story.

Despite the tragedies that beset the expedition, it should be remembered as one of the most extraordinary of the eighteenth century. Lapérouse had taken the precaution of sending copies of journals and other documents home to France from ports he visited and,

through them, we have the record of most of the voyage. Lapérouse set out to follow in the steps of Cook and is one of the few individuals who stands comparison with the British explorer.
SEE ALSO: France and French reaction to Cook, Pacific exploration after Cook

Latitude

Latitude is the angular distance on its meridian of any place on the earth's surface, north or south from the Equator (from the Latin *latus*, meaning wide). Lines of latitude circle the earth parallel to the Equator and are denoted in degrees. The Equator is therefore 0° latitude, while the poles are at 90° N and S. The Tropic of Cancer (23° 27' N), the Tropic of Capricorn (23° 27' S), the Arctic Circle (66° 32' N) and the Antarctic Circle (66° 32' S) are other significant lines of latitude.

By the mid-eighteenth century, sailors were able to calculate latitude with considerable precision. Quadrants and sextants had been developed to take observations of celestial bodies such as the sun, the moon, or stars and, from the resulting angle between the horizon and that body, the latitude could be determined.
SEE ALSO: Navigation

Law, John (?–1786?)

John Law sailed on the third voyage on the *Discovery* as surgeon until 3 August 1778 when Anderson died. He then transferred to become the surgeon on the *Resolution*. After the voyage he remained in touch with James King and attended him when King had gone to Nice in the south of France to recuperate. Law was attached to HMS *Trusty* at the time, based at Civita Vecchia in Italy. Law may himself have died in 1786 leaving a will (FRC 11/1147?).
SEE ALSO: King (James), Third voyage

Ledyard, John (1751–1788)

John Ledyard sailed on the third voyage on the *Resolution* as the Marine corporal. He was later promoted to sergeant in 1780. He was born in Groton, Connecticut in 1751. His father died in 1762 and John was placed under the care of his grandfather, who sent him to train for the law. The grandfather died in 1771 and Ledyard's mother sent John to Dartmouth College in New Hampshire to study theology. Ledyard rebelled though and ran away (he actually paddled away in a canoe!). He joined a ship, which took him to Gibraltar, the West Indies and back to America. In 1774, he sailed to Britain to seek out family connections but nothing resulted and, in 1776, he joined the Marines at Plymouth and was posted aboard the *Resolution*.

In this way, Ledyard joined Cook's voyage in which he played a prominent part, including going as envoy to the Russians on Unalaska. After the voyage, Britain was at war with America and Ledyard refused to fight Americans so was confined to barracks in Britain. However, he sailed to America in 1782 and deserted onto Long Island. He wrote an account of the third voyage, which was published in Hartford, USA, in 1783. It drew heavily on an anonymous account (usually attributed to Rickman) published earlier.

Ledyard realised the possibilities of the sea otter fur trade on the north-west coast of America so in 1784 he revisited Europe to organise an expedition. He became friends with John Paul Jones, the privateer, and Thomas Jefferson, the newly-appointed American ambassador to France. Both men showed interest but would not invest in Ledyard's project. Having failed in his attempts to interest major backers, he set off to walk across Europe and Asia. Sir Joseph Banks provided some of the funding. He walked right round the Gulf of Bothnia from Stockholm to St Petersburg, arriving in March 1787.

Ledyard continued on toward Siberia, carrying supplies for Joseph Billings, with whom he had sailed on Cook's third voyage and who was now employed by the Russians. In Irkutsk, Ledyard was arrested (as a spy!) and deported back to Poland. He made his way to London and once more sought out Banks.

A new expedition was mooted by Banks and the African Association to explore overland routes from Alexandria to the Niger. Ledyard departed on 30 June 1788 and reached Cairo in August. However, he died in November 1788, either from dysentery or an excessive dose of tartar emetic. There is a short biography in the *DNB*, v11, pp 782–3.
SEE ALSO: Marines, Published accounts, Third voyage

Libraries and archives

The libraries and archives discussed here are those holding research collections of unique manuscript material, as well as published books, relating to the life and voyages of James Cook.

Australia possesses two such major repositories. Both contain extensive collections of manuscripts and other unpublished material as well as extensive holdings of books about all aspects of Cook's life. Both libraries have benefited from bequests by individuals that have formed the basis of their present holdings. The State Library of New South Wales in Sydney has two special sections, the Mitchell Library and Sir William Dixson Research Library, and both have printed books and manuscripts collections of interest to Cook scholars. The library has the Corner copy of Cook's *Endeavour* journal and also Banks' *Endeavour* journal. It published Beddie's *Bibliography of Captain James Cook* in 1970 and has created a website making its holdings of the papers of Sir Joseph Banks available online. The National Library of Australia's special collection was based on bequests and sales by Rex Nan Kivell. It presents a combination of pictorial, manuscript and printed material relating to Australia, New Zealand and the Pacific region with many items relating to the three voyages by Captain Cook, including drawings and paintings by John Webber and William Ellis. The library has published their copy of Cook's *Endeavour* Journal as a CD-ROM.

In Wellington, **New Zealand**, the Alexander Turnbull Library, part of the National Library, holds New Zealand's documentary research collections. These contain original material such as drawings and prints, manuscripts and archives relating to New Zealand and the Pacific. They also contain the largest collection of early printed books and maps in New Zealand, including early voyages. The library holds much unique material pertaining to Cook.

The two principal Cook research collections in the **United Kingdom** are housed in the British Library and the Public Record Office (PRO). The British Library on Euston Road in London has taken over the material previously housed in the Library of the British Museum in Bloomsbury. It holds the logs from the *Endeavour* and *Resolution* (second and third voyages) plus journals from the second and third voyages. The journals, log books, muster rolls and pay books belonging to the Admiralty were lodged with the PRO, now located in Kew. The PRO and the Historical Manuscripts Commission (HMC) have now joined together as The National Archives. A large number of the documents written on Cook's voyages are held here. The wills of James and Elizabeth Cook and over a hundred men who sailed with Cook are lodged here as well. The United Kingdom Hydrographic Office (UKHO) Archive in Taunton, Southwest England, contains charts, sailing directions, coastal views and ships' remark books from the 1700s including material by James Cook and his crews. The Natural History Museum Library in South Kensington, London contains scientific material from the voyages, especially botanical and relating to Banks' *Florilegium*. Among the collection at the Library at the National Maritime Museum in Greenwich are copies of Cook's *Endeavour* and *Resolution* (second voyage) journals

Lind, James (1716–1794)

James Lind was born in 1716 in Edinburgh where he attended grammar school. He entered the Navy as a surgeon's mate in 1739, serving in the Mediterranean, West Africa and the West Indies. Lind was appointed surgeon on HMS *Salisbury* in 1746 and conducted a controlled trial of six treatments for scurvy in 1747. The next year, Lind retired from the Navy, graduated MD and opened a practice in Edinburgh. He published his *A Treatise of the scurvy* in 1753, in which he summarised knowledge of the disease and suggested ways of avoiding it. He was appointed Chief Physician at the Royal Naval Hospital at Haslar in Portsmouth in 1758 and remained in the position until 1783. Lind proposed a simple method of supplying ships with fresh water by distillation and also described a means of producing lemon and orange juice concentrates, recommending that they be carried on all vessels of the Royal Navy. He died at Gosport in 1794.

Lind's *Treatise* was a confusing work and contemporary readers of his work could have found passages to support almost any view of the disorder. His conclusions and recommendations were not clear and, for these reasons, the Admiralty procrastinated for over 40 years before accepting Lind's findings that oranges and lemons were the best option. Not until 1795 was lemon juice issued to sailors. It is not surprising therefore that Cook, in attempting to prevent scurvy, did not follow what turned out to be the best advice.

See Also: Medical aspects of Cook's voyages, Scurvy

Literature of Cook's voyages

It is interesting to speculate what the outcome of Cook's first voyage would have been had Joseph Banks and his retinue not sailed with him on the *Endeavour*. While there is every reason to believe Cook would still have observed the Transit, searched for the southern continent and brought the ship home, his reception back in Britain would have been very different, as would his subsequent career. Banks's position in British society at the time ensured that the voyage received a much higher profile than recent expeditions by Byron, Wallis and Carteret. Indeed, when the *Endeavour* reached Britain in 1771, the glory was all for Banks and the voyage was described as his, not Cook's. Without Banks, Cook's fame would possibly have remained on a par with Wallis and Carteret and he might not have been offered a second voyage.

Another difference, and the one that interests us here, was Banks's role in the education and development of Cook as the *Endeavour* voyage progressed. Cook was an intelligent man but lacked a formal education. One of the most obvious manifestations of his development on the voyage is seen in his journal-keeping, which changes from being a typical seaman's record of weather and other factors of the ship's progress to one where Cook writes at length, offering opinions and making acute observations.

Cook was no stranger to keeping a log and journal. Part of a log exists that Cook wrote when he served on HMS *Eagle* in 1756. However, it was during his time in eastern Canada and Newfoundland that Cook, by now a master, learned to keep an official record. The Royal Navy had decreed in 1731 that all their ships would maintain a detailed record (log) of all occurrences on board. The logs remained the property of the Navy and were handed in at the completion of a voyage or tour of duty. Perhaps 999 out of 1000 were very routine documents, devoid of anything exciting or interesting and would be filed away in naval archives, never to be seen again.

An early example of Cook's writing is from 13 August 1762, *en route* to Placentia in Newfoundland in HMS *Northumberland*. It is little more than sailing directions: 'From St Peters to Cape St Marys the Course is ESE¼E distce. 29 leags. From St Peters to Placentia, is E½S distance 32 leagues. All the north side of the Bay of Placentia is very high mountainous land; the most remarkable is the Mountain of the Red Hatt, which is very high and lies ENE¾E, 17 leagues from St Peters; This Mountain is of a redish colour and the top makes like the crown of a hatt from whence it takes its name'.

On 20 May 1767, off the west coast of Newfoundland, the entry is still a very straightforward and unembellished record of events. (This piece may have actually been written by Michael Lane, Cook's deputy at the time): 'Moderate and fair weather. At 1 PM Cape St George NNW. Point of Beach E by N½N. At 8 came to in St Georges Harbour in 10 fathoms water. Both boats employed on the survey. Found here a tribe of the Mickmak Indians'.

Before Cook's time, there was little tradition of Royal Navy records being written up and published for public consumption. For ordinary readers, the maritime parts of naval narratives were rather boring and repetitious as, for long stretches, they dwelled upon the routines of shipboard life. Travel literature up till that time usually was based on the voyages of buccaneers and privateers, such as Dampier and Shelvocke. Dampier's work was an inspiration for Swift's *Gulliver's Travels* while Shelvocke's writing was one of Coleridge's sources for his *Ancient Mariner*. Things changed in 1771, when John Hawkesworth was commissioned by the Earl of Sandwich to edit and collate the journals of Wallis, Byron, Carteret, Banks and Cook.

Cook's literary development had not progressed far by the time he took charge of the *Endeavour*. He probably somewhat resented having to share the great cabin, normally the captain's preserve, with Banks, Solander and other members of Banks's party but he was astute enough to realise that he could learn much from the situation. For example, he was able to read books from the library that Banks brought with him. While logs were written up straight away, journals were written more at leisure and often in several drafts. Cook would sometimes leave spaces and fill them in later. There is reason to believe he wrote his journal following discussions with Banks and others and that he had sometimes read the entries in Banks's own journal before composing his own. However, it was not just one way and Cook also influenced Banks.

It is perplexing that Banks, having written a journal while on *Endeavour*, wrote so little else in the course of his life and, given his close friendship with and knowledge of Cook, it is to be regretted that he did not write anything about Cook. Cook's journals with their tendency to report facts reveal little about Cook himself. Only occasionally does he let slip and write of his feelings and emotions. On his second voyage in January 1774, after being thwarted by Antarctic ice, Cook wrote: 'I who had ambition not only to go farther than any one had done before, but as far as it was possible for man to go, was not sorry at meeting with this interruption...'

While in Cape Town in March 1775 on learning what had happened to some of the *Adventure*'s crew in Queen Charlotte Sound at the hands of Māori: 'I shall make no ref[l]ections on this Melancholy affair until I hear more about it. I must however observe in favour of the New Zealand[er]s that I have always found them of a Brave, Noble, Open and benevolent disposition, but they are a people that will never put up with an insult if they have an opportunity to resent it'.

At the beginning of the *Endeavour* voyage, Cook would not have expected that his journals would ever to be published. He never claimed to be a writer, describing his work later: '. . . that it would be exceptable to the Public, in the Author's words, than in any other persons, and that the Candid and faithfull manner in which it is written would counterbalance the want of stile and dullness of subject. It is a work for information and not for amusement, written by a man, who has not the advantage of Education, acquired, nor Natural abilities for writing... he hopes the Public will not consider him as an author, but a man Zealously employed in the Service of his Country and obliged to give the best account he is able of his proceedings'.

As the voyage continued, Cook's entries increased in length and expanded to include observations on all matters, not just to do with sailing *Endeavour*. At the end of the voyage, Cook would still not have expected to be the author of any narrative submitted for publication. As such, he would not have been surprised or offended when his and Banks's journals were passed to John Hawkesworth for editing. It was only later, in 1775, that Cook had reservations. Hawkesworth's work was published in 1773 after Cook had left Britain on his second voyage and Cook only saw a copy at the Cape of Good Hope during his passage home. Cook, like many others, was unhappy at Hawkesworth's work in which the editor had rewritten and misrepresented Cook's original text. While the work was a popular success, Hawkesworth was particularly hurt by the criticism and died shortly afterwards.

On subsequent voyages, aware now that his journals would be published, Cook kept and edited the records believing he could do better than Hawkesworth. The Navy agreed and, after the second voyage, Cook was appointed to a position at Greenwich Hospital, a sinecure that would allow him time to write. As Cook still lacked confidence in some aspects of writing, Canon John Douglas (an early ghost writer) was engaged to give literary and editorial assistance, but without Hawkesworth's freedom to rewrite.

The third voyage to the Pacific took Cook away from Britain before the narrative of the second voyage was published and he would never see it or that of the third voyage. James King, a lieutenant on the third voyage and a man educated at Oxford, was entrusted with writing the narrative of that voyage with Douglas being used again for editorial purposes. By the third voyage, Cook was writing long descriptions of places and people. For example, in several pages of text about Nootka, Cook wrote of the inhabitants: 'Their face is rather broad and flat, with highish Cheek bones and plump cheeks. Their mouth is little and round, the nose neither flat nor prominent; their eyes are black little and devoid of sparkling fire'. It hard to imagine the Cook of Newfoundland using a phrase such as 'devoid of sparkling fire' but his descriptions, when added to Webber's paintings, provide an excellent impression of the people of Nootka. Cook had no scientists on this voyage but he had developed sufficiently to partly fill the role himself.

The value of the literature of Cook's voyages is enhanced by the fact that Cook was not the only person keeping a journal. Many others on board were writing and so we often have a range of viewpoints on events. Most of the supernumeraries kept journals and the majority survived with several of them eventually being published despite the Admiralty's jealous protection of anything written on its voyages. The Admiralty regarded anything written on their ships as their property and required Cook to acquire all logs and diaries for handing-in at the end of a voyage. Officers and midshipmen were encouraged to maintain journals though most of them copied freely from each other. It appears they were written communally in the mess room and offer little that is individual or different. Some people, the Forsters for example, objected to handing over their work, feeling the opportunity to publish it independently was their right. Several seamen also saw it as a right to be able to publish and hid their work to avoid handing it over. Richard Rollett is supposed to have hidden his in his Bible. Anonymous journals were hurried out after each voyage ahead of the authorised version.

From the first voyage, Parkinson's journal was published by his brother while Banks's journal (incorporated into Hawkesworth) eventually appeared in the twentieth century, edited by Beaglehole. The second voyage was notable for the writings of the two Forsters. Reinhold Forster had joined the voyage in the expectation (on his part) that he would be able to write about it afterwards. Forster was angry when he was told his material would be incorporated into the official version and would not appear under his own name. His son Georg, however, did not feel the directive applied to him, and assisted by his father, used their diaries to quickly write and publish a narrative that appeared ahead of Cook's version. Reinhold would later publish his own observations, while his journal appeared in the twentieth century, edited by Michael Hoare. The Forster writings offer a rich source of scientific information but also provide an alternative view to the usual naval perspective.

The literature of the third voyage is virtually all drawn from naval personnel. No extra naturalists travelled on this voyage (Surgeon Anderson covered this role) so opportunities for other viewpoints were limited. King used his own journal and that of Clerke to supplement that of Cook after Cook's death. The confusion of Cook's death was described by many on board, including Samwell and Gilbert, whose versions were published separately. Ellis, Rickman (anonymously) and Ledyard (largely derived from Rickman) published works independently. The two astronomers, Wales and Bayly, wrote up the astronomical observations of the second and third voyages.

The Historical Records of New South Wales, and of New Zealand, reproduce portions of logs and journals not published elsewhere but Cook scholarship was given a huge boost in the 1950s when the Hakluyt Society commissioned J C Beaglehole to edit Cook's journals for publication. The result, which appeared between 1955 and 1967, provided access as never before to Cook's three voyages as Beaglehole not only used Cook but regularly provided text in the notes field from other journal-writers on board. He also reproduced large parts of those journals.

The literature of Cook's voyages remains a valuable source, which continues to be picked over for new information by researchers from many disciplines. It provides descriptions for people such as those studying culture contact, weather patterns in the Pacific, and evidence of homosexuality in the region. It also continues to be reworked and reassessed in light of present knowledge and current attitudes. In recent years, people have begun to study Cook's role in creating the voyage records. The original journals together with corrections, rewrites by Cook and his editors have been examined to try to discover not just Cook's own development but what he understood the purpose of writing the journals to be.

Very little, if any, of the writing emanating from Cook's voyages would ever be described as 'literature'. There had been no real tradition prior to Cook's time and few of the persons involved had been educated with a view to writing. Even James Burney, whose sister Fanny would achieve fame as a writer, escaped to sea before receiving a formal education. Cook's voyages did, however, establish the tradition and the realisation that future narratives needed to be well written. Bare facts would no longer suffice. The nineteenth century would see numerous attempts published, some of which succeeded.

SEE ALSO: Published accounts

Littleboy family, and Timothy Rarden

The Littleboy brothers, Richard (born 30 November 1744) and Michael (born 3 October 1748), who were sons of Richard and Susannah Littleboy of Woolwich, sailed together on the *Endeavour* voyage, both as AB. Richard was punished during the voyage on 2 December 1769 for theft.

Richard Littleboy was apprenticed as a waterman from 1758 until 1765. In 1765, he married Rebecca Neale at St Magdalene Church, Bermondsey. They had five sons, only one of whom survived beyond infancy. Rebecca died in 1778 but it is unknown when Richard died. Their surviving son, another Richard Littleboy, petitioned Banks describing himself as an orphan.

Michael was also apprenticed as a waterman, this time from 1761 until 1771. He married Sarah Chappell at St Alfege's Church, Greenwich in June 1775 and they had a son and three daughters. Sarah died in 1781 and Littleboy remarried in 1783 to Hannah Large. He had another son and two more daughters. Michael fell on hard times, having lost his boat and petitioned Joseph Banks on 3 February 1787.

The family was friendly with Timothy Rarden (Rearden), who sailed on the *Grenville* as an AB with Cook in Newfoundland in 1766 and 1767. He was discharged into sick quarters on 11 January 1767, but rejoined using the surname Bearden on 7 March 1767. Rarden then followed Cook onto the *Endeavour* as an AB.

Rarden was born in Cork in 1743. He died during the *Endeavour* voyage in Jakarta on 24 December 1770. He left a will (FRC 11/969). In the will, he leaves his 'Worldly Estate and Effects' to his 'beloved friend Richard Littleboy and Susannah his wife', the parents of the brothers who sailed on the *Endeavour* with him.

SEE ALSO: First voyage, Newfoundland

Logs, journals and muster rolls

The ship's log or logbook was the official record of the progress and management of a ship. The name was derived from the 'log', an instrument used to estimate the speed of the ship. It was originally a navigational account in which the speed, course and location of the vessel were carefully recorded on a daily, often hourly, basis. By 1730, the Admiralty identified the need for consistency and issued the order in their Naval Instructions of 1731 that a logbook be maintained.

The day of the week and the date were recorded. Then, at regular, sometimes hourly, intervals, information was collated about wind direction, especially when there was a significant change (the wind direction being the point of the compass from which the wind was blowing); the ship's course; and the distance sailed. In a remarks section, shipboard activities and any remarkable incidents, which covered a large range of activities and observations, including setting and reduction of sails, sightings of land, icebergs and other ships, meteorological information such as squalls, rain, snow or fog, as well as the state of the sky and the sea were recorded.

Ships were on ship's time (the nautical day) so the date changed at noon. Noon was, therefore, the most important time of the day and the ship's estimated position and a summation of the distance travelled and the course taken in the previous 24 hours were recorded at this time. The latitude, north or south of the equator, was determined by an observation of the sun or the pole star, while the longitude, the ship's position either east or west of a fixed or zero meridian, was recorded after computation using marine chronometers or the method of lunar distances.

Below is part of a sample day's log for the *Grenville* at the end of 1765 as Cook is rounding the Isle of Wight after spending the summer in Newfoundland. The figures in brackets in the remarks column are times. The first row refers to observations made at 1.00pm.

When at anchor, the log entry would be brief, recording the weather and a brief summary of activities on board.

Whereas the log was the bare record of the ship's progress, a ship's journal offered an officer the opportunity to expand at length, make observations and provide explanations concerning all matters that had happened to the ship and its crew. They provided the space to describe places visited and people met, together with recommendations for future action such as colonisation, exploitation of fishing resources, etc. Journals were maintained by the captain and by other members of the crew.

Cook and many of his men kept journals on the voyages. As well as giving us a complete story of the voyages, they now provide valuable descriptions of the first contacts with Pacific peoples. The ships' clerks made several copies of the official journals and logs, which could be returned separately to Britain if another ship was encountered. The French explorer, Lapérouse, did this and it is thanks to those copies that we have a record of his voyage as his two ships were lost in a hurricane. All logs and journals were deemed to belong

Day	Date	Wind	Remarks
		WNW	(1) Light breezes and clear weather.
		W	(4) Light airs. Dunnose NE½E, distance 7 or 8 miles.
			(8) Light breezes and clear weather. Dunnose NE by E, 9 or 10 miles.
			(10) Tacked and sounded 23 fathoms, stony bottom. Dunnose then NNE 4 leagues.
			(12) Tacked. Dunnose N by W 2 or 3 leagues.
Saturday	30th Nov. 1765		(2) Anchored with the small bower in 22 fathoms water. Dunnose N by W, 2 or 3 leagues.
			(4) Moderate breezes and fair.
			(6) Weighed and came to sail in first reef of the mainsail and main and foretopsail.
			(8) Fresh gales and cloudy. Culver Cliffs N by W 4 or 5 miles.
			(10) Anchored at Spithead. Found here the *Guernsey* and the *Aquilon*.

to the Navy and were required to be handed in to the captain before reaching home port. Some men such as Rickman (third voyage) and Marra (first) did secrete their personal journals and used them as the basis of unauthorised works published privately.

The muster records provided a listing of all the people on board a ship. The Clerk of the Cheque would inspect the muster book when a ship returned to port in Britain. It would then be used for payroll purposes. They now provide a useful source for the age and place of birth (sometimes recruitment) of the ships' crews.
SEE ALSO: Literature of Cook's voyages

London

Most of Cook's early experience with London occurred east of London Bridge. The North Sea colliers on which he served discharged their coal at the wharves in Wapping and Shadwell, and he, himself, stayed in accommodation such as the Bell Alehouse in that area. After his marriage, he and Elizabeth lived first in Shadwell and later, just to the north, in Mile End.

In 1756, when Cook was on HMS *Eagle* he went to Trinity House in Water Lane near London Bridge to sit his master's examination. As he gained experience in Newfoundland, Cook was required to attend the Admiralty in Whitehall and the Navy Board near Tower

A view of the Thames with London Bridge; the bridge effectively blocked the upstream passage of ships and so the river to its east supported the wharfs and docks familiar to Cook. (Print published by John Bowles 1746)

Hill when he was home during the winter months. Under Governor Palliser's patronage, Cook also began to meet influential people. His obvious ability saw him carrying out duties in London not normally associated with ship's masters, such as finding evidence in London bookshops to disprove French claims about Newfoundland. His other haunts were the dockyards at Deptford and Woolwich, down river from London Bridge. Deptford Dockyard fitted out all of Cook's ships and they all sailed from there.

Cook submitted papers to the Royal Society and he was elected a Fellow of the Society in 1775. Cook attended some meetings at their premises in Crane Court off Fleet Street and was a guest at several dinners in The Mitre Tavern nearby. His good friend, Joseph Banks, who later became the President of The Royal Society lived in New Burlington Street in Mayfair and Cook, no doubt, visited the house. Cook may have also visited the Banks' family home on Paradise Row in Chelsea while Banks took Cook to meet King George III at Kew, south-west of London after the *Endeavour* voyage.

After the second voyage, Cook was appointed Captain at Greenwich Hospital in south-east London. It was a nominal posting as Cook chose to continue living with his family in Mile End. However, Cook is remembered in Greenwich by displays at the National Maritime Museum and a statue near the Queen's House. The Museum has many original documents relating to Cook's voyages in its archives and many art works, including Hodges' paintings. Nearby, the Royal Observatory collections hold Harrison's chronometers, which Cook took on his voyages.

The British Museum in Bloomsbury holds collections of ethnographic material brought back from Cook's voyages while the Natural History Museum (NHM) in South Kensington has many of the botanical and zoological specimens brought back. Both museums hold original documents, including journals. The NHM holds all the originals of Banks' *Florilegium*. In Kew, the Public Records Office holds many of the original journals, log books and muster rolls from the voyages, and many of the wills for Cook and other people associated with Cook while the Herbarium at the Royal Botanical Gardens has specimens brought back on Cook's voyages.

There is statue of Cook in Central London in the Mall outside the Admiralty. At the other end of Whitehall, Cook is one of three Navigators remembered by a memorial in Westminster Abbey.

After Cook's death Elizabeth Cook left Mile End in 1788 to live in Clapham on the High Street just north of the Common. She lived there and at nearby Merton Abbey with her cousin Isaac Smith until her death in 1835.

Longitude

Longitude is the distance east or west on the earth's surface, measured by the angle which the meridian of a particular place makes with the prime meridian at Greenwich. It is reckoned to 180° east or west, and is expressed in degrees. A line of longitude or meridian is a line running from pole to pole linking all places with same longitude.

For ships sailing east to west or vice versa, knowledge of longitude was essential but it had always been a problem for sailors to fix their exact position at sea, away from the sight of land. In the eighteenth century, the development of sextants and octants had enabled latitude, the distance north or south of the Equator, to be determined reasonably correctly but longitude remained a problem. To calculate longitude required knowing the local time and knowing the time at the same moment at the prime meridian at Greenwich. The difference in time gave the longitude. Cook wrote that 'The longitude is counted west from the meridian of Greenwich where no other place is specifically mentioned'.

At the beginning of the eighteenth century, the scale of this problem had been demonstrated when the British flagship, *Association*, and three other warships were wrecked on the Scilly Isles in 1707 with the loss of over 2000 men. They had completely miscalculated their longitude. The disaster prompted the British government to offer a prize to the person who solved the longitude problem and they created the Board of Longitude to oversee the matter.

Through the eighteenth century, various methods of determining longitude were proposed. Some were far-fetched and totally impractical while others offered more potential. The two favoured options were the lunar distance method and the use of marine chronometers and the two methods shared some of the prize money. The Astronomer Royal, Nevil Maskelyne, was a champion of the lunar distance method but it involved many calculations and eventually lost out to the chronometers. John Harrison developed chronometers so that they became very accurate, dependable, and easy to use.

See Also: Chronometers, Harrison (John), Navigation

Lono and Makahiki

Lono was the Hawaiian god of agriculture and fertility, who Hawaiians honoured to ensure peace and productivity. Lono was associated with clouds, rain and the winter season during which the land and the gardens are nourished. His worship was gentle, without human sacrifice as happened for the war god Ku. Any man might set up a temple to Lono. The time when Lono was honoured was known as Makahiki and marked the traditional celebration of the harvest and was a time of personal rest and spiritual and cultural renewal. Makahiki began with the Autumn rising of the constellation Pleiades (Makali'i, or little eyes) above the horizon in the evening sky. The Makali'i is much revered in the Hawaiian tradition as the place from which, according to legend, the first Hawaiian people came to Earth. During Makahiki, a procession travelled clockwise round parading images of Lono throughout coastal districts and gathering tribute in the form of produce for the ali'i (chiefs).

It was with this background that James Cook arrived off the coast of Hawai'i during the celebration of Makahiki in 1778. He finally landed on 17 January 1779 at Kealakekua Bay. Like Lono, Cook had come to the Hawaiian people from the sea. The shapes of the English ships were reminiscent of the kapa cloth and upright standards used in the Makahiki parades. Also, Cook's ships had sailed around Hawai'i clockwise, the same direction followed by Lono's processions. In addition, Kealakekua, where Cook's ships anchored, was the site of the important Hikiau Heiau. Cook was welcomed ashore and British accounts of the event report that the word 'Orono' (Lono) was used when addressing Cook.

The heiau at Kealakekua was a luakini heiau ornamented with the skulls of Maui warriors, and the central carved image was that of Ku-nui-akea (Ku the great, spreading over all). The heiau was therefore dedicated to Ku, but Ku as the patron of *all* men's works (not just warfare) but also the material arts, crafts, fishing, men's agricultural work, and the arts of governance and politics, was in abeyance during Makahiki. War could not be waged during this time, nor any large public works undertaken that had to be done under the auspices of Ku. The king, Kalaniopu'u, as representative of men, also went into abeyance during Makahiki, leaving a power vacuum so Lono could return and take the land as his wife and fertilise it with the insemination of spring rains.

Cook's return on 11 February came at the most inopportune time, when Makahiki was being concluded, and the king was carrying out rituals to re-appropriate the land so men could use it and make a living on it. Thus Lono had to be displaced. At this time, the king was in a very vulnerable situation, which is why he was so angry when Cook returned. Kalaniopu'u, refused to believe that the reason lay in a broken foremast. The thefts began, as the chiefs encouraged commoners to steal and make trouble, and this led to the events of 14 February. As Clerke took the British away on the 22nd, they wondered why the heiau was burning. It was then the time when the house, fence, tower, all the structures upon the rock platform, were burned off and rebuilt for the new season of Ku.

Debate still continues as to whether the Hawaiians believed Cook to be a manifestation of Lono or whether this is how the British chose to interpret the situation in order to increase Cook's status. American Christian missionaries who arrived in Hawai'i in the nineteenth century were critical of Cook and accused him of willingly playing the part of a false god.

SEE ALSO: Cook as god and Cook's death, Hawai'i, Colour plates 15 & 16

Louisbourg

The island of Île Royale (Cape Breton) became a base for fishermen from France, England, Spain, and Portugal, who crossed the Atlantic to exploit the vast stocks of cod on the Grand Banks, off Newfoundland. Most fished during the summer months and returned to Europe each winter. In 1713, the *Semslack* called at Havre à l'Anglois and landed approximately 160 men, who began the settlement of Louisbourg. A fort was constructed. Louisbourg (45° 55' N, 59° 58' W) enjoyed three peaceful decades as a French colonial seaport. As well as protecting the fishing fleets it commanded the approaches to the Gulf of St Lawrence and France's colonies in North America.

In 1745, troops from New England besieged the fort and captured it for Britain during the War of the Austrian Succession. However, the Treaty of Aix-La-Chapelle in 1748 returned the Île Royal to France, which reoccupied it in 1749. War was resumed in 1756 and in early 1758 James Cook, aboard the *Pembroke,* was part of the British force that crossed the Atlantic to attack French Canada.

Cook and the *Pembroke* arrived while the British, under General Wolfe, were still besieging Louisbourg. The French finally surrendered on 27 July 1758. Cook played little part in the attack but later he met Samuel Holland, an army engineer in Kennington Cove, as he was surveying on the beach. Cook expressed interest and Holland began showing him how to the survey. It was a pivotal moment in Cook's life. Louisbourg's fortifications were destroyed in 1760.

SEE ALSO: Canada, Nova Scotia and Halifax, Seven Years War

Lunar distance method and lunar tables

One of the methods used to calculate a ship's longitude before the development of accurate marine chronometers was the lunar distance method. Lunar distance is the angular distance of the moon from a chosen body – the sun, a star, or a planet. In the lunar method, the local time of taking a given lunar distance (by means of a sextant or repeating circle), was compared with the Greenwich time corresponding to the same distance. This was computed using lunar tables

The rock at Kennington Cove where Wolfe is believed to have landed prior to the sacking of Louisbourg, and where Cook began his career as a surveyer. (David Gary Fisher)

in a nautical almanac. The difference between these times gave the longitude for the location of the ship.

Tobias Mayer, a German mathematician, worked as a cartographer in Nürnberg and later became professor of mathematics at Göttingen in 1751. He began calculating lunar tables in 1753 and, in 1755, he sent them to the British Government. These tables were good enough to determine longitude at sea with an accuracy of half a degree. Nevil Maskelyne incorporated Mayer's work in publications that appeared in the 1760s. Maskelyne had become convinced that the lunar method was the best when he had gone to Saint Helena in 1761 to observe the Transit of Venus. It led to his reluctance to accept the marine chronometer.

In 1763 Maskelyne published the *British Mariner's Guide*, a handbook for the determination of the longitude at sea by the method of lunar distances. Next came his *Nautical Almanac and Astronomical Ephemeris*, which, among other data, included pre-calculated lunar distances to five well-selected bodies for every three-hour interval of Greenwich time. The companion piece to the *Almanac* was Maskelyne's *Tables Requisite to be Used with the Nautical Ephemeris for Finding the Latitude and Longitude at Sea*. This volume contained 30 tables needed for correction of observations and calculation of latitude and longitude and, in addition, it contained an explanation of the tables. Although the lunar method could be used to find longitude, it was complex, time-consuming and usually involved more than one observer. A number of corrections (or clearings) had to be applied. It also depended on a calm sea and clear visibility to sight the moon and stars. Chronometers soon replaced the lunar distance method as the accepted method of calculating longitude.

SEE ALSO: Chronometers, Maskelyne (Nevil), Navigation

M

Magra (Matra), James (1746–1806)

James Magra sailed on the *Endeavour* as an AB until 27 May 1771. He then became a midshipman. He was falsely accused of the attack on Orton, the ship's clerk, on 23 May 1770 but he was pardoned on 13 June. Magra changed his surname to Matra in 1775. Matra corresponded with Joseph Banks and, in 1783, produced a pamphlet entitled *A Proposal for establishing a settlement in New South Wales*. He was the British Consul in Tenerife from 1772 until 1775 and was on the staff of British Embassy in Constantinople from 1778 to 1780. Matra filled a consular post in Tangier from 1787 until his death on 29 March 1806. He was born in New York in 1746. Magra Islet off the north Queensland coast is named for him.

SEE ALSO: First voyage, Published accounts

Mai (Omai) (1753?–1780s)

Mai (Omai) was a native of Raiatea who had fled to live in Tahiti when his own island was attacked by Puni, the leader of Bora Bora. He was present at Matavai Bay when Wallis, in the *Dolphin,* and Cook, in the *Endeavour,* visited Tahiti. During Cook's first island sweep on his second voyage, the British called at Huahine in September 1773. Mai, who had moved to that island, persuaded Tobias Furneaux, captain of the *Adventure,* to take him back to Britain, despite reservations expressed by Cook. Mai appeared on the muster as Tetuby Homy. Cook and Furneaux separated shortly after and the *Adventure* headed back to Britain alone, arriving in July 1774.

Mai was taken to London and became a celebrity, being seen as personification of the Noble Savage. Mai (or Omai as he was usually known) was placed under the care of Joseph Banks, who introduced him to the King at Kew. Mai's behaviour on this occasion guaranteed his acceptance in British society. Mai for his part revelled in his time in Britain. Those that met him were impressed and he showed himself to be a sophisticated man with a culture of his own. He dined with the Royal Society on several occasions, stayed at Hinchingbrooke with Lord Sandwich, and went to Yorkshire with Banks. In London, Mai often visited the theatre, and was keenly sought after by Society hostesses. His portrait was painted by several artists, including Sir Joshua Reynolds and Nathaniel Dance.

He always expressed a desire to return to the Pacific and plans were made to take him home. Cook, who had returned to Britain in 1775 to find Mai a famous man, was appointed to lead the voyage, which departed in July 1776. Mai wished to be left on Raiatea after the British would have recaptured his family's land on that island. Cook, though, insisted on Huahine, not wishing to become involved in fighting with Raiatea. They arrived at Huahine in October 1777. Land was purchased near Fare where a house was built for Mai. The many gifts that had been transported to help him re-establish himself were put ashore, including horses and cattle. The British departed in early November leaving behind a tearful Mai.

Mai, still harbouring plans to return to Raiatea, survived for a few years but he was exploited by local Huahine people and by relations in Raiatea so that most of his possessions soon disappeared. Lieutenant John Watts, who had sailed as a midshipman with Cook, visited Huahine in the *Lady Penrhyn* in 1788 and heard about Mai's last days. Mai had died some years before. Raiateans had attacked Huahine after his death to retrieve Mai's belongings. The house and one horse survived.

SEE ALSO: Second voyage, Tahitians

Manley, Isaac George (1756–1837)

Isaac George Manley sailed on the *Endeavour* as master's mate until 4 February 1771 when he was made a midshipman. He was promoted to lieutenant in 1777, commander in 1782, and captain in 1790. Later in 1809 he became a rear-admiral in 1809, a vice-admiral in 1814, and an admiral in 1830. Manley was born in London in 1756 and died in Checkendon, Oxfordshire (west of Henley) on 29 July 1837, leaving a will (FRC 11/1886). Manley Island, an islet off the north

Queensland coast is named for him.
SEE ALSO: First voyage

Māori

The Māori, part of the Polynesian diaspora, were the first inhabitants of New Zealand or Aotearoa. They are believed to have arrived between AD 1000 and 1200 from an island known to them as Hawaiki and often equated with Raiatea in the Society Islands. Evidence suggests that there were several waves of migration over the period of a few hundred years in ocean-going canoes or waka. It is now thought that Polynesian migration was planned with many waka making return journeys to Hawaiki. Modern replicas of waka, such as *Te Aurere*, have successfully journeyed throughout the Pacific, using traditional navigation methods. Present-day Māori iwi (tribes) identify with particular waka and trace their whakapapa (genealogies) back to them.

The original settlements were founded on the north and east coasts but gradually people spread to occupy all corners of the islands and adapted to the new climate and environment. The islands proved colder and less hospitable than the islands they had come from and the Māori developed a unique culture accordingly. The settlers introduced animals such as the dog and the small Polynesian rat, the kiore. They also brought vegetables but the colder climate meant some such as taro were difficult to grow while others such as kumara thrived.

Fish was an important source of food so people mostly lived near the coast. Māori wove fishing nets from harakeke (flax), and carved fishhooks from bone and stone. They also hunted the many flightless birds they found. Trading took place throughout the country, especially in pounamu (greenstone), which was highly valued and used for special carvings. The Māori had no form of writing but added to an oral tradition the ability to record information through their art. Moko (tattooing), waiata (songs), carvings and woven artefacts were all used to store and recount information, genealogies and creation stories. Strong religious beliefs and customs brought with them were maintained. Marae were the religious and cultural focal points of settlements.

As the population grew and Māori spread, the iwi began to split into smaller sub-tribes, hāpu. Competition increased for land and resources and the people became more warlike. Inter-tribal fighting became common and settlements were fortified and known as pa. Only men fought, using weapons such as the spear-like taiaha. Other weapons included the mere (club). Haka (challenges) would be given to visitors and utu (revenge or payback) would be extracted after a wrong was committed.

The manner in which New Zealand Warriors defy their enemies. Engraved by R Godfrey after Parkinson. (Parkinson pl 17, fp 92)

The isolation of the islands meant the Māori were the last major human group to be affected by the wider world. The first reported contact was that of Abel Tasman, the Dutch explorer in 1642. The name Māori originally meant 'the local people'. New arrivals, the Europeans, were called Pakeha. Tangata whenua, signifying the people of the land, is another term used for the first inhabitants of Aotearoa. Eventually, through immigration of Europeans and by inter-marriage, Māori have become a minority. Cook's first meetings with Māori in Turanga Nui (Poverty Bay) in 1769 resulted, through misunderstandings on both sides, in the deaths of several Māori. In 1995, the visit to Gisborne of the *Endeavour* replica was opposed by sections of local Māori. For some Māori, tino rangatiratanga (self-rule and Māori sovereignty) remains the goal to strive for. Cook is blamed, not just for those deaths but for all the wrongs that Māori are believed to have suffered since his arrival.

Cook's other contacts with Māori were generally much friendlier, though sometimes with incident. He enjoyed returning to the country and respected the Māori people. The documents from his voyages represent a resource for studying Māori culture as it was until the arrival of the Europeans.
SEE ALSO: Indigenous peoples and Cook, New Zealand, Polynesian diaspora

Marines

Detachments of Marines travelled on all of Cook's Pacific voyages, with the number on board being in proportion to the ship's complement of sailors. The Marines had been formed in 1664 as the Lord High Admiral's Maritime Regiment of Foot. They later disbanded and reformed on two occasions, the last time being in 1755 when three Grand Divisions were based at Chatham, Plymouth and Portsmouth under the control of the Admiralty.

On board, the Marines were ship-based infantry, who were not expected to take part in sailing the ship. Their principal role on Cook's ships was to maintain discipline on board and enforce regulations. Marines kept distinct quarters from the sailors and formed a buffer between the officers and the rest of the crew. When Cook arrived at new locations, the Marines were expected to perform guard duties and escort crew members when they went ashore. They also prevented men from deserting. Cook even used the Marines to impress islanders by having them parade in uniform and formation.

On the *Endeavour*, the complement of Marines numbered 12, comprising a sergeant, a corporal, a drummer and nine privates. They went aboard at Plymouth from its division. John Edgcumbe was the sergeant whose good relationship with Cook ensured he was promoted to lieutenant for the second voyage. One private drowned on the voyage while two others died after the visit to Jakarta. Three privates needed to be punished for various misdemeanours during the voyage even though they were supposed to be the law on board. Two other men attempted to desert on Tahiti.

The Chatham Division provided most of the Marines for the second voyage and they went on board at Sheerness on 29 May 1772. Lieutenant John Edgcumbe led 20 men on the *Resolution*, comprising a sergeant, two corporals, a drummer, a bagpiper and 15 other privates. Lieutenant James Scott was in charge of 11 men on the *Adventure*. That ship had a sergeant, a corporal, a drummer and eight privates. As on the first voyage, some of the Marines needed to be punished. Two privates died on the voyage.

For the third voyage, Plymouth again provided most of the Marines. Lieutenant Molesworth Phillips led a sergeant, two corporals, a drummer and 15 privates on the *Resolution*. The *Discovery* carried a sergeant, a corporal, a drummer and nine privates. Three men tried to desert while three men drowned. Four Marines died with Cook at Kealakekua Bay where Phillips' actions have subsequently been questioned.

John Ledyard, a corporal on the third voyage, later had his journal published. He was the main advocate for American involvement in the sea otter trade, having seen the possibilities in the voyage. Samuel Gibson sailed on all three voyages, starting as a troublemaking private who tried to desert on the first voyage and ending up as a trusted sergeant and friend of Cook on the third. Sadly, he drowned on the last leg between Orkney and London having just married during the stopover in Orkney.

Marquesas Islands

The Marquesas Islands (Te Henua te Enata) (09° 50′ S, 139° W) lie between 373 and 621 miles (600 and 1000km) south of the equator and approximately 870 miles (1400km) north-east of Tahiti. They fall naturally into two geographical divisions: the northern group centred around the large island of Nuka Hiva and the two smaller islands of Ua Pou and Ua Huka, and the southern group of Tahuata, Moho Tani and Fatu Hiva, clustered around the main island of Hiva Oa. With a combined area of some 404 square miles (1049 sq km), the Marquesas are among the largest island groups of French Polynesia and were formerly a major centre of east Polynesian civilisation.

Recent archaeological findings suggest that the Marquesas were settled some 2200 years ago by people probably of a western Polynesian origin. The first European to visit the Marquesas was Alvaro de Mendaña, who arrived in 1595, named the islands Las Islas de Marquesa de Mendoza and claimed them for Spain. As with many early Spanish discoveries the location of the islands was not precisely fixed and James Cook decided to find them again.

In early April 1774, Cook, who was ill at the time, brought the *Resolution* west along latitude 10° S. On the 6th, Fatu Huku was sighted. Cook sailed through the strait between the islands of Hiva Oa and Tahuata searching for a harbour described by Mendaña on the west coast of Tahuata. He anchored in Vaitahu Bay on the 8th. Water and provisions were available and trade began but misunderstandings arose and a Tahuatan was shot dead. Trade continued but with suspicion on both sides. Cook decided it was time to leave. The *Resolution* sailed from Vaitahu on 12 April, heading for Tahiti. Surprisingly, nobody had apparently noticed the other islands of the Marquesas further to the north. Despite

the short stay and limited contact, the Marquesan people and islands left a very favourable impression on Cook. Few women had been seen but the men were held to be the most handsome in the Pacific.
SEE ALSO: Polynesian diaspora, Second voyage

Marra, John (1744 or 1747–1783)

John Marra (Mara) joined the first voyage on the *Endeavour* as an AB at Jakarta in November 1770. He re-enlisted for the second voyage on the *Resolution* as a gunner's mate. During this voyage Marra was punished four times. The first two occasions on 3 August 1772 and on 30 August 1773 were for insolence. He attempted to desert on 14 May 1774. Finally, he was punished on 3 November 1774 for disobedience.

Marra wrote an account of the second voyage that was published anonymously in 1775. Robert Anderson, who was suspected of its authorship persuaded Marra to own up. He was born in Cork in 1744 or 1747, and died in 1783. He left a will (FRC 11/1101).
SEE ALSO: First voyage, Published accounts, Second voyage

Martin, John Henry (1753–1823)

John Henry Martin sailed on the third voyage. He began on the *Discovery* as midshipman until 31 October 1777 when he became master's mate on the *Resolution*. He kept a log. Martin became a lieutenant in December 1780 and a commander in February 1800. He was in charge of HMS *Xenophon*, 22 guns, in the North Sea in 1800. He was the commander of HMS *Explosion*, a bomb ship, in Nelson's unsuccessful attack on Boulogne on 15/16 August 1801. He was born 1753 and died on 10 May 1823. Martin was buried at St Elidyr's Church, Ludchurch, Pembrokeshire, Wales. He left a will (FRC 11/1676).
SEE ALSO: Third voyage

Marton

Marton (54° 32' N, 1° 12' W), is a village in Northeast England, 2.5 miles (4km) south of the centre of Middlesbrough. It is now completely engulfed by the industrial conurbation of Teesside. In the eighteenth century, however, it was still a rural settlement where on 27 October 1728, James Cook was born. Cook was baptised at nearby St Cuthbert's Church in Marton, on 3 November. The church register is still displayed in the church and the entry reads: 'Nobr. 3 James ye son of James Cook daylabourer baptized'. The church has a stained-glass window depicting Cook and one wall bears a memorial to him.

The Cook family moved around Cleveland during this period and settled briefly in Marton in 1728. James Cook senior had obtained a position there working for George Mewburn, a local farmer. They left the village again but by 1733 they had returned to Marton and their fourth child, Mary, was born there. The Cooks were still poor and the children were put to work as soon as they were able. It is believed, therefore, that young James was already tending stock, watering horses and running errands for local people by the age of five. A story exists that in return a Dame Walker taught him his alphabet and how to read. In 1736, when Cook was eight the family left Marton to live at Aireyholme Farm in Great Ayton.

It is thought that the Cooks lived in two separate homes in Marton but nothing remains of either of them. The original cottage where Cook was born was demolished by the Rudd family in 1786, when they creating parkland surrounding their new house, Marton Lodge. Almost 70 years later, H W F Bolckow bought the ruins of the Lodge and built a new mansion in its place. In 1858, Bolckow erected the granite vase which now marks the site of the cottage. Nearby is the modern Captain Cook Birthplace Museum opened in 1978 on land purchased and donated by Thomas Stewart to Middlesbrough in 1924.
SEE ALSO: Cleveland, Cook's early years

Mary

The *Mary* was a small vessel working on the North Sea and in the Baltic trade. Cook had completed his apprenticeship as a seaman for the Walkers at the end of 1749 and, after wintering with his family in Great Ayton, Cook signed on with the *Mary* under her master, William Gaskin, at North Shields in February 1750. It is believed that the *Mary* and Cook sailed to Christiania (Oslo) and the Baltic (Cook may have reached St Petersburg). Cook was discharged from the *Mary* on 8 October 1750 in London. Cook is thought to have possibly returned to the north-east on board the *Hopewell*, a Stockton-registered collier.
SEE ALSO: North Sea and the coal trade, Walker (John), Whitby

Maskelyne, Nevil (1732–1811)

Nevil Maskelyne was born on 6 October 1732 in London, the third son of Edmund and Elizabeth

Maskelyne. The family had property in Purton in Wiltshire. He attended Westminster School. His father died in 1744 and his mother in 1748. The eclipse of 25 July 1748 awakened Maskelyne's interest in astronomy.

Maskelyne entered Cambridge University in 1749 where he studied mathematics. He graduated in 1754 and became a fellow of Trinity College in 1756. Maskelyne was ordained a minister in 1755 and obtained various clerical positions in Barnet (1755), Shropshire (1775), and Norfolk (1782). Astronomy, though, had become his main interest and, in 1757, Maskelyne became assistant to the then Astronomer Royal, Bradley. He was elected Fellow of the Royal Society in 1758.

In 1761, The Royal Society sent him to the island of St Helena to observe the Transit of Venus, with the aim of using this information to calculate the distance of the Earth from the Sun. Bad weather prevented any useful observations being made. However, Maskelyne used his journey to develop a method of calculating longitude called the lunar distance method. He returned to Britain and, in 1763, published *The British Mariner's Guide*, in which described how to determine longitude using lunar tables and a reflecting quadrant. The Board of Longitude sent Maskelyne to Barbados in 1764 to test John Harrison's timepiece H4, a rival method of determining longitude.

Soon after his return, in 1765, he was appointed the fifth Astronomer Royal. He published the first volume of the *Nautical Almanac* in 1766 and continued to work on this project up to the time of his death. His time as Astronomer Royal was spent making improvements to existing apparatus and installing new equipment. In 1769, he used this improved apparatus along with his improved method of observation to observe the Transit of Venus at Greenwich. Maskelyne carried out an experiment in 1774 on Schiehallion, a mountain in Perthshire, Scotland, to calculate the Earth's density. From his observations, Maskelyne computed the density to be approximately 4.5 times that of water. He was awarded the Copley Medal of the Royal Society in 1775 for this work. Maskelyne married Sophia Rose in 1785. They had one daughter, Margaret. He died on 9 February 1811 and was buried at St Mary the Virgin, Purton, Wiltshire. He left a will (FRC 11/1520). There is a short biography in the *DNB*, v12, pp1299–1301.

SEE ALSO: Astronomical results of Cook's voyages, Lunar distance method and lunar tables, *Nautical Almanac*

A view of Matavai Bay in Otaheite from One Tree Hill. An engraving by John James Barralet copied from Sydney Parkinson. (Hawkesworth II fp 80)

Matavai Bay

Matavai Bay is situated on the north coast of Tahiti, 6.2 miles (10km) east of present-day Papeete. The bay, 1.5 miles (2.5km) wide, lies between two headlands, Points Venus and Tepane, and is fringed by a reef, the Dolphin Bank. Gaps in the reef allowed sailing ships to anchor safely in the bay before Papeete became the main port of call. Matavai Bay and the Tahitians impressed Cook so much that it became one of his favourite places in the Pacific and he would visit four times.

The first European to visit Tahiti was Samuel Wallis in the *Dolphin*, who anchored at Matavai Bay in 1767. On his return to London in 1768, he reported positively about the location and it was selected as the site from which to observe the Transit of Venus in 1769. On 13 April 1769, James Cook anchored the *Endeavour* in Matavai Bay, having been welcomed by a flotilla of local people in canoes. The British had seven weeks to prepare for the Transit of Venus and Cook negotiated the use of a site ashore on which to build an observatory. It was constructed on the headland, renamed Point Venus. Several tents were erected on the point to house observation equipment and to provide living quarters ashore for Green, Banks and others. A wooden stockade termed Fort Venus was constructed around the tents. Cook, having observed the Transit and having made a tour of the island, left Matavai Bay on 13 July 1769.

Cook returned for the first time in August 1773 after a short visit to Tautira on Tahiti Iti. A civil war had taken place since Cook's last visit and provisions were in short supply. Cook, realising the situation would not improve, decided to leave and sailed on 1 September. He returned again in April 1774 but, as he remembered the lack of supplies the previous August, he did not intend to stay long. He was surprised to find pigs and other supplies in plenty and, after restocking, he left Tahiti on 14 May. Cook made his last visit during his third voyage in August 1777 when he transferred to Matavai Bay from Tautira. Cook left finally on 29 September 29.

Parkinson drew sketches, especially of One Tree Hill (Mt. Taharaa) overlooking the bay, while Hodges' paintings recorded the *Resolution* and the *Adventure* at anchor in the bay.

SEE ALSO: Tahiti, Transit of Venus

Medals and money

In early 1772, Joseph Banks commissioned the Birmingham company of Boulton and Fothergill (metal castings and fabrication) to design and produce a medal that he could take to the Pacific with him for distribution, as Bougainville had done on his expedition. Matthew Boulton created the '*Resolution* & *Adventure* Medal', of which 2 gold, 142 silver and 2000 platina copies were struck. The medals show King George III on the obverse and the *Resolution* and the *Adventure* on the reverse. Banks withdrew from the voyage but Cook took the medals, which he handed out as gifts to islanders. Not all were used up and some were given out during the third voyage. Most have disappeared but occasionally examples are found.

The Royal Society, which had bestowed its Copley Medal on Cook in 1776, met on 27 January 1780, shortly after the news of his death had reached London. The Committee resolved to have a medal struck in memory of Cook, 'expressive of his desserts'. This was the only occasion the Society did this, no doubt reflecting Banks' close friendship with Cook. In June 1780, Lewis Pingo, the Chief Engraver at the London Mint, was selected to design and produce the medal but the medals did not appear until 1784. They depict Cook in profile, looking left, on the obverse and a Britannia on the reverse. A total of 22 gold, 322 silver and 577 bronze medals were struck, mostly going to members of the Royal Society who had subscribed. Copies of the gold medals were given to King George and Queen Charlotte, King Louis XVI of France and Catherine the Great of Russia. Belatedly Elizabeth Cook was also given a gold medal.

Captain Cook medal, 1780. This bronze medal was seemingly rushed out in 1780 to commemorate Cook. The design, a bust of Cook and the words 'Capt. James Cook' on the obverse and the inscription 'Courage and Perseverance' on the reverse, shows minimal design and poor workmanship. (Museum of New Zealand Te Papa Tongarewa)

In 1771 Josiah Wedgwood had started a series of small medallions of famous people, fashioned in a white jasper clay attached to a coloured jasper background. He produced a Cook medallion in 1777 based on Hodges' portrait of Cook. Cook is shown front on, looking left. After Cook's death, Wedgwood commissioned another medallion in 1784. This was designed by John Flaxman, possibly after an engraving by Thomas Cook. Cook is shown in profile, looking right.

Subsequently Cook has been the subject of many medals, mostly commissioned in the 1960s and 1970s when Cook anniversaries were being celebrated. Full listings can be found in Allan Klenman's *The Faces of Captain Cook*. Klenman's book also records most of the coins that have been issued, either commemorating or using Cook.

During the 1970s, several Pacific nations issued commemorative high-denomination coins aimed more at collectors than for use as normal currency. The New Zealander, James Berry, designed coins for New Zealand, Samoa and the Cook Islands. Berry also designed the 50-cent coin, which is still in every day use in New Zealand after 37 years with the *Endeavour* on the reverse.

Cook also featured on the banknotes of New Zealand issued by the Reserve Bank. Prior to decimalisation in 1967, the 10/- (1940–55), 1.00, 5.00 (1967), and 10.00 (1956–67) notes all featured Cook, based on Dance's portrait. He did not survive to appear on dollar notes. In 1988, Cook appeared on an Australian $10.00 note.

Medical aspects of Cook's voyages

James Cook had no formal education though he had, it is true, a good early grounding thanks to schooling provided by his family benefactor Thomas Skottowe but his knowledge thereafter was garnered 'on the job'. His ideas about health were those of the practical seaman who knew the conditions under which the humblest sailor survived the stresses of wet, cold, poor nutrition and homesickness.

When he came to prepare for his pioneering first voyage he may have read what various medical pundits of his day had written about the prevention of scurvy but there is no evidence that he studied Lind's book concerning a scientific trial of alleged anti-scorbutics. He was however impressed by the ideas and writings of D MacBride, which is why he set such store on preparing malt wort and making fresh beer from it. In common with most of his contemporaries he attributed illness to foul air or miasmas, lack of cleanliness and feeble ship's discipline. Therefore, his measures for preserving crew health on long voyages were based on personal cleanliness, deck-scrubbing and fumigation by controlled fires between decks. His emphasis on maintaining morale and psychological well-being was typified by his encouragement of music and dancing. Most importantly he aimed to make regular stays in secure harbours and to encourage his crewmen to gather shore-greens while recreating themselves ashore. Though apparently abstemious himself, his attitude towards the heavy drinking prevalent among both officers and men was ambiguous.

Scurvy

It is impossible to make sense of the conflicting and erroneous ideas about scurvy in the eighteenth century without first reviewing what we know today. The final elucidation of the scurvy mystery did not occur until the middle of the twentieth century. Ascorbic acid, the Vitamin C of earlier years, is an essential substance which man's body cannot manufacture and which must be taken in his diet to maintain health. The reserves we normally carry in our body can last from eight to twelve weeks after which symptoms and signs of scurvy develop. Ascorbic acid, otherwise known as ascorbate because it is ionised in solution, is present in the blue-green algae which were the predominant life-form three billion years ago. Its function in such proto-life forms was to mop up free radicals produced in the process of photosynthesis. Chemically, ascorbic acid is composed of only twenty atoms and has four less hydrogen atoms than glucose, the universal energy-provider of living organisms. Knowing these facts allows us to deduce that ascorbate must be present in all germinated seeds and young vegetable shoots. This has been confirmed by chemical analysis. The cause of scurvy, therefore, is the consumption of a diet free of germinated seed, green shoots, certain fruits and raw flesh of healthy animals. What the eighteenth-century scientist did not know was that the anti-scorbutic principle (ascorbate) was destroyed by boiling heat, vinegar and strong alcohol. This ignorance led to great confusion, because potential anti-scorbutics were destroyed in the processing or storage. Thus, malt wort which is very rich in ascorbate is rendered useless by boiling or high alcohol levels, just as cabbage hearts are not effective anti-scorbutics when stored in vinegar. Even potatoes, which are rich in ascorbate when raw, are useless when boiled relentlessly for half an hour.

We can therefore see with the benefit of hindsight that eighteenth century sailors were prevented by ignorance from discovering the way to prevent scurvy at sea. The Chinese, four centuries earlier, had germinated soya bean shoots aboard their ocean-going vessels to add to the crew's diet. Some sea-captains in the East India trade are reported to have had success by growing and consuming legume shoots on board. What eighteenth-century sailors probably knew, but their medical advisors did not, was that ascorbate was present in the flesh and livers of animals, so that lightly-cooked seal meat if consumed by the whole crew, could cure incipient scurvy. Fresh beef from killed animals on board or by purchase in inhabited areas such as Kamchatka was even better as it was eaten eagerly by the crew. Best of all was the eating of fresh shore-greens during stop-overs for ship repairs and astronomical observations. This subject will be dealt with more fully below.

Cook's measures for scurvy prevention

Cook encouraged a whole variety of measures to prevent scurvy and to maintain his crews' psychological health, but it was a hotch-potch. He never made an attempt at a controlled trial of any single substance, and the only trial was a fortuitous one between the crews of *Resolution* and *Adventure* in 1773 (see below).

Here are recorded Cook's general disciplinary measures for the prevention of scurvy. Of these it can be said today that none would have prevented scurvy but all would promote the psychological well-being of the crew. His measures were a three-watch system giving eight hours of rest between four-hour spells of deck duty, cleanliness and dry, warm clothing, regular firing between-decks (using wood and sprinkled gunpowder as fuel) to promote ventilation, and recreational activities such as music and dancing both afloat and ashore. Cook's list of possibly anti-scorbutic dietary additions are long and confusing. Only those which could have contained ascorbate have been printed in bold type while the really important ones have been underlined as well: portable soup; **sauerkraut**; sugar; sago; marmalade of carrots; mustard; salop (ground-up orchid roots); vinegar; **spruce beer**; **malt wort**; **raw onion**; **rob of lemon** (in surgeon's store) and **shore greens**, often floating in portable soup.

Because of the heat used in the preparation of rob of lemon and malt wort and because of the vinegar used to preserve sauerkraut the amounts of ascorbate would have been low and variable between batches. The same caveat applies to spruce beer, but the amount allowed per day (one gallon) ensured that the crew imbibed between 1 and 5 mgms of ascorbate per day, enough to keep scurvy at bay as long as the brew lasted. The methods of making spruce beer in Dusky Sound, N.Z. were derived from Cartier's experience of curing a scorbutic crew frozen in the St Lawrence River in 1536. They had made an infusion of the twigs and buds of a prevalent tree (probably sassafras). Cook's method involved stripping the shoots of evergreens such as rimu (*Dacrydium cupressinum*) and manuka (*Leptospermum scoparium*) plunging them into boiling water and leaving them for up to four hours before adding five gallons of inspissated malt wort and one gallon of molasses, bringing the mixture to the boil and sealing it in wooden casks.

In Tierra del Fuego Cook used the stripped bark of *Drimys winteri* and in north-west America, spruce, thuja and western hemlock greenery. The word spruce in spruce beer is derived from the German word 'Sprossen', meaning a green shoot. The question mark over the beer's effectiveness derives from the doubt as to how much ascorbate was destroyed by the heating process, but both Cook's and the later Vancouver's experience suggest that it was effective in keeping the ascorbate levels in the crews' blood just high enough to prevent clinical scurvy.

The importance of the consumption of shore-greens during Cook's long stays in secure anchorages such as within Queen Charlotte Sound, NZ, during the second and third voyages has been thoroughly explored by Professor Cuppage in his 1994 publication 'James Cook and the conquest of scurvy'. I shall quote extensively from the results of his on-the-spot researches and his conclusions which are those of an experienced medical scientist. Shore-greens varied from place to place but the main components were scurvy grass (*Cochlearia sp*), wild celery (*Apium sp*), and fat hen (*Chenopodium sp*). Additionally, in New Zealand, the men ate the heart of the cabbage palm (*Cordyline australis*) which was a favourite food of the Māori, fern root (*Freycineta banksias*), glass wort (*Anthrocremium austaliasicum*) and various fruits. Cook himself attached great importance to the gathering and consumption of shore-greens as shown by his letter to the Admiralty of July 1775 quoted by Cuppage. 'We came to a few places w[h]ere ye art of man or nature had not provided some sort of refreshments or other in ye animal or vegitable way, and it was first care to procure them by every means in my power and obliged ye people to make use of them, both by example and by authority'.

We must now consider the events of April–August 1773 when the differences between the attitudes of Cook in *Resolution* and Furneaux in *Adventure* were to prove by fortuitous trial the virtues of 'example and authority' in compelling crews to eat shore-greens. Furneaux arrived at Queen Charlotte Sound in April 1773 after a voyage from Tasmania where he had not insisted on his men gathering and eating shore-greens. Many of his men were scorbutic on arrival in New Zealand. Both ships set sail for Tahiti at about the same time in June, arriving in August. The crew of the *Resolution* were fit and healthy on arrival whereas at least 20 per cent of *Adventure*'s complement were disabled by scurvy, but were soon cured by the shore diet of Tahiti. This fortuitous dietary trial between the two ships provided with the same standard victuals is a truly proof that Cook's achievements in the conquest of scurvy were largely due to his 'example and authority' in caring for his crew's health by insisting on their eating fresh greenery even if they scattered it in their portable soup. From what we know about scurvy this was sound common sense, as was that of Bering's men marooned on a bleak Aleutian island who grazed the scant herbage like sheep.

The problem of venereal disease

The purpose of the *Endeavour*'s voyage was to observe the Transit of Venus, an appropriate planet for the sexual permissiveness of the inhabitants which not only enabled the young men to enjoy their recreation ashore as sexual tourists but exposed the population to an epidemic of gonorrhoea. Yaws, closely related to syphilis, was endemic in Polynesia so the record as to syphilis transmission is blurred, as is that of the rarer lymphogranuloma venereum.

On subsequent voyages the inhabitants of Tahiti and Tonga repaid their visitors with interest, so much so that Cook was driven to distraction when his men, even the actively-infected ones, proceeded to inflict the downside of Western Civilisation on the Hawaiians. Sir James Watt believes that Cook's dismay over this was a major factor in his errors of judgement and the disillusion of the Hawaiians during the return of *Resolution* to repair its foremast (see below).

The tragedy of Batavia

The success of Cook in maintaining crew-health in *Endeavour* during the first two years of the voyage was tarnished by an essential but unhappy stay at Batavia where ship repairs were made before the voyage home. At that time Batavia was a canal-lined town close to the anchorage so that both those on board and those living ashore were exposed to malaria-carrying mosquitoes and a water supply contaminated by sewage. Even the privileged such as Joseph Banks who rented homes ashore were dangerously exposed to disease. Munkhouse, the none-too efficient surgeon who lived ashore, died in a high fever almost certainly due to falciparum malaria. When in 1770 *Endeavour* sailed for home five of her complement were already dead and many desperately ill. An anchorage at Prince's Island did not help, and Solander found mosquito larvae in the ship's casked water. Altogether, 22 died on the voyage from Prince's Island to the Cape of Good Hope, most of them apparently from dysentery. As to what type of dysentery, the present author, who was a practising hospital physician with experience of tropical medicine, believes it may have been the amoebic form so easily carried in contaminated water. He does not agree with Sir James Watt's suggestion that some of the deaths were due to typhoid fever; the reported symptoms just do not fit with such a diagnosis.

However, at this point I must acknowledge the great contribution made by Surgeon Vice-Admiral Sir James Watt in his splendid historical works on the health of the crews of Pacific explorers. His writings were, at the time, ground-breaking but, as nearly 25 years have rolled by, so modern botanical and biochemical research can now more readily underpin our views on maritime medical history.

Health records

Due to the Batavia catastrophe, the health record of *Endeavour* was not really good. Deaths from malaria and dysenteric diseases accounted for 31 out of the 41 deaths. Three died from tuberculosis, three from alcoholic excess and three from drowning. On the second voyage there were again no deaths from scurvy in *Resolution*, but one in *Adventure*. Eight of *Adventure*'s crew were murdered by Māori, while on the third voyage Cook himself and four others were slain by the Hawaiians.

We must agree that Cook deserved the Copley Medal of the Royal Society, though we also agree with Watt that the combination of Cook's immense prestige and his conviction that the answer to scurvy prevention was boiled malt wort delayed the acceptance by the Admiralty of Lind's proof that citrus fruit juices were the best dietary supplement for inclusion in HM ships' victuals.

Cook's deteriorating health

For a masterly account of Cook's increasing irritability and failure of judgement during the third voyage the reader is referred to Sir James Watt. The present author has to reject Watt's hypothesis that Cook was suffering from a deficiency of thiamine and niacin, as his symptoms of depression, constipation and irritability do not accord with the likely consequences of Vitamin B-complex deficiency.

Cook's physical symptoms of abdominal colic, constipation and possible anaemia match best those of chronic lead poisoning which was known to be prevalent among naval officers due to the habit of storing wine in pewter vessels and sweetening it with lead acetate ('sugar of lead'). Cook, however, was reputedly abstemious with alcohol and driven to distraction by his men's sexual misdeeds in transmitting venereal diseases throughout the Pacific. We can only safely conclude that Cook's later failures of command were largely due to stress-related depression and the premature onset of old age.

By John M Naish

See Also: Scurvy, Sex, sexuality and venereal disease

Melanesia

Anthropologists and historians have divided the islands of the Pacific into three broad groupings. One of them, Melanesia, covers the islands in the region from Maluku (Indonesia) in the west, through the islands of New Guinea, the Solomons, Vanuatu, New Caledonia, to Fiji in the east. The term, meaning 'black islands', was coined by the French explorer Dumont d'Urville in 1832 to describe the darker-skinned people who lived on these islands in the western Pacific and to differentiate them from the fairer Polynesians. The people, known as Melanesians, moved into the region from Southeast Asia. Their development has lasted longer than that for Polynesians and their languages, part of the Austronesian stock, show more variety.

Cook encountered Melanesians on his second voyage during his second sweep of the Pacific. He had been used to meeting Polynesians and, on his arrival in the New Hebrides (Vanuatu) in July 1774, he realised that the inhabitants were different. Cook and his men had acquired a basic ability to speak and understand Polynesian languages but it was useless here.

Cook landed on Mallikolo and Erromango but the local people were very suspicious and gave cool receptions that caused Cook to leave immediately. He did stay for two weeks on Tanna but only on sufferance. Cook visited the island of New Caledonia next and the people there were found to be similar to Vanuatu. Cook went ashore at Balade and to a more friendly reception. He stayed for eight days. Forster and Cook made descriptions of the people and Forster assembled vocabularies.

See Also: New Caledonia, Second voyage, Vanuatu

Memorials to Cook

The years 1969 and 1970 marked the 200th anniversaries of Cook's visits to New Zealand and Australia. Celebrations were held in both countries and to mark the events many cairns, plaques and assorted memorials were erected. The euphoria of that time has passed and some of those memorials no longer exist or are now in poor repair. A few of the more interesting memorials will be mentioned below.

The Cook monument erected by Sir Hugh Palliser at his house, The Vache, in Chalfont St Giles, Buckinghamshire. (The author)

About 20 statues of Cook exist around the world though one of the most famous statues of 'James Cook' is not of Cook at all. The statue on Kaiti Hill overlooking Gisborne, erected to celebrate Cook's visit to Poverty Bay, turned out to be one of an Italian naval officer. Two more copies exist including one in central Auckland. Gisborne has redeemed itself by displaying one of Anthony Stones' fine bronzes produced for the New Zealand Pavilion at Expo '92 in Sevilla, Spain. The National Maritime Museum at Greenwich also has a Stones.

Another famous statue was sculpted by Sir John Tweed and stands high on East Cliff in Whitby. Copies have been erected in Waimea, Kaua'i and in Victoria, British Columbia. Sir Thomas Brock was responsible for the statue near the old Admiralty building in The Mall in London (1914). Several statutes of Cook exist in Australia. Thomas Woolner produced the statue in Hyde Park in central Sydney while a red sandstone statue stands in Randwick. Further north, Cooktown's statue is by Stanley Hammond. Christchurch in New Zealand has a statue by William Trewethey (1932). All of the above statues depict Cook as a man in naval uniform and are derived from the portraits of Cook by Dance, Hodges and Webber. Great Ayton has one of him as a boy sculpted by Nicholas Dimbleby.

Several obelisks are scattered around the world. They include the Captain Cook Monument on Easby Moor overlooking Great Ayton, one by the Endeavour River at Cooktown, and Cook's monument, erected in 1874 at Ka'awaloa near the spot on the shore in Kealakekua Bay where he died (it is theoretically on a small patch of British soil). Two other obelisks mark the arrival of Cook in New Zealand and Australia. One stands behind a timber yard in Gisborne, the other where Isaac Smith stepped ashore in Botany Bay. Stewart Park in Marton has a Birthplace Vase to mark the location of the cottage where Cook was born.

One of the most elaborate memorials is in the Parc du Jeurre at Etampes, south of Paris, where the Captain Cook Memorial stands proudly in the gardens. It was commissioned by the French banker, Laborde. Cook's friend, Hugh Palliser, erected an equally unique memorial at his estate, The Vache, in Buckinghamshire. A different type of memorial, the modern 'Bottle of Notes' sculpture by artists, Claes Oldenburg and Coosje van Bruggen, stands in Middlesbrough as a tribute to Cook.

Cook is one the navigators honoured in Westminster Abbey by the Navigators' memorial while his bust sits atop a large memorial facing the Arctic Ocean at Cape Shmidta on the Chukotskiy peninsula. In Canberra on Lake Burley Griffin, the Captain Cook Memorial Water Jet spurts out opposite the National Library, home of many original Cook manuscripts.

Two New Zealand locations associated with Cook are still very much as Cook would have known them. A simple plaque marks the spot in Dusky Sound where the *Resolution* anchored and the stumps of trees cut down by Cook's crew are a natural surviving memorial to him. At Queen Charlotte Sound in unspoilt Ship Cove, a more elaborate memorial stands to mark Cook's visit. Sydney Town Hall has a beautiful stained-glass window designed by Lucien Henry in 1889 while St Cuthbert's Church in Marton, the site of Cook's christening has a more simple stained-glass window.

Mercury Bay/Te-Whanganui-a-Hei

Mercury Bay (36° 48' S, 175° 46' E) is an inlet on the eastern side of the Coromandel Peninsula on Te Ika a Maui, the North Island of New Zealand. The bay is 3.1 miles (5km) deep and 1.8 miles (3km) wide at its mouth.

Cook, who had been sailing across the Bay of Plenty was aware that a Transit of Mercury was approaching. He needed to be ashore in order to observe it. On 4 November 1769, Cook reached a small inlet suitable for this purpose, Te-Whanganui-a-Hei, where he anchored the *Endeavour*. The observation of the Transit of Mercury would allow Cook to calculate longitude and know his position more precisely. An observatory was set up on the south shore, 164 yards (150m) west of the mouth of the Purangi River (Oyster River). Clear skies on 9 November allowed a good sighting of the event, which gave the bay its new name, Mercury Bay. The bay was charted carefully and trips were made to all corners including deep into Whitianga Harbour (Mangrove River). Two pa (Māori fortified settlements) on the north shore, Te Puta o Paretauhinau (the site of Spöring's Grotto) and Wharetaewa, were visited and relations with the local Māori, Ngati Hei, were very friendly. The visit was described by Te Horeta Te Taniwha from a Māori point of view many years later.

Having restocked, Cook left Mercury Bay on 15 November after a visit of 11 days. The *Endeavour* skirted some islands, the Mercury Islands, before regaining the coast and sailing north to round Cape Colville (named after his old captain but now with an extra e) and enter the Firth of Thames. There is a memorial to Cook on Shakespeare's Cliff at the west end of Cook's Beach, while another memorial marks the site of the observatory. Whitianga Museum has a small Cook exhibit.

SEE ALSO: New Zealand, Transit of Mercury

Molyneux, Robert (1746–1767)

Robert Molyneux (Molineux) sailed on the first voyage on the *Endeavour* as master. He kept a journal and a log, and drew charts. Molyneux had previously sailed as a master's mate with Wallis on the *Dolphin* to Tahiti in 1767. He was born in Hale, near Liverpool in 1746 and died in Table Bay off Robben Island on 16 April 1771, leaving a will (FRC 11/969). Molyneux's Harbour in New Zealand was named after him but the name is no longer used.

SEE ALSO: First voyage

A View of Aimeo harbour (Oponohu Bay), by John Webber. Cook only visited Moorea on the third voyage and anchored in this bay, not Paopao Bay, now also known as Baie de Cook. (British Library)

Moorea

Moorea (17° 32' S, 149° 50' W) is the westernmost of the Windward Society Islands in the South Pacific. The island, 48 square miles (125 sq km), is 10.5 miles (17km) west of Tahiti and now forms part of the territory of French Polynesia. It is a popular destination spot for tourists seeking a tropical island.

Moorea had been sighted in 1767 by Samuel Wallis, who had called it The Duke of York's Island. When Cook arrived in 1769 he himself did not visit Moorea but one of the parties under Gore, deputed to observe the Transit of Venus, did so from Motu Irioa, an islet situated in Moorea's lagoon at the north-west corner of the island. Banks visited the settlement at Papetoai. Cook recorded the island's name as Eimo.

Cook finally visited the island in 1777 on his third voyage. Cook left Tahiti on 29 September 1777 and crossed to Moorea where he anchored in Opunohu Bay. He was not received by Chief Mahine, who probably thought Cook had been helping To'ofa and other Tahitian leaders in their war against Moorea. The ordinary people were more friendly though and much fruit and wood were obtained. Mahine then appeared and asked for some goats. Two animals were stolen, leading to a series of incidents. One goat disappeared completely and with it, Mahine. Cook was informed they had gone to the south of the island and dispatched two midshipmen to recover the goat. They returned empty-handed so Cook, by now angry, marched over the island's central hills himself to Maatea. Even he could not find the goat so he returned via the west coast burning houses and destroying several canoes along the way in an uncharacteristic display of bad temper. Cook went on to Paopao Bay (now known as Baie de Cook) and destroyed more canoes before, eventually, the goat was recovered. Cook was ready to leave and did so on 11 October. Cook's visit to Moorea must be regarded as one of his least productive and most regrettable anywhere.

See Also: Society Islands, Third voyage

Mouat, Alexander (1761–1793)

Alexander Mouat sailed on the *Discovery* as a midshipman until 20 August 1779. He then became an AB until 29 April 1780 when he resumed as a midshipman. Mouat attempted to desert on Raiatea in the Society Islands in November 1777. He became a lieutenant in November 1780 and a commander in November 1790. From 1793 to 1794, Mouat was in command of HMS *Rattlesnake,* 16 guns. At his death, he was attached to HMS *Marlborough,* and listed as coming from Stock in Essex. He was born in Greenwich in 1761, the son of Captain Patrick Mouat, who had commanded the *Tamaron* on Byron's world voyage in 1764. He died on 11 October 1793, leaving a will (FRC 11/1245).

See Also: Third voyage

Munkhouse brothers, Jonathan (?–1771), and William Brougham (1732–1770)

William Munkhouse (Monkhouse) sailed on the first voyage on the *Endeavour* as surgeon. He kept a journal of which only a small part survives. William had previously sailed as surgeon aboard HMS *Niger* on the Newfoundland station from 1763 to 1767. During this time he saved Joseph Banks' life when the botanist, who was visiting Newfoundland, was 'very ill with ague and fever and at one time not expected to recover'. Munkhouse died at Jakarta on 5 November 1770.

His younger brother Jonathan, who was a midshipman on the voyage, only survived him by a few weeks. He died in the Indian Ocean on 6 February 1771. Jonathan, who kept a log, had taken charge of fothering the *Endeavour* when the ship struck the Barrier Reef and his actions saved the ship. He had served in the Navy in

the West Indies before joining the *Endeavour*. Both the Munkhouses were born in Penrith, Cumberland. William Munkhouse left a will (FRC 11/970).
SEE ALSO: First voyage

Museums

Zoological, botanical and ethnological material was brought back to Europe by people who sailed on Cook's voyages. Some of the material was subsequently traded around between collectors and museums for over two hundred years and, as a result, many museums around the world now possess 'Cook collections'. Joseph Banks played an important role in the dispersal, firstly receiving items from people such as Forster, Clerke and Anderson, and then passing on material to others. He also brought home items himself on Cook's first voyage. Much of Banks' collection eventually found its way to the Natural History and British Museums in London.

Many collections at the time were in the hands of private individuals such as the Duchess of Portland, though some operated museums where members of the public could view the specimens. George Humphrey was a dealer and collector, who as well as having his own museum, passed on material to collectors. Among the museums were the Leverian (belonging to Sir Ashton Lever), the Bullock (owned by William Bullock), and the Hunter (John Hunter). Lever's collection later was housed in the Rotunda in London and was dispersed at auction in 1806. When the Bullock Museum was auctioned off in 1819 substantial purchased were made by museums in Paris, Vienna, Edinburgh and Vienna.

Unfortunately, as material changed hands, items often went missing as did the documentation allowing provenance so that collections now contain specimens of doubtful authenticity. The long history of sales, loans, gifts and transfers has created a web that will probably never be unravelled.

Some collections remain where they were first lodged and are named after the people who gathered them: Forster in Pitt Rivers Museum in Oxford; Sparrman in the National Museum of Ethnography in Stockholm; King in Trinity College, Dublin; and Webber in the Bernisches Historisches Museum, Bern. Many other museums simply have collections labelled 'Cook collection'; they include the Museum fur Völkerkunde in Vienna and the Kunstkammer in St Petersburg.

Another group of museums is devoted to Cook himself. Several museums are located in Cleveland devoted to Cook's early life: Marton has the Birthplace; Great Ayton has the Schoolroom; and Whitby has the Memorial Museum.

The house, both family home and place of business, which belonged to the Walker family in the mid-eighteenth century, and where Cook lodged 1746-49. A typical Whitby shipowner's residence, with its slipway down to the water, it is now the site of the Captain Cook Memorial Museum. (Captain Cook Memorial Museum, Whitby)

Music, Cook and

Cook was not a music aficionado like Lord Sandwich, who collected examples of Pacific music, or the guitar-playing Joseph Banks, who planned to take a liveried band of musicians to Tahiti on Cook's second voyage. Cook had no formal musical instruction and lacked such enthusiasms. He would probably have considered shanty-singing a sign of poor discipline on board ship and prohibited it in keeping with Georgian naval regulations. Music-making was nonetheless an institutional as well as recreational aspect of shipboard life. The boatswain's whistle piped orders for each watch and the seamen passed their time doing country-dances and hornpipes to the fiddle, fife and drum. In addition, Cook's ships included formally-trained musicians in their complements of marines. Among those associated

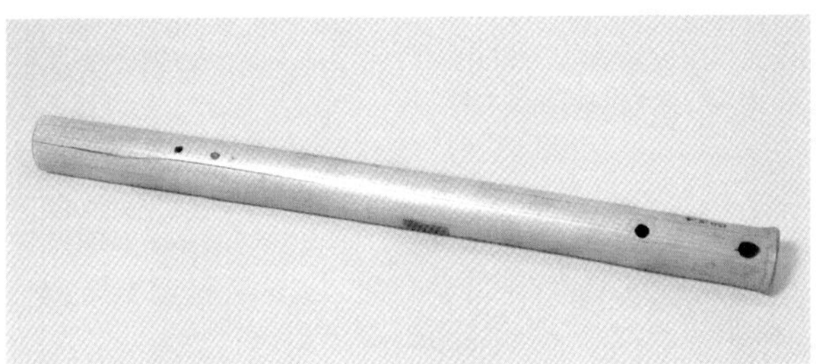

A Vivo, a nose flute collected in Tahiti on the first voyage. (Banks Collection, Pitt Rivers Museum, Oxford)

with the voyages were Philip Brotherson, a drummer and violinist, and the bagpipers Archibald McVicar and Thomas McDonald.

In keeping with a centuries-old tradition of using musicians at sea, Cook was instructed by the President of the Royal Society that indigenous people should be 'entertained near the Shore with a soft Air,' rather than frightened by the sound of guns, drums or trumpets. The Admiralty too instructed bagpipers, fife and fiddle players to be trained and dispatched on Cook's ships bound for 'making Discoveries'. This suggests that music was part of the official conception of the Cook voyages and that music, like gift-exchange and trade, was seen as a means of facilitating cross-cultural contact. Various groups of Pacific islanders performed on behalf of the voyagers and the naturalist Johann Reinhold Forster reported that the Tahitians composed topical songs that referred to the arrival of Cook's men. The seamen and supernumeraries reciprocated with songs of their own, and Cook had the bagpipes performed to a mixed reception in New Zealand, Tahiti and Tonga. Within a short time of Cook's visits, such instances of cross-cultural musical exchange gave rise to the assimilation of European forms such as the hornpipe.

The Cook voyages generated some of the earliest ethnomusicological reflection on the Pacific. Cook, the naturalists Anders Sparrman and Georg Forster, the astronomer William Wales, and Lieutenant James Burney all reflected on indigenous music-making. While this commentary did not give a particularly detailed account of non-European music, it did provide some of the first European accounts of certain musical instruments and practices, and included transcriptions of Māori and Tongan music. These reports were particularly significant because they demonstrated that harmony was not an exclusively European invention, as was believed at the time. Such observations about the 'complexity' of indigenous music complicated the common hierarchical ordering of Pacific peoples according to somatic and social criteria. Cook's artists, in particular John Webber, depicted numerous examples of musical instruments and music-making in Polynesia, including the nose flute (vivo), conch trumpet (pū), drums (pahu) and panpipes (mimiha). Webber's depiction of the 'night dance' is noteworthy because it is one of the few visual representations to show 'ceremonial' music-making within the context of voyager-islander encounters.

By Vanessa Agnew

See Also: Ethnographic results of Cook's voyages

Music, Cook in

In 1970 RCA Australia released a record, *James Cook's First Voyage around the World, HM Bark Endeavour, 1768-1771*, featuring shanties and pieces about Cook from a group called 'Black plus red'. It is one of a very small number of recordings that have been issued for Cook. Only a small number of pieces of music have been written for or about Cook though they have appeared in a variety of forms. Performances appear to have been extremely limited.

As early as 1785, William Shield set to music the words of J O'Keefe for the pantomime, *Omai, or, a trip around the world,* which used Mai and other characters from the Pacific to tell the story of Cook's voyages. J Devlin produced *The Captain Cook march* in Australia about 1900 as piece of stirring nationalistic music while George M Cohan wrote *If Captain Cook should come to life* in 1906 as part of the musical *The Girl behind the counter.*

Other works include: Jim Parker, *All aboard: a musical voyage with Captain Cook* (1983); Gilbert Vinter, *James Cook - circumnavigator* (1969 - brass band music); Bo Lawergren, *Captain Cook: a chamber opera in 3 scenes* (1978); David Farquhar, *O Captain Cook!: musical based on Giradoux play*; George Dreyfus, *Reflections in a glass-house: an image of Captain James Cook for speaker, children's chorus and orchestra* (1972); and Anne Boyd, *The Death of Captain Cook: an oratorio for soprano, tenor, baritone, three small choirs, large chorus and orchestra* (1978).

Andrew Cantrill and the Orpheus Choir in Wellington, New Zealand, commissioned John Psathas to write a musical work for the choir's 50th birthday. His *Orpheus in Rarohenga* received its premiere in 2002. The libretto, which used Cook as a theme, was by Robert Sullivan and later appeared as a poem.

Nan Kivell, Sir Rex (1898–1977)

Nan Kivell was born on 8 April 1898 in Christchurch, New Zealand. He was born Reginald Nankivell. He served in the First World War, mostly in England and not seeing action as he later claimed. In fact, his service was undistinguished and he was disciplined on several occasions.

After the war, he created a new persona, changing his name to Rex de Charembac Nan Kivell, and inventing a false past for himself. He stayed on in Britain and began to visit galleries and exhibitions, and to collect books, manuscripts, maps, paintings and the like, concentrating on material relating to the European exploration, discovery and colonisation of Australia, New Zealand and the Pacific.

In 1925, he joined the Redfern Gallery in London and by 1931 was its managing director. He remained associated with the gallery until his death. His personal collection grew to over 14,000 items and, in 1946, Nan Kivell negotiated with the Commonwealth National Library in Canberra to take charge of it in return for unlimited public access. Eventually, in 1959, the collection was purchased. The National Library of Australia (as it became) now possesses one the best collections of material relating to Cook in the world, largely based on the Nan Kivell material.

In 1976, the Australian Government bestowed a knighthood on Nan Kivell for services to the Arts. He died on 7 June 1977 in London, never having visited Australia or having returned to New Zealand.

See Also: Libraries and archives, Museums

Native Americans

Cook met Native Americans on both coasts of North America. In Eastern Canada he met them in Nova Scotia while serving there as master on the *Northumberland* and afterwards in Newfoundland when he was surveying there. Later, he encountered them as he sailed up the Canadian and Alaskan coasts looking for the Northwest Passage.

When Cook arrived in Newfoundland in the 1760s, two groups of Native Americans were living on the island. The Beothuk were the indigenous people of the island. They were Algonkian-speaking hunter-gatherers but at the time of European contact their numbers were much reduced and they had moved inland from the coast. There is no direct evidence from Cook's logs that he met Beothuk. In 1768, the governor, Hugh Palliser, attempted to make contact with the Beothuks and to draw them into a peaceful relationship but without success. Unfortunately, this increased concern about the welfare of the Beothuk would have little real effect and they became extinct.

Cook possibly had some contact with Inuit when he visited the Labrador coast to chart Chateau Bay in 1763. Another group, the Mi‘kmaq had only moved into south-western Newfoundland from Nova Scotia in about the sixteenth century. During the war, the Mi‘kmaq sided with the French so when the French were defeated in 1763, the Mi‘kmaq in Newfoundland were regarded with suspicion by British authorities. Cook encountered them in 1768 in St George's Bay. This and encounters he may have had with other Mi‘kmaq in Nova Scotia were only brief but probably represent his first contact with non-European people.

Over the next ten years, Cook had extensive contact with Pacific people and met Americans only briefly on two visits to Tierra del Fuego. In 1778 when he entered Nootka Sound on the Canadian west coast he met North Americans once more. People had been living on the north-west coast for about 12,000 years. Their ancestors had travelled from Asia and crossed into North America in the Bering Strait region, possibly at a time when there was a land bridge. Over thousands of years they spread and diversified to occupy most corners of the American continents. Several broad ethnic and linguistic groupings developed, with each of these broad groupings comprising a number of tribes. Over several months in 1778, Cook encountered members of three groups.

The first group Cook met were members of the Northwest Coast people, who occupy the coastal mainland and offshore islands from Washington in the

A Man of the island of Unalaschka (Unalaska, the island at the western end of the Alaskan peninsula). Engraved by J Colyer after Ellis. (Ellis 1782 II fp 45)

south as far north as Yakutat Bay in Alaska. At Nootka Sound on Vancouver Island, Cook met members of the Mowachaht and Muchalaht peoples of the Nuu Chuh Chah. Their culture was based on whaling and fishing. The Spanish had made a very brief visit in 1774, but Cook's ships were the first to enter the Sound and have prolonged contact. On their arrival, over 30 canoes full of local people paddled around the ships and trading for animal skins, especially those of the sea otter, began immediately. Cook quickly realised that the people were not Polynesian but Native Americans. Communication was difficult but gradually some was established and Surgeon Anderson produced a vocabulary of the local language. Cook visited Yuquot in Friendly Cove where he met Chief Maquinna, the leader of the Nootka people. A detailed description of the Nootkans was produced. The British visit to Nootka Sound had a profound effect as news of the sea otter skins obtained at Nootka and its suitability as a base soon sparked the fur trade. From 1785, Nootka was host to many European and American fur traders, and the local people's way of life was changed for ever.

Cook sailed north and met more Native Americans in Alaska. Their dress, their canoes or kayaks, and small language and cultural differences all suggested they were different from the Nootka people to the south. In Cook Inlet, Cook met members of the second grouping on this coast. The Subarctic or Athabascan tribes occupy inland Alaska and Canada but also live at Cook Inlet and on parts of the Kenai Peninsula. The Dena'ina (Tanaina) are one of the few Athabascan tribes that live close to the sea. Cook had very brief contact with them near present-day Anchorage in the upper part of Cook Inlet.

The third of the groupings were the Eskimo-Aleuts who occupy most of Alaska and the Aleutian Islands. The Eskimo-Aleuts themselves comprise several sub-groups and it was members of the Pacific Eskimo (Alutiiq or Sugpiaq) whom Cook met first. They inhabit Prince William Sound, Kodiak Island and the eastern end of the Alaskan Peninsula. Several names are applied to these people. Anthropologists have used the term Pacific Eskimo to show the relationship to the broader grouping, Eskimo. Another name is Alutiiq, which is derived from the name Aleuts used for these people (interestingly, Alutiiq was the source of the name Aleut). The third name is Sugpiaq, the name the people call themselves. Two distinct sub-groups of the Sugpiaq are recognised Chugach and Koniag. Entering Prince William Sound, Cook anchored in Snug Corner Bay where he traded with Chugach people. Moving on, Cook met Koniag near the mouth of Cook Inlet and possibly saw them again on Kodiak Island and the Alaskan Peninsula.

The Unangan or Aleut are the native people of the Aleutian chain of islands stretching across the North Pacific Ocean between Alaska and Kamchatka. They also live on the western end of the Alaskan Peninsula. The name Aleut itself is not of Aleut origin. It was introduced by Russian explorers and fur traders who conquered the Aleutian Islands from 1745. The people's historic and traditional name for themselves is Unangan, probably derived from una, which refers to the seaside. Prior to the coming of the Russians, the Unangans lived on the wildlife of the sea and some food gathering. The Russians had begun a process of enslaving the Unangans to provide furs for them. When Cook arrived in the Aleutians, he met Unangans at the

Shumagin and Sanak Islands and at Unalaska. Contact was brief but Cook wrote a detailed description of the Unangans he met at Unalaska.

The final group that Cook met were the Eskimo of the Bering Sea and Strait where several sub-groups were spread over a huge area. Cook only went ashore on a few occasions but saw evidence of these peoples on shore. Opportunities for contact were limited but he met some Mainland Eskimo near Cape Newenham on 21 July 1778 and in September met some Bering Strait Eskimo in Norton Sound.

In the Arctic region, Cook also had contact with another group of people, who were not Native Americans. These were the Chukchi, a Siberian people who came to live on the Asian side of the Bering Sea later than the Eskimo. Cook put in for three hours at St Lawrence (Lavrentiia) Bay on the Chukotskiy peninsula. He noted differences with Americans and remarked that 'these...appeared to be quite a different Nation'.

Cook and his men collected artefacts from the Northwest Coast while the descriptions written and John Webber's paintings provide one of the earliest sources of information about all these peoples.

SEE ALSO: Alaska, Indigenous peoples and Cook, Nootka Sound

Nautical Almanac

Nevil Maskelyne, the fifth Astronomer Royal, proposed and helped create the *Nautical Almanac.* Under an Act of Longitude in 1765, the Board of Longitude was instructed to produce a *Nautical Almanac*. Maskelyne lost no time in drawing up plans for the ephemeris, which he presented on 30 May 1765 and which were approved by the board. The *Nautical Almanac and Astronomical Ephemeris*, known familiarly as the *Nautical Almanac*, was to be published annually giving data relating to a particular year. The main purpose of the *Almanac* was to simplify finding longitude at sea and hence it contained tables of lunar distances tabulated for every three hours of every day. It also contained other astronomical data of use to both the navigator and the astronomer.

It was divided into four sections: The preface explained the rationale behind the *Nautical Almanac* and indicated which tables had been used in its preparation. Next came a page containing a key to the symbols used in the almanac, a list of the expected eclipses of the year, and other astronomical data. The third section contained the ephemeris for each month of the year and the last section explained what the tables contained and how they could be used in practice, often with examples. The tables for any particular month were given in 12 pages. This format remained largely unchanged until 1834 and was a testament to Maskelyne's practical experience of both astronomy and observing and calculating at sea.

To produce the *Almanac,* Maskelyne needed people who could perform astronomical calculations under his supervision. In June 1765, Israel Lyons and George Witchell were appointed as computers and later John Mapson and William Wales were also chosen. The computers were expected to carry out the work in their own homes. Wales, who would later accompany Cook on the second voyage, continued computing at Hudson Bay when he went there to observe the Transit of Venus in 1769.

The first *Nautical Almanac* was published in January 1767 and gave data for that same year. Subsequently, the *Almanac* was computed and published sufficiently in advance to be useful to sailors on long voyages. For example, on his first voyage of exploration, Cook was able to take with him only the *Nautical Almanacs* for 1768 and 1769, but on his second voyage he was able to take with him the editions for 1772, 1773, 1774, and the few sheets of 1775 that were ready. Maskelyne edited 49 editions of the *Nautical Almanac* covering the years 1767 to 1816.

SEE ALSO: Astronomical results of Cook's voyages, Maskelyne (Nevil)

Navigation

The term navigation describes the ability to determine and plan a ship's position and course by means of geometry, nautical astronomy, and instruments, and being able to sail the ship on open water from Point A to Point B. Most sea journeys in the early days of European sailing were made close to land so that bearings could be made to establish the ship's position. As voyages became longer, involving passages across oceans out of sight of land, it became vital to develop navigational skills in order to fix position. Through the seventeenth and eighteenth centuries, huge improvements were made in navigational instruments. Other developments took place in the understanding of scientific principals underlying navigation, especially in astronomy.

An integral part of navigation was the use of charts. For known regions, existing charts were indispensable, provided they were correct. For new regions, fixing and recording positions and the preparation of charts was crucial. In Cook's time, navigation duties rested with the ship's master but Cook's background ensured that on his Pacific voyages he retained a direct interest. The charts of the Pacific were among the most important outcomes of Cook's voyages and helped future navigators.

For many years, long voyages were hit and miss. Compasses gave ships an idea of the direction they were sailing and the distance sailed was calculated after estimating the ship's speed using a log, and taking into account the wind's speed and direction. This was dead reckoning and details of speed, sailing course, wind direction and strength would be regularly recorded. Traverse tables would be used so that the ships net change in latitude and longitude could be calculated. At the end of 24 hours, usually at noon, the results were summarised in the ship's record book or log. This provided the net change over the day.

A ship's position involved two components. The distance north or south of the equator was the latitude, which was relatively easy to measure by Cook's time. The astrolabe had given way in turn to the back-staff, quadrant and sextant, which enabled angles to be measured accurately and thus allowed for a more precise determination of latitude. The other component was longitude. The British had selected Greenwich as the prime meridian and the longitude of any other location was its difference east or west of Greenwich. However, in the mid-eighteenth century, measurement of longitude was still difficult.

Marine chronometers were developed in the eighteenth century, which allowed navigators to compare local time with that on an accurate chronometer, keeping the time at a known point, usually Greenwich, and, from the difference, the navigator could determine his longitude. An alternative method used astronomical observations. The sun, moon, planets and stars had long been used for navigation but the development of lunar tables allowed more calculations to be made of longitude. The ease of use and accuracy of the chronometers saw them displace the lunar table method and become the accepted method of determining longitude.

SEE ALSO: Astronomical results of Cook's voyages, Seamanship, Surveys and running surveys

Navy Board

The Navy Board oversaw the administrative affairs of the Navy, while subordinate to the Admiralty. Various departments carried out the day-to-day activities of operation including supervision of shipbuilding and repair, the purchase of ships, the purchase of naval stores and the administration of the dockyards. The control of naval expenditure fell under its control. Other activities were looked after by related boards such as the Victualling Board and the Sick and Hurt Board but the Navy Board oversaw their financial control.

By the late eighteenth century, the Navy Board comprised the Controller (sometimes spelled Comptroller), the Surveyor, the Clerk of the Acts, and the Controllers of the Treasurer's, Victualling and Storekeepers' Accounts. The Controller was the senior naval officer represented on the Board and was usually in charge. George Cockburn and Cook's friend, Hugh Palliser, were the Controller through most of Cook's career. The Surveyor, who amongst other duties designed ships, was usually a master shipwright and Thomas Slade occupied the position from 1755 until 1771. All the other positions were invariably occupied by civilians.

It was the Navy Board that acquired and arranged the fitting out of Cook's ships through the naval dockyards. While officers at the yards were appointed by the Board of Admiralty, the yards were under the administration of the Navy Board, represented at the yard by a resident commissioner. Another junior official that Cook had regular dealings with was the Clerk of the Cheque. All ships' captains were required to maintain muster rolls listing their crews and this official would check the records on return to British ports.

SEE ALSO: Admiralty, Dockyards, Royal Navy

New Caledonia

New Caledonia (21° 30' S, 166° 30' E) is a series of islands in the Southwest Pacific Ocean just north of the Tropic of Capricorn. Grande Terre is by far the largest island, accounting for 85 per cent of the total land area of 7334 square miles (19,060 sq km). It runs 248.5 miles (400km) north-west to south-east with a central mountain range, which reaches 5250ft (1600m) in height.

The people of New Caledonia are Melanesian, who first arrived on the island from Vanuatu in about 1500 BC. These original people developed the Lapita pottery and culture that spread to other parts of the Pacific. The Melanesian people now call themselves Kanaks and their country Kanaky, though it remains French territory.

*A New Caledonian night heron (*Nycticorax caledonicus*) (annotated* 'Aredea ferruginea'*) drawn by George Forster on the second voyage. (Natural History Museum)*

The name New Caledonia was given by Cook when he landed on Grande Terre in September 1774. The coast apparently reminded him of Scotland, Caledonia being an ancient name for part of Scotland. Cook was the first known European visitor when he anchored at Balade on the north-west coast, staying there for eight days. Relations between the British and local people were good though communication was difficult. Forster compiled a short vocabulary. Cook then sailed slowly south and rounded the Île des Pins (Cook's Isle of Pines), being intrigued by the tower-like trees that could be seen on shore. He anchored at Amere (Botany) Island and the botanists examined the trees, now called the New Caledonia Pine (*Araucaria columnaris cooki*). Cook left on 1 October 1774.

SEE ALSO: Melanesia, Second voyage

New Zealand

New Zealand (41° S, 174° E) comprises a group of isolated islands in the Southwest Pacific, 2000km (1243 miles) east of Australia. Two of the islands, Te Ika a Maui (North Island) and Te Wai Pounamu (South Island) make up the majority of its 103,378 square miles (268,680 sq km). The long isolation (about 80 million years) of New Zealand has allowed a unique environment and fauna and flora to evolve. The total absence of land mammals and the presence of only a small number of reptiles left birds with few predators. Many became flightless but suffered when man finally arrived at the islands and began hunting them.

The islands were one of the last sizeable land-masses to be inhabited by man. Polynesians discovered the islands about AD 1000 and, through a succession of visits by canoe, settled the country. These people, who later became known as Māori, developed their own culture over the next 800 years. The Māori's exclusive tenure of Aotearoa, as they called New Zealand, was interrupted by the arrival of Europeans. Abel Tasman led a Dutch expedition, which arrived in late 1642. Tasman sailed up the west coast and met Māori in what is now called Golden Bay. A fight resulted. Tasman sailed on without ever setting foot on what he called Staten Landt (it was later changed to Nieuw Zeelandt by Dutch mapmakers). It is possible that Spanish, Portuguese, Chinese and Malay ships also visited before James Cook reached New Zealand in 1769. Over the next five months, Cook circumnavigated the islands and, after carrying out a running survey with only a few landings, produced a chart of exceptional quality and accuracy. The British later annexed and colonised New Zealand.

Cook and the *Endeavour* made landfall on 8 October 1769 at Turanganui a Kiwa, a location now also called Poverty Bay. Cook and a party landed near the mouth of Turanganui River (the site of Gisborne) where they

River Thames and Mercury Bay in New Zealand. Engraved after Cook and Smith. (Hawkesworth II fp 323)

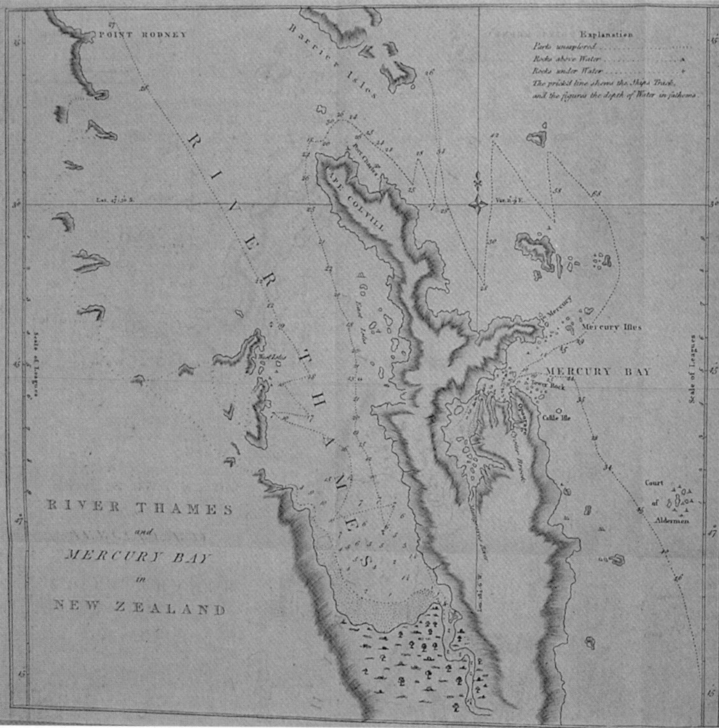

A View in Queen Charlottes Sound, New Zealand, by John Webber. This was published in 1809 by Boydell as part of Views in the South Seas. *It shows Māori at the British camp at Ship Cove. (National Library of Australia, NK4120)*

met local Māori. It was realised that Tupaia, the Raiatean on board, could converse with them but, even so, misunderstandings arose and some Māori were killed. Over the next six months Cook circumnavigated New Zealand, showing it to be islands and not part of the Southern Continent. He made landings at several locations (Anaura Bay, Tolaga Bay, Mercury Bay, Firth of Thames and the Bay of Islands) as he sailed around Te Ika a Maui. On 14 January 1770, Cook entered a large inlet hoping to find a safe harbour. The inlet was Totaranui or, as Cook called it, Queen Charlotte Sound. The *Endeavour* was towed into Ship Cove (Meretoto) where Cook remained for three weeks.

Queen Charlotte Sound was discovered to be part of Te Wai Pounamu and Cook set off to investigate this island. He sailed between the two large islands through the strait that Banks called Cook Strait. The *Endeavour* sailed around Te Wai Pounamu without landing. Cook made two rare mistakes during this passage. He saw land which he called Banks' Island though it is really a peninsula. A few days later, he made his second mistake when he did not realise Stewart Island was an island, separated from Te Wai Pounamu by the Foveaux Strait. On the west coast, Banks, who had not been ashore for several weeks, tried to persuade Cook to enter one of the fiords but Cook refused being unsure whether they would be able to sail out again. Cook had circled Te Wai Pounamu when he anchored in Admiralty Bay off D'Urville Island. Cook left New Zealand on 31 March 1770, heading west into the Tasman Sea.

Cook returned to New Zealand on his second voyage. On 26 March 1773, Cook brought the *Resolution* into Dusky Sound on the west coast of Te Wai Pounamu after being separated from the *Adventure,* the companion vessel. It was one of the inlets he had refused to take Banks into three years earlier. The British had been in Antarctic waters and needed somewhere to recover. After six weeks, Cook was ready and on 11 May he sailed back out into the open sea and north up the coast. He entered Queen Charlotte Sound and was relieved to find the *Adventure* safely anchored in Ship Cove. Cook was not about to sit idly over the winter months and gave instructions to prepare for a sweep of the Central Pacific. The reunited *Resolution* and *Adventure* set sail on 7 June.

The ships returned to New Zealand in October 1773 but, off Cape Palliser, gales separated them again. The *Resolution* made it into Queen Charlotte Sound on 3 November and waited for the *Adventure*, which did not appear. Cook remained in the sound for three weeks but by 25 November the *Resolution* was ready and Cook could not wait any longer. He sailed for the Antarctic again. Meanwhile, the *Adventure* had spent several days buffeted by gales before being blown well to the north where it put into Tolaga Bay. Finally, on 30 November, the *Adventure* reached Queen Charlotte Sound to find the *Resolution* had already departed. On 17 December, Furneaux sent the cutter, manned by 11 men, to cut fresh greens but it did not return. A search party found remains of the cutter and, more ominously, remains of the cutter's crew at Whareunga Bay (Grass Cove). Furneaux, hearing the news, decided to leave and set off for Britain on 23 December 1773. Cook made his third visit to New Zealand during the second voyage on 18 October 1774. He anchored in Queen Charlotte Sound where he found evidence that the *Adventure* had been there since the *Resolution*'s previous visit. Cook met local Māori from whom he heard stories, some contradictory, about killings and sinking ships. The Māori themselves were nervous. Cook sailed on 10 November, this time across the Pacific, heading for Britain and home.

On the third voyage in 1777, Cook made his final visit to New Zealand. The *Resolution* and the *Discovery* crossed the Tasman Sea after a short visit to Tasmania. Rocks Point on the west coast of Te Wai Pounamu was sighted on 10 February and the ships sailed round Cape Farewell to anchor in Queen Charlotte Sound on the 12th. Local Māori visited the ships but were very wary. The attack carried out at Grass Cove on some of the *Adventure*'s crew in 1773 was in everyone's mind. Cook's crew, Mai, the Raiatean on board, and the Māori all expected Cook to retaliate or extract 'utu' (the Māori term). However, he surprised them all by doing nothing except entertaining Kahura, the local chief suspected of leading the attack. Cook departed on 24 February 1777, sailing from New Zealand for the last time.

Cook liked New Zealand and respected the Māori. He saw the value of Queen Charlotte Sound as a base where he could repair his ships, restock them, and rest his crew. Ship Cove became a second home. Cook returned to New Zealand four times and spent over 300 days either ashore or in New Zealand waters. Cook's relations with the Māori were complex. He made every effort to avoid bloodshed and yet Māori were killed on several occasions. The worst incidents took place during the *Endeavour* voyage, especially shortly after arriving in Poverty Bay when the two sides were still unsure of each other. The British possessed firearms, making them more powerful than Māori, who would always come off worse in any confrontation. Cook, though, developed a contact policy, which allowed his crew to perform their duties with minimal impact on Māori. To this end Cook severely punished members of his crew who knowingly stole from the Māori or interfered with their material possessions. Through the logs and journals of Cook and other members of the voyages, New Zealand and its people were extensively described at the time of contact. Added to which, the paintings of Parkinson, Hodges and Webber, and Cook's own charts have produced a detailed visual record. The result is a carefully documented and detailed body of work, which has kept researchers busy ever since.

Early in the twenty-first century, Cook occupies a confused position in New Zealand. The euphoria at the time of the 200th anniversary of his visit in 1769 has gone. Many memorials remain from that time but Cook's role in New Zealand has been downplayed. Until that time, New Zealand history was largely European. It was also short and, in a search for heroes, Cook had been an obvious choice. Since the 1980s, however, at academic and government level, the emphasis has been more on the events since colonisation and more recognition has been shown to Māori history. Cook and other elements of earlier British history have been largely erased. A Government-sponsored Historical Atlas deemed, in 1997, that Cook did not hold a sufficiently important place in New Zealand's history for his achievements to be featured. A similar attitude is held by the major museums, which rarely mention Cook or display material related to his voyages.

At a more general level, Cook still receives a high level of interest. The *Endeavour* replica has drawn large crowds on its visits while many towns have streets named after him. Everywhere there are schools, public houses and products, including wine, that have used his name and the *Endeavour* still adorns the 50 cent coins. It is fitting that Cook's foremost scholar and biographer has been J C Beaglehole, a New Zealander. The map of New Zealand is proof of Cook's impact on the country; still carrying many names bestowed by him or in his honour.

See Also: First voyage, Māori, Second and Third voyages

Newfoundland

The island of Newfoundland (49° N, 56° W) is situated off the east coast of the Canada. It is separated by the Strait of Belle Isle and the Gulf of St Lawrence River from the mainland. The island is triangular-shaped with an area of 43,093 square miles (112,000 sq km). Its coastline is convoluted and stretches over more than 10,500 miles (17,000km). Newfoundland only joined Canada in 1949.

The first inhabitants were the now extinct Beothuk people. Other Native Americans, the Mi'kmaq, crossed over from Cape Breton Island in the eighteenth century. The first Europeans to visit Newfoundland were Norsemen, who arrived in the late tenth century. In 1497, John Cabot landed on the island and claimed it for Henry VII of England. Other Europeans, mainly Basques, Portuguese, British and French, followed from about the sixteenth century to exploit the nearby rich fishing grounds on the Grand Banks. The British and French fought over Newfoundland during the 1600s and 1700s. In 1662, France established a fort and colony at Placentia while the British were based at St John's.

James Cook was based in Halifax, Nova Scotia, in August 1762 when news reached the port that the French had captured St John's, the capital of Newfoundland. His ship, HMS *Northumberland*, under Captain Lord Colvill, sailed to Placentia on the west side of the Avalon Peninsula to rendezvous with other forces, prior to recapturing the island. Cook prepared

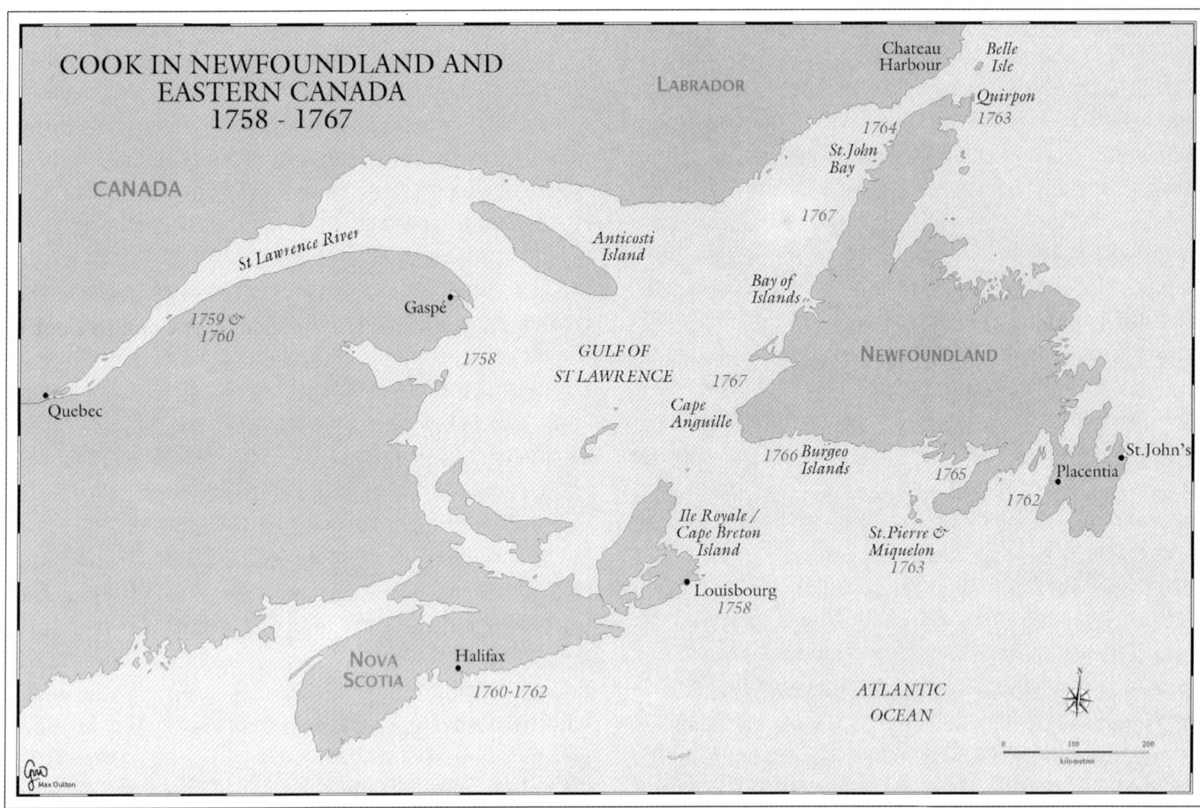

charts there. The small fleet then sailed round to Cape Spear. St John's was quickly retaken and Cook set about making surveys and charts of Carbonnear and St John's harbour. In October 1762, Cook and the *Northumberland* left Newfoundland for London. The Treaty of Paris was signed in February 1763, in which France retained the islands of St Pierre and Miquelon, off the south coast of Newfoundland, but gave up all other claims to Canada. The Governor of Newfoundland, Thomas Graves, realised the need to have good charts of the coast, including the islands about to be passed back to France. Cook was the ideal choice to carry out the surveys and so, in May 1763, he accompanied Graves back to Newfoundland aboard the *Antelope*.

Cook transferred to HMS *Tweed* under Captain Douglas and, in less than two months, completed the survey of St Pierre and Miquelon, which were handed over to the French Governor. Cook transferred to St John's where Governor Graves had a schooner, the *Grenville*, ready for him to begin his surveys of the Newfoundland coast. Graves first dispatched Cook north to Petit-Nord (the Northern Peninsula), part of an area known as the French Shore. In September and October 1763, Cook charted the harbours of Croque, Noddy and Quirpon as well as Chateau Bay on the nearby Labrador coast before heading back to St John's and on to London. Cook spent the winter drawing up his charts and plans.

Cook had begun what would be a regular schedule for the next few years: sail to Newfoundland in April; spend until October surveying; and return to London for the winter to produce final versions of the charts and associated sailing instructions and descriptions. Hugh Palliser, Cook's Captain on the *Eagle*, replaced Graves as Governor of Newfoundland in 1764. He and Cook sailed together on the *Lark* in May 1764 for St John's.

Cook collected the *Grenville* and sailed back up to Petit-Nord to resume surveying near Quirpon. He worked his way meticulously along the coast past Cape Onion, Pistolet Bay and Cape Norman as far as Pointe Ferolle before turning back in October. In August, Cook had an accident at Unfortunate Cove when a powder horn exploded damaging his hand (it was the scars from this injury that helped identify his remains after his death in Hawaii in 1779). Cook was rushed to Noddy Bay for treatment.

In 1765, Cook, instead of continuing where he left

off in 1764, was directed to the south of Newfoundland. The British were concerned about renewed French activity out of their base at St Pierre and Miquelon. In June, Cook began surveying at St Lawrence on the Burin Peninsula and proceeded round the Peninsula into Fortune Bay. The *Grenville* ran aground in Long Harbour at the head of Fortune Bay and needed repairs. Cook carefully sailed the brig into Bay d'Espoir (Despair Bay) where repairs were carried out. He then sailed for London.

Cook crossed the Atlantic in 1766 to Bonne Bay, next to Bay d'Espoir where he had finished the previous year. He continued to survey west along the South Coast to Cape Ray and Cape Anguille, the southwest points of the island. Numerous bays were investigated, as were the offshore island groups of Penguin, Ramea and Burgeo. At the Burgeo Islands an auspicious event took place for Cook. Arriving at the islands in fog, it cleared just in time for Cook to observe a solar eclipse, the details of which he wrote up as a paper that Dr John Bevis read to the Royal Society in London in April 1767. In this way Cook's name was brought to the attention of the Royal Society, the body that would be involved with sending the expedition to the South Pacific in 1768. On his way back to London Cook called in at St John's where the frigate *Niger* was in port with Joseph Banks (Cook's *Endeavour* passenger) on board. Cook sailed for London.

Cook returned for what would be his last season in Newfoundland in 1767. He began at Cape Anguille in the southwest and worked up the west coast towards Pointe Ferolle (previously charted in 1764), thus filling in the gap on this coast. Cook made his way back down the west coast to the Bay of Islands, where he stayed for a month. He even made a rare trip inland, rowing up the Humber River to Deer Lake. Leaving the Bay in September he sailed via St John's to be in London by November 1767.

Cook did not return to Newfoundland and his assistant, Matthew Lane, completed the survey. Their combined charts were published in 1770. Newfoundland proved a very crucial stage in Cook's career. He developed his surveying and charting skills and learned to record detailed sailing instructions and other useful information. Added to which, his astronomical observations brought him to the attention of important people. Newfoundland offered him the opportunity to develop his leadership skills and realise the need for a healthy and happy crew. Cook had also met local Beothuk and Mi'kmaq people giving him his first experiences of communicating with non-European peoples.

Newfoundland has several features and localities with Cook connections. Cook, though, did not bestow names during his time there. Cook's Harbour at the top of Petit-Nord and Cook's Brook and the Cook Ponds in the Bay of Islands are named for him. There is a memorial to Cook on Crow Hill overlooking the Humber River in the Bay of Islands. A Captain Cook's Trail runs west along the south side of the Humber as far as Bottle Cove near Lark Harbour where a small memorial to Cook marks the end of the trail.

SEE ALSO: Canada

Niue

Niue (19° 02' S, 169° 55' W) is an isolated island in the central South Pacific. It is about 310 miles (500km) east of Tonga and 310 miles (500km) south of American Samoa. The island is a raised coral atoll of 96 square miles (250 sq km). The Niuean people are Polynesian, who first arrived at the island about 1000 years ago, possibly from Tonga or Samoa.

Cook approached the island on 22 June 1774 during the second island sweep on his second voyage. He attempted to land near Tuapa and later near Alofi on the north-west coast. The landing party was thwarted by islanders and Cook decided to sail away. He termed the island 'Savage Island' after the reception given to him.

SEE ALSO: Polynesian diaspora, Second voyage

'Noble Savage'

The term 'Noble Savage' gained prominence in the eighteenth century following the writings of Jean-Jacques Rousseau. In 1756, Rousseau's *The Discourse on Inequality* was published, in which he argued that the happiest state of humankind was a middle state between completely wild and completely civilised, symbolising the innate goodness of one not exposed to the corrupting influences of (western) civilisation. The concept was a highly romanticised one. Attributes of the noble savage supposedly included: living in harmony with nature; innocence; moral courage; physical health; and a lack of sexual inhibitions.

For some of the Europeans who visited Tahiti in the eighteenth century, the island represented a form of paradise and its inhabitants were the epitome of the noble savage as described by Rousseau. The reports of men such as Philibert Commerson (naturalist on

Bougainville's voyage) and Joseph Banks did much to perpetuate the idea of the Noble Savage, though Cook and Bougainville were far more prosaic in their descriptions. The concept was very much in the eye of the beholder and the act of contact soon removed any innocence that may have existed before.

Two Tahitians did much to keep the Noble Savage debate going when they accompanied ships returning to Europe, thereby providing society there with examples to inspect first hand. As Bougainville left Tahiti in April 1768, he was persuaded by the local chief, Ereti, to take his brother, Ahu-toru (Aotourou), away with them. Back in France in March 1769, Bougainville took Ahu-toru to the Court at Versailles and then to Paris. Ahu-toru became an instant celebrity and, having been presented to the King, he was taken under the wing of the Duchesse de Choiseul, who showed him off in Paris society. He was a regular at Versailles and at the Opera and was often seen walking around Paris. In 1770, Ahu-toru set off for home but contracted smallpox in Mauritius and died off Madagascar.

In September 1773, Furneaux, on Cook's second voyage, followed Bougainville's example when he allowed Mai (Omai) on board the *Adventure* at Huahine and took him to Britain. Like Ahu-toru before him Mai was a celebrity, this time in London. Mai was eventually returned to Huahine.

SEE ALSO: Polynesia

Nootka Sound

Nootka Sound (49° 36' N, 126° 37' W) is an inlet located on the west coast of Vancouver Island, British Columbia, itself on the west coast of Canada. The original residents of Nootka Sound were Mowachaht and Muchalaht peoples of the Nuu Chuh Chah. Their culture was based on whaling and fishing. In 1774, the Spanish sailor, Juan Perez, anchored near Estevan Point, south of the mouth of Nootka Sound, where he traded with local people. He did not enter the sound or go ashore but claimed the discovery for Spain.

In 1778, James Cook reached the north-west coast of North America at the start of his search for the Northwest Passage. As he approached land on 29 March 1778, he described a stretch of coast between Point Estevan and Woody Point as Hope Bay (a name no longer used) and steered into an inlet near Point Estevan. Cook's Woody Point was later renamed Cape Cook. It lies on the Brooks Peninsula where there is also a Cape Clerke and a Solander Island.

A woman of Nootka Sound. Engraved by W Sharp after Webber. (Cook & King (Atlas) pl 39)

Cook had left Hawai'i nearly eight weeks before and needed to go ashore for fresh water and to repair the ships. A large inlet near Point Estevan looked suitable and Cook took HMS *Resolution* and HMS *Discovery* in, though a lack of wind necessitated the ships being towed. They were the first European ships to enter the inlet and on the 31st, they anchored in Ship Cove (later Resolution Cove) on Bligh Island. Over 30 canoes full of local people paddled around the ships as they arrived and trading commenced immediately. The local people were selling animal skins, especially those of the sea otter.

For two very wet weeks, the crews worked to replace rigging and masts using timber that was felled from coniferous forests growing down to the water's edge. The local people were, for once, not Polynesian but Native Americans and communication was difficult. Gradually though communication was established and Surgeon Anderson produced a vocabulary of the local language. A mistake was made with the name of the inlet and the people. Cook thought they had replied Nootka (or Nutka) so the inlet became Nootka Sound (Cook called it King George's Sound but the name soon lapsed). It is believed now that they were saying 'itchme nutka', meaning go around as they wanted the British to visit their village at Yuquot. Nootkans continued to visit the ships, serenading the British with music from their canoes.

On 20 April, Cook set off to explore and went first to the village of Yuquot in Friendly Cove near the mouth of the inlet. The British were made very welcome and shown all around the village and into houses. The artist, John Webber, recorded the visit with a series of fine paintings. At Yuquot, Cook met Chief Maquinna, the leader of the Nootka people. From Yuquot, the British rowed up Cook Channel past the Saavedra Islands and across the mouths of the Kendrick and Tahsis Channels. Cook remarked that the trees here were the tallest he had ever seen (they were probably Douglas Firs). They landed at another village where they received a much cooler reception. Continuing on, they realised that they had rounded an island (Bligh Island) against which they were anchored. Midshipman Trevenen accompanied Cook on this trip and recorded some observations: 'We were fond of such excursions, although the labour of them was very great… . Captain Cook also on these occasions would sometimes relax from his almost constant severity of disposition now and then to converse familiarly with us. But it was only for a time; as soon as on board ship he became again the despot'.

On 26 April, after four weeks in the inlet, Cook sailed from Nootka Sound. It would never be the same again as news of the sea otter skins obtained at Nootka and its suitability as a base soon sparked a fur trade. From 1785, Nootka was host to many profit-hungry Europeans and Americans. Friction between the Spanish and the British led to the Nootka Sound Incident in 1789 and nearly brought the two countries to war. Many features in Nootka Sound now carry names associated with people from Cook's visit.

See Also: Native Americans

North Sea and the coal trade

The North Sea is a branch of the North Atlantic Ocean. It separates the British Isles from the coastal countries of continental Europe, namely Norway, Denmark, Germany, the Netherlands, Belgium and France. The North Sea is linked to the Atlantic in the south by the narrow English Channel, but it is open to the ocean in the north. It is approximately 596 miles (960km) north to south and 398 miles (640km) wide, with an area of 221,239 square miles (575,000 sq km). The North Sea was known as the German Ocean until the early twentieth century.

The North Sea coal trade developed to meet the ever-expanding need London had for coal. The South Northumberland coalfield, close to the coast and with good port facilities at the mouth of the River Tyne, was the most suitable to satisfy that need and fleets of ships

Shipping, with perhaps a collier in the foreground, in a calm off Flamborough Head. The seven-mile long promontory, just south of Whitby, was a natural confluence for North Sea merchant ships making their way up and down the East Coast. (Etched and published by Robert Dodd, 1797)

sprang up to transport the coal down the east coast of England to the capital. As early as the thirteenth century coal mining was well established along the Tyne and coal was being shipped to London as early as 1305. By 1378 Newcastle shipped 15,000 tons of coal per year and exported coal to many parts of Europe. The phrase 'Coals to Newcastle', meaning an unnecessary pursuit, was first recorded in 1538. By 1615, 200 ships carried coal to London and another 200 supplied coal to other parts of the country. Newcastle had a virtual monopoly on exporting coal.

Whitby, situated along this trade route, became a major factor in the coal trade. Whitby shipyards built many of the ships used to transport coal. The harsh weather conditions and sandbanks along the coast demanded ships capable of manoeuvrability in shallow water and adverse winds, yet able to carry a large cargo. The shallow-draught collier, known as the cat or bark, was developed. It was this type of vessel that Cook sailed on in his time on the North Sea and the Royal Navy chose the same type for Cook's Pacific voyages. Whitby businessmen, such as John Walker (for whom Cook sailed), owned many of the ships, which were manned by men from the Whitby region.

For Whitby ships, each round-trip could take over a month; a week to load the coal at North Shields, a week to unload at Wapping on the Thames and a week each way sailing along the East Coast. As the weather and conditions in the North Sea could be treacherous, the crew would be given a break of 2–3 months over the winter.

James Cook began sailing on the North Sea in 1747 but it is not known in which ships he sailed during his first year. In 1747, a new Act of Parliament was passed that decreed that all ships must keep Muster Rolls. From that time, therefore, there is a near complete record of the Whitby (and other) vessels on which Cook sailed. Cook is known to have sailed on the *Freelove* (1747–48), the *Three Brothers* (1748–51) and the *Friendship* (1751–55), all owned by the Walkers. After his apprenticeship finished in 1749 he also spent some months on other vessels, the *Mary* and the *Hopewell*.

The coal was delivered to wharves close to the centre of London, affording Cook his introduction to the capital as the colliers sailed up the Thames to discharge the coal at the wharves along the north bank of the river, east of London Bridge. The Walkers dealt with Quaker families in Wapping and Shadwell.

While the majority of Cook's experience was on the Tyne-Thames coal route he also crossed the North Sea to Norway on the *Three Brothers* and he sailed into the Baltic Sea on the *Mary*. This period was crucial in Cook's life as he learned the skills in seamanship that would serve him well in the future. Cook was prepared to study and learn, which obviously impressed Walker so that a lasting friendship developed between the two men. Cook's abilities singled him out and enabled him to progress from seaman to mate and he would have become a master of one of Walker's ships had he not surprised everyone by volunteering for the Royal Navy in 1755.

See Also: Walker (John), Wapping, Whitby

Northumberland, HMS

Cook joined HMS *Northumberland* in late 1759 as master. The vessel had just been designated the flagship of a small squadron under Commodore Alexander, Lord Colvill. Captain William Adams was the ship's captain. While Admiral Charles Saunders took the rest of the fleet back to Britain, Colvill was to take his squadron to Halifax and remain on the North American station.

The *Northumberland* was built at Plymouth Dockyard in 1750. She was a Third Rate of 1414 tons, 160ft 1in by 44ft 11in (48.8m by 13.7m), carried 70 guns, and was the largest ship that Cook would sail on. In 1760, Colvill and the *Northumberland* returned to Quebec to assist General Murray who had been besieged by the French attempting to retake the city. The French finally surrendered Canada in September 1760 and the British ships prepared to retire once more to Halifax. Nicholas Bateman replaced Adams as captain before they left Quebec.

The *Northumberland* stayed in Halifax harbour from October 1760 until August 1762, when she sailed via Placentia to help retake St John's in Newfoundland. After a successful mission, the British fleet sailed from Newfoundland in October and anchored at Spithead. Cook was laid off and went home to get married. The *Northumberland* became a storeship and was renamed *Leviathan* in 1777. She foundered in 1780.

See Also: Canada, Nova Scotia

Northwest Passage

The American continent was rediscovered by Europeans in the late fifteenth century when they were looking for new routes to China and the Indies. No sooner had they found it than they began looking for ways around it, still trying to reach the East. Routes

Resolution *with* Discovery *in the distance, depicted by John Webber in the ice somewhere north of the Bering Strait, probably off Icy Cape, August 1778. (National Maritime Museum, London)*

were established round the south of South America in the sixteenth century but it was felt that a sea route must also exist round the north of the continent. Over the next 300 years various attempts were made to locate what became known as the Northwest Passage but the cold and ice of the frozen lands of northern Canada thwarted them all. The passage, however, remained a most important goal, and the search for the passage continued even though at that time such a route had no commercial value. A route was finally demonstrated between 1903 and 1906 by the Norwegian explorer Roald Amundsen.

The earliest attempts by Frobisher in 1576–78, Davis in 1585–87, Hudson in 1610, and Baffin in 1615, all used the eastern approach between Greenland and Canada. The location and naming of Davis Strait, Hudson Bay and Baffin Island all result from these explorations but none of them came close to finding the passage. Samuel Hearne, a British explorer with the Hudson's Bay Company, went overland in 1771 as far as the mouth of the Coppermine River on the Arctic Ocean. In doing so he effectively demonstrated that there was no short passage to the Pacific. The British government, though, continued to encourage searches for the passage and James Cook was instructed to make an attempt at locating the passage from the Pacific.

The problem was not helped by unsubstantiated or fictitious accounts of sailing through between the Atlantic and the Pacific. Among these were the supposed voyages of Juan de Fuca and Bartholomew de Fonte. The reports of both of these voyages appeared in British publications. In 1625, the popular *Purchas, His Pilgrims* carried the account of a Greek pilot, Apostolos Valerianos, sailing to the north-west coast of America. This man, more commonly known as Juan de Fuca, is supposed in 1592 to have found a large inlet on the North American coast near 50° N, which led to the Northwest Passage. Cartographers believed the story and the feature began appearing on maps. Interestingly, a large strait existed where de Fuca had stated and, when it was eventually identified in 1787, it was called the Strait of Juan de Fuca after him. Juan de Fuca possibly did exist but Bartholomew de Fonte was most probably fiction. His story appeared in London in 1708 in *Memoirs for the curious*. Fonte was supposed to have found the Northwest Passage in 1640. Cartographers gave it credence by including a 'Rio de los Reyes' or 'Fonte's Strait' on their maps at about 55° N.

One of the principal objectives, therefore, for Cook's third voyage was finding the still elusive Northwest Passage. In 1778, Cook left Nootka Sound on Vancouver Island and headed north up the coast. For much of the time he was too far from the coast to see possible openings but he did investigate Prince William Sound and Cook Inlet, which proved not to be the passage. He entered the Arctic Ocean in August 1778 but ice stopped his progress and forced his retreat. Clerke, who had taken over from Cook, tried again in 1779 but with the same negative result. While Cook and Clerke were trying on the west coast, Richard Pickersgill, who had sailed with Cook, was given command of HMS *Lyon* and sent up the Davis Strait, theoretically to meet up with Cook. Pickersgill was forced back by ice at 68° N.

George Vancouver, one of Cook's ablest pupils, demonstrated between 1791 and 1794 in his methodical charting of the Northwest Coast that no passage existed south of 60° N.

SEE ALSO: Alaska, Cook and the geographers

Nova Scotia and Halifax

Nova Scotia (45° N, 64° W), now one of the Maritime Provinces, is a peninsula of mainland Canada, extending into the North Atlantic Ocean. It has an area of 21,349 square miles (55,487 sq km) and extends south-west to north-east for 342 miles (550km). Norsemen may have sailed here but the first recorded contact by Europeans occurred about 1497 when John Cabot visited the region. Mi'kmaq people, had, however, been long-term residents. The French were also early visitors and they and the British would claim and fight over the territory until 1763 when it was finally declared to be British.

In 1605, the French established the first successful European settlement in what is now Canada at Port Royal. The name Arcadia was applied, but to a much larger region. Later, it was modified to Acadia and applied more specifically to the peninsula, but, in 1621, the British renamed it Nova Scotia. Eight years later groups of Scots settled at Charlesfort.

During the War of the Austrian Succession, the French and British again battled over Nova Scotia, with British provincial forces from New England capturing Louisbourg. When Louisbourg was returned to the French at war's end, the British founded Halifax as a fishing port and naval station. In 1749, Edward Cornwallis landed with some 2500 settlers and established the port, naming it after Lord Halifax, the President of the Board of Trade. The harbour, called Chebookt by the Mi'kmaq, became the base for the Royal Navy on the North American station.

The Seven Years War saw more hostilities between France and Britain. James Cook, on the *Pembroke*, was part of the British force, which captured Louisbourg again in 1758, securing Nova Scotia and neighbouring Cape Breton Island. For the next four years, Halifax would be Cook's base. In 1759 and 1760, he went to Quebec but winters and most of 1761 and 1762 were spent in and around Halifax. During this time, Cook mapped and prepared sailing instructions for the harbour and for parts of the southern Nova Scotia coast. There is a memorial to Cook in Fort Needham Park, Halifax.

SEE ALSO: Canada, Louisbourg

O / P

Other Cooks

By a very strange coincidence, three different James Cooks were employed by the Royal Navy on the North America Station in the early 1760s. All of the three were masters at some point and all carried out surveys and drew charts. Two of them, including the famous Cook, may have even met in St John's Harbour, Newfoundland in October 1762.

James Cook #1 is the subject of this Encyclopaedia. From 1759 until 1762, Cook #1 was master of HMS *Northumberland*, the flagship of Alexander, Lord Colvill, based in Halifax, Nova Scotia. During this time Cook surveyed Halifax Harbour and produced sailing instructions for the Nova Scotian coast thereabout. The French attacked Newfoundland in 1762 and Cook was part of the force that went to recapture the island. From then until 1767, Cook #1 was occupied in surveying Newfoundland.

James Cook #2 was commissioned as a lieutenant in 1760. He had been master of HMS *Mercury* but he was now posted to HMS *Gosport*, one of the other ships based in Halifax under Lord Colvill. After the fall of St John's, Captain John Jervis brought the *Gosport* into the harbour and Cook #2 is recorded as having brought communications across to the *Northumberland* where Cook #1 was master. Cook #2 then moved to the West Indies where he took part in actions to carry dispatches across the Yucatan peninsula, which formed the basis of a small book (*Remarks on a Passage from the River Balise, in the Bay of Honduras, to Merida; The Capital of the Province of Jucatan in the Spanish West Indies.* London, 1769). In the 1770s he was back in Britain where he produced a chart of Fowey Harbour in Cornwall, published in 1779. He disappeared from the Navy Lists in 1800.

James Cook #3 is known from three charts published in London in 1766 by Emmanuel Bowen. He arrived at Halifax in October 1762 as master of HMS *Mars*, just weeks after the other two Cooks had left the port. He was based there until April 1763 and used the time to survey Halifax Harbour. On his return to Britain, Cook #3 transferred to the *Alarm* and sailed to Jamaica. In 1764, he was at Port Royal, South Carolina, which he also surveyed. However, in August 1765, he was court-martialled for disobedience (apparently taking too much effort and time on surveying) and he was dismissed in January 1766. Cook #3 returned to America where he had acquired land. He became a land surveyor and several of his plans of the Carolinas and Florida remain. Cook #3, however, disappears from the record in 1776.

Pacific exploration after Cook

Europeans sailing to the Pacific after Cook fell into three broad categories: commercial, religious and scientific. Exploration, *per se*, became less important as, to a certain extent, there was a feeling that Cook had seen all there was to see. The accounts of Cook's voyages had been translated into all the major European languages and his exploits were well known. However, there were still a few gaps to fill on the charts and much to learn about the ocean and its inhabitants.

The first voyages prompted by Cook were purely commercial. The success of sea otter pelt sales in Canton soon caused a rush to the north-west coast. In 1785, James Hanna was the first trader to reach the coast and others soon followed. Many of the traders used Hawai'i as a wintering retreat and played a significant role in events there, including helping Kamehameha gain control of the island group. In 1788, whalers and sealers entered the Pacific and they would make various discoveries over the next 50 years.

1788 was also the year when the First Fleet landed in Botany Bay to establish Britain's first settlement and penal colony. Several of the ships used as transports for that fleet went on to discover islands. Captains Thomas Gilbert and John Marshall discovered the island groups named after them (the Gilberts later became Kiribati).

European governments soon realised the value of sending out scientific expeditions. Ships would undertake hydrographic charting while scientists on board would study the zoology, botany and ethnology of the Pacific. The first of these was led by the

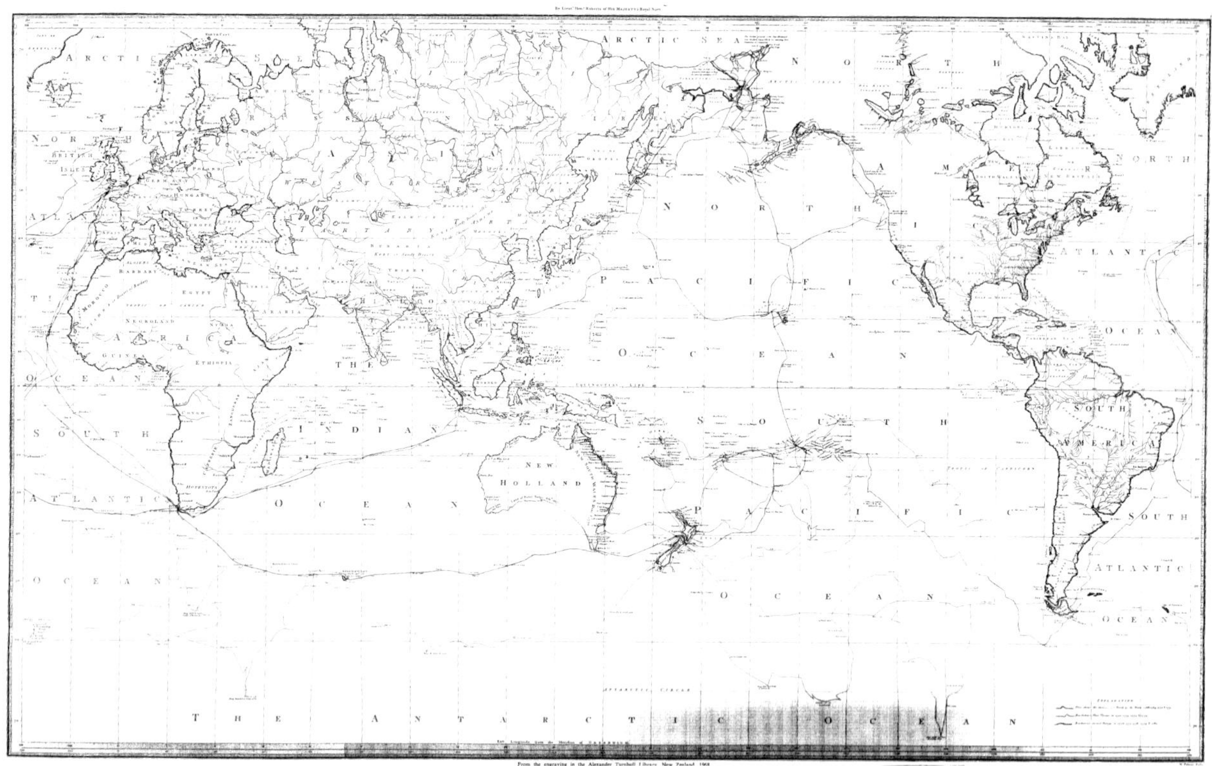

A General Chart exhibiting the discoveries made by Capt. James Cook in this and his preceding Voyages with the Tracks of the ships under his command, by Henry Roberts. Engraved by W Palmer after Roberts. (University of Waikato Map Collection)

Frenchman, Jean-François de Galaup de Lapérouse. Lapérouse was given charge of an expedition in 1785, which proved one of the great voyages of exploration. It ended in tragedy, however, during a hurricane at Vanikoro in the Santa Cruz Group in 1788. In 1791, Bruny d'Entrecasteaux was dispatched to search for Lapérouse. He scoured the south-west Pacific without finding any trace of Lapérouse, though he did fix various islands in New Guinea and New Caledonia. It was not until 1826 that Peter Dillon found evidence on Vanikoro of Lapérouse's demise. In 1789, Fletcher Christian led the mutiny on the *Bounty* in the Tongan Group when William Bligh, the ship's captain, and 17 others were put in a small boat that Bligh managed to sail to Timor. The *Bounty* mutineers settled on Pitcairn Island. Bligh made some discoveries on this voyage and on a later one in 1793.

Two important voyages took place in the 1790s when Malaspina led a Spanish expedition and Vancouver led a British one. Vancouver formed a close friendship with Kamehameha, which led to Hawai'i being placed notionally under British protection. He also charted most of the Northwest Coast of America. Malspina's voyage was more ambitious and covered Alaska, Tonga and Manila. The Spanish had always had priests on board their ships, part of whose role was to convert the islanders. In the 1790s, a new wave of missionaries began to arrive to spread Christianity and James Wilson, in the *Duff*, brought the first missionaries to Tahiti in 1797. Ships transporting missionaries also made island discoveries.

The Russians entered the Pacific in the 1800s when Krusenstern led the first expedition in 1803, followed by Kotzebue (1815), Bellingshausen (1819), Kotzebue (again in 1823), and Litke (1826), who all made significant contributions to knowledge of the Pacific. The French returned to the Pacific in the 1810s and, over the next 30 years, sent many expeditions. The French, like the British, used the early contacts they made to claim territory, many of which remain under French control. Freycinet (1817), Duperrey (1823) and Bougainville (Louis-Antoine's son Hyacinth in 1824) all led successful voyages. Dumont d'Urville was one of the great expedition leaders and he made two very successful voyages, the first in 1825 and the second in 1837. He was the first to use the terms Melanesians and Micronesians to differentiate those people from Polynesians.

The Royal Navy had ignored the Pacific somewhat until Beechey led a lengthy scientific expedition in 1825. This was followed by FitzRoy's voyage in the *Beagle* in 1831 when Charles Darwin was a passenger on board and made the observations, especially in the Galapagos Islands, that led to his work, *On the Origin of Species.* Belcher (1837) and Stanley (1838) continued the British tradition. The 1830s also saw the arrival of Americans. Downes led an American voyage in the *Potomac* in 1831 and Wilkes led the United States Exploring Expedition in 1838 on a three-year voyage.

By 1840, virtually every island in the Pacific had been visited, contact had been made if there were inhabitants, and the island's position plotted exactly on the map. Cook had only left a small number to locate and the map of 1840 bore a strong resemblance to Cook's.

SEE ALSO: France and French reaction to Cook

Pacific exploration before Cook

The first known exploration of the Pacific was undertaken by Austronesian people, who moved east from Southeast Asia, about 4000 BC. They gradually spread to occupy most of the Pacific Islands by AD 1000. The last major landmass to be settled was New Zealand, when people arrived about AD 1200 from the Society Islands far to the north-east. These movements were mostly planned as a sophisticated method of navigation had evolved, which enabled these people to sail back to their starting point.

Asian inroads to the Pacific remain unclear. Sailors from Japan sailed east from Asia and reached America, though whether this was intentional or by accident is not certain. The Chinese fleet of Zheng He may possibly have ventured into parts of the Pacific in the early fifteenth century. Ships from Southeast Asia certainly visited Australia.

Things, though, would change after Europe entered the Pacific in the early sixteenth century, not long after Columbus had reached America. This had prompted the Treaty of Tordesillas, which was signed in 1494 dividing the New World between Portugal and Spain. Portugal received the Moluccas while most of the rest of the, as yet unknown, ocean fell to Spain. The Spanish explorer, Vasco Nuñez de Balboa, crossed the Isthmus of Darien in 1513 and sighted the Pacific from east. He named it the 'South Sea' and claimed it in the name of the King of Spain. The Portuguese navigator, Ferdinand Magellan sailing for Spain on a voyage to find a western passage to the Spice Islands in Indonesia, reached the ocean, which he called the 'Mar Pacifica', the Pacific Ocean. He went on to become the first European to cross the Pacific, reaching Guam in March 1521. Magellan was killed while involved in inter-island fighting in the Philippines. Juan Elcano assumed command and brought the *Victoria* home to Spain in 1522, completing the first circumnavigation of the world. For the next eighty years, the Pacific remained essentially a Spanish preserve. Portugal made a few sorties from the Moluccas to the New Guinea and Micronesia region through Diogo de Rocha in 1525 and Francesco de Castro in 1538.

In the meantime Loaysia (1525), de Saavedra (1527), Grijalva (1537), Lopez de Villalobos (1542), and Gaetan (1543) led voyages across the Pacific. Loaysia's ships were separated as they emerged into the Pacific and one of them, the caravel, *San Lesmes*, which has been called the Lost Caravel, is believed by some to have reached the Tuamotus or even New Zealand. In 1564, Miguel de Legazpi, accompanied by Alonso de Arellano and Andreas de Urdaneta, led an expedition from Mexico in the *San Pedro* and *San Lucas.* He founded the first Spanish settlement in the Philippines at Cebu. De Arellano sailed back to North America becoming the first European to cross the Pacific from west to east. De Urdaneta followed using a similar route and is credited with finding the Galleon route, which allowed Manila Galleons to return to Mexico. The Spanish began their regular sailings of Manila Galleons across the Pacific between Manila and Acapulco in 1593.

Alvaro de Mendaña led the next major expedition when he sailed from Peru in 1567 to find the islands of Solomon. He reached islands in the western Pacific and believing he had found his goal called them the Solomon Islands. In 1595, Mendaña sailed on second voyage from Peru and discovered the Marquesas, before proceeding on to Santa Cruz, where he died. His widow led the expedition on to the Philippines before the navigator, Quiros, brought the expedition back to Peru.

Pedro Fernandez de Quiros led his own expedition from Peru in 1605, looking for a southern continent. He was accompanied by Luis Vaez de Torres. Quiros 'discovered' Espirtu Santo in present-day Vanuatu. The expedition broke up with Quiros returning to Peru. Meanwhile, Torres sailed west through the strait now

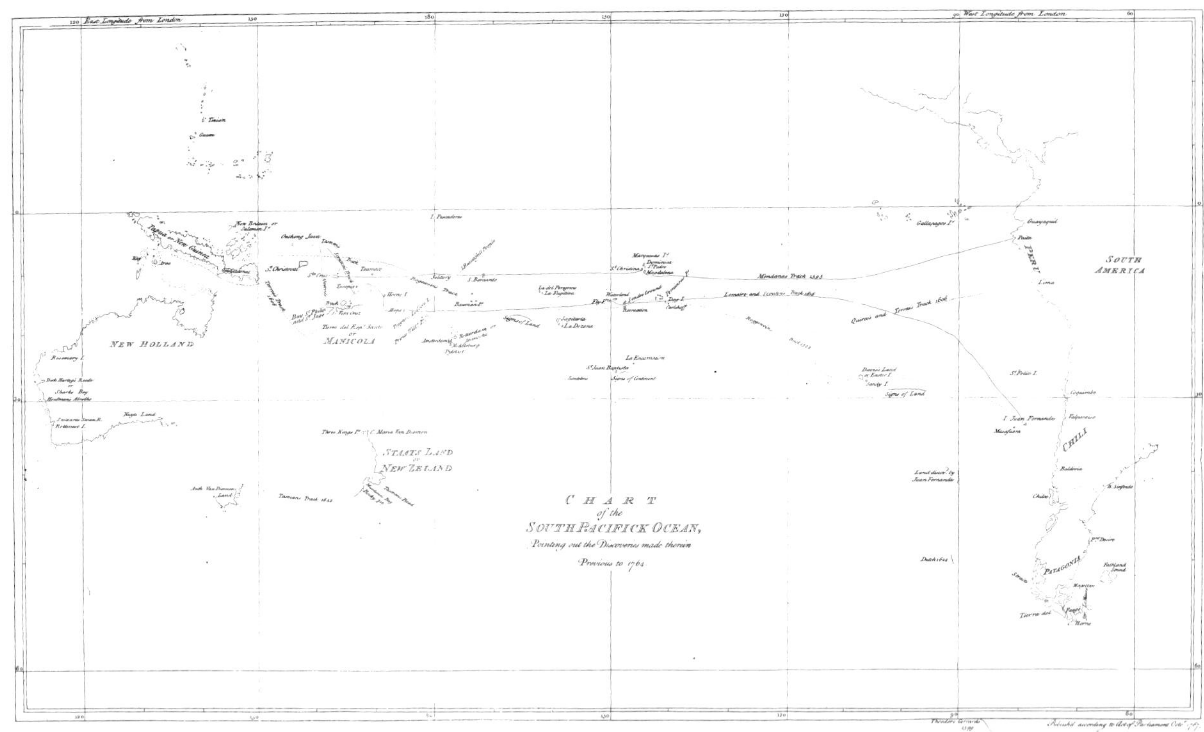

Chart of the South Pacifick Ocean, pointing out the Discoveries made therein previous to 1764. From Dalrymple's An Historical Collection of the several Voyages and Discoveries in the South Pacific Ocean. *(University of Waikato Map Collection)*

bearing his name between New Guinea and Australia in 1606.

Quiros marked the end of Spanish dominance in the Pacific. Many islands had been visited but the inability of early explorers to fix locations precisely meant that the Spanish did not know exactly where some of those islands were. Mendaña had been unable to find the Solomons again. Towards the end of the sixteenth century, the British, in the form of the privateers Francis Drake (1577–80) and Thomas Cavendish (1586–88), entered the Pacific. They were more intent on robbing Spanish galleons than exploring but Drake did make the first British circumnavigation.

The Dutch became the next European power in the Pacific. The Dutch East India Company (VOC), based in Jakarta exerted wide control and sent ships off to explore the possibilities of trade. Their ships visited Japan and New Zealand. Jacques Mahu (1598), Olivier Van Noort (1598), Joris van Silbergen (1614), and Jacob Le Maire and Willelm Schouten (1615) led Dutch expeditions to the Pacific, all representing companies in competition with the VOC. Mahu's expedition was the first Dutch crossing of the Pacific while Van Noort made the first Dutch circumnavigation. Le Maire's voyage was notable for naming Cape Horn at the southern end of South America. In 1642, Abel Tasman led an expedition for the Dutch East India Company in the *Heemskerck* and *Zeehaen*. He was accompanied by the navigator, Visscher. They sailed from Java to Mauruitus, then sailed south of New Holland (later Australia) and reached Tasmania, which was called Van Diemen's Land. They sailed on to become the first Europeans to visit New Zealand, southern Tonga and Fiji.

For about 40 years from 1680 until 1720, British buccaneers patrolled the south-east Pacific. However, like Drake a hundred years earlier, they spent little time exploring. Many of them did keep journals that have been published. They included Charles Swan, Edward Davis, John Clipperton and George Shevlocke. Shevlocke is credited with being one of the sources of Coleridge's poem about the Ancient Mariner. William Dampier was another buccaneer but one with loftier ambitions. He was the first Briton to visit Australia and also explored through New Britain and New Ireland.

Jean-Baptiste Langerie was the first Frenchman of

note in the Pacific. He sailed the *Comtesse de Pontchartrain* across the Pacific in 1715 from China to South America and on to France, becoming the first person to circumnavigate the world from west to east. The Dutch were not quite finished and, in 1722, Jacob Roggeveen, visited Easter Island (Rapa Nui).

Jonathan Swift's novel *Gulliver's Travels* was published in London in 1726. It was partly based on Dampier's journals and events in the Pacific. 1741 marked the entry into the Pacific of Royal Navy vessels, when George Anson's expedition arrived there in the *Centurion*. He was followed by John Byron in the *Dolphin* in 1765. Neither Anson nor Byron found any land of note and Anson continued the British role of plundering Spanish ships. The *Dolphin*, commanded by Samuel Wallis, and accompanied by the *Swallow*, commanded by Carteret, returned to the Pacific in 1767. The two ships separated and the *Swallow* limped very slowly back to Britain. Wallis though made the first visit to Tahiti and returned to Britain in time to inform the Admiralty, who chose it as the location they would use to observe the Transit of Venus.

The French historian, Charles de Brosses wrote his *Histoire des navigations aux terres australes*, which was published in Paris in 1756. It summed up the history of exploration of the Pacific to that time and he was the first to use the terms 'Polynesia' and 'Australasia'. He influenced Alexander Dalrymple, who wrote a similar work, and a young Frenchman, Louis-Antoine de Bougainville. Bougainville led a French expedition to Tahiti, Vanuatu, Solomon Islands and New Guinea. It can claim to be the first scientific expedition as naturalists and scientists were on board. Reports from the voyage promoted the concept of the 'Noble Savage' and the Pacific as an earthly paradise. Jeanne Baret, who had travelled as naturalist Philibert Commerson's valet, became the first woman known to circumnavigate the world. Before Bougainville had returned to France, Cook had embarked on his first Pacific voyage.

SEE ALSO: Cook and the geographers, Dutch explorers, Spanish explorers

Pacific Ocean

The Pacific Ocean is the world's largest body of water. It encompasses a third of the Earth's surface, having an area of 6902 million square miles (179.7 million sq km). From north to south it extends 9631 miles (15,500km) from the Bering Sea to Ross Sea, while from west to east it is 12,303 miles (19,800km) from Indonesia to Colombia. The Ocean contains about 25,000 islands, the majority of which are found in the south-west quarter (this region is sometimes called Oceania).

The Pacific islands were settled by people moving originally from Southeast Asia. Moving on from New Guinea about 4000 years ago, through canoe journeys and island-hopping they had reached virtually every island before the arrival of the Europeans in the sixteenth century. Though they did not draw maps as such on paper, Micronesian people in the central-west Pacific produced stick charts, which clearly showed their knowledge of the geography of their region. It also showed their ability to reproduce voyages. Polynesian people also had a good understanding and maintained the geography as part of their oral tradition.

The explorer Ferdinand Magellan entered the ocean in 1520 from the Straits of Magellan at the southern end of South America. He encountered calm conditions causing him to called the ocean 'Pacific' meaning peaceful. The European explorers who followed Magellan suffered from a lack of suitable instruments with which to determine their position in the ocean so their 'discoveries' were often lost as soon as they had been made. The Spanish, who carried out most of the early expeditions, did little to build up an accurate and full map. The Dutch who followed had more success, fixing the positions of New Zealand and Tonga amonst others.

It was left to James Cook to define the Pacific. In his three voyages from 1769 to 1779, Cook 'discovered', 'rediscovered' and/or fixed the locations of virtually all the islands and island groups of the south and central Pacific. The chart that Henry Roberts drew after Cook's death is nearly identical to any chart produced today.

SEE ALSO: Polynesian diaspora

Palliser, Sir Hugh (1722–1796)

Hugh Palliser was born at Kirk Deighton, West Yorkshire, England on 22 February 1722. He entered the Royal Navy on the *Aldborough*, his uncle's ship, at age eleven. In 1741 he became a lieutenant, and in 1746 he became a captain, commanding several ships during the War of the Austrian Succession. He commanded the *Eagle* during the Seven Years War and then that his and Cook's paths first crossed. Palliser next commanded the *Shrewsbury*.

In 1762, Palliser was sent to Newfoundland to help expel the French, who had captured St John's, but arrived the day after the French surrendered. Two years

Portrait of Sir Hugh Palliser, by George Dance. (National Maritime Museum, Greenwich, Greenwich Hospital Collection)

later, he was appointed to succeed Graves as Governor of Newfoundland and arrived there in April 1764. He and Cook crossed the Atlantic together on HMS *Lark*. For much of his term, Palliser was concerned with French access to fisheries around Newfoundland and St Pierre and Miquelon. Palliser had to keep the French within the limits set by the Treaty of Paris, and keep the English from disrupting them. Palliser actively encouraged Cook in his survey of Newfoundland from 1764 until 1767, and the two men became good friends. Palliser did much to champion Cook's career.

Palliser left Newfoundland in 1768. From 1770 until 1775, he was Comptroller of the Navy. He was created a baronet in 1773 and elected to parliament in 1774. In 1778 he was promoted vice-admiral and governor of Greenwich Hospital in 1780. In 1787, he was promoted admiral. In 1778, Palliser took part in a battle off Ushant, which led to accusations and courts-martial. Even though he was acquitted, Palliser fared badly and was forced to retire from public life. He had a house and estate at The Vache, near Chalfont St Giles in Buckinghamshire. He died there, unmarried, in March, 1796. Palliser erected a monument to Cook at The Vache. Cook, in his turn, named a point in New Zealand, some islands in the Tuamotus and an inlet on Kerguelen after his friend. There is a short biography in the *DNB*, v15, pp114–6. A portrait by Dance is held at the National Maritime Museum in Greenwich.

SEE ALSO: Admiralty, Newfoundland

Parker, Sir William (1743–1802)

William Parker was part of the compliment of HMS *Guernsey*, which carried James Cook to Newfoundland to begin surveying that island's coastline in 1764. He was transferred to the *Grenville* and became the master's mate and assistant surveyor for the next three years. As mate, Parker's role was to sail the schooner and make soundings and coastal observations while Cook went off in small boats to carry out inshore and onshore work. Parker maintained the log and journal and, as such, is rarely mentioned himself. In August 1764, while Cook was recovering from an injury, Parker had a more prominent role when he led the survey of Griquet.

Parker was born on 1 January 1743 at Harburn, Warwickshire, the son of Augustine and Elizabeth Parker. William entered the Navy at an early age, about 1756. He sailed on the *Centurion*, captained by William Mantell, and was present during the captures of Louisbourg in 1758 and of Quebec in 1759. After six years service as a midshipman and master's mate, he passed an examination in 1762.

Parker left the *Grenville* at the end of 1766 when he was promoted to lieutenant and went aboard HMS *Niger*. For a time, he continued to serve in Newfoundland waters and was promoted to commander in 1773, before, in 1777 and now a captain, he went to the West Indies in command of HMS *Deal Castle* under the command of Barrington and later under Byron. From 1787 to 1790, he served as commodore and commander-in-chief on the Leeward Islands station, on board the *Jupiter*.

During the early 1790s he served in the Channel fleet under Admiral Richard Howe. In 1794, he was promoted to rear-admiral and served in Jamaica. In 1797, Parker, aboard the *Prince George,* took part in the battle at Cape St Vincent when the British fleet under

Sir John Jervis defeated the Spanish fleet. Parker was knighted for his contribution. He became a vice-admiral in 1799.

William Parker died on 31 December 1802 aged 59. He had married, in 1766, Jane Collingwood, and together they had seven daughters and one son, William George, born in 1787, who rose to be a vice-admiral.
SEE ALSO: *Grenville* (HM Schooner), Newfoundland

Parkinson, Sydney (1745–1771)

Sydney Parkinson sailed on the first voyage on the *Endeavour* as artist. His primary role was to draw natural history specimens and he is best known for his botanical work. He also drew landscapes, portraits and coastal views.

He was born in 1745 in Edinburgh, the son of Joel and Elizabeth Parkinson. The family, which also included an older brother Stanfield and a sister Britannia, were staunch Quakers. His father was a brewer and, after his father's death, Sydney was apprenticed to a wool draper. However, his real ability was drawing and painting and, when the family shifted to London, he exhibited flower paintings at the Society of Artists exhibition of 1765.

Parkinson was employed by James Lee, from the Vineyard Nursery at Hammersmith, to give painting lessons to his daughter, Ann, who became a very good natural history painter Parkinson would leave his painting utensils to Ann in his will. By early 1767, Lee had introduced Parkinson to Joseph Banks, who employed him to draw the insects and birds collected during Banks' Newfoundland voyage. Parkinson joined the *Endeavour* as part of Banks' retinue to draw botanical and zoological specimens in the course of the voyage. He also kept a journal during the voyage, which later became a bone of contention as to ownership, between Banks and Sydney's brother Stanfield. After Buchan's death in Tahiti, Parkinson was expected to take on his duties, drawing landscapes and coastal views.

Parkinson became ill during the stay at Java while the *Endeavour* was being repaired and died during the passage to the Cape of Good Hope, on 26 January 1771. He was just 25 years of age. He produced a self-portrait. Parkinson's output during the voyage was prodigious, completing 280 botanically accurate paintings and over 900 sketches and paintings, which are now at the British Museum (Natural History) London. *Ficus parkinsonii* was named in his honour. In 2000, a reef was named after Parkinson, just north of Cape Grenville in northern Queensland.

Sydney Parkinson, a self portrait. Engraved by J Newton after Parkinson. (Parkinson 1773 fp title page)

After the voyage, his brother, Stanfield, claimed all Sydney's written and painted work and a dispute ensued with Banks, as Parkinson's employer, and Hawkesworth, as author of the official account of the voyage. Even though he was paid for the papers, Stanfield secretly arranged for Sydney's journal to be published in 1773.
SEE ALSO: Art of Cook's voyages, Artists on Cook's voyages, Botanical results of Cook's voyages, First voyage

Patten, James (1744–1797)

James Patten sailed on Cook's second voyage on the *Resolution* as surgeon. Patten is believed to have been born in Streamville in County Antrim, Ireland, about 1744, one of six sons of the Reverend William Patten. James trained as a surgeon and is so described in a 1770 property document for Boynagh, County Meath, signed by him. His early naval career is not known but he joined the *Resolution* from HMS *Senegal* in December 1771 and helped stock the ship with medical supplies.

During the voyage he is credited, among other

things, with nursing Cook back to health after his serious illness in early 1774, with the assistance of Johann Reinhold Forster. Sir John Pringle gave a paper to the Royal Society in November 1776 on the prevention of scurvy, drawing information from the medical journal of Patten. Unfortunately, the journal is now lost. After the voyage, Patten moved to Dublin where he married Elizabeth Greene on 6 September 1777 and set up as a surgeon and 'Practioner in Midwifery'. He gave his collection of 'curiosities', acquired in the Pacific, to Trinity College Dublin and, in return, the College bestowed an honorary degree of Doctor of Physick in August 1780.

Patten died on 3 March 1797. He and Elizabeth had three daughters (Jane, Mary and Susan) and a son (John). Various features in New Zealand are named after Patten. Mount Patten overlooks Acheron Passage, linking Dusky and Breaksea Sounds. Patten Passage is located in Queen Charlotte Sound.
SEE ALSO: Second voyage

Peckover, William (1748–?)

William Peckover sailed on all three voyages with Cook. He sailed on the *Endeavour* voyage as an AB, on the second voyage on the *Resolution* as a gunner's mate, and on the third voyage on the *Discovery* as the gunner. He later went with Bligh on the *Bounty* voyage as gunner and accompanied Bligh in the longboat when the mutiny took place and the mutineers sailed off near Tofoa, in Tonga in 1788. He survived the arduous long row to Timor. Peckover was born in Aynho, Northamptonshire, on 17 June 1748, the only son of Daniel and Mary Peckover. The Peckovers were poor so William left home to join the Navy. In 1772, he wrote to Joseph Banks, unsuccessfully seeking help to become a midshipman. Instead, he saw service as gunner on a long list of ships until HMS *Gelykheid* in 1801. He later lived in Wapping.
SEE ALSO: First, Second and Third voyages

Pembroke, HMS

Cook's third Navy ship was HMS *Pembroke,* which he joined in Portsmouth in late 1757. The *Pembroke* was still a new ship having just been launched from Plymouth Dockyard earlier the same year. She was not well built, however, as the ship had problems over the next years. She was a Fourth Rate of 1247 tons, 155ft 10in (47.5m) long, 41ft 11in (12.8m) wide and carried 60 guns.

The captain of the *Pembroke* was John Simcoe, who took the ship to sea in December 1757 to patrol in the Bay of Biscay. In February 1758, they returned to Plymouth where the ship was readied for action. Later that month, the *Pembroke* was part of Admiral Boscawen's fleet that sailed across the Atlantic to Canada. The *Pembroke* reached Halifax on 9 May but was in need of repairs and stayed in port when the rest of the fleet sailed on to lay siege to Louisbourg. In June, Simcoe finally arrived at Louisbourg. The ship next took part in activities around the Gulf of St Lawrence in late 1758 before returning to Halifax for the winter.

In May 1759, the British fleet, including the *Pembroke,* left Halifax and sailed up the River St Lawrence to attack Quebec. Sadly, Captain Simcoe died off Anticosti Island and was replaced by John Wheelock. The *Pembroke* remained in The Basin, below Quebec, from May to the city's surrender in September. James Cook was then transferred to HMS *Northumberland.* The *Pembroke* returned to Halifax, where she was hulked in 1776 and eventually broken up in 1793.
SEE ALSO: Canada, Cook's ships

Perry, William (1747–1807?)

William Perry sailed on the first voyage on the *Endeavour* as surgeon's mate until 6 November 1770. When William Munkhouse died in Jakarta, Perry replaced him as surgeon and treated the others who had caught malaria. Towards the end of the voyage, he wrote a report on the health of the crew and the success of attempted preventions and cures. The report was sent to the Victualling Board, with Cook's comments. He later served on the ships *Scorpion*, *Dispatch*, *Salisbury* and *Superbe*, which he left when he retired in 1782. He went to live and practice in Chiswick. His name appears in local records until 1795. Perry was born in Chiswick, West London in 1747 and died in 1807, leaving a will (FRC 11/1472). In the will he is listed as coming from Christchurch in Hampshire and living in Soho, London. He left all to his wife Lydia.
SEE ALSO: First voyage, Medical aspects of Cook's voyages

Philately

James Cook has been featured on many postage stamps and this number increases greatly if one includes those who are associated with him, his ships, the places he visited and/or named, the places named after him and the flora and fauna first seen. All the known portraits of Cook have been reproduced on stamps, the first in 1888 with the reproduction of the Dance portrait on the

4d stamp of the New South Wales Centenary issue. Also featured on stamps are some of those who sailed with him – Banks, Bligh, the Forsters, Hodges, Omai, Solander, Sparrman, Parkinson, Vancouver, and Wales.

New Zealand first paid tribute in 1898, featuring Mount Cook on two stamps, and in 1906, and again in 1935, depicted Cook's landing at Poverty Bay. In 1940 their Centennial issue included a 1d stamp showing Cook's chart of the islands, the *Endeavour* and Cook as seen in the statue on the Mall, London. Between 1920 and 1950 Cook Islands, Penrhyn, Niue and Aitutaki issued stamps using the Dance portrait of Cook; showing the landing and also featuring charts and a statue. These include the rarest Cook stamp, a Cook Islands 1d stamp with the head of Cook inverted.

In 1968, the bicentenary of Cook's first voyage was celebrated by the issue of stamps (and often associated postmarks) by several countries, including Great Britain, the first time Cook's home country had afforded him such a tribute. Since that time the number of stamps has grown in number considerably as various countries, particularly those visited by Cook, feature aspects from the three voyages. Many reproduce the work of the artists, Parkinson, Hodges and Webber. Anniversaries of major events, such as the first sighting or landing, and the death of Cook, brought the issue of many stamps, usually accompanied by specially designed First Day Covers and postmarks. The launch of the *Endeavour* replica in 1997 and her subsequent voyages have brought further contributions to the philatelic story of Cook's life. By the beginning of 2004 over 500 stamps related to Cook had been issued by more than 80 stamp issuing countries. In addition there are stamps from private post services, many postmarks and cachets, and postal stationary. Helpful lists and details can be found via the links pages of the Captain Cook Society website.

There is a Captain Cook stamp checklist compiled by Brian Sandford at: http://www.captaincooksociety.com/ccsu32.pdf

BY ALWYN PEEL

SEE ALSO: Captain Cook Society

Alaska 1778
13c USA
FIRST DAY OF ISSUE
1978
FATEFUL RETURN TO HAWAII
"As we drew near the shore, the Natives came to us; they were a little shy at first."

First day postal cover from Hawai'i. (The author)

Phillips, Molesworth (1755–1832)

Molesworth Phillips sailed on the third voyage on the *Resolution* as second lieutenant of the Marine, in charge of nine men. He was part of the shore party at Kealakekua Bay when Cook was killed. Phillips himself was wounded but managed to save one of his privates, John Jackson. He is reported to have fought duels with John Williamson in connection with Williamson's perceived inaction and failure to save Cook at Kealakekua Bay. After the voyage, Phillips was promoted to captain in 1780.

Phillips was born in Swords, near Dublin on 15 August 1755. He married Susan Burney, sister of James in 1782. They moved in 1784 to live in Mickleham in Surrey, where they had three children. By 1787, the marriage had begun to deteriorate, and it had all but collapsed by the end of 1795, when Phillips left England to live at his estate at Belcotton, Co. Louth. His wife was obliged to join him there the following year but he was openly conducting an affair with his cousin. Phillips had proved to be a dissolute gambler and womaniser who mistreated his wife. She died from dysentery in 1800. Phillips married a second time to Ann Maturin.

In the Marines, Phillips rose to the rank of brevet lieutenant-colonel in 1798 and visited France where he was detained by Napoleon from 1802 until 1814. He then returned to England where he became friends with the poet Southey and with Charles Lamb. Lamb described Phillips as 'the high minded associate of Cook, the veteran colonel with his lusty heart still sending cartels of defiance to old Time'. Phillips eventually died of cholera at his home in Lambeth,

London, on 11 September 1832. He is buried in St Margaret's, Westminster. There is a short biography in the *DNB* Supp, pp1135–6. The National Portrait Gallery in London has two portraits of him.
SEE ALSO: Marines, Third voyage

Pickersgill, Richard (1749–1779)

Richard Pickersgill, who sailed on two of Cook's voyages, was a Yorkshireman, like Cook, having been born in West Tansfield in 1749. Aged 17, he sailed around the world in the *Dolphin* under Captain Wallis, and had hardly returned from that voyage in 1768 when he was appointed as master's mate to the *Endeavour.* Under Cook's tutelage he developed his sailing skills so that when Robert Molyneaux, the master of the *Endeavour*, died, Cook appointed Pickersgill to this post. He kept a journal and a log but was punished on 12 October 1768 for disobedience.

Pickersgill rejoined Cook for the second voyage as third lieutenant. He kept a log, a section of which is reproduced in the *Historical records of New South Wales, vol. 1, part 1: Cook 1762-1780.* Cook had a high opinion of his skills as a surveyor, his handling of the native peoples they came across and his judgement. In fact, Cook often sent him exploring the coastal areas in one of the small boats, or used him as an ambassador when arriving at ports of European colonies, getting Pickersgill to visit the dignitaries. At Easter Island, Pickersgill led the exploring party. At Tierra del Fuego, Cook 'sent Lieutenant Pickersgill, who I frequently employed on these occasions, to Examine and draw a sketch of the Channel'. Cook named several features in his honour.

He did not accompany Cook on his third voyage round the world, but was promoted to be the captain of a ship that would, hopefully, meet Captain Cook as he appeared round the top of Canada. In 1776, Pickersgill was sent up Davis Strait on the east coast of Canada, whilst Cook was sent to the west coast to find the Northwest Passage back to Britain. Nobody had found the passage from the Atlantic so it was hoped they would find it from the Pacific. Unfortunately, Pickersgill's ship, the *Lyon,* was sent late in the season and Pickersgill's leadership was wanting. He returned in disgrace and was court-martialled, though some of the blame lay with the Admiralty.

It is not clear what happened to him after that, but Johann Forster, the German scientist on Cook's second voyage, later wrote that he had become a privateer. He died in 1779, the same year as Cook, from falling over while boarding a ship and drowning in the River Thames. He was 30 years old. Pickersgill was described by another of Cook's crew as 'a good officer and astronomer, but liking ye Grog'. He left a will (FRC 11/1057).

BY IAN BOREHAM

SEE ALSO: First and Second voyages

Poetry, Cook in

Many poems have been written about Cook over the years. Most are forgettable and few have ever been good enough to be published. They were usually written for specific occasions such as centenaries. The early poems were invariably laudatory, portraying Cook as hero.

One of the first was by Thomas Perry, who sailed with Cook and at some point composed the *Antarctic Muse* about the second voyage, replete with lines such as:

'Brave Captain Cook he was our commander
Has conducted the Ship from all eminent danger'

Anna Seward's *An Elegy on Captain Cook,* which appeared in London in 1780 was the first published poem that actually dealt with Cook. A reviewer in *The Gentleman's Magazine* wrote 'With the assistance of the Muse, she has raised a trophy worthy of one of the greatest men this or any age or nation has produced'. Poems linked to Cook's voyages had been published earlier but they were satirical and dealt more with Joseph Banks and his supposed liaisons with Purea (Oberea) and other Tahitian women. Other odes followed by many forgotten authors, including Alexander Schomberg, Richard Cooksey and Robert Colvill.

The first poet of note to deal with Cook was William Cowper who touched on Cook in his poem *Charity*, written in 1781. In this he wrote:

'When Cook – lamented, and with tears as just
As ever mingled with heroic dust,
Steer'd Britain's oak into a world unknown,
And in his country's glory sought his own,
Wherever he found man, to nature true,
The rights of man were sacred in his view:'

The most famous poem with links to Cook is *The Rime of the Ancient Mariner* by Samuel Taylor Coleridge. Bernard Smith and others have shown that Cook and William Wales were among the influences and sources from which Coleridge derived inspiration.

In recent years Jean Latham (*Far voyager: the story of James Cook,* 1970), Alex Galloway (*A Transit of Venus: poems of passage*, 1993), Catherine Fisher (*The*

Unexplored Ocean, 1994) and Robert Sullivan (*Captain Cook in the Underworld,* 2002) are some of many poets who continue to use Cook's voyages as inspiration or cause for comment. Sullivan's long poem was originally commissioned as a libretto for the oratorio, *Orpheus in Rarohenga*, composed by John Psathas. In the poem, Sullivan sets out what he sees as the 'damage his [Cook's] expeditions inflicted on the indigenous peoples of the Pacific'.

SEE ALSO: Literature of Cook's voyages

Polynesia

The term Polynesia, meaning 'many islands', was coined by Charles De Brosses in his 1756 *Histoire des Navigations aux Terres Australes*, where it was applied to all of the islands of the Great South Sea. De Brosses divided the Pacific into three broad regions; Australasia (the west), Polynesia (the centre) and Magellanica (the south-east).

Dumont d'Urville later split Polynesia into two separate regions, Polynesia and Melanesia. Polynesia is now applied to a region described as the Polynesian triangle, stretching from Hawai'i to Easter Island and New Zealand. The people are called Polynesians. The similarity and close relationship among the peoples of Polynesia was first recognised by Cook. Forster, who published a comparative table of Polynesian words in 1778, on the second voyage developed the concept further. Linguistic studies confirm that the 36 documented Polynesian languages form a single branch of the Austronesian language stock. They can all be traced back to a Proto-Polynesian language, for which more than 4000 words have now been reconstructed.

Most of Cook's contact with Pacific peoples was with Polynesians. He never encountered Micronesians and only met Melanesians in New Caledonia and Vanuatu.

SEE ALSO: Pacific Ocean

Polynesian Diaspora

James Cook, in sailing around the Pacific, soon realised that the people he met on many disparate islands shared a similar language, and similar customs and beliefs. He wondered how they had managed to spread so far and wide without navigational instruments and using only the canoes he had seen. Tupaia, the priest Cook met at Tahiti, was able to demonstrate some of the navigational skills and knowledge possessed by Polynesians and showed that movement was planned and not random.

It is believed the peoples now grouped as Polynesian had their origins in Southeast Asia. About 4000 BC people of the Austronesian language stock moved west into the Pacific through the chain of islands now known as Indonesia. Some continued on to New Guinea while others turned north through the Philippines. These people moved on from Philippines to Guam and Mariana Islands about 1500 BC.

Meanwhile, between 1500 and 1000 BC people moved east from New Guinea to the Solomon Islands, Santa Cruz, Vanuatu and New Caledonia. A type of pottery, known as Lapita from a site in New Caledonia where it was first described, was developed and has helped to identify the continued spread east from Vanuatu to Fiji and Samoa. About 200 BC, people headed east from Fiji to Tonga, the Cook, the Society and the Marquesas Islands. It is these people, the people who left them later to settle other islands, and their descendants who are known as Polynesians.

The last part of the dispersal began about AD 300 in the Society Islands. People moved south-east to Easter Island (Rapa Nui) followed in AD 400 by the first migrations north from the Society or Marquesas Islands to Hawai'i. The final part happened between AD 1000 to 1200 when people sailed southwest from the Society Islands to New Zealand (Aotearoa). Virtually all the islands of the Pacific had been settled, or at least visited, by people long before Europeans entered the region. Polynesians had spread to occupy islands in what is now termed the Polynesian triangle, stretching from Hawai'i to Easter Island and New Zealand.

Portlock, Nathaniel (1749–1817)

Nathaniel Portlock sailed on the third voyage on *Discovery* as a master's mate until 23 August 1779 when he was transferred to the *Resolution* as master's mate. Beaglehole attributes to Portlock a log, which he describes as 'a good log, in which there sounds an individual voice'. Portlock was discharged from *Resolution* at the Cape and was sent ahead by Gore to Britain with copies of the ships' Journals, etc for the Admiralty on board the faster ship, HMS *Sybil.*

He was made lieutenant in September 1780 and served in the English Channel. Portlock next commanded a private fur trading expedition to North Pacific in 1785 in the *King George* (George Dixon, who had been the armourer on the *Discovery,* commanded the *Queen Charlotte,* the companion vessel). He rejoined the Royal Navy and commanded HMS *Assistant* on Bligh's 1791 breadfruit voyage. They carried breadfruit to St Vincent in the West Indies before reaching Britain in late 1793.

Portlock was promoted to commander and gave him the command of HMS *Reliance,* about to depart for Australia. However, he was replaced at the last moment. In 1797, he was in charge of *HMS Arrow,* a 20-gun sloop, on the Downs station. Two actions mark this period; in September 1799 the *Arrow* destroyed a Dutch frigate, the *Draak;* and on the night of 9–10 October 1799, the frigate HMS *Lutine* was wrecked in the Zuyder Zee, Netherlands. The *Arrow* picked up the lone survivor. The bell of the *Lutine* was salvaged in 1858 and it is this bell that is rung in Lloyd's of London (the insurance organisation) whenever a ship sinks. Portlock was made captain in 1799 after these actions.

Portlock was born in Virginia in 1749. The family owned a brig that traded between Norfolk, Virginia, and Liverpool, England, so Nathaniel was destined for a maritime life. In 1771, when employed as sailing master on a ship in the West Indies trade, he was threatened with being pressed on to HMS *St Albans.* Portlock volunteered and within two years had made warrant officer and midshipman. In 1775, he joined the *Resolution.* By choosing to stay with the Royal Navy, Portlock alienated his family in America and relinquished land left to him.

Portlock died in Greenwich Hospital on 12 September 1817. He left a will (FRC 11/1600). Portlock Island in south-east Alaska is named for him. There is a portrait in the National Maritime Museum.

See Also: Third voyage

Portraits of Cook

The first known portrait of Cook was painted by William Hodges (1744–1797) about 1775–76. Hodges had been the artist for the second voyage and had produced many fine landscapes and some chalk portraits of Pacific Islanders during the voyage. His portrait of Cook is an oil on canvas measuring 30in x 25in (762mm x 635mm). It is a head and shoulders portrait to left of Cook in captain's undress uniform. The arrangement of his buttons in pairs shows the sitter to be a captain of under three years' seniority. Cook was promoted to the rank of captain on 9 August 1775, which suggests that Cook sat for Hodges after that date and before 12 July 1776, when Cook set out on his last voyage. Some of the preliminary sketches for the portrait may been drawn by during the return part of the second voyage. He was re-employed by the Admiralty immediately on his return to work up his sketches for publication in the voyage proceedings. The painting's first owner was probably Sir Hugh Palliser, Cook's friend and patron, who, it is believed, displayed it at The Vache, his Buckinghamshire house. It then disappeared and for years this portrait was only known from an engraving. It resurfaced when it was spotted in an auction in Ireland in 1986 and was purchased by the National Maritime Museum, Greenwich where it still resides.

The second portrait was commissioned by Joseph Banks and painted by Nathaniel Dance in 1775–76. Cook sat for this portrait on 25 May 1776 but it is not known whether he did so again before he left London on 24 June for his third voyage, never to return. Dance was a portrait painter, born in London in 1736. He went to Rome where he trained under Pompeo Batoni. On his return to London in 1764, Dance became one of the most prestigious of British portrait and history painters and was a founding member of the Royal Academy in 1768. His Cook portrait is one of his best and most famous. It proved, however, to be one of his last works as he stopped painting after inheriting a fortune in 1776. The painting is an oil on canvas measuring 50in x 40in (1270mm x 1016mm). It is a three-quarter-length portrait of Captain Cook, seated to the left, facing the right. He is wearing captain's full-dress uniform, 1774–87, consisting of a navy-blue jacket, white waistcoat with gold braid and gold buttons and white breeches and a grey wig. He holds his own chart of the Southern Ocean on the table and his right hand points to the east coast of Australia on it. His left thumb and finger lightly hold the other edge of the chart over his knee. His hat sits on the table behind him to the left on top of a substantial book, perhaps his journal, itself resting on the chart. The portrait was presented to Greenwich Hospital by Banks' executor in 1829 and remains at the National Maritime Museum in the Greenwich Hospital Collection. David Samwell, surgeon's mate and later surgeon on the third voyage thought Dance's portrait 'a most excellent likeness ... and ... the only one I have seen that bears any resemblance to him'.

John Webber, who sailed on Cook's third voyage as official artist, painted at least four portraits of Cook, of which three were from life (two in 1776 and one in 1777). The first painting is in the National Portrait Gallery, London. It is an oil on canvas, in oval spandril, and measures 14.5in x 12in (370mm x 300mm). It was painted at the Cape in late 1776, probably as they waited for Clerke and the *Discovery.* It is head and shoulders, turned towards the right, wearing a dark blue captain's uniform. The second of Webber's portraits is in the National Art Gallery, Wellington, New Zealand. The Wellington portrait originally belonged to Elizabeth Cook, who disliked it because it made Cook look severe. It is almost full length of Cook standing in captain's uniform with sword, holding a telescope in his left hand and his hat in his right hand, which is gloved, presumably to hide the scar. It is an oil on canvas, measuring 43.5in x 27.4in (1105mm x 698mm). The painting was purchased by the New Zealand Government in 1960. The third portrait, painted in Tahiti, was given by Cook to his friend Tu. John Watts mentions seeing it still in Tu's proud possession when he visited Tahiti in 1788. Vancouver also saw the painting in 1792 but it later disappeared. On his return to Britain, Webber painted another portrait in 1782, which is derived from the Wellington portrait. This one is three-quarter with Cook standing in captain's uniform with sword. His right hand is gloved. It is an oil on canvas, measuring 45in x 36in (1143mm x 914mm). In 2000, the painting was purchased by the Australian Government and it hangs in the National Portrait Gallery in Canberra.

John Flaxman (1755–1826) while establishing his reputation as a monumental sculptor, produced wax reliefs for the Wedgwood company. White mouldings taken from the wax were applied to blue jasperware. In 1784, Flaxman produced a relief of James Cook. Using an original cast, Wedgwood re-issued 200 copies in 1968 on the bicentenary of Cook's first voyage.

The National Library of Australia possesses a painting by John Hamilton Mortimer from 1771. The Library maintains that it shows a group of James Cook, Joseph Banks, the Earl of Sandwich, Daniel Solander and John Hawkesworth. It is by no means certain, however, that James Cook is one of the characters depicted.

SEE ALSO: Artists on Cook's voygages, Hodges (William), Webber (John)

Captain James Cook, by John Webber. Cook sat for this portrait in late 1776 in Cape Town at the beginning of the third voyage. (Museum of New Zealand Te Papa Tongarewa)

Poverty Bay/Turanga Nui and Gisborne

Gisborne, (38° 39' S, 178° 1' E) is a town located on Poverty Bay, an inlet on the east coast of Te Ika a Maui, the North Island of New Zealand. The town is at the mouth of the Turanganui River. It was the first landfall in New Zealand made by James Cook when he arrived in October 1769. Cook gave the bay its name because he could find little food for his crew. It was known to the local Māori, whom Cook met, as Turanganui. The mouth of Poverty Bay extends 4.9 miles (8km) from Tuahine Point to Young Nick's Head, named after the first of Cook's crew to sight land (he most probably sighted a mountain inland rather than this headland).

Cook and the *Endeavour* anchored on 8 October 1769

off Turanganui. Cook, Banks, Solander and some marines landed near the mouth of Turanganui River and seeing people across the river crossed to meet them. However, the people quickly disappeared and only empty huts were found. In the meantime, some crew had met four Māori and in the encounter one Māori had been shot dead. The next day Cook took another party ashore and this time about 100 Māori performed a haka on the opposite bank of the river. It was realised that Tupaia could converse with them and, after he had made an initial breakthrough, a Māori and Cook waded into the water to meet on a sand bank in the middle of the river. They greeted each other, which encouraged more Māori to come forward, and exchanges were made. However, Green's sword was taken and Surgeon Munkhouse shot the thief so the British retired back on board the *Endeavour* for safety.

Cook still needed fresh water so he tried to land further round the bay but surf stopped them reaching the shore. They met more Māori in canoes near the mouth of the Kohututea River and another skirmish occurred. Three young Māori were taken captive. The next day, 10 October, Cook landed again and, as the botanists collected plants, 200 Māori assembled including the uncle of one of the captive boys. Negotiations were held but, surprisingly, the boys preferred to stay on board. Cook, though, was ready to leave and the boys were put ashore.

These events highlighted the problems of two peoples with completely different cultures coming together. The nervousness and suspicions of both parties led to actions and gestures being misinterpreted, with tragic results. In his journal Cook expressed sadness at the shootings and deaths. Cook took the *Endeavour* south.

A monument marks the spot where Cook landed in New Zealand, while up on Kaiti Hill a statue (supposedly of Cook but actually an Italian naval officer) looks out over Poverty Bay. There is also a more authentic statue of Cook and a statue of Young Nick near Waikanae Beach.

SEE ALSO: New Zealand

Prince William Sound

Prince William Sound (60° 30' N, 147° W) is an inlet on the central south coast of Alaska. Hinchinbrook and Montagu Islands disguise the inlet's existence but the narrow Hinchinbrook Entrance between these islands leads into a bay 77.6 miles (125km) wide and about 46.6 miles (75km) deep. It consists of many smaller inlets and numerous islands. Glaciers discharge directly into the sound. The people inhabiting the sound when Cook arrived were a subgroup of Sugpiaq or Pacific Eskimo called Chugach. They were, therefore, different to the Native Americans he had met earlier at Nootka Sound, to the south-east.

A view of Snug Corner Cove, in Prince William Sound, Alaska. Engraved by W Ellis after Webber. (Cook & King (Atlas) pl 45)

In May 1778, James Cook was sailing in the Gulf of Alaska in search of an opening for the Northwest Passage. The coast had started trending east-west much to Cook's concern, when he expected to be still sailing north. A map they had on board, by Stählin, showed northward-running channels linking to a northern ocean in this region and Cook was hoping to find one of them. On 12 May, Cook rounded Cape Hinchinbrook and found the opening to a large inlet, which he entered. He put into a cove just inside the inlet and was surrounded by the local Chugach people paddling kayaks, who were keen to trade otter furs. The next day, Cook transferred to another anchorage, Snug Corner Bay, deeper in the inlet in Port Fidalgo. Repairs were carried out while more people visited the ships to trade furs. Gore and Roberts rowed up the Valdez Arm to check for the Passage but returned unsuccessfully, although Roberts thought he had seen a channel.

The ships sailed on 17 May and waited off Bligh Island before heading south-west, having given up on the inlet being the Northwest Passage. Cook called the inlet Sandwich Sound but the Earl of Sandwich later changed it to Prince William Sound. Cook sailed through the Montague Strait past Green Island and between Montague Island and the mainland. Cook had been the first European known to have entered the sound. Soon, though, Russian and British fur traders

would arrive and the lives of the Chugach would be irretrievably changed.
SEE ALSO: Alaska

Pringle, Sir John (1707–1782)

Sir John Pringle, a British physician, was President of the Royal Society from 1772 until 1780. He was born on 10 April 1707 in Stitchel, Roxburghshire in Scotland, the younger son of Sir John Pringle. Pringle was educated at St Andrews, at Edinburgh, and at Leiden, receiving a degree of doctor of physic at Leiden in 1730. He settled in Edinburgh as a physician. In 1742, he became physician to the Earl of Stair, then commanding the British army in Flanders, and in 1744 was appointed by the Duke of Cumberland as physician-general to the forces in the Low Countries. Pringle co-invented the Red Cross concept when he helped establish a neutral field hospital to provide the wounded with a safe haven within easy reach of the battlefield.

In 1745, he was elected Fellow of the Royal Society. The regular publication of papers through the Society gave him a great reputation in the scientific world and one, on septic and antiseptic substances, led to his being awarded the Copley Medal in 1752. He became President of the Society in 1772 and was in office when Cook was awarded the Copley Medal. Pringle wrote of Cook and his work in fighting scurvy that the Society had 'never more cordially nor more meritoriously bestowed that faithful symbol of their esteem and affection'.

He moved to London in 1749 when he was made physician to the Duke of Cumberland. In 1752, he married Charlotte Oliver but she died a few years later. They had no children. Subsequently he received other court appointments as physician, and in 1766 was made a baronet. In 1768, he became physician to the King's mother, the Princess of Wales, followed in 1774 by his final appointment as Physician to King George III. He retired in 1778 and resigned his presidency of the Royal Society in 1780. He died on 18 January 1782. There is a monument to him in Westminster Abbey.
SEE ALSO: Royal Society

Published accounts

As James Cook sailed up the Atlantic at the end of the *Endeavour* voyage, he called in all of the journals and logs that crewmembers had written so he could hand them in to the Admiralty when they reached Britain. For most Royal Navy ships that would be the end of the story with the material being sent into storage. However, for some more high-profile voyages, narratives were produced from the raw material and published for public consumption. Cook's voyage fell into this category and the *Endeavour*'s journals, together with those from three other voyages, were handed over to John Hawkesworth for him to turn into a literary narrative. It appeared in 1773 as *An Account of the voyages undertaken by the order of His Present Majesty for making discoveries in the southern hemisphere, and successively performed by Commodore Byron, Captain Wallis, Captain Carteret, and Captain Cook, in the Dolphin, the Swallow, and the Endeavour. Drawn up from the journals which were kept by the several commanders, and from the papers of J. Banks, by J. Hawkesworth, ...in three volumes. Illustrated with cuts, and a great variety of charts and maps relative to countries now first discovered, or hitherto but imperfectly known*, published in London by W Strahan and T Cadell. A second edition soon followed together with a Dublin edition, both published in 1773. In 1774 a German, Dutch and two French editions came out. Various further editions followed. Cook had no part in the publication and was already well into his second voyage when the Hawkesworth edition appeared.

Cook was made a captain at Greenwich Hospital at the end of his second voyage. The appointment was a sinecure, which would give Cook the opportunity to write his own narrative of his voyage. Canon John Douglas was commissioned to assist Cook and ensure the work had a literary quality. However, the Earl of Sandwich persuaded Cook to lead the third voyage and Cook sailed for the Pacific before the narrative was completed. It was published in two volumes as *A Voyage towards the South Pole, and round the world, performed in His Majesty's Ships the Resolution and Adventure, in the years 1772, 1773, 1774, and 1775; written by James Cook, Commander of the Resolution. In which is included Captain Furneaux's narrative of his proceedings in the Adventure during the separation of the ships. In two volumes. Illustrated with maps and charts, and a variety of portraits ...and views ...drawn during the voyage by Mr. Hodges, and engraved by the most eminent masters* by W Strahan and T Cadell, in London in 1777. The work was an immediate success and a second edition and two Dublin editions appeared the same year. In 1778, a Dutch, three French, and a German edition were published. A Swedish (1783), Italian (1794), Swiss (1796), and a Russian (1796) edition appeared later.

Cook and Clerke both died on the third voyage and

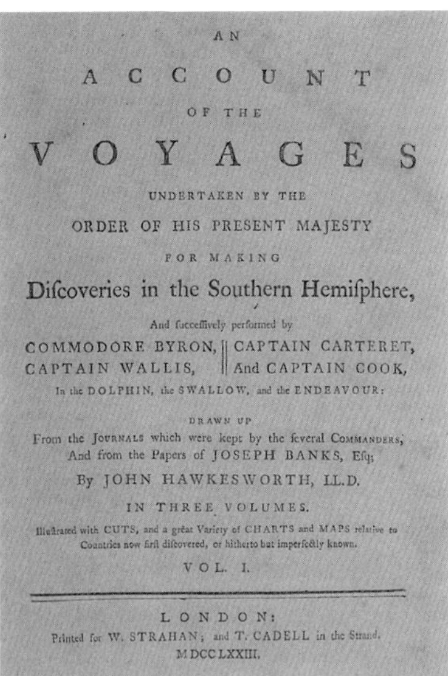

AN
ACCOUNT
OF THE
VOYAGES
UNDERTAKEN BY THE
ORDER OF HIS PRESENT MAJESTY
FOR MAKING
Difcoveries in the Southern Hemifphere,
And fucceffively performed by
COMMODORE BYRON, | CAPTAIN CARTERET,
CAPTAIN WALLIS, | And CAPTAIN COOK,
In the DOLPHIN, the SWALLOW, and the ENDEAVOUR:
DRAWN UP
From the JOURNALS which were kept by the feveral COMMANDERS,
And from the Papers of JOSEPH BANKS, Efq;
By JOHN HAWKESWORTH, LL.D.
IN THREE VOLUMES.
Illuftrated with CUTS, and a great Variety of CHARTS and MAPS relative to
Countries now firft difcovered, or hitherto but imperfectly known.
VOL. I.

LONDON:
Printed for W. STRAHAN; and T. CADELL in the Strand.
MDCCLXXIII.

Part of the title page of An Account of the Voyages undertaken … for making Discoveries in the Southern Hemisphere, *by John Hawkesworth, printed in 1773.*

Gore brought the ships home. However, Gore had no pretensions as a writer and James King, who had captained the *Discovery* home, was commissioned to write the narrative. Once again Canon Douglas was brought in to assist. King was not well and the project took a considerable time. Henry Roberts was used to draw a portfolio of charts, much to the anger of William Bligh, the *Resolution*'s master, who later maintained he had drawn the charts and was not credited. The narrative was published in three volumes and an atlas by Nicol and Cadell in London in 1784 as *A Voyage to the Pacific Ocean, undertaken, by the command of His Majesty, for making discoveries in the northern hemisphere, to determine the position and extent of the west side of North America, its distance from Asia, and the practicability of a northern passage to Europe, performed under the direction of Captains Cook, Clerke, and Gore, in His Majesty's ships the Resolution and Discovery, in the years 1776, 1777, 1778, 1779, and 1780. In three volumes: vol. 1 and 2 written by Captain J. Cook, vol. 3 by Captain J. King. Illustrated with maps and charts, from the original drawings made by Lieut. Henry Roberts under the direction of Captain Cook; and with a great variety of portraits of incidents, drawn by Mr. Webber during the voyage, and engraved by the most eminent artists.* As with earlier voyages, the account was a tremendous success and numerous editions (and abridged editions) appeared in London and Dublin over the next two years. Foreign-language editions appeared in French, German, Dutch, Swedish, Russian and Italian.

J C Beaglehole edited Cook's journals, which were published by the Hakluyt Society as *The Journals of Captain James Cook on his voyages* in four volumes plus a map portfolio between 1955 and 1967. They were republished by Boydell Press, 1999. In 1999, Penguin published *The Journals of Captain Cook*, a further condensation of Beaglehole's work, edited by Philip Edwards.

SEE ALSO: Literature of Cook's voyages, Logs, journals and muster rolls

Purea (also known as Te Vahine Airoro atua i Ahurai, and Oberea)

Purea was a high-ranking Tahitian at the time of Wallis' visit to Tahiti in 1767. She lost much of her power before Cook's arrival but still maintained sufficient status to feature in Cook's visits to the island. Wallis had not realised that Purea was only one of several chiefs and that her base was Papara at the southwest corner of the island. The daughter of chief Terii Vaetua, she married Tevahitua, the chief of Papara and together they had a son, Teri'irere, in about 1762. Purea and Tevahitua (who changed his name to Amo (Oamo)) then lived apart, as was the custom, but caused a large pyramid to be created at the Mahaiatea marae to honour their son. This was resented by people in other parts of the island and they combined to fight Purea, who was defeated in December 1768.

When she visited the *Endeavour* in late April 1769, Purea was recognised by Molyneux, the ship's master, who had sailed with Wallis. Cook perpetuated Wallis' error that Purea was queen of the whole island and accorded her that status. However, Cook was puzzled as he realised that Tutaha, who resented the attention paid to Purea, was chief of the district which included Matavai Bay where they were anchored. Purea and her family were only visitors.

In August 1773, Pickersgill went to Papara where he met Amo and Teri'irere. Purea, who was living apart in the district, entertained him. On Cook's next visit in May 1774, Purea appeared on board the *Endeavour* at Matavai Bay with gifts of pigs and fruit. However, when Cook arrived in August 1777, he learned that Purea had died in 1775 or 1776. In Britain, plays and satires were written about Banks and his supposed liaison with Purea during the first voyage.

SEE ALSO: Tahitians

Q / R

Quakers

The Quakers is the popular name for the Society of Friends. The named is supposed to have originated with Justice Bennet at Derby in 1650 as they 'tremble (or quake) at the word of the Lord'. The Society, a protestant dissenting sect, was founded in the English Midlands in 1647 by George Fox. The introduction of the Clarendon Code, which severely limited the freedom of nonconformists, particularly affected Quakers. People were required to take an oath but Friends believed that they should speak truthfully at all times and oaths were unnecessary. They were, therefore, excluded from the universities, government, and most professions.

In their early days, the Quakers were persecuted as members were fervent and radical but the Toleration Act 1689 improved matters and, by the mid-eighteenth century, it had emerged as an accepted religious movement. Its members became successful in many commercial ventures such as banking and manufacturing and gained social respectability. A number of Quakers became rich through their values of honesty, hard work and aversion to frippery and luxury. The Society insisted on good and humane business practices.

James Cook encountered Quakers when he was apprenticed to the Walkers in Whitby. When not at sea, Cook lived in the Walkers' house and thereby encountered first hand the Quaker way of life. Although not subscribing to the religion, Cook took on board some of their ideals. His marriage and family events were nevertheless celebrated in the Anglican church. John Walker's commitment to Quakerism was tested in Cook's time as he agreed to carrying guns on his ships against Friends' teaching. Walker dealt with other Quaker businessmen in London, notably James Sheppard, who owned wharves in the Wapping area. Sheppard was a friend of the Batts family and Walker's crews, including Cook, stayed at the Batts' public house, The Bell. Elizabeth Batts was staying with the Sheppards prior to her marriage to Cook in Barking.

Sydney Parkinson, the artist, was a Scottish Quaker. When he went to London, he worked for James Lee at the Chelsea Physic Garden and also for John Fothergill. Through these men he met Joseph Banks and went as a member of his party on the *Endeavour* voyage.

John Cookworthy, a Plymouth chemist and Quaker, discovered the kaolin or china-clay deposits of Cornwall and developed its use for porcelain. He trained in London and became acquainted with the Swedish community, leading to him translating Swedenborg's *Doctrine of life*. Cook joined Solander and Banks to visit Cookworthy in Plymouth prior to the *Endeavour* voyage.

John Fothergill (1712–80) was a physician and Quaker. He settled in London in 1740, where he gained an extensive practice. In his leisure he made a study of conchology and botany; and at Upton, near Stratford, he had an extensive botanical garden where he grew many rare plants obtained from various parts of the world. Fothergill had employed one of Banks' servants, Thomas Richmond, prior to Cook's first voyage. He was a friend and patron of Sydney Parkinson before the artist set out on the same voyage. Fothergill purchased the copyright to Parkinson's journal after its first publication and also his shell collection. The collection is now at Glasgow University's Zoology Museum.

SEE ALSO: North Sea and the coal trade, Religion and Cook, Wapping, Whitby

Quebec

Quebec (46° 47' N, 71° 15' W) occupies a strategic position on the St Lawrence River in Canada. The Huron-Wendat people had established a settlement called Stadacona on the site before the French arrived. The French explorer Jacques Cartier visited in 1534 but it was Samuel de Champlain who founded Quebec City in 1608. The name Quebec comes from 'Kebec', an Algonquin word meaning 'There where the river narrows'. It would become the capital of New France and an important centre of trade.

Quebec was seen as a prize, crucial to the future of Canada. Whoever controlled Quebec controlled the St Lawrence and access to the remainder of the country.

French-British rivalry in North America culminated with the Seven Years War, which saw the siege of Quebec. The British captured Louisbourg, the fort that controlled the mouth of the St Lawrence in 1758 but delayed in pressing on to attack Quebec.

James Cook was aboard HMS *Pembroke* as part of the British fleet under the command of Admiral Saunders that sailed up the St Lawrence to Quebec, arriving in June 1759. Cook had been active in establishing a route up the river. Dislodging the French from Quebec proved more difficult and the British tried many times over the next 11 weeks. Cook played a back-up role helping to ferry troops and charting the river. Finally, on 13 September, the British, led by James Wolfe, made an audacious ascent to the Plains of Abraham and successfully attacked the French, under General Montcalm, from the rear. Both generals died in the battle. Bougainville, the future French explorer of the Pacific, was aide-de-camp to Montcalm throughout the campaign.

Cook came to the attention of Admiral Saunders and was transferred, on Saunders' orders, to the 70-gun HMS *Northumberland*, under Lord Colvill. Saunders took most of the fleet back to Britain where he arranged for Cook's charts to be published. Cook was back in Quebec in 1760 when the French surrendered at Montreal. In 1763, the Treaty of Paris was signed, in which France gave up Canada.

SEE ALSO: Canada, Seven Years War

Queen Charlotte Sound/Totaranui

Queen Charlotte Sound (41° 15' S, 174° 9' E) is part of the Marlborough Sounds, a labyrinth of inlets, islands and bays on the north-eastern coast of the South Island of New Zealand. The inlet was inhabited by Māori, who called it Totaranui.

James Cook brought the *Endeavour* into the sound in January 1770. He rounded Motuara Island and sailed into what is now known as Ship Cove (Meretoto). It offered fresh water and food including a native plant (*Lepidium Oleraceum*), which along with a beer brewed from young rimu branches, produced a good infusion of Vitamin C for the crew. Today this is commonly known as Cook's scurvy grass.

Cook enjoyed good relations with local Māori, though the killing of men from the *Adventure* in 1773 did sour matters. Cook landed pigs, planted vegetables, and gave seeds to the Māori. He used the cove to careen his ship and carry out general maintenance. On 30 January 1770, Cook climbed to the highest point of Motuara and claimed the lands and waters surrounding for 'king and country'. He named the waterway Queen Charlotte Sound after the king's consort, Queen Charlotte Sophia. Cook would return to Ship Cove on four occasions between 1773 and 1777 during his explorations. Cook established from here the existence of the passage of water between the two main islands of New Zealand. Banks proposed that it be called Cook Strait. Cook learned from Māori the names of the two islands; he recorded 'Tovy-poenammu' (Te Wai Pounamu) for South Island and 'Aeheino mouwe' (Te Ika a Maui) for North Island.

During the second voyage, the two ships lost contact in November 1773 and visited the sound separately. Cook learned later that during the *Adventure*'s visit a shore party had all been killed at Grass Cove, Wharehunga Bay. Furneaux had left immediately. When Cook returned on his third voyage in February 1777, everyone expected him to seek revenge for the killings. His crew and local Māori were surprised though when Cook did nothing.

There are monuments commemorating Cook's visits at Ship Cove and on Motuara Island. Cook bestowed several of the names used in the sound and others honouring Cook, his men and ships have appeared since.

SEE ALSO: New Zealand

Quiros, Pedro Fernándes de (1565–1615)

Pedro Fernándes de Quiros was born in Evora, Portugal in 1565. He travelled to Peru about 1591 and saw service in the Manila Galleons sailing across the Pacific, becoming an experienced navigator. In 1595, he served as pilot aboard the *San Jerónimo* on the second voyage of Alvaro de Mendaña de Nehra, from Peru to the Marquesas Islands and the Santa Cruz Islands in search of the Solomon Islands. After the death of Mendaña, Quiros led the survivors to Manila in January 1596, and subsequently returned to Peru in June 1597.

Quiros visited Europe where he obtained the support of Pope Clement VIII and King Philip III of Spain to undertake more exploration in the Pacific. He returned to Peru in 1603 with the intention of finding and settling the mythical Terra Australis. Quiros left Callao in Peru in the *San Pedro y Paulo* on 21 December 1605, accompanied by the *San Pedrico* (under Torres) and *Los Tres Reyes*, In May 1606, Quiros reached land, which he called La Austrialia del Espiritu Santo (now Espiritu Santo in Vanuatu), and began the settlement of Nova

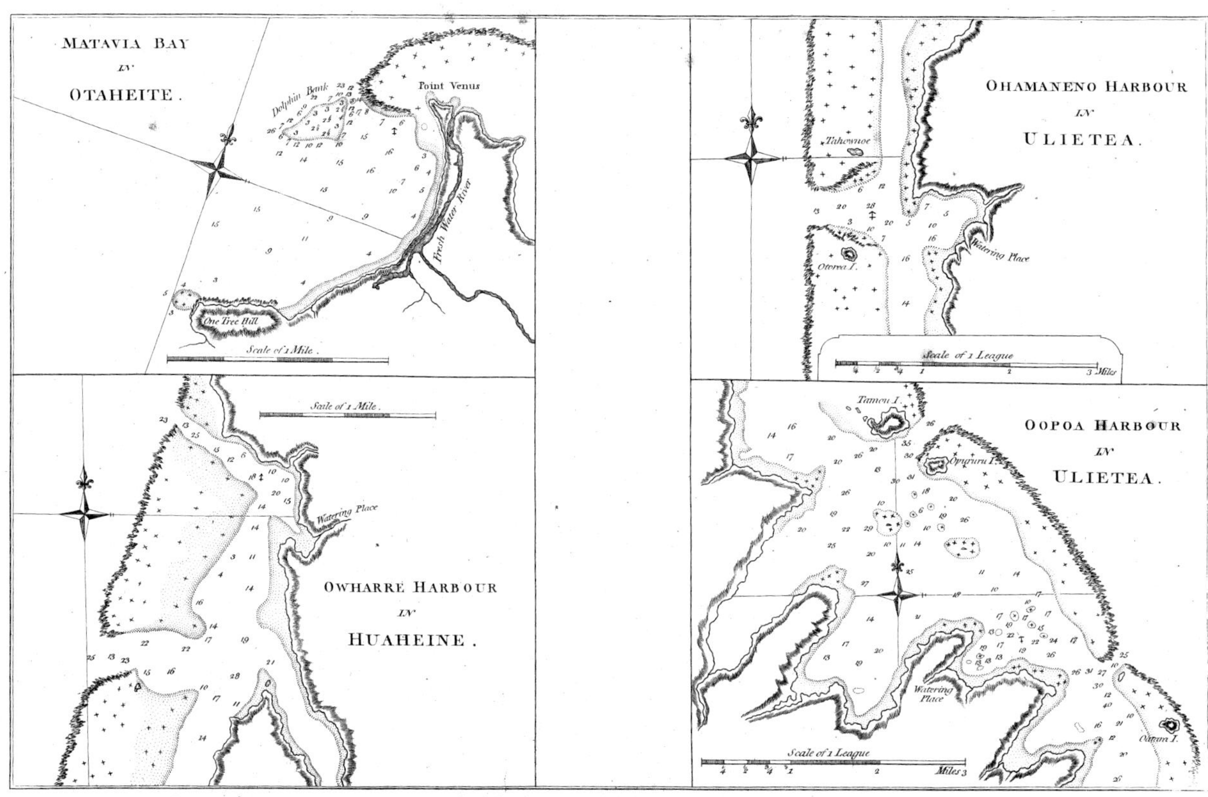

Four harbours in the Society Islands. After Cook. 1784. The marae at Taputaputea on Raiatea is on the headland to the east of the watering place on 'Oopoa Harbour in Ulietea' (bottom right). (University of Waikato Map Collection)

Jerusalem. The colony was soon abandoned due to native hostility and disagreements among the crew. The *San Pedro y Paulo* became separated from the other ships in bad weather and sailed to 38° N, before returning via the North Pacific to Acapulco, arriving there on 23 November 1606. Torres led the other ships east past New Guinea.

Quiros returned to Madrid in 1607, where he spent the next seven years in poverty, trying to gain support for further voyages. Philip III dispatched him back to Peru with false orders for further voyages but Quiros died *en route* in Panama, late in 1615. Quiros had shown himself to be a very able navigator. Unfortunately, the lack of good instruments at the time made it difficult for him to record the locations of his 'discoveries' with any certainty. Cook was able to fix some of Quiros' islands, especially the Marquesas and Vanuatu, during his second voyage.

SEE ALSO: Pacific exploration before Cook, Spanish explorers

Raiatea

Raiatea (16° 48' S, 151° 25' W) is one of the Leeward Society Islands in the South Pacific. The island is 124 miles (200km) WNW of Tahiti and now forms part of the territory of French Polynesia. Raiatea was the cultural, religious and historical centre of the Society Islands and the marae at Taputapuatea near Opoa was one of the most sacred sites in Polynesia. Tupaia, who joined the *Endeavour*, came originally from Raiatea. It is believed that several of the canoes that populated the Pacific, including New Zealand, originated in Raiatea.

Cook visited the island on each of his voyages. On his first visit in July 1769, he began at Opoa on the east coast. Cook then rounded the island and anchored inside Passe Rautoanui on the west coast. They repaired a leak there and took on fresh water, and rocks for ballast. Bora Bora controlled these islands at the time and its Chief, Puni, was present on Raiatea so Cook went to pay his respects. Tupaia was of great value as he led the British through Polynesian protocol. Cook also made short trips to Baie Hurepiti on Tahaa and south down the west coast of Raiatea as far as Pointe Pautu. After a week on Raiatea, Cook was ready to head south to explore the Southern Ocean so he left on 9 August.

On the second voyage, Cook anchored again at Passe Rautoanui. Orio, the local chief, welcomed him lavishly with entertainments, dancing, theatre and music every day of the visit. Pickersgill was charged with obtaining fresh supplies and even went north to Tahaa for fresh pigs. The ships left Raiatea on 17 September 1773. During the second sweep in June 1774, Cook was received by Orio, who put on more elaborate entertainments, this time featuring his daughter Poetua. They were able to trade as provisions were plentiful and they left the island on 4 June. Cook visited for the last time in November 1777 on his third voyage. Orio welcomed Cook, who stayed for a month, prolonged by the desertion of crew members and the time taken for search parties to locate them. Cook went after two men to Tahaa only to find they had gone on to Tupai. Cook left on 7 December.

SEE ALSO: Society Islands

Religion and Cook

J C Beaglehole famously characterised Cook as a secular rational humanist: '[h]e had, so far as one can see, no religion'. This judgement is not borne out by detailed scrutiny of Cook's upbringing, naval career and encounters with cultural 'others'.

To begin with, he was clearly raised in the Protestant tradition and participated in it via the usual rites of passage. He was baptised in the village church of St Cuthbert's at the age of one week and as a rising naval star married Elizabeth Batts in her parish church of St Margaret's in the parish of Barking, Essex on 21 December 1762. Established religion was therefore part of his cultural background. Young James learned 'writing, arithmetic and his catechism' at the Postgate School in Great Ayton. At the age of 18, he was apprenticed to John Walker, 'a Quaker ship-master, ship-owner, and coal-shipper' of Whitby and a man to whom he maintained a strong connection after joining the Royal Navy, possibly even being recommended by him 'to the London Quaker connection'. Quakers, it should be noted, are sceptical of organised and established churches and tend not to talk much about their religious beliefs – but they are still clearly religious.

Heinrich Zimmermann, who accompanied Cook on the third voyage (but on the *Discovery* rather than the *Resolution*), stated that Cook 'never mentioned religion and would have no priests on his ships; and, although he seldom celebrated the Sabbath, he was a just and upright man in all his dealings. He never swore, not even when in a rage'. This characterisation, probably based mostly on hearsay and written in the aftermath of Cook's death, is unconvincing. First, Cook almost certainly did swear; and, second, a man who *rejects* priests is likely to be more exercised by religion than one who is merely indifferent to them. The 'ban' on clerics may have stemmed more from unwillingness to share shipboard authority than from anti-clericalism *per se*. Even if Cook were less religious than most of his contemporaries, such an assessment can only be made in relation to his environment. Religion was an ever-present and taken-for-granted backdrop of eighteenth-century English life. It would not take much questioning to appear anti-religious in such a setting.

At most, then, it might be possible to say that Cook did not seek out church involvement in his projects or in his personal life; but all the indications are that he tolerated and occasionally welcomed it. For example, he collaborated with educated churchmen on a number of occasions. The Reverend Dr John Douglas, Canon of Windsor and St Paul's, worked with Cook to help prepare the journal of the first and second voyages for publication and also edited the third after the captain's death. Beaglehole mentions that Cook's gratitude to Douglas was 'great and unfeigned'. Another cleric, the Reverend Dr Richard Kaye, provided the navigator with a number of silver two-penny pieces ('Maundy money') to leave sealed in bottles at various sites of discovery in the course of the third voyage. In turn, 'as a mark of... esteem and regard', an island was named after him.

Cook sometimes resorted to quite a conventional vocabulary of Christian belief in his writings: 'creation' crops up at least once and 'Providence' several times. When the *Endeavour* narrowly averted shipwreck in waters of the Great Barrier Reef in August 1770, Cook named the opening through which they escaped 'Providential Channell' and wrote, 'It pleased GOD at this very juncture to send us a light air of wind', a view that Beaglehole dismisses as a momentary lapse of reason. It is more likely that his world view had, for those moments when scientific causation failed, a fallback position of divine intervention, a reading bolstered by a letter of 20 November 1772 to John Walker, before the second voyage: 'When I think of the inhospitable parts I am going to, I think the Voyage dangerous, I however enter upon it with great cheerfullness, providence has been very kind to me on many occasions, and I trust in the continuation of the divine protection'.

There are also Biblical echoes in the published journals: for example, a reference to the story of Lot's wife in his account of the 'inasi ceremony at Tongatapu, when he disobeyed a 'commandment' not to look behind him. The same entry approvingly states that the ritual 'was conducted with Ceremonious solemnity, and that it was mixed with a great deal of Religion is evident not only from the place where it was performed, but from the manner of performing it... . These to me were a sufficient testimony that they looked upon themselves to be acting under the immediate eye of a Supreme Being'.

Given that his vessels were generally too small to have qualified for an onboard chaplain, the performance of religious offices, as required by the Naval Instructions of 1731, would have rested on Cook or his nominee. There are scattered references to a low-key atmosphere of religious observance, perhaps because Sunday worship was so taken for granted. Sometimes secular and sacred intertwined, as with the institution of 'banyan' (meatless) days on Mondays, Wednesdays and Fridays: no doubt introduced for reasons of economy but still resonant with Christian tradition. And even though there could never be a day of rest and religious observance under sail in the same way as at anchor, evidence suggests that the Sabbath was marked by better food (when available) and at least occasional services. By navy tradition, Sunday seems to have been the day for regular inspection of the ship and its crew. One of the onboard diarists noted that, for Cook, 'every day was a Sunday' in this sense. According to Zimmermann, Cook insisted his seamen 'should put on clean clothes every Sunday'. The ritual element of such practices should not be underestimated.

Moreover, the important 'pagan' maritime ceremonies such as 'crossing the line' were always marked. The bacchanalia of equatorial crossings seems to have been outdone only by Christmas, a festival arguably pagan in many of its manifestations (another 'Ancient Custom of the Sea', as Beaglehole puts it), not yet having acquired the Victorian aura of sentimentality or its status as a time of more sober indulgence. Christmas was renowned for the crew's eating, drinking and 'drunken fighting'. As evidence of Christmas's cultural and emotional salience, any nearby landmark, anchorage or island ran the risk of being commemorated by that name. During his exploration of the north-west coast, too, Cook named an inlet Cross Sound, after the church festival of the 'Invention of the Cross', and a nearby mountain and cape after Saints Augustine and Bede.

A View of a Morai [Heuai] at Owhyhee. Engraved by W Walker after Ellis. (Ellis. 1782. II FP 180)

In short, Cook tolerated religion. He may not have shared all the ideals or beliefs of those whom he wrote about or worked with. He may even have felt superior to those whose lives were more ruled by religion than his. Yet he was sufficiently imbued with religious empathy to claim to recognise its various manifestations – Christian and otherwise – and to interpret them as signs of social development. The extended descriptions of Tongan and Tahitian ceremonies are testimony to this.

The Europeans on the three great voyages commanded by Cook often participated, wittingly and unwittingly, in the rituals of the people they encountered (eg Joseph Banks at Tahiti in 1769). Cook, too, engaged in such role-play though he sometimes revealed himself to be as impatient or ill at ease with organised Polynesian religion as he was reputed to be with the English variety. He disobeyed protocol at the Tongan 'inasi ceremony in July 1777 referred to earlier. He also appears to have transgressed in January 1779 after ceremonies he took part in at the heiau or shrine called Hikiau at Kealakekua Bay on the island of Hawai'i though the reasons behind his order to have the heiau fence broken up for firewood are the subject of dispute. Beaglehole sees it as a pragmatic act while Obeyesekere sees it as Cook's atonement for a sense of Christian guilt.

Obeyesekere argues that Cook was no humanist because he did not live up the ideals of that philosophy, but he does not question the conventional wisdom that eighteenth-century rationalists were indeed humanists. Arguably *none* of the humanists of the time, Cook included, were as rational and agnostic as stereotypically portrayed.

By Michael Goldsmith

See Also: Cook as god and Cook's death, Quakers

Resolution, HMS

The Navy Board purchased two ships for Cook's second voyage. The larger ship, intended for Cook, was the *Marquis of Granby*, built by the Fishburn yard at Whitby in 1770. She was renamed the *Drake* but it was soon realised that this name might offend the Spanish so the ship became HMS *Resolution*. She cost the Admiralty £4151. The *Resolution* impressed Cook greatly and he called her 'the ship of my choice, the fittest for service of any I have seen'. She was of 462 tons, 110ft 8in (33.7m) long, with a breadth of 35ft 1in (10.7m). The ship was fitted out at Deptford and classed as a sloop.

The Resolution *at anchor in the Marquesas Islands, in a sketch by William Hodges. (National Maritime Museum, London)*

Joseph Banks had intended to sail again with Cook and modifications were made to accommodate him and his extensive entourage. An additional upper deck and a raised poop were built to Banks' instructions but they made the ship top-heavy, as was found in short sea trials. The Admiralty ordered that the offending structures be removed at Sheerness, much to Banks' anger and he refused to sail. The conversion bills came to a further £6565.

Resolution's voyage began on 13 July 1772 and was completed on 30 July 1775. The ship had performed adequately and was selected to sail again on Cook's third voyage to the Pacific in 1776. However, she was not properly repaired and did not handle as well on that voyage, which began on 12 July 1776 and finished on 7 October 1780. Cook began both voyages as ship's captain, the second as commander and the third as post captain.

Like the *Endeavour*, the probable later history of the *Resolution* has only recently been determined. The *Resolution* was converted into an armed transport in late 1780 and sailed for the East Indies in March 1781. She was captured by a French squadron on 9 June 1782 *en route* for Trincomalee. The French realised they had captured Cook's old ship and changed her name to *Marie Antoinette*. In 1783, she sailed to France where she was sold and became a whaler, making several voyages to the Arctic between 1785 and 1787. In 1789, she was sold to W Haydon and renamed, in light of the French Revolution, *La Liberté*. She made further whaling voyages to the Pacific and was seen by Admiral John Barrow in the Cape Verde Islands in 1793. *La Liberté* went to Newport, Rhode Island, where she sank at her moorings in the harbour in 1793 and was abandoned. She now lies under a carpark. The ship therefore ended up in the same resting-place as the *Endeavour* and the *Lark*. Not all of this later history has been confirmed and may never be.

The *Resolution* was the first ship to cross both the Antarctic (17 January 1773) and Arctic Circles (12 August 1778). The name *Resolution* has been used for various geographical features in Canada, Vanuatu, New Zealand and on Mercury. The Resolution Trust was formed in 1999 to build a replica of the vessel but no

A modern cutaway model of the Resolution, *demonstrating a collier's great loading capacity. Cook described the* Resolution, *his ship on his second and third voyages, as 'the ship of my choice'. (Captain Cook Memorail Museum, Whitby)*

progress had been made in early 2004.

SEE ALSO: Cook's ships, Second and Third voyages

Rickman, John (?–1818)

John Rickman sailed on Cook's third voyage. He began the voyage as second lieutenant on the *Discovery* and was transferred to second lieutenant on the *Resolution* on Clerke's death in August 1779. He kept a log, on which he based an account of the third voyage, which was published anonymously in 1781.

Very little is known about Rickman, especially his early life. He joined the *Discovery* from the *Carcass,* a bomb vessel. After Cook's third voyage, Rickman transferred to the *Sally,* a storeship, in 1781. Rickman was on board HMS *Goliath,* a Third Rate of 74 guns, in 1787. From 1798 to 1799, John Rickman was in command of HMS *Victory,* a First Rate of 100 guns, being used as a hospital ship at Chatham. (The *Victory* was rebuilt in 1801 and used by Nelson as his flagship at Trafalgar in 1805.)

Rickman died in 1818, having been wounded and spending his last months from 1817 at the Greenwich Hospital. He left a widow and two sons.

SEE ALSO: Published accounts, Third voyage

Rio de Janeiro

Gaspar de Lemos set sail from Portugal for Brazil in 1501 and entered a huge bay in January 1502. Mistaking it for a river, he named it Rio de Janeiro (22° 53' S, 43° 17' W). It remained a small port for the next 200 years. Gold was found in the Brazilian interior in Minas Gerais at the start of the eighteenth century and this changed Rio's role. It became an important port. In 1710, the French, who were raiding the Portuguese colonies, attacked the city.

The Portuguese authorities decided to replace Salvador de Bahia with Rio de Janeiro as the colonial capital in 1763. The Viceroy moved south to his new capital. In 1808 the entire Portuguese monarchy and court arrived in Rio, and so it was that the city came to house what was left of the Portuguese Empire.

Cook brought the *Endeavour* to Rio on 13 November 1768, only to receive an unexpectedly hostile reception. Portugal was regarded as an ally of Britain but the Viceroy was suspicious of the *Endeavour*'s purpose and Cook was given a torrid baptism in diplomacy. After restocking, Cook left on 7 December. Peter Flower, who had worked with Cook in Newfoundland, had drowned in the harbour. Banks and Solander managed to get ashore and collect some botanical specimens.

SEE ALSO: First voyage

Riou, Edward (1762–1801)

Edward Riou sailed on the third voyage on the *Discovery* as a midshipman until 6 September 1779. He was then transferred to the *Resolution.* He kept a log, and made surveys and drew charts. During the voyage Riou, or 'Young Neddy' as he was known, acquired a native dog at Queen Charlotte Sound. The dog apparently bit several of Riou's colleagues so when he was ashore one day the dog was given a mock trial, found guilty, killed and cooked. This was referred to as the 'Trial of the Cannibal Dog'. The instigator of the episode was Alexander Home, whose memoirs provide details.

Riou had served on the *Barfleur* at Portsmouth and on the *Romney* on the Newfoundland station before he joined Clerke on the *Discovery* for the third voyage. He was promoted to lieutenant in October 1780, serving first in the West Indies on HMS *Scourge.* This was followed by a spell on HMS *Ganges,* a guardship at Portsmouth. Riou next experienced two years on half-pay before from 1786 until 1788 he served on HMS *Salisbury* on the Newfoundland station. In 1789, he was given charge of HMS *Guardian* to transport convicts to Australia. While attempting to obtain ice for fresh drinking water, the ship hit an iceberg near Prince Edward Island on 24 December 1789. Riou managed to nurse the sinking vessel back to the Cape, which he reached on 21 February 1790. He was commended and promoted commander in September 1790 and captain in June 1791.

In 1793, Riou took command of HMS *Rose* and sailed to the West Indies. In 1795, he transferred to HMS *Beaulieu*. However, his health was not good and he returned to Britain. When Riou recovered he had a short period in charge of the royal yacht, *Princess Augusta,* before he was given command of HMS *Amazon,* a Fifth Rate of 38 guns, in 1799 and joined the Baltic Fleet in 1801. The *Amazon* and Riou took part in the Battle of Copenhagen on 2 April 1801, where he was killed. Nelson wrote later 'In my poor dear Riou the country has sustained an irreparable loss' and 'In that case, poor dear Riou might have been saved; but his bravery attempted what I directed three sail of the line to assist him in'.

He was born in Faversham, Kent, on 20 November 1762. He left a will (FRC 11/1356). There is a memorial to Riou in St Paul's Cathedral, London, while Point Riou in south-east Alaska is named for him. There is a brief biography in the *DNB*, v16, pp1201–2.

SEE ALSO: Third voyage

Roberts, Henry (1757–1796)

Henry Roberts sailed on the second voyage on the *Resolution* as an AB. He drew charts and coastal views. Roberts sailed again on the third voyage on the *Resolution* as a master's mate during which he made a painting of the *Resolution*. He kept a log and drew charts. He was given the task of preparing the charts of the third voyage for the published official account and worked on this from 1781 until 1784. Roberts was made lieutenant in October 1780 and served as second lieutenant on HMS *Dragon*. He was given the command of an expedition to the north-west coast of America in 1790 but, before he could sail, the expedition was postponed. Command was then given to Vancouver and Roberts was given instead a command of a voyage to Africa. Roberts was made a commander in January 1790 and captain in August 1794. He was captain of HMS *Undaunted* in 1796 and took the ship to the West Indies where he died of yellow fever on 25 August 1796 (his ship was wrecked two days later!).

He was born in Shoreham, Sussex on 17 March 1757, one of six sons and two daughters of Henry and Susannah Roberts. He and his wife Harriet had seven children. Floors Castle, near Kelso in Scotland has a portrait of Roberts by Thomas Gainsborough. The National Maritime Museum has another portrait. Roberts was a capable artist himself as shown by his watercolour of HMS *Resolution*.

SEE ALSO: Cartographic results of Cook's voyages, Third voyage

Rollett, Richard (1750–1821)

Richard Rollett sailed, apparently reluctantly, on the second voyage on the *Resolution* as the sailmaker. He wrote to Joseph Banks asking Banks to get him excused from the voyage. During the voyage Rollett kept a journal, hiding it in his Bible.

He was born in King's Lynn, Norfolk where he was baptised in St Margaret's Church on 10 June 1750. After the voyage with Cook, Rollett married Susanna Hart on 16 October 1777 in Boston. They had one daughter, Susanna. Rollett died on 20 January 1821 and is buried in All Saints Church, Gainsborough, Lincolnshire. There is a memorial in St Botolph's Church, Boston, in part dedicated to Rollett.

SEE ALSO: Second voyage

Royal Navy

The Royal Navy, which James Cook joined in the mid-eighteenth century, was a huge organisation with some of the largest industrial complexes in the period. It designed and built warships in its own dockyards, supplied victuals for the ships though its own yards, as well as raising seamen to man the ships. Some of the administration for this traced its origins to the mediaeval office of Lord High Admiral, while other parts had been created in the middle of the sixteenth century.

At the top of the hierarchy was the Admiralty Board, which had taken over the office of the Lord High Admiral. Therefore, instead of one person exercising office alone, it was carried out by a board made up, at this period, of seven people. Each member of the Board had a commission from the sovereign, and in theory had equal weight on the Board. In practice one of them, called the First Lord, carried more weight than his colleagues; sometimes this person was a sea officer, although when Cook entered the Navy the First Lord was the Fourth Earl of Sandwich. In fact, the First Lord was quite often a civilian and much of the board was made up of civilians rather than sea officers.

The Board functioned as the strategic director of naval operations, converting the orders of the King – in practice the Secretaries for the North and South departments – into orders and directions. They also appointed officers, called Sea Officers to differentiate them from officers of the Navy Board, who were naval officers. The Admiralty Board also had a hand in raising men for the Navy. They gave orders and directions to the Navy Board, which built the ships and supplied the food to those ships. To support the Board, which met in the afternoon six days a week, was the Secretary of the Admiralty and he handled all the correspondence to and from the Board. Eight senior clerks supported him and, in time of war, upward of a dozen more temporary clerks were hired. It was the Secretary who read all the letters out to the Board. At least four members of the Board were required to be present for their decisions to be binding.

As well as matters of high strategy, the Admiralty oversaw the appointment and examination of officers, especially the first and most important step up the ladder, that for lieutenant, which was the lowest commissioned rank in the Navy. In theory all subsequent promotions were based on the date of this first appointment. However, officers could be promoted on foreign stations by their commander-in-chief, although always subject to confirmation by the Board. Patronage was one of the strongest weapons in their administrative arsenal. Officers kept journals as much to prove service as for the information on where and what they and their vessel were doing. Another oddity of the eighteenth-century Navy was that officers were given commissions for a certain vessel and, although retaining their seniority, gained another for their subsequent vessels. When not serving, an officer was not under military discipline and could, if he so chose, turn down a commission, even in wartime. This happened during the War of American Independence when many officers disagreed with the policy of the Government towards the Americans. Another part of the Admiralty's patronage came through the boroughs it controlled in the dockyard towns. The Members of Parliament returned for those seats were either Sea Officers or Naval Officers from the yards meaning there were quite a number of sea officers who sat in Parliament throughout the eighteenth century.

The other main part of naval administration at the time was the Navy Board, which had been formed in the middle of the sixteenth century. This Board was charged with overseeing the work of the dockyards and supplying the timber, hemp, tar and all the necessaries to build and fit out a warship. It also looked after the feeding and health of seaman, as well as the transport service and victualling of overseas expeditions. Although the Admiralty Board was nominally senior to the Navy Board, their relationship was a contentious one for most of the eighteenth century. The Admiralty issued orders to the Navy Board for anything which fell under their jurisdiction. This could and sometimes did lead to disputes between the two boards as to who should be ordering what and these matters of precedent could slow down the fitting out and sailing of warships. However, by and large, the two boards worked well together.

Commissioners of the Navy Board oversaw this work with the principal members based in central London, though every dockyard had its own Commissioner. The Board had officers who managed different aspects of its work. The Surveyor of the Navy was in charge of ship design, the Comptroller of the Navy oversaw the finances of the Navy, and the Clerk of the Acts acted as the secretary to the Navy Board.

It was the Navy Board who brought in Cook's vessels, such as *Endeavour,* from the merchant marine and fitted them out for the voyages. The largest part of the Navy Board's responsibilities lay with the dockyards. In the eighteenth century, there were five home yards ranked, according to seniority, Deptford, Woolwich, Chatham, Portsmouth and Plymouth. The latter had only been founded in the late seventeenth century in response to the change in threat from the Dutch to the French.

Whilst the Principal Commissioners administered the Board from London, it was their colleagues in the yards who would have surveyed and fitted out *Resolution* and *Endeavour*, or any of Cook's ships. Experienced officers would have overseen the survey and subsequent fitting of the vessel. The master shipwright would have surveyed the vessel and would have overseen its fitting out. In this, he would have been assisted by the master attendant, who looked after all of the vessels moored in the yard and its surroundings.

Within the yard there were a large number of craftsmen at work, from shipwrights to bricklayers, and carpenters to coopers. All of these craftsmen helped to build, fit out or refit vessels for the Navy. It has rightly been said that the Royal Dockyards, to give them their full appellation, were the largest industrial complexes of their time. Several other activities were carried out within the confines of the dockyard walls as an aid to security by keeping workers in and controlling pilfering. There could be found the manufacture of rope, a smithy to forge fixtures and fittings from hanging knees to anchor flukes, a colour loft for flags, a pond in which

A sheer hulk lifting a mast into a ship at Portsmouth Dockyard, 1772. (National Maritime Museum, London)

pine was kept for masts, as well as stacks of timer for frames and planking of ships. Most of those employed by the Navy Board in the yards were skilled artisans, many of whom would spend their whole working life in the yards, often remaining on the books long after their working life was over. This was not corruption but paternalism as there were no pensions for these men once they retired. They would be put on light duties, such as watchman until they died.

The Royal Dockyards would build major warships, major meaning First, Second and Third Rate ships of the line. Smaller ships such as frigates and bomb vessels would be built in commercial yards with fittings supplied from the Royal Dockyards. Once these vessels were built they would be fitted out for naval service in the Royal Dockyards. As well as the home yards, the Navy Board had yards overseas, at Antigua, as well as facilities at Gibraltar, Halifax in Canada, and in Jamaica. Not all of these locations had full dockyard facilities such as dry-docks, but had some repair and refitting capabilities, as well as storehouses and hospitals.

The Navy Board was also required to feed all seaman serving at the time. This could be, in time of war, upward of 45,000 men, all of whom were given an established diet, such as salt pork or beef, peas, butter, cheese, and bread, the latter a baked biscuit. The bread was baked in the Navy Board's own baking houses, under the control of the Victualling Board, itself part of the Navy Board. The Victualling Board had its own yards, usually part of, or adjacent to, the Royal dockyards. As well as baking bread there, beef and pork were salted and packed in barrels and beer was brewed, using its own coopers as well as brewers and slaughter men. Beer was carried on board ships as a staple in addition to water which became brackish within a matter of weeks.

In addition to building and repairing ships and supplying them with victuals, the Navy Board appointed some of the officers aboard a ship. One of these was the master, the rank to which Cook was appointed in 1757. Masters where not commissioned officers, as were lieutenants, captains and the like, but warrant officers appointed by warrant from the Navy Board. Masters had control over the sailing of the vessels, as well as the navigation when under way. They were highly skilled individuals, who also taught the midshipman these arts. The Navy Board also appointed standing officers to ships of the Navy. They were called standing officers because unlike most other officers, once appointed, they stayed with the same vessel whether it was in service or in Ordinary, ie reserve (so called because they were carried on the Ordinary vote of the Navy, granted by Parliament). The standing officers were the boatswain and the carpenter. When a vessel was not in service it was laid up, either in the dockyard, or in the harbour or river adjacent to a yard. The Navy Board was responsible for them, and the master attendant of the yard, as well as the standing officers, maintained the vessels whilst they were in Ordinary.

Whilst officers, both commissioned and warrant, were important, they could have achieved little without a crew which was capable of handling a ship under sail. Nor could Cook have achieved what he did without skilled seamen as part of his crew. The common conception about the eighteenth-century Navy, still prevalent today despite the best effort of some distinguished scholars, is of poorly paid men swept up by the press gang willy-nilly and dumped aboard ship, only to see their homes years later. So much for the myth: the reality was that the Navy needed trained seamen to work these complex machines called warships and the best place to get them was from was the pool of merchant seamen. It was they whom the press gang targeted and it was especially those rated as seaman, whom the Navy most needed. It must be remembered that the Navy had no system for the wholesale training of seaman until the nineteenth century. Those who volunteered, and there were more than might be thought, gained a bounty or extra pay. The rest were pressed under an Admiralty warrant for the duration, and the duration was up to the Admiralty. If so-called 'landsmen' volunteered, they had to be trained aboard the ships to which they were sent, imposing an additional strain on the experienced seaman. They were usually given the least skilled jobs such as weighing anchor, bracing round the yards etc, sparing the highly skilled seamen for the jobs aloft.

The need for skilled seamen would be even greater on Cook's vessels. They were few in number and everyone was important, leaving no one spare to train up willing but inexperienced landsmen. From the muster books, it is clear that all of those who sailed with Cook were experienced men, many of whom had sailed to the Pacific before. Cook was lucky in as much as his voyages were, at the start, undertaken in peacetime, which meant he could virtually hand-pick his crew from the very best men. In wartime, captains seldom had that luxury having often to make up their crews from a mixture of volunteers, seamen, and pressed men. Sometimes even this was not enough and troops were embarked to make up the numbers. In this case, the unskilled soldiers were treated in the same way as landsmen and give the heavy jobs.

Another of the Navy Board's functions was to care for sick and wounded seamen. The Navy for most of the eighteenth century saw the health of its seamen as an administrative problem and sought administrative solutions to it. They did build hospitals and large ships did carry surgeons but the overall impression given is more of loss management than of positive care for those who became sick. Much debate about Cook is rightly focused on his role in combating scurvy. In many ways, Cook was lucky, for in addition to his own proclivities about seamen's health, he had a small, hand-picked crew whose health he could closely manage. In wartime, by contrast, the huge numbers of men entering and leaving ships, made it difficult, but not impossible, to give the same attention as did Cook.

The Royal Navy in the eighteenth century was a vast and complex organisation, administered, by modern standards, by a very small number of professional officers. It would be ludicrous to say that there was no inefficiency or corruption in either the administration or the dockyards. On the whole though, it managed to build, fit out, and send to sea fleets which were the equal and, more often than not, superior to the French or Spanish. It fed and clothed its men, and paid them, albeit in arrears, sometime many years so. Cook's ships were surveyed and fitted out by an organisation, which was used to sending tens of thousand of seamen and hundreds of ships to sea year after year. That his first expedition made little impact initially on the Navy should be no surprise when it is remembered that it was only one of that huge number of craft sent to sea by the Navy. It considered itself as a professional and proficient organisation, so it is wholly fitting then that a man of Cook's talents should have been part of it.

By Christopher Ware

See Also: Admiralty, Discipline and punishment, Navy Board

Royal Society

The Royal Society of London for the Improvement of Natural Knowledge was founded in 1660 though people had been meeting since the 1640s. As such, the Royal Society is the world's oldest scientific academy still operating. King Charles II granted it its Royal title. In the beginning, the Society met weekly to witness experiments and discuss scientific topics. In 1665, the first issue of the Society's *Philosophical Transactions* appeared and it is now the oldest scientific journal in continuous publication.

The Society has had several homes. At first it met at Gresham College but after the Fire of London in 1666 it moved to Arundel House. In 1710, under the presidency of Isaac Newton, the Society acquired its own home in Crane Court, off Fleet Street. It was here that Cook attended meetings. The Society moved again in 1780 to premises at Somerset House provided by the Crown, an arrangement made by Sir Joseph Banks, who had become the President.

Members or Fellows of the Society had to be elected, though the majority of early Fellows were not professional scientists but 'gentlemen amateurs' interested in science. In 1731, a new rule established that candidates for election had to be proposed in writing and this written certificate signed by those who supported his candidature.

The Society has awarded various medals and prizes over the years to recognise achievement and contributions to the advancement of science. The premier medal of the Society is the Copley Medal; it is also the oldest, having been first awarded in 1731. It is awarded annually for outstanding achievements in research in any branch of science. During its long history it has been awarded to such luminaries as Charles Darwin and Albert Einstein. James Cook won the Copley in 1776 for his work on fighting scurvy.

In Cook's time of contact with the Royal Society the Presidents were James, Earl of Morton (1764–68), Sir James Burrow (1768), James West (1768–72), Sir John Pringle (1772–78), and Sir Joseph Banks (1778–1820).

Cook submitted his observations of a solar eclipse at the Burgeo Islands in Newfoundland in 1766. Dr. John Bevis presented it as a paper on 30 April 1767 and it appeared in the *Transactions*.

The Royal Society was instrumental in organising the *Endeavour* voyage to Tahiti to observe the Transit of Venus. Cook, as a tribute, named the island group of which Tahiti is a member, the Society Islands. He also named various features in southern Queensland after the Society's President, the Earl of Morton (the names have since acquired an 'e' to become Moreton). In return, at Banks' behest, the Society commissioned a Cook medal in 1784, designed by Lewis Pingo, the chief engraver at the Royal Mint.

Cook was nominated to be a Fellow in late 1775. His nomination was signed by 25 eminent Fellows, including Banks, Solander, Johann Reinhold Forster, Maskelyne and Philip Stephens. Cook was admitted on 7 March 1776. Cook also attended the Royal Society Dining Club, of which Banks was a prominent member, at the Mitre Tavern off Fleet Street.

SEE ALSO: Copley Medal, First voyage

Russians

James Cook is thought to have visited St Petersburg on the *Mary* around 1750 as an ordinary seaman. Thirty years later, material collected on his last voyage was being appropriated by the Russian Government for display in the city. On that last voyage, Cook had sailed north in search of the Northwest Passage, aware of Bering's visits to the Gulf of Alaska on behalf of Russia. He was also aware of a Russian presence in Alaska but it was only on his return to Unalaska in October 1778 that he met any Russians when three fur traders accompanied Ledyard to Samgoonoodha after the marine had been sent by Cook to visit their post. Another Russian, the Factor Gerassim Gregoriev Ismailov, who had been carrying out a census of Aleuts on Umnak, came later with charts for Cook to copy. Ismailov also gave Cook letters of introduction to the Governor of Kamchatka while Cook wrote a letter to the Admiralty, which he asked Ismailov to forward to London.

After Cook's death, Charles Clerke took over command, intent on returning to the Arctic despite his own failing health. The British ships entered Avacha Bay in Kamchatka in April 1779. Clerke sent King, with their letters of introduction from Ismailov in Unalaska, to meet the Russians in their post at Petropavlovsk. They found that Magnus Behm (1727–1806), the Governor of Kamchatka, resided in Bol'sheretsk on the far side of the peninsula and only a sergeant was based in Avacha Bay. Emissaries arrived from the Governor inviting them to visit but, given Clerke's poor health, it was King, Gore and Webber who left on 7 May for Bol'sheretsk, where Behm met them on the 12th. They returned, accompanied by the Governor who met Clerke on board the *Resolution* on 16 May. The British set off for the Arctic on 19 June but arrived back on 24 August having failed once more to find the Northwest Passage. Unfortunately, Clerke had died of consumption two days earlier. Gore was now in command.

Clerke was buried in Petropavlovsk at the site of its future church. A Russian sloop arrived with letters and supplies from Governor Behm. In return copies of letters and journals were sent to Behm, with the request that, as he was returning to St Petersburg, he take them and forward them to London. Behm was as good as his word and it was through him that the first news of Cook's death reached Europe in January 1780. Behm travelled to London where he sought help from Joseph Banks. There is still a memorial to Clerke in Petropavlovsk.

The British were grateful for their treatment by the Russians in Kamchatka and gave Behm a collection of Pacific artefacts in return. Behm transported them back to St Petersburg but, by Catherine the Second's order of 27 March 1780, this collection was handed over to the Emperor's Academy of Sciences. They were incorporated into Peter the Great's Museum of Anthropology and Ethnography (Kunstkammer) in St Petersburg. Cook's collection now occupies a particularly significant place among the extremely valuable ethnographical and artistic eighteenth-century exhibits.

Cook's reputation was as high in Russia as it had become throughout Europe. Any link with Cook guaranteed employment and at least two men who had sailed with Cook obtained positions. James Trevenen died fighting for the Russians against the Swedes at Viborg in 1790 and Joseph Billings led a Russian expedition into the Gulf of Alaska in 1790. Many Russian naval officers trained in Britain, among them Ivan Krusenstern and it was Krusenstern who named the Cook Islands after the British explorer. Vancouver in turn had named the Behm Canal in north-west America after Magnus Behm.

SEE ALSO: Alaska, Billings (Joseph), Trevenen (James)

S

Saint Helena

St Helena is a lone island on the mid-Atlantic ridge in the South Atlantic. The island, 9.9 miles by 6.2 miles (16km by 10km), and 46.9 square miles (122 sq km) in area is situated at 15° 55′ S and 5° 45′ W. It lies 1950 miles (3138km) west of Angola, the nearest mainland. The island's capital is Jamestown. St Helena was discovered by the Portuguese on 21 May 1502, feast day of St Helena, mother of the Roman emperor Constantine.

In 1659 the English East India Company (EIC) took possession of the island under charter from Charles II. It remained under their control until 1834, except for a few months in 1672 when the Dutch captured the island. A resident governor ran the island for the EIC. From 1764 to 1782, the governor was John Skottowe, the son of Thomas Skottowe, who had been Lord of the Manor of Great Ayton when Cook was growing up there. Governor Skottowe, who had married Mary Greentree on the island on 30 September 1766 retired to Britain in 1782.

By the late seventeenth century the island had become a regular and welcome stopping-off point for ships sailing to and from India and the East Indies. Like many others, Cook stopped at the island on the return legs of his first two voyages. On both occasions Skottowe was the governor. Cook brought the *Endeavour* to anchor at St Helena on 1 May 1771 but there is no record that he met Skottowe on this occasion. Cook returned again on 15 May 1775 in the *Resolution* but by this time Hawkesworth's account of Cook's first voyage had been published in which Cook was uncomplimentary about St Helena. A copy had reached the island causing Cook to receive a torrid reception. Misunderstandings were soon resolved and Cook was entertained by Governor Skottowe.

SEE ALSO: Great Ayton, Skottowe family

Saint Lawrence River and Gulf

The St Lawrence River is one of the most important in North America. It is divided into three main sections: the river proper down from Lake Ontario to Quebec; the estuary down to Ste-Anne-des-Monts on the Gaspé Peninsula; and the Gulf, including the Cabot Strait. The river is navigable for large parts of the year but ices over most winters. It affords access to Canada's interior and the principal cities such as Quebec and Montreal. In the eighteenth century, whoever controlled the river was likely to control the country.

At the outbreak of the Seven Years War in 1756, France controlled the river. Forts at Louisbourg, on the Île Royal, which protected the Gulf and lower reaches of the river, and at Quebec, which controlled the upper reaches, gave France the upper hand. Britain set out to capture both and rest control of Canada from the French. James Cook was part of the British fleet that attacked Louisbourg in 1758. The French finally surrendered on 26 July. The British hesitated about pressing on to attack Quebec and, instead, made forays into the Gulf of St Lawrence to attack other French positions. Cook was present during General Wolfe's attack on Gaspé and he surveyed the Harbour and Bay afterwards. This was his first known chart.

The British then returned to Halifax to spend the winter away from the ice and cold of the St Lawrence. Ice detained the British fleet in Halifax in early 1759 but by May the fleet had set off up the St Lawrence for Quebec, under the command of Admiral Saunders. Tragedy struck the *Pembroke* on 16 May off Anticosti Island when Captain Simcoe died suddenly. He was replaced as Captain by Captain John Wheelock. The St Lawrence was largely unknown to the British, except through captured charts. It was thought to be difficult to navigate so a vanguard of ships, including the *Pembroke*, was sent ahead to establish a route. Cook is believed to have played a significant role. Progress proved surprisingly quick and the British fleet anchored in The Basin just below Quebec in June to begin its offensive. Quebec finally fell in September and Montreal, and with it Canada, the next year 1760. Cook's charts of the St Lawrence were published later.

SEE ALSO: Canada, Louisbourg, Quebec

Samwell, David (1751–1798)

Samwell was a surgeon's mate and then surgeon on Cook's third and last voyage. He was born in Nantglyn, North Wales where his father and grandfather were both clergymen. Little is known of his early life but he was probably educated in a local school or privately by his father. His subsequent career as a surgeon and a highly-regarded Welsh poet suggest that he was well educated.

Samwell probably studied medicine at sea. In 1771, he went on a voyage to Greenland. In the eighteenth century, largely for the convenience of the Navy, prospective ship's surgeons were examined at the Surgeons' Hall and success led the candidate being classed as surgeon's mate (assistant surgeon) of various grades. A surgeon's mate was allowed to practice as an assistant to a ship's surgeon. Because many voyages lasted some years an assistant surgeon could be promoted to the rank of surgeon by the ship's captain. In October 1775 Samwell appeared before the Court of Examiners at the Surgeons' Hall and qualified with the rank of second mate third rate. Alternatively, qualification as a ship's surgeon could be achieved by an exit examination at the Surgeons' Hall.

In 1776 Samwell sailed with Cook as assistant to Anderson on the *Resolution*. On 3 August 1778 Anderson died of consumption. The following day Cook appointed Law, surgeon of the *Discovery*, as surgeon of the *Resolution* and Samwell was appointed surgeon of the *Discovery*. He was popular with the sailors of the *Discovery* and amused them with his anecdotes and poems. Surprisingly as a son of the church he spoke and wrote of the dear girls. Williams wrote '...(he, Samwell) revelled in the nymphs of the South Seas laying any personable female he could...'.

On 14 February 1779 Samwell witnessed the death of James Cook and provided an eye witness account in his journal. His journal also reflected on the introduction of syphilis to the South Seas. Cook and King (captain of the *Discovery*) believed '...that the distemper was received from our people...', presumably during the second Cook voyage. Samwell did not agree for a Hawaiian had told him that syphilis was prevalent at O'ahu – an island not visited by the third voyage.

Samwell returned to London in 1780. He was also a poet, who wrote verse in English and Welsh, and a member of the Gwyneddigion Society. He was a ship's surgeon on at least six further voyages, including time on HMS *Crocodile* under James King, and for part of the last year of his life was surgeon to the British prisoners of war at Versailles. He died, possibly of venereal disease, at his home in Fetter Lane, London, in 1798. He was buried in London at St Dunstan's, Fleet Street.

By John Morris

See Also: Cook as god and Cook's death, Medical aspects of Cook's voyages, Third voyage

Sanderson, William (1711–1773)

Sanderson, Cook's employer in Staithes from 1745, was 'a big fish in a small pond'; his shop on the seafront at Staithes was also an indication of his status and prosperity. Cook's biographers describe him as a shopkeeper, but this term demeans his role as a merchant, as well as his social position within the close-knit community. When he was not travelling around the country on business, he was acting as a local Constable keeping the peace in and around Staithes. When trustees were needed for rebuilding Easington Parish Church Sanderson was appointed. And when gentlemen came ashore at Staithes from passing vessels, it was Sanderson who provided them with horses to enable them to continue their journey inland.

William Sanderson and his wife Elizabeth had a large family of nine boys and two girls. Whilst some died in infancy, two of his sons, Thomas and William, died in the service of the British East India Company (EIC). It is thought that Sanderson's family connections with Thomas Scottowe of Great Ayton enabled him to place his sons within the service of the EIC, as in 1755, one of Thomas Scottowe's sons, Augustine, had married Sanderson's sister-in-law, Ann Gill. In subsequent years the two families became more closely entwined. Two of Scottowe's sons had also entered the EIC, John Scottowe rose to be the Governor of St Helena, and Nicholas Scottowe was captain of the East Indiaman *Royal George* when the ship's surgeon, William Sanderson, died at sea in February 1767.

Such was Scottowe's confidence in his friend that in his will dated 24 December 1770, he nominated Mr William Sanderson of Staithes as one of the trustees responsible for securing the education of his granddaughter, Elizabeth Scottowe.

Sanderson's various connections also helped the young James Cook. It was through Sanderson's friendship with Thomas Skottowe of Great Ayton that Cook acquired his job in Staithes, and eighteen months later, it was through Sanderson's acquaintance with John Walker that Cook moved on to Whitby.

The shop where Cook briefly worked was just one of Sanderson's business interests, and at his death he owned not only the shop but warehouses in Staithes as well as properties at Hinderwell, Loftus and Whitby. His land holdings ran into hundreds of acres, including a farm. Sanderson was buried in the churchyard of Hinderwell Parish Church, the memorial inscription on the family tombstone recording his name and those of his departed family. Today the site of the Sanderson shop lies underwater, some 20 yards off-shore. The shop and other harbourside properties were extensively damaged during rough seas and high tides around 1800, although building materials from the shop were salvaged and used to construct new premises in Church Street, which stand there to this day.

By Clifford E Thornton

See Also: Cook's early years, Staithes

Sandwich, John Montagu, 4th Earl of (1718–1792)

John Montagu was born on 3 November 1718 and succeeded his grandfather, Edward, the 3rd Earl, as Earl of Sandwich in 1729. He was educated at Eton and at Trinity College, Cambridge, before spending time travelling in Europe. On his return to England in 1739 he took his seat in the House of Lords. Sandwich took part in the negotiations for peace leading to the treaty of Aix-la-Chapelle in 1748.

He was appointed a Lord Commissioner of the Admiralty and, in February 1748, he became First Lord of the Admiralty, retaining this post until he was dismissed by the king in June 1751. He had instigated inspections of naval shipyards and written code of discipline in 1749. Sandwich later became one of the principal secretaries of state. Sandwich was a leading member of the Hellfire Club and acquired a reputation for his hedonistic lifestyle. He took a leading part in the prosecution in 1763 of John Wilkes, a fellow hedonist, which made him very unpopular, and he became known as 'Jemmy Twitcher' after a character in the *Beggar's Opera*.

He was postmaster-general in 1768, secretary of state in 1770, and resumed his post as First Lord of the Admiralty from 1771 to 1782. He was First Lord when Cook returned from the first voyage and the two formed a strong if unlikely friendship. Their backgrounds were very different and Sandwich's reputation for hedonism

The Earl of Sandwich was First Lord of the Admiralty from 1771. A man of some notoriety for his personal life, he worked well with Cook, who named many features after him. (Captain Cook Memorial Museum, Whitby)

could not be further from Cook's sober behaviour. Sandwich ensured Cook's second voyage took place even though it strained his own friendship with Joseph Banks. It was later Sandwich who prevailed on Cook to undertake the third voyage. Cook, in return, named many features around the world after the First Lord, using both his Montagu and Sandwich names and also that of Sandwich's country estate, Hinchingbrooke, near Huntingdon.

Sandwich proved an able, if corrupt, administrator, and his naval policy was generally sound. However, his retirement in March 1782 was hailed with joy as he had become very unpopular. Sandwich had a son John with his wife Dorothy. By 1755, Sandwich and Dorothy had separated, with Lady Sandwich, who was having mental problems, living in an apartment in Windsor Castle. Martha Ray became Sandwich's mistress around 1762, when she was 17 years old and they had several children together. The murder of Miss Ray by a rejected suitor in April 1779 increased the earl's unpopularity, He died on 30 April 1792. The sandwich was also named after him, supposedly after his tendency to eat food in that form rather than leave the gaming table.

See Also: Admiralty

Scotland

Scotland is the part of the United Kingdom, lying between 54° and 61° N, and 0° and 6° W and making up the northern portion of the island of Britain. It borders its neighbour, England, to the south. In AD 843, Kenneth MacAlpine was crowned the first king of Scotland, uniting the Picts and the Scots, though Southern Scotland was still under different rule. In 1016, the Scots defeated the English and gained Lothian and Borders, establishing the country's present-day boundaries. An ancient name for part of Scotland was Caledonia.

King James of Scotland became king of England in 1603, uniting the two countries. In 1715, the son of James II attempted to win back the throne for the Stuarts by raising an army, but popular support for the Jacobite cause evaporated and he had to escape to France. Kelso, in the Scottish Borders, was a rallying point for the Jacobite uprising. James Cook's father was born and brought up at Ednam, near Kelso and it has been suggested that Cook senior may have been a Jacobite, explaining why, when the uprising failed, he needed to leave home quickly and head south to Cleveland.

After James Cook had passed his master's examination in 1756, he was assigned to HMS *Solebay*, a 24-gun frigate commanded by Captain Robert Craig and currently in harbour at Leith near Edinburgh in Scotland. Cook joined his new ship on 30 July. HMS *Solebay* sailed from Leith on 2 August on a patrol up the east coast of Scotland to Orkney and Shetland. The voyage kept close to the coast and the ship put in at Stonehaven and Peterhead on the mainland, Copinsay in Orkney and Fair Isle before reaching Lerwick in Shetland on 9 August. After a few days in Lerwick, the *Solebay* returned via Stromness in Orkney to reach Leith towards the end of the month.

Cook did not sail again with the *Solebay* as he received a warrant transferring him to HMS *Pembroke* in Portsmouth as master. His short stay in Scotland, the country of his father, made an impression as he later used the names New Caledonia and New Hebrides for islands in the Pacific.

SEE ALSO: *Solebay* (HMS)

Scurvy

Scurvy is a disease that results from insufficient intake of Vitamin C (ascorbic acid), taking about three months of Vitamin C deprivation to begin inducing the symptoms. It leads to the formation of livid spots on the skin, spongy gums and bleeding from almost all mucous membranes. Other symptoms include weakness, joint pain, black-and-blue marks on the skin and gum disease. Eventually death results. The disease did not emerge as a significant problem for sailors until vessels started sailing on much longer voyages and spending more time away from land. In 1520, Magellan lost more than 80 per cent of his crew while crossing the Pacific. By Cook's time, scurvy was a major concern for any crew setting sail on a long voyage.

Some of the problems suffered by ships' crews were not just caused by scurvy but other similar conditions caused by vitamin deficiencies. Diets at sea in the eighteenth century consisted chiefly of refined carbohydrates in the form of sea biscuits, dried cereals and legumes, and dried or salt meat. They were typically deficient in thiamin as well as ascorbic acid. This resulted in other diseases such as beriberi (caused by a lack of thiamin (Vitamin B) and other vitamins of the B complex) taking hold.

Various remedies for scurvy were tried without anyone really knowing which, if any, were being successful. Portable soup (a preparation of dried vegetables), malt, sauerkraut, rob (concentrated fruit juice), vinegar, mustard, molasses and beans were all used. They were aimed at repelling any sign of scurvy from the outset, since it was impossible to control it, once it had gained a footing, other than by going ashore. For his first voyage, Cook was supplied with 40 bushels of malt, 1000lb of portable soup, vinegar, mustard and wheat. He then took on large amounts of onions at Madeira.

Despite his efforts Cook was not scurvy-free. He had five cases of scurvy on his first voyage but on his next two voyages Cook's good management, or luck, persisted, and no deaths from scurvy were reported. As a result, Cook has been mistakenly credited with conquering scurvy. Some of his actions gave no benefit at all. Rob, which was carried on board Cook's ships, had been boiled to reduce it and, in the process, all its beneficial Vitamin C had been lost.

However, Cook paid strict attention to cleanliness, both of the ship and the men. The ship was regularly cleaned and aired, while the crew were expected to wash themselves and their clothes on a regular basis. These measures did not in themselves prevent scurvy but did ensure his crews were healthier and more able to resist illness. Cook always brewed when he reached land and

ensured that his crews drank quantities of beer. He used the plant known as scurvy grass, which acquired its name as it appeared to cure scurvy. It is most unfortunate that the discovery by James Lind of the means to prevent and treat scurvy by eating citrus fruit such as lemons and limes was not more widely known and acted upon earlier by the Navy.
SEE ALSO: Medical aspects of Cook's voyages

Sea otter fur trade

The sea otter (*Enhydra lutris*) is the only member of the genus Enhydra and the largest member of the family Mustelidae, which also includes weasels, skunks and badgers. It is the smallest marine mammal and hunts, sleeps and mates in the sea. It is found around the coast of the North Pacific Ocean from the Kurils to California where it forms a close relationship with the great kelp beds in which it spends most of its life. The sea otter dives for sea urchins and other bottom-dwelling marine life that it then kills using rocks as tools before eating. The coat of the animal is extremely dense to act as insulation in the cold water and, as such, is very warm. The indigenous peoples of the North Pacific region used the pelt of the sea otter as clothing and, when Europeans arrived in the eighteenth century, the pelts became one of the main items of trade.

James Cook's third voyage to the Pacific visited the north-west coast of America, Alaska and Kamchatka. During the course of the voyage, his crew traded with local people and the expedition acquired many sea otter pelts. When the ships reached Macao, the pelts were sold in Canton for a considerable sum of money. The news of this transaction, in 1780, quickly spread and soon companies were forming plans to sail to the North Pacific to exploit this new bonanza. Portlock, Dixon and Colnett, who had sailed with Cook, were among the sailors who took part. This trade in sea otter pelts nearly lead to the extinction of the animal. Fortunately, an international treaty halted the trade in 1911 but considerable damage had already been done. Millions of animals had died to grace the backs of rich Asians, Europeans and Americans. The sea otter had been killed off in huge stretches of the north-west coast and it only remained in very small numbers in isolated colonies. With help numbers have been restored in many places but close to populous areas, such as California, numbers are still very low.
SEE ALSO: Colnett (James), Portlock (Nathaniel), Third voyage

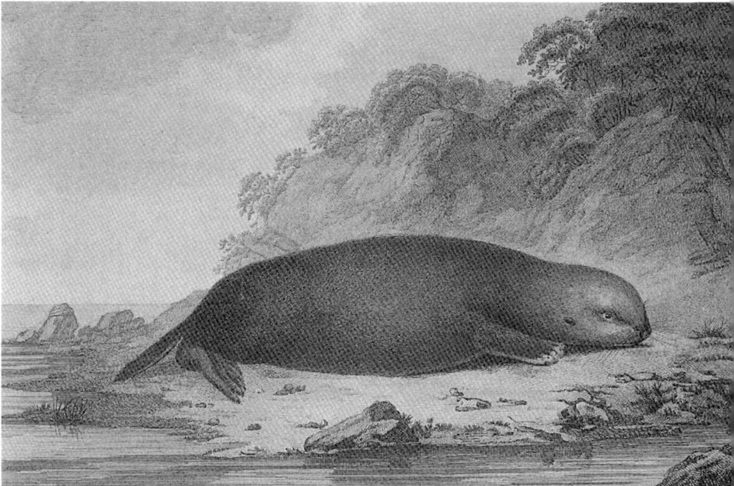

Sea otter. Engraved by P Mazell after Webber. (Cook & King (Atlas) pl 43)

Seamanship

Seamanship in the days of sail amounted to the daily management of a ship at sea. It involved managing the ship's gear, anchors, rigging, sails and small boats. It included keeping the watches both at sea and in port. The ship's boatswain was responsible for the crew and ensuring that the basic duties involved in running the ship took place. Under him, able seamen (ABs) were the sailors who performed the work, handling the sails, rigging, etc.

Cook learned his seamanship on North Sea colliers, which carried small crews, so all hands became familiar with all aspects of sailing a ship. Sailing close to the east coast of England over sandbanks and in the variable weather conditions found there, gave him invaluable training for his time later on *Endeavour* and *Resolution*. It also meant that when he became captain of his own ship he had a rare understanding of all operations on board. His crews knew that Cook had performed all the duties at some time, however menial, and knew how hard much of the work was and how tedious other aspects could be.
SEE ALSO: Navigation

Second voyage (1772–1775)

The idea of the existence of a Great Southern Continent had still not been totally dispelled when Cook returned from his *Endeavour* voyage in 1771. Cook believed he was the person to resolve the problem and submitted plans to the Admiralty. He, himself, would

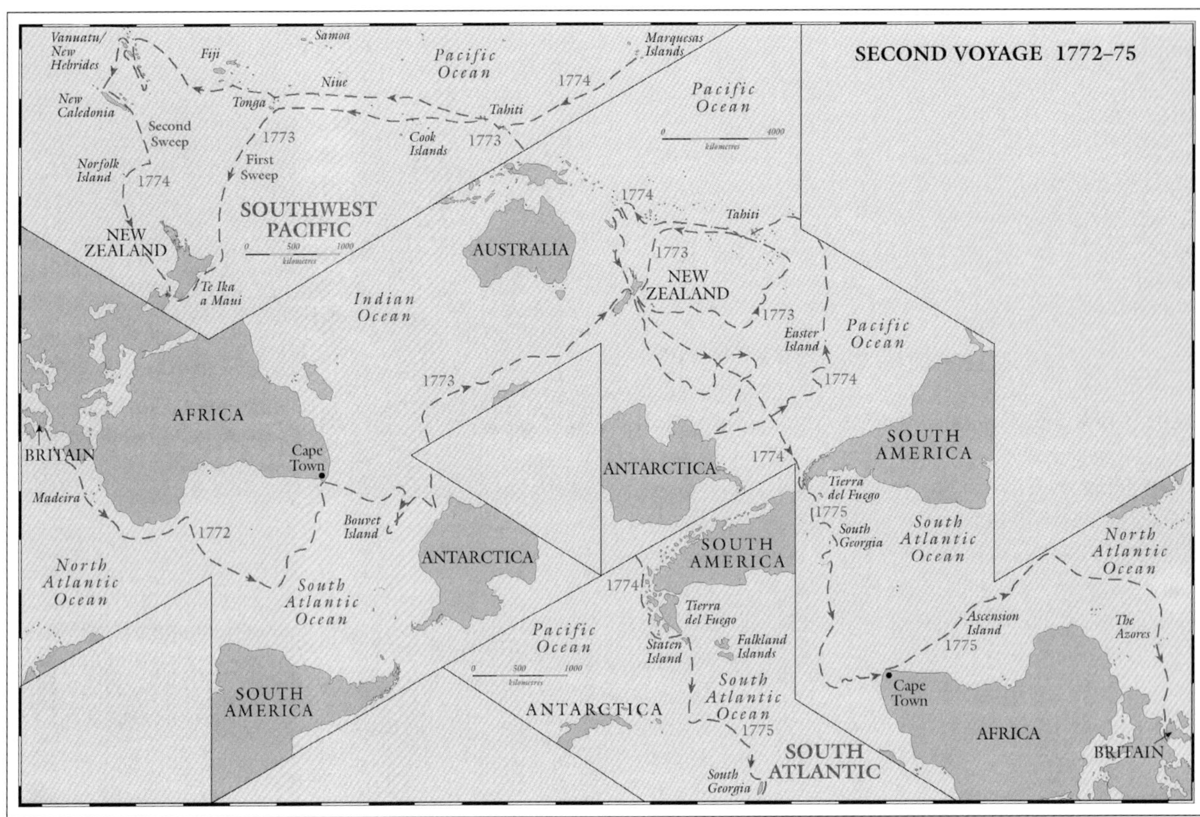

circumnavigate the South Pole as far south as conditions would allow and, if land existed, he would find it. The Admiralty agreed and appointed Cook, now promoted to Commander, to lead an expedition. Two ships, renamed HMS *Resolution* and HMS *Adventure,* were bought and fitted out for the voyage.

Joseph Banks expected to sail again but demanded that extensive alterations be made to the *Resolution* to accommodate him and his party. This took time, delaying the voyage, but also making the ship unsafe. Finally, the Navy said no and had the ship returned to its previous seaworthy state. Banks was angry and refused to sail. Johann Reinhold Forster was taken on as scientist in Banks' place, assisted by his son George. Williams Wales and Bayly were appointed astronomers and William Hodges travelled as artist.

The experience of the *Endeavour* on the Barrier Reef had shown the need to Cook for two ships. The *Resolution,* under Cook, accompanied by the *Adventure,* captained by Tobias Furneaux, left Plymouth on 13 July 1772. They sailed down the Atlantic together and reached Cape Town in October. Sailing on to the south, they looked, unsuccessfully, for land sighted by Bouvet, a French explorer. In January 1773, Cook became the first person known to cross the Antarctic Circle before pack ice and fog blocked his way and forced him back north. The two ships became separated but Cook sailed on returning south and then east through more ice and fog. In March he relented and headed to New Zealand where he and his crew recovered in Dusky Sound for a month. Moving on to Queen Charlotte Sound he found the *Adventure* waiting.

It was the wrong time of year to return south but Cook did not want to waste time so he decided to explore the Central Pacific. The two ships left New Zealand in June 1773 and sailed east for several weeks, finding no land, before heading north to Tahiti. The island was short of supplies so Cook only stayed for two weeks before sailing west. Furneaux took a Raiatean called Mai on board at Huahine. The ships next reached the southern islands of Tonga. Cook was impressed by the Tongan people, even in a short visit of a few days. As the ships approached New Zealand again, a storm separated them and the *Resolution* reached safety by itself in Queen Charlotte Sound. Cook waited for Furneaux for one month before sailing. He could wait no longer as he needed the warmer, summer conditions when he sailed south.

Over the next three months, Cook ploughed through the Southern Ocean finding no sign of land. He went south, crossing the Antarctic Circle on two occasions, before ice and cold drove him back. He was convinced that land did, indeed, lie further south and was the source of the ice. Cook became ill as they sailed north. In March 1774, the *Resolution* reached Easter Island and stopped briefly before sailing on via the Marquesas to arrive once more at Tahiti. The island had recovered and the ship could be restocked. After three weeks on Tahiti, Cook sailed west via Raiatea, Palmerston Atoll and Niue to arrive at the central Tongan Islands, north of his earlier visit.

The Spanish, under Quiros, were known to have visited some islands in the western Pacific 170 years earlier but their exact location was uncertain. In July 1774, Cook arrived at these islands and proceeded to chart them in only a few weeks. He called them the New Hebrides though they are now known as Vanuatu. Cook landed on several islands but communication was difficult as the people were different from those met on other islands. They were Melanesians, not Polynesians. In September, Cook pressed on to the south-west and came to another island, which he called New Caledonia. After three weeks there, he headed south for New Zealand and entered Queen Charlotte Sound. There were signs that Furneaux and the *Adventure* had been and gone. Cook, therefore, quickly stocked up with water and wood and set sail for home. He crossed the Pacific and reached South America in time for Christmas, which was celebrated in Christmas Sound, Tierra del Fuego.

Cook still wanted to check the South Atlantic and, early in 1775, he landed on South Georgia, a cold and desolate island. Nearby to the east, Cook found some other tiny islands, which he called the South Sandwich Islands. Cook found no other land and headed for Cape Town. He had circumnavigated the Southern Ocean near latitudes 55–60° S and there was no large landmass, only a few small islands and lots of ice. The *Resolution* sailed up the Atlantic calling in at St Helena, Ascension Island and the Azores before anchoring at Spithead on 30 July 1775. Cook learned that the *Adventure* had arrived back safely the previous year. Mai had become a celebrity in London society.

The voyage was a triumph for Cook and this time he received the acclaim of the general public. It had been one of the greatest voyages of all time. The crew was healthy though Cook himself had been ill and was now ready for a long rest. He had criss-crossed the South Pacific, locating many new islands and producing detailed charts of them all. He had left no large landmass undiscovered and had shown that a Southern Continent could only exist so far south as to be completely uninhabitable. The Forsters added much to scientific knowledge and Hodges returned with many paintings. For the moment Cook could enjoy time with his family.

Family in Dusky Bay, New Zealand. Engraved by D Lerpernière after Hodges. (Cook I fp 76)

View in the Island of New Caledonia. Engraved by W Byrne after Hodges. (Cook II fp 110)

SEE ALSO: *Adventure* (HMS), Forster family, *Resolution* (HMS), Colour plate 14

Seven Years War (1756–1763)

This war was fought in Europe, North America, and India between France, Austria, Russia, and (after 1762) Spain on the one side and Prussia and Great Britain on the other. Colonial rivalry between France and England in India and North America had continued even after the Treaty of Aix-la-Chapelle in 1748 and fighting resumed in 1755 with renewal of the French and Indian War in North America. This proved a spark for general war that was declared in Europe in 1756.

Britain sent a fleet across to North America in 1758 where they recaptured Louisbourg. In 1759, they continued up the St Lawrence River and captured Quebec. The French finally surrendered at Montreal in 1760, though they made a belated effort to regain some territory in 1762 when they captured St John's in Newfoundland. After protracted negotiations between the war-weary powers, peace was made on 10 February 1763 between England, France, and Spain at Paris. France handed over North America to the British, though St Pierre and Miquelon, off Newfoundland, were ceded to France.

Cook took part in many of the naval operations of the Seven Years War. He joined the Royal Navy in mid-1755 when war was imminent. For three years, he was involved in patrols in the English Channel, the Bay of Biscay and the North Atlantic, in which the British undertook to blockade the French navy in its ports. Supplies were blocked from entering France while French troops were prevented from easily reaching North America. This achieved its ultimate success at the Battle of Quiberon Bay off the French west coast in 1759. In 1758, Cook sailed to North America. He was present at the sieges of Louisbourg (1758) and Quebec (1759). For the next three years, Cook was based at Halifax and not involved in actions. However, he took part in one of the last acts of the war when the British recaptured St John's, Newfoundland, in late 1762.

SEE ALSO: Canada, Louisbourg, Quebec

Sex, sexuality and venereal disease

Cook and his men spent insufficient time with different Pacific peoples for them to understand clearly the way those societies functioned, the relationships between people and the nature of their sexual habits. Though surprised by the different sexual mores, the British sailors were quick to take advantage of the willingness of women to have sexual intercourse with them. For men who had been confined to a ship for months, such a situation must have seemed like paradise. For Cook, it represented a problem of massive proportions as it soon became obvious that venereal diseases (syphilis and gonorrhoea) were being transmitted by the contact.

Cook's surgeons were supposed to check seamen for signs of venereal diseases and any man showing signs of infection was supposedly quarantined. However, policing this measure was nearly impossible and the diseases continued to spread. The British and French later accused each other of introducing syphilis though both were probably guilty, together with the Spanish. However, the problem was complicated by the presence of yaws, an endemic disease. Yaws (caused by the spirochaete, *Treponema pertenue*) and syphilis (by *Treponema pallidum*) are very closely related and, though transmitted differently, exhibit similar effects. It is not known whether any sexual diseases were endemic to the Pacific. In recent years, some Hawaiians and other Pacific Islanders have condemned Cook, blaming him for introducing to the region diseases which killed many people.

Cook and others described the sexual relations between his men and Pacific women and, though Hawkesworth did his best to edit out explicit references, such passages did much, no doubt, to ensure the popularity of the published narratives. While Cook held back, Banks had no qualms and after a woman had danced in front of him he 'took her by the hand and led her to the tents accompanied by another women her freind'. Banks described Otheathea, an attendant of Purea as his special 'flame', while his supposed liaisons with Purea made him the butt of satires and cartoons on his return to Britain.

Cook remained an observer and was generally tolerant of what he saw. Sometimes his background and own mores came to the fore and he was more judgmental. For instance, he wrote at Tahiti during the first voyage: '…more than one half of the better sort of the inhabitants have enter'd into a resolution of injoying free liberty in love without being troubled or disturbed by its consequences… . Chastity indeed is but little Valued'.

Homosexuality was expressly banned on British ships of the time and was punishable by death. It is improbable therefore that any Briton would have described having a homosexual relationship with a Pacific Island man. However, though there were descriptions of homosexuality in Hawai'i. King and Samwell describe young men, aikāne, attached to

Kalaniopu'u. Samwell (known to have had sexual relations with several Hawaiian women) could still write: 'Another Sett of Servants of whom he [Kalaniopu'u] has a great many are called Ikany [aikāne]... Of this class are Parea [Palea] and Cani-Coah [Kānekoa] and their business is to commit the Sin of Onan upon the old King'.

Christian missionaries soon clamped down on most of the sexual practices of the Pacific.

SEE ALSO: Medical aspects of Cook's voyages

Sextants, quadrants and octants

Navigation and the ability of sailors to determine their position at sea depended on instruments, with which sightings of celestial bodies such as the sun, moon and stars could be made. Huge progress was made in developing these instruments during the eighteenth century. The backstaff and cross-staff were made redundant by a new instrument, the quadrant, which John Hadley invented in 1731. Hadley's quadrant, also called an octant, had an arc which measured one-eight of a circle and two mirrors which allowed the sun (or another star) and the sea horizon to be seen simultaneously. This allowed for much more accurate measurements at sea and easier observations of the lunar-distance method. John Bird improved the quadrant further in 1757 when he invented the sextant. This added a telescope sight and had a greater arc (one-sixth of a circle), allowing a far more precise determination of latitude.

In the sextant, the telescope or sight, mounted rigidly to the framework, is lined up with the horizon. The radial arm, on which a mirror is mounted, is then moved until the star is reflected into a half-silvered mirror in line with the telescope and appears, through the telescope, to coincide with the horizon. The angular distance of the star above the horizon is then read from the graduated arc of the sextant. From this angle and the exact time of day as registered by a chronometer, the latitude can be determined by means of published tables.

SEE ALSO: Astronomical results of Cook's voyages

Ships' time or the nautical day

Until an Admiralty order of October 1805, ships kept ship's time. A ship's day began and ended at midday when the major observations were recorded for position, course and distance run in the preceding 24 hours and the log was written up to cover these along with the weather and significant events. The ship's day began at noon *before* the civil reckoning, in which the day commenced at midnight, and was named for the day upon which it completed. Thus, the example from the *Grenville*'s log below covers the period from noon Thursday 11 September 1766 to noon 12 September 1766 in the civil day and is referred to as Friday. Any events occurring in the pm of 12 September in the log would, if translated into the civil day, have happened in the afternoon of 11 September; while occurrences in the morning of 12 September would have been in the morning of 12 September in both systems.

For the purposes of the ship's log, the nautical day was divided into three parts: the first part consisted of the afternoon watch and the two 'dog watches' (12.00 to 20.00); the middle part consisted of the first and middle watches (20.00 to 04.00); and the latter part was made up of the morning and forenoon watches (04.00 to 12.00).

The example below is taken from the *Grenville's* log from September 1766 at Port-aux-Basques in Newfoundland. It shows the use of the three parts of the day in recording weather. It also shows the afternoon coming before the morning, a reflection of the day starting at midday.

When a ship entered a port it immediately reverted to the time of a normal civil day at that port.

SEE ALSO: Astronomical results of Cook's voyages

Simcoe, John (?–1759)

Captain John Simcoe was Cook's captain on board HMS *Pembroke* from 1758 until his death in 1759. Simcoe had taken over this command in 1757. When Cook met Samuel Holland after the siege of Louisbourg in 1758, Simcoe encouraged Cook to learn from the

Day	Date	Winds	Remarks
	12th	ENE	The first and middle parts strong gales with rain. The later light airs and clear.
Friday	Sept.		PM Employed overhauling the sails and repairing them.
	1766	variable	AM Employed fitting the rigging.

surveyor and provided the time and resources for him to develop his skills. Simcoe was one of a line of benefactors who helped Cook.

Simcoe had married Catherine Stamford in Cotterstock on 8 August 1747 and they had four sons. One of them, John Graves Simcoe, later became lieutenant-governor of Upper Canada. Captain Simcoe died of pneumonia on 15 May 1759 aboard the *Pembroke* as they passed Anticosti Island near the mouth of the St Lawrence River. The ship was part of the British fleet under Admiral Saunders heading to attack Quebec.

SEE ALSO: Canada, *Pembroke* (HMS)

Skelton, Raleigh Ashlin (1906–1970)

R A Skelton, the cartographical historian, was born in Plymouth in 1906. He was known as Peter by his friends. He studied at Cambridge before joining the British Museum in 1931 as an assistant keeper in the Department of Printed Books. This brought him into contact with the narratives and atlases from early voyages. Skelton served in the Royal Artillery during the Second World War, and then returned to the British Museum, this time in the map room. He reorganised and improved the collection to the extent that, when he retired in 1967, it was without equal.

Skelton was an active member of many societies, including the Hakluyt Society, for whom he was for many years secretary and a member of its council. He oversaw the publication of over 40 volumes. Of special note was his contribution to J C Beaglehole's Hakluyt edition of Cook's journals, for which Skelton selected the portfolio of charts. Skelton published extensively both in monographs and in journals. He was involved with *Imago Mundi,* the journal for the history of cartography, and worked with Nico Israel in Amsterdam on the *Theatrum Orbis Terrarum* series of facsimile atlas reprints. Skelton became the pre-eminent map historian and librarian of his time. He died in 1970 from injuries received in a road accident.

SEE ALSO: Cartographic results of Cook's voyages

Skottowe family

Thomas Skottowe, the Lord of the Manor for Great Ayton, lived in Ayton Hall, having brought his family north from Little Melton Manor, outside Norwich, in 1725. Skottowe's father had married Elizabeth Coulson and, through her, Thomas inherited property in Cleveland, including Ayton. Skottowe had married in 1717 but his wife Rebecca had died after the birth of a son, Coulson. With his second wife, Ann, Thomas had four more sons and two daughters.

Among the Ayton properties was Aireyholme Farm, where James Cook Senior became Hind or Foreman in 1736. Thomas Skottowe would then play a pivotal role in shaping James Cook's life. As well as providing the secure setting for Cook's childhood, he enabled young James to begin his formal education at the Postgate School in Ayton. Skottowe sat as a Justice of the Peace in the local Assizes and it is believed he became acquainted with William Sanderson, a merchant and haberdasher at Staithes, through this activity. Indeed, Skottowe's youngest son, Augustine, and Sanderson would become related when they both married the daughters of Samuel Gill, the Customs Officer in Staithes. Through this connection, Skottowe arranged for Cook to be employed in Sanderson's shop in Staithes in 1745.

John Skottowe, the second son of Thomas, was born in 1725. He had a short army career before, in 1764, becoming Governor of St Helena in the South Atlantic. In 1766, he married a local woman, Margaret Greentree. Skottowe was Governor when Cook called at St Helena in the *Endeavour,* in 1771 but there is no mention of the two men meeting. However, Cook and Banks' descriptions of the short visit were written up, somewhat distortedly, in Hakesworth's narrative and the unflattering words would haunt Cook on his return in the *Resolution* in 1775.

On this occasion, Cook met the Skottowes and Margaret led the light-hearted attack on Cook with several jokes being made at his expense. Cook spent a few pleasant days in Governor Skottowe's company. John Skottowe returned to Britain and died in Chesham in 1784.

John's father Thomas had died in Great Ayton in 1771 and is buried at All Saints Church close to Cook's mother Grace. Another son, Nicholas, maintained Ayton Hall until 1780 when he sold it to Commander William Wilson. Augustine Skottowe, the last of the family to be associated with Ayton, as the rest of the family had moved away, lived in Ayton Grange before he died in 1789 (1777?).

SEE ALSO: Cook's early years, Great Ayton, Saint Helena

Smith, Bernard (1916–)

Bernard Smith, the Australian art historian was born in 1916. In 1934, Smith entered Sydney Teachers' College where his interest in art was stimulated by May

Marsden. Between 1935 and 1944, he combined teaching about art with his own painting and drawing. About 1944, Smith decided to give up painting and concentrate on being an art historian. The following year he published his first art history text, *Place, Taste and Tradition*, which he has described as the first structured history of Australian art.

Smith spent several years in Europe including time at the Courtauld Institute in London, where he worked with Anthony Blunt. At this time Smith became interested in the art of European explorers, especially the work of Cook's artists. This led to his work, *European Vision and the South Pacific,* published in 1960. During this period, he also showed the links between Cook's second voyage, William Wales and Coleridge's *Rime of the Ancient Mariner.*

He returned to Australia in 1951 and embarked on an academic, research and writing career that has made him one of the leading figures in Australian art. It led to the publication in 1962 of *Australian Painting 1788–1960*. Smith was not finished with Cook though and he has been at the forefront of the debates that have taken place since the 1970s in which Cook and his achievements have been reassessed. He worked with Rüdiger Joppien, to produce the definitive works, *The Art of Captain Cook's Voyages,* published between 1985 and 1987.

Developing Australians' interest in, and knowledge of, their artistic traditions has been the focus of Bernard Smith's life. He was one of the founders of the discipline of art history in Australia and among its most distinguished practitioners. He has continued to write, in recent years producing his memoirs.

SEE ALSO: Art of Cook's voyages, Coleridge (Samuel Taylor)

Smith, Isaac (1752–1831)

Isaac Smith was a cousin of Elizabeth Cook. He sailed to Newfoundland as an AB on the *Grenville* in 1767. Smith then joined Cook on the *Endeavour* as an AB. On 23 May 1770, he was made a midshipman and then on 26 May 1771, after Hicks' death, he became a master's mate. Smith was the first to land at Botany Bay; Cook is reported to have said 'Isaac, you shall land first' and to have followed him ashore.

He sailed on the second voyage on the *Resolution* as master's mate. He kept a log. Smith made surveys and Cook used him frequently to draw and copy charts. In 1775, after the second voyage, Smith, now a lieutenant, joined the sloop, *Weazle,* 16 guns. He was promoted to commander in May 1781 and captain in December 1787. Smith commanded a ship on the East Indies station. He was listed as a superannuated rear-admiral in 1807.

Smith was born in London in 1752. After retiring from active naval service, he retired to south London where he lived with his cousin, Cook's widow Elizabeth, at her house in Clapham High Street. Smith inherited nearby Merton Abbey in 1827 from his brother Charles, and he and Elizabeth moved there. He died on 2 July 1831, leaving a will. (FRC 11/1788). Elizabeth, who moved back to Clapham, erected a memorial to him in St Mary the Virgin Church, Merton.

SEE ALSO: Cartographic results of Cook's voyages, First and Second voyages

Society Islands

The Society Islands (17° S, 150° W) are an archipelago in the central South Pacific, about 1118 miles (1800km) south of the Equator, 2237 miles (3600km) north-east of New Zealand, and about 4350 miles (7000km) west of South America. The archipelago is divided into two smaller groups, the Windward (to the east), of which Tahiti and Moorea are the main islands, and the Leeward, of which Raiatea, Huahine and Bora Bora are the main islands. The islands are now part of the territory of French Polynesia.

The islands were peopled about 1300 years ago by Polynesians. Since then, it is believed that people from the Society Islands dispersed to settle Hawai'i and New Zealand. Cook learned from Tupaia, a Raiatean, about the navigational skills of Tahitians and their knowledge of the existence of, and means of sailing to and from, many other islands. Cook first visited the islands in 1769 in order to observe the Transit of Venus. Matavai Bay on Tahiti would prove one of Cook's favourite places in the Pacific and one he returned to several times as it usually offered him fresh water and supplies and great hospitality from the people.

The name Society is one of Cook's and probably represents a pun. Cook's mission to the islands had been partly sponsored by the Royal Society while he had found the people very friendly and sociable. However, they were less friendly to each other on occasions. Cook returned to Tahiti in 1773 just after a civil war had taken place. Inter-island rivalry was also a way of life and, at the time of Cook's visits, Bora Bora exerted control over several other islands, especially its neighbours in the Leeward group. Te To'ofa, a Tahitian chief, tried to

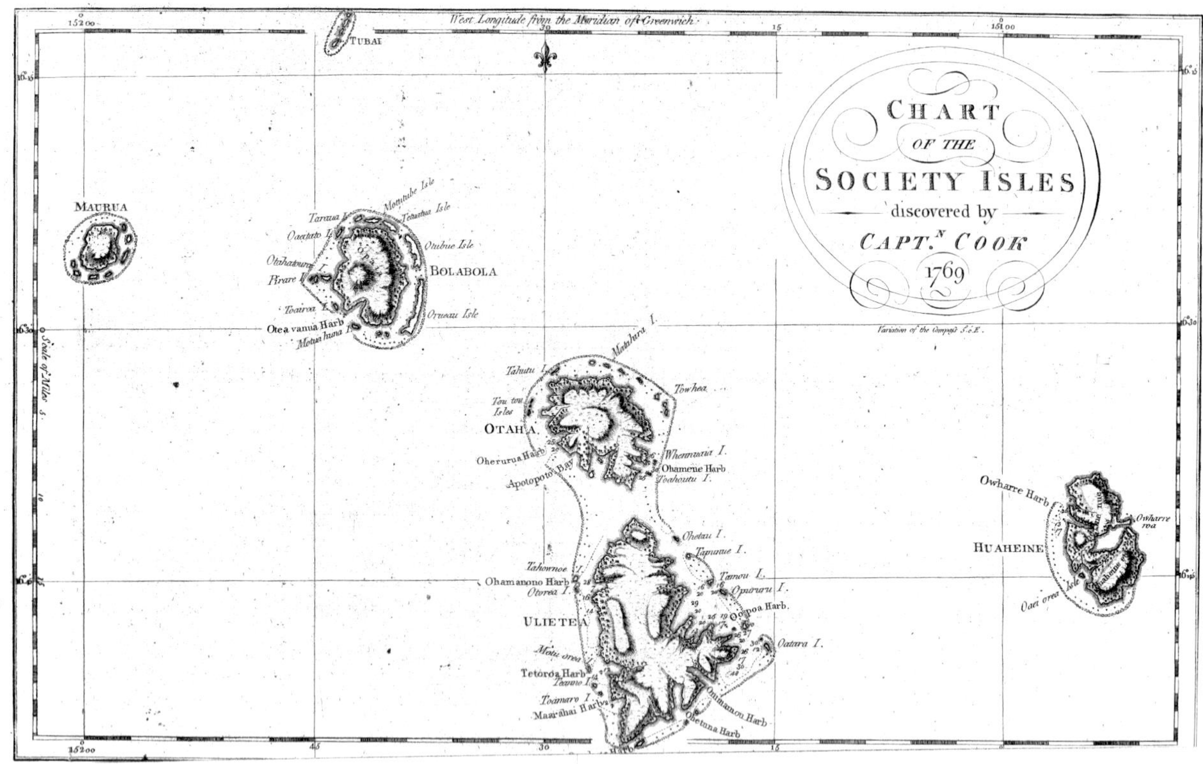

Chart of the Society Isles discovered by Cook in 1769. After Cook. 1784. (University of Waikato Map Collection)

enlist Cook in his attacks on Moorea, which continued for several years during the 1770s.

SEE ALSO: Huahine, Moorea, Raiatea, Tahiti

Solander, Daniel Carl (1733–1782)

Daniel Solander was a close friend and scientific colleague of Joseph Banks, accompanying Banks on Cook's first voyage on the *Endeavour* as a naturalist. Solander was born in Piteå Gammelstad (now Öjebyn) in northern Sweden on the Gulf of Bothnia on 19 February 1733. He travelled south to Uppsala in 1749 and enrolled in the university in 1750, staying with his uncle who had been its rector. Solander changed in 1752 to study botany under Carl Linnaeus, becoming one of his best students and disciples.

Solander undertook collecting tours visiting Lapland in the north and the Malmo region in the south. John Ellis and other naturalists in Britain contacted Linnaeus asking for someone to go over to explain Linnaeus' system of classification. Solander was chosen and he reached London in June 1760. Although he never gained a doctorate, he assumed the title of Doctor on his arrival in Britain. Over the next two years, he met important people and travelled on collecting trips. He was also an agent for the Swedish Government trying to secure new inventions and technology for Sweden.

The British Museum employed him in 1763 to catalogue and classify its large botanical and other natural history collections. His system of recording and description on slips stored in small boxes is in various forms still used today. The boxes were designed by him and this type are still referred to as Solander boxes. Hermann Spöring, whom he met through the Swedish community in London, became his assistant in 1766. Solander was elected a Fellow of the Royal Society in 1764.

Solander met and became friends with Joseph Banks in 1764. When Banks received permission to go on Cook's *Endeavour* voyage, it was agreed that Solander would go as well. The voyage, however, would take its toll on Solander's health. Already a plump man with a history of malaria, he suffered from hypothermia on a collecting trip at Terra del Fuego. Solander was very ill in Jakarta, in November 1770, when he again caught malaria and dysentery. Finally, at the Cape, he was confined to bed for two weeks with a recurrence of the Jakarta illness.

On their return to Britain in July 1771, Solander and

Banks were feted by society and scientific circles and invited to meet King George III. Solander returned to his work at the British Museum. When Banks withdrew from Cook's second Pacific voyage, Solander joined the consolation voyage to Iceland and Orkney in 1772, later producing the *Flora Islandica*. Solander became Banks' secretary and librarian at Soho Square, as well as becoming keeper of natural history at the British Museum. He also sat on the Council of the Royal Society from 1774. While he was at breakfast at Banks' home in Soho Square on 8 May 1782, Solander suffered a massive cerebral haemorrhage, and died five days later. He was buried at the Swedish Church in East London on the 19th. When the church was demolished in 1913 his coffin was removed and reburied in the Swedish section of Brookwood Cemetery in Woking, Surrey. Several features around the world are named for Solander: Solander Island off South Island, NZ, Solander Island off Vancouver Island, Cape Solander at Kurnell, Botany Bay, plus a Solander Memorial at Kurnell. The plant genus *Solandra* and Solander's petrel (*Pterodroma solandri*) honour him. A portrait of Solander by Johann Zoffany is held by the Linnean Society in London.

SEE ALSO: Banks (Joseph), Botanical results of Cook's voyages, First voyage

Solar eclipses

A solar eclipse (eclipse of the Sun) occurs when the Moon passes between the Earth and the Sun thereby obscuring all (total eclipse) or part (partial eclipse) of the Sun from the Earth. This can only occur at New Moon. If the Moon's shadow happens to fall upon Earth's surface at that time, we see some portion of the Sun's disk covered or 'eclipsed' by the Moon. The Moon's orbit around Earth is tilted 5 degrees to Earth's orbit around the Sun so it is only twice a year that the geometry lines up so that some part of the Moon's shadow falls on Earth's surface and an eclipse of the Sun is seen from that region. The total phase of a solar eclipse is very brief, lasting only for several minutes.

On 5 August 1766, a solar eclipse occurred, which is now known as Captain Cook's Eclipse. It was an annular solar eclipse, where the body of the moon was seen projected upon the sun's disk with a ring of light visible all round. The optimum location to view the greatest extent of this eclipse was eastern Canada and Cook was in the Burgeo Islands on the south coast of Newfoundland at the time.

Cook made an observation and forwarded the results to Britain where they were presented at the Royal Society in April 1767, thus bringing him to the attention of members of that body. It proved to be a pivotal moment for Cook. It showed him to be a capable astronomer and it helped the Royal Society accept him when the Navy nominated him to lead the *Endeavour* voyage.

SEE ALSO: Astronomical results of Cook's voyages

Solebay, HMS

In 1757, Cook joined HMS *Solebay*, the third vessel to carry the name, which commemorated the Battle of Solebay that had taken place on 28 May 1672, marking the opening of the Third Anglo-Dutch War (1672–74). This *Solebay* was a Sixth Rate, built in the Plymouth Dockyard in 1742 and was of 442 tons, 105ft 11in (32.3m) long, 29ft 10in (9.1m) wide and carried 24 guns.

Britain was not at war at the time and the *Solebay* was being used for general duties and reconnaissance, including the prevention of smuggling, based in Leith in Scotland. Cook travelled north in July 1757 to join the vessel on the 30th as master, his first appointment at that rank. The *Solebay* was under the command of Captain Robert Craig.

They left Leith on 2 August to make a patrol north to Orkney and Shetland before returning to Leith at the end of the month. In early September, Cook was transferred to HMS *Pembroke*. The Navy sold the *Solebay* in 1763.

SEE ALSO: Cook's ships, Scotland

South Georgia

South Georgia is an island situated in the South Atlantic Ocean located at 37° W, 54° S, about 870 miles (1400km) ESE of the Falkland Islands. The island is about 106 miles (170km) long and trends north-west to south-east. Mountain ranges form its spine, rising to nearly 9800ft (3000m) while huge glaciers and snowfields cover about 75 per cent of the island. There are many offshore islands, including Willis Island, Bird Island, Cooper Island and Clerke's Rocks.

The island was possibly first sited by Antonio de la Roche, an English merchant, who had been blown off course while rounding Cape Horn, in April 1675. One hundred years later, on 17 January 1775, James Cook, who was crossing the South Atlantic to confirm or deny sightings reported on earlier charts, arrived at the island.

Possession Bay, South Georgia. Engraved by S Smith after Hodges. (Cook II fp 212)

He passed between Willis Island (named after Thomas Willis, a midshipman) and Bird Island to reach the north coast.

Cook reported the inhospitable nature of the place, the lack of vegetation and animals, and the glaciers, after he investigated Possession Bay on the north side of the island (Cook took possession of the country there). He sailed east along the north coast and rounded the south-east corner on the 20th. Cook named this Cape Disappointment as from here he could see the point to the north-west where he had first sighted land a few days earlier. He had therefore established it was an island and not part of Antarctica.

Cook headed east and, in thick fog on 25 January, negotiated his way carefully around the Clerke's Rocks, which Cook named after his lieutenant. Cook had named several other features after his crew and members of the Royal Navy. Cook Bay and Cook Glacier honour his visit there.

SEE ALSO: Second voyage

South Sandwich Islands

The South Sandwich Islands consist of a 249-mile (400km) long chain of eleven volcanic islands, which trends north-south. The islands lie 472 miles (760km) south-east of South Georgia and are almost 80 per cent covered by glaciers. The inhospitable climate and nature of the terrain renders them uninhabitable, except by birds and sea mammals.

Captain Cook discovered the most southerly islands on 30 January 1775 and named them Sandwich Land, later South Sandwich Islands, after John Montagu, the 4th Earl of Sandwich and First Lord of the Admiralty. Cook sailed north in thick fog past the other southern members of the group without landing, before heading east on 3 February. The foggy conditions had prevented Cook being able to discern if they were separate islands or headlands of a larger landmass. He sailed south again on 6 February and felt confident the land had only been small islands.

Cook named Candlemas, Saunders, Montagu, Bristol and Southern Thule islands. He also named Freezland Rock after Samuel Freezland, the sailor who had first sighted the islands. Another rock was named after midshipman Richard Grindall and the passage of water between Bristol and Thule Islands was named Forster Passage. One of the Southern Thule islands was later called Cook Island.

SEE ALSO: Second voyage

Space, Cook in

James Cook, who became a proficient astronomer in his lifetime, would have been proud that his name has since been associated with space, both factually and in fiction.

Cook is one of several terrestrial explorers who has been honoured in space.

The Moon. A small crater in the southeast quarter of the near side of the Moon (18° S, 49° E) is named Cook Crater. The crater, 29.3 miles (47km) across, is situated between the Mare Nectaris and the Mare Fecunditatis, near the Pyrenees Mountains. The name was ratified in 1935.

Mercury has three rupes (ridges) all named after Cook's ships. Adventure, Resolution and Discovery rupes are all situated about 60° S in the southeast sector of the planet.

Space Shuttles. The United States Space Program developed the use of the Space Shuttle Orbiters in the 1980s. Two of the shuttles, Orbiter Vehicles OV-103 and OV-105, have been named after ships used by Captain Cook on his voyages of exploration. In 1989, President George W. Bush Snr confirmed that, after a competition to choose a name, vehicle OV-105 would be called *Endeavour* after Cook's first ship. This *Endeavour* made its first flight in 1992 and has since (as at January 2004) made 19 journeys into space. Cook's *Endeavour* was 368 tons, 100ft (30.5m) long and 20ft (6m) wide; the Space Shuttle *Endeavour* is 78 tons, 122ft (37m) long and 78ft (23.7m) wide. The *Discovery*, OV-103, was named after the ship that accompanied Cook on his third voyage. It made its first flight in 1984 and has since made 30 successful journeys into space.

Star Trek. The last connection between Cook and space is speculative. It has been suggested that the American television series has some features that bear a striking resemblance to Cook and his exploits. The similarities will never be confirmed as the developer of the series, Gene Roddenberry, died in 1991.

The original series, begun in 1966, centred on a starship, the USS *Enterprise*, whose commander was Captain James Kirk. These names bear strong similarities to *Endeavour* and James Cook. At the beginning of each episode Captain Kirk would say, 'These are the voyages of the Starship *Enterprise*. Its five-year mission...to boldly go where no man has gone before'. Compare that with Cook's statement during his second voyage after just failing to reach Antarctica, 'I who had ambition not only to go farther than any one had done before, but as far as it was possible for man to go'.

Spanish explorers

The Treaty of Tordesillas was signed by Portugal and Spain at Tordesillas in Spain on 7 June 1494 after mediation by the Pope. It divided the world outside of Europe in a exclusive duopoly between the Spanish and the Portuguese along a north-south meridian 1099 miles (1770km) west of the Cape Verde Islands or roughly 46° 37' W. The lands to the east would belong to Portugal and the lands to the west to Spain. The remaining exploring nations of Europe such as France, England, and the Netherlands were excluded and refused access to any new lands. It followed Columbus having recently reached America in 1492 and foreshadowed Vasco Núñez de Balboa, in September 1513, becoming the first European to sight the Pacific Ocean, naming it the South Sea. This new sea fell into the region ascribed to Spain and for the next 150 years the Pacific would effectively be the 'Spanish Lake'. Ferdinand Magellan (Fernao de Magalhaes) entered the Pacific for Spain in 1520 and crossed to the Philippine Islands in 98 days, though making no major discoveries *en route*. He was killed on Cebu but one of his ships went on to complete the first circumnavigation of the world.

Spain conquered most of Latin America, especially the west coast, and had already claimed the Philippines in the west. Spanish ships began to cross the ocean and for a period they had the ocean to themselves. Manila Galleons started transporting gold, silver and other riches from Peru across the South Pacific to Manila in the Philippines. The ships would follow prevailing currents back via the North Pacific to Acapulco in Mexico and on to Peru.

In 1567, Alvaro de Mendaña set sail from Callao in Peru and early in 1568 sighted one of the islands of Tuvalu and Ontong Java before reaching the Solomon Archipelago. Mendaña sailed on a second voyage from Callao in 1595 to colonise the Solomon Islands. In May, he discovered a group he named Las Marquesas de Mendoza (now known as the Marquesas). He died in the Santa Cruz group in the Solomons on 18 October 1595.

Pedro Fernández de Quirós, one of Mendaña's captains, set sail again from Callao in December 1605 in search of new lands and the unknown southern continent (Terra Australis Incognita). In April 1606, he sighted La Australia del Espiritu Santo (now Espiritu Santo) in the New Hebrides. The voyages of Quiros marked the end of Spain's domination of the Pacific but they still retained a presence in the region through their South and Central American colonies. Russian movement into Alaska in the mid-1700s provoked Spanish reaction and several voyages went north to investigate. In an effort to restore some prestige to

Spain, Malaspina led a major scientific expedition around the Pacific in the 1790s but his imprisonment on his return to Spain led to the achievements of the voyage being ignored.
SEE ALSO: Pacific exploration before Cook

Sparrman, Anders (1748–1820)

Anders Sparrman was a botanist and doctor taken on by Johann Reinhold Forster at Cape Town to assist with the scientific side of the second voyage. Sparrman, a Swede born in Tensta, Uppland, on 27 February 1748, had only recently arrived at the Cape in April 1772 to be tutor to the children of the Dutch resident at False Bay. The prospect of joining Cook's voyage was most attractive to Sparrman, who had already sailed in 1765 to Canton with the Swedish East India Company (EIC) as a surgeon. He studied medicine at Uppsala University and learned botany under Linnaeus at Uppsala. He wanted to travel and the Swedish EIC had arranged for Sparrman to travel on the *Castle of Stockholm* to explore and collect botanical specimens in South Africa. Sparrman put this on hold and set off with Cook and Forster.

Sparrman was on the *Resolution* when the ship sailed for Antarctic waters on 23 November 1772. In January 1774, when the *Resolution* reached 71°10′ S, Sparrman vied with Vancouver for the honour of having been furthest south. When the *Resolution* returned to the Cape, Sparrman left the voyage and set off on a nine month expedition of his own as far as the Eastern Cape, north of present-day Port Elizabeth. He returned to Sweden in late 1776 where he wrote up a narrative of his African expedition, including descriptions of Hottentots and Kaffirs.

In his absence he had been conferred with a degree of Doctor of Medicine. He set up in practice. Sparrman was elected to the Swedish Academy of Sciences, which also bestowed a reward of 1000 crowns on him. He was appointed Keeper of the Academy's cabinet of curiosities, to which Sparrman had contributed. Sparrman was persuaded to take part in an expedition to Senegal in 1787 to assess its potential for a Swedish colony. Back in Sweden, he was appointed professor of natural history in Stockholm. Sparrman eventually wrote a narrative of Cook's voyage, which was published in two parts in 1802 and 1818. In his later years he worked as a parish doctor for the poor and he died without marrying on 9 August 1820. Mount Sparrman in New Zealand is named after him.
SEE ALSO: Botanical results of Cook's voyages, Second voyage

The Head of a Canoe, by Hermann Spöring, who has captured the intricate detail of the carving. (Banks' Journal II pl 4a)

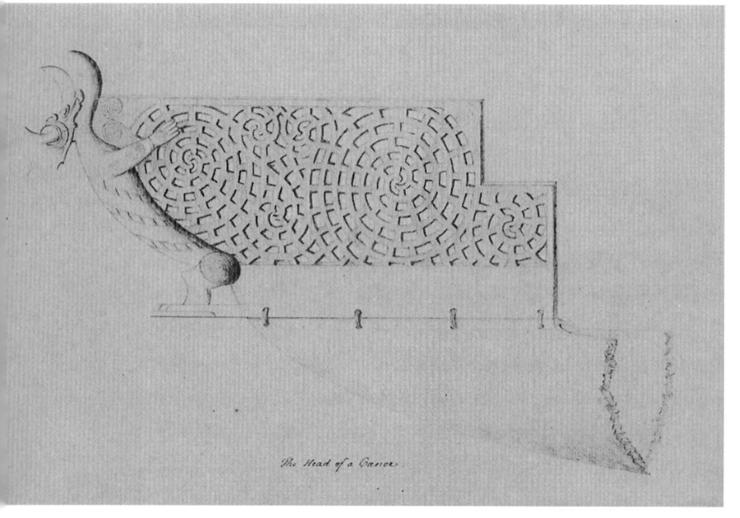

Spöring, Herman Dietrich (1733–1771)

Herman Dietrich Spöring was born in Turku, Finland (then Åbo and part of Sweden), in 1733. His father, who held the chair of medicine at the University of Turku and corresponded with Linnaeus, died in 1747. His mother died in 1754. Spöring had begun studying at the University of Turku in 1748 but moved to Stockholm in 1753 to continue his studies. He then went to London in about 1755 and worked as a draughtsman and watchmaker before becoming Daniel Solander's personal clerk.

Solander was invited by Joseph Banks to sail on the *Endeavour* and Spöring was taken on as secretary to Banks, also transcribing Solander's notes on the flora and fauna they collected. After the death of the artist Buchan, Spöring took on a crucial role drawing many delightful and accurate coastal profiles. He also drew careful studies of the prows of Māori waka (canoes), bringing the meticulous eye for detail of the watchmaker to his drawings.

During the voyage, Cook used Spöring's other talents to repair various defects in the ship's instruments, and in Tahiti he restored the quadrant after it had been stolen and damaged. Like many others he fell seriously ill after Batavia and died of dysentery on the voyage to the Cape. He was buried at sea on 25 January 1771. Cook named Spöring's Island off Cook's

Cove at Tolaga Bay, New Zealand but it has reverted to its Maori name, Pourewa. A memorial to Spöring was unveiled in Turku in 1990.
SEE ALSO: Botanical results of Cook's voyages, Coastal views, First voyage

Staithes

Staithes (54° 33' N, 0° 48' W), is a fishing village on the North Sea coast of Cleveland at the mouth of Roxby Beck. The old village nestles at the foot of cliffs, about 7.5 miles (12km) west of Whitby. It was settled by the Vikings who gave the village its name, which means 'The Landing Place'.

In 1745, when James Cook was ready to leave home and get a job, it was arranged that he should work in a haberdashery and grocery shop at Staithes belonging to William Sanderson. Cook's father's employer, Thomas Skottowe, was also a Justice of the Peace for the North Riding of Yorkshire and would have attended sessions at Guisborough where it is probable he would have met Sanderson, who also acted as a Constable in the district. The two men became friends and later even became related when their sons married sisters named Gill.

Staithes was always a very close community and it took a long time for newcomers to be accepted. For a young boy like Cook, away from home for the first time, it would have been a strange and lonely place. He soon realised that shopwork was not for him and the sea beckoned him instead. Sanderson, aware that Cook was unsettled, used his connections to introduce the boy to the Walker family in Whitby. In 1746, Cook moved to Whitby and began his life as a seaman.

The shop where Cook worked fell into the sea but stones from the shop were later used to build the present 'Captain Cook's shop'. There is also now a Captain Cook and Staithes Heritage Museum.
SEE ALSO: Cleveland, Cook's early years, Sanderson (William)

Stephens, Sir Philip (1725–1809)

Philip Stephens was Secretary to the Lords Commissioners of the Admiralty from 1763 until 1795. As such much of the correspondence concerning Cook's voyages emanates from Stephens or is addressed to him. Cook also worked and corresponded with Stephens during his time in Newfoundland. Many business letters between the two men survive.

Stephens was born in 1725 in Alphamstone in Essex, the son of the rector. He was educated at the Free School in Harwich before becoming a clerk at the Victualling Board. Anson befriended him and made him his secretary. In 1759, he became second secretary to the Admiralty, under John Clevland. While the title 'Secretary' implies a junior role, the position actually carried considerable power and Stephens made some decisions without referring to the Lords Commissioners.

He was elected FRS in 1771 and from 1768 until 1806 he was MP for Sandwich. On his retirement he was knighted and made a Lord Commissioner himself. He died on 20 November 1809 and is buried in Fulham. He was married and had one son, who predeceased him. He had property in St Faith's, Norfolk. He left a will (FRC 11/1507). There is a short biography in the *DNB*, v18, p1067. Cook named several features after Stephens. Stephens Island and Point Stephens near the northern tip of South Island, New Zealand, and Port Stephens on the New South Wales Coast honour him.
SEE ALSO: Admiralty

Surveys and running surveys

Seamen rely on good charts to tell them where they are and where danger in the form of rocks and coasts lie. In the eighteenth century, many regions remained uncharted and it was a responsibility of explorers to generate accurate charts of the places they visited. Few sailors of the time though were capable of carrying out surveys and producing charts.

Cook learned his surveying and charting in the waters of Eastern Canada and Newfoundland. Under the patronage of his captain on HMS *Pembroke*, John Simcoe, Cook was taught by Samuel Holland, whom he met after the fall of Louisbourg. Simcoe let Cook use his copies of works such *The Young Mathematician's Companion* and Leadbetter's *Compleat System of Astronomy*. The charts he produced were a mixture of information gathered at sea and on land. In Newfoundland, he developed the practice whereby Parker, the master's mate, kept the *Grenville* offshore and made observations at sea, including depths and sightings of prominent features onshore. In the meantime, Cook would go ashore himself to set up a base line and determine the direction of north. Those same prominent features would be chosen for triangulation points and bearings would be taken using a plane table and sextant. He would also survey the inlets and other features close to the shore.

The resulting charts would be composite, bringing all the information gathered together on one sheet.

Coastal views and sailing directions would be added, together with any other information that could be gleaned, such as fisheries and potential for settlements. Such experience stood Cook in good stead when he entered the Pacific. For Cook, the preparation of charts was one of the most important duties that he was required to perform. They recorded his achievements and the places he had visited. They also recorded the open sea where he had found no land and in doing so had shown such features as the Great Southern Continent did not exist.

However, at sea, he usually did not have the time to be as methodical as he would have wished and his Pacific surveys were not as precise as those in Newfoundland. It was usually not possible to go ashore to set up a base line. Instead, Cook used the practice of running survey for many of his charts in the Pacific. That of Vanuatu (New Hebrides) is a prime example. Cook was only able to go ashore at a few selected places in Vanuatu and had to rely on observations made as he sailed along the coast. At a starting point (point A), Cook made sightings, involving compass bearings and horizontal sextant angles, of selected prominent features onshore. The ship would sail on, the distance and direction being carefully calculated, before the same features would be observed from point B. This procedure would be repeated many times and triangles created to form the basis of a chart. Considering they way in which they were produced, Cook's charts of Vanuatu and New Zealand are still wonderful examples of the surveying art. Good weather and the ability to see the shore were crucial.

The value of surveys and hydrographic charts was finally acknowledged by the Admiralty when the Hydrographic Office was established in 1795 and Alexander Dalrymple was appointed its first hydrographer.

See Also: Cartographic results of Cook's voyages

Surville, Jean-François-Marie de (1717–1773)

Jean-François-Marie de Surville was born on 18 January 1717 at Port-Louis, Brittany, France. Surville went to sea at the age of 10 for the French India Company and served mostly in the Indian Ocean and the China seas. During the War of the Austrian Succession and the Seven Years War he served in the French navy. On 24 September 1750 he married Marie Jouaneaulx at Nantes. Surville became captain and part owner of the *St Jean-Baptiste*, a 650-ton French merchant ship built in Nantes in 1767. Surville took the ship to the Ganges River in Bengal arriving in November 1768. He heard of Wallis' voyage to the Pacific and determined to sail there, hoping to find new land and trading possibilities.

The *St Jean-Baptiste* sailed from the Hooghly River on 3 March 1769. After calling at Pondicherry, it crossed to Malacca and then north to the Philippines and the Bashi Islands between Luzon and Formosa (Taiwan). It next sailed south-west until, on 8 October, it arrived in the Solomon Islands. On 22 October, they continued south through the Coral Sea and into the Tasman Sea. After two months, during which scurvy ravaged the crew, the ship turned east, hoping to find shelter in New Zealand, then known only from Tasman's 1642 voyage.

On 12 December, Surville reached land near Hokianga on the west coast of New Zealand. He sailed north and rounded North Cape at the same time as Cook was doing the same in the other direction. It is estimated that the two ships missed one another by as little as 25 miles (40km). Surville put in at Doubtless Bay on 17 December. The Māori proved helpful and the surviving crew soon regained their strength. After discussing the available options, Surville decided to cross the Pacific rather than return to India. He sailed on 31 December 1769.

The crossing, at about 35° S, took its toll and many of the crew died. Most of the crew were sick when they finally reached the Peruvian coast on 7 April. Landfall was made at Chilca but Surville drowned in the surf when his boat capsized as he went ashore. The ship went to Callao, where the French were arrested and held for three years. Eventually, the *St Jean-Baptiste* sailed and arrived back at Port-Louis, Brittany, on 20 August 1773. The voyage had been a disaster, and the ship and what cargo remained were auctioned. At Patia Point, Doubtless Bay, there is a commemorative plaque marking Surville's visit. The Surville Cliffs, the northernmost part of New Zealand, are named after him.

See Also: First voyage, France and French reaction to Cook

T

Tahiti

Tahiti (17° 40' S, 149° 28' W) is the largest of the Windward Society Islands in the South Pacific. It is 1118 miles (1800km) south of the Equator and now forms part of the territory of French Polynesia, of which it is the principal island. The capital of French Polynesia, Papeete, is located on the north-west coast of the island. Tahiti has become synonymous with the concept of tropical paradise and is a popular destination spot for tourists seeking a tropical island. Tahiti comprises two parts, Tahiti Nui (to the northwest) and Tahiti Iti, separated by a narrow isthmus.

Cook visited the islands on each of his voyages. Matavai Bay was one of his favourite places in the Pacific while he also anchored at Tautira at the eastern end of Tahiti Iti on two occasions. Samuel Wallis returned to London in 1768 having visited Tahiti on a voyage round the world and he recommended Tahiti as a suitable location from which to observe the Transit of Venus. Cook anchored the *Endeavour* in Matavai Bay on the north coast of Tahiti on 13 April 1769. Cook was welcomed by Tutaha, the ari'i or chief of the district, who allowed him to build a camp ashore. Good relations existed between Cook and Tutaha. Later, Cook met Purea, who had welcomed Wallis. Cook had seven weeks to prepare for the Transit and decided to build the observatory on the promontory causing it to acquire the name Point Venus. In early June, Cook sent two groups to other locations to provide back-up observations. Hicks took a party east to an islet, Motu Taaupiri, while Gore's rowed west across to Moorea to a rock named Motu Irioa. The day of the Transit, 3 June, was clear, bright and very hot, which augured well for a good sighting. Green and the two other groups were pleased but Cook had distinct reservations about his own readings.

Chart of the Island Otaheite by Cook 1769. Engraved by J Cheevers after Cook and Smith. (Hawkesworth II fp 79)

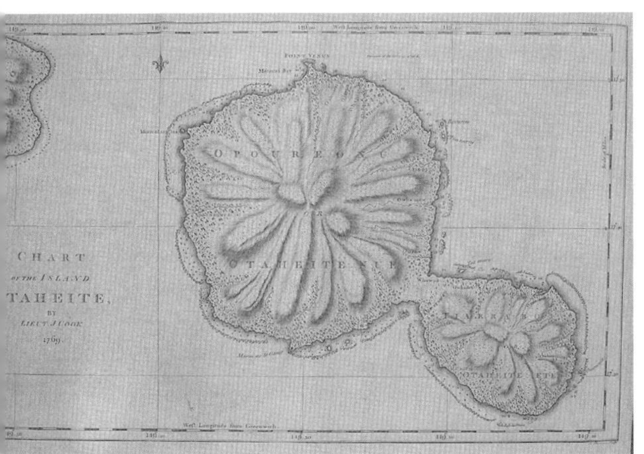

Cook was not yet ready to leave Tahiti as it was too soon in the year to venture south in search of the Southern Continent. Instead, he decided to make a tour of the island and he, Banks and a small party set out on 26 June. They made the tour in a clockwise direction in six days. They visited Hitia'a where they were shown where Bougainville, the French explorer, had landed the previous year. At Taravao they realised Tahiti was two parts linked by a narrow isthmus before proceeding on to Tahiti Iti. At Tautira they met the local ari'i and his son accompanied them as far as Pari. Back on Tahiti Nui they saw near Papara, the marae at Mahaiatea, which impressed Banks greatly. The party made its way up the West Coast to Faaa and Pare and finally back to Matavai Bay.

The restocked and repaired *Endeavour* sailed from Matavai Bay on 13 July 1769. Banks persuaded Cook to take Tupaia on board and this proved to be a beneficial move as Tupaia's navigational, translating and diplomatic skills were to be used often. Tahiti had had a considerable effect on Cook and all others on board. The drawings of Parkinson and the descriptions by Cook, Banks and others all contributed to the idyllic picture of the South Seas that soon developed in Europe. The concept of the 'Noble Savage' as a description for the Polynesians stemmed partly from Banks' writings. Cook though was more practical and saw Tahiti as an ideal base from which to explore the Pacific. It was central, possessed an equitable climate and afforded all the fruit, vegetables, water and other supplies that Cook could need.

He therefore returned to Tahiti on his second voyage. The ships approached from the south-east on 15 August 1773 and nearly ran onto the fringing reef. They managed to sail through a gap in the reef but not without difficulties and several anchors were lost. On the 17th, the ships anchored at Cook's Anchorage near Tautira in Vaitepiha Bay on Tahiti Iti and the British were received warmly. The local ari'i was now Vehiatua, who had accompanied Cook on his tour in 1769. Hodges recorded the visit by painting scenes of the Vaitepiha River and Valley. Cook left Tautira on the 24th and two days later arrived at Matavai Bay.

Things had changed since Cook's last visit. A war had taken place and Vehiatua had been victorious, defeating and killing Tutaha. Tu, based in Pare, was now ari'i. As a result of the war, provisions were in short supply so Cook decided to leave. The ships sailed on 1 September. Cook, though, was back in Matavai Bay on 22 April 1774. Remembering the lack of supplies the previous August, he did not intend to stay long but was surprised to find pigs and other supplies in plenty. Cook was also amazed by the spectacle he saw at Pare a few days later where over 300 double canoes were assembled. Cook counted 160 war canoes and 170 smaller support canoes with about 7000 men on board. To'ofa was in control of the fleet, which had been assembled to attack Moorea. Cook could not be persuaded to help the attack and left Tahiti on 14 May.

On his final voyage, Cook once more returned to Tahiti. On 12 August 1777, the southernmost end of Tahiti Iti was sighted and the ships anchored near Tautira the next day. Cook was welcomed warmly. Vehiatua, the previous ari'i had died and had been replaced by his brother. The British learned that Spanish ships from Peru had made two visits since their own last visit and that the Spanish had made attempts to convert islanders to Christianity.

On 23 August, Cook transferred to Matavai Bay where crews set about general repairs and restocking. Tu was still ari'i. At the time of Cook's previous visit a war fleet of canoes had been assembled to attack Moorea and the conflict was still under way. The fleet's commander To'ofa again tried to involve Cook but, to To'ofa's disgust, Cook declined. Instead Cook accepted an invitation to attend a ceremony at Atehuru marae where a human sacrifice was made to the gods to gain assistance against Moorea. To'ofa went across to Moorea and engaged in a short battle before a peace was declared, prompting another ceremony that Cook, being ill, was unable to attend. Tu's female relatives gave Cook a series of massages and he recovered.

Cook had Webber paint his portrait and gave the painting to Tu, who carried it around with him for many years. Tahiti had had a profound affect on Cook and was probably his favourite place in the Pacific. Despite some problems with theft, he maintained a good relationship with the Tahitians and formed close friendships with many of them. Cook left Tahiti for the final time on 29 September 1777.

SEE ALSO: Matavai Bay, Society Islands, Transit of Venus, Colour plate 12

Tahitians

When the British arrived in Tahiti in 1769, they found a people who had inhabited the islands for over 1000 years, having come from islands to the west. They were Polynesians and had organised themselves into a well-functioning social structure. However, the British found it difficult to grasp how the political and social life of Tahiti was organised and tried to understand it by imposing European models on it. For example, they expected that there would be one overall ruler on the island and, given they had dealings with Purea on the first voyage, assumed she was the ruler of the whole island. This was despite Tutaha's obvious status at Matavai Bay. The real situation at the time of Europeans' arrival was that a set of families ruled, each in particular districts. No one chief was able to control all tribes. Intermarriage by members of the ruling families created alliances. These rulers were called ari'i and they were sacred.

The ari'i were at the top of a pyramid structure. Just below them and nearly as important were tahu'a, approximating to priests, who held spiritual power. They also had special skills and knowledge. Tupaia, who sailed with Cook was a tahu'a, versed in navigation. Below them were ra'atira, minor nobility holding limited power and able to own land. At the bottom were the manahune, who were the ordinary people. Religious custom was transmitted from one generation through the tahu'a. Ceremonies were held on marae. Relationships needed to be shown between gods and ari'i in order to legitimise the power of the ari'i. Human sacrifices were even made to obtain prophecies and protection. The whole society had to respect tabu, which had the power of law.

Potatow, an ari'i from Punaauia on Tahiti. Engraved by John Hall after Hodges. (Cook I fp 159)

The Tahitians retained the ability to sail between islands and had extensive knowledge of many of their locations. Tupaia demonstrated this when he drew a map for Cook, which showed the Marquesas to the north-east and the Cook Islands to the west. They used two main types of canoes. Large double-hulled canoes, used for migrations or war, could reach 98ft (30m) in length and transport up to 300 people. Hodges depicted these canoes in the fleet To'ofa assembled to attack Moorea. Smaller single canoes with an outrigger were used for fishing.

The early European visitors believed the Tahitians were the epitome of the 'Noble Savage', a concept put forward by Rousseau. To the Europeans, they appeared to live easy, idyllic lives in a wonderful climate in a beautiful location. However, despite appearances and the alliances between districts, war was common on the islands. Not long before Cook arrived, Puni from Bora Bora had captured Raiatea and Huahine. This had caused the Oro religious cult based at the Taputapuatea marae on Raiatea to leave that island and several tahu'a, including Tupaia, moved to Tahiti, taking their beliefs with them and becoming advisors to Purea. In 1773, when Cook returned to Tahiti, he found the island devastated after a civil war. Tutaha, who had received Cook in 1769 had attacked Vehiatua, the ari'i of Tahiti Iti and had been killed. Vehiatua, in reprisal, then destroyed much of the crops and houses of north-west Tahiti near Matavai Bay where Cook visited. To'ofa tried to persuade Cook to help attack Moorea on both the second and third voyages.

SEE ALSO: Indigenous peoples and Cook, Polynesia

Tasman, Abel (1603–1659)

Abel Janszoon Tasman was born in the village of Lutjegast, near Groningen in the Netherlands, in 1603. He joined the Dutch East India Company (Verenigde Oostindische Compagnie or VOC) in 1633. Tasman was first mate of the *Weesp* in 1634 and later that year skipper of the *Mocha*, patrolling in the Dutch East Indies (Indonesia). He was back in the Netherlands in 1637.

He left again in 1638 for Batavia (present-day Jakarta), in command of the ship *Engel* on a 10-year contract. He would make several trading and exploring voyages in the Pacific and Indian oceans. He sailed to the north-west Pacific between 1639 and 1642 visiting the Philippines and Taiwan, followed the coast of Japan, and discovered several small islands.

In 1642, the Governor, Antony van Diemen, approved a voyage to the Southwest Pacific and Tasman was put in charge. Two ships were prepared for the voyage, the *Zeehaen*, an armed transport, and the *Heemskerck*, the flagship. He was accompanied by Frans Visscher, an able navigator, hydrographer and surveyor, who had suggested the voyage. They sailed first to Mauritius in the Indian Ocean then allowed currents to take them east. They reached land, which was named Van Diemen's Land (it was later called Tasmania) after the VOC governor. They sailed on and sighted the west coast of South Island, New Zealand, in the Hokitika area on 13 December 1642. It was the first recorded sighting of New Zealand by Europeans. Tasman sailed northward, following the coast, before entering Golden Bay. He anchored at Wharewharangi Bay and soon encountered Māori of the Ngati Tumatakokiri tribe. Māori double canoes began visiting the ships. Tasman sent a small boat out to greet the local canoes. A Māori canoe rammed the boat and three of the Dutch were killed. The Māori retreated while Dutch guns fired, killing a Māori.

Tasman now considered the Māori as hostile. No more contact was attempted as he sailed up the west coast. On 6 January 1643, he left Staten Landt, as he called the land. It was renamed 'Nieuw Zeeland' (New Zealand) some years later. Tasman headed north-east and arrived at Tonga on 21 January, where he finally obtained ample supplies of food and water by trading with the islanders. Sailing on, in early February they sighted some of the northern islands of Fiji but did not land. They turned westwards, survived a prolonged storm, and experienced an earthquake at sea. Reaching New Guinea in mid-April, they navigated its northern coastline and reached Batavia on 15 June 1643.

Tasman had circumnavigated Australia and had demonstrated that it was not part of the southern continent. In 1644, he made a short expedition into the Gulf of Carpentaria. By 1653 Tasman had retired. He owned 288 acres of town land in Batavia. He died in October 1659. Various features in the south-west Pacific are named for him, including Tasmania and the Tasman Sea.
SEE ALSO: Dutch explorers, Pacific exploration before Cook

Tasmania/Van Diemens Land

Tasmania (42° S, 147° E) is an island off the south-east coast of Australia. When Abel Tasman, the first European to do so, visited the island in 1642, he found it inhabited by Aboriginal people. Tasman called it Van Diemen's Land.

When Cook left New Zealand in 1770, he was heading for Van Diemen's Land but his course was too far north and he reached the Australian mainland instead. On his second voyage, Cook contemplated sailing to Van Diemen's Land after his spell in Antarctic waters but chose to go to Dusky Sound. It was therefore in 1777 that Cook finally reached Van Diemen's Land.

A composite illustration by Peter Fannin, master of the Adventure *in 1773. It shows a chart of Adventure Bay and local birds. (Admiralty Library Manuscript Collection, Royal Navy Museum)*

He had left Kerguelen Island and sailed east in latitudes, 45–50° S, as far as 110° E before heading north. Cook still thought Van Diemen's Land was part of the mainland of New South Wales. In 1773, Furneaux, in the *Adventure*, had visited a bay on the south coast and Cook now made for that bay. On 24 January 1777 he was off Southwest Cape. He then sailed along the south coast past rocks that were named Mew Stone and Eddystone after similar rocks in Devon and Cornwall. Cook crossed a large bay, now known as D'Entrecasteaux Channel but called Storm Bay by Cook, before rounding Penguin Island to anchor in Adventure Bay on 26 January. Cook and the crew went ashore and obtained plenty of wood and water from around the bay and Penguin Island. After three days, Palawah people from the local Aboriginal tribe visited the parties ashore but communication was nearly impossible. Cook realised that these people were similar to those he had met further north seven years earlier but he described various differences. Tasmania had been separated from the mainland for 12,000 years causing isolation. More locals visited the next day, including women and children. On the 30th Cook sailed, crossing (modern) Storm Bay and past Tasman Peninsula before making for New Zealand. He had not realised that his landing spot had been on a small island, later to be called Bruny Island (the aboriginal name is Lunawannaalonna).

In 1773, Furneaux had only sailed along the south and east coasts and Cook had reproached him for not investigating the possibility of Tasmania being an island. Now when he himself had the chance to explore, he sailed off instead to New Zealand. This was, perhaps, the first indication that, on this voyage, Cook had lost some of his drive and curiosity. He never actually landed on the island of Tasmania.

Bass and Flinders, in the late 1790s, showed that Tasmania, as the land was later named, was indeed an island. Various names around Adventure Bay remember Cook's visit. Bligh, the *Resolution*'s Master, would return later in his own ship and a museum records that and visits by other European explorers, including Cook.
SEE ALSO: Aborigines, Australia

Taylor, William (1761–1842)

William Taylor sailed on the third voyage on the *Resolution* as an AB until 23 March 1778 when he appointed midshipman. He kept a log. Taylor was promoted to lieutenant in October 1780, commander in January 1783, and captain in September 1793. In 1795, Taylor took command of HMS *Prompte,* 20 guns, before taking over HMS *Andromeda,* a Fifth Rate of 32 guns, which he sailed off Scotland and Newfoundland until 1799. In 1800, he took HMS *Magnanime,* a Third Rate of 64 guns, as escort for a merchant convoy to Africa and the East Indies. He then went to the West Indies before returning to Plymouth in 1802 and was laid off. In 1803, Taylor commanded *Sparrow,* a 12-gun cutter. Taylor became a rear-admiral in 1811, a vice-admiral in 1819, and an admiral in 1830. He was born in Woolwich in 1761 and died on 19 July 1842, leaving a will (FRC 11/1968). He was buried at St Alphage's Church, Greenwich.

SEE ALSO: Third voyage

Te To'ofa (also known as Towha and Te'towha) (??–??)

Te To'ofa was chief of Atehuru on the west coast of Tahiti. After the battle of 1773 between the forces of Vehiatua and Tutuha in which Te Pau, a chief of Faaa was killed, Te To'ofa achieved power. His genealogy is uncertain.

Te To'ofa was one of several Tahitian chiefs keen to attack Moorea but Tu refused to participate, leading to animosity between the two men. Cook was amazed in April 1774 when he observed a force of 330 canoes that had been assembled to attack Moorea. Te To'ofa was in command of the force and Cook referred to him as 'The Admiral'. It is believed that the Tahitians began their attack against Moorea shortly after Cook left in May 1774. The war lasted for over three years and was still in progress when Cook returned in August 1777. About this time, Te To'ofa and Mahine, the chief of Moorea, finally agreed peace terms, though on terms not advantageous to Tahiti.

Te To'ofa expressed resentment towards Tu but Cook, when he left at the end of September, warned against taking any action. Te To'ofa and others waited five years before attacking and defeating Tu in 1782.

SEE ALSO: Tahitians

Theatre, Cook in

As with other literary forms, there have been comparatively few examples of drama and theatre being used to portray Cook or events in his life. Indeed, in several twentieth-century plays inspired by his life, Cook is silent or even absent. A number of plays appeared in the years following his death but since then plays have only occasionally been written, usually associated with an anniversary of an event associated with Cook. If these later plays have been produced at all, it will have only have been as a single performance. No plays have entered the dramatic repertoire.

However, there have been a few interesting plays. The first of note was the 1785 stage spectacle *Omai: Or A Trip Round the World.* Written by John O'Keefe, with music by William Shield, *Omai* is best known for its apotheosis scene and the set designs. This remarkable spectacle functioned both as pantomime and travelogue, as well as exhibition, with extensive use of scenery and costume, including a procession of about eighty people, representing thirteen ethnic groups. Phillip de Loutherbourg was the designer and he worked closely with John Webber, the artist on Cook's third voyage, to ensure authenticity. *Omai* was one of the most popular theatrical pieces of the decade and helped fuel popular interest in travel and exploration of the Pacific. The apotheosis set depicted Cook ascending to heaven, attended by 'Fame and Britannia'. The image was published in 1794 and contributed to the development of Cook's posthumous reputation.

A French play by Jean Arnould, *La Mort du Capitaine Cook,* opened in Paris in October 1788. Set in Hawai'i, the play is an unhistorical account of Cook's death. It proved extremely popular and was produced in several translations in Britain as *The Death of Captain Cook: a grand serious-pantomimic-ballet in three parts.* Performances related to Cook and his death continued into the nineteenth century.

In the twentieth century, the play of note was that by Giraudoux. *Supplément au voyage de Cook,* which was first performed in 1935, has been described as a one-act romp in which a middle-aged, missionary-minded British couple, Mr and Mrs Banks, disembark from the frigate of the explorer Captain Cook. They plan to civilise the islanders but their plans go wrong when a Tahitian maiden almost seduces Mr Banks. Cook himself does not appear in the farce, except off-stage. Giraudoux mixes characters from Cook and Bougainville's voyages in his critical commentary on the clash of cultures.

Plays by Yarrington in Australia in 1901 and Fairfax-Blakeborough in the UK in 1928 are examples of the anniversary-based pieces of commissioned drama that glorify Cook. *Captain James Cook,* by Aldyth Morris, appeared in 1978 as part of the 200th anniversary of Cook's visit to Hawai'i. It is a monologue in which Cook retraces his life.

Third voyage (1776–1780)

On Cook's return from his second voyage, he was given a hero's welcome as, by now, his fame had spread. His portrait was painted by Hodges and Dance, he was a frequent dinner guest and he was elected a Fellow of the Royal Society. While the voyage had been successful, Cook was pleased to be home with his wife and children. Elizabeth, especially, hoped that, after so many years at sea, Cook would retire and he was appointed a captain of Greenwich Hospital so he could write up the narrative of the second voyage. It was not long, however, before Cook found this new work boring in comparison with sailing the world.

Sketch of Nootka Sound. Engraved by M Smith after Cook. (Cook & King II pl 37, fp 279)

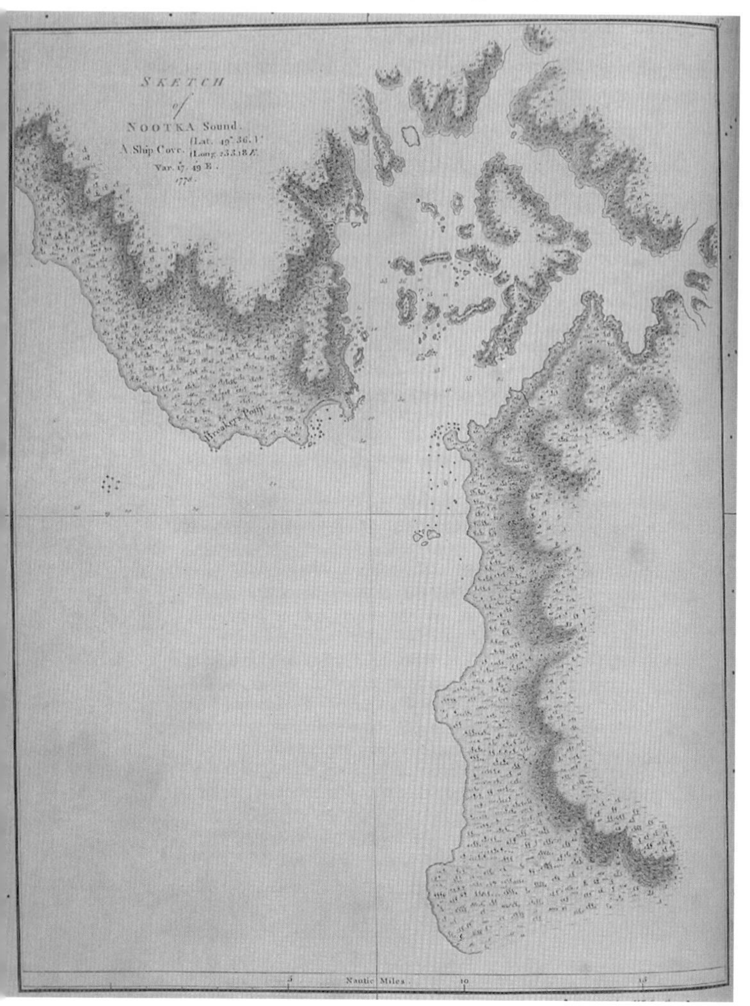

It became even more boring when he learned the British Admiralty was planning a new voyage of exploration. The goals were to return Mai to Huahine and to find the elusive navigable Northwest Passage round the north of America. The latter was a challenge that would appeal to Cook. The Earl of Sandwich, First Lord of the Admiralty, asked Cook for advice on who should lead the expedition though it was well known he wanted Cook for the role. Cook put his own name forward and was snapped up by the eager Earl so that his family's hopes of his retirement were shattered. Promoted to captain, Cook began preparations for the voyage.

By mid-1776, Cook was ready to sail again. It had been decided to use HMS *Resolution*, which had served him well on the second voyage but HMS *Adventure* would not be used again. A replacement, another collier, was purchased and renamed HMS *Discovery*. She was put under the captaincy of Charles Clerke, who had already completed three Pacific voyages, two of them with Cook. Before the voyage, Clerke, who had stood as guarantor for his brother, was arrested and placed in debtor's prison. This delayed the departure of *Discovery* and sowed the seeds of tuberculosis that would kill him four years later off Kamchatka.

Cook himself was now 47 years old and, though much recovered from the second voyage, he was no longer the fit man who had sailed in the *Endeavour*. He was sailing against the wishes of his wife Elizabeth, who had just given birth to their sixth child, Hugh, in May 1776. Some of the crew had sailed with Cook before. No scientists were taken and Surgeon William Anderson doubled as naturalist and ethnologist. John Webber sailed as artist. The most famous person on board, other than Cook, was William Bligh, the master, who would later gain notoriety as captain of HMS *Bounty* and Governor of New South Wales.

The *Resolution* and the *Discovery* sailed separately to Cape Town as Clerke was still in prison. The *Discovery* caught up on 10 November 1776. Cook had the ships repaired and restocked before they sailed together into the Indian Ocean via the Prince Edward Islands to Kerguelen Island. The British briefly examined the desolate island and then made for Tasmania, where the ships put into Adventure Bay. Cook was keen to keep going and left for New Zealand to spend two weeks in Queen Charlotte Sound. He paid a visit to Wharehunga

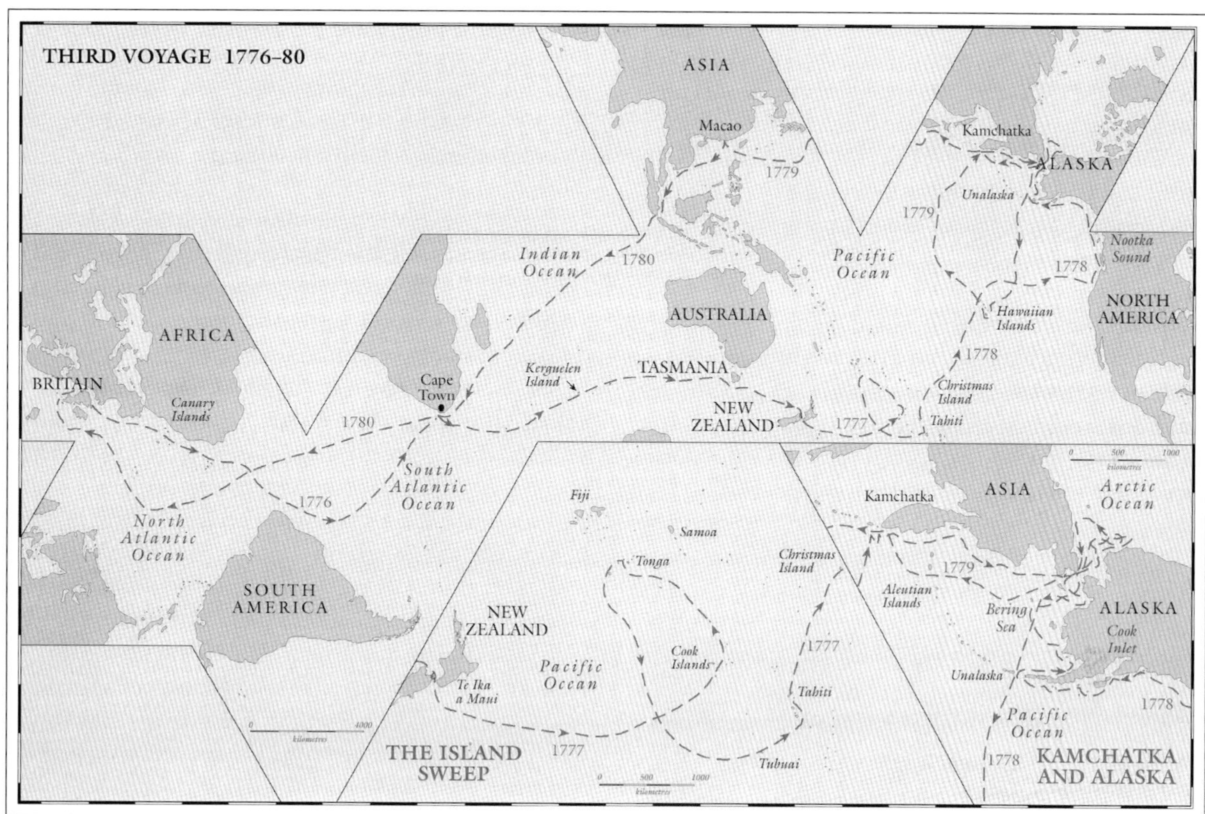

Cove, the site of the massacre of part of the *Adventure*'s crew on the previous voyage, and surprised his crew and local Māori by not extracting 'utu' (revenge). He then sailed out into the Pacific.

In March, Cook reached the islands that would be later named after him, touching on several of them. Tonga was the next port of call and the ships anchored at Nomuka. Cook met Finau, a chief, who joined the British when they set off to examine other islands in the Ha'apai group. At Lifuka, they were joined by the Tu'i Tonga. In June, Cook moved south to Tongatapu, showing, for him, a strange lack of urgency, passing up opportunities to visit nearby Samoa and Fiji. He finally left Tonga on 19 July.

On the way to Tahiti, Tubuai, an island in the Austral Group, was visited. Cook spent ten days at Tautira near the eastern end of the island before transferring to Matavai Bay, where he was welcomed by Tu and To'ofa. Cook was ill during his time on Tahiti. In late September, Cook made his first visit to Moorea where he showed uncharacteristic overreaction, burning houses and canoes after a goat was stolen. Next, Mai was deposited on Huahine, fulfilling one of the goals of the voyage.

The other major goal was to search for the Northwest Passage so in December 1777, Cook sailed for the North Pacific. They crossed the Equator and arrived at an island, named Christmas Island after the time of year. The ships continued north and in mid-January 1778 reached a new group of islands, Hawai'i. Cook anchored at Kaua'i for a few days, then crossed to Ni'ihau. Cook was realised that the Hawaiians not only resembled those people found in such faraway places as Tahiti and New Zealand, they had similar customs and spoke a similar language.

Cook left Hawai'i to continue north-east across the North Pacific to America, which he reached at Oregon in March 1778. Cook sailed north missing the Strait of Juan de Fuca and put into Nootka Sound on Vancouver Island on 29 March. The British remained in the sound for most of April while the ships were repaired and the inlet was explored. They also traded for sea otter pelts. The ships resumed their voyage north but at a distance from the coast and outside the Queen Charlotte and Baranof Islands.

The coast trended west and Cook entered a large inlet, Prince William Sound. Shortly after, they arrived at the entrance to a larger bay, Cook Inlet, into which they sailed. Neither proved to be the Northwest Passage. The coast forced Cook to sailed south-west past Kodiak Island and the Alaskan Peninsula. Finally, in early July, Cook found a pass that allowed him to enter the Bering Sea and sail north. The ships passed through the Bering Strait and crossed the Arctic Circle. They reached 70° 14' N near Icy Cape when further progress was blocked by ice. Cook crossed over to the Russian shore and followed it back to the Bering Strait.

Cook examined Norton Sound before returning to Unalaska. Winter was approaching and he wanted to sail south to Hawai'i for rest and restocking. On the way south Cook celebrated his 50th birthday. They reached Maui on the 26th, then headed for the neighbouring large island of Hawai'i. However, Cook puzzled his crew by spending the month sailing slowly round the island and making no apparent attempt to land. Finally, on 16 January 1779, Cook put into Kealakekua Bay on the island's west coast. The British were received well but probably outstayed their welcome. The ships departed on 4 February but a mast, damaged in a storm, forced them back to Kealakekua. This time the reception was much cooler. Cook tried to take the Hawaiian Chief hostage, and, in the ensuing fight, Cook and many others were killed. Clerke assumed overall command and worked hard to restore peace between the two sides. He moved to the *Resolution* while John Gore took over the *Discovery*. Relations were good again when the ships sailed on 22 February.

Clerke put in at Kaua'i and Ni'ihau, then set off for Arctic waters to resume the search for the Northwest Passage, reaching Avacha Bay in Kamchatka on 24 April. They departed again on 19 June and headed north up the coast. Clerke took the ships through the Bering Strait and across the Arctic Circle into the Chukchi Sea only for the ice to foil him close to where Cook had been a year earlier. The ships sailed south but a few days out from Avacha Bay, Clerke died. Gore took over command and James King became captain of the *Discovery*. They began their return to Britain on 9 October, sailing via Japan and Macao. King visited Canton for supplies and to sell the sea otter pelts. They crossed the Indian Ocean to the Cape, then sailed up the Atlantic. In August 1780, gales forced the ships to the west of Ireland and Scotland and Gore put in at Orkney on 22 August. He managed to leave Orkney on 20 September and the ships finally sailed up the River Thames in early October.

The voyage had not found the Northwest Passage and the ships had returned to Britain without their captains, Cook and Clerke. Even so, the voyage was not a failure. They had explored and charted a large section of the North American coast from Oregon to Alaska and a similar stretch of the Asian coastline from Kamchatka northwards. In the Pacific Ocean, the Hawaiian Island Group had been located, together with islands in the Cook, Tonga and Austral Groups while Kerguelen Island in the Indian Ocean had been better described.

In hindsight, Cook probably should not have sailed on the voyage, never mind lead it. He had been ill on his previous voyage and was now close to 50 years of age. He had spent most of the previous ten years away at sea and retirement, or a long period of relaxation, would have served him better. His age, declining health and tiredness led to erratic behaviour not witnessed before. He had lost some of his drive and was much harder on his crew, and less tolerant of island people. Outbursts of anger and violence had not been seen before and may have contributed to his death on Hawai'i, where he reacted in a way that a younger Cook would not have. His death at Kealakekua Bay on 14 February 1779 has remained a source of scholarly controversy.

SEE ALSO: *Adenture* (HMS), *Resolution* (HMS), Clerke (Charles)

Three Brothers

The *Three Brothers* was a collier in the North Sea coal trade. James Cook left the *Freelove* on 22 April 1748 to work on fitting out a new ship belonging to the Walkers, the *Three Brothers*, and Cook sailed on its maiden voyage, which left Whitby on 14 June 1748. John Walker was master at first but John Jefferson transferred to take command. The first voyage lasted four months.

On 14 October 1748, the *Three Brothers* was requisitioned to help transport troops and horses from the Netherlands back to Britain and Ireland at the end of the War of the Austrian Succession. In April 1749, the *Three Brothers* resumed normal duties transporting coal from the Tyne to London. Cook was discharged when the ship berthed at Whitby in December 1749. He had completed his apprenticeship and was free to sign on with any ship. Cook rejoined the *Three Brothers* on 19 February 1751. He served under a new master, Robert Watson until 30 July 1751. He and most of the crew then transferred to the *Friendship*.

SEE ALSO: North Sea and the coal trade, Walker (John), Whitby

Tierra del Fuego, Cape Horn and Staten Island

Tierra del Fuego (54° S, 69° W) is an archipelago at the southern extremity of South America, from which it is separated by Strait of Magellan. Magellan sailed through the strait in 1520 and called the land to the south Tierra del Fuego (land of fire), for the fires maintained by the local people. In 1616, the Dutch navigators, Schouten and Le Maire sailed through the Strait of Le Maire between Tierra del Fuego and Staten Island. They then rounded the southernmost headland, Cape Horn (55° 55' S, 67° 20' W), which they named after one of their ships. Staten Island (55° S, 64° 30' W) lies 18.6 miles (30km) east of Tierra del Fuego, separated by the Strait of La Maire. This island was uninhabited.

The largest island is Tierra del Fuego, or Isla Grande, with an area of 18,507 square miles (48,100 sq km). Numerous small islands lie to its south. People moved to the islands around 10,000 years ago. Several different groups occupied the area when Cook visited. The Haush, a sub-group of the Selk'nam lived at the south-east corner of Tierra del Fuego, while Yamanas or Yaghanes lived on the south coast of Tierra del Fuego and its offshore islands. None of these Fuegans now survive.

The *Endeavour* approached Tierra del Fuego on 11 January 1769. Cook decided not to sail through the Strait of Magellan and approached the Strait of Le Maire instead. It proved difficult to sail through the Strait and Cook stood the *Endeavour* off Thetis Bay allowing Banks to go ashore where he collected over 100 new plant species. Two days later they successfully negotiated the Strait and anchored in the Bay of Good Success on the 15th for an eventful stay of five days. On the 17th Cook, ashore looking for water, met local Haush, a Fuegan people. Banks was more ambitious and organised an expedition to go inland to collect botanical specimens. Buchan, the artist, suffered an epileptic fit and, while he was being tended, the temperature dropped and snow fell. Efforts were made to return to the ship but some of the party were in no state to do so and spent the night in the open. Search parties the next day found Banks' two servants dead, either from the cold or from the rum they had drunk to keep warm. Meanwhile, Cook had surveyed the bay and replenished the fresh water. They left on 21 January to round Cape Horn in a westerly direction against prevailing currents and winds. They passed the Cape on the 25th heading

Christmas Sound, Tierra Del Fuego. Engraved by W Watts after Hodges. (Cook II fp 185)

south-westerly through Drake Passage to latitude 60° 10' S. Cook then turned north into a new ocean, the Pacific.

Cook returned to Tierra del Fuego on his way home on the second voyage. Having crossed the Pacific, Cook arrived at Cape Desado on Desolation Island on 17 December 1774. He headed south-east, following the coast, which comprised hundreds of small islands, making for Cape Horn. The *Resolution* was kept at a safe distance from the shore. The ship passed a large inlet on the 19th, which is now called Cook Bay. Cook needed provisions and a harbour to check the state of the *Resolution*. He found a suitable inlet into which he took the ship. Cook stayed there for eight days over Christmas, which earned the inlet the name Christmas Sound (55° 25' S, 69° 40' W). Fresh water and vegetables were obtained while Cook, the Forsters, Pickersgill and Clerke made sorties exploring the inlet. Local Fuegan people, this time probably Yamanas, visited the ship and gifts were exchanged.

The *Resolution* sailed on 28 December and rounded Cape Horn safely the next day before making for the Bay of Good Success to check for signs of the *Adventure*. Pickersgill went ashore but found no trace of the other ship having been there. Cook passed through the Strait of Le Maire and turned east along the north coast of Staten Island. He came to a group of small islands, the New Year's Isles, on the 31st. Cook anchored the ship in the lee of the largest island, Observatory Island, and sent Gilbert to explore an inlet on Staten Island. Gilbert charted what proved to be a good harbour and named it New Year's Harbour and some isles at its mouth, Gull Isles. Two days later they sailed east passing a bay, later called Cook Bay, and rounding Cape St John before heading off to explore the South Atlantic.

SEE ALSO: First voyage, Indigenous peoples and Cook, Native Americans, Third voyage

Tonga

Tonga (20° S, 175° W) is an archipelago situated in the central South Pacific, south of Samoa and south-east of Fiji. It consists of four island groups. From south to north, they are: Tongatapu, Ha'apai, Vava'u and the Niuas. Tonga is made up of 170 islands of which 36 are inhabited. The land area of Tonga is 269 square miles (699 sq km).

People arrived in Tonga about 3000 years ago. They were part of the Lapita culture, who had travelled east through Fiji and would become Polynesians. Gradually a formal social structure developed on the islands with a king or Tu'i Tonga as the overall ruler. An elite class, hou'eiki, ruled over districts which were then divided into smaller units under chiefs or mu'a. They sublet land to ordinary people. Tongans developed a complex family ranking system whereby the eldest female (and her descendants) held higher rank within the family than the brothers, while a paternal inheritance system meant the eldest son received all property and titles.

Various Europeans, including Tasman and Wallis, visited the islands before Cook, who visited Tonga on three occasions on his second and third voyages. His first visit occurred in October 1773. Cook was aware that Tasman had visited islands in the region in 1643 and Cook was keen to fix the islands' position. The ships approached 'Eua (Tasman's Middelburg) from the east and anchored off the island's west coast. Cook went ashore at Ohonua to meet Chief Taione. The Tongans showed no desire to trade so Cook decided to move across to another island, visible to the north-west.

Chart of the Friendly Isles showing the tracks from all of Cook's visits. Engraved by W Harrison after Bligh and Cook. (Cook & King I pl 12, fp 225)

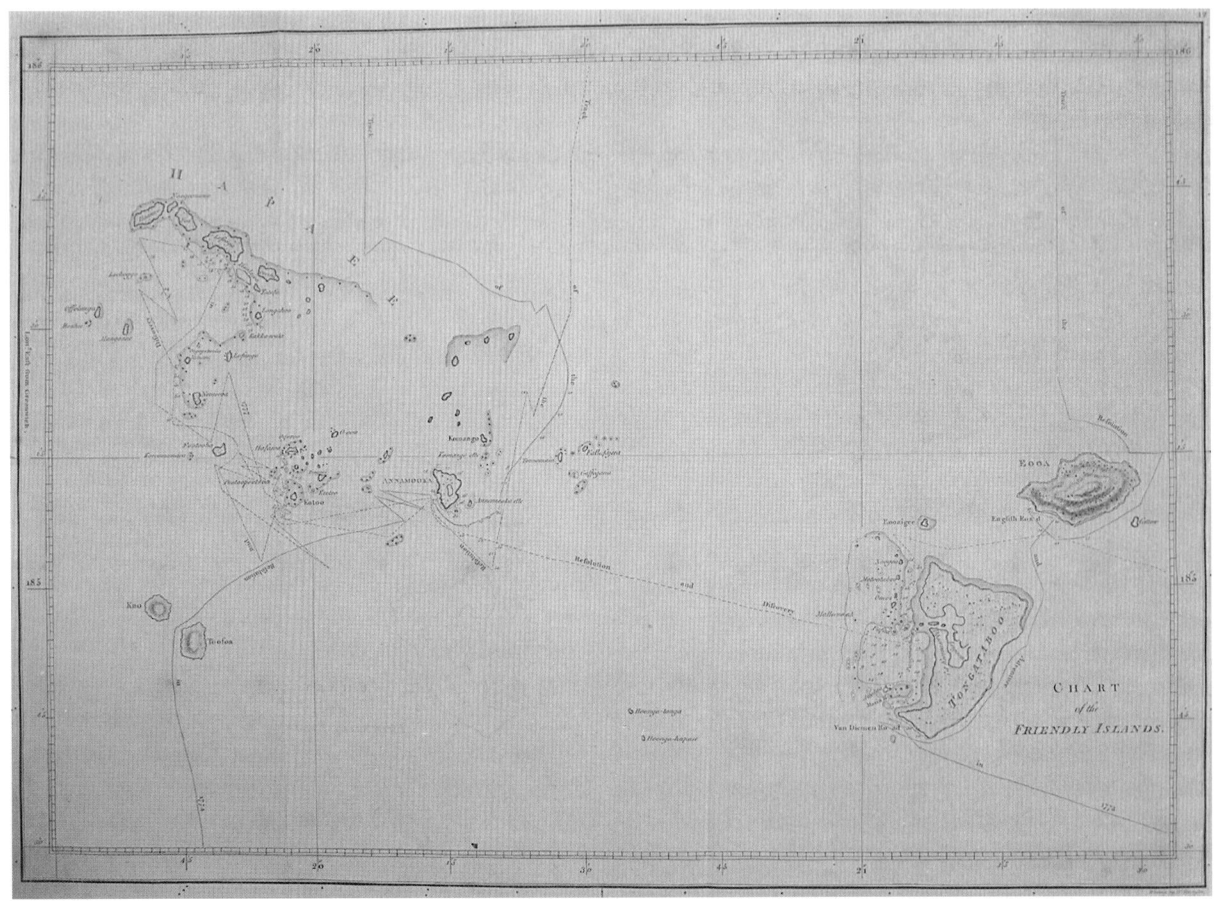

Boats of the Friendly Islands, by John Webber. This was published in 1791 by Webber as part of Views in the South Seas. *Cook was impressed by the speed of Tongan canoes and their seamanship. (National Library of Australia, NK4859)*

They sailed across to Tongatapu (Tasman's Amsterdam) on 3 October to an anchor at the north-west point of the island. Cook was soon introduced to a Chief, Ataongo, who looked after him during his stay The reception was so cordial that Cook gave the name Friendly Islands to the group. The visit was only short but for those four days trade was brisk in coconuts, bananas, pigs and Cook, despite the short time, gave a detailed and favourable description of Tongatapu and 'Eua. He learned also about more islands to the north. The British departed on 8 October heading for New Zealand. They passed the tiny island of 'Ata the next day.

In June 1774, Cook returned, this time to the northern islands he had heard about in Tongatapu in 1773. He reached the Ha'apai Group on 25 June, aiming for Nomuka (Tasman's Rotterdam). Cook anchored on its north coast. The island was able to supply provisions and fresh water in plenty so trade was brisk. Cook sailed north on the 29th, heading for two islands. On the 30th Cook sailed through the channel between Kao and Tofua, an active volcano. On the passage from Nomuka to Tofua, Cook had been able to watch Tongan canoes and admire how they were sailed, together with their capabilities for speed and manoeuvrability. The mutiny on the *Bounty* would take place off Tofua in 1789.

Cook's third visit took place in April 1777 on his third voyage. Cook anchored briefly off Mango before moving on to Nomuka on 1 May. Cook went ashore to be welcomed by the island's Chief, Tupoulangi. Five days later a High Chief, Finau, arrived from Tongatapu to see Cook. Cook sailed north on 14 May to explore the other islands in the Ha'apai Group. Finau accompanied Cook on the *Resolution*. Reefs and shoals forced Cook round Kotu. He then sailed between Fotuha'a and Lofanga to anchor off the northern end on Lifuka where Cook went ashore near Kuolo. Over the next few days there were feasts and entertainments. The Tongans made exhibitions of dancing, boxing and wrestling, and the British let off fireworks. Afterwards, it emerged that the entertainments had been part of a plot to kill Cook but the Tongans could not agree about the time or the method so Cook escaped. Finau left to go north to the Vava'u Group of islands but lied to Cook about suitable anchorages there for Cook's ships when Cook wanted to accompany him. Cook, instead sailed south and made a stop at the southern end of Lifuka.

Fatafehi Paulaho, the Tu'i Tonga (king), suddenly arrived and, after gift exchanges and ceremonies, both parties sailed south. Cook arrived back at Nomuka on 5 June, where he was rejoined the next day by Finau and, on the 7th, by the Tu'i Tonga. Cook was now able to observe the hierarchy of Tongan society more closely and its protocols. On the 8th they all departed for Tongatapu. Tongan pilots on board helped Cook bring the ships through the reefs to a safe anchorage off Holeva Point on the north coast of the island. The British were welcomed by the Tu'i Tonga. Cook arranged for repairs to be carried out on the ships. A change in Cook's character manifested itself here as he stayed on the island for a month doing little except taking part in feasts and being entertained. His drive to explore seemed to have evaporated and stories about nearby and yet unvisited island groups, such as Samoa and Fiji, failed to fire Cook's imagination. Also, Cook's tolerance and good nature were not in evidence, as he reacted to the prevalent thieving by having offenders flogged and taking hostages until items were returned.

On 12 June, Cook was taken, in the Tu'i Tonga's canoe, to visit Maealiuaki (the King's father) at Mu'a on the central lagoon. A banyan tree (Captain Cook's Tree) and a monument mark the visit. All repairs had been completed by 25 June but Cook decided to wait to observe a solar eclipse on 5 July, which was only partly successfully recorded. Finally, on 10 July, the ships sailed but only to 'Eua. Cook left Tonga on 17 July 1777.

Cook spent close to 14 weeks in Tonga but made little progress in understanding the Tongans and their culture. He was unaware of plots to kill him and left still believing them to be the Friendly Isles. He did not visit Vava'u Group or the far northern islands.

SEE ALSO: Polynesia

Toponymy, Cook's

By the time of his death near the end of his third voyage, James Cook had probably bestowed more names on geographical features than any other person before or since. Several hundred of Cook's names are still used while many more have disappeared, replaced by original local names as they were determined or by later people choosing to use their own. Cook usually attempted to find out local names but translation problems, lack of local people or the fact that he remained at sea whilst passing a feature often left him inventing a name of his own.

The names fall into several broad categories:

Honouring persons in authority – Cook's background and lack of standing rendered him vulnerable so it was prudent of him to honour prominent politicians, nobility and senior officers of the Admiralty as he did on the first voyage. The east coast of Australia is strewn with such names, for example Rockingham Bay, Cape Hawke and Cape Grafton. Even on the third voyage, Cook was still careful and named Norton Sound and Bristol Bay in this manner. Interestingly, Cook rarely honoured royalty but the king and queen received their dues with South Georgia and Queen Charlotte Sound.

Persons on board – Cook was very frugal in using the names of his crew though he occasionally named features after the first person that sighted them. The scientists and officers were more likely to be honoured and the names of Banks, Solander, Hicks, Clerke and Gore are scattered around. Some of the masters did well (Gilbert and Bligh especially) while artists fared badly. A few midshipman were honoured (Willis and Grindall) while Freezeland and Young Nick were the only ordinary crew remembered.

Descriptive of features – Names such as Flat Island, East Cape, Woody Island and White Island are typical of this group.

Descriptive of events – The stay in Dusky Sound during the second voyage provided many instances of such names. Luncheon and Supper Coves describe the meals eaten while Woodhen, Parrot and Petrel Islands describe the birds shot at those locations. Capes Kidnappers, Runaway and Farewell are self-explanatory examples from the first voyage in New Zealand.

Dates and festivals – Religion never makes an overt presence in Cook's actions and writings but several names reflect the Christian calendar. Christmas and Whitsun are both used on several occasions (though not Easter). While sailing on the American coast in early 1778, Cook uses several saints' days (Bede and Gregory) while Cross Sound was sighted on the day celebrating the 'Stations of the Cross'.

Reminiscent – Cook was happy to reuse existing names and the Bay of Islands in New Zealand reminded him of a similar bay in Newfoundland. Rocks off the south coast of Tasmania were reminiscent of rocks near Plymouth and were named accordingly (Eddystone, Mew, Swilly). The Waihou River in New Zealand was evocative of the mouth of the Thames and the Firth of Thames resulted. New Caledonia was named because its coast looked similar to Scotland, Caledonia being an old name for part of Scotland.

Interestingly, Cook never named anything after members of his own family. Cook Strait in New Zealand, which was named at Banks' insistence, is the only feature named after Cook himself in his lifetime. The Cook Islands were named by the Russian explorer Krusenstern.

SEE ALSO: Cartographic results of Cook's voyages, Appendix V.

Torres, Luis Váez de (?–?)

Luis Váez de Torres accompanied Pedro Fernándes de Quiros in 1605 on his expedition to find the Solomon Islands and Terra Australis. He was captain of the *San Pedrico,* which left Callao, in Peru, and reached La Austrialia del Espiritu Santo (now Espiritu Santo in Vanuatu) in May 1606. Disagreements between the expedition leaders caused Quiros to leave in the *San Pedro y Pablo* and separate from the other two ships.

Torres made an unsuccessful search for Quiros but only discovered that Espiritu Santo was an island not a continent. He led the two ships south-west to 21° S before being forced north-west, reaching Tagula in the Louisiade Archipelago off New Guinea in July 1606. They anchored at Basilaki Island. Unable to sail north, Torres coasted southern New Guinea (called Magna Margarita) and sighted Long Reef off Cape York (called Volcan Quernado). He then continued west passing through a strait (later named Torres Strait in 1769 by Alexander Dalrymple, who discovered Torres' reports in Manila in 1762) between New Guinea and Australia. The ships cleared the western end of New Guinea in October and put into Ternate. Torres proceeded to Manila, which he reached in May 1607. Diego de Prado y Tovar, who accompanied Torres, wrote an account of the voyage. Little is known of Torres' life before and after this voyage.

Cook passed through Torres Strait in late 1770 keen to reach Java where he could have the *Endeavour* repaired but also intent on proving the existence of the strait.

SEE ALSO: Pacific exploration before Cook, Spanish explorers

Transit of Mercury

The transit of a planet occurs only when one of the inner planets, Mercury and Venus, which lie between the Sun and Earth, passes across the face of the Sun, as seen from Earth. On the average, there are 13 Transits of Mercury each century. The first ever observed was in 1631 by the French astronomer Gassendi.

All Transits of Mercury fall within several days of 8 May and 10 November. The plane of the Earth's orbit round the sun is known as the plane of the ecliptic. Since Mercury's orbit is inclined seven degrees to Earth's, it intersects the ecliptic at two points or nodes which cross the Sun each year on those dates. In 1716, Edmond Halley published a paper describing exactly how transits could be used to measure the distance from the Earth to the sun, and consequently calculate many other astronomical values. Unfortunately, his method proved somewhat impractical since contact timings of the required accuracy were difficult to make.

In early November 1769, Cook was sailing along the Bay of Plenty coast in New Zealand aware that a Transit of Mercury was due on the 9th. He entered an inlet on the 4th so he could establish a base on shore to make observations. This was carried out successfully near the mouth of the Purangi River in Te Whanganui-a-Hei, which Cook called Mercury Bay.

SEE ALSO: Astronomical results of Cook's voyages, Mercury Bay

Transit of Venus

The transit of a planet occurs only when one of the inner planets, Mercury and Venus, which lie between the Sun and Earth, passes across the face of the Sun, as seen from Earth. Transits of Venus occur in a clear pattern of recurrence at intervals of 8, 121.5, 8 and 105.5 years and are only possible during early December and June when Venus's orbital nodes pass across the Sun. In 1639, Jerimiah Horrocks and William Crabtree became the first to observe a Transit of Venus scientifically.

In 1716, Edmond Halley published a paper describing exactly how transits could be used to measure the distance from the Earth to the Sun. Halley had realised that that a Transit of Venus could be use to estimate the parallax to the Sun and that, having observed the transit from many widely-separated locations on the Earth, the combined data would provide an excellent way to measure the parallax of the Sun, and hence its distance from the Earth with unprecedented precision. Halley formulated a detailed plan for how the next transits of 1761 and 1769 should be observed.

A Transit occurred on 6 June 1761 and observations were made from selected points around the world. The next Transit was scheduled for 3–4 June 1769 and bodies such as the Royal Society dispatched astronomers around the world. William Wales, who would sail on Cook's second voyage was sent to Fort Churchill on Hudson Bay in Canada. The Royal Society negotiated with the Royal Navy to organise an expedition to take an astronomer to the central South Pacific, which had been determined to be an optimum location for observations. At that time, Wallis returned from the Pacific with news about the island of Tahiti, which was then selected.

James Cook led the expedition to Tahiti in the *Endeavour*, with Cook himself and Charles Green being the astronomers (during the voyage, Green trained several officers in making observations). They reached Tahiti in April 1769 and set up an observatory at Point Venus in Matavai Bay. Cook arranged for two other parties to make observations elsewhere in case Matavia Bay was cloudy. Hicks went east to Motu Taaupiri and Gore took a party across to Motu Irioa on Moorea. The observations were made relatively successfully.

The analysis of the transit data proved to be worth the great price paid by the astronomers who travelled the world to observe it. In 1771, the French astronomer, Lalande, used the combined 1761/1769 transit data to compute a distance of 95 million miles (153 million km), which compares with a modern radar measurement of 92.9 million miles (149.6 million km).

SEE ALSO: Astronomical results of Cook's voyages, Charles Green, Matavai Bay, Royal Society, Tahiti

Trevenen, James (1760–1790)

James Trevenen sailed on the third voyage on the *Resolution* as a midshipman until 3 April 1778. He then became an AB until 16 February 1779 when he resumed as a midshipman. After the voyage, Trevenen was made lieutenant in October 1780 and joined HMS *Conquestador.* He then sailed with James King on HMS *Crocodile* to the West Indies in 1781. Trevenen followed King to HMS *Resistance* in July 1782 as first lieutenant and they sailed to the West Indies, where, in 1783, they took part in Nelson's attempt to capture Turk's Island. Back in Britain in 1783 when peace was restored, Trevenen was without a position and went, with his brother, for a tour of Scotland. King's health had worsened so he went to Nice in France with his friend in September 1784. King died that November but Trevenen remained on the continent travelling in Italy, France and Switzerland until late 1785.

Trevenen was considered for commander of two historical voyages but was given neither. They were the First Fleet to Botany Bay and Bligh's *Bounty* voyage. He had seen the success of the north Pacific fur trade and suggested a plan to the Russian Ambassador in London. He was engaged by the Russian navy in 1787 but on his arrival in St Petersburg found that his plan had been shelved. Instead, he fought for the Russian navy against the Swedes from 1788. He had command of the *Rodislav,* 64 guns. This ship was wrecked in 1789 and Trevenen transferred to the *Netron Menya*. He took part in further actions against the Swedes before, on 3 July 1790, Trevenen was present at the Battle of Viborg Bay, during which he was fatally wounded.

Trevenen had attended Heston Grammar School as a young boy then went to the Naval Academy at Portsmouth from 1772 until 1775 where he became a close friend of James Ward. They joined Cook's third voyage together. Trevenen married Elizabeth Farquharson in Kronstadt in 1789. They had one daughter. (His widow married Thomas Bowdler, the literary sanitiser, in 1806.) Trevenen left memoirs, which provide insights into events and colleagues from the third voyage, including some observations about Cook.

He was born in Camborne, Cornwall on 1 January 1760. He died on 9 July 1790. He left a will (FRC 11/1199) and there is a brief biography in the *DNB*, v19, pp1137–8. Samwell wrote an obituary that appeared in the August 1790 edition of the *Gentleman's Magazine.* The poet Donald Davie wrote a poem entitled 'Trevenen'. There is a portrait of Trevenen in the uniform of the Russian navy.

SEE ALSO: King (James), Russians, Tahitians, Third voyage

Tu (also known as Otoo, Tunuieaaite atua i Tarahoi, Tynah and Pomare-Vairatoa) (1743?–1803)

Tu was the son of Teu (Happai) and Tetupaia i Raiatea. After the defeat of Purea and Amo, Tu was ruler designate of Tahiti but Tutaha was appointed his regent. At the time of Cook's first visit Tu was a shadowy figure and Cook did not realise the exact nature of the relationship between Tu and Tutaha. Tu was

Tu (Otoo), King of O-Taheite. Engraved by John Hall after Hodges. (Cook I fp 154)

already 25 years old, and married but could not go to Matavai as it lay in the domain of Tutaha.

After the death of Tutaha in 1773, various chiefs existed on Tahiti as equals, with Tu being one of the least powerful. The district of Haapape came under the control of Tu so he was able to welcome Cook at Matavai Bay when Cook returned in September 1773. Though he suspected that, in reality, Tu enjoyed only limited power and status, Cook accorded Tu the rank of overall chief or king. Tu, therefore, greatly to the disgust of the other chiefs, got most of the gifts, and all the social civilities of the British. Tu asked Cook to help him against Vehiatua and he complained that the chiefs of Ahurai and Paea were not his friends.

A war against Moorea was being organised under the command of Te To'ofa but Tu showed no inclination to take part or to support it. The war began in late 1774 after Cook's departure and was still in progress when he returned in 1777. Te To'ofoa eventually made peace with Mahine, the chief of Moorea, in terms not advantageous to Tahiti. Cook had Webber paint his portrait and gave the painting to Tu.

Tu's inaction and his alienation of other chiefs led to his downfall when he was defeated by an alliance of Moorea and other Tahitian chiefs, including Te To'ofa, in 1782. He fled to the mountains and changed his name to Tynah. His own name passed to his son, who became Tu. Both John Watts and William Bligh met Tu when they visited Tahiti several years later. His family became the Pomare dynasty that became the first rulers of all Tahiti.

Tuamotu Archipelago

The Tuamotu Archipelago (17° S, 144° W) is an assemblage of atolls and coral islands in the central South Pacific, 1056 miles (1700km) south of the Equator. The chain of about 75 atolls, one raised coral atoll (Makatea), and innumerable coral reefs covers 1243 miles (2000km) and has a total land area of only about 265 square miles (690 sq km). The chain runs WNW to ESE and is situated about 186 miles (300km) northeast of Tahiti. It now forms part of the territory of French Polynesia. Most of the islands have been inhabited at some time by Polynesian people, the Paumotu. Europeans first visited the islands in 1521 when Magellan led a Spanish expedition that passed through the chain.

Cook had entered the Pacific via Cape Horn and was *en route* for Tahiti when, on 4 April 1769, the *Endeavour* reached Vahitahi (Cook called it Lagoon Island), the first of the Tuamotu Archipelago. They saw but had no contact with a few people on the islands. Cook sailed on past several other islands in the group including Akiaki, Hao and Anaa towards Tahiti.

On the second voyage, in August 1773, Cook sailed through the southern edge of the archipelago, once more on his way to Tahiti. In April 1774, the *Resolution* visited the Northern Tuamotus after leaving the Marquesas. The atolls and reefs required careful navigation so Gilbert, the master, was dispatched in a small boat to guide the ship through the maze. On the 17th they arrived at Takaroa where Cook and Forster went ashore but local people did not make them welcome and they moved on to neighbouring Takapoto. After a quick inspection there Cook continued to a cluster of small atolls to which he gave the name Palliser's Isles; they include Apataki, Arutua and Toau.
SEE ALSO: Polynesia

Tupaia (?–1770)

Tupaia was a tahu'a or priest on Tahiti at the time of the visits of Wallis and Cook. He was originally from

The lad Taiyota (Taiata), Native of Otaheite in the dress of his country. Taiata is shown playing a nose flute. Engraved by R Godfrey after Parkinson. (Parkinson pl 9, fp 66)

Raiatea, the religious centre of the Society Islands but had fled, probably when Bora Bora defeated that island about 1760. Tupaia and others introduced the Oro cult to Tahiti. When Wallis arrived in 1767, Tupaia was seen as an adviser to Purea. Tahu'a were men who lived in constant communication with the gods and spirits, usually but not exclusively within the precinct of the marae. Some of them had spiritual power grounded in a particular skill and, for Tupaia, this was as a navigator.

At the time Cook arrived at Tahiti, Tupaia was aware that Purea had lost much of her power and was concerned for his own future. It is believed that Tupaia had previously advised Purea to kill Tutaha, the chief at Pare, and Tutaha was aware of this. Tupaia impressed Banks, who persuaded Cook to take the priest and his servant Taiata with them on the *Endeavour*. Tupaia demonstrated his knowledge to Cook by drawing a map on which the relative positions of islands from the Marquesas to the Cooks were indicated. He followed this by predicting the *Endeavour*'s arrival at Rurutu after the ship left the Society Islands. This navigational skill helped Cook understand the Polynesian diaspora.

Tupaia's other great benefit to Cook occurred in New Zealand where he was able to understand the Māori and so could translate and mediate between the two sides. It has been suggested that Tupaia was perceived by the Māori as the leader of the *Endeavour* as he was the person with whom they had most contact. The Māori attempted unsuccessfully to snatch Taiato at the southern end of Hawke's Bay causing Cook to call the headland Cape Kidnappers.

Tupaia was less successful in Australia where he was unable to understand the people and could not serve as a translator. Both Tupaia and Taiato died of dysentery soon after reaching Batavia, Taiato on 17 December and Tupaia, stricken with grief, on 20 December 1770. In recent years it has been shown that paintings previously attributed to the unknown 'Artist of the Chief Mourner' were done by Tupaia.

SEE ALSO: First voyage, Raiatea, Tahitians

Tutaha (also known as Tootahah and Hercules) (?–1773)

When Cook anchored at Matavai Bay on 13 April 1769, he met Tutaha (Tootahah), the chief of the district. Tutaha had been one of the principal agents in the fall of Purea and Amo in December 1768. His base was Paea on the island's west coast but when Cook arrived he had extended control to include the north-west, including Matavai Bay so it was under Tutaha's protection that Cook set up his tents on Point Venus.

Tutaha was the second son of an older Tutaha and Tera'iatua, a woman of chiefly rank in the district of Atehuru. Banks called him Hercules because of his stature. Cook misunderstood Tutaha's status and believed him to be chief of the whole island in 1769. Tutaha was a chief but was acting as regent for Tu (Otoo), the son of Amo's brother Teu (Happai). Tu had been designated a future chief.

Tutaha's ambitions led him to attack Vehiatua, the chief of Tahiti Iti. In naval and land battles in March 1773, his forces were comprehensively beaten and Tutaha was killed.

SEE ALSO: Tahitians

U / V

Unalaska and the Aleutian Islands

Unalaska Island (53° 40' N, 166° 40' W) is one of the Aleutian Chain, which stretches south-west from the Alaskan Peninsula. The Aleutian Islands separate the Bering Sea, to the north, from the Pacific Ocean. They extend in an arc for 1118 miles (1800km) to Attu Island. The islands were inhabited by Aleut people, a branch of the Eskimo-Aleut group. The name Aleut itself is not of Aleut origin. It was introduced by Russian explorers and fur traders who conquered the Aleutian Islands. The people's name for themselves is Unangan. From 1758, Russian fur hunters led by Glotov spent three years trading on Umnak and Unalaska. After an initial attempt to defeat the Russian intruders, the Aleut were forced to hunt fur seal and sea otter. Then in 1772 a permanent Russian settlement was established at Unalaska by Solov'ev.

Cook approached the Aleutians in June 1778. He was looking for the Northwest Passage but the landmass of Alaska had forced him south. He had then followed the coast of the Alaskan Peninsula in poor, foggy conditions. The British had met local people, Aleuts, who had approached them in kayaks and passed on notes written in Russian near the Sanek Islands. Fog had slowed their progress but on the 21st a volcano, Shishaldin, on Unimak Island, the first island in the Aleutians was seen. Cook steered south of Unimak and the Krenitzin Islands and was lucky to anchor off Sedanka Island having narrowly avoided large rocks in thick fog. Cook sailed north through Unalga Pass before taking shelter in Samgoonoodha Harbour (English Bay) on Unalaska Island. More Aleuts, with whom they traded, visited the ships before Cook sailed north out into the Bering Sea on 2 July 1778.

After spending three months unsuccessfully searching for the Northwest Passage, Cook arrived back at Unalaska on 2 October. They entered Unalaska Bay on the north coast where the Russians had a post at Dutch Harbour/Unalaska but Cook left straight away without attempting contact. He moved back to Samgoonoodha at the eastern end of the island. Work began refitting both ships. Notes in Russian were received and on the 8th Cook sent John Ledyard to Unalaska to make enquiries. Ledyard returned with three Russians with whom communication was possible although difficult. Another Russian, the Factor, Gerassim Gregoriev Ismailov, came with charts from which Cook made copies, especially of the Aleutian Islands. Cook pointed out the errors in Muller's and Stählin's maps that he had been using. Ismailov gave Cook letters of introduction to the Governor of Kamchatka while Cook wrote a letter to the Admiralty, which he asked Ismailov to forward across Russia (it reached London!).

Canoes of Oonalashka. Kayaks are shown from the south coast of Alaska. Engraved by W Angus after Webber. (Cook & King (Atlas) pl 50)

SEE ALSO: Alaska, Russians, Third voyage

United Kingdom

In the United Kingdom, Cook is primarily associated with Cleveland in the north-east of England, where he spent his early life, and with London, where he was based during his adult years. However, there are other places in the UK that can claim some connection with Cook.

An inspection of the crew list in Appendix III shows that Cook's voyages drew upon men from throughout the British Isles (as well as Europe and America). Given that the muster rolls often only gave the last residence of the men, which was often Deptford or other places along the River Thames and not necessarily their home town, we do not know the whole range of places involved. Nor did the voyages just use men from ports and coastal towns as many inland towns were represented. Cemeteries in many places carry tombstones with inscriptions proudly stating that the man buried there sailed with Cook. A typical example is that of Joseph Poole, a marine on the *Discovery* on the third voyage, who is buried in St John's Church, Staplegrove in Somerset. His inscription states 'Sacred to the memory of Joseph Poole, who after sailing round the globe with Captn Cooke departed this life Octr 3rd 1791'.

Cook himself had few direct links to other places but some are connected with his family and close friends. Cook spent time in the naval ports of Plymouth (especially) and Portsmouth and also made one journey to Edinburgh in 1757. Both Joseph Banks (at Revesby in Lincolnshire) and the Earl of Sandwich (at Hinchingbrook near Huntingdon) possessed country houses. Cook definitely visited Hinchingbrook but it is uncertain whether he ever visited Revesby.

Cook's youngest child, Hugh, attended Christ's College, Cambridge but died from fever in December 1793, aged 17. He was buried in St Andrew the Great Church in Cambridge. A few months later, Hugh's brother, James, died in strange circumstances in Poole Harbour near the Isle of Wight. He was aged 31 and also buried in Cambridge. When Elizabeth Cook died in 1835, she was buried with her two sons. Cambridge possesses one of the major collections of artefacts brought to Britain by Cook's voyages in the Museum of Archaeology and Anthropology. Oxford has a similar collection in the Pitt Rivers Museum.

Other repositories outside London include the Hunterian Museum in Glasgow with its collection of artefacts and the Hydrographic Office in Taunton with many original charts. Cook's friend, Hugh Palliser, retired to Chalfont St Giles, west of London, where he built a monument to Cook in the grounds of his house, The Vache. Further north, Stowe School has a monument in its grounds.

Vancouver, George (1757–1798)

George Vancouver sailed on the second voyage on the *Resolution* as an AB. He drew some charts but only two survive. He then sailed on the third voyage aboard the *Discovery* as a midshipman. He again drew charts but only one survives. After the third voyage, he was made a lieutenant in December 1780 and posted to HMS *Martin*, a 14-gun sloop. The *Martin* patrolled in the North Sea and English Channel before sailing to the West Indies in early 1782. Vancouver transferred to HMS *Fame*, a Third Rate of 74 guns, as fourth lieutenant. *Fame* returned to Plymouth in 1783 and Vancouver went on half pay. In November 1784, he was posted to HMS *Europa*, a Fourth Rate of 50 guns, in which he returned to Jamaica. He made second lieutenant in 1787 and first lieutenant in 1788. The *Europa* and Vancouver returned to Britain in 1789.

An expedition to the North Pacific had been mooted and, in December 1789, Vancouver was appointed first lieutenant. However, the expedition was postponed and Vancouver went to HMS *Courageux*, a Third Rate of 74 guns, in the English Channel. In late 1790, the Pacific expedition was resurrected but with different objectives and Vancouver was appointed its commander in December 1790.

From 1791 until 1795, Vancouver led the expedition, which charted most of the north-western American coast from California to Alaska. The voyage was undertaken by HMS *Discovery* (not the same ship as Cook's) and HMS *Chatham*. The achievements of the voyage rank with those of Cook, Vancouver's mentor. He was made a captain in 1794. He was a sick man when he returned to Britain and spent the next few years writing up the official account of the voyage. He died before its completion and publication.

He was born in King's Lynn on 22 June 1757 and died in Petersham, south-west London on 12 May 1798. Vancouver left a will (FRC 11/1312). He was buried in St Peter's Church, Petersham. Various geographical features are named for him including Vancouver Island, the city in British Columbia, Canada and mountains in New Zealand and on the Canada-Alaska border.

SEE ALSO: Pacific exploration after Cook, Third voyage

Vanuatu (New Hebrides)

Vanuatu (17° S, 168° E) is a group of 83 islands in the south-west Pacific, north-east of New Caledonia and north-west of Fiji. The islands occupy 5000 square miles (13,000 sq km) and form a Y-shaped archipelago, stretching 528 miles (850km) from north to south. They are inhabited by the Ni-Vanuatu people, Melanesians, who arrived from the northwest by canoes about 3500 years ago. The country became independent in 1980 and the name Vanuatu, meaning land eternal, replaced the earlier name, New Hebrides, bestowed by James Cook.

Quiros, the Spanish explorer, visited these islands in 1606 and called them Tierra Austrialia del Espiritu Santo. Unfortunately, he did not fix their location exactly so future explorers were not sure which islands he had seen. Bougainville visited the northern islands in 1768 and named them the Grandes Cyclades. Then in 1774, James Cook, who had sailed west from Tonga, reached the island of Maewo on 16 July. Over the next six weeks Cook sailed through the island chain, surveying as he went and producing a marvellous chart. He rounded Maewo and headed southwest for the island of Malekula where he found an inlet and anchored the *Resolution* on the 22nd. Cook went ashore only to find that the people were Melanesian not Polynesian so communication was extremely difficult. Cook thought it wise to leave. They sailed from the inlet, Port Sandwich, and turned south.

They passed to the east of Efate and worked their way to Erromango. Cook came to a large bay and anchored in Polenia Bay on 4 August. He attempted to land but his reception was cool if courteous. As he was invited to step ashore Cook became suspicious and gave orders to return to the ship. A fight broke out and marines fired their muskets, killing four locals. Cook issued instructions to leave.

Cook sailed on to the next island, Tanna, where he anchored the *Resolution* in an inlet, Port Resolution, near the south-eastern corner of the island. They were met by a large crowd of local people but the reception was lukewarm and, although the ship stayed for two weeks, relations remained distant. The crew was able to fish and get fresh water, wood and some supplies but Cook always set a guard of marines when anyone went ashore. One Tanna man, Paowang, did become friendly and he was entertained on the ship.

Cook now felt he had reached the end of the island chain and returned north to be off Malekula by 23 August. Cook passed east through the Bougainville Strait between Malekula and Malo and changed course north along the coast of a larger island. Cook correctly identified this island with Quiros' Tierra Australis del Espiritu Santo and honoured the Spanish explorer by naming a headland Cape Quiros. The *Resolution* rounded the island before leaving the islands on 1 September.

Man of the Island of Tanna, Vanuatu (New Hebrides). Engraved by J Basire after Hodges. (Cook II fp 78)

There had only been minimal contact with local people. The Melanesian languages and customs were different from the Polynesian to which Cook and his crew had become accustomed. Cook called the islands the New Hebrides.

SEE ALSO: Melanesia, Second voyage

Wales, William (1735–1798)

William Wales sailed on the second voyage on board the *Resolution* as astronomer. He also made surveys and drew charts. Wales was baptised in Warmfield, outside Wakefield in Yorkshire on 1 March 1735. William was the eldest of three children. Little is known of his early life and he appeared in London in the 1750s writing articles and contributing mathematical problems to the magazine, *Ladies Diary*.

Wales married Mary Green, the sister of astronomer Charles Green, in 1765. They had six children. Wales began working with the Astronomer Royal, Nevil Maskelyne, on the first edition of the *Nautical Almanac*, published in 1767. Wales' brother John was also employed and remained with the *Almanac* until 1796. The Royal Society chose Wales to be one of its observers of the 1769 Transit of Venus, sending him to Prince of Wales Fort (now Churchill) on Hudson Bay in Canada. He was then chosen for Cook's second voyage. During the voyage, Wales formed an acrimonious relationship with the Forsters, which continued after the voyage.

After the voyage, Wales wrote an account of his observations for the Board of Longitude and helped John Douglas to write the official account of the second voyage. He secured a position in 1775 at Christ's Hospital School in London, teaching mathematics. Samuel Taylor Coleridge, the poet, was a pupil at Christ's Hospital when Wales was teaching there and it is believed Wales' tales of Cook's voyage was one stimulus for Coleridge's famous poem, *The Rime of the Ancient Mariner*. Many passages in the poem bear a striking resemblance to the descriptions in Cook's journals. In November 1776, Wales was elected as a Fellow of the Royal Society.

Wales died on 29 December 1798 and was buried in the grounds of Christ's Hospital. He left a will (FRC 11/1318). There is a short biography in the *DNB*, v20, pp490–1. Various geographical features were named after Wales. Vancouver named Wales Point and Wales Island at the entrance to Portland Canal after his friend; Mount Wales on Resolution Island, north of Dusky Sound in New Zealand; and Wales Peak on the border between Alberta and British Columbia in Canada.

SEE ALSO: Astronomical results of Cook's voyages, Coleridge (Samuel Taylor), Second voyage

Walker, John (1706–1785)

John Walker, to whom James Cook was apprenticed in 1746, lived in Grape Lane in Whitby, in the house which is now the Captain Cook Memorial Museum. It is a substantial town house, backing on to the upper harbour, and had its own slipway, and gave John Walker a wide view of the often crowded upper harbour, and Whitby's busy boat- and ship-yards. It was exactly the house which a man deeply involved with the shipping industry in Whitby would have chosen. John Walker was a substantial investor in shipping, though he still described as a master and mariner. He would not have described himself as a ship-owner. There were still multiple shareholders in shipping, before marine insurance became routine, so he would have been described as 'ship's husband', or managing owner, of those vessels known to be 'John Walker's ships'. He probably held more shares in these vessels than did anyone else.

William Sanderson, for whom Cook worked as a grocer's assistant in Staithes, chose Walker with care. Walker was a Quaker, one of the strong and influential members of the Society of Friends who formed the Whitby Monthly Meeting, established by George Fox himself around 1654. It was the integrity and plain-dealing of the Quaker participants in Whitby's important merchant fleet which gave it such a high reputation, to which non-Quakers also had to aspire. The Society of Friends also informed the daily life of the Walker household, in which Cook and the other servants who lived there outside the sailing season would benefit from the example of steadiness, sobriety and humanity which prevailed.

The young James Cook would be placed in whichever of John's ships was most suitable. At 17 years old, James would have been more use, even at the outset, than the child of anything from 10 to 13 who was a normal new 'servant'. John Walker's shipping was engaged chiefly in the coal and Baltic trades, so that the destination of most of his cargoes was London. There his agent was probably James Sheppard of Wapping, a fellow Quaker, who also owned shares in several of Walker's ships. This was a common practice in Whitby's merchant fleet, since it gave the agent a vested interest in providing labour for unloading cargo, and loading ballast, in the congested Port of London, and thereby ensured a swift turn-around for the vessel.

Walker was related by blood or by marriage to most of the other wealthy Quaker shipping families of his day, such as the Chapmans, Linskills, Yeomans and Simpsons, so that he was part of a considerable controlling nexus in the town. As Quakers they were conscientious about their civic duty, although there were often clashes which they were quite ingenious at resolving. Whitby was administered by the Select Vestry of the parish church, using the income from *church* rates, which the Quakers refused in conscience to pay. However, civic and harbour improvements were dealt with by private Acts of Parliament, which inevitably required their own taxes, and a Board of the Trustees to take charge of these, and the Quakers provided the bulk of these public servants, and paid their *state*-imposed taxation without a murmur.

The same pragmatic approach was used in dealing with the pressure to arm shipping in time of war. Whenever a war began, the London Yearly Meeting sent strictures against arming vessels, and against taking out Letters of Marque, to the meetings at all ports. The Whitby Monthly Meeting distributed their copies of these documents to those Friends involved with shipping, and enquired no further. The Monthly Meeting was supposed to 'deny', or expel, such Friends as disobeyed, but it was not until the American War of Independence that such a drastic step was taken, and then only because there might be Quakers among the crews of American vessels. But by then John Walker was in his seventies, and as far as is known, was never denied, despite the dilemmas he must have faced during the War of the Austrian Succession and the Seven Years War. As an owner of shipping he was bound, by the Law of the Sea, to protect the cargo, and the vessel and crew, from violence, yet he was not allowed, by his religious laws, to defend them.

After James Cook left Walker's employment to join the Navy, he corresponded with his old master, and came back to Whitby to visit him, and other northern friends, between the first and second voyages.

John Walker married twice, and had eight children, two daughters from his first marriage, and three sons and three daughters from his second. Both of his wives died young, so that John was twice left to care for very young children. It must have been a very bustling household, with eight children and a number of apprentices during the winter months. All three sons followed their father to sea, as he had followed his father before him. He died in 1785, aged 79, after a widowhood of 33 years.

By Rosalin Barker

See Also: North Sea and the coal trade, Quakers, Whitby

Wallis, Samuel (1728–1795)

Samuel Wallis was born in April 1728 at Fentonwoon in Cornwall. He joined the Navy and had made lieutenant by 1748. In 1755, he was aboard HMS *Torbay*, the flagship of Vice-Admiral Boscawen. He was given command of HMS *Swan* in 1756 and spent most of the Seven Years War in North American waters.

John Byron, who had taken HMS *Dolphin*, a Sixth Rate of 508 tons, to the Pacific in 1764, returned to the Downs in May 1766. The *Dolphin* was still in excellent condition due mostly to the fact that before her sailing, her hull was sheathed in copper against teredo worms. Almost immediately, *Dolphin* was fitted out for a second voyage, under Samuel Wallis. The companion vessels were HMS *Swallow*, under Lieutenant Samuel Carteret, and the storeship *Prince Frederick*. The Admiralty was keen to explore the South Pacific, and when the two ships sailed on 22 August 1766, it was to find 'Land or Islands of Great extent ... in the Southern Hemisphere between Cape Horn and New Zeeland ... in Climates adapted to the produce of Commodities useful in Commerce'. Several men, who would later sail with Cook were on board the *Dolphin*, including Clerke, Furneaux, Gore, Wilkinson and Molyneux.

The ships arrived at the Strait of Magellan on 17 December but took four months to negotiate the strait. The *Prince Frederick* sailed instead for the Falkland Islands. The other ships entered the Pacific on 11 April 1767, but immediately were separated. The *Swallow* would have a very long journey back to Britain, finally reaching Spithead in May 1769.

The *Dolphin* reached the Tuamotus, and, on 18 June, arrived at Tahiti, the first European vessel to do so. After skirmishes on arrival, Wallis established excellent relations with Purea, a Tahitian leader, and the crews spent six weeks on the island. They sailed on 26 July having made one of the most important discoveries by Europeans in the Pacific. Tahiti would play a significant role in future events, providing a base for Cook and firing the concept of the 'Noble Savage'.

From Tahiti, Wallis sailed west, landing on Niuatoputapu and Tafahi, the northernmost Tongan islands, and on Wallis Island, in Wallis and Futuna, in August. He reached Batavia, then sailed on to the Cape and finally to the Downs where he arrived on 20 May 1768. The Admiralty was preparing for the *Endeavour* voyage to observe the Transit of Venus and Wallis' report about Tahiti offered the best location for this to take place.

Wallis was given a gratuity and two years' leave. On resuming his career he served on the *Torbay* (again) and the *Queen*. His active service finished in the early 1780s and he died in London in 1795.

SEE ALSO: Pacific exploration before Cook, Tahiti

Stained glass window in Sydney Town Hall. Designed by Lucien Henry, the window showing Cook was manufactured by Goodlet and Smith in 1889. (Sydney Town Hall)

Wallpaper and stained glass, Cook in

Two of the more esoteric art forms in which James Cook has been celebrated are wallpaper and stained glass. One of the most remarkable pieces is the panoramic wallpaper *Les Sauvages de la Mer Pacifique.* Designed by Jean-Gabriel Charvet, the wallpaper was created in 1805 in Mâcon, France by Joseph Dufour et Cie using woodblocks, stencils and handpainting. The design was divided into 20 separate strips that could be assembled as one long panorama or in smaller groupings depending on the size of the room where they were hung. Each strip is 8ft 2in (250cm) long and 1ft 9in (54cm) wide.

The design, being French, derives from the images reproduced in the published narratives of Lapérouse and Bougainville as well as Cook. It shows people from most islands in the Pacific but with a strong classical influence. It also shows the influence of the *Tableau des découvertes du Capitaine Cook, et de la Pérouse,* engraved by Antoine Phelippeaux and published by Jacques Grasset de Saint-Sauveur in Paris in 1797. The design had an educational purpose as well as a decorative one.

Cook is also remembered by some beautiful stained glass. Sydney Town Hall has a beautiful stained-glass window by its northern staircase. It was designed by Lucien Henry and manufactured by Goodlet and Smith in 1889 to mark the centenary of the founding of the state of New South Wales in 1788. Cook stands on the deck of one of his ships, telescope in hand, in the central panel. St Cuthbert's Church in Marton, the site of Cook's baptism, has a more simple stained-glass window.

Wapping

James Cook is most closely connected with the area of London north of the River Thames and east of London Bridge known as Wapping and Shadwell. He also became closely involved with the Quakers of the area. At the close of the seventeenth century, the Quakers in East London, the Ratcliff Friends, found their meeting house overcrowded. They resolved to erect a new one in Wapping for the use of Friends residing in the city-ward of their district. Accordingly, a piece of ground was leased for £6 a year. It was situated behind a house with a court, about 96ft (29.2m) in length leading to it from the north side of Wapping High Street and south of a Rope Walk belonging to one Marmaduke Bushel.

The Wapping Friends, largely tinctured with a nautical element, worked as mariners, shipwrights, riggers, sailmakers, sea biscuit bakers, coopers, carpenters, clockmakers, cheesemongers, and nautical instrumental makers, etc. They participated in the thriving commercial activity that depended on the demands of the river traffic, especially the servicing of the north-east coastal colliers. The Friends' foothold in local communities was widespread as their network was structured around their travels back and forth from local meetings around the country. While on these excursions, they combined their religious lives with their trade and business. They wrote to each other, exchanged and discussed publications, and used each other's houses as forums for considering mutual commercial interests, where business advice was proffered and accepted, deals were struck and opportunities pursued. To secure their personal and business interests, they carefully arranged marriages of their sons and daughters into other appropriate families. In 1738, Zachariah Cockfield removed from Whitby to Wapping for the purpose of marrying Sarah Sheppard, the daughter of Joseph Sheppard, a timber merchant and ships' chandler. Such marriages themselves did not guarantee success, but their well-being was invariably cemented by access to family networks.

The servicing of Whitby coastal colliers had been organised by Friends for some years, and it proved a profitable arrangement for both parties. The Sheppard family especially benefited from these alliances and clinched business deals with the Whitby ship owners. James Sheppard, the son of Joseph, subsequently invested in part ownership of Captain John Walker's ships, Walker being one of the Whitby Quakers. James Sheppard was aware that the rapidly-expanding shipbuilding industry required a steady flow of top-quality wood from Norway. He foresaw a profitable business opportunity and, through his mother's (Ann Sheppard, née Harle) family connections in the Norwegian timber trade, he was quick to capitalise commercially on the price of Norwegian timber, which was rising steeply. Sheppard needed to arrange transportation for the timber with fellow Quakers to bring it from Norway to his timber yards and wharves in Wapping.

In 1748, John Walker sailed to Wapping in the *Three Brothers,* John Jefferson being mate and James Cook listed as servant. When Walker discharged himself, Jefferson thereafter took command. On this visit, Walker would have discussed with Friends the pending war with France and the pressing need to transport quality timber from Norway for rebuilding and fitting out ships. These timbers were crucial not only to stock up the market for the shipbuilding industry but also to rebuild the dilapidated Wapping meeting house, as recorded in their minutes. Walker would have also discussed the arrangements for necessary repairs to his ships and, of course, it was in their interest, being co-owners, to fulfil this agreement. Thus Friends would replace damaged sails, supply fresh victuals and find lodgings for the young apprentices, including James Cook.

The *Three Brothers*, under the command of Jefferson, was fitted out in Deptford with stalls for horses and was engaged for about a year in evacuating British troops from Middleburg in the Netherlands, just as the war between Britain and France was coming to an end. Some of the soldiers and horses were taken to Dublin and others to Liverpool. By April 1749, the *Three Brothers* was back in London and immediately set sail to start trading with Norway. The *Three Brothers* undertaking appeared to have been successful, as court records for the year 1750 show Zachariah Cockfield and Joseph Sheppard being accused by Charles Hiller of stacking so much timber against his chimneys that they collapsed. Consequently, Cockfield and Sheppard were sentenced to Marshalsea prison. The news of this unfortunate affair reached the Friends network and they were subsequently released for the sum of £600. Joseph Sheppard only survived for a few months after his terrible ordeal in prison. His son James and his son-in-law Zachariah Cockfield subsequently carried on his ministerial duties within the Friends community, as well as taking care of his combined interests in the coastal trade, and the refitting, rigging and overhauling of the colliers.

James Cook would have been familiar with the coastal trade routes while employed as servant on John Walker's ships. He would have engaged himself amongst the men listening to their traditional abuse and chaff. He was no different to any red-blooded male who desired a seafaring life. His rank onboard ship would have been one of an 'underdog', to use a modern expression. However, his natural ability and keenness proved him to be a worthy seaman. Each year, during the spring and summer months, the colliers sailed from the Tyne. There was a race as they sailed through the narrow channels of Yarmouth roads and as many as 300 colliers, heavily laden with coal, could be bunched together near the mouth of the Thames, waiting for the tide to turn. Cook's spirit of adventure opened his mind, taking in what he had heard and seen on board. He was part of those huge coal fleets that sailed up the Thames, their forests of blackened masts dominating the skyline.

From Gravesend to the Pool of London, the Thames twisted and turned between mudflats, with the navigable channel offering a depth of less than 12ft (3.6m) at low tide. Scores of small ships could be left high and dry on these mud banks waiting for the tide to float them off. At these times, there were many opportunities for every kind of wrongdoing involving the spiriting away of cargo, smuggling, and even piracy. The river was a vast floating warehouse containing everything that Londoners needed: food, clothes, hides, coal, timber, liquor and tobacco. Luxury items such as silk, china, and spices could find a market among the newly rich living in other parts of London. The vessels, which were able to navigate through the Thames avoiding the menace of the unseen mudflats, moored up in the centre of the river at Wapping or Shadwell.

Friends in Wapping knew the dangers posed by the unseen obstacles under the Thames, as well as the nefarious activities carried out by the various miscreants that used the Thames to finance their criminal activities. However, they still found the river was the safest way for them to begin their travels around the country to attend their various Meeting Houses. There was a ready market in Wapping for items plundered from ships but Friends were more concerned employing their own craftsmen and looking after the poor. Despite the image of the Friends to the outside world being one of sober, sedate, thoughtful, diligent and honest people, many of the poor Friends in Wapping followed pleasure, drunkenness and gaming. In the Wapping Minutes, Zachariah Cockfield is mentioned as visiting these unruly Friends and bringing them to heel.

Quakers dominated businesses around Execution Dock in Wapping. From the Land Tax Records, their Meeting House was in a narrow alley called Blackmore Alley. In Old Gravel Lane, there was a sea biscuit baker named Joseph Curtis and next door to him was Daniel and Lewis Weston, coopers. Next door to them was Daniel Day, block and tackle maker. Across the road, down Brewhouse Lane, was Jonathan Eade who was a nautical instrument maker. In Cinnamon Street was the business of James Sheppard and Zachariah Cockfield, timber merchants, sailmakers and master mariners. The closest alehouse, near Execution Dock Stairs, was The Bell, owned by Samuel Batts. In their wills, which can be found at the Public Records Office, it can be seen that they left legacies of substantial amounts of money, property and investments in Britain and North America. They were all co-owners of merchant ships and also shared in the ownership of John Walker's ships and colliers.

The Friends serviced all the colliers that Cook sailed on when he was an apprentice for John Walker. Consequently Cook's master, John Jefferson, would have introduced him to the Friends when he first sailed to Wapping. (There is no firm date when Cook first sailed to Wapping as the muster roll for the *Freelove* in 1747 shows that he had sailed previously.) They would have found lodgings for him at the local alehouse, namely The Bell. Victuallers' Records and Land Tax Records show that Samuel Batts was the landlord of The Bell Alehouse from 1722. This was an unusual achievement as, from Victuallers' Records, alehouses in Wapping were lucky to survive a year or more before changing hands. The Bell must have been a very well-run establishment and the Friends recognised it as a secure place to do business. Samuel Batts established good relations with visiting sea captains. The *Daily Post* for the 22 September 1735 carried an article as follows: 'Yesterday morning a sailor, formerly a master of a collier, who with two others of the same fraternity lodged at the Bell ale house the corner of Execution Dock, got privately out of bed and hanged himself at the catch of the door. At dawn of day his chums waked and missed him, but discovering him on his knees they imagined he was at his devotion, and therefore would not disturb him. In this posture he remained so long without motion, that they concluded he was fallen asleep, and therefore resolved to wake him, but upon examination he was found dead and cold'.

The Bell was probably used as a 'house of call', which was a sort of employment exchange. Different trades went to certain inns to find work and be paid. Lumpers and coal heavers would have attended The Bell alehouse at which there was a pay table set up on Saturday evenings. Therefore, Samuel Batts would have been known as an undertaker or a labour agent. Samuel Batts and his wife, formerly Mary Smith, had a daughter Elizabeth baptised in 1741 at St John's, Wapping. Unhappily however, Samuel Batts died suddenly in the year 1741. In his will he mentions another daughter, Sarah, who was married to Peter Ford. He left his wife Mary in a good financial position with her now the leaseholder and freeholder of properties in and around London. At this time, there is evidence to suggest that young Elizabeth was sent to be looked after by the Sheppard family who owned property in Barking, leaving Mary free to continue running Samuel's businesses and The Bell.

There is a story that Captain Cook stood sponsor for

a little girl at her baptism in Barking Church. He is supposed to have said that if the infant lived he would marry her. This story came about from a letter written by the artist, John Constable, to his friend C R Leslie in 1833. It seems that Constable was wrong to suppose that it was Elizabeth Batts that Cook stood sponsor for as research has shown that she was in fact baptised in St Johns, Wapping in 1741 when Cook was still a young lad in Great Ayton. The fact remains that Cook was certainly in Wapping while Elizabeth Batts was growing up. Constable may have heard the story about Cook's wife from his uncle John Watts, who entered the Royal Navy at the age of 13 and served as a midshipman on Cook's third voyage in HMS *Resolution,* together with William Bligh of the *Bounty* fame. Watts's career did not end with Cook's death as he sailed to Australia, as part of the First Fleet on the *Lady Penrhyn* convict ship, which was part-owned by William Curtis, the son of Joseph Curtis the sea biscuit baker in Wapping.

Mary Batts remarried in 1745. Her new husband was John Blackburn, a 40-year-old mariner who had lodged at The Bell and he subsequently became landlord of the alehouse until 1750, when the family moved to Upper Shadwell. In the early 1750s, Cook was on the coal ships and, during his visits to London, because he knew John Blackburn well, he probably stayed at the Ship and Crown, the alehouse next door to the Blackburn family's house in Shadwell. By this time, Elizabeth had moved back to stay with her family, which gave Cook and Elizabeth ample time to become acquainted. In 1755, Cook joined the Royal Navy at Wapping. Seven years later he married Elizabeth at St Margaret's Church, Barking. On the Vicar General's Licence, Elizabeth was listed as being resident for four weeks at Barking, probably staying with the Sheppard family. However, as soon as they were married the couple moved to 126 Upper Shadwell into John Blackburn's house. From the Land Taxes, James Cook was resident in Shadwell from the year 1763 to 1765. In this time, his first child, James, was born and baptised in St Paul's, Shadwell. In 1765, Cook appears at Mile End Old Town in a recently built house at 7 Assembly Row.

In conclusion, James Cook's early life revolved around his apprenticeship to John Walker and the people he met in East London. The connections he made at this time stayed with him to the end of his life. He was still writing to the Friends he had met in Wapping on the return from his first voyage of discovery onboard the *Endeavour*. One letter survives, dated 10 December 1771, in which he wrote to Joseph Cockfield, the son of Zachariah, at Upton, informing Joseph to come and look at the rare plants that he had brought back with him and that he would meet Mr Banks and Doctor Solander. The Quakers and East London had a profound effect on James Cook.

SEE ALSO: Cook (Elizabeth), North Sea and the coal trade, Quakers

BY JULIA RAE

Ward, James (1758–1801 or 1806)

James Ward sailed on the third voyage on the *Resolution* as an AB until 1 November 1777. He then became a midshipman until 2 November 1779 when he reverted to being an AB. He was the first aboard to sight the Hawaiian Islands in January 1778.

Ward attended the Naval Academy at Portsmouth from 1772 until 1775 where he became a close friend of Trevenen. After the voyage, he became a lieutenant in August 1782 and saw service in the East Indies under James Burney. He was born in 1758 and died on 29 August 1801 (there is a will for a James Ward of Sevenoaks in Kent (FRC 11/1375)) or 28 September 1806. There is a portrait of Ward at the National Maritime Museum.

SEE ALSO: Third voyage

Watts, John (?–1801)

John Watts sailed on the third voyage on the *Resolution* as a midshipman until 1 November 1777. He was then made an AB until 2 November 1779 when he became a midshipman again. He wrote a proceedings. Watts joined the voyage from HMS *Barfleur*. He was promoted to lieutenant in December 1781 and commander in December 1796.

John Watts was born in London, the son of William Watts, a cooper. His sister, Ann, was the mother of the artist, John Constable. Lieutenant Watts sailed to Australia on the *Lady Penrhyn,* in 1787, as part of the First Fleet, carrying 100 female convicts. He is listed as a passenger on the voyage. The *Lady Penrhyn* left Sydney in early 1788 and sailed to Tahiti, where it was the first European ship to visit since Cook in 1778. Watts has provided a short description of life on the island, including various people such as Tu, remembered from Cook's time. From Tahiti, the *Lady Penrhyn* sailed to Macao, passing on the way an island that was named Penrhyn Island after the ship. The island is now one of the Cook Islands.

Watts took command of the *Osprey*, 18 guns, in 1799 and patrolled in the North Sea but died on 4 March 1801 while in command. He left a widow, Mary, and a will (FRC 11/1361). They are recorded as living in Deal, Kent. Watts described a species of shark at Sydney, which was named Watts' shark but is now known as the Wobbegong shark.
SEE ALSO: Third voyage

Webber, John (1751–1793)

John Webber was the official artist on Cook's third and last voyage aboard the *Resolution* and it is for his connection with Cook that he is known, especially his images of early Alaska, British Columbia and Hawai'i. During the voyage, he painted landscapes, portraits, and coastal views.

Webber was born in London on 6 October 1751, the son of an immigrant Swiss sculptor, Abraham Wäber, who had moved to London and, in 1744, married Mary Quant. Together they had six children. John (or Johann) was the second child and he was sent to Switzerland to be raised by an aunt when he was six. Webber was apprenticed from 1767 to 1770 to one of the foremost Swiss landscape artists, Johann Aberli, in Bern. After three years' training with Aberli, he continued his studies at the Académie Royale in Paris, making many sketches of rural landscapes and learning to paint in oils. From Paris, he returned to London, aged 24, and was admitted to study at the Royal Academy, where he first exhibited in 1776.

Daniel Solander, the Swedish naturalist who had sailed on Cook's first voyage, saw and admired Webber's works at this exhibition. Solander was aware that no artist had been appointed for Cook's forthcoming third voyage and he recommended Webber. The young man was appointed by the Admiralty on 24 June and joined the *Resolution* at Plymouth on 5 July just before the expedition sailed. The choice was a good one, as Webber produced an astounding number of high quality images. It was Webber's job to make drawings and paintings of people and objects encountered on the journey, and to 'observe the genius, temper, disposition and number of the natives . . . shewing them every kind of civility and regard'. He painted Cook's portrait during the voyage.

After the voyage, he was retained to supervise the production of the engravings that were to illustrate the published journal of the voyage. He also exhibited paintings and drawings relating to the *Resolution* expedition at the Royal Academy, and over the ensuing years he made a modest income from reworking drawings for sale on commission. Webber was elected a member of the Royal Academy in 1791. Apart from the Cook-related material, Webber was best known for landscapes but he continued to produce portraits until the time of his death. A self-portrait hangs in Bern. He died in London of kidney disease on 29 April 1793, leaving a will (FRC 11/1233), which William Hodges witnessed. Webber was unmarried. There is a short biography in the *DNB*, v20, pp1023–4.
SEE ALSO: Art of Cook's voyages, Artists on Cook's voyages, Portraits of Cook, Third voyage

Weather

For eighteenth-century sailors, the weather was a fundamental and constant matter of concern. Too little wind and a ship became becalmed while too much in the form of a gale could damage or even sink a ship. Fog and ice offered different perils while heavy rain made the ship wet and unhealthy. Too much sun affected the supplies of fresh water but too much cloud cover restricted the ability to take navigational observations to determine the ship's position.

We have a very good idea of the weather experienced by Cook as it was a requirement to record the weather in the ship's log. The direction of the wind and a description of its strength would be noted at least every four hours and more often if there were appreciable shifts. No scale of wind speed had been developed but terms such as airs, squalls, breezes and gales would be used with modifiers like light, fresh and strong. In his Newfoundland logs, Cook often had to put 'foggy' or 'hazy' to describe visibility. The table opposite is part of the *Grenville* log for September 1765 showing the weather records (the schooner was anchored in Hermitage Bay while Cook was surveying so the record is abbreviated).

Cook was able to use the features of the weather to assist his navigation. By observing indicators such as cloud formations, offshore breezes and currents, he received clues to the presence of land nearby.

When Cook experienced lack of wind, it left him at the mercy of tides as happened when he left Queen Charlotte Sound in New Zealand in February 1770. He rounded Cape Koamaru and as he approached two rocks, The Brothers, the tide took hold. Cook wrote 'At this time we had it nearly calm and the tide of Ebb makeing out we were carried by the rapiditty of the

Monday	16th	W	Almost calm and fair these twenty four hours.
Tuesday	17th	W then calm	Light breezes and fair weather the first and later parts. The middle thick fog.
Wednesday	18th	W	The major part fresh breezes and fair weather.
Thursday	19th	W	The first and later parts fresh gales. The middle strong gales and rain.

stream in a very short time close upon one of the Islands where we narrowly escaped being dashed against the rocks'. Danger did not always result. Sometimes it was only inconvenient and the crew went out in small boats to tow the ships. As Cook approached Nootka Sound on the third voyage where 'at 5 o'clock we reached the west point where we were becalmed for some time, during which hoisted out all the boats to tow the Ship in'.

Cook experienced gales often. Perhaps the most crucial took place off Hawai'i in February 1779. On the 8th, Cook was forced to return to Kealakekua Bay to repair the *Resolution* after 'at 6 AM the same [fresh gales], found the head of the Foremast badly sprung...so very defective as to make it Absolutely necessary to replace them with others'. A contrary wind or the conditions on a lee shore, such as Cook encountered on the *Endeavour* voyage off Dusky Sound, were equally dangerous. Cook was under pressure from Banks to anchor so he could go ashore to botanise but Cook refused. He wrote 'I saw clearly that no winds could b[l]ow there but what was either right in or right out... and it certainly would have been highly imprudent in me to have put into a place where we could have not got out but with a wind that we have lately found does not blow one day in a month. I mention this because there were some on board who wanted me to harbour'.

Sailors feared fog as, when it was thick, it was easy to lose bearings and run onto rocks. Fog was responsible for the *Resolution* and the *Adventure* separating in Antarctic waters on 8 February 1773. Cook wrote 'the *Adventure* was about a point or two upon our larbd quarter...about half an hour after a thick Fogg came on so that we could not see her. At 9 o'Clock we fired a gun and repeated it at 10 and at 11...but neither this last signal or any of the former were answered by the *Adventure*'.

Extremes of weather took their toll. In March 1774, the *Resolution* sailed north after several weeks in the freezing cold around Antarctica only to encounter the heat of the tropics. William Wales wrote 'it's scarcely 3 weeks ago we were miserable on acco of ye cold: we are now wretched with ye heat: the latter is I think less supportable of ye two'. Descriptions like these influenced Coleridge for his poem about the Ancient Mariner.

Cook used the weather for place names: Cape Foulweather in Oregon and Calm Point in Alaska are examples.

Websites and CD-ROMS

The internet has radically changed research methods by providing access to many online databases containing journal articles and other information (much full-text), allowing research from many places in the world. It soon also discovered James Cook and hundreds of websites quickly sprang up. Unfortunately, like much of the internet, the majority of sites are very poor and would do more good by closing down. Many of these sites are self-indulgent, offering little in the way of original research and show that, while the owners know how to host a website, they know little about Cook, no matter how much they admire him. They have often plagiarised material from better sites without permission or acknowledgement.

However, some sites are worth exploring. The following provide information or have themselves created links to good sites:

The website of the Captain Cook Society (http://www.CaptainCookSociety.com) is the best starting point on the internet for finding out about James Cook. It contains much information on its own pages and provides the most comprehensive set of links to other Cook-related sites.

Mark Winthrop in Denmark (http://www.winthrop.dk/jcook.html) hosts his own website devoted to Cook. It contains the online version of Cook's family tree. Of interest is the discussion list devoted to Cook that he hosts. To subscribe to this free facility visit the relevant web site at:
(http://groups.yahoo.com/group/captcook).

The *Endeavour* Replica has its own website (http://www.barkendeavour.com.au/) where you can find out where the ship is at present and where is going next. It also carries a host of other information about the ship.

Other sites worth investigating include:

1: The Papers of Sir Joseph Banks (http://www.sl.nsw.gov.au/banks/);

2: *Endeavour* botanical illustrations (http://internt.nhm.ac.uk/cgi-bin/perth/cook/);

3: The Cook Collection at the Pitt Rivers Museum, Oxford (http://www.prm.ox.ac.uk/cook.html);

4: Captain Cook Voyages of Discovery from the Hunterian Museum, Glasgow (http://www.hunterian.gla.ac.uk/museum/cook/cook.html);

5: Captain James Cook (1728–1779): Celebrated North Country Navigator (http://www.captcook-ne.co.uk/);

6: 1768 – The voyage of the *Endeavour* (http://www.nhm.ac.uk/museum/tempexhib/voyages/endeavour.html).

The internet is a constantly evolving entity so be warned that it is possible that by the time this work is published some of the links above will not work and other websites will have been created. John Robson has a website supporting this *Captain Cook Encyclopaedia*: (http: //pages.quicksilver.net.nz/jcr/~capcookencl.html). The site contains a short biography, some bibliographies, wills of Cook's crews, and lists of memorials, as well as material that could not be included in the printed encyclopaedia.

The medium of CD-ROM has not been taken up by many with regards Cook but a good one was published by the National Library of Australia in 1999. This was *Captain Cook's journal, 1768-71, Endeavour,* which offered Cook's original manuscript journal plus a transcript with comments and many other related items.
SEE ALSO: Captain Cook Society

Whitby

Whitby lies on the North Yorkshire coast, at 54° 30′ N and 0° 34′ W. The town straddles the estuary of the River Esk, which enters the sea in a northerly direction. By the middle of the eighteenth century it was a thriving port, with protective piers, and was a legally-designated harbour of refuge, which entitled it to levy dues from passing vessels should money be needed for the repair of its harbour installations, or of the bridge which led through to the sheltered upper harbour.

The river was spanned by a drawbridge, in the centre of the town, the position of whose supporting piers gave added protection to the upper harbour, although they made the passage of vessels from the thriving shipyards and dry-docks within the upper harbour a skilled task. However, the gap between the piers was wider near the surface of the river, so that it accommodated the hulls of most of the larger vessels which had to pass through.

The town itself was mediaeval in layout, established by Whitby's Benedictine Abbey around 1128, with a skewed grid plan which followed the line of the principal thoroughfare, the river itself, with as many houses as possible fronting both the river and a street. Linking the streets, and leading through to the river itself were the yards or *ghauts* which are still a feature of the town. Each is wide enough for a porter, for a pack-animal or for a hand-cart, while the streets are just wide enough for two horse-drawn wheeled vehicles to pass each other.

Whitby was a frontier town, as are all ports, and in time of war was relatively easy to blockade, since the harbour approach was restricted on the east by the triangular shale reef known as Whitby Rock, which stretches out into the sea for a mile. Maps and surveys made in 1782 and 1794 by Francis Gibson, Customer and Captain of Militia, show batteries and other defences designed to protect the vital Baltic traders and colliers. John Paul Jones still succeeded in blockading the town during the War of American Independence, as had the Dutch and French during previous wars of the seventeenth and eighteenth centuries.

At the time when James Cook first became acquainted with Whitby, probably when he was working in Staithes, around 1746, the town's fleet numbered some 200 vessels, ranging from single-masted sloops to fully rigged three-masted ships. They were largely locally-owned, and usually, but not always, Whitby-built, in the town's thriving shipyards. It was formerly thought that shipbuilding in Whitby did not really start until the turn of the seventeenth and eighteenth centuries, but evidence from Privy Council and other archives indicates that the shipyards were already well-known by 1640, and were capable of building large merchantmen.

The principal trades of Whitby's vessels were for timber and coal, but there was also coastal shipping all round the northern seas. The town's fleet was a service industry, plying between other ports rather than serving Whitby itself. Whitby is a very isolated town, cut off from the rest of England by high and inhospitable moorland, with poor roads, and served by a short, and very fast-flowing river, the Esk, which is navigable for

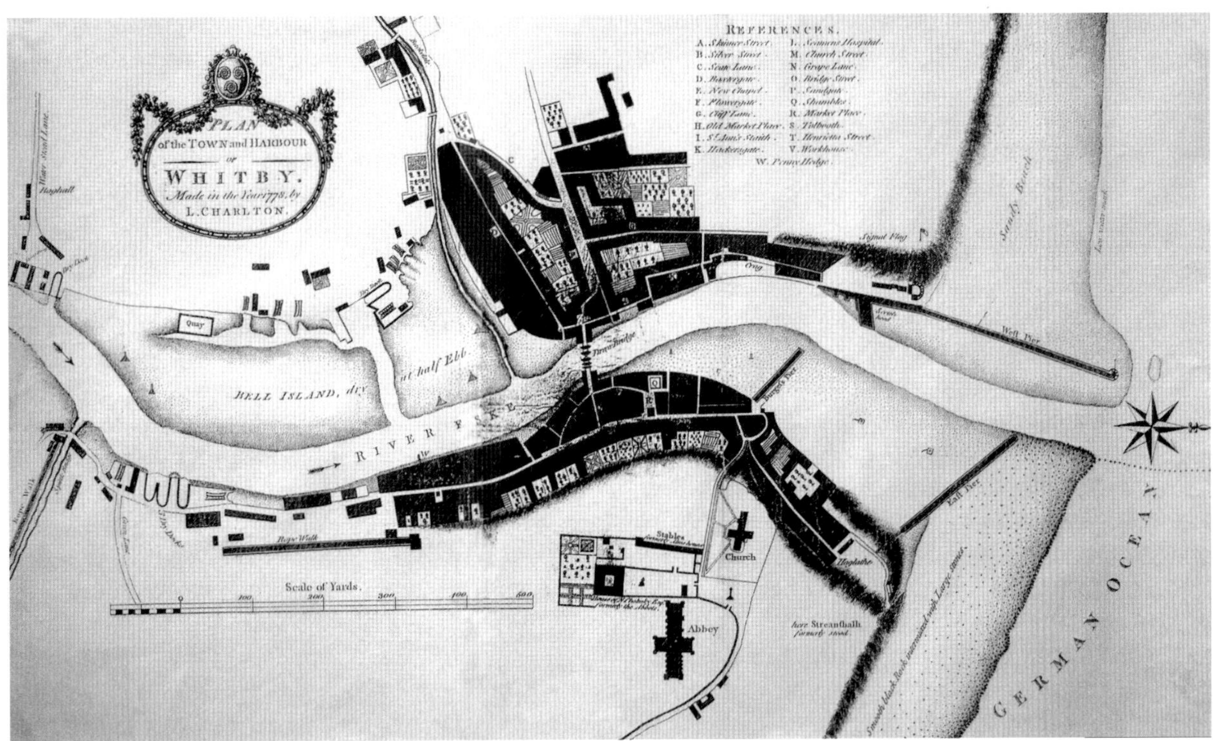

A plan of the town and harbour of Whitby drawn by Lionel Charlton in 1778. It shows the port nestling alongside the River Esk, which flows into the North Sea (German Ocean) to the right. (R Barker)

only a mile up-stream. There was little primary produce to export from the pastoral farming of the hinterland, and the only mineral exploited locally was alum, mined since the start of the seventeenth century, but exported in strictly limited quantities to avoid sharp reductions in the price per ton. The exported alum, and the coal imported to service the processing works, absorbed a very small percentage of Whitby's shipping capacity. There were imports, of mixed household goods and of grain, coal, salt and other necessaries not available locally. Timber, tar, pitch, hemp, and flax were imported for the ship-building, rope-making and sail-cloth manufacturing which made up the rest of the town's industry. Whitby, which had been a 'company town' of her great Benedictine Abbey in the Middle Ages, was once more effectively a single-industry, town for the seventeenth, eighteenth and much of the nineteenth centuries.

Whitby's involvement with the timber trade was extensive. Ralph Davis, in his *Rise of the English Shipping Industry*, calculated that in the middle of the eighteenth century, Whitby vessels carried half of the timber imported from Norway to English ports, and by the end of the century Whitby's large, sturdy vessels carried 20 per cent of all the trade from the Baltic to England. Later, during Cook's service in Whitby ships, the town's shipowners entered the northern whaling trade, at which, although the proportion of the fleet involved in whaling was small, the industry was exceptionally successful. Whenever there was a war, and the Navy required shipping for troop transport, or as store-ships, or even as hired armed vessels, Whitby vessels were greatly in demand, and indeed, when Cook was an apprentice, the port would be filling up with vessels returning from naval service during the War of the Austrian Succession, which ended in 1748. It was no doubt a feature of harbour life that returning seamen would exaggerate the drama of such service, particularly to impressionable apprentices.

Always, in the background, there was the coal trade. It was Whitby's 'cash crop', the trade to which the fleet always turned when other trades were slack. The returning whaler did not rest on its laurels at the end of the season, in August; there was still time for two coal voyages up to the Tyne and down to London before the seamen were paid off. Only the whaling specialists, the specksioneers, boatsteerers and harpooners, were able to go ashore and spend their 'fish money'. The sailing season in the North Sea ran from early March to the end of October, eight months, into which could be crammed, in a good year, eight to ten coal trips, or three to five trips to the Baltic. Even the naval transports, returning after three or more years away, would find themselves, not reunited with their families, but off to the Tyne and down to London before being laid up for 'winter work', the repairs which every vessel needed after the North Sea season.

Cook entered the shipping industry as a servant, apprenticed to John Walker, himself a master mariner turned ship-owner, though he would not necessarily have recognised the latter definition, which belongs to a later period of effective sole ownership. In the mid-eighteenth century, when routine marine insurance was in its infancy, risk was still covered by multiple share-holding. Most vessels were held in 64ths, although at times these might be held in bundles of up to eight, so that it could seem that there were only eight shares in a vessel. On the other hand, a contemporary schedule of returns from shares in shipping, sadly without the owner's name, shows that even 64ths could be subdivided, perhaps among siblings after an intestacy. The smallest denominator found so far is the 1/512th share in Robert Middleton's *Lark*, which in 1744 yielded a return of 11s.

John Walker was a leading member of Whitby's strong Quaker community, and his house in Grape Lane, in which Cook would have lodged during the winter season, had its own private landing place, and commanded a good view of the upper harbour. During the winter months Cook would have helped, as did most of the servants, with winter-work and with rigging his master's vessels, and would have attended the classes in navigation, mathematics and accounting which are known to have been available. Indeed, Lionel Charlton, surveyor, mathematician and historian of Whitby, whose map illustrates this chapter, was such a teacher in the town. Whitby was clearly a magnet port for training aspirants to the merchant service.

In 1747 the Seamen's Sixpence system, which charged all merchant seamen sixpence per month at sea to pay for the support of Greenwich Hospital, was extended to cover a named range of other seafaring charities, including Whitby's Seamen's Hospital Charity. This resulted in the creation of detailed muster rolls, and large volumes into which the rolls were copied. Few ports still have these rolls, but Whitby is remarkable in having both rolls and volumes. When the first of Whitby's detailed Seamen's Sixpence rolls was made up, there were over 1200 servants listed on Whitby vessels, aged from 10 to 27, but of an average age of 16–17 years old. They came from all round the British coastline, though mainly from the north-east. Some would become practical seamen, able to 'hand, reef and steer'. Some would be carpenter's apprentices, and some with culinary flair would become cooks. All would have to learn basic seamanship. The brightest, such as James Cook, would become mariners, skilled in seamanship, and in both pilotage and blue water navigation.

Servitude lasted anything from three to nine years, basically depending on the age at which the boy joined. No-one would be willing to pay him a man's wage until he could 'pull his weight'. Cook, entering at 17, was apprenticed for three years. Thereafter a boy destined to become a ship's officer or 'mariner', capable of standing a watch and of navigating the vessel, would serve one or more years as a seaman, before, if he showed promise, becoming a second mate or even the only mate on a smaller vessel. Thereafter he might be offered command of his own vessel, and possibly the opportunity to invest in her as well. There is evidence that he would feel himself ill-done by if he had not made enough money as a master to retire and become an owner himself, with shares in a range of different vessels to spread the risk, by the time he was 40. One such master, contemp-orary with Cook, who was treated somewhat shabbily by his first owner, complained that he had 'been born under a twopenny planet' when he was still at sea at 47.

Seafaring was an extremely hard life, since men in the merchant fleet might find themselves handling up to 30 tons of vessel, compared with the three or four tons handled by a man in the much larger crews of the Navy. However, merchant crews were considerably better paid than those of the Navy. Whitby's considerable and important shipping archive, an almost unique survivor of the Second World War, when most of the accounts and logs of the days of sail were destroyed in the bombing of shipping offices and other port installations in the larger ports, gives a very clear picture of the diet, pay, welfare and working conditions of the shipping in the fleet. They also make clear the careful adherence to the principles of the Laws and Customs of the Sea which protected the industry and the rights of its workforce. While the causes in the Vice-Admiralty courts for the region make clear that the actuality did

A view of Whitby Harbour from Cook's time showing the drawbridge linking the east and west banks of the River Esk. The bridge built in 1766 was replaced in 1833. (R Barker)

not always live up to the ideal, nonetheless there is a level of protection and care, in the provision of a good diet, in the cleanliness, particularly of the boys, in the medical care after illness or injury, and ultimately in the provisions of Whitby Seamen's Hospital Charity which, founded in 1675, provided for 'decayed and distressed seamen' and their families. The Hospital, bound by its rules to put the orphaned children of seamen to apprenticeship, was also an instrument of social mobility by allowing the son of an illiterate seaman to rise through his own efforts to become a master, shareholder and gentleman.

However, the Hospital was also an instrument of social control. Sobriety was insisted upon for the residents of the charity's houses. So too was the care of servants at sea. The Law of the Sea insisted that injured and sick seamen should receive care, if necessary ashore, and there is clear evidence that this was done. However, masters of Whitby vessels could reclaim from the charity any medical expenses involved, with the proviso that the master could supply two witnesses willing to swear that any injury or illness was not caused by negligence or assault. Petitions for reimbursement were refused if this stricture was not met.

Social control in the Whitby fleet also emanated from the influence of the Quakers, whose reputation for integrity and plain dealing made their vessels popular with merchants who had cargoes to ship. Such an influential body within the ship-owning community forced, to a large extent, conformity on non-Quaker shipping, since competition for cargoes was intense. The whole of the town's shipping benefited from this high reputation. Ironically, it was this reputation for good building and well-found and well-crewed vessels which made Whitby shipping so popular with the naval transport industry, yet the Quakers were apparently banned by the Society of Friends from benefiting from this industry. They were not supposed to arm their vessels, or apply for the Letters of Marque and Reprisal which would allow them to attack and take enemy shipping as prizes. Yet the law of the land, and the law of the sea, to which they were also bound, even by the Society itself, expected them to take all care during wartime for their crews and their cargoes. It was a veritable tight-rope, which the Whitby Monthly Meeting walked with great delicacy, coming to grief only during the War of American Independence, when the fear that Whitby Friends might fire upon American

Friends led to the 'denial' or expulsion of those Whitby Friends who armed their vessels.

Shipping was always subject to booms and slumps, especially during the eighteenth century when wars might raise seamen's wages far above anything that could be earned ashore, and when the transport trade, with its protection from the press gang, was a huge source of fairly safe profit to Whitby's fleet. However, the ending of each war produced an often catastrophic slump, when the cessation of the need for shipping armies overseas threw hired transports, and sold-off naval vessels, back into the mercantile fleet, and when discharged seamen flooded the labour market. Nevertheless, an analysis of the profits of Whitby's fleet over a run of a century and a half shows a fairly consistent operating profit of well above the level that might be obtained by putting capital out at interest rather than investing it in shipping. The high reputation of the fleet clearly paid its dividends.

In Cook's day there were many changes afoot in Whitby, changes that may have made him, and other enterprising young men, restive. The practice of laying-up in Whitby, and doing the winter-work 'in-house', was coming to an end for the larger brigs and ships. It was better by far for the collier to be laid-up in the Tyne or the Wear and be first in the queue for a cargo of coal at high post-winter selling prices in London. Coal and other high-bulk cargoes were generally factored by the master; they were bought at the quayside and sold in Billingsgate by the master himself. For the Baltickers, constrained by the freezing of the Gulf of Riga into a much shorter season than in the coal trade, a lay-up in the Thames meant a saving of several days, and an early entry into the newly ice-free ports of the Baltic meant first choice of the season's timber, hemp, sail-cloth, tar and pitch which were so necessary for the shipyards in England. Whitby itself, though thriving financially, would be less busy in the winter than in earlier days. But times were also unstable elsewhere; Cook would have been at sea at the end of the second Jacobite rebellion, but there were those in Whitby who had given discreet refuge to Jacobites. Between the end of the War of the Austrian Succession and the Seven Years War there were but eight years, and in that time Cook, in search of opportunities that were not available in Whitby, made his choice between the merchant and the naval fleet. Who could possibly say that he made the wrong decision?

By Rosalin Barker

See Also: North Sea and the coal trade, Quakers, Walker (John)

Williamson, John (?–1798)

John Williamson sailed on Cook's third voyage. He began the voyage as third lieutenant on the *Resolution* and was promoted to second lieutenant in the reshuffle that happened after Cook's death in February 1779. In the second major reshuffle that occurred six months later at Clerke's death Williamson was transferred to the *Discovery* as first lieutenant.

Very little is known about Williamson but what is portrays him as an unpopular member of the crew, at odds with everyone including Cook. Unlike Cook, he was prepared to shoot to kill and disapproved of many aspects of island life, finding them improper. Trevenen described him as 'a wretch, feared & hated by his inferiors, detested by his equals, & despised by his superiors; a very devil, to whom none of our midshipmen have spoke for above a year'. Griffin wrote that he was 'a very bad man & a great Tyrant'. Williamson was in command of the launch at Kealakekua Bay when Cook died. He claimed to have misunderstood Cook's signals, which led to him being blamed by some for not doing sufficient to save his colleagues. He is supposed to have fought duels as a result. Williamson kept a log and proceedings from February 1776 until June 1778.

Williamson was made post-captain in June 1782. He was appointed captain of HMS *Agincourt,* a Third Rate of 64 guns, in 1796. He took part in the Battle of Camperdown (Camperduin) against the Dutch off the Dutch coast in October 1797. Williamson was charged with cowardice, negligence and disaffection that he had held *Agincourt* back from the fight and not done his utmost to bring the enemy ships to battle. He was court-martialled at Sheerness for his unsatisfactory behaviour. Cowardice only was proven. He was sentenced to be placed at the bottom of the captain's list and rendered incapable of ever serving on board a ship of the Royal Navy. This ended his naval career and he died in 1798. Williamson Passage in Nootka Sound is named for him.

See Also: Third voyage

Young, George (1777–1848)

George Young, the theologian, biographer and geologist, was born on 15 July 1777 on a farm near Edinburgh, Scotland. Since he was born with only one hand (his right), agriculture was ruled out as a future vocation. Instead, George began four years of literary and philosophical studies at the University of Edinburgh in 1792. He was especially interested in natural science, studying James Hutton's old-Earth uniformitarian geological theory. He followed this by taking a five-year course in theology at Selkirk.

In 1801, he was licensed to preach by the presbytery of Edinburgh. After a brief visit in the summer of 1805 to Whitby, North Yorkshire, the next year he became the pastor of the Presbyterian chapel there, which he served for 42 years until his death in 1848. Young became a founding member and the first secretary of the Whitby Literary and Philosophical Society in 1823, a position he held until his death and which included the establishment of the Whitby Museum. He wrote 21 books, including a respected two-volume *History of Whitby* and his biography of Captain James Cook, published in 1836. Young had to publish the book at his own expense and he was responsible for adding some Whitby material to our information on Cook.

Young married Margaret Hunter, a daughter of the prominent Robert Hunter of Whitby in 1826. They had no children. After contracting influenza in early 1848 at the age of 71, he died on 8 May.

SEE ALSO: Biographies of Cook

Young, Nicholas (?–?)

Nicholas Young is a shadowy figure on Cook's first voyage on the *Endeavour* where he appeared as one of Banks' retinue and later as cabin boy. He was the first on board to sight New Zealand and Cook named the southern point of Poverty Bay, Young Nick's Head, in his honour, punning his age and name. The headland was not, however, the piece of land first sighted by Young. That was higher land further inland. Young was also the first to see land on their return to Britain. He later accompanied Banks to Iceland. Karen Hesse has written a fictional account of Young's part in the *Endeavour* voyage. There is a statue of 'Young Nick' at Gisborne, looking out to his headland.

SEE ALSO: First voyage

Zimmermann, Heinrich (1741–1805)

Heinrich Zimmermann sailed on the third voyage on the *Discovery* as an AB. He wrote an account of the voyage, *Reise um die Welt mit Capitain Cook,* which was published in Mannheim in 1781 and subsequently appeared in several English translations. The book has many interesting descriptions, including some of Cook, but, as he sailed on the *Discovery,* their authenticity is open to question.

He was born on 25 October 1741 in Wiesloch, 9.3 miles (15km) south of Heidelberg in Germany, the son of a surgeon. Leaving home in 1770, Zimmermann had a variety of jobs around Europe before arriving in London in 1776. He had trained as a belt-maker and spent time as a metalworker in Geneva, bell-maker in Lyon and a swordmaker in Paris. Zimmermann never married and died on 3 May 1805 in Starnberg, 12.4 miles (20km) south-west of Munich, where he had been working as a shipmaster on the Starnbergersee.

SEE ALSO: Published accounts, Third voyage

Zoological collections from Cook's voyages

Before Cook's first circumnavigation in *Endeavour* (1768–72), natural history observations as an official and integral part of European voyages of exploration had depended almost entirely on whether or not ships' commanders had any interest in such matters. Men such as William Dampier and Willem de Vlamingh, for instance, had collected plant specimens and made amateur records of flora and fauna during their voyages, but there were no dedicated personnel to make systematic collections or observations. Cook's voyages were to change all this. They were remarkable not only for their geographical and navigational discoveries but also for the vast amount of scientific knowledge they consciously accumulated. In particular, they resulted in the most comprehensive natural history collections of the Pacific region to date.

In 1768, when Cook set sail on the first of his three circumnavigations, the sciences of zoology, botany and entomology were still in their infancy, but the time was ripe for the huge influx of biological data these voyages would bring. New methods recently devised by the Swedish naturalist, Carolus Linnaeus, gave the proto-biologists of the day an efficient, and more importantly, universal system of naming and cataloguing the myriad new species that were to be discovered. But it is unlikely there would have been any of this scientific effort on this, or Cook's subsequent voyages, without the presence on *Endeavour* of the gentleman botanist Joseph Banks.

When news of Cook's planned voyage to observe the Transit of Venus reached the ears of Banks, a rich young landowner with a passion for natural history, he lobbied the Royal Society and the Admiralty for permission to go on the voyage to make natural history observations. Banks was duly accepted and he funded and equipped a suite of seven artists, scientists and servants at an expense estimated at £10,000, or virtually the entire annual income from his estates in the north of England. This inclusion of artists and scientists on the voyage set a precedent for future expeditions, both British and European, and was the necessary precursor to later voyages, such as those of the *Beagle* and *Challenger*.

Although Cook himself was no natural historian he appears to have welcomed the party on board and he forged a lifelong friendship with Banks. He borrowed heavily from Banks's observations to supplement his own journal with basic descriptions of flora and fauna. It was Cook who made the first zoological observations of Australia's east coast, noting on 29 April 1770 that the native people were eating oysters and mussels and that there were innumerable stingrays in the water – so many that he originally named Botany Bay, Stingray Bay.

Natural history collections were made on all three of Cook's circumnavigations. While Cook himself cannot be personally credited with these, it is a tribute to his seamanship and the dedication of his crews, that all the collections were safely brought back to England.

The first voyage

Banks's party included his great friend and protégé of Linnaeus, the Swede Daniel Solander. He also took two artists; Sydney Parkinson for natural history and Alexander Buchan for landscapes and figures; a draftsman, Herman Spöring (also Swedish); two servants and two black slaves. The Royal Society had recommended Banks to the Admiralty as a gentleman 'well-versed in Natural History' and he went prepared to collect and preserve anything from bird and mammal skins to fish and invertebrates. But Banks and Solander's primary interest, was botany and, although Banks made both botanical and zoological collections, the zoological specimens were ultimately to suffer from this preference.

Banks and his team began collecting as soon as the voyage got underway. Their first acquisitions were seabirds and fish of which Parkinson made many detailed drawings. This was the first and virtually only time he had the leisure to make finished paintings. Once they made landfall, the sheer number of plant specimens collected meant that Parkinson often did not have time to finish his drawings. The scientists and artists worked in the captain's great cabin. Conditions were cramped and they could only work when the table was not being used for dining or for Cook's own purposes. Parkinson would often just make sketches and colour notes planning to work them up once they got home. Sadly Parkinson died on the return voyage, so never got the chance to complete his drawings.

Parkinson worked mainly from dead specimens and made fewer drawings of mammals than he did of fish, birds and invertebrates. In Australia, for instance, he only made sketches of a kangaroo and a quoll. This reflects the fact it was far easier to catch fish, birds and invertebrates than fast-moving mammals for study and illustration later.

Both Cook and Banks mention birds in their journals. Banks went on shooting expeditions to acquire birds for specimens and also for food – mammals and birds were likely to be eaten by the crew. Banks later explained that they simply did not have enough spirit to preserve whole animals and birds, so the specimens they did bring back tended to be simply heads with skins and feet, the remainder having been discarded or eaten. Some lorikeets they shot in Botany Bay were 'made into a pie and they ate very well', Banks records. Many of the birds they saw can be identified from Banks's descriptions and from Parkinson's sketches. There is also a fascinating record of one live specimen which survived the journey home – a rainbow lorikeet brought back from Botany Bay. Banks gave it to Marmaduke Tunstall and an illustration of it, by Peter Brown, was published in 1776

– the earliest published illustration of an Australian parrot.

According to the contemporary naturalist John Ellis, Banks and Solander returned 'laden with the greatest treasure of Natural History that ever was brought into any country at one time by two persons'. The listings of the zoological specimens are not complete, but it can be estimated with some confidence that at least 500 fishes were collected and roughly the same number of birds. The shell and invertebrate collections were also considerable. Parkinson's drawings amount to 164 fish, 32 birds, 5 reptiles, 24 crustaceans, 7 insects, 7 molluscs and 51 other, mainly marine, invertebrates.

The second voyage

Banks and Cook had got on well on *Endeavour* and Banks had every intention of accompanying the captain on his next voyage. However, due to a disagreement about the fitting-out of the two expedition ships for scientific purposes, Banks pulled out at the last minute, and his place was taken by the father-and-son team, Johann Reinhold Forster and George Forster. A third naturalist, Anders Sparrman, joined the voyage at the Cape of Good Hope. Unlike Banks, the Forsters and Sparrman were professional natural historians, who earned their living through their skills as naturalists. The Forsters were diligent collectors and excellent exponents of natural history. George, a talented artist, recorded their finds in hundreds of paintings and drawings, 139 on birds alone. In total some 260–270 zoological specimens (birds, fishes, quadrupeds, cetaceans, amphibians) were brought back from the voyage, plus two live secretary birds (*Sagitarrius serpentarius*), and a springbok (*Antidorcas marsupialis*) from Africa destined for Queen Charlotte. Solander talked of four casks containing zoological material being earmarked for Banks. He selected specimens from the entomological collections for Banks, the British Museum, the Royal Society, Marmaduke Tunstall and Sir Ashton Lever. Banks himself wrote that the Forsters presented him with many animal specimens. All the shells from the voyage were also offered to Banks but there is evidence that he refused them, and they were probably then sold as the Forsters were perilously short of money at the time. Reinhold also sent at least one parcel, thought to have contained shells and dry material, to Linnaeus.

The Forsters were undoubtedly the most professional and diligent of all the naturalists who sailed with Cook.

*Poe Bird, New Zealand. A Tui (*Prosthemadera novaseelandiae*). After a painting by George Forster. (Cook I fp 97)*

They published more than all of Cook's other scientists put together and were far more than simply 'species hunters', to quote Samuel Johnson. In their lectures and published works, the Forsters analysed their observations, looked at cause and effect; extrapolated and experimented and used analogy to integrate their discoveries and observations into a more holistic, and undoubtedly more modern, understanding of natural history.

The third voyage

Despite the undoubted skills of the Forsters as naturalists, Reinhold, in particular, was a volatile character and Cook experienced a number of problems dealing with him on the second voyage. As a consequence, Cook declined to take an official scientific party on his third expedition, the role of naturalist/ collector being taken by his Chief Surgeon William Anderson. The task of natural history illustration fell to the official artist, John Webber, and William Ellis, Surgeon on Cook's second ship, *Discovery*. Ellis and Anderson thus began a tradition of ships' surgeon-naturalists which reached its pinnacle with Thomas Huxley's work on the *Terror*, almost 100 years later. Anderson had sailed on Cook's previous voyage and had learnt a lot from the Forsters. Cook recorded that Anderson had a 'great proficiency in natural history, [and] was as willing as he was well qualified, to describe every thing in that branch of science which should occur worthy of notice'. Cook referred to him as 'the ingenious Mr Anderson' but he was still an amateur, albeit an enthusiastic one, and had other duties to occupy him, so perhaps not surprisingly the natural history discoveries of this expedition suffered as a result of not having dedicated scientist on board. A small notebook containing 13 pages of bird descriptions and 13 of animals observed on Cook's second and third voyages, does survive in the Natural History Museum in London but was never published. Anderson's journal, however, was used along with Cook's in the compiling of the official account of the voyage. Anderson tantalisingly also referred to a manuscript of his account of the second voyage but this has been lost. Anderson died on the voyage but his Surgeon's Mate, David Samwell, took over from him and continued to make collections and natural history notes.

It is difficult to estimate the numbers and types of specimens collected on this voyage, as records are scant. It is likely that as on previous voyages, zoological specimens would have found their way to Banks. Jonas Dryander, Banks's librarian, lists 220 birds (some 96 bird drawings from the voyage are known) and 3 mammals, but whether these actually came to Banks, is unclear. Unfortunately, Anderson and Samwell were not as expert at the organising and preservation of specimens as their predecessors. The contemporary naturalist, Thomas Pennant observed with some horror that 'It was a great misfortune, in this voyage, that the fishes were promiscuously thrown into one common cask, so that it was impossible to ascertain the species belonging to each country'.

Impact on contemporary society

When Cook and Banks returned from the first voyage it was the plants collected that aroused the most intense interest, the zoological collections being received with less enthusiasm. There were no spectacular specimens, either in size or form, to seize the public imagination. Even of the new species, many were sufficiently similar to known forms to make little impact. The one exception, however, was the kangaroo. Banks brought back two kangaroo or wallaby skulls, and also a marsupial skin, of either a young grey kangaroo, or a wallaby. The famous painting of Captain Cook's (or more correctly) Banks's kangaroo, by George Stubbs, modelled on this skin (apparently inflated, which explains the rather bloated appearance of the animal), and on Parkinson's sketches was exhibited in 1773. Although marsupials had been noted by early Dutch explorers of the west coast of Australia, no large marsupial specimens had been seen in Europe before. However, the first descriptions of the material, made by Zimmerman in 1777 did not recognise them as marsupials (the specimens were either male or immature, so there was no obvious pouch). Banks had recognised a possum, collected in the Endeavour River area as a marsupial, but had not realised that kangaroos were marsupials too.

There was a great expectation that Banks would publish his natural history findings. An early anonymous account of the voyage stated that 'Mr Banks and Mr Solander will hereafter abundantly gratify the curiosity of those who delight in the study of nature' by publishing their finds. And, indeed, Banks had great plans on his return to produce fantastic publications on his collections, of a quality and detail never before seen. He spent thousands of pounds on the engraving of Parkinson's plant drawings for publication as a *Florilegium*, and Daniel Solander dedicated much of the rest of his life to writing up their scientific descriptions. But the zoological collections were largely ignored. Banks ran out of money and steam on his great *Florilegium* project; perhaps he had intended to turn his attention to the zoological specimens once this was completed, but the premature death of Solander in 1783, put paid to his great ambition. The *Florilegium* was never completed in Banks's lifetime and the zoological collections remained neglected. Seven years after their return, Banks had still not unpacked some of his zoological specimens. Prophetically, back in 1770 Linnaeus had expressed a heartfelt worry that there would be a delay in publishing details of the collections and that in the interim they might decay, be destroyed or that their collectors might die before they could publish.

By contrast, the Forsters were very keen to publish their zoological findings as soon as possible. They worked up their observations both on the voyage and immediately afterwards and had the bulk of their zoological descriptions ready for publication very quickly. But Cook was concerned that their publication would come out before his and ordered that they should delay. In the event George summarised their natural history collections in the chapter 'Remarks on the Organic Bodies' in J R Forster's *Observations made during a Voyage round the world* published in 1778 and Reinhold gave short diagnoses of birds, fishes and as well as plants in *Enchiridion historiae naturali inserviens* (1788). *Descriptiones Animalium Quae in Itinere ad Maris Australis Terras*, the fuller zoological account, was finally published posthumously in 1844 and contained 200 original descriptions of birds, fish, insects, and mammals. The delay in its publication was a tragedy. Had it been published immediately after the voyage it would have been unsurpassed in its depth and breadth.

With the unofficial naturalist, William Anderson, dying of tuberculosis in the course of the third voyage there was far less of an impact on the natural history world when Cook's ships finally made it home. In his will, Anderson left 'to Joseph Banks Esquire the Natural Curiosities I have collected during this voyage with some Manuscript Notes relating to them'. These notes were nothing like as detailed or extensive as Banks, Solander and the Forsters' records on the previous voyages, and they were never published, although some of Anderson's observations were included in the official account of the voyage.

The fate of the collections

It was not just the naturalists who collected material on the voyages. Anyone, from Cook himself down to the lowliest crewman, could have brought specimens back. Selling curiosities from voyages was a source of extra income for poorly-paid seamen and there is no doubt that dealers bought shells off ordinary sailors on Cook's second and third voyages. George Humphrey, for instance, acquired a huge number of shells from ordinary crew members on the second voyage. He sold some to the Duchess of Portland, whose shell collection was legendary, and some to the Literary and Philosophical Society of Danzig. Here they were worked on by Friedrich Zorn von Plombsheim whose descriptions were the first published account of Cookian shells. Humphrey also bought shells from the third voyage, in particular those collected by David Samwell. Most of these were sold on to Thomas Martyn who published some in *The Universal Conchologist* (1784–87). Substantial collections can also be attributed to the more prominent members of the expeditions, such as Solander and Parkinson. Parkinson's shells were bought by naturalist and collector John Fothergill (1712–80). These ended up at the University of Glasgow.

The fate of the major collections, however, is inextricably linked to Banks. Peter Whitehead has described him as the hub around which the natural history of Cook's voyage revolves. As the financier of the natural history aspects of the first voyage Banks quite rightly claimed ownership of the *Endeavour* collections and many specimens from the other voyages also found their way into his hands. But Banks appears to have been in possession of only a fraction of this zoological material at his death. It seems that the great majority of Cook zoological specimens were dispersed by Banks during his lifetime. Perhaps because zoology was not his primary interest, Banks was generous in giving away zoological material and in allowing others access to work on it, but less concerned about doing anything with it himself. Many famous naturalists of the day came to see and study his collections which he housed in a kind of salon-museum in his great London house in Soho Square. The Linnaean entomologist Johan Christian Fabricius spent some time at Banks's house and described about 400 arthropods from the *Endeavour* voyage in his *Systema Entomologiae* (1775). Pierre-Marie-Auguste Broussonet (1761–1807) came to England for two years in 1780 to work on Cook fishes at Soho Square. He published separate descriptions of dogfish and a sailfish, and then a further 10 Cook fishes in his *Icthyologia* (1782). Banks made a gift of at least 44 fish specimens to Broussonet, most from Cook's voyages. Forty-two of these still survive in the Musée Nationale d'Histoire Naturelle, in Paris. Other gifts include a number of shells going to naturalist John Fothergill and to the Duchess of Portland.

The birds from Cook's voyages generated a lot of interest and many in Banks's possession as well as examples in the British Museum and the Leverian Museum were examined and described by ornithologist John Latham (1740–1837). Latham also used drawings from all three voyages and Anderson's notes to describe new specimens.

It is not unexpected that the numbers of mammals collected on all three voyages was small. Landfalls were made in areas with relatively low numbers of mammal species. In total, only some 40 mammals were figured by Cook's artists. Banks explained the difficulties of preserving mammal specimens and it would just not have been feasible for large ungulates or cetaceans to have been collected.

In 1792, some 20 years after the *Endeavour* voyage, Banks cleared out a huge amount of zoological material. About half went to the British Museum and the rest to the Scottish surgeon, John Hunter, who had a burgeoning museum of natural curiosities which would eventually become the museum of the Royal College of Surgeons. Hunter's aim was to illustrate anatomy, and as a consequence was inclined to dissect specimens or boil them up to extract their skeletons. It seems likely that this is the fate that befell some of Banks's poorly-preserved zoological material.

Another museum notable for receiving of Banks specimens was Sir Ashton Lever's massive collection of natural curiosities housed in Leicester Square. The museum received material, particularly birds, from the second voyage directly from the Forsters, as well as insects via Solander. Lever eventually had to sell his museum and, although it survived as a going concern until 1806, it was finally auctioned off in lots, and material was spread throughout Europe. Some Cook specimens have been tracked down from that sale, such as a small collection of fish in the Cuming Museum, Southwark, and a few fish and bird skins now in the Naturhistorische Museum in Vienna. Other material is now in the Liverpool Museum.

Similarly William Bullock's Museum in Piccadilly also boasted Cook material, including birds from the first voyage. Bullock seems to have acquired specimens from the Royal College of Surgeons and the Leverian sale. In 1829 he also decided to sell up, and although the British Museum was offered the collections, it refused, and they were auctioned. Tracing Cook material from this sale is near impossible, but six birds are known to be extant, one in Liverpool Museum, four in Leiden and one in Vienna.

A collection of some 3000 Banks insects, some of which originated from Cook's was given to Linnean Society of London along with some shells by Banks in 1815. The Society presented this collection to the British Museum (Natural History) in 1863. Despite its age and the fact it had been kept for so many years in a badly fitting cabinet, it was noted that the insect specimens were in a very fair state of preservation. This remains as a separate collection at the Natural History Museum to this day. In the same year, the museum received some Banksian arachnids from the Entomological Society.

In the end several societies, museums and many individuals too numerous to mention here all benefited in the short term from Banksian zoological gifts, donations and sales, but specimens were often passed on again or sold with such rapidity, and with so little documentation, that it is now almost impossible to trace them. If it seems strange that Banks and other contemporary holders of Cook material did not simply donate everything to the British Museum, it should be remembered that the this was not the august institution we know today. It was newly founded and its department of natural productions (which would eventually become the Natural History Museum), certainly not the most obvious nor the only possible repository for material from the voyages. Indeed the museum often rejected Cook material offered to it, and specimens which did come to the museum from Banks in 1792 were neglected in a basement for the next 17 years.

So the odds against the survival of Cook's zoological specimens have stacked up over the years. Banks's lack of interest meant that the large collections in his possession were neglected or dispersed. Subsequent donations, sales and a general lack of accompanying documentation make it difficult to track specimens once they left Banks's hands. In addition, many of the specimens were poorly preserved and curated. *The History of the Collections contained in the Natural History Department of the British Museum* (1906) recognised that many had simply perished. The birds in particular were 'inadequately prepared, were always mounted, and, from a lack of appreciation of their priceless value, were allowed to decay, through a want of proper curatorial knowledge'. Birds probably suffered more than any other group from poor preservation techniques and although several hundred were brought back on the three voyages, fewer than twenty now survive. These include two birds from Hawai'i and New Zealand, unusually preserved in spirit from the second or third voyage which are now in the Natural History Museum, London, having been transferred from the Royal College of Surgeons in 1845. This was fortuitous as much of the College's collections was destroyed by bombing in the Second World War.

The importance of the collections

The main importance of the collections at the time was that they brought to light not only species new to European science, but that they hinted at the scale of numbers of species on earth that had never before been dreamt of. They also inspired others to find out more. Scientists from all over Europe followed in his footsteps, and the corpus of biological knowledge burgeoned as a consequence.

But what of the relevance of the collections today? The shells and insects have fared the best but the mammals and birds are severely diminished through loss and decay, and much of those remaining are poorly preserved. Are these collections really still of any importance to modern zoology? Undoubtedly they are. Whether or not the specimens are still extant, records of their existence, including the artworks of Parkinson, Forster and others provide an invaluable benchmark, a snapshot of world ecosystems of over 200 years ago. Zoologists and ecologists can infer much from these records about the natural world in these regions before the arrival of Europeans. Surviving Cook material is also very much in demand by modern workers – new techniques such as DNA analysis are now squeezing even more information from these elderly specimens.

The specimens and the drawings based on them are still a vital reference for untangling problems of nomenclature and taxonomy. Often these are the type specimens (the first examples on which a species has been determined) and will always be the primary source of reference for that species. The systematic study of zoology relies heavily on type specimens so the loss of so much of Cook's zoological material in the intervening years, which included type specimens is a source of deep regret. Sadly some of the species collected are now extinct so these records and extant specimens provide a unique record of a life-form that is no longer in existence. The specimens also have a historical significance as well as a scientific one. They provide a tangible link with the past and the history of science enabling modern discoveries to be put into historical context.

New discoveries

Because of the way that collections from the three voyages have been dispersed over the last two hundred years, it is, perhaps, not surprising that material has languished unseen, unidentified or misidentified, and that things occasionally come to light once more. For instance, two bird lice, collected by the Forsters from an albatross they shot in 1772 were recently been identified in the Macleay Museum, University of Sydney. These were probably purchased by Alexander Macleay as part of a larger collection of insects from the Leverian Museum sale in 1806.

In 1983 a superb eighteenth-century cabinet of shells came up for auction which included four drawers of specimens connected to the Cook voyages. The collection was studied by scientists from the Natural History Museum but the cabinet was subsequently sold, and its current whereabouts are not known.

New bird specimens also occasionally come to light. The Berlin Museum archives for instance, list at least 20 specimens that could be from Cook's voyages while Cook material known to have been used for teaching purposes in Frankfurt am Main just after the Second World War may still be extant in the collections at Gottingen. Five Cook birds have been identified in Turin's natural history museum which came to it from sale of the Bullock Museum collections. Researchers are hopeful that more Cook material may yet be found.

Summary of extant collections

CORALS: Examples from the first voyage are held by Glasgow University.
JELLYFISH: Examples were illustrated by Parkinson and Forster, but no specimens are known.
SEA URCHINS: No extant specimens known, one specimen was recorded in the Leverian Museum.
MOLLUSCS: Cook shells are widely dispersed and have been identified in many collections including substantial collections in the Natural History Museum, London, and the Cambridge Museum of Zoology. The Royal College of Surgeons holds part of a likely Cook squid. A fine cabinet of Cook shells was auctioned in the 1980s, but the current location is not known.
CRUSTACEANS: Fabricius described at least 30 species. Some 40 Banks specimens exist in the NHM collections but these may not all derive from Cook's voyages.
INSECTS AND ARACHNIDS: 50 drawers of Banksian insects are held by the Natural History Museum, London. One possible Cook specimen is known in Glasgow. Macleay Museum, University of Sydney has insects from the Leverian sale.
FISH: Natural History Museum, London, Musée Nationale d'Histoire Naturelle, Paris, Vienna, Cuming Museum, London.
REPTILES AND AMPHIBIANS: Few specimens were collected on the voyages and no extant specimens are known.
BIRDS: Natural History Museum, London, Liverpool, Gottingen, Leiden, Vienna, Stockholm, Amsterdam, Edinburgh, Cambridge, Paris, Turin, Berlin.
MAMMALS: No extant specimens known.

BY JULIA BRUCE

SEE ALSO: Anderson (William), Forster family, Solander (Daniel)

Appendix I: A Listing of Logs, Journals, etc associated with Captain James Cook's ships

HMS *Eagle* (1755–1757)
Hamar, Joseph, Captain's Log, PRO, Adm 51/292
Palliser, Hugh, Captain's Log, PRO, Adm 51/292
Bisset, Thomas, Master's Log, PRO, Adm 52/578
Cook, James, Log, ATL

HMS *Solebay* (1757)
Craig, Robert, Captain's Log, PRO, Adm 51/908
Cook, James, Master's Log, PRO, Adm 52/1033

HMS *Pembroke* (1757–1759)
Simcoe, John, Captain's Log, PRO, Adm 51/686
Wheelock, John, Captain's Log, PRO, Adm 51/686
Cook, James, Master's Log, PRO, Adm 52/978

HMS *Northumberland* (1759–1762)
Colvill, Alexander, Admiral's Journal, PRO, Adm 50/22
Adams, William, Captain's Log, PRO, Adm 51/3925
Bateman, Nathaniel, Captain's Log, PRO, Adm 51/3925
Cook, James, Master's Log, PRO, Adm 52/959

HMS *Tweed* (1763)
Douglas, Charles, Captain's Log, PRO, Adm 51/1016

***Grenville* (14 June 1764 – 15 November 1767)**
Cook, James, Log and Journal, PRO, Adm 52/1263

HM Bark *Endeavour* (1768–1771)
Muster, PRO, Adm 36/8569
Log books etc, PRO, Adm 51/4545-8, Adm 55/39-41
Banks, Joseph, Journal, ML, Safe 1/12-13
Banks, Joseph, Miscellany, APL, Grey MS 48-9, 51-2
Bootie, John, Journal, PRO, Adm 51/4546/134-5
Bootie, John, Log, PRO, Adm 51/4546/136-9
Clerke, Charles, Journal, PRO, Adm 51/4548/143-4
Cook, James, Log, BL, Add MS 27955, 27885
Cook, James, Journal, PRO, Adm 55/40, Admiralty MS
Cook, James, Journal, NLA, MS 1, Canberra MS
Cook, James, Journal, ML, Safe 1/71, Mitchell MS
Cook, James, Journal, NMM, Greenwich MS
Forwood, Stephen, Journal, PRO, Adm 51/4545/133
Gore, John, Journal, PRO, Adm 51/4548/145-6
Green, Charles, Log-Journal, PRO, Adm 51/4545/151
Hicks, Zachary, Journal, PRO, Adm 51/4546/147-8
Hicks, Zachary, Log, ATL
Molyneux, Robert, Journal, PRO, Adm 51/4546/152
Molyneux, Robert, Log, PRO, Adm 55/39
Munkhouse, Jonathan, Log, ML
Munkhouse, William, BL, Add MS 27889
Pickersgill, Richard, Journal, PRO, Adm 51/4547/140-1
Pickersgill, Richard, Log, PRO, Adm 51/4547/142
Wilkinson, Francis, Journal, PRO, Adm 51/4547/149-50
Anon., Ship's Log, BL, Add MS 8959
Anon., Journals and Logs, PRO, Adm 51/4547/153-5

HMS *Resolution* (R) (1772–1775) and HMS *Adventure* (A) (1772–1774)
Muster (A), PRO, Adm 36/7550
Muster (R), PRO, Adm 36/7672
Log books etc, PRO, Adm 51/4520-4; 4553-6
Log books etc, PRO, Adm 55/1; 103-9
Bayly, William (A), Log, RO, Brd of Longitude Papers Vol XLIV
Bayly, William (A), Observations, RO, Brd. of Longitude Papers. Vol XLV
Bayly, William (A), Journal, ATL
Brown(e), Robert (A), Journal, PRO, Adm 51/4521/9-10
Burney, James (A), Log, PRO, Adm 51/4523/1-2
Burney, James (A), Journal, PRO, Adm 51/4523/3-4
Burney, James (A), Journal, NLA, MS 3244, Ferguson MS
Burr, John (R), Log, PRO, Adm 55/106
Clerke, Charles (R), Log, BL, Add MS8951-3, original
Clerke, Charles (R), Log, PRO, Adm 55/103, fair copy
Constable, Love (A), Journal, PRO, Adm 51/4520/7-8
Cook, James (R), Log, PRO, Add MS 27956
Cook, James (R), Log Book and Journal, BL, Add MS 27886, JCB's "text"
Cook, James (R), Journal, BL, Add MS 27888, JCB's "B"
Cook, James (R), Journal, PRO, Adm 55/108, JCB's "A", Admiralty MS
Cook, James (R), Journal, NMM, J.C.B's "G", Greenwich MS
Cook, James (R), Journal, P H Hudson, JCB's "H", Palliser Hudson MS
Cooper, Robert (R), Journal, PRO, Adm 55/104, 109
Dyke, Thomas (A), Log, PRO, Adm 51/4521/12
Elliott, John (R), Log, PRO, Adm 51/4556/208
Elliott, John (R), Memoirs, BL, Add MS 42714
Falconer, John (A), Log, PRO, Adm 51/4524/1-2
Furneaux, Tobias (A), Journal and Log, PRO, Adm 55/1
Furneaux, Tobias (A), Narrative, BL, Add MS 27890
Furneaux, Tobias (A), Holograph letters etc, ATL, Portion of Journal
Gilbert, Joseph (R), Log, PRO, Adm 55/107
Harvey, William (R), Journal, PRO, Adm 51/4553/184-7
Hawkey, William (A), Log, PRO, Adm 51/4521/11
Hergest, Richard (A), Journal, PRO, Adm 51/4522/13
Hood, Alexander (R), Journal, PRO, Adm 51/4554/181-3
Kempe, Arthur (A), Log, PRO, Adm 51/4520/1-3
Kempe, Arthur (A), Journal, PRO, Adm 51/4520/4-5
Lightfoot, Henry (A), Log, PRO, Adm 51/4523/5
Loggie, Charles (R), Journal, PRO, Adm 51/4554/207
Maxwell, James (R), Log, PRO, Adm 51/4555/2-6
Mitchel, Bowles (R), Log, PRO, Adm 51/4555/194-5
Pickersgill, Richard (R), Log, PRO, Adm 51/4553/205-6
Price, Joseph (R), Log, PRO, Adm 51/4556/190
Price, Joseph (R), Journal, PRO, Adm 51/4556/188-9
Smith, Isaac (R), Log, PRO, Adm 55/105
Wales, William (R), Journal, ML, MSS, Safe PH 18/4
Wales, William (R), Log-Book, RO, Brd of Longitude Papers Vol XLVI
Willis, Thomas (R), Log, PRO, Adm 51/4554/201-2
Willis, Thomas (R), Journal, PRO, Adm 51/4554/199-200
Anon., Logs, PRO, Adm 51/4555/218-9

HMS *Resolution* (R) (1776–1780) and HMS *Discovery* (D) (1776–1780)
Muster (D), PRO, Adm 36/8013
Muster (R), PRO, Adm 36/8048-9
Log books etc, PRO, Adm 51/4528-32; 4557-61
Log books etc, PRO, Adm 55/20-4; 110-24
Anderson, William (R), Journal, PRO, Adm 51/4560/203-4, (vol 3 is missing)
Anderson, William (R), Botanical compilation, NHM
Bayly, William (D), Log and Journal, PRO, Adm 55/20
Bayly, William (D), Log, ATL
Burney, James (D), Journal, PRO, Adm 51/4528/45
Burney, James (D), Journal, BL, Add MS 8955
Burney, James (D), Journal, ML, Safe 1/64, 79, Burney M
Charlton, William (R), Journal, PRO, Adm 51/4557/191-3

Clerke, Charles (D), Log and Proceedings, PRO, Adm 55/22
Clerke, Charles (R), Log and Observations, PRO, Adm 51/4561/217
Clerke, Charles (R), Log, PRO, Adm 55/124
Cook, James (R), Journal, BL, Egerton MS 2177A
Cook, James (R), Log, BL, Egerton MS 2177B, Fragment 7-17 January 1779
Cook, James (R), Journal or Log, PRO, Adm 55/111-2
Cook, James (R), Proceedings, PRO, Adm 55/113
Edgar, Thomas (D), Journal, BL, Add MS 37528
Edgar, Thomas (D), Log, PRO, Adm 55/21, 24
Gilbert, George (RD), Journal, PRO, Adm 51/4559/213-5
Gilbert, George (RD), Narrative, BL, Add MS 38530
Gilbert, George (RD), Narrative, DL
Gore, John (RDR), Log, PRO, Adm 55/120
Gore, John (DR), Log, PRO, Adm 51/4532/49
Griffin, William (R), Short narrative, DL, MS
Harvey, William (RDR), Log, Adm 55/110, 121
Home, Alexander (D), Account, NLA
King, James (RD), Log and Proceedings, PRO, Adm 55/116, 122
King, James (D), Running Journal, HO
King, James (RD), Log, DL, MS, King D
Lanyon, William (RD), Log, PRO, Adm 51/4558/196-8
Law, John (DR), Journal, BL, Add MS 37327
Martin, John (DR), Journal, PRO, Adm 51/4531/47
Paul, Mathew (R), Log, PRO, Adm 51/4560/209
Portlock, N. (DR), Log, PRO, Adm 51/4531/67-9
Portlock, N. (DR), Log, PRO, Adm 51/4532/70
Rickman, John (DR), Log, PRO, Adm 51/4529/46
Riou, Edward (DR), Log, PRO, Adm 51/4529/41-4, vol 4 missing
Roberts, Henry (R), Log, DL
Samwell, David (RD), Some account of a ..., BL, Egerton MS 2591
Shuttleworth, W. (R), Proceedings, PRO, Adm 51/4561/210-1
Shuttleworth, W. (D), Journal of Proceedings, PRO, Adm 51/4531/48
Taylor, William (R), Log, PRO, Adm 51/4561/216
Watts, John (R), Proceedings, PRO, Adm 51/4559/212
Williamson, John (R), Log and Proceedings, PRO, Adm 55/117
Anon., Logs, PRO, Adm 51/4561/64, 65-6, 71-2
Anon., Logs, PRO, Adm 51/4561/220, 221
Anon., Log, PRO, Adm 55/114, Possibly James Trevenen

Key to abbreviations used in table

Add MS	Additional manuscript
ADM	Admiralty
APL	Auckland Public Library, Auckland
ATL	Alexander Turnbull Library, Wellington
BL	British Library, Euston, London
DL	Dixson Library, State Library of New South Wales, Sydney
HO	Hydrographic Office, Taunton
JCB	J C Beaglehole, Cook's biographer
ML	Mitchell Library, State Library of New South Wales, Sydney
NHM	Natural History Museum, London
NLA	National Library of Australia, Canberra
NMM	National Maritime Museum, Greenwich
PRO	Public Records Office, London
RO	Royal Observatory, Greenwich

Appendix II: Libraries, Archives and Museums

LIBRARIES AND ARCHIVES

Australia

National Library of Australia, Canberra, ACT 2600, Australia. (http: //www.nla.gov.au/).

State Library of New South Wales, Macquarie Street, Sydney, NSW 2000, Australia. (http://www.sl.nsw.gov.au/).

New Zealand

Alexander Turnbull Library, National Library of New Zealand, PO Box 1467, Wellington 6001, New Zealand. (http://www.natlib.govt.nz/).

United Kingdom

The British Library, 96 Euston Road, London, NW1 2DB, UK. (http://www.bl.uk/).

The Caird Library, National Maritime Museum, Greenwich, London, SE10 9NF, UK. (http://www.nmm.ac.uk/).

The National Archives (formerly Public Record Office), Kew, Richmond, Surrey, TW9 4DU, UK. (http://www.nationalarchives.gov.uk/).

The Natural History Museum Library, Cromwell Road, London, SW7 5BD, UK. (http://www.nhm.ac.uk/library/).

United Kingdom Hydrographic Office Archive, Admiralty Way, Taunton, Somerset, TA1 2DN, UK. (http://www.hydro.gov.uk/).

MUSEUMS

The following is a list of museums holding significant collections of Cook material:

Museums devoted to Cook:

United Kingdom

The Captain Cook Schoolroom Museum, 10 High Street, Great Ayton, TS9 7HB, North Yorkshire, UK

The Captain Cook Birthplace Museum, Stewart Park, Marton, Middlesbrough, TS7 8AT, UK

The Captain Cook and Staithes Heritage Centre, High Street, Staithes, Saltburn-By-The-Sea, TS13 5BQ, UK. (http://www.staithes.co.uk/museum1.htm).

The Captain Cook Memorial Museum, Grape Lane, Whitby, YO22 4BA, North Yorkshire, UK. (http://www.cookmuseumwhitby.co.uk/).

Museums with significant Cook collections:

Australia

The James Cook Museum, crnr of Furneaux and Helen Streets, Cooktown, Queensland, Australia.

Austria

Cook collection, The Museum of Ethnology (Museum für Völkerkunde), A-1010 Wien - Neue Burg, Austria. (http://www.ethno-museum.ac.at/en/museum.html).

Germany

Cook/Forster collection, Institute of Ethnology, Goettingen University, Theaterplatz 15 – 37073 Göttingen, Germany. (http://wwwuser.gwdg.de/~ethno/sammle.htm).

Ireland

National Museum of Ireland – Archaeology & History, Kildare Street, Dublin 2, Republic of Ireland.

Italy
National Museum of Anthropology and Ethnology, Via del Proconsolo, 12 50122 Florence, Italy. (http://www.unifi.it/unifi/msn/main_eng.htm).

Russia
Cook collection from Cook's third voyage, Kunstkammer Museum, 3 University Emb., St Petersburg, Russia. (http://www.kunstkamera.ru/english/).

Sweden
Etnografiska museet (National Museum of Ethnography), Djurgårdsbrunnsvägen 34, Box 27140, 102 52, Stockholm, Sweden. (http://www.etnografiska.se/etnoweb/index.htm). (The Sparrman Collection).

Switzerland
Bern Historical Museum (Bernisches Historisches Museum), Helvetiaplatz 5, Bern, Switzerland. (http://www.bhm.ch/). (The Webber Collection).

United Kingdom
The British Museum, Great Russell Street, London, WC1B 3DG, UK. (http://www.thebritishmuseum.ac.uk/).
The Museum of Archaeology and Anthropology, University of Cambridge, Downing Street, Cambridge, CB2 3DZ, Cambridgeshire, UK. (http://museum.archanth.cam.ac.uk/).
The Cuming Museum, 155-157 Walworth Road, London, SE17 1RS, UK. (http://www.southwark.gov.uk/CultureHeritage/MuseumsAndArtGalleries/TheCumingMuseum/).
The Hunterian Museum & Art Gallery, University of Glasgow, Glasgow, G12 8QQ, UK. (http://www.hunterian.gla.ac.uk/).
The Natural History Museum, Cromwell Road, London, SW7 5BD, UK. (http://www.nhm.ac.uk/).
The National Maritime Museum, Park Row, Greenwich, London, SE10 9NF, UK. (http://www.nmm.ac.uk/).
The Pitt Rivers Museum, South Parks Road, Oxford, OX1 3PP, UK (http://www.prm.ox.ac.uk/).
The Herbarium, The Royal Botanic Gardens, Kew, Richmond, Surrey, TW9 3AB, UK. (http://griffin.rbgkew.org.uk/herbarium/).
The Whitby Museum, Pannett Park, Whitby, YO21 1RE, North Yorkshire, UK. (http://www.durain.demon.co.uk/).

United States
Bishop Museum, 1525 Bernice Street, Honolulu, HI 96817, USA. (http://www.bishopmuseum.org/).

Appendix III: Cook's Crews

This list includes all the men who sailed with Cook on his ships. Entries indicate which ship the men sailed on, their muster number (in brackets), and their rank. Punishments and any other irregularities are also given. Further information is included, if known, about place and date of birth, place and date of death, and whether wills have been located. Details which are uncertain are denoted by a question mark.

Abraham, Mahomet. 3rd (167) on *Resolution* as AB. (Joined Macao on December 1779). Born in Bengal, India in 1756.
Adams, Francis. 2nd (202) on *Resolution* as AB. (Joined Cape Town 1775). Born in Cork in 1737.
Aires, Christopher. 3rd (168) on *Resolution* as AB. (Joined Macao on December 1779). Born in Putney, south-west London in 1752.
Aitken, Aneas. 3rd (10) on *Discovery* as Boatswain. Died in 1806. FRC will (11/1452). He had been on HMS *Favourite*.
Allden, William. 2nd (M6) on *Adventure* as Marine Private. Died in 1780. FRC will (11/1068).
Allen, John. 3rd (M14) on *Resolution* as Marine Private. Died with Cook at Kealakekua Bay on 14 February 1779. Punished 3 times; on 10 January 1777 for drunkenness; on 12 September 1777 for theft; and on 28 September 1778 for theft. FRC will (11/1095).
Anderson, David. 2nd (111) on *Resolution* as Boatswain's mate. Born in Dalkeith, Scotland (south-east of Edinburgh) in 1748.
Anderson, Robert *see* Main listing.
Anderson, William. 2nd (134) on *Adventure* as AB. (Joined Cape Town March 1774).
Anderson, William *see* Main listing.
Andrews, Thomas. He sailed on the second voyage on the *Adventure* (32) as surgeon. He died in 1813 in Gillingham, Kent, leaving a will (FRC 11/1551).
Armstrong, Robert. 3rd (101) on *Discovery* as AB. (Joined Cape Town 12 November 1776). Born in 1738.
Arrowsmith, Noble. 2nd (61) on *Adventure* as AB. Born in London in 1749. Died in 1781? FRC will (11/1077).
Asget, John. AB on *Grenville* in 1766. Born in North Colden, Devon in 1742. Ran on 8 March 1767.
Atkin, Anthony. 2nd (140) on *Resolution* as Quartermaster. Born in Fife, Scotland in 1742.
Atkinson, William. 2nd (194) on *Resolution* as AB. Born in Westmoreland in 1742. Died in Kendal, Westmoreland in 1829? FRC will (11/1755)? Punished on 16 February 1773 for theft.

Baldy (Baldie), Richard. 2nd (M8) on *Resolution* as Marine Private. Punished on 8 May 1774 for neglect of duty. (Possibly born Falmer, Sussex in 1744).
Banks, Joseph *see* Main listing.
Baptista (Baptisto), John. 1st (116) on *Endeavour* as AB. (Joined Jakarta November 1770). Died in 1797. FRC will (11/1296).
Barber, George. 3rd (73) on *Resolution* as Carpenter's mate. Born in Dublin in 1743. Died in 1800? FRC will? (11/1346). Punished on 1 May 1777 for disobedience.
Barber, Robert. 2nd (23) on *Adventure* as Quartermaster to 31 December 1772; then AB. Born in Kilkenny, Ireland in 1749. Died in 1783. FRC will (11/1105).
Barrett, Edward. 2nd (152) on *Resolution* as Cook's mate; 3rd (13) on *Discovery* as AB. Born in London in 1756. Died 1796 or 1801? FRC will? (11/1284 or 11/1361?).
Barrow, Richard. AB on *Grenville* in 1765. Born in Ross, Hereford in 1748. Discharged on 17 February 1766 at Deptford.
Bates, William. 3rd (75) on *Discovery* as AB. Born in Yorkshire in 1758.
Bayly, William *see* Main listing.
Bazil, Antony. 2nd (28) on *Adventure* as AB. Born in 1750.
Beach, Mathew. 3rd (47) on *Resolution* as AB. Born in London in 1757. Punished on 31 August 1779 for insolence.
Bean (Baines), Thomas. 3rd (36) on *Discovery* as AB. Born in Deptford in 1753. Died in 1775? FRC will? (11/1015).
Beard, Robert. 2nd (M4) on *Resolution* as Marine Corporal. Died on HMS *Thunderer* in West Indies in 1780. FRC will (11/1080). Sergeant of Marines on *Thunderer*.
Bee, William. 2nd (72) on *Resolution* as Quartermaster's mate. Born in Barton, North Yorkshire (near Croft) in 1747. Died in Deptford in 1799. FRC will (11/1326).
Bell, Michael. 2nd (39) on *Adventure* as AB. Born in Deptford in 1751. Died at

Wharehunga Bay (Grass Cove) on 17 December 1773.

Bennett, Peter. 3rd (42) on *Resolution* as AB to 14 January 1780; then Quartermaster. Born in Plymouth in 1755.

Bentham, Gregory. 3rd (8) on *Discovery* as Clerk.

Bevan (Bevans), William. 2nd (118) on *Resolution* as Carpenter's crew. Born in Glamorgan in 1747. Died in 1781 or 1783? FRC will? (11/1087 or 11/1107).

Biddon, James. AB on *Grenville* in 1763. (Surveying assistant).

Billings, Joseph *see* Main listing.

Bishop, Samuel. 3rd (126) on *Resolution* as AB. Born in Bristol in 1756. Died in 1802? FRC will (11/1386). Punished on 21 January 1778 for neglect of duty.

Blackburn, John. 2nd (63) on *Resolution* as AB. Born in London in 1746.

Bligh, William *see* Main listing.

Bloom, William. 3rd (55) on *Discovery* as AB. Born in Hampton in 1756. Fell overboard and rescued in Bashi Channel on 24 November 1779.

Bode, Johan. 1st (135) on *Endeavour* as AB. (Joined Cape Town March 1771).

Bootie, John. He sailed on the *Endeavour* as a midshipman (32). He died in the Indian Ocean on 4 February 1771. He kept a journal and a log. A section of his journal is reproduced in the *Historical records of New South Wales, vol 1, part 1: Cook 1762-1780.* Bootie islet off the north Queensland coast is named for him.

Bordall, Samuel. 2nd (141) on *Resolution* as Quartermaster. Born in Topsham, Devon (south of Exeter) in 1751.

Bostock, John. 3rd (145) on *Resolution* as AB. Born in 1751.

Bowles, Daniel. 3rd (100) on *Discovery* as Quartermaster. Deserted at Cape Town 27 November 1776.

Bowles, John. 1st (M13) on *Endeavour* as Marine Private. Punished on 7 April 1770 for disobedience.

Boyd, John. 3rd (38) on *Resolution* as AB. Born in Greenwich in 1758. Punished twice; on 8 June 1778 for theft; and on 27 August 1778 for neglect of duty.

Bradley, William. 3rd (66) on *Resolution* as Gunner's mate. Born in Deptford in 1751. Died 1784 or 1802. FRC will? (11/1126 or 11/1385). Punished 3 times; on 26 November 1776 for being absent without leave; on 2 November 1777 for insolence; and on 25 January 1779 for sexual relations with a native.

Bremer, Michael. 1st (M6) on *Endeavour* as Marine Private.

Brewer, John. 1st (117) on *Endeavour* as AB. (Joined Jakarta November 1770).

Briscoe, Peter. 1st (S10) on *Endeavour* as Banks' servant. Born in Revesby Abbey, Lincolnshire.

Briscoe, William. 2nd (119) on *Resolution* as Ship's tailor. Born in Scarborough in 1751. Punished on 16 February 1773 for theft.

Broom, William. 3rd (M13) on *Discovery* as Marine Private.

Brotherson, Philip. 2nd (M5) on *Resolution* as Marine Drummer. Punished on 16 February 1773 for theft.

Brown, John. 3rd (77) on *Resolution* as AB to 31 December 1776; then Quartermaster. Born in St Ives, Huntingdon in 1738. Punished on 23 June 1777 for hitting a native.

Brown, Matthew. 2nd (164) on *Resolution* as Armourer. Born in York in 1746.

Brown, Michael. AB on *Grenville* in 1766. Born in Dublin in 1738. Ran on 31 October 1766 at St John's.

Brown, Richard. 3rd (M8) on *Resolution* as Marine Private.

Brown, Robert. 2nd (98) on *Adventure* as AB (Kept journal).

Brown, William. 3rd (M9) on *Discovery* as Marine Private. Deserted at Cape Town 26 November 1776.

Brown, William. 3rd (7) on *Resolution* as Gunner's mate. Born in Stromness, Orkney, in 1752.

Buchan, Alexander *see* Main listing.

Burn, William. 1st (125) on *Endeavour* as AB. (Joined Jakarta November 1770).

Burney, James *see* Main listing.

Burr, John Davall. He sailed on the second voyage on the *Resolution* as a master's mate (68). He kept a log. He became a lieutenant in August 1775, joining Cooper on HMS *Hawke.* He was in charge of HMS *Milford,* 28 guns, in 1777. Burr was born in London in 1745 and died in 1784.

Butcher, Thomas. 3rd (72) on *Resolution* as AB. Born in Coleshall, Kent (north of Sittingbourne) in 1751.

Butler, William. 3rd (99) on *Resolution* as AB. Born in Deptford in 1757. Punished on 11 June 1777 for losing part of a french horn.

Buttall (Buttal), John. 2nd (M18) on *Resolution* as Marine Private. Died in 1799? FRC will (11/1335). Punished twice; on 16 February 1773 for theft; and on 30 August 1773 for rioting.

Campbell, James. 1st (128) on *Endeavour* as AB. (Joined Jakarta November 1770).

Cant, Jacobus. 1st (137) on *Endeavour* as AB. (Joined Cape Town March 1771).

Carley (Carly), Isaac. 3rd (M18) on *Resolution* as Marine Private. Died in 1786? FRC will (11/1143). Punished on 2 November 1777 for neglect of duty.

Carlo (Carlow), Thomas. 2nd (75) on *Adventure* as AB. Born in London in 1740. Died in 1789? FRC will (11/1183).

Carpenter, Richard. 2nd (M10) on *Resolution* as Marine Private.

Carr, William. 2nd (119) on *Adventure* as Master-at-arms.

Cater, Thomas. 3rd (144) on *Resolution* as AB. Born in Chatham in 1750.

Cavanagh, John. 2nd (90) on *Adventure* as AB. Born in Kilkenny, Ireland in 1742. Died at Wharehunga Bay (Grass Cove) on 17 December 1773.

Cave, John. 2nd (38) on *Resolution* as Quartermaster's mate; 3rd (16) on *Resolution* as AB. Born in Durham in 1747. Deserted at Macao on 13 January 1780. Died 1784? FRC will (11/1113).

Cawn, Edward. 3rd (41) on *Resolution* as AB. Born in Greenwich in 1757. Punished on 3 January 1777 for leaving bed on deck.

Chapman, William. 2nd (11) on *Resolution* as AB; from 23 July 1773 Cook on the *Adventure.* Born in Gravesend, Kent in 1733. Died in 1800? FRC will (11/1350).

Charlton (Charleton), John. Master's servant on *Grenville* in 1765, 1766, 1767. Born in London in 1753. 1st (104) on *Endeavour* as Captain's servant. Died in 1783. FRC will (11/1109).

Charlton, William *see* Main listing.

Childs, Joseph. 1st (70) on *Endeavour* as AB From 1 February 1771 Cook. Born in Dublin in 1739.

Clark, Daniel. 2nd (133) on *Resolution* as Master-at-arms. Born in Essex in 1740. Died in 1782. FRC will (11/1091).

Clay, Job. 3rd (107) on *Resolution* as AB. Born in Bow, East London, in 1735. Punished 3 times; on 16 July 1777 for neglect of duty; on 7 February for neglect of duty; and on 1 June 1779 for insolence.

Clerke, Charles *see* Main listing.

Cleveley, James. 3rd (4) on *Resolution* as Carpenter (He made drawings, later developed into paintings by his brother John). Died in 1821. FRC will (11/1644). (There is a short biography for his brother John Cleveley in the *DNB*, v4, p504).

Coal, William. AB on *Grenville* in 1767. Born in London in 1749.

Coghlan (Coglan, Coughlan), John. He sailed on the second voyage on *Resolution* as AB (179). He was punished twice; he was sent before the mast on 1 February 1773 for quarrelling; and on 18 March 1775 for threatening violence to the cook. Coghlan was born in Glamorgan in 1757. He never became a lieutenant so probably left the Navy.

Coleman, James. 3rd (40) on *Discovery* as Quartermaster. Born in Dorking, Surrey in 1751.

Collett, Joseph *see* Main listing.

Collett, Richard *see* Main listing.

Collett, William *see* Main listing.

Colnett, James *see* Main listing.

Command, James. AB on *Grenville* in 1766. Born in Cork in 1715. Discharged on 5 January 1767.

Commena, —. 2nd (M7) on *Resolution* as Marine Private.

Connelly, John. 3rd (137) on *Resolution* as AB to 20 September 1780; then Quartermaster. Born in Kerry, Ireland in 1754. Died in 1807? FRC will (11/1457).

Constable, Love. He sailed on the second voyage on the *Adventure* as an AB (12) until 17 December 1773 when he became a midshipman. He kept a journal. He was made a lieutenant in March 1781 and a commander in October 1793. He was married to Elizabeth and died in 1794, leaving a will (FRC 11/1254).

Cook, James *see* Encyclopaedia.

Cook, Peter. AB on *Grenville* in 1764. Volunteer at St John's. Born in Kilmair, Ireland in 1744. Discharged 16 April 1765 at Deptford.

Cooper, Peter. 1st (136) on *Endeavour* as AB. (Joined Cape Town March 1771).

Cooper, Robert Palliser *see* Main listing.

Corbett, Richard. 2nd (175) on *Resolution* as AB – Barber. Born in Limehouse, East London, in 1746. Died in Deptford in 1795? FRC will (11/1259).

Cox, Joseph. 3rd (74) on *Discovery* as Quartermaster. Born in Sunderland in 1740. Died 1784? FRC will?

Cox, Matthew. 1st (66) on *Endeavour* as AB. Born in Gillingham, Dorset in 1746. Punished twice; on 30 November 1769 for theft; and on 1 December 1769 for disputing previous sentence. Started court action against Cook for that punishment but did not pursue action.

Cravan, James. 2nd (93) on *Adventure* as AB. Born in Dublin in 1750.

Crispin, William. 2nd (116) on *Adventure* as Carpenter's mate.

Cronean (Croneen), John. 2nd (118) on *Adventure* as AB. Born in Limerick, Ireland in 1749. Died in 1783? FRC will (11/1105).

Crotch, William. 3rd (146) on *Resolution* as AB. (Joined Cape Town October 1776). Died 1807? in Needham, Suffolk? FRC will (11/1460). Punished on 8 June 1778 for theft.

Cunningham, John. AB on *Grenville* in 1765, 1766. Born in Dublin in 1739. Discharged 27 March 1767.

Dailey, Mathew. 3rd (147) on *Resolution* as AB. (Joined Cape Town November 1776). Punished on 27 August 1778 for theft.

Davies, Robert. 3rd (104) on *Resolution* as Surgeon's mate. He qualified as surgeon's mate on 7 March 1776. Born in Mold, North Wales, in August 1752.

Davis, John. 3rd (85) on *Resolution* as Quartermaster. Born in Halifax, Canada in 1755. Died at sea off Scotland on 20 September 1780. Punished on 3 April 1779 for neglect of duty.

Dawson, Edward. 2nd (93) on *Resolution* as Carpenter's mate. Born in Scotland in 1742.

Dawson, William. 1st (12) on *Endeavour* as AB; 2nd (25) on *Resolution* as Clerk. Born in Deptford in 1749. Petitioned Joseph Banks on 2 July 1788.

Day, James. 2nd (96) on *Resolution* as AB. Born in Scotland in 1745. Died in 1777. FRC will (11/1032).

De Beecker, Jan Arno. 3rd (59) on *Resolution* as AB. Born in Bremen, North Germany, in 1750.

Dermot, James. 3rd (130) on *Resolution* as AB. Punished 3 times; on 12 September 1777 for theft; on 24 April 1778 for theft; and on 25 January for being absent without leave.

Dewar, Alexander. 2nd (30) on *Adventure* as Clerk; 3rd (20) on *Resolution* as Clerk. Born in Dunbar, south-east Scotland, in 1748. Died in 1792. FRC will (11/1218).

Dixon, George *see* Main listing.

Dorlton, George. 1st (S12) on *Endeavour* as Banks' servant. Died 16 January 1769.

Doughty, Simon. AB on *Grenville* in 1767. Born in Wilton, Wiltshire (west of Salisbury) in 1739.

Doyle, William. 3rd (138) on *Resolution* as Boatswain's mate. Born in Waterford, Ireland in 1756. Died 1823? FRC will? Punished twice; on 10 September 1777 for neglect of duty; and on 29 September 1777 for hitting a native.

Dozey, John. 1st (83) on *Endeavour* as AB. Born in Brazil in 1748. Died 7 April 1771 at Cape Town.

Drawwater, Benjamin. 2nd (89) on *Resolution* as Surgeon's mate. Born in 1748. He died in 1815 and is buried in Greasley, near Eastwood, Nottinghamshire. FRC will (11/1581).

Drew, William. 2nd (163) on *Resolution* as Armourer's mate. Born in London in 1751.

Driver, Thomas. 2nd (98) on *Resolution* as AB. Born in Orkney in 1741.

Dunn, John. AB on *Grenville* in 1766. Born in Falmouth in 1736. Discharged on 9 March 1767.

Dunster (Dunister), Thomas. 1st (M11) on *Endeavour* as Marine Private. Died in the Indian Ocean on 25 January 1771. FRC will (11/971). Punished on 16 September 1768 for disobedience.

Dyer, William. AB on *Grenville* in1766. Born in Devon in 1741. Ran on 3 March 1767.

Dyke, Thomas. He joined from HMS *Torbay* and sailed on the second voyage on the *Adventure* (112) as a master's mate until 30 November 1773. He then became an AB He kept a log. He never became a lieutenant so probably left the Navy.

Edes, Abraham. 2nd (200) on *Resolution* as AB. Born in Warwickshire in 1752.

Edgar, Thomas *see* Main listing.

Edgcumbe, John. He sailed on the on *Endeavour* (M1) as sergeant of Marines and on the second voyage on the *Resolution* (M1) as Marine second lieutenant.

Elliott, John *see* Main listing.

Ellis, William *see* Main listing.

Ellwell (Elwell), John. 2nd (156) on *Resolution* as Quartermaster. Born in London in 1727. Died in 1784? FRC will (11/1114).

Elmes, James. 2nd (203) on *Resolution* as AB. (Joined Cape Town 1775). Born Suffolk in 1753. Died in 1800 in Rotherhithe. FRC will (11/1349).

England, John. 3rd (61) on *Discovery* as AB. Born in Lincolnshire in 1758. Died in 1787. FRC will (11/1159).

English, George. AB on *Grenville* in 1767. Born in Limerick, Ireland in 1733.

Evans, Evan. 3rd (39) on *Resolution* as AB. Born in London in 1758. Died in 1780. FRC will (11/1071). Punished on 21 October 1776 for being absent without leave.

Evans, Samuel. 1st (95) on *Endeavour* as Quartermaster. From 5 February 1771 Boatswain. Died in 1800 in Bristol?

Evans, William. 3rd (78) on *Discovery* as Carpenter's crew. Born in Worcester in 1749.

Ewin, William. 2rd (29) on *Resolution* as Boatswain's mate; 3rd (2) on *Resolution* as Boatswain. Born in Pennsylvania in 1744.

Facey, William. 2nd (113) on *Adventure* as AB. Born in Lancaster in 1747. Died 17 December 1773.

Fagan, John. 2nd (94) on *Adventure* as AB. Born in Woolwich in 1752.

Falconer, John Richard. He sailed the second voyage on the *Adventure* (55) as an AB until 31 March 1773. He then became a master's mate. Falconer kept a log. He joined the voyage from HMS *Somerset*. He became a lieutenant in November 1779. He died in 1784?

Fannin, Peter *see* Main listing.

Fatchett, Thomas. 3rd (M15) on *Resolution* as Marine Private. Died with Cook at Kealakekua Bay on 14 February 1779. FRC will (11/1075).

Fenton, Thomas. 2nd (153) on *Resolution* as AB. Born in London in 1754.

Fick, Closs. 1st (131) on *Endeavour* as AB. (Joined Cape Town March 1771).

Finley, John. 2nd (104) on *Adventure* as AB to 17 December 1773; then Quartermaster. Born in Fife, Scotland in 1746.

Fish, John. 2nd (69) on *Adventure* as AB. Born in Epping, Essex in 1750. Died 1785?

Fisher, John. 3rd (14) on *Resolution* as AB. Born in Findon, West Sussex (north of Worthing) in 1756. Died in London in 1816? FRC will (11/1578). Punished on 14 September 1779 for drunkenness.

Fitzgerald, Thomas. 2nd (73) on *Adventure* as AB. Born in Ireland in 1752.

Flatman, John. 3rd (118) on *Resolution* as AB. Born in London in 1756.

Flood, James. 3rd (83) on *Discovery* as AB. Born in Honiton, Devon in 1753. Injured at sea in South Atlantic on 4 June 1780.

Flower, Peter *see* Main listing.

Forester, Henry. He sailed on the third voyage on the *Discovery* as AB (90) until 25 August 1779. He then became a midshipman. He was born in London in 1757. He never became a lieutenant so probably left the Navy.

Forster, Johann Georg. 2nd (S38) on *Resolution* as Naturalist (kept journal and drew landscapes and natural history specimens). Born in Hochzeit, West Prussia on 26 November 1754. Died in Paris on 10 January 1794. *DNB* v7, p455.

Forster, Johann Reinhold. 2nd (S37) on *Resolution* as Naturalist. Born Dirschau,

West Prussia in 1729. Died in Halle on 9 December 1798.
Forwood, Stephen. 1st (62) on *Endeavour* as Gunner (Kept Journal).
Frazer, John. 2nd (180) on *Resolution* as Ship's corporal. He petitioned the Earl of Sandwich after the voyage. Sandwich consulted Cook who recommended him for a master-at-arms position. He had experience as a soldier with the East India Company. Born in London in 1731. Died in 1798? FRC will (11/1319).
Freeman, Thomas. 2nd (11) on *Adventure* as AB. Born in Plymouth in 1750.
Freezland (Freeland), Samuel. 2nd (138) on *Resolution* as AB. Born in Holland in 1749. Died in 1811? FRC will (11/1528). Rock in South Shetlands named after him.
Furneaux, Tobias *see* Main listing.

Gameson, James. 2nd (77) on *Adventure* as Armourer.
Gardner (Gardiner), James. 2nd (129) on *Adventure* as AB. (Joined Cape Town March 1774). Died 1779 in London? FRC will (11/1061).
Garratty, T. 3rd on *Resolution*. Not on muster roll but listed as Marine who was punished twice; on 5 May 1777 for neglect of duty; and on 6 July 1777 for neglect of duty. (Possibly a confusion with the name Girley).
Garrett, Abraham. 2nd (131) on *Adventure* as AB. (Joined Cape Town March 1774).
Gatenby, John. 3rd (91) on *Discovery* as AB
Gathman (Gahtman), Francis sailed on the *Grenville* in 1764 as an AB He returned to Newfoundland with Cook as a midshipman on the *Grenville* in 1765 and 1766. Gathman was discharged on 23 February 1767 and joined HMS *Scarborough*. He was born in Salem, Massachusetts in 1744, the son of Samuel Gahtman, a seafarer. The surname underwent a change. Francis probably joined the American navy at or after the War of Independence.
Gathrey, John. 1st (47) on *Endeavour* as Boatswain. Died in the Indian Ocean on 4 February 1771.
Gerring, Thomas. Master's servant on *Grenville* in 1764. Discharged 27 March 1765.
Gibbs, James. 2nd (27) on *Adventure* as Boatswain's mate. Born in Perth, Scotland in 1743. Died in 1828? FRC will (11/1739).
Gibson, Samuel *see* Main listing.
Gilbert, George *see* Main listing *under* Gilberts.
Gilbert, Joseph *see* Main listing *under* Gilberts.
Gilbert, Richard. 2nd (196) on *Resolution* as AB. (Joined Cape Town on 27 November 1772, discharged Cape Town on 30 April 1775). Born Boston, Lincolnshire. Lieutenant 1790 (?).Died in 1798? FRC will (11/1317). *See also* Main listing *under* Gilberts.
Gilliard, William. AB on *Grenville* in 1766, 1767. Born in Queensferry, Scotland in 1713. Discharged into sick quarters on 12 January 1767.
Gilpin, George. 2nd (S12) on *Resolution* as Servant. Died 1810. Clerk of the Royal Society from 1785 until 1809. Secretary of the Board of Longitude from 1801 until 1809. Made studies of magnetic dip and variation.
Girley (Garratty?), Thomas. 3rd (M10) on *Resolution* as Marine Private.
Gloag, Andrew. 2nd (24) on *Adventure* as Gunner.
Goldsmith, Thomas. 1st (108) on *Endeavour* as AB. (Joined Jakarta November 1770).
Goodjohn, John. 1st (88) on *Endeavour* as AB. Petitioned Joseph Banks on 7 December 1791.
Goodman, Thomas. 3rd (47) on *Discovery* as AB. Born in London in 1755.
Gore, John *see* Main listing.
Goulding, Robert. 2nd (32) on *Resolution* as Carpenter's crew; 3rd (12) on *Discovery* as Cook. Born in Birmingham in 1748.
Goulston, William. 3rd (86) on *Discovery* as AB. Born in Southwark in 1753.
Grant, John. 3rd (134) on *Resolution* as AB to 23 August 1779; then Quartermaster. Born in Waterford in 1749.
Gray, James. 1st (53) on *Endeavour* as AB From 5 February 1771 Quartermaster; 2nd (81) on *Resolution* as Boatswain. Born in Leith in 1744.
Green, Charles *see* Main listing.
Green, George. AB on *Grenville* in 1765. Born in Ipswich in 1733. Discharged on 22 December 1765 at Deptford.
Greenslade, William. 1st (M9) on *Endeavour* as Marine Private. Drowned (suicide) 26 March 1769 after stealing a colleague's seal skin .
Griffin, William. 3rd (27) on *Resolution* as Ship's corporal (Kept a short narrative). Born in London in 1755. Died in 1839 in Watford.
Griffiths, James. AB on *Grenville* in 1764, 1765, 1766. Born in Carmarthen, West Wales in 1730. Discharged into sick quarters on 16 March 1767. A James Griffiths joined the *Endeavour* as Clerk on 27 May 1768 but was discharged as unsuitable on 29 June 1768.
Griffiths, T. 3rd on *Resolution*. Not on muster roll but listed as being punished on 19 June 1777 for neglect of duty. Probably meant to be Griffin above.
Grimshaw, William. AB on *Grenville* in 1767. Born in Liverpool in 1745.
Grindall (Grindle), Richard *see* Main listing.

Haite, Francis. 1st (14) on *Endeavour* as AB and carpenter's crew. Born in Rochester, Kent in 1726. Died in the Indian Ocean on 30 January 1771. Had sailed to Pacific with Byron on *Dolphin*.
Haley, John. 2nd (42) on *Adventure* as Boatswain's mate. Born in Cork in 1745.
Hamilton, John. 2nd (M21) on *Resolution* as Marine Sergeant.
Hanson, Turkel. 1st (129) on *Endeavour* as AB. (Joined Cape Town March 1771).
Harding, James. 3rd (91) on *Resolution* as Quartermaster to 23 August 1779; then AB. Born in London in 1735. Died in 1805. FRC will (11/1431).
Hardman, Thomas. AB on *Grenville* in 1767. 1st (10) on *Endeavour* as Boatswain's mate to 25 March 1769; AB to 1 February 1771; then Sailmaker. Born in Shadwell, East London in 1734. Died in 1786? FRC will (11/1142).
Harford, Thomas. 3rd (M19) on *Resolution* as Marine Private. Punished 4 times; on 1 December 1776 for selling necessaries; on 14 July 1777 for disobedience; on 17 July 1777 for neglect of duty; and on 6 April 1778 for neglect of duty.
Harper, John. 2nd (M12) on *Resolution* as Marine Private.
Harrison, George. 3rd (M2) on *Discovery* as Marine Corporal. Drowned in South Atlantic on 23 September 1776.
Harrison, John. 2nd (192) on *Resolution* as AB. Born in North Shields, Northumberland in 1751.
Harrison, John. 3rd (M6) on *Resolution* as Marine Private. Punished twice; on 30 October 1777 for neglect of duty; and on 16 November 1777 after having attempted to desert on Raiatea.
Harrison, Robert. 2nd (103) on *Adventure* as AB. Born in Prestonpans, Scotland (east of Edinburgh) in 1748.
Hart, Edward. 2nd (17) on *Adventure* as AB. Born in 1754. Died in 1784 in Wapping? FRC will (11/1118).
Hart Thomas. AB on *Grenville* in 1765. Born in Mais Island, Essex in 1745. Ran on 23 February 1766 at Deptford.
Harvey, William *see* Main listing.
Hatley, John *see* Main listing.
Hawkey, William. He sailed on the second voyage on the *Adventure* (33) as a master's mate until 31 December 1773. He then became an AB He kept a log. Hawkey became a lieutenant in September 1775. He died in 1778?
Hayes, James. 2nd (178) on *Resolution* as AB. Born in Bridgwater, Somerset in 1747.
Heideman, William. 3rd (33) on *Resolution* as AB. Born in London in 1758.
Hendrick, John. 2nd (204) on *Resolution* as AB. (Joined Cape Town 1775). Born in Hanover, Germany in 1747.
Herbet, Ruben. AB on *Grenville* in 1765. Joined 1 October at St Lawrence. Born in Maison, Somerset in 1748. Discharged on 27 March 1766 at Deptford.
Hergest, Richard *see* Main listing.
Herold (Harrod), William. 3rd (65) on *Resolution* as AB. Born Westminster in 1733. Died in 1781. FRC will (11/1086). Discharged Cape Town November 1776. Punished on 5 August 1776 for neglect of duty.
Herriott, John. 3rd (M8) on *Discovery* as Marine Private.
Hetherton, Augustin. 3rd (129) on *Resolution*

as AB. Born in Kingston, Surrey in 1755.
Hicks, Zachary *see* Main listing.
Hill, Andrew. 2nd (64) on *Adventure* as Sailmaker.
Hill, Richard. 1st (120) on *Endeavour* as Master's servant. (Joined Jakarta November 1770).
Hill, Thomas. 2nd (49) on *Adventure* as AB. Born in Portsmouth in 1745. Died at Wharehunga Bay (Grass Cove) on 17 December 1773.
Hillsey (Hilsey), William. 3rd (98) on *Discovery* as Sailmaker. Born in Portsmouth in 1747. Died in 1784? FRC will (11/1122).
Hinks, Theophilus. 3rd (M7) on *Resolution* as Marine Private. Died with Cook at Kealakekua Bay on 14 February 1779. Punished on 24 November 1777 for neglect of duty.
Hodges, William *see* Main listing.
Hogg, Alexander. 3rd (10) on *Resolution* as AB. Born in Polwarth, south-east Scotland (near Duns) in 1755.
Hollamby (Hollanby), William *see* Main listing.
Holloway, Jeremiah. 3rd (M12) on *Discovery* as Marine Drummer. Tried to desert in Petropavlovsk. Died in 1811? FRC will (11/1521).
Home, Alexander *see* Main listing.
Hood, Alexander *see* Main listing.
Horn, Andrew. 2nd (54) on *Resolution* as AB. Born in Kildare, Ireland in 1751.
Howson, William. Supposedly on *Grenville* in Newfoundland; 1st (2) on *Endeavour* as Captain's servant. Born in London in 1752. Died in St Mary Newington, Surrey in 1819? FRC will (11/1623).
Hughes, Richard. 1st (36) on *Endeavour* as AB and Carpenter's mate. Born in London in 1746. Died in Deptford in 1785? FRC will (11/1127).
Hunt, William. 3rd (81) on *Resolution* as Armourer. Punished on 22 October 1776, discharged and sent home from Cape Town for 'coining bad money'.
Hutchins, Richard. 1st (67) on *Endeavour* as AB to 1 September 1769; then Boatswain's mate to 5 February 1771; then Boatswain. Born in Deptford in 1741. Died in Portsmouth in 1785? FRC will (11/1132). Punished on 16 April 1769 for disobedience.
Hutchinson, Alexander. 2nd (128) on *Adventure* as AB. (Joined Cape Town March 1774).
Hutchison, Isaac. AB on *Grenville* in 1767. Born in London in 1745.

Innell, John. 2nd (71) on *Resolution* as AB. Born in London in 1754. Punished twice; on 22 February 1774 for drunkennness; and on 6 April 1774 for insolence.
Irvin (Ervin), Richard. 3rd (58) on *Resolution* as Carpenter's crew. Born in Deptford in 1755. Punished on 21 October 1776 for being absent without leave.

Jackson, George. 2nd (122) on *Resolution* as Carpenter's mate. Born in London in 1751.
Jackson, John. 3rd (M12) on *Resolution* as Marine Private. Wounded at Kealakekua Bay on 14 February 1779. Punished on 23 December 1776 for fighting.
James, James. 3rd (101) on *Resolution* as Boatswain's mate. Born in Wales in 1751. Punished on 1 May 1777 for neglect of duty.
James, John. 3rd (M5) on *Resolution* as Marine Private.
Jeffs, Henry. 1st (46) on *Endeavour* as AB and ship's Butcher. Died in the Indian Ocean on 27 February 1771. FRC will (11/969). Punished on 29 April 1769 for aggression.
Johns, Edward. 2nd (15) on *Adventure* as Boatswain.
Johnson, Isaac. 1st (43) on *Endeavour* as AB. Born in Knutsford, Cheshire in 1742.
Jones, James. 2nd (108) on *Adventure* as AB. Born in Gosport, Hampshire in 1747. Died 17 December 1773.
Jones, Samuel. 1st (18) on *Endeavour* as AB. Born in London in 1746. Punished twice; on 12 April 1769 for disobedience; and on 13 November 1769 for disobedience. Petitioned Joseph Banks on 26 January 1786.
Jones (Johns), Thomas. 1st (73) on *Endeavour* as Surgeon's servant. His widow, Elizabeth, petitioned Joseph Banks in June 1791.
Jones, Thomas. 1st (77) on *Endeavour* as AB. Born in Bangor, North Wales in 1741.
Jordan, Benjamin. 1st (15) on *Endeavour* as AB. Born in Deptford in 1738. Died in the Indian Ocean on 31 January 1771.
Jordan (Jorden), Thomas. 1st (48) on *Endeavour* as Boatswain's servant to 5 February 1771; then AB Deserted in Thames on 12 September 1771. Died in 1805? FRC will (11/1427).
Joyce, James. 1st (107) on *Endeavour* as AB. (Joined Jakarta November 1770).
Judge, William. 1st (M4) on *Endeavour* as Marine Private. Punished on 30 November 1768 for insolence.

Kearney, William. 2nd (M8) on *Adventure* as Marine Private.
Kempe, Arthur *see* Main listing.
Kempe (Kempes), Samuel *see* Main listing.
Kent, John. 2nd (80) on *Adventure* as Surgeon's mate.
Keplin, J. 2nd on *Resolution*. Not on muster roll but listed as being punished twice; on 20 July 1773 for 'putting old tobacco into ship's meal'; and on 6 November 1774 for disobedience.
Kerwin, Christopher. 3rd (M4) on *Discovery* as Marine Private.
Kich, James. 3rd (M1) on *Discovery* as Marine Sergeant. Fell overboard and rescued off Kaua'i on 27 January 1778.
King, James *see* Main listing.
King, James. 3rd (57) on *Resolution* as AB. Born in Deptford in 1755. Punished twice; on 21 October 1776 for going absent without leave; and on 11 June 1777 for drunkenness.
Knight, Thomas. 1st (75) on *Endeavour* as AB

Lamb, William. AB on *Grenville* in 1765, 1766. Born in Great Ayton, North Yorkshire in 1750. Discharged on 31 March 1767.
Lambrecht, John. He sailed on the second voyage on *Adventure* as AB (51). He was born in 1754 and died at sea in the Atlantic on 24 August 1772 from sunstroke.
Lane, John. 2nd (M3) on *Adventure* as Marine Drummer. Died 1780? FRC will?
Lane, Michael *see* Main listing.
Langford, John. 2nd (45) on *Adventure* as AB. Born in Shepton Mallet, Somerset in 1752.
Lanyon, William *see* Main listing.
Law, John *see* Main listing.
Lear, David. 2nd (M4) on *Adventure* as Marine Private.
Ledyard, John *see* Main listing.
Lee, Richard. 2nd on *Resolution* – not on muster roll but listed as seaman being punished 3 times; on 11 September 1772 for insolence; on 22 November 1773 for theft; on 22 February 1774 for drunkenness. 3rd (28) on *Resolution* as AB. Born in London in 1752. Punished on 29 August 1778 for drunkenness.
Legg, John. 1st (121) on *Endeavour* as AB. (Joined Jakarta November 1770). Died 1809? FRC will?
Lett, John. 3rd (S2) on *Discovery* as Bayly's servant.
Leverick, J. 2nd on *Resolution*. Not on muster roll but listed as seaman being punished on 22 February 1774 for drunkenness.
Lewis, David. 2nd (107) on *Adventure* as Carpenter's crew. Born in North Wales in 1747. FRC will.
Lightfoot, Henry. He sailed on the second voyage on the *Adventure* as a midshipman (47). He kept a log. Lighfoot became a lieutenant in November 1782. He died on 24 December 1790?
Lind, Alexander. Midshipman on *Grenville* in 1767. Born in Aberdeen in 1727 or 1753?
Lindsay, Alexander. 1st (109) on *Endeavour* as AB. (Joined Jakarta November 1770). Died in the Indian Ocean on 14 February 1771. FRC will.
Littleboy, Michael *see* Main listing.
Littleboy, Richard *see* Main listing.
Lock, Thomas. AB on *Grenville* in 1765. Born in London in 1748. Discharged on 8 March 1766 at Deptford.
Lockton, John. 2nd (190) on *Resolution* as Quartermaster. Born in Bristol in 1729.
Loggie, Charles. He sailed on the second voyage on the *Resolution* as an AB (102). He kept a journal. Loggie was sent before the mast on 6 January 1773 for arguing and disrated on 2 January 1774 for assaulting James Maxwell. He was also punished on 18 March 1775 for threatening violence. Loggie became a lieutenant in March 1776. He was born in Plymouth in 1755 and was killed in duel in 1782.
Lohman (Lowman), Barthold (Bartholomew). 3rd (37) on *Discovery* as AB to 23 August 1779; then quartermaster. He became lost on Christmas Island, 29 December 1779.

Born in Hessen-Kassel, Germany in 1749. He returned to Germany where he was a baker until his death in April 1812.

Lorrain, John. 1st (113) on *Endeavour* as AB. (Joined Jakarta November 1770). Died 4 April 1771 at Cape Town.

Low, Fulke. 3rd (72) on *Discovery* as AB. Born in Webbery, Devon (east of Bideford) in 1753.

Loye, John. 3rd (99) on *Discovery* as AB

Lungley, Nathaniel. AB on *Grenville* in 1765, 1766. Born in Toston Dowsey, Essex in 1743. Discharged on 2 March 1767.

Lyon, Benjamin. 3rd (128) on *Resolution* as AB. Born in Southwark, London in 1735. Punished on 25 January 1779 for being absent without leave.

Lyon, Stephen. AB on *Grenville* in 1766. Born in Shadwell, East London in 1749. Discharged on 6 March 1767.

McAllister, Dugal. 2nd (121) on *Adventure* as AB

McDonald, John. 3rd (M11) on *Resolution* as Marine Private. Died 1786? FRC will (11/1143). Punished twice; on 17 July 1777 for neglect of duty; and on 7 September 1779 for insolence.

McIntosh, Alexander. 3rd (8) on *Resolution* as Carpenter's mate. Born in Perth, Scotland in 1746. Died in Petropavlosk on 16 May 1779. FRC will.

McIntosh, John. 3rd (27) on *Discovery* as AB. Born in Perth in 1757. Died on 28 October 1778 off Maui (after main tack gave way). FRC will (11/1070)?

McKenzie, Daniel. 3rd (9) on *Resolution* as AB. Born in Inverness in 1744.

McKenzie, James. AB on *Grenville* in 1764. Born in Perth, Scotland in 1739. Punished for mutiny at St John's, 17 October 1764. Discharged on 19 March 1765. His name appears as McHensey in the Log entry detailing his punishment.

Mackie (Mackay, Mackey), Robert. He sailed on the third voyage on the *Resolution* as a midshipman (86) until 1 September 1777. He was then made an AB He was sent before the mast at Huahine on 31 October 1777. Mackie joined the voyage from the *Nonsuch*. He was born in Stirling in 1755. A Robert Mackie became a lieutenant in November 1780. He died in 1789 while serving on HMS *Carron*?

Mackrell, William. 3rd (142) on *Resolution* as Sailmaker's mate. Born in Chichester, West Sussex in 1744.

Macky, Robert. 2nd (S19) on *Adventure* as Bayly's servant.

McLeod, John. 3rd (M17) on *Resolution* as Marine Private.

McVicar, Archibald. 2nd (M20) on *Resolution* as Marine Private. (Bagpiper).

Magra (Matra), James *see* Main listing.

Mahony, Mortimer. 2nd (101) on *Adventure* as Cook. Died of scurvy in South Pacific on 23 July 1773.

Mai (Omai) *see* Main listing.

Manley, Isaac *see* Main listing.

Markham, David. 3rd (23) on *Discovery* as Sailmaker's mate. Born in Guernsey in 1739.

Marra (Mara), John *see* Main listing.

Marshall, James. 3rd (45) on *Discovery* as AB. Born in Sandwich, Kent in 1757. Punished on 18 March 1775 for threatening violence.

Martin, John Henry *see* Main listing.

Mason, Peter. 3rd (51) on *Resolution* as Carpenter's crew. Born in London in 1757. Died 1797? FRC will?

Masson, Francis. 2nd (S33) on *Resolution* as Gardener. Born in 1741. Died 1805. He left the ship at Cape Town on 22 November 1772. A plant collector from Kew, he made expeditions at the Cape and in the West Indies. FRC will. *DNB* v13, p16.

Mathews, James. AB on *Grenville* in 1765. Born in Wexford, Ireland in 1745. Ran on 27 April 1766 at Deal, Kent.

Mathias, Thomas. 1st (115) on *Endeavour* as AB. (Joined Jakarta November 1770). Died 1784? FRC will?

Matthews, Thomas. 1st (58) on *Endeavour* as Cook's (Thompson's) Servant.

Maxwell, James. He sailed on the second voyage on the *Resolution* as AB (177). He kept a log. Maxwell was confined 1 February 1773 for threatening the ship's cook. He was sent before the mast on 6 February 1774 for damaging a sail. Maxwell was born in London in 1751 and may have died 1812?, leaving a will? (FRC 11/1530). He never became a lieutenant so probably left the Navy.

Mayley, James. 3rd (120) on *Resolution* as AB. Born in London in 1751.

Medberry, William. 2nd (53) on *Adventure* as Carpenter's crew. Born in London in 1753.

Medd (Midd), William Plaistred. He sailed on the third voyage on the *Resolution* as midshipman (32) until 23 March 1778. He was then made an AB He was born in Little Shutton, Leicestershire (?) in 1758. He never became a lieutenant so probably left the navy.

Millett, James. 3rd (125) on *Resolution* as Quartermaster. Born in London in 1745.

Mills, Alexander. 2nd (M2) on *Adventure* as Marine Corporal.

Mills, John. 2nd (165) on *Resolution* as AB. Born in Banff, north-east Scotland in 1748.

Milton, William. 2nd (115) on *Adventure* as AB. Born in Azores, North Atlantic in 1753. Died 17 at Wharehunga Bay (Grass Cove) on December 1773.

Mitchell (Mitchel), Bowles. He sailed on the second voyage on the *Resolution* as a midshipman (114) until 1 July 1773. He then became an AB Mitchell kept a log, and drew a few charts and coastal views. He was promoted lieutenant in May 1777 and was listed as a superannuated commander in August 1810. He was born in Deptford in 1752 and died in Ramsgate, Kent on 18 January 1824, leaving a will (FRC 11/1681).

Mollonex (Mollineux, Molyneux), John. 2nd (M1) on *Adventure* as Marine Sergeant. Died 1778. FRC will (11/1049).

Molloy, Richard. 2nd (97) on *Adventure* as AB. Born in Dublin in 1733.

Molyneux (Molineux), Robert *see* Main listing.

Monk, Simon. 2nd (148) on *Resolution* as AB. Born in Brentford, West London in 1742. Died at New Caledonia on 6 September 1774 after falling down hatchway.

Monk, William. 2nd (M19) on *Resolution* as Marine Private.

Moody, George. 3rd (M5) on *Discovery* as Marine Private. Drowned in the Tasman Sea on 4 February 1777.

Moody, Robert. 2nd (4) on *Adventure* as Quartermaster. Born in Dundee, Scotland in 1745. Died 1783? FRC will?

Moody, Samuel. 1st (42) on *Endeavour* as Carpenter's crew. Born in Worcester in 1728. Died in the Indian Ocean on 30 January 1771. FRC will (11/969).

Morey (Moorey), George. He sailed on the *Adventure* as an AB (40) until 1 January 1773. He then became a midshipman. Morey became a lieutenant in March 1781 and a superannuated commander in January 1816. He may have died in Portsea, Hampshire in 1827, leaving a will (FRC 11/1727) or in 1821?

Morey, Nathaniel. 1st (91) on *Endeavour* as Gore's servant.

Morgan, Peter. 1st (111) on *Endeavour* as AB. (Joined Jakarta November 1770). Died in the Indian Ocean on 27 February 1771.

Morris, Robert. 3rd (5) on *Resolution* as Cook.

Morris, Thomas. 3rd (M13) on *Resolution* as Marine Private. Punished over 3 days on 30 October to 1 November 1777 for neglect of duty in letting a prisoner escape.

Morrison, Robert. 3rd (166) on *Resolution* as AB. (Joined Macao December 1779). Born in Glasgow in 1755.

Mouat, Alexander *see* Main listing.

Moulton, William. 1st (114) on *Endeavour* as AB. (Joined Jakarta November 1770).

Munkhouse (Monkhouse), Jonathan *see* Main listing.

Munkhouse (Monkhouse), William *see* Main listing.

Murphy, Francis. 2nd (26) on *Adventure* as Quartermaster. Born in Dublin in 1741. Died at Wharehunga Bay (Grass Cove) on 17 December 1773.

Nash, William. 3rd (18) on *Resolution* as AB. Born in London in 1755. Punished twice; on 31 October 1776 for neglect of duty; and on 25 January 1779 for disobedience.

Nelson, David. 3rd (S3) on *Discovery* as Gardener. A plant collector from Kew. On *Bounty* voyage. Went in longboat with Bligh to Timor where died of fever.

Newman, Michael. 3rd (M14) on *Discovery* as Marine Private.

Nicholls, —. 2nd (130) on *Adventure* as AB. (Joined Cape Town March 1774).

Nichols, Peter. 1st (127) on *Endeavour* as AB

Nicholson (Nicolson), James. 1st (24) on *Endeavour* as AB. Born in Inverness in 1747. Died in the Indian Ocean on 31 January 1771. FRC will (11/970). Punished on 12 June 1769 for theft.
Norris, Edward. AB on *Grenville* in 1767. Born in Sutton Cotten, Hampshire in 1739.
Nowell (Knowel), George. 1st (87) on *Endeavour* as Carpenter's crew to 12 February 1771; then Carpenter. To *Scorpion* August 1771.

Offord, William. 2nd (59) on *Adventure* as Carpenter. Died 1799? FRC will?
Olafson, Canute. 1st (133) on *Endeavour* as AB. (Joined Cape Town March 1771).
Orton, Richard. 1st (80) on *Endeavour* as Clerk. Attacked by Saunders, 23 May 1770.

Parker, Isaac. 1st (26) on *Endeavour* as AB until 25 March 1769; then Boatswain's mate. Born in Ipswich in 1741. Died 1784? FRC will?
Parker, William *see* Main listing.
Parkinson, Sydney *see* Main listing.
Passmore, William. 3rd (79) on *Discovery* as AB. Born in Tiverton, Devon in 1754.
Patten, James *see* Main listing.
Paul, Henry. 1st (M5) on *Endeavour* as Marine Private.
Paul (Pall), Mathew. 3rd (34) on *Resolution* as AB (kept log). Born in 1758.
Peckover, William *see* Main listing.
Pereira (Parreyra), Manuel. 1st (98) on *Endeavour* as AB. (Joined Rio December 1768). Kidnapped on Tahiti, 23 June 1769. Punished on 30 November 1769 for theft. Died in the Indian Ocean on 27 February 1771. FRC will.
Perkins, John. 3rd (M16) on *Resolution* as Marine Private. Died 1783? FRC will? Punished on 14 November 1776 for neglect of duty.
Perry, Thomas. 2nd (193) on *Resolution* as AB. Born in London in 1733. Wrote a song about the second voyage.
Perry, William *see* Main listing.
Petterson (Peterson), Emmanuel. 2nd (82) on *Resolution* as AB. Born in Bombay, India in 1751. Died 1781? FRC will? Punished on 30 August 1773 for rioting.
Phillips, John. 2nd (M9) on *Resolution* as Marine Private.
Phillips, Molesworth *see* Main listing.
Pickersgill, Richard *see* Main listing.
Pirie, John. 2nd (7) on *Resolution* as AB. Born in Aberdeen in 1739.
Ponto, Antonio. 1st (82) on *Endeavour* as AB. Born in Venice, Italy in 1744.
Poole, Joseph (James). 3rd (M15) on *Discovery* as Marine Private. Died 3 October 1791. Buried at St John's Church, Staplegrove, Somerset.
Portlock, Nathaniel *see* Main listing.
Portsmouth, Michael. 3rd (M20) on *Resolution* as Marine Drummer.
Poulter, William. 3rd (92) on *Discovery* as AB. Born in Swaffham, Norfolk in 1750. Died 1821? FRC will?
Praval (Provall), Charles. 1st (122) on *Endeavour* as AB. (Copied earlier drawings by Parkinson, Spöring, etc. Joined at Jakarta on 19 December 1770).
Preston, Daniel. 1st (M7) on *Endeavour* as Marine Private. Died in the Indian Ocean on 15 February 1771. FRC will.
Price, Joseph. He sailed on the second voyage on the *Resolution* as a midshipman (41). He kept a log and a journal. He became a lieutenant in September 1777 and a superannuated commander in June 1811. He was born in Westminster in 1752.
Price, Walter. AB on *Grenville* in 1765. Born in Westminster in 1742. Ran on 16 December 1765 at Deptford.
Price, Thomas. 3rd (84) on *Resolution* as Armourer's mate. Born in 1754. Punished twice; on 21 October 1776 for going absent without leave; and on 28 September 1777 for theft.
Pryor, Henry. 2nd (71) on *Adventure* as AB. Born in Alton in 1736.

Quin (Quinn), Thomas. 3rd (78) on *Resolution* as Boatswain's mate. Born in Limerick in 1750. Died 1783? FRC will?

Ramsay, John. 1st (11) on *Endeavour* as AB; 2nd (8) on *Resolution* as Cook; 3rd (45) on *Resolution* as AB. Born in Plymouth or Perthshire? in 1732.
Randall, William. 3rd (M7) on *Discovery* as Marine Private. Died 1781? FRC will?
Rarden (Rearden), Timothy *see* Main listing *under* Littleboys.
Ravenhill, John. 1st (59) on *Endeavour* as Sailmaker. Born in Hull in 1719. Died in the Indian Ocean on 26 January 1771.
Rayside, John. 2nd (123) on *Adventure* as AB. (Joined as stowaway at Madeira August 1772).
Reading (Redding, Readon), John. 1st (30) on *Endeavour* as Boatswain's mate. Born in Kinsale, Ireland in 1744. Died from drinking too much rum on 28 August 1769. FRC will. Punished on 30 November 1768 for neglect of duty.
Reading (Redden), Solomon. 2nd (62) on *Resolution* as Boatswain's mate. Saved Thomas Fenton from going overboard. Wounded at Erromanga. Born in London in 1747. Petitioned Joseph Banks 3 times.
Reed, Richard. 2nd (M7) on *Adventure* as Marine Private.
Reynolds, John. 1st (S5) on *Endeavour* as Green's servant. Died in Jakarta on 18 December 1770.
Reynolds, Peter. 2nd (9) on *Resolution* as Carpenter's mate; 3rd (11) on *Discovery* as Carpenter. Born in Deptford in 1750.
Rice, Thomas. 3rd (52) on *Resolution* as AB. Born in Wales in 1756.
Richardson, John. 3rd (87) on *Discovery* as Boatswain's mate. Born in Yorkshire in 1748.
Richmond, Thomas. 1st (S11) on *Endeavour* as Banks' servant. Died at Tierra del Fuego on 16 January 1769. Had worked previously for John Fothegill.
Rickman, John *see* Main listing.
Riou, Edward *see* Main listing.
Roberts, Charles. AB on *Grenville* in 1765. Born in London in 1733. Discharged into sick quarters on 1 January 1766 at Portsmouth.
Roberts, Daniel. 1st (63) on *Endeavour* as Gunner's servant. Died in the Indian Ocean on 2 February 1771.
Roberts, Henry *see* Main listing.
Roberts, James. 1st (S9) on *Endeavour* as Banks' servant. Born in Mareham le Fen, Lincolnshire (west of Revesby, Banks' home) in 1752. Died 8 July 1826. Memorial in St Botolph's Church, Boston.
Roberts, Thomas. 1st (130) on *Endeavour* as AB. (Joined Cape Town March 1771).
Roberts, Thomas. 3rd (102) on *Resolution* as Quartermaster to 31 December 1776; then AB. Born in Bermuda in 1748. Died off Nihau on 27 January 1778.
Roberts, William. 2nd (114) on *Adventure* as Sailmaker's mate. Born in Beaumaris, Anglesey in 1743.
Rollett, Richard *see* Main listing.
Ross, Alexander. 2nd (M12) on *Adventure* as Marine.
Rossiter, Thomas. 1st (M3) on *Endeavour* as Marine Drummer. Punished twice; on 2 December 1769 for theft; and on 21 February 1771 for drunkenness.
Rowe, John. He sailed on the second voyage on the *Adventure* (19) as a master's mate until 31 October 1773. He then became an AB until 30 November 1773 when he became a master's mate again. Rowe joined the voyage from HMS *Torbay*. He was born in 1746 and was killed at Wharehunga Bay (Grass Cove) on 17 December 1773.
Ryan, William. 2nd (132) on *Adventure* as AB. (Joined Cape Town March 1774).

Sake, Antonio van. 1st (134) on *Endeavour* as AB. (Joined Cape Town March 1771).
Salmon, William. 3rd (117) on *Resolution* as AB. Born in Yarmouth in 1729.
Samwell, David *see* Main listing.
Sanderson, William. 2nd (65) on *Adventure* as Gunner's mate. Born in Hull in 1743.
Satterley, John. 1st (3) on *Endeavour* as Carpenter. Helped with fitting out of ship. Died in the Indian Ocean on 12 February 1771. FRC will.
Saunders, Lowrand. 1st (138) on *Endeavour* as AB. (Joined Cape Town March 1771).
Saunders, Patrick. He sailed on the *Endeavour* as a midshipman (78) until 23 May 1770. He was then disrated to an AB It was believed that Saunders had been responsible for the attack on Orton, the ship's clerk. Saunders deserted at Jakarta on 25 December 1770, which was taken as proof of his guilt in the Orton incident. He never became a lieutenant so probably left the Navy.
Scarnell, Francis. 2nd (87) on *Resolution* as

Quartermaster. Born in Portsmouth in 1750.
Scholient, Ernest. 2nd (S39) on *Resolution* as Servant.
Scott, James. 2nd (M13) on *Adventure* as Marine 2nd lieutenant.
Scruse, William. 3rd (M9) on *Resolution* as Marine Private. Punished on 17 July 1777 for neglect of duty.
Seymour, James. 2nd (15) on *Resolution* as Carpenter's crew. Born in Thame, Oxfordshire in 1750.
Shank, Joseph. He was appointed first lieutenant on HMS *Adventure*, Cook's companion vessel on the second voyage. On the voyage south in the Atlantic, Shank became ill and was sent home ill from the Cape in November 1772. Shank had become a lieutenant in 1759.
Shaw, Thomas. 2nd (34) on *Resolution* as AB; 3rd (34) on *Discovery* as Gunner's mate. Born in London in 1754. Attempted to desert on Raiatea in November 1777.
Sheath, Thomas. 3rd (76) on *Discovery* as Quartermaster. Born in Boston, Lincolnshire in 1758.
Shortnell, Morris. AB on *Grenville* in 1765. Born in Waterford in 1733. Ran on 3 June 1765 at Great St Lawrence on arrival in Newfoundland.
Shuttleworth, William. He sailed on the third voyage on the *Resolution* as a midshipman (124) until 16 February 1779. He was then transferred to be a midshipman on the *Discovery*. He kept a journal of proceedings. He never became a lieutenant so probably left the Navy. There is a will for a William Shuttleworth of Ingatestone in Essex for 1784 (FRC 11/1113).
Simmonds, Thomas. 1st (29) on *Endeavour* as AB. Born in Brentford, West London in 1744. Died 1780? FRC will?
Simms, James. 2nd (55) on *Resolution* as AB. Born in London in 1752.
Simms, John. AB on *Grenville* in 1767. Born in London in 1718.
Simpkins, James. AB on *Grenville* in 1767. Born in London in 1748.
Simpson, Alexander. 1st (71) on *Endeavour* as AB Died in the Indian Ocean on 21 February 1771. FRC will. Punished on 2 December 1769 for theft.
Smallpiece, John. 3rd (59) on *Discovery* as AB. Born in Deptford in 1753.
Smally, John. 2nd (147) on *Resolution* as AB. Born in Deal, Kent in 1746.
Smart, Edward. Draughtsman on *Grenville* in 1763. He died in London on 8 March 1764.
Smith, Isaac *see* Main listing.
Smith, John. 1st (126) on *Endeavour* as AB. (Joined Jakarta November 1770).
Smith, John. 2nd (201) on *Resolution* as AB. (Joined Cape Town 1775). Born in Bristol in 1739.
Smith, Joseph. 3rd (132) on *Resolution* as AB. Born in Greenwich in 1752. Punished on 31 October 1776 for neglect of duty.
Smith, Samuel. 1st (124) on *Endeavour* as AB. (Joined Jakarta November 1770).
Smith, Thomas. Carpenter's mate on *Grenville* in 1765, 1766, 1767. Born in Shadwell in 1734.
Smock, Henry. 2nd (154) on *Resolution* as AB. Born in Portsmouth in 1742. Died at sea near Cape Town on 29 October 1772. He had been working over the side in the scuttles.
Snagg (Spagg?), James. 3rd (33) on *Discovery* as Surgeon's mate. Died 1785? FRC will?
Snowden Thomas. 2nd (191) on *Resolution* as Sailmaker's mate. Born in Whitby in 1750.
Soby, William. 3rd (133) on *Resolution* as AB. Born in Newark, Nottinghamshire in 1750.
Solander, Daniel *see* Main listing.
Sommerfield, Bonaventure. 2nd (M9) on *Adventure* as Marine Private.
Sowrey, William. 2nd (109) on *Adventure* as AB to 31 December 1772; then Quartermaster. Born in Lancaster in 1748.
Sparrman, Andreas *see* Main listing.
Spencer, Michael. 3rd (50) on *Resolution* as AB (Deserted at Macao on 13 January 1780). Born in Buckinghamshire in 1757. Punished on 12 October 1777 for theft.
Spilsbury, William. 3rd (108) on *Resolution* as AB. Born in Isleworth, Midlesex in 1743.
Spöring, Herman *see* Main listing.
Stainsby, Robert. 1st (52) on *Endeavour* as AB (Tattooed on Tahiti – first man to be done). Born in Darlington in 1741.
Stalbone, Christopher. 1st (132) on *Endeavour* as AB. (Joined Cape Town March 1771).
Stalker, John. 2nd (51) on *Resolution* as AB. Born in Ayrshire in 1741.
Stanley, John. 3rd (94) on *Resolution* as AB. Born in Wilton in 1755. Died 1783? FRC will?
Stephens (Stevens), Henry. 1st (76) on *Endeavour* as AB. Born in Falmouth in 1740. Punished 2 times; on 16 September 1768 for disobedience; and on 30 November 1769 for theft.
Stevens, William. 3rd (64) on *Discovery* as Quartermaster. Born in Maidstone in 1741.
Stewart, Donald. 2nd (M5) on *Adventure* as Marine Private.
Stewart, George. 3rd (139) on *Resolution* as AB. Born in Charleston, South Carolina in 1747.
Still, John. 1st (143) on *Endeavour* as Gunner's servant. Died 1781? FRC will?
Stirling, William. 3rd (60) on *Resolution* as Gunroom servant. Born in Chichester, West Sussex in 1754.
Stringer, Zachariah. AB on *Grenville* in 1766. Ran on 26 November 1766 at Woolwich.
Surridge (Surrage), James. AB on *Grenville* in 1767. Born in Chipping Ongar, Essex in 1732. Died in Newfoundland in 1767.
Sutherland, Forby. 1st (25) on *Endeavour* as AB. Born in Orkney in 1739. Died at Botany Bay on 1 May 1770. Memorial to him at Kurnell near Sutherland Point.
Swilley, James. 2nd (2) on *Adventure* as Furneaux's servant. Died at Wharehunga Bay (Grass Cove) on 17 December 1773.
Taiata. 1st (S66) on *Endeavour* as Tupaia's servant. Born in Tahiti. Died in Jakarta on 17 December 1770.
Taylor, Francis. 2nd (M17) on *Resolution* as Marine Private. Punished twice; on 11 September 1772 for insolence; and on 16 February 1773 for theft.
Taylor, Isaac. 2nd (M17) on *Resolution* as Marine Private. Died at Tahiti on 18 August 1773.
Taylor, Robert. 1st (54) on *Endeavour* as Armourer. Died 1771? FRC will?
Taylor, William *see* Main listing.
Thomas, James. 3rd (M3) on *Resolution* as Marine Corporal. Died with Cook at Kealakekua Bay on 14 February 1779.
Thomas, Richard. 1st (112) on *Endeavour* as AB. (Joined Jakarta November 1770). Died 15 March 1771 at Cape Town.
Thomas, William. 2nd (29) on *Adventure* as AB. Born in London in 1751.
Thompson, Hamlet. 3rd (M6) on *Discovery* as Marine Private.
Thompson, John. 1st (57) on *Endeavour* as Cook. (One-handed). Died in the Indian Ocean on 31 January 1771.
Thompson, John. 3rd (165) on *Resolution* as AB. (Joined Macao December 1779). Born in Tralee, Ireland in 1748.
Thurman, John. 1st (97) on *Endeavour* as AB (Pressed at Madeira September 1768). Born in 1748. Died in the Indian Ocean on 3 February 1771. FRC will. Punished twice; on 19 November 1768 for disobedience; and on 12 June 1769 for theft.
Tickle, James. 3rd (71) on *Discovery* as AB. Born in London in 1756.
Tow, William. 2nd (M11) on *Resolution* as Marine Private. Punished on 18 August 1774 for trading with natives.
Treneer, Francis. 2nd (96) on *Adventure* as Quartermaster. Born in Falmouth in 1747.
Tretcher, Thomas. 3rd (89) on *Discovery* as AB. Born in London in 1758. Became lost on Christmas Island, 29 December 1779.
Trevenen, James *see* Main listing.
Truslove, John. 1st (M2) on *Endeavour* as Marine Corporal. Died in the Indian Ocean on 24 January 1771.
Tunley, James. 1st (85) on *Endeavour* as AB. Born in Blackwall, East London in 1744. Punished on 19 June 1769 for theft.
Tupaia *see* Main listing.
Turner, Robert. AB on *Grenville* in 1766. Born in Bafield, Suffolk in 1733. Ran on 1 February 1767.
Turrell (Terrell), Edward. 1st (4) on *Endeavour* as Carpenter's mate and AB; 2nd (146) on *Resolution* as AB. Born in Spitalfields, London in 1750. Died in Folkestone in 1823. No listed family. (FRC will 11/1677).
Twitty, Charles. 2nd (M16) on *Resolution* as Marine Private. Died 1831? FRC will?

Upton, John. 2nd (92) on *Adventure* as Gunner's mate. Born in Deptford in 1746. FRC will?

Vancouver, George *see* Main listing.
Vandome, Abraham. AB on *Grenville* in 1767. Born in London in 1746.
Vincent, John. AB on *Grenville* in 1767. Born in Newton Poppleford, Devon (east of Exeter) in 1741.
Vowell, Cornelius. 2nd (95) on *Adventure* as AB. Born in Cork in 1737.

Wales, William *see* Main listing.
Walker, William. 3rd (22) on *Discovery* as Carpenter's crew. Born in Glasgow in 1756. Injured at sea in South Atlantic on 4 June 1780.
Wallis (Wallace), James. 2nd (5) on *Resolution* as Carpenter. Died 1791? FRC will?
Walsh, William. AB on *Grenville* in 1764, 1765. Born in Waterford in 1747. Discharged to sick quarters on 1 January 1766 at Portsmouth.
Ward, James *see* Main listing.
Waterfield, Richard. 2nd (M14) on *Resolution* as Marine Private.
Watman (Whattman), William. 2nd (158) on *Resolution* as AB; 3rd (68) on *Resolution* as AB. Born in Reigate, Surrey in 1732. Died at Kealakekua Bay, Hawai'i on 1 February 1779.
Watson, William. 3rd (169) on *Resolution* as AB. (Joined Macao December 1779). Born in London in 1755.
Watts, John *see* Main listing.
Weaver, Robert. 2nd (62) on *Adventure* as AB. Born in London in 1748.
Webb, Clement. 1st (M12) on *Endeavour* as Marine Private. Punished on 14 July 1769 for desertion at Tahiti. Petitioned Joseph Banks on 21 March 1808.
Webber, John *see* Main listing.
Wedgeborough, William. 2nd (M13) on *Resolution* as Marine Private. Drowned (drunk) at Christmas Sound on 22 December 1774. Fell overboard and rescued off Erromanga 1 August 1774. Punished twice; on 18 March 1774 for drunkenness; and on 19 August 1774 for shooting a man on Tanna.
Weir, Alexander. 1st (5) on *Endeavour* as Quartermaster. Born in Fife in 1733. Drowned at Madeira, dragged down by buoy-rope and anchor on 14 September 1768. FRC will.
Whelan (Wheilon), Patrick. 2nd (91) on *Resolution* as Quartermaster; 3rd (12) on *Resolution* as Quartermaster. Born in Limerick in 1732 or London in 1742. Punished twice; on 18 February 1777 for insolence; and on 5 April 1778 for neglect of duty.
White, George. 2nd (84) on *Adventure* as AB. Born in Chichester in 1748.
White, Stephen. 2nd (124) on *Resolution* as AB. Born in London in 1740. Died 1778? FRC will?
White, Thomas. 2nd (6) on *Resolution* as AB. Born in Scotland in 1746.
Whitehouse, John. He sailed on the second voyage on the *Resolution* as a master's mate (45). Whitehouse was promoted to lieutenant in August 1775. He was born in London in 1741 and may have died in 1780, leaving a will (FRC 11/1070).
Whitton, Benjamin. 3rd (19) on *Resolution* as Carpenter's mate. Born in Boston, Lincolnshire in 1739. Punished on 28 October 1777 for theft.
Widdall, William. 3rd (106) on *Resolution* as Sailmaker.
Wight, Henry. 2nd (124) on *Adventure* as AB. (Joined Cape Town November 1772).
Wilby, John. He sailed on the second voyage on the *Adventure* as AB (88) until 31 January 1774. He then became a midshipman. He kept a journal. He was promoted to lieutenant in November 1776. Wilby became a naval Knight of Windsor. He died in 1803.
Wilkinson, Francis. He sailed on the *Endeavour* (79) as a master's mate. He kept a journal). He was born in Bangor, North Wales and died in London in August 1771, leaving a will (FRC 11/971). Wilkinson died a few days after the *Endeavour* had tied up in the Thames at the end of the voyage. He had sailed to the Pacific with Wallis in the *Dolphin*. A section of his journal is reproduced in the *Historical records of New South Wales, vol 1, part 1: Cook 1762–1780.*
Willard, Nathaniel. 2nd (106) on *Adventure* as Carpenter's mate. Born in Maidstone in 1727.
Williams, Charles. 1st (68) on *Endeavour* as AB. Born in Bristol in 1730.
Williams, Charles. 2nd (145) on *Resolution* as AB. Born in Wapping in 1752. Punished on 28 May 1774 for losing tools.
Williams, John. AB on *Grenville* in 1766. Ran on 31 October 1766 at St John's.
Williams, Robert. 3rd (97) on *Discovery* as AB
Williams, William. 3rd (102) on *Discovery* as Carpenter's crew. (Joined Cape Town November 1776). Born ? in 1740.
Williamson, John *see* Main listing.
Willis, Thomas. He sailed on Cook's second voyage on the *Resolution* (79) as a midshipman. He kept a log and a journal. He was promoted to lieutenant in February 1778. Willis was born in Holywell, Flintshire, North Wales, in 1755. He may have died in Pagham, Sussex in 1797?, leaving a will (FRC 11/1295). Willis Island at the west of South Georgia was named for him.
Willoughby, James. AB on *Grenville* in 1765. Born in Portsmouth in 1746. Discharged on 26 March 1766 at Deptford.
Willoughby, John. AB on *Grenville* in 1766. Born in Deal, Kent in 1750. Discharged on 20 March 1767.
Wilshire, William. 1st (M8) on *Endeavour* as Marine Private. Petitioned Joseph Banks on 23 June 1802.
Wilson, Thomas. 2nd (133) on *Adventure* as AB. (Joined Cape Town March 1774).
Wolf (Wolfe), Archibald. 1st (60) on *Endeavour* as AB. Born in Edinburgh in 1729. Died in the Indain Ocean on 31 January 1771. Punished on 4 June 1769 for theft.
Woodfield, Philip. 3rd (85) on *Discovery* as Carpenter's mate. Born in Woolwich in 1754. Broke leg on 24 April 1777, east of Tonga.
Woodhouse, Thomas. He sailed on the second voyage on the *Adventure* as a midshipman (3). He was one of the party killed at Wharehunga Bay (Grass Cove) in Queen Charlotte Sound, New Zealand on 17 December 1773. He left a will (FRC 11/1000).
Woodruff, Simon. 3rd (65) on *Discovery* as Gunner's mate. Born in America in 1746.
Woodward, George. 2nd (M15) on *Resolution* as Marine Private. Died 1784? FRC will? Punished on 30 August 1773 for rioting.
Woodworth, John. 1st (89) on *Endeavour* as AB. Died in Jakarta on 24 December 1770. FRC will.
Wybrow, John. 2nd (35) on *Resolution* as AB. Born in Edinburgh in 1753.

Young, John. AB on *Grenville* in 1764. Born in London in 1741. Punished for theft at St John's on 17 October 1764. Ran 27 February 1765 at Deptford.
Young, John. 2nd (81) on *Adventure* as Surgeon's mate.
Young, Nicholas *see* Main listing.
Young, Richard. 3rd (44) on *Resolution* as Cook's mate. Born in Kenson in 1753. Punished twice; on 14 November 1776 for neglect of duty; and on 2 May 1777 for neglect of duty.

Zimmermann, Heinrich *see* Main listing.

Appendix IV: Cook Chronology

The chronology lists all events in the life of James Cook together with his immediate family. Significant events in British history of the time are also listed, especially those that impacted on Cook.

1693
January John Cook and Jean Duncan, Cook's paternal grandparents, were married at Ednam, Roxburghshire, Scotland on 19 January.
1694
March James Cook, Cook's father was baptised in Ednam on 4 March.
1695
November John Pace and Deborah Butler, Cook's maternal grandparents, were married on 29 November.
1702
Grace Pace, Cook's mother, was born in Thornaby, Cleveland.
Anne became Queen of Great Britain.
1707
Act of Union between England and Scotland.
1714
King George I became King of Great Britain.
The Board of Longitude set up.
1715
The first Jacobite Rebellion.
1719
Daniel Defoe's *Robinson Crusoe* published.
Sometime before 1725, James Cook moved south from Ednam to live and work in Cleveland, North Yorkshire.
1725
October James Cook and Grace Pace, Cook's parents were married in Stainton-in-Cleveland Parish Church on 10 October.
1726
Jonathan Swift's *Gulliver's Travels* published.
1727
King George II became King of Great Britain.
The Cooks were living in Morton, Cleveland. Their first child, John, was born and baptised on 10 January.
1728
Bering passed through Bering Strait.
The Cook family moved a few miles west to live in Marton.
The Cook's second child, James, was born at Marton, Cleveland on 27 October. He was baptised at the Parish Church of St Cuthbert, Marton on 3 November.
1730
The Cook family moved east to nearby Ormesby.
1731
John Hadley developed the quadrant.
January Christiana, the first daughter, was born and baptised in Ormesby on 31 January.
1732
The Cook family returned to Marton.
1733
May Mary Cook, the second daughter was born and baptised on 13 May.
1736
The Cook family moved a few miles south to Great Ayton where Cook's father had been made foreman at Aireyholme Farm.
1737
June Cook's sister Mary died on 30 June. Cook began attending the Postgate School, Great Ayton.
1738
May Another sister, Jane, born on 21 May.
October Cook was 10 years old on 27 October.
1740
December Another sister, Mary (number 2), born and baptised on 7 December.
War of the Austrian Succession began.
George Anson began his voyage to the Pacific.
1741
Bering reached south-east Alaska.
June Mary (number 2) died on 17 June.
Elizabeth Batts, Cook's future wife, was born in the Bell Alehouse, Wapping where James Cook would later stay. She was baptised at nearby St John's Church.
1742
Tasman reached Tasmania and New Zealand.
May Jane died on 12 May on 12 May.
July Another sister, Margaret was born and baptised on 20 July.
1743
Joseph Banks born.
1745
Second Jacobite Rebellion.
January Another brother, William, was born on 12 January. Cook left home and went to work for Mr William Sanderson, a grocer and haberdasher at Staithes on the Cleveland coast.
1746
Cook left Staithes and moved to Whitby. He became an apprentice in John Walker's shipping company that operated in the North Sea Coal Trade between North Shields, on the River Tyne, and London.
1747
James Lind showed that eating citrus fruit prevented scurvy.
September Cook sailed as an Apprentice aboard the *Freelove* on 29 September.
December Cook was discharged at Whitby on 17 December.
1748
John Montagu, Earl of Sandwich, became First Lord of the Admiralty.
War of Austrian Succession ended. Treaty of Aix-la-Chapelle.
January Cook's brother, William, died on 29 January.
February Cook sailed on 26 February on board the *Freelove*.
April He was discharged at Whitby on 22 April to work on rigging a new ship, the *Three Brothers*.
June On 14 June, Cook sailed on board the *Three Brothers*.
October The *Three Brothers* returned to Whitby on 14 October and sailed again, the same day as a transport ship for the Government moving troops and horse between Middelburg (Netherlands), Dublin and Liverpool.
Cook was 20 years old on 27 October.
1749
April Cook returned to Whitby and sailed again, the same day (20 April), in the *Three Brothers*, now as a Seaman. He may have visited Norway on this voyage.
September Cook returned to Whitby on 26 September and left again the next day.
December The *Three Brothers* returned to Whitby on 8 December. Cook probably went to Great Ayton to spend Christmas with his family.
1750
Cook travelled to the River Tyne and joined the *Mary*.
February The *Mary* sailed on 8 February, possibly to the Baltic.
September Cook's elder brother, John died on 20 September.
October On 8 October, the *Mary* put into London where Cook was discharged. He possibly returned to the North East on the *Hopewell*.
1751
First volume of the *Encyclopedie* published in France.
February Cook rejoined the *Three Brothers* on 19 February and sailed from Whitby.
June Lord Anson became First Lord of the Admiralty.
July The *Three Brothers* returned to Whitby on 30 July. The next day Cook transferred to the *Friendship*, which sailed from Whitby.
October Cook temporarily left the *Friendship* at Whitby on 28 October.
November Cook rejoined the *Friendship* on 21 November and sailed from Whitby.
1752
January On 7 January the *Friendship* berthed at Whitby for the winter.
March Cook was now the Mate of the *Friendship*, when it left Whitby on 30 March.
November The *Friendship* returned to Whitby on 10 November for the winter.
1753
James Lind published his *Treatise on the Scurvy*.
February Cook sailed again on board the *Friendship* as Mate on 2 February.
1754
Thomas Pelham, Duke of Newcastle, became Prime Minister.
February The *Friendship* returned to Whitby on 4 February. Cook went on leave.
April On 2 April, Cook left Whitby as Mate

on the *Friendship*.
July The *Friendship* voyage finished at North Shields on 25 July
August The *Friendship* left Shields again on a new voyage on 9 August.
December The voyage finished at Whitby on 18 December. Cook possibly went home on leave.
1755
February Cook sailed from Whitby as Mate on the *Friendship* on 15 February.
June Cook discharged himself at London on 14 June 1755. It was the end of his time working on the colliers in the North Sea. Three days later, on 17 June, Cook joined the Royal Navy at Wapping. He joined HMS *Eagle* at Spithead on 25 June.
Cook's parents left Aireyholme Farm and moved to a new cottage in Great Ayton.
July Cook was quickly promoted to Master's mate.
August HMS *Eagle*, under Captain Hamar, sailed and went out on patrol in St George's Channel.
September The *Eagle* returned to Plymouth on 5 September.
October Now under Captain Hugh Palliser, the *Eagle* went out on 1 October to patrol in the western approaches to the English Channel.
November Palliser took the *Eagle* back to Plymouth where it spent the winter.
1756
William Cavendish, Duke of Devonshire, became Prime Minister.
Seven Years' War began.
Rousseau published his *Discourse on Inequality*, promoting the debate about the 'Noble Savage'.
Charles de Brosses published his *Histoire des Navigations aux Terres Australes* in France.
February Cook spent a few days in hospital in Plymouth.
March The *Eagle* returned to sea on 13 March, crossing to the Cherbourg Peninsula in Normandy. By 19 March, the ship was off Cape Barfleur. She worked her way west toward Brittany.
April Cook was given command of a cutter, which began patrolling off Brittany. He was off Morlaix on 5 April and the Tragoz rocks on 8 April. Cook returned to Plymouth as a passenger on HMS *Falmouth* on the 21st but three days later he returned to sea aboard HMS *St Albans*.
May On 3 May, Cook rejoined HMS *Eagle*, which captured two prize ships. Cook was given command of one, the *Triton*, and instructed to return it to Plymouth and then London.
June Cook took the *Triton* to London and then returned to Plymouth.
July Cook rejoined HMS *Eagle* at Plymouth on 1 July.
August The *Eagle* sailed from Plymouth on 4 August to patrol in the Channel and the Bay of Biscay.
November The *Eagle* returned to Plymouth on 11 November.
Richard Grenville, Earl Temple became First Lord of the Admiralty.
December On 29 December, Palliser took the *Eagle* out again and headed up the English Channel.
1757
Thomas Pelham, Duke of Newcastle, became Prime Minister again.
John Bird developed the sextant.
January The *Eagle* was in a storm off the Isle of Wight on 4 January and put into Spithead before it returned to Plymouth. On 30 January, the *Eagle* sailed from Plymouth into the Bay of Biscay.
April The *Eagle* anchored in Plymouth on 15 April.
Daniel, Earl Winchilsea became First Lord of the Admiralty.
May The *Eagle* once more left Plymouth on 25 May. Five days later, in company with HMS *Medway*, the *Eagle* fought and captured a French East Indiaman, the *Duc d'Aquitaine*. The prize, which was dismasted, was towed to Plymouth.
June On 29 June, Cook sat the examination at Trinity House near the Tower of London, which qualified him to be a Master. He was discharged from HMS *Eagle* the next day.
Lord Anson became First Lord of the Admiralty.
July Cook was posted to HMS *Solebay* in Leith, Scotland. On his way north to Scotland, Cook probably called in to see his family and friends at home in Cleveland. On 30 July, Cook joined the *Solebay* at Leith, as Master. Robert Craig was Captain of the Sixth Rate.
August The *Solebay* sailed north on 2 August from Leith to Orkney and the Shetlands. It was at Lerwick in the Shetland Islands on 9 August and ten days later anchored at Stromness, Orkney. By the end of the month, the *Solebay* had returned to Leith.
September On 7 September, Cook was discharged from HMS *Solebay*.
October Cook was appointed Master of HMS *Pembroke*, a Fourth Rate under Captain John Simcoe on 18 October. He joined the ship at Spithead on the 27th.
December The *Pembroke* left Spithead on 8 December to patrol in the Bay of Biscay and close to Cape Finisterre.
1758
February The *Pembroke* put into to Plymouth on 9 February left again on the 22nd as part of the Fleet under Admiral Boscawen bound for North America, via Tenerife and Bermuda.
May On 9 May, the *Pembroke* arrived in poor condition at Halifax, Nova Scotia and in need of repairs. It was unable to sail with the rest of the Fleet, which left for Louisbourg, Cape Breton Island.
June The *Pembroke* sailed on 7 June to rejoin the Fleet at Louisbourg, where it arrived on the 12th.
July The French garrison at Louisbourg surrendered on 26 July and the next day Cook landed at Kennington Cove, where he met Samuel Holland, an Engineer with General Wolfe's army. Holland began instructing Cook in the skills of surveying.
August Cook and the *Pembroke* remained at Louisbourg for most of August before they sailed into the Gulf of St Lawrence on the 28th.
September Cook made of his first surveys and drew his first charts, including one of Gaspé Harbour.
October The *Pembroke* arrived back at Louisbourg on 2 October
Cook was 30 years old on 27 October.
November The *Pembroke* left Halifax on 14 November and anchored in Halifax, where it spent the winter.
1759
January Cook worked with Holland on charts of the St Lawrence and sailing directions for the Cape Breton area.
May The *Pembroke* sailed from Halifax on 5 May as part of the British fleet heading to attack the French stronghold of Quebec. Captain Simcoe died on the 15th and was buried at sea off Anticosti Island in the Gulf of St Lawrence. Captain John Wheelock transferred from HMS *Squirrel* to be the new Captain of the *Pembroke*. The ship was part of the advance guard finding a route and charting the river as it went. They had reached Ile St Barnabe by the 20th.
June The *Pembroke* reached The Traverse at the northern end of Ile d'Orleans, near Quebec on 5 June. The Traverse was navigated and the British fleet anchored in the Basin below Quebec on the 27th.
September The British attacked successfully on 13 September and the French surrendered on the 18th. On 23 September, Cook was appointed Master of HMS *Northumberland* under Captain Lord Alexander Colville.
October The *Northumberland* returned to Halifax where it passed the winter. Cook began surveying Halifax Harbour.
1760
April Colville sailed the *Northumberland* out of Halifax on 22 April bound for Quebec.
May The *Northmberland* arrived back at Quebec on 18 May.
September The French surrendered at Montreal on 7 September.
October Cook and the *Northumberland* sailed from Quebec on 10 October. They were back at Halifax on the 25th and remained here until August 1762. Cook resumed charting Halifax Harbour and the coast of Nova Scotia.
Kew Gardens were founded outside London.
George II died, succeeded by his grandson as King George III.
1761
A Transit of Venus took place.
HMS *Northumberland* was careened and overhauled. Cook continued his duties as

Master of the ship and continued charting.

1762

John Stuart, Earl of Bute, became Prime Minister.

June George Montagu, Earl of Halifax became First Lord of the Admiralty.

Cook and the *Northumberland* remained in Halifax until August when news arrived from Newfoundland that the French had attacked and captured St John's.

August Colville was dispatched to retake St John's. He sailed to Newfoundland, landing at Placentia on the other side of the Avalon Peninsula fron St John's.

September The British attacked and captured St John's. Cook spent the rest of the month surveying local harbours, including Carbonear.

October Cook sailed from St John's for England.

George Grenville became First Lord of the Admiralty.

December Cook arrived back in Britain and was paid off. He presented his charts to the Admiralty. On 21 December, Cook married Elizabeth Batts, aged 21, at St Mary's Parish Church, Barking, Essex. The Cooks went to live in Shadwell.

1763

Rio de Janeiro was made capital of Brazil.

George Grenville became Prime Minister.

January Treaty of Paris signed, ending the Seven Years' War.

April Appointed Surveyor in Newfoundland.

John Montagu, Earl of Sandwich, became First Lord of the Admiralty.

May Cook joined HMS *Antelope* and sailed for Newfoundland.

June The *Antelope* arrived off Cape Race. Cook transferred to HMS *Tweed*, which carried him to St Pierre and Miquelon Islands to begin surveying.

July Cook made a quick but full and proper survey of St Pierre and Miquelon Islands, which were handed over to the French.

August HMS *Tweed* took Cook to St John's. The *Grenville*, a schooner, had been made available for Cook. He sailed his first command to the north of Newfoundland and began surveying.

September Cook surveyed several harbours and returned to St John's. He joined HMS *Tweed*, which transported him back to Britain.

John, Earl of Egmont became First Lord of the Admiralty.

October The Cook's first son, James, was born on 13 October

November The *Tweed* arrived at Spithead. Cook saw his son and the family moved to a new house in Mile End, Stepney.

1764

John Byron sailed for the Pacific in HMS *Dolphin*.

April Cook was appointed Master of the *Grenville*.

May HMS *Lark* carried Cook and Hugh Palliser to Newfoundland from Portsmouth.

July Cook rejoined the *Grenville* and sailed from St John's back to the northern peninsular of Newfoundland. He began that year's survey in Sacred and Pistolet Bays.

August They worked west past Cape Norman. Cook injured a hand when a powder horn exploded in Unfortunate Bay.

September St Genevieve and St Margaret Bays were surveyed.

Margaret Cook married James Fleck, a Redcar fisherman.

October Cook had surveyed as far as Point Ferolle. He then set sail for St John's.

November Cook sailed across the Atlantic in the *Grenville*.

December The *Grenville* was docked at Deptford for an overhaul and refit. Cook went home.

The Cook's second son, Nathaniel, was born on 14 December.

1765

Charles Wentworth, Marquis of Rockingham, became Prime Minister.

Nevil Maskelyne became the Astronomer Royal.

February Cook's mother died on 15 February in Great Ayton.

April Cook sailed the *Grenville* from the Downs for Newfoundland.

June Cook arrived at St Lawrence on the Burin Peninsula and began surveying the south coast.

July The survey continued in Fortune Bay.

August The *Grenville* ran aground in Long Harbour.

September Cook managed to take the *Grenville* into Bay d'Espoir where he repaired the ship in Ship Cove.

October The *Grenville* sailed from Ship Cove to St John's.

November Cook left St John's for England.

December Cook arrived at Deptford and rejoined his family.

1766

Byron returned in the *Dolphin*.

Bougainville set off on his Pacific voyage.

William Pitt became Prime Minister.

January Cook prepared his charts and sailing directions for Labrador and Newfoundland for publication.

April Cook left Deptford once more bound for Newfoundland.

May The *Grenville* reached Cape Race and started again close to Bay d'Espoir where he had finished the previous year.

June Cook moved to Bonne Bay and began working west.

July Cook surveyed the Penguin and Ramea Island, and the nearby coast.

August Cook had reached the Burgeo Islands where he observed a solar eclipse. He continued past Connoire Bay toward Port-aux-Basques.

Captain Samuel Wallis left Britain in the *Dolphin* for the Pacific.

September Cook rounded Cape Ray before turning at Cape Anguille to retrace his route.

The Cook's daughter, Elizabeth, was born in Mile End and christened in St Dunstan's, Stepney.

Sir Charles Saunders became First Lord of the Admiralty.

October That year's survey finished at La Poile Bay. Cook sailed for St John's. Joseph Banks was in St John's at this time but there is no evidence that he and Cook met at the time.

November Cook sailed for Britain where he rejoined his family.

Sir Edward Hawke became First Lord of the Admiralty.

1767

Alexander Dalrymple published his *Account of the Discoveries made in the South Pacifick Ocean*.

Augustus Fitzroy, Duke of Grafton, became Prime Minister.

Nevil Maskelyne published the first *Nautical Almanac*.

Cook once more prepared his charts. He wrote up his observation of the solar eclipse and forwarded it to the Royal Society.

April The *Grenville* sailed for Newfoundland but was involved in a collision in the Thames with a collier. After quick repairs it sailed again.

May Cook returned to Cape Anguille to resume the survey where he had finished in 1766. He proceeded into St George's Bay.

June The survey continued up the west coast of Newfoundland past the Bay of Islands.

Samuel Wallis arrived at Tahiti in the *Dolphin*.

July Cook surveyed Bonne Bay and northward.

August Ignornachoix and St John Bays were surveyed. Cook had reached Point Ferolle, his finishing point in 1764, so he returned south to investigate the Bay of Islands.

September Still in the Bay of Islands, Cook made a thorough survey of the many inlets. He even made a rare journey inland up the Humber River. Cook left the Bay of Islands for St John's.

October Cook set off for Britain after a quick visit to St John's.

November Cook arrived back at Deptford. He returned home where he began drawing his charts. He also started planning for the next year's survey.

1768

February The Royal Society proposed British involvement in scientific plans to observe the Transit of Venus expected in June 1769. The King granted money for an expedition and the Admiralty agreed to provide a ship.

April The Admiralty purchased the *Earl of Pembroke*, a collier, to be the expedition's ship. The ship's name was changed to HM Bark *Endeavour*. Alexander Dalrymple expected to captain the ship but the Admiralty objected, insisting that a Navy man would command. James Cook was

plucked from relative obscurity by the Admiralty to lead the voyage.
May Cook was presented to the Royal Society for their approval.
Samuel Wallis anchored the *Dolphin* in the Downs with news of Tahiti.
Tahiti was identified as the most suitable location to observe the Transit of Venus.
June Joseph Banks, a member of the Royal Society and a naturalist, paid for himself and a retinue to sail on board the *Endeavour*.
July The Admiralty issued Cook with his instructions – to observe the Transit of Venus on Tahiti and to search for the Great Southern Continent. Cook sailed the *Endeavour* from Gallions Reach on the Thames.
August The *Endeavour* arrived at Plymouth. Cook sent for Banks and his party. Cook's First Voyage began as the *Endeavour* sailed from Plymouth on 25 August. The ship sailed across the Bay of Biscay.
The Cooks' third son, Joseph, was born 26 August.
September The ship passed Cape Finisterre to anchor at Madeira. It continued past the Canary Islands to reach the Cape Verde Islands.
Joseph Cook died 13 September.
October The ship crossed the Equator and approached Brazil.
Cook was 40 years old on 27 October.
November Cook put into Rio de Janeiro and stayed close to one month.
December Cook left Rio de Janeiro and continued down the South Atlantic.
1769
January The *Endeavour* approached Tierra del Fuego on 11 January. It then passed through the Strait of Le Maire to anchor in the Bay of Good Success. Cape Horn was rounded and Cook entered the Pacific Ocean.
February The *Endeavour* sailed north-west across the Pacific.
March The *Endeavour* continued north-west across the Pacific.
April The *Endeavour* turned west across the Pacific and reached the Tuamotu Archipelago. Cook sailed past several atolls before reaching Tahiti on 13 April. He anchored at Matavai Bay.
May Cook prepared to observe the Transit of Venus.
June The Transit of Venus was observed on 3 June. At the end of the month, Cook and Banks made a tour round the coast of Tahiti.
July The *Endeavour* left Tahiti with Tupaia, a local priest, on board. The ship transferred to the island of Huahine, to the west. After a few days, Cook moved on to Raiatea. The ship remained here for six days before leaving. The *Endeavour* then sailed around Tahaa and stood off Bora Bora.
August The ship anchored on Raiatea's west coast, inside Passe Rautoanui. Cook left the Society Islands and sailed south. He arrived at Rurutu (as Tupaia had predicted) and continued south to search for the Great Southern Continent.
September Cook continued looking for the Great Southern Continent but at 40° S he turned west and headed for New Zealand.
October The *Endeavour* reached Te Ika a Maui (the North Island of New Zealand) in early October. Tupaia helped the communication between the local Māori and the British but there were still problems and some Māori died. Cook sailed, going south at first before returning north and rounding East Cape.
November Cook sailed west across the Bay of Plenty and put into Mercury Bay to observe a Transit of Mercury. He investigated the Firth of Thames then reached the Bay of Islands by the end of the month.
December After a few more days in the Bay of Islands, Cook continued north and rounded North Cape.
1770
Frederick North, Lord North, became Prime Minister.
Jefferys published *A Collection of Charts of the coasts of Newfoundland*, produced by Cook, Lane and Gilbert.
January The *Endeavour* worked its way south down the west coast of New Zealand from Cape Maria van Diemen. The ship rounded Taranaki and crossed to enter Queen Charlotte Sound at the northern end of Te Wai Pounamu (South Island). It anchored in Ship Cove.
February Cook left Queen Charlotte Sound, then sailed through Cook Strait. He proceeded down the east coast of Te Wai Pounamu as far as Otago.
March The ship rounded the south of the country and worked its way up the west coast to anchor at d'Urville Island. Cook had shown New Zealand to comprise two large islands and that it was not part of the Great Southern Continent. Cook sailed west from Cape Farewell across the Tasman Sea.
April Cook arrived at New Holland (Australia) at its southeastern corner in mid-April. He began sailing up the east coast, finally landing in Botany Bay. Cook charted the coast all the way north.
May The *Endeavour* left Botany Bay and continued north up the coast as far as the Northumberland Islands and Thirsty Sound (Queensland).
June Cook continued north through the Whitsunday Islands only to ground on the Great Barrier Reef on 11 June. Cook managed to limp the Endeavour into the mouth of the Endeavour River for repairs.
July The *Endeavour* was being repaired all month.
August Repairs completed, the ship left the Endeavour River on 4 August. Cook took the ship out through the reef to open sea. However, he could not see the coast and returned inside the reef. He rounded Cape York and took possession of New South Wales, as he called the coast he had just traversed. The *Endeavour* passed through the Torres Strait and sailed into the Arafura Sea.
September The *Endeavour* touched on the south coast of New Guinea. It sailed on past Timor to anchor at Savu. Cook continued along the south coast of Java to reach the entrance to the Sunda Strait.
October Cook took the ship through the Sunda Strait and round to Jakarta (Batavia). The *Endeavour* was in dire need of repair and the Dutch authorities agreed to carry them out.
November Cook and the *Endeavour* were stuck in Jakarta. Unfortunately, Jakarta was most unhealthy and members of the crew began to die. Seven men died there.
December Finally, on 26 December, the ship left Jakarta.
1771
January John Montagu, Earl of Sandwich, became First Lord of the Admiralty again. The ship passed through Sunda Strait and began its crossing of the Indian Ocean.
February The *Endeavour* slowly crossed the Indian Ocean, during which time 24 more men died.
March Cook reached Africa and brought the ship to anchor at Cape Town. They remained there a month to resupply the ship. Three more men died there.
April Cook left Cape Town and sailed north up the Atlantic.
The Cooks' daughter, Elizabeth, died on 9 April.
May Cook reached St Helena and joined a British convoy for the next passage north. They passed Ascension Island and crossed the Equator.
June The ship made a large sweep round the Azores and headed for Britain.
July Land's End was sighted and the *Endeavour* began sailing up the English Channel. Cook anchored the ship in the Downs off Deal on 13 July. He went ashore and immediately travelled to London. He had been away just under three years.
August Cook was promoted. He was introduced to King George III at St James's Palace and the King gave him his commission as Commander. Cook was appointed to command HMS *Scorpion* in order to do survey work.
September After prompting by Cook, the Admiralty determined to make another voyage to the Pacific to settle, once and for all, the question of the Southern Continent. The Navy Board was instructed to purchase two suitable vessels.
October Cook located three possible ships, all colliers like the *Endeavour*.
November The Navy Board purchased the *Marquis of Granby* and the *Marquis of Rockingham*, both from Whitby. They were renamed the *Drake* and the *Raleigh* respectively with Cook to command the former and Tobias Furneaux to command the latter.
December The Cooks went north to Yorkshire to visit his family and friends in

Great Ayton and Whitby.

1772

January The Cooks were still in Yorkshire. Cook's father was persuaded to go to live with his daughter Margaret in Redcar. Cook then arranged to sell the Great Ayton cottage. The Cooks returned to London.

February To avoid offending the Spanish, the ships' names had been changed again. The *Resolution* (ex-*Drake*) was being prepared at Deptford while the *Adventure* (ex-*Raleigh*) was at Woolwich. Joseph Banks expected to sail again and began having the *Resolution* refitted to suit his own wishes and demands.

March The refit demanded by Banks (and against Cook's wishes) delayed the departure.

April The refit continued.

May On 14 May, a pilot took the *Resolution* down the Thames to the Nore but pronounced it unfit to go to sea. The Admiralty saw reason and sent the ship to Sheerness to be restored to its original state. Banks was furious and withdrew from the voyage. The *Adventure* sailed on ahead to Plymouth.

June Johann Forster was selected to travel as naturalist in place of Banks. The *Resolution* was finally ready and Cook joined the ship at Sheerness on the 21st. They sailed for Plymouth.

July The Cooks' fourth son, George, was born 8 July.

Cook arrived at Plymouth on the 3rd. His Second Voyage began when the *Resolution* and the *Adventure* sailed from Plymouth on 13 July 1772. The ships crossed the Bay of Biscay and sailed down to anchor in Madeira at the end of the month.

August After restocking, the ships left Madeira and continued down the Atlantic passed the Canary Islands to reach the Cape Verde Islands. Cook sailed onto the south.

September The ships crossed the Equator and passed Ascension Island.

October George Cook died 1 October.

On 30 October, the ships anchored at Cape Town.

November Most of November was taken up with repairing and restocking the ships, which left Cape Town to sail south toward the Antarctic.

December Cook began looking for Cape Circumcision as described by the French explorer Bouvet.

1773

John Hawkesworth's retelling of the voyages of Wallis, Byron, Cook and Carteret was published as *An Account of the voyages undertaken in London*.

John Harrison finally awarded Longitude prize for his development of marine chronometers.

January Cook gave up looking for Cape Circumcision, which he felt had been an iceberg. He sailed off to the southeast and became the first person to cross the Antarctic Circle. He reached 67° 15' S before ice and cold forced the ships back north.

February The ships became separated in thick fog on 8 February. Furneaux took the *Adventure* towards Tasmania. Cook, though, headed back south-east towards Antarcitca and sailed east parallel to the Antarctic coast at about 60° S.

March Furneaux reached Tasmania. After a short stopover, he set course for New Zealand, the appointed rendezvouz. Cook, having sighted no land at high latitudes headed northeast and reached Dusky Sound in New Zealand.

April Furneaux reached Queen Charlotte Sound in New Zealand and anchored to wait for Cook. Cook spent the month exploring Dusky Sound.

May Cook left Dusky Sound and transferred to Queen Charlotte Sound where he rejoined Furneaux. The two ships were prepared for a sweep round the Pacific.

June The *Resolution* and the *Adventure* left together on 7 June and sailed out into the South Pacific on an easterly course.

July After sailing east, Cook headed north at the end of the month for Tahiti.

August The ships passed Pitcairn Island and encountered islands in the Tuamotu Archipelago, east of Tahiti. On 15 August, the ships were nearly wrecked on reefs at the eastern end of Tahiti. The ships made it through the reef to anchor at Tautira. Cook later transferred to Matavai Bay.

September Cook left Tahiti on 2 September and crossed to Huahine and Raiatea. Mai (Omai), a Huahine man, was taken on board by Furneaux. Cook next sailed for Tonga. Manuae and Te Au o Tu (the Hervey Islands), part of the Cook Islands, were inspected late in the month.

October The ships reached 'Eua in the Tongatapu Group on 2 October. After a week on 'Eua and neighbouring Tongatapu, Cook sailed southwest for New Zealand. Table Cape on Te Ika a Maui was reached but severe gales separated the ships before they could enter Cook Strait.

November Cook finally made it into Queen Charlotte Sound and waited for Furneaux, who had put into Tolaga Bay instead. Cook could wait no longer and left for another larger sweep of the South Pacific. Furneaux reached Queen Charlotte Sound after Cook's departure.

December Cook headed southeast toward Antarctica again. The *Resolution* reached 67°31' S before Cook turned north. A party of *Adventure*'s men were killed at Wharehunga Bay. Furneaux decided to sail home and left New Zealand aiming across the South Pacific for Cape Horn.

1774

January Cook performed a sweep in the central southern Pacific before disappointing his crew when he sailed south once more. The Resolution again crossed the Antarctic Circle to reach 71°10' S at 106°54' W. Cook headed north. Meanwhile, Furneaux was rounding Cape Horn and entering the South Atlantic.

February The *Resolution* headed north looking for land claimed by Juan Fernandez and Edward Davis. Cook was taken seriously ill.

March The ship anchored at Easter Island in mid-March. Cook still too ill to join the party that went ashore. Furneaux reached Cape Town.

April Cook reached the southern Marquesas Islands in early April. After a brief stay, he continued through the Tuamotu Archipelago to Matavai Bay in Tahiti. Furneaux left Cape Town to sail up the Atlantic.

May On 16 May, Cook left Tahiti and crossed to Huahine. After a week, he moved on to Raiatea.

June Cook left Raiatea for Tonga on a more northerly course than the previous year. The *Resolution* stopped at Palmerston Atoll (one of the Cook Islands) and Niue before arriving in the Ha'apai Group of Tonga. Cook anchored at Nomuka.

July Cook briefly called at Vatoa, a southern outlier of the Fiji Islands. He then reached Vanuatu (New Hebrides) and began charting that island group. He had approached Erromanga by the end of the month. Furneaux returned home, having anchored at Spithead.

August Cook remained in Vanuatu, charting from Erromanga south to Tanna and back north to Espiritu Santo.

September The *Resolution* left Vanuatu heading south-west. A few days later, it arrived at another island, New Caledonia. Cook spent the rest of the month charting there.

October From New Caledonia, Cook sailed south where he discovered Norfolk Island. After a very brief stop, Cook returned to Queen Charlotte Sound in New Zealand. He found signs that the *Adventure* had been there since his last visit.

November On 10 November, Cook left New Zealand to sail home via Cape Horn. He sailed across the Pacific close to 55° S.

December Cook reached South America on 17 December. He then followed the outer coast of Tierra del Fuego southeast. The *Resolution* spent Christmas in Christmas Sound. Cook pressed on round Cape Horn to anchor at Staten Island.

1775

Start of American War of Independence. Sayer and Bennett published the *North American Pilot*, containing many of Cook's charts.

January Cook set off from Staten Island to examine the South Atlantic. He arrived at South Georgia in the middle of the month and discovered the South Sandwich Islands at the end.

February The *Resolution* sailed past the South Sandwich Islands in thick fog before Cook sailed off to the north-east to make another search for Cape Circumcision. He was looking in the wrong location. He gave up and sailed for Cape Town.

March Cook reached Cape Town on 22 March.

April Cook left Cape Town on 27 April.

May The *Resolution* made a short visit to St Helena, followed by one to Ascension Island. He made a quick search for St Matthew, another mythical island.

June Cook visited Fernando de Noronha, then sailed north crossing the Equator.

July Cook called in at the Azores. The *Resolution* continued on to enter the English Channel. It anchored at Spithead on 30 July. Cook landed at Portsmouth and made his way to London.

August Cook was presented to the King at St James Palace. He was promoted to Post Captain and appointed to HMS *Kent*. That appointment was immediately cancelled and Cook was posted to Greenwich Hospital as Fourth Captain. He began attending the Royal Society Club.

September The *Resolution* went into the Dockyard at Deptford for a major overhaul. Unfortunately, Cook was rarely on hand and a very poor job was done.

December John Marra's *Journal* was published, the first account of the Second Voyage.

In late 1775, Charles Clerke was committed to King's Bench Prison in St George's Fields, Southwark after standing surety for his brother's debts.

1776

During 1776, Cook's portrait was painted by Hodges, Dance and Webber.

January Cook was involved in finding a companion vessel for the *Resolution* for a future voyage. A collier, the *Diligence* was located and purchased by the Navy Board. Its name was changed to the *Discovery* and it was sent for alterations.

February Cook was busy writing up his journals from the Second Voyage and working with Canon John Douglas, who was editing them for publication. Cook applied to go on the planned voyage to the Northwest Passage and to return Mai to the Pacific. He was immediately appointed and given his commission on the *Resolution*. Charles Clerke was transferred to command the *Discovery*.

March The *Resolution* came out of Deptford Dockyard. Cook was elected a Fellow of the Royal Society and read a paper to the Society.

April Cook was admitted as a Fellow of the Royal Society.

May Nathaniel Dance painted Cook's portrait.

The Cooks' fifth son, Hugh, was born 23 May.

June Cook joined the *Resolution* at the Nore and sailed it round to Plymouth. As Clerke was still detained, James Burney had already taken the *Discovery* there.

July Cook and the *Resolution* sailed from Plymouth on 12 July to begin the Third Voyage. The *Discovery* was left behind as Charles Clerke was still in prison. The *Resolution* passed Cape Ortegal near the end of the month. Clerke appeared at Southwark Town Hall on 29 July and obtained his release. He hurried immediately to Plymouth to join his ship. Unfortunately, the time in prison affected Clerke's health.

America declared itself independent on 4 July.

August The *Discovery* finally left on 1 August with instructions to meet the *Resolution* at Cape Town. Cook put in at Tenerife and later passed through the Cape Verde Islands.

September Cook crosssed the Equator then passed the Brazilian coast.

October The *Resolution* reached Cape Town. Cook had the ship repaired and restocked while he waited for Clerke. He learned he had been awarded the Copley Medal of the Royal Society.

November The *Discovery* arrrived on 10 November. A small group made an expedition to the Drakenstein Hills.

December The ships sailed together on the 1st. They sailed through the Prince Edward Islands and reached Kerguelen Island. The ships anchored in two locations and Cook examined the desolate island.

1777

January Cook headed east across the souther Indian Ocean and arrived at Tasmania. The ships anchored in Adventure Cove where Furneaux had been three years earlier. Cook left and headed for New Zealand.

February The *Resolution* and the *Discovery* spent two weeks in Queen Charlotte Sound. Cook paid a visit to Wharehunga Cove, the site of the massacre four years earlier. He then sailed out into the Pacific.

March At the end of the month, the ships stood off Mangaia, the southernmost island in the Cook group.

Georg Forster's *A Voyage around the world* was published.

April Cook continued north through the Cook Islands, visiting Atiu, Takutea, Manuae and Palmerston Atoll. He sailed on to reach Tonga. The ships anchored at Nomuka in the Ha'apai Group.

May Cook met Finau, a chief, and the Tu'i Tonga. Finau joined the British when they set off to examine Lifuka, Uoleva and other islands in the group.

Cook's *Voyage towards the South Pole* was published in London.

June The ships returned to Nomuka but encountered a storm off Kotu. From Nomuka Cook headed south to Tongatapu and anchored off Holeva Point on 10 June. The ships were ready to sail by the 25th but Cook remained. He passed up opportunities to visit nearby Samoa and Fiji.

July Cook continued to linger on Tongatapu, being entertained by the Tu'i Tonga and other dignitaries. He observed a solar eclipse. Finally on the 10th, Cook sailed across to 'Eua. Cook sailed south away from Tonga on 19 July.

August Tubuai, an island in the Austral Group, was visited before Cook arrived at Tahiti. He spent ten days at Tautira near the eastern end of the island then transferred to Matavai Bay. He was welcomed by Tu and To'ofa. Cook was ill at this time.

September Cook made his first visit to Moorea.

October A goat was stolen. Cook set off in pursuit, burning houses and canoes in an uncharacteristic overreaction. He then crossed to Huahine where Mai was returned to his home island.

November Cook sailed over to Raiatea. During the stopover, three men tried to desert.

December Cook left Raiatea for the last time and stood off Bora Bora while he bartered for an anchor recovered after a visit by Bougainville a few years earlier. The *Resolution* and the *Discovery* next headed north for the North Pacific. They crossed the Equator and arrived at an island, named Christmas Island for the time of year.

1778

Johann Forster's *Observations made during a voyage round the world* was published during 1778.

Sir Joseph Banks was elected President of the Royal Society.

Cook's old ships *Endeavour* (now the *Lord Sandwich*) and the *Lark* were sunk in Newport Harbor, Rhode Island, to thwart the French navy.

January The ships continued north and in mid-January encountered a new group of islands, Hawai'i. Cook anchored at Waimea on Kaua'i. After a few days, Cook moved the ships across to Ni'ihau.

February Ni'ihau provided many yams before Cook left, heading north-east across the North Pacific to America to look for the Northwest Passage.

March Cook reached the American coast at Oregon. Bad weather hindered progress for a few days before the ships sailed north up the coast. Cook missed the Strait of Juan de Fuca but put into a large inlet on the 29th. This was Nootka Sound on Vancouver Island.

April The British remained in Nootka Sound for most of April. The ships were repaired and the inlet was explored. They also trade for sea otter pelts. The fur trade that this engendered would flourish for a few years, nearly led to a war between Britain and Spain, and the near-extinction of the sea otter. Cook left at the end of the month.

May The *Resolution* and the *Discovery* continued north but at a distance from the coast and outside the Queen Charlotte and Baranof Islands. They followed the coast as it trended west and entered a large inlet, Prince William Sound. After a few days, they left to head southwest before they found an even larger inlet, into which they sailed. Now able

to sail north, Cook was hopeful that this was the Northwest Passage.
June The inlet, Cook Inlet, proved not to be the Passage and Cook had to retrace his route back into the open sea. He next sailed past Kodiak Island, the Shumagin and Sanak Islands and the Alaskan Peninsula. They ships put into Samgoonoodha on the island of Unalaska at the end of the month.
July Cook found a pass that allowed him to enter the Bering Sea and he was able to sail north-east. Cook explored Bristol Bay but found no sign of a Passage. He sailed on past St Matthew Island.
August The ships approached the Bering Strait but Cook put in at St Lawrence Bay on the Chukotskiy Peninsula before he passed through the Strait. He crossed the Arctic Circle and reached 70° 14' N near Icy Cape when ice blocked progress. Cook crossed over to the Russian shore and followed it back to the Bering Strait.
September Cook sailed south through the strait then entered Norton Sound, again without any sign of the Northwest Passage. Cook returned toward Unalaska. He needed to sail south to avoid the winter.
October After a stopover of nearly a month at Unalaska, where he met Russian fur traders, Cook left to sail south for warmer climes.
Cook was 50 years old on 27 October.
November Cook's objective was the Hawaiian Group of islands that he had visited in January. He reached Maui in the group on the 26th. After a couple of days, Cook headed for the neighbouring large island of Hawai'i.
December Cook puzzled his crew by sailing slowly round the island and making no apparent attempt to land.

1779
January Finally, on 16 January, Cook put into Kealakekua Bay on the west coast of Hawai'i. The British were received well but probably outstayed their welcome.
February The *Resolution* and the *Discovery* left on 4 February but damage in a storm forced them back to Kealakekua. This time the reception was much cooler. Cook tried to take the Hawaiian Chief hostage after a theft, and, in the ensuing fight, Cook was killed. Clerke assumed overall command and worked hard to restore peace between the two sides. He moved to the *Resolution* while John Gore took over the *Discovery.* Relations were good again when the ships sailed on 22 February. They worked their way through the islands to reach O'ahu.
March Clerke put in at Kaua'i and Ni'ihau, then set off for Arctic waters to resume the search for the Northwest Passage.
April The ships reached Avacha Bay in Kamchatka on 24 April. They anchored off Petropavlovsk.
Cook's father, James Cook senior, was buried at Marske on 1 April.
May The British remained in Kamchatka all month. Gore and King led a party to visit Governor Behm who resided on the other coast of the peninsula.
June The ships left Avacha Bay on 19 June and headed north up the coast. By the 30th, they had sailed as far as Cape Navarin.
July Clerke took the ships through the Bering Strait and across the Arctic Circle into the Chukchi Sea only for the ice to foil him close to where Cook had been a year earlier. He returned south.
August The ships sailed south but a few days out from Avacha Bay, Clerke died. Gore took over command and James King became captain of the *Discovery.* Clerke was buried in Petropavlosk.
September The British remained in Avacha Bay all month.
October Gore left on 9 October and headed south along the Kuril Islands. They were off Japan on the 26th
November The ships continued down the coast of Japan then made a sweep of the Pacific past Iwo Jima to pass through the Bashi Channel between Taiwan and the Philippines.
December They reached Macao on 4 December. King visited Canton for supplies and to sell the sea otter pelts.

1780
January The ships left Macao on 13 January. They crossed the South China Sea and approached Sumatra. News of Cook's death reached London independently after Governor Behm's journey from Kamchatka across Russia. Elizabeth Cook was granted a pension.
February Gore took the ships through the Sunda Strait and set off across the Indian Ocean.
March The ships continued their slow passage across the Indian Ocean.
April On 12 April, Gore anchored the ships in Sim on's Bay, south of Cape Town, for supplies.
May Gore sailed on 10 May and headed up the Atlantic. He had decided to sail all the way without stopping.
June The ships were sailing north.
July The ships were still sailing north.
August Gales forced the ships to the west of Ireland and Scotland. Gore put in at Orkney on 22 August. Gore delayed their departure. King was dispatched to London with their news.
September Gore finally left Orkney on 20 September. The ships sailed south down the east coast of Scotland and England but stopped at Yarmouth for some repairs.
October In early October, the *Resolution* and the *Discovery* sailed up the River Thames at the end of their voyage, both without their original captains.
Nathaniel Cook died on 5 October. His ship, HMS *Thunderer*, was lost in a hurricane in the Caribbean.

1782
Daniel Solander died.
April Augustus, Viscount Keppel, became First Lord of the Admiralty.

1784
June *A Voyage to the Pacific Ocean in the years 1776, 1777, 1778, 1779 and 1780. Vol I and Vol II written by Captain J. Cook, Vol III by Captain J. King*, edited by Canon John Douglas, was published in London.

1785
James Hanna became the first sea otter fur trader to reach Nootka Sound.
A Coat of arms was granted to Elizabeth Cook in memory of James Cook.
The French explorer, Laperouse, set off on his Pacific voyage.

1788
Elizabeth Cook left Mile End and moved across the river to live in the High Street,Clapham.
Andrew Kippis' *The Life of Captain James Cook* published.

1789
The Mutiny on the *Bounty* took place involving William Bligh who had been master on the *Resolution.*

1793
The *Resolution* (now *La Liberte*) sank at its moorings in Newport Harbor, Rhode Island.
Hugh Cook went to Christ's College, Cambridge University.
December Hugh Cook died in Cambrdige on 21 December.

1794
January The Cook's first son, James Cook, died on 25 January. He died in unexplained circumstances, perhaps drowned, in Poole Harbour while on his way to his ship, HMS *Spitfire.*

1795
Christiana Cocker, Cook's sister, died.
The Hydrographic Office established in London.

1798
Coleridge's *Rime of the Ancient Mariner* published.

1804
October Margaret Fleck, Cook's sister, was buried on 17 October.

1820
Sir Joseph Banks died.

1827
Elizabeth Cook went to live with her cousin, Isaac Smith, at his home at Merton Abbey, south of London.

1831
Isaac Smith died. Elizabeth Cook returned to live at her house in Clapham.

1835
May Elizabeth Cook died on 13 May, aged 94. She had been a widow for 56 years and had outlived all her six children.

Appendix V: Gazetteers of places named after James Cook, his ships and men who sailed with James Cook on his ships

A: PLACES BELIEVED TO HAVE BEEN NAMED AFTER JAMES COOK

Bahia de Cook, Tierra del Fuego, Chile, 55°10'S 70°15'W
Baie de Cook, Huahine, French Polynesia, 16°43'S 151°02'W
Baie de Cook, Moorea, French Polynesia, 17°30'S 149°48'W
Big Cook Pond, Newfoundland, Canada, 48°51'N 58°04'W
Cape Cook, Tanna, Vanuatu, 19°32'S 169°29'E
Cape Cook, Vancouver Island, Canada, 50°07'N 127°55'W
Captain Cook, Hawai'i, United States, 19°30'N 155°55'W
Captain Cook Point, Oregon, United States, 44°16'N 124°07'W
Captain Cook's Rock, Pentecost, Vanuatu, 15°57'S 168°11'E
Cook (suburb), Canberra, ACT, Australia, 35°16'S 149°04'E
Cook Bay, Cairns, Queensland, Australia, 16°46'S 145°41'E
(Cook Bay) Hanga Roa, Easter Island, Chile, 27°08'S 109°26'W
Cook Bay, South Georgia, 54°03'S 37°08'W
Cook Bay, Erromango, Vanuatu, 18°48'S 169°13'E
Cook Bay, Malekula, Vanuatu, 16°30'S 167°47'E
Cook Bluff, Mercury Bay, New Zealand, 36°50'S 175°46'E
Cook Calotte (Glacier), Kerguelen Island, 49°25'S 69°10'E
Cook Channel, Dusky Sound, New Zealand, 45°46'S 166°44'E
Cook Channel, Nootka Sound, Canada, 49°45'N 126°37'W
Cook Crater, The Moon, 18°00'S 49°00'E
Cook Creek, Tasmania, Australia, 43°22'S 147°20'E
Cook Glacier, South Georgia, 54°26'S 36°10'W
Cook Inlet, Alaska, United States, 60°00'N 152°00'W
Cook Island, New South Wales, Australia, 28°12'S 153°35'E
Cook Island, South Sandwich, 59°27'N 27°08'W
Cook Island, Christmas Island, Kiribati, 1°57'N 157°28'W
Cook Islands, Cook Islands, 10-22°S 157-166°W
Cook Mountains, Antarctica, 79°25'N 158°00'E
(Cook Point) Houma Toloa, Tongatapu, Tonga, 21°18'S 175°07'W
Cook Point, Easter Island, Chile, 27°08'S 109°26'W
Cook Point, Hawai'i, United States, 19°29'N 155°56'W
Cook Reef, Queensland, Australia, 10°22'S 141°35'E
Cook Reef, Emae, Vanuatu, 17°05'S 168°16'E
Cook Reef, New Caledonia, 20°00'S 164°00'E
Cook River, Te Wai Pounamu, New Zealand, 43°27'S 169°46'E
Cook Rock, Cook Strait, New Zealand, 41°02'S 174°25'E
Cook Rock, Candlemas Islands, South Sandwich, 57°04'S 26°50'W
Cook Shoal, Queensland, Australia, 10°04'S 141°23'E
Cook Strait, New Zealand, 41°20'S 174°22'W
Cook Stream, Dusky Sound, New Zealand, 45°48'S 166°34'E
Cook's Anchorage, Tahiti, French Polynesia, 17°45'S 149°09'W
Cook's Bay, Ontario, Canada, 79°30'N 44°15'W
Cook's Bay, Mercury Bay, New Zealand, 36°50'S 175°44'E
Cook's Bay, New Guinea, Indonesia, 6°20'S 138°20'E
Cook's Beach, Mercury Bay, New Zealand, 36°51'S 175°44'E
Cook's Brook, Newfoundland, Canada, 48°55'N 58°04'W
Cook's Chasm, Oregon, United States, 44°17'N 124°07'W
Cook's Cove, Bay of Islands, New Zealand, 35°15'S 174°09'E
Cook's Cove, Tolaga Bay, New Zealand, 38°23'S 178°20'E
Cook's Harbour, Newfoundland, Canada, 51°36'N 55°51'W
Cook's Island, Palmerston Atoll, Cook Islands, 18°05'S 163°11'W
Cook's Look, Queensland, Australia, 14°40'S 145°27'E
Cook's Lookout, Queen Charlotte S., New Zealand, 41°13'S 174°13'E
Cook's Passage, Queensland, Australia, 14°32'S 145°33'E
Cook's Point, Newfoundland, Canada, 51°37'N 55°50'W
Cook's Pyramid, Tanna, Vanuatu, 19°32'S 169°29'E
Cook's River, Botany Bay, Australia, 33°57'S 151°10'E
(Cook's River), Alaska, United States, *see* Cook Inlet
Cook's Stream, Botany Bay, Australia, 34°01'S 151°13'E
Cook's Tooth, Te Ika a Maui, New Zealand, 40°23'S 176°37'E
Cooktown, Queensland, Australia, 15°28'S 145°15'E
Little Cook Pond, Newfoundland, Canada, 48°52'N 58°04'W
Mount Cook / Aoraki, Te Wai Pounamu, New Zealand, 43°36'N 170°09'E
Mount Cook (village), Te Wai Pounamu, New Zealand, 43°44'S 170°06'E
Mount Cook, Tasmania, Australia, 43°25'S 147°21'E
Mount Cook, Alaska / Yukon, USA / Canada, 60°11'N 139°59'W
Mount Cook, Cooktown, Queensland, Australia, 15°30'S 145°16'E
Mount Cook, Magnetic Island, Queensland, Australia, 19°08'S 146°50'E
Mount Cook (suburb), Wellington, New Zealand, 41°18'S 174°46'E
Puerto Cook, Staten Island, Argentina, 54°45'S 64°03'W
Recif de Cook, New Caledonia, 20°00'S 164°00'E
Small Cooks Islands, Palmerston Atoll, Cook Islands, 18°03'S 163°07'W
Teluk Cook, New Guinea, Indonesia, 6°20'S 138°20'E

B: PLACES BELIEVED TO HAVE BEEN NAMED AFTER CREW MEMBERS OR SHIPS

Anderson Point, Nootka Sound, Canada, 49°47'N 126°27'W
Adventure Bay, Tasmania, Australia, 40°00'S 148°10'E
Banks' Island, British Columbia, Canada, 53°30'N 130°20'W
Banks' Islands, Vanuatu, 14°00'S 167°30'E
Banks' Peninsula, Te Wai Pounamu, New Zealand, 43°43'S 173°08'E
Banks' Strait, Tasmania, Australia, 40°50'S 148°00'E
Bankstown, Sydney, Australia, 33°55'S 151°02'E
Bligh Island, Nootka Sound, Canada, 49°48'N 126°30'W
Bligh Island, S. Alaska, United States, 60°49'N 146°46'W
Bootie Island, Queensland, Australia, 11°51'S 143°18'E
Buchan Isle, Queensland, Australia, 11°51'S 143°18'E
Burney's Beach, Queen Charlotte S., New Zealand, 41°11'S 174°17'E
Cabo Colnett, Staten Island, Argentina, 54°42'S 64°22'W
Cabo Furneaux, Staten Island, Argentina, 54°42'S 63°52'W
Cape Banks, Botany Bay, Australia, 34°01'S 151°15'E
Cape Colnett, New Caledonia, 20°30'S 164°45'E
Cape Solander, Botany Bay, Australia, 34°02'S 151°14'E
Cape Vancouver, Western Australia, Australia, 34°55'S 118°11'E
Cape Vancouver, Alaska, United States, 60°32'N 165°28'W
Clerke Island, Queensland, Australia, 11°58'S 143°17'E
Clerke Peninsula, Nootka Sound, Canada, 49°45'N 126°30'W
Clerke Point, Vancouver Island, Canada, 50°05'N 127°48'W
Clerke's Rocks, South Georgia, 55°00'S 34°50'W
Cooper Bay, South Georgia, 54°48'S 35°54'W
Cooper Island, Dusky Sound, New Zealand, 45°43'S 166°50'E
Cooper's Island, South Georgia, 54°49'S 35°53'W
Discovery Point, Nootka Sound, Canada, 49°40'N 126°32'W
Endeavour Inlet, Queen Charlotte S., New Zealand, 41°08'S 174°11'E
Endeavour Reef, Queensland, Australia, 15°47'S 145°35'E
Endeavour River, Queensland, Australia, 15°28'S 145°14'E
Endeavour Strait, Queensland, Australia, 10°45'S 142°15'E
Endeavour Stream, Magnetic Island, Australia, 19°07'S 146°51'E
Forster's Passage, South Sandwich, 59°15'S 26°50'W
Freezland Rock, Montagu Island, South Sandwich, 59°03'S 26°45'W
Furneaux Isles Group, Tasmania, Australia, 43°18'S 147°22'E
Gilbert Islands, Breaksea Sound, New Zealand, 45°35'S 166°40'E
Gore Bay, Te Wai Pounamu, New Zealand, 42°52'S 173°19'E
Gore Island, Queensland, Australia, 11°59'S 143°15'E
Gore Island, Nootka Sound, Canada, 49°48'N 126°18'W
Gore Point, S. Alaska, United States, 59°11'N 150°57'W
Grindle Rock, Montagu Island, South Sandwich, 59°03'S 26°40'W

Hicks Bay, Te Ika a Maui, New Zealand, 37°35'S 178°18'E
Hicks Island, Queensland, Australia, 11°59'S 143°16'E
Islas Gilbert, Tierra del Fuego, Chile, 55°00'N 71°10'W
King Island, W. Alaska, United States, 64°59'N 168°03'W
King Passage, Nootka Sound, Canada, 49°47'N 126°18'W
Lake Forster, Dusky Sound, New Zealand, 45°48'S 166°33'E
Little Solander Island, Te Wai Pounamu, New Zealand, 46°34'S 166°51'E
Magra Islet, Queensland, Australia, 11°52'S 143°17'E
Manley Island, Queensland, Australia, 11°51'S 143°18'E
Mount Clerke, Dusky Sound, New Zealand, 45°41'S 166°41'E
Mount Colnett, New Caledonia, 20°31'S 164°41'E
Mount Edgecumbe, Dusky Sound, New Zealand, 45°45'S 166°52'E
Mount Forster, Dusky Sound, New Zealand, 45°41'S 166°46'E
Mount Gore, Nootka Sound, Canada, 49°43'N 126°18'W
Mount Hodges, Te Wai Pounamu, New Zealand, 45°42'S 166°46'E
Mount Patten, Dusky Sound, New Zealand, 45°39'S 166°45'E
Mount Sparrman, Dusky Sound, New Zealand, 45°48'S 166°38'E
Mount Vancouver, Alaska / Yukon, USA / Canada, 60°21'N 139°41'W
Mount Wales, Dusky Sound, New Zealand, 45°38'S 166°40'E
Orton Island, Queensland, Australia, 11°59'S 143°14'E
Patten Passage, Queen Charlotte S., New Zealand, 41°11'S 174°15'E
Pickersgill Cove, Tierra del Fuego, Chile, 55°25'S 69°50'W
Pickersgill Harbour, Dusky Sound, New Zealand, 45°48'S 166°35'E
Pickersgill Island, Queen Charlotte S., New Zealand, 41°10'S 174°17'E
Pickersgill Island, South Georgia, 54°40'S 36°45'W
Pickersgill Reef, Queensland, Australia, 15°52'S 145°35'E
Point Banks, S. Alaska, United States, 58°38'N 152°17'W
Point Hicks, Victoria, Australia, 37°48'S 149°16'E
Point Riou, S. Alaska, United States, 59°53'N 141°30'W
Port Resolution, Tanna, Vanuatu, 19°32'S 169°29'E
Puerto Clerke, Tierra del Fuego, Chile, 55°25'S 69°50'W
Puerto Vancouver, Staten Island, Argentina, 54°48'S 64°05'W
Resolution Bay, Te Wai Pounamu, New Zealand, 41°07'S 174°13'E
Resolution Cove, Nootka Sound, Canada, 49°42'N 126°30'W
Resolution Island, Te Wai Pounamu, New Zealand, 45°39'S 166°35'E
Solander Island, Te Wai Pounamu, New Zealand, 46°34'S 166°54'E
Solander Island, Vancouver Island, Canada, 50°07'N 127°56'W
Sutherland Point, Botany Bay, Australia, 34°01'S 151°13'E
Tupaia Head, New South Wales, Australia, 33°58'S 151°16'E
Vancouver, British Columbia, Canada, 49°13'N 123°06'W
Vancouver Island, British Columbia, Canada, 49°30'N 126°00'W
Vancouver Island, Chile, 51°20'S 74°10'E
Wales Island, British Columbia, Canada, 54°45'S 130°30'E
Wales Point, British Columbia, Canada, 54°42'S 130°28'E
Wales Point, Dusky Sound, New Zealand, 45°48'S 166°35'E
Williamson Passage, Nootka Sound, Canada, 49°49'N 126°18'W
Willis Island, South Georgia, 54°00'S 38°15'W
Young Nick's Head, Te Ika a Maui, New Zealand, 38°45'S 177°59'E

Appendix VI: Royal Navy ships on which James Cook served or sailed

Eagle, Fourth Rate, 58 guns, 1124bm, 44.8 x 12.8, built at Harwich by Barnard 1745, Capt Joseph Hamar/Hugh Palliser, Cook on board 1755-57 as AB/Master's mate.

Falmouth, Fourth Rate, 50 guns, 1052bm, 43.9 x 12.5, built at Woolwich by Dockyard 1752, Cook on board 1756 as passenger.

St Albans, Fourth Rate, 60 guns, 1191bm, 45.7 x 13.1, built at Deptford by West 1747, Cook on board 1756 as passenger.

Solebay, Sixth Rate, 24 guns, 442bm, 32.3 x 9.1, built at Plymouth by Dockyard 1742, Capt Robert Craig, Cook on board 1757 as Master.

Pembroke, Fourth Rate, 60 guns, 1247bm, 47.5 x 12.8, built at Plymouth by Dockyard 1757, Capt John Simcoe/John Wheelock, Cook on board 1757-59 as Master.

Northumberland, Third Rate, 70 guns, 1414bm, 48.8 x 13.7, built at Plymouth by Dockyard 1750, Capt William Adams/Nicholas Bateman, Cook on board 1759-62 as Master.

Antelope, Fourth Rate, 54 guns, 853bm, 40.8 x 11.6, built at Woolwich by Dockyard 1741, Capt Thomas Graves, Cook on board 1763 as passenger.

Tweed, Fifth Rate, 32 guns, 661bm, 39 x 10.4, built at Hull by Blaydes 1759, Capt Charles Douglas, Cook on board 1763 as Surveyor.

Grenville, Schooner, 12 guns, 69bm, 16.8 x 5.2, built at Massachusetts 1763, ex-*Sally*, purchased, Cook on board 1763-67 as Captain.

Lark, Fifth Rate, 32 guns, 646bm, 38.7 x 10.4, built at Rotherhithe by Bird 1762, Capt Thompson, Cook on board 1764 as passenger.

Endeavour, Bark, 6 guns, 368bm, 29.7 x 8.9, built at Whitby by Fishburn 1764, ex-*Earl of Pembroke*, purchased 1768, Cook on board 1768-71 as Captain.

Resolution, Sloop, 12 guns, 462bm, 33.8 x 10.8, built at Whitby by Fishburn 1770, ex-*Marquis of Granby/Drake*, 1771, Cook on board 1772-75 and 1779-79 as Captain.

Adventure, Sloop, 10 guns, 336bm, 29.7 x 8.7, built at Whitby by Fishburn 1770, ex-*Marquis of Rockingham/Raleigh*, purchased 1771, Capt Tobias Furneaux, Cook on board 1772-74.

Discovery, Sloop, 299bm, 27.9 x 8.4, built at Whitby by Langbourn 1774, ex-*Diligence*, purchased 1774, Capt Charles Clerke, Cook on board 1776-80.

Notes

1. Dimensions are length by width in metres.
2. In tonnage, bm means builder's measurement.
3. Type - rate refers to the number of guns carried. The lower the rate, the more guns.

Sources

1. Lyon, David. *The Sailing Navy List: all the ships of the Royal Navy - built, purchased and captured - 1688-1860* (London 1993)
2. Colledge, J J. *Ships of the Royal Navy* (London 2003)

BIBLIOGRAPHY

A fuller bibliography can be found on the supporting website, Captain Cook Encyclopaedia, at http://www.CaptainCookEncyclopaedia.com

NARRATIVES

First voyage

Hawkesworth, John, *An Account of the voyages undertaken by the order of His Present Majesty for making discoveries in the Southern Hemisphere, and successively performed by Commodore Byron, Captain Wallis, Captain Carteret, and Captain Cook, in the Dolphin, the Swallow, and the Endeavour: drawn up from the journals which were kept by the several commanders, and from the papers of Joseph Banks, Esq. Illustrated with cuts, and a great variety of charts and maps relative to countries now first discovered, or hitherto but imperfectly known.* 3 vols (London: Strahan and Cadell, 1773).

Second voyage

Cook, James, *A Voyage towards the South Pole, and round the world. Performed in His Majesty's ships the Resolution and Adventure, in the years, 1772, 1773, 1774, and 1775. Written by James Cook, commander of the Resolution. In which is included, Captain Furneaux's narrative of his proceedings in the Adventure during the separation of the ships. Illustrated with maps and charts, and a variety of portraits and views drawn during the voyage by Mr. Hodges.* 2 vols (London: Strahan and Cadell, 1777).

Third voyage

Cook, James, and James King, *A Voyage to the Pacific Ocean, undertaken, by the command of His Majesty, for making discoveries in the northern hemisphere, to determine the position and extent of the west side of North America, its distance from Asia, and the practicability of a northern passage to Europe, performed under the direction of Captains Cook, Clerke, and Gore, in His Majesty's ships the Resolution and Discovery, in the years 1776, 1777, 1778, 1779, and 1780. In three volumes: vol. 1 and 2 written by Captain J. Cook, vol. 3 by Captain J. King. Illustrated with maps and charts, from the original drawings mad by Lieut. Henry Roberts under the direction of Captain Cook; and with a great variety of portraits of incidents, drawn by Mr. Webber during the voyage, and engraved by the most eminent artists.* 3 vols (London: Nicol and Cadell, 1784).

MONOGRAPHS

Abbott, John Lawrence, *John Hawkesworth: eighteenth-century man of letters* (Madison: University of Wisconsin Press, 1982).

Adams, Brian, *The Flowering of the Pacific: being an account of Joseph Banks' travels in the South Seas and the story of his Florilegium* (Sydney: Collins, 1986).

Alexander, Michael, *Omai: "Noble savage"* (London: Collins & Harvill Press, 1977).

Archbishop Herring's visitation returns, edited by S L Ollard, and P C Walker. 5 vols (Wakefield: Yorkshire Archaeological Society, 1928–31).

Augustin, Stephan, *Kunstsachen von Cooks Reisen - Die Sammlung und ihre Geschichte im Volkerkundemuseum Herrnhut* (Dresden: Museum fur Volkerkunde. 1993).

Badger, Geoffrey, *The Explorers of the Pacific* (Kenthurst, NSW: Kangaroo Press, 1996).

Baker, Simon, *The Ship: retracing Cook's Endeavour voyage* (London: BBC, 2002).

Ballantyne, R M, *The Cannibal Islands; or Captain Cook's adventures in the South Seas* (London: Nisbet, 1869).

Banks, Joseph, *The Endeavour journal of Joseph Banks: 1768–1771*, edited by J C Beaglehole (Sydney: The Trustees of the Public Library of New South Wales in association with Angus and Robertson, 1962).

_____, *Journal of Joseph Banks in the Endeavour* (Genesis Publications, 1980).

Barrow, Terence, *Captain Cook in Hawaii* (Norfolk Island: Island Heritage, 1978).

Bassani, Ezio, *Cook, Polinesia a Napoli nel Settecento* (Bologna: 1982).

Bauman, Richard, *Let Your Words Be Few: Symbolism of Speaking and Silence Among Seventeenth-Century Quakers* (Cambridge: Cambridge University Press, 1983).

Baume, Eric, *Devil Lord's daughter* (New York: Dodd, Mead, 1948).

Bayfield, Henry Wolsey, *The St. Lawrence Survey Journals of Captain Bayfield, 1829–1853*, edited by Ruth McKenzie 2 vols (Toronto: The Champlain Society, 1984, 1986).

Beaglehole, John Cawte, *Cook the writer* (Sydney: Sydney University Press, 1970).

_____, *The Death of Captain Cook* (Wellington: Alexander Turnbull Library, 1979).

_____, *The Exploration of the Pacific* (London: A & C Black, 1966).

_____, *The Life of Captain James Cook* (London: A & C Black, 1974).

Begg, A Charles, *Dusky Bay* (Christchurch, NZ: Whitcombe & Tombs, 1968).

_____, and Neil C Begg, *James Cook and New Zealand* (Wellington: Government Printer, 1969).

Besant, Walter, *Captain Cook* (London: Macmillan, 1890).

Betts, Jonathan, *John Harrison* (London: National Maritime Museum, 1993).

Between belief and transgression: structuralist essays in religion, history and myth, edited by Michel Izard & Pierre Smith (Chicago: Chicago University Press, 1982).

Bibliography of Captain James Cook, R.N., F.R.S., circumnavigator (New York: Burt Franklin, 1968).

Bibliography of Captain James Cook, R.N., F.R.S., circumnavigator, edited by M K Beddie. 2nd ed (Sydney: Council of the Library of New South Wales, 1970).

Bligh, William, *A Voyage to the South Sea...in His Majesty's Ship the Bounty* (London: Nicol, 1792). [reprinted Adelaide: Libraries Board of South Australia, 1979]

Blunden, Godfrey, *Charco Harbour* (London: Weidenfeld & Nicolson, 1968).

Bolton King, John, *James King R.N.* ([Plymouth]: South West Maritime History Society, 2004).

Boswell, James, *Boswell: Laird of Auchinleck, 1778–1782,* edited by Joseph W Reed. (New York: McGraw-Hill, 1977).

_____, *Boswell: the Ominous years, 1774–1776*, edited by Charles Ryskamp (London: Heinemann, 1963).

Bottle of notes: public sculpture for Middlesbrough by Claes Oldenburg & Coosje Van Bruggen (Middlesbrough: Middlesbrough Borough Council, 199?).

Bougainville, Louis-Antoine de, *Pacific Journal of Louis-Antoine De Bougainville, 1767–1768,* edited by John Dunmore. Third series, no 9 (London: Hakluyt Society, 2003).

_____, *A Voyage round the World. Performed by Order of His Most Christian Majesty, in the Years 1766–9*, translated from the French by John Reinhold Forster. Bibliotheca Australiana, vol 12. (Amsterdam: N Israel, 1967). [London: J Nourse, 1772.]

Bowen, E G, *David Samwell* (Cardiff: University of Wales Press, 1974).

Broc, Numa, *La Géographie des Philosophes: Géographes et Voyageurs Français au XVIIIe-Siècle* (Paris: Éditions Ophrys, 1974).

Brosses, Charles de, *Histoire des Navigations aux Terres Australes. Contenant ce que l'on sçait des moeurs et des productions des Contrées découvertes jusqu'e à ce jour.* Bibliotheca Australiana, vol 1–2. 2 vols (Amsterdam: N Israel, 1967 [Paris: Durand, 1756]).

Brown, Nigel, *The Cook inventory, compiled by Nigel Brown, from 100 works 'dealing' with Captain James Cook by the Artist* (Auckland, NZ: N Brown & Susan McLaughlin, 1998).

Burke, Edmund, *The Correspondence of Edmund Burke. Volume VII, January 1792–August 1794* (Cambridge: Cambridge University Press, 1968).

Burney, James, *A Chronological History of the North-Eastern Voyages of Discovery; and of the early Eastern Navigations of the Russians.* Bibliotheca Australiana, vol 49. (Amsterdam: N Israel, 1969 [London: 1819).

_____, *A Chronological History of Voyages and Discoveries in the South Sea, or Pacific Ocean.* Bibliotheca Australiana, vol 3–7. 5

vols (Amsterdam: N Israel, 1967 [London: Luke Hansard, 1803–17]).
_____, *With Captain James Cook in the Antarctic and Pacific: the journal of James Burney, Second Lieutenant of the Adventure on Cook's second voyage, 1772–1773* (Canberra: National Library of Australia, 1975).
Burnicle, Ada, *Genealogical study of the family of Captain James Cook, R.N., F.R.S., 1728–1779* (Middlesbrough: Middlesbrough Borough Council, 1988).
Bushnell, O A, *The Return of Lono: a novel of Captain Cook's last voyage* (Honolulu: University Press of Hawaii, 1979).
Byron, John, *Byron's Journal of his Circumnavigation, 1764–1766*, edited by Robert E Gallagher. Second Series, no 122 (Cambridge: Hakluyt Society, 1964).
Callegari, Dennis, *Cook's cannon and anchor: the recovery and conservation of relics from HMB Endeavour* (Kenthurst, NSW: Kangaroo Press, 1994).
Campbell, Gordon, *Captain James Cook, R.N., F.R.S.* (London: Hodder and Stoughton, 1936).
Captain Cook: navigator and scientist, Papers presented at the Cook Bicentenary Symposium Canberra, 1 May 1969, edited by G M Badger (Canberra: Australian National University Press, 1970).
Captain Cook and the South Pacific, edited by T C Mitchell (London: British Museum, 1979).
Captain Cook Country Tour (Middlesbrough: Captain Cook Tourism Association, 1994).
Captain Cook's second voyage: the Journals of Lieutenants Elliott and Pickersgill (London: Caliban, 1984).
Captain Cook's South Sea Island vocabularies, edited by Peter A Lanyon-Orgill (Byfleet, UK: the editor, 1979).
Captain James Cook: image and impact, South Seas discoveries and the world of letters, edited by Walter Veit. 2 vols (Melbourne: Hawthorn Press, 1972, 1979).
Captain James Cook and his times, Simon Fraser University, British Columbia, International and interdisciplinary conference, April 26–30, 1978, edited by Robin Fisher & Hugh Johnston (Vancouver: Douglas & McIntyre, 1979).
Captain James Cook, navigator: the achievements of Captain James Cook as a seaman, navigator and surveyor, edited by David Cordingly (London: National Maritime Museum, 1988).
Captain James Cook, R.N. (1728–1779): a bibliography of his voyages, to which is added other works relating to his life, conduct, & nautical achievements, compiled by Sydney A Spence (Mitcham, UK: S A Spence, 1960).
Captain James Cook, R.N., F.R.S,: a bibliographical excursion, compiled by Sir Maurice Holmes (London: F Edwards, 1952).
Carpenter, Kenneth J, *The History of Scurvy and Vitamin C* (Cambridge: Cambridge University Press, 1986).
Carrington, Hugh, *Life of Captain Cook* (London: Sidgwick & Jackson, 1939).
Carter, Harold B., *Sir Joseph Banks, 1743–1820* (London: British Museum [Natural History], 1988.
Carteret, Philip, *Carteret's Voyage Round the World, 1766–1769*, edited by Helen Wallis. 2 vols. Second Series, no 124–125 (Cambridge: Hakluyt Society, 1965).
The Charts & Coastal views of Captain Cook's Voyages. Volume one: The Voyage of The Endeavour 1768–1771, edited by Andrew David (London: Hakluyt Society, 1988).
The Charts & Coastal views of Captain Cook's Voyages, Volume three: The Voyage of The Resolution and Discovery 1776–1780, edited by Andrew David (London: Hakluyt Society, 1997).
The Charts & Coastal views of Captain Cook's Voyages, Volume two: The Voyage of The Resolution and Adventure 1772–1775, edited by Andrew David (London: Hakluyt Society, 1992).
Coleridge, Samuel Taylor, *The Rime of the Ancient Mariner* (New York: Dover, 1970).
A Collection of Charts of the Coasts of Newfoundland and Labradore…from Original Surveys taken by James Cook, Michael Lane, Surveyors (London: Thomas Jefferys, 1769–70).
Colledge, J J, *Ships of the Royal Navy: the complete record of all fighting ships of the Royal Navy from the fifteenth century to the present*. Rev ed (London: Greenhill, 2003).
Collinge, J M, *Navy Board Officials 1660–1832* (London: University of London, 1978).
Collingridge, Vanessa, *Captain Cook: obsession and betrayal in the New World* (London: Ebury Press, 2002).
Colnett, James, *A Voyage to the northwest side of America: the journals of James Colnett, 1786–89*, edited by Robert Galois (Vancouver, BC: University of British Columbia Press, 2003).
_____, *A Voyage to the South Atlantic and round Cape Horn into the Pacific Ocean, for the purpose of extending the Spermaceti Whale Fisheries, and other objects of commerce, by ascertaining the ports, bays, harbours, and anchoring berths in certain islands and coasts in those seas at which the ships of the British merchants might be refitted*. Bibliotheca Australiana, Vol 36 (Amsterdam: N Israel, 1968 [London: J Colnett, 1798]).
The Commissioned sea officers of the Royal Navy, 1660–1815, edited by David Syrett, R L DiNardo (Aldershot, UK: Scolar Press for the Navy Records Society, 1994).
Conner, Daniel, *Master mariner: Capt. James Cook and the peoples of the Pacific* (St Lucia, Queensland: University of Queensland Press, 1979).
Cook & Omai: the cult of the South Seas (Canberra: National Library of Australia, 2001).
Cook's sites: revisiting history, Photographs by Mark Adams; text by Nicholas Thomas (Dundein: University of Otago Press, 1999).
Cook's voyages and the peoples of the Pacific, edited by Hugh Cobbe (London: British Museum, 1979).
Cook, James, *Captain Cook in Australia: extracts from the journals of Captain James Cook, giving a full account in his own words of his adventures and discoveries in Australia*, edited by A W Reed (Wellington: A H & A W Reed, 1969).
_____, *Captain Cook in New Zealand: extracts from the journals of Captain James Cook, giving a full account in his own words of his adventures and discoveries in New Zealand*, edited by A H & A W Reed. 2nd ed (Wellington: A H & A W Reed, 1969).
_____, *Captain Cook's voyages, 1768–1779*, selected and introduced by Glyndwr Williams (London: Folio Society, 1997).
_____, *A Journal of a Voyage round the World in H.M.S. Endeavour, in the years 1768–71. Containing all the various occurrences of the voyage with descriptions of several newly discovered countries in the Southern Hemisphere (etc.). To which is added a concise vocabulary of the language of Otaheite*. Bibliotheca Australiana, vol 14 (Amsterdam: N Israel, 1967 [London: 1771]).
_____, *The Journal of H.M.S. Endeavour 1768–1771*. Facsimile edition (Guildford, United Kingdom: Genesis Publications, 1977).
_____, *The Journal of H.M.S. Resolution 1772–1775*. Facsimile edition (Guildford, United Kingdom: Genesis Publications, 1981).
_____, *The Journals of Captain Cook*, edited by Philip Edwards (London: Penguin, 1999).
_____, *The Journals of Captain James Cook on his Voyages of Discovery. Volume one: The Voyage of The Endeavour 1768–1771*, edited by J C Beaglehole (Cambridge: Hakluyt Society, 1955).
_____, *The Journals of Captain James Cook on his Voyages of Discovery. Volume two: The Voyage of The Resolution and Adventure 1772–1775*, edited by J C Beaglehole (Cambridge: Hakluyt Society, 1961).
_____, *The Journals of Captain Cook*, edited by J C Beaglehole. 5 vols (Woodbridge, UK: Boydell & Brewer, 1999).
_____, *Seventy north to fifty south: the story of Captain Cook's last voyage*, edited by Paul W Dale (Englewood Cliffs, New Jersey: Prentice-Hall, 1969).
_____, *The Voyage of the Resolution and Adventure, 1772–1775. Addenda and corrigenda to the first edition, 1961* (Cambridge: Hakluyt Society, 1969).
_____, *A Voyage towards the South Pole and round the World, performed in His Majesty's Ships the Resolution and Adventure in the years, 1772, 1773, 1774 and 1775*. Facsimile edition (Adelaide: Libraries Board of South Australia, 1970).

_____, and James King, *The Journals of Captain James Cook on his Voyages of Discovery. Volume three: The Voyage of The Resolution and Discovery 1776–1780*, edited by J C Beaglehole. 2 vols (Cambridge: Hakluyt Society, 1967).

Cowley, Gordon, *In the wake of Captain Cook: the life and times of Captain Charles Clerke, R.N., 1741–79* (Boston, UK: Richard Kay, 1997).

Cowper, William, *The Poems of William Cowper. Volume 1: 1748–1782* (Oxford: Oxford University Press, 1980).

Coxe, William, *Account of the Russian discoveries between Asia and America: to which are added the conquest of Siberia, and the history of the transactions and commerce between Russia and China*. 3rd ed rev (London: T Cadell, 1787).

Cuppage, Francis E, *James Cook and the conquest of scurvy* (Westport, Connecticut: Greenwood Press, 1994).

Dalrymple, Alexander, *An Account of the Discoveries made in the South Pacifick Ocean* (London: 1769; reissued with an essay by Andrew Cook, Sydney: Hordern House, 1996).

_____, *An Historical Collection of the several Voyages and Discoveries in the South Pacific Ocean*. Bibliotheca Australiana, vol 11. 2 vols in 1 (Amsterdam: N Israel, 1967 [London: A. Dalrymple, 1770–71]).

Darby, Madge, *William Peckover of Wapping: gunner of the Bounty* (Colchester, UK: Conner and Butler, 1989).

Day, Marele, *Mrs Cook: the Real and Imagined life of the Captain's Wife* (Sydney: Allen & Unwin, 2002).

The Dictionary of National Biography, edited by Sir Leslie Stephen and Sir Sidney Lee. 22 vols (London: Oxford University Press, 1917).

Dixon, George, *A Voyage round the World; But more particularly to the North-west coast of America*. Bibliotheca Australiana, vol 37 (Amsterdam: N Israel, 1968 [London: Geo Goulding, 1789]).

Dunmore, John, *Who's Who in Pacific Navigation* (Honolulu: University of Hawaii Press, 1991).

Duyker, Edward, *Nature's argonaut: Daniel Solander 1733–1782, naturalist and voyager with Cook and Banks* (Melbourne: Miegunyah Press, 1998).

Edmond, Rod, *Representing the South Pacific: colonial discourse from Cook to Gauguin* (Cambridge: Cambridge University Press, 1998).

Edwards, Philip, *Story of the voyage: sea-narratives in eighteenth-century England* (Cambridge: Cambridge University Press, 1994).

Eisler, William, *The Furthest shore: images of Terra Australis from the Middle Ages to Captain Cook* (Cambridge: Cambridge University Press, 1995).

Ellis, William, *An Authentic narrative of a voyage performed by Captain Cook and Captain Clerke, in His Majesty's ships Resolution and Discovery, during years 1776, 1777, 1778, 1779, and 1780; in search of a northwest passage between the continents of Asia and America, including a faithful account of all their discoveries, and the unfortunate death of Captain Cook. Illustrated with a chart and a variety of cuts, by W. Ellis, assistant surgeon to both vessels.* 2 vols. (London: Printed for G Robinson, J Sewell and J Debrett, 1782).

_____, *An Authentic Narrative of a Voyage performed by Captain Cook and Captain Clerke, in H.M. Ships Resolution and Discovery during the years 1776–1780; in search of a North-West passage between the continents of Asia and America. Including a faithful account of all their discoveries, and the unfortunate Death of Captain Cook.* Bibliotheca Australiana, vol 55–56. 2 vols (Amsterdam: N Israel, 1970 [London: 1782]).

Employ'd as a discoverer: papers presented at the Captain Cook Bi-Centenary Symposium Sutherland Shire, 1–3 May, 1970, edited by J S Megaw (Sydney: A H & A W Reed, 1971).

Enlightenment and exploration in the North Pacific, 1741–1805, edited by Stephen Haycox, James K Barnett, Caedmon A Liburd (Seattle: University of Washington Press, 1997).

Enlightenment and New Zealand: Essays Commemorating the Visit of Johann Reinhold Forster and George Forster with James Cook to Queen Charlotte and Dusky Sounds, edited by Michael E Hoare Wellington: National Art Gallery, 1979).

The Expedition of the St Jean-Baptiste to the Pacific, 1769–1770; From Journals of Jean de Surville and Guillaume Labé, translated and edited by John Dunmore. Second Series, no 158 (London: Hakluyt Society, 1981).

Exploration in Alaska: Captain Cook commemorative lectures, June-November, 1978 (Anchorage: Cook Inlet Historical Society, 1980).

Fairfax-Blakeborough, J, *The Bi-centenary of Captain James Cook: an historical play to celebrate a great Yorkshireman and benefactor of the Empire* (Whitby: Horne & Son, 1928).

Finch, Roger, *Coals from Newcastle: the story of the North East coal trade in the days of sail* (Lavenham, UK: Terence Dalton, 1973).

Forbes, David W, *Encounters with paradise: views of Hawaii and its people, 1778–1941* (Honolulu: Honolulu Academy of Arts, 1992).

Forster, Georg(e), *George Forsters Werke: Sämtliche Schriften, Tagebücher, Briefe*, edited by the Deutschen Akademie der Wissenschaften zu Berlin. 18 vols (Berlin: Akademie-Verlag, 1958–1985).

_____, *Reply to Mr. Wales's remarks* (London: B White, J Robson, and P Elmsley, 1778).

_____, *A Voyage round the world in His Britannic Majesty's sloop, Resolution, commanded by Capt. James Cook, during the years 1772, 3, 4, and 5*. 2 vols (London: B White; J Robson; P Elmsly; and G Robinson, 1777).

_____, *A Voyage round the World*, edited by Nicholas Thomas and Oliver Berghof, assisted by Jennifer Newell. 2 vols (Honolulu: University of Hawai'i Press, 2000 [1777]).

Forster, Johann Reinhold, *Observations made during a voyage round the world, on physical geography, natural history, and ethic philosophy. Especially on: 1. The earth and its strata; 2. Water and the ocean; 3. The atmosphere; 4. The changes of the globe; 5. Organic bodies; and 6. The human species* (London: G Robinson, 1778).

_____, *Observations made during a voyage round the world*, edited by Nicholas Thomas, Harriet Guest, and Michael Dettelbach; with a linguistics appendix by Karl H Rensch (Honolulu: University of Hawai'i Press, 1996 [1778]).

_____, *The Resolution Journal of Johann Reinhold Forster, 1772–1775*, edited by Michael E Hoare. 4 vols. Second Series, no 152–155 (London: Hakluyt Society, 1982).

From maps to metaphors: the Pacific world of George Vancouver (Vancouver: University of British Columbia Press, 1993).

Frost, Alan, *The Precarious life of James Mario Matra: voyager with Cook; American loyalist; servant of empire* (Melbourne: Miegunyah Press, 1995).

_____, *Voyage of the Endeavour: Captain Cook and the discovery of the Pacific* (St Leonards, NSW: Allen & Unwin, 1998).

Furneaux, Rupert, *Tobias Furneaux, Circumnavigator* (London: Cassell, 1960).

Galloway, Alex, *A Transit of Venus: poems of passage* (Katoomba, NSW: Quadrat & Quoin, 1993).

Gathercole, Peter, *"From the islands of the South Seas 1773–4". An exhibition of a collection made on Capn. Cook's Second Voyage of discovery by J.R. Forster* (Oxford: Pitt Rivers Museum, [1970]).

Gilbert, George, *Captain Cook's Final Voyage: The Journal of Midshipman George Gilbert*, introduced and edited by Christine Holmes (Horsham, Sussex: Caliban Books, 1982).

Giraudoux, Jean, *Supplément au voyage de Cook* (Paris: Grasset, 2000).

Gordon, Joseph Stuart, *Reinhold and Georg Forster in England, 1766–1780*. Duke University PhD Thesis (Durham, North Carolina: 1975).

Gough, Barry M, *Distant dominion: Britain and the Northwest coast of North America, 1579–1809* (Vancouver: University of British Columbia Press, 1980).

Gould, Rupert, *Captain Cook* (London: Duckworth, 1935. Republished 1978).

Graham, J Geoffrey, *Muster rolls of Whitby ships in which James Cook sailed, 1747–1755*, compiled by Harold Brown (Whitby: Whitby Literary and Philosophical Society, 1990).

Graves, John, *The History of Cleveland in the North Riding of the County of York.* (Carlisle: F Jollie, 1808).

Gray, William R, *Voyages to paradise: exploring in the wake of Captain Cook* (Washington DC: National Geographic Society, 1981).

A Guide to Captain Cook country (Middlesbrough: Captain Cook Tourism Association, 1993).

Gurney, Alan, *Below the convergence: voyages toward Antarctica, 1699–1839* (New York: W W Norton, 1997).

Handbook of North American Indians, Volume 5: Arctic, edited by David Damas (Washington: Smithsonian Institution, 1984).

Handbook of North American Indians, Volume 7: Northwest Coast, edited by Wayne Suttles (Washington: Smithsonian Institution, 1990).

Hauptman, William, *John Webber, 1751–1793: Landschaftsmaler und Sudseefahrer [Pacific voyager and landscape artist]* (Bern: Kunstmuseum Bern, 1996).

Heavisides, Michael, *Rambles in Cleveland and peeps into the Dales on foot, cycle and rail* (Stockton-on-Tees: Heavisides & Son, 1901 [Republished: Guiseley, UK: M T D Rigg, 1988]).

Hesse, Karen, *Stowaway* (New York: Simon & Schuster, 2000) (UK version published as *Young Nick's Head.* London: Simon & Schuster, 2001).

Historical records of New South Wales, Volume 1, Part 1, Cook, 1762–1780 (Mona Vale, NSW: Lansdown, Slattery & Co, 1978).

Historical records of New Zealand, edited by Robert McNab (Wellington: Government Printer, 1908).

The History of the Collections contained in the Natural History Departments of the British Museum, Vol II (London: British Museum [Natural History], 1906).

Hoare, Michael E, *Enlightenment and New Zealand 1773–1774* (Wellington: National Art Gallery, 1979).

_____, *The Tactless philosopher: Johann Reinhold Forster [1729–98]* (Melbourne: Hawthorn Press, 1976).

_____, *Three men in a boat. The Forsters and New Zealand Science* (Melbourne: Hawthorn Press, 1975).

Hooker, John, *Captain James Cook* (Ringwood, UK: Penguin, 1987).

Horwitz, Tony, *Blue latitudes: boldly going where Captain Cook has gone before* (USA: Henry Holt, 2002).

Hough, Richard, *Captain James Cook* (London: John Curtis, 1994).

_____, *The Murder of Captain James Cook* (London: Macmillan, 1979).

Howe, K R, *The Quest for origins: who first discovered and settled New Zealand and the Pacific Islands?* (Auckland: Penguin, 2003).

_____, *Where the waves fall: a new South Sea Islands history from first settlement to colonial rule* (Sydney: George Allen & Unwin, 1984).

Howse, Derek, *Nevil Maskelyne. The Seaman's Astronomer* (Cambridge: Cambridge University Press, 1989).

_____, and Hutchinson, B, *The Clocks and Watches of Captain James Cook 1769–1969* (London: Antiquarian Horological Society, 1969).

Implicit understandings: observing, reporting, and reflecting on the encounters between Europeans and other peoples in the early modern era (Cambridge: Cambridge University Press, 1994).

Innes, Hammond, *The Last voyage: Captain Cook's lost diary* (London: Collins, 1978).

James Cook, F.R.S., R.N.: the first record; the facts behind the myth; St, Cuthbert's Church, Marton, Middlesbrough (Middlesbrough: Middlesbrough Borough Council, 1993.

James Cook: Gifts and Treasures from the South Seas, edited by Brigitta Hauser-Schäublin and Gundolf Krüger. Munich and New York: Prestel, 1998).

James Cook, surveyor of Newfoundland: being a collection of charts of the coasts of Newfoundland and Labradore, &, Drawn from original surveys taken by James Cook and (San Francisco: David Magee, 1965).

John Cawte Beaglehole: a bibliography, Wellington: Alexander Turnbull Library, 1972.

Joppien, Rudiger, *Philippe Jacques de Loutherbourg, R.A., 1740–1812* (London: Greater London Council, 1973).

_____, and Bernard Smith, *The Art of Captain Cook's Voyages. Volume one: The Voyage of The Endeavour 1768–1771* (Melbourne: Oxford University Press, 1985).

_____, *The Art of Captain Cook's Voyages. Volume three: The Voyage of The Resolution and Discovery 1776–1780* (Melbourne: Oxford University Press, 1987).

_____, *The Art of Captain Cook's Voyages. Volume two: The Voyage of The Resolution and Adventure 1772–1775* (Melbourne: Oxford University Press, 1985).

Kaeppler, Adrienne L, *"Artificial Curiosities" being An exposition of Native Manufactures Collected on the Three Pacific Voyages of Captain James Cook, R. N.* (Honolulu: Bishop Museum Press, 1978).

_____, *Cook Voyage Artifacts in Leningrad, Berne, and Florence Museums* (Honolulu: Bishop Museum Press, 1978).

Kāne, Herb Kawainui, *Voyagers* (Bellevue, Washington: Whalesong, 1991).

King, J C H, *Artificial curiosities from the Northwest Coast of America: Native American artefacts in the British Museum collections* (London: British Museum, 1981).

Kingston, William Henry, *Captain Cook: his life, voyages, and discoveries* (London: Religious Tract Society, 1871).

Kippis, Andrew, *The Life of Captain James Cook.* London: G Nicol, G G J & J Robinson, 1788.

Kitson, Arthur, *Captain James Cook R.N., F.R.S.: the circumnavigator* (London: John Murray, 1907).

Klenman, Allan, *The Faces of Captain Cook: a record of the coins and medals of James Cook. A numismatic memoir* (n.p.: Klenman, 1983).

Koivukkangas, Olavi, *From the midnight sun to the long white cloud: Finns in New Zealand* (Turku, Finland: Institute of Migration, 1996).

La Pérouse, Jean-François de la Galaup de, *The Journal of Jean-François de Galaup de la Pérouse, 1785–1788,* translated and edited by John Dunmore. 2 vols. Second Series, no 179–180 (London: Hakluyt Society, 1994–95).

_____, *A Voyage round the World, performed in the years 1785, 1786, 1787, and 1788, by the Boussole and Astrolabe, under the command of J.F.G. de la Pérouse: published by order of the National Assembly, under the superintendence of L. A. Milet-Mureau.* Bibliotheca Australiana, vol 27–29. 2 vols + atlas (Amsterdam: N Israel, 1968 [London: A Hamilton, 1799]).

Latham, Jean Lee, *Far voyager: the story of James Cook* (New York: Harper & Row, 1970).

Law, Joy, *"Captain Cook's Florilegium": a note on its production* (London: Lion and Unicorn Press, 1976).

Ledyard, John, *A Journal of Captain Cook's last voyage to the Pacific ocean, and in quest of a North-west passage between Asia & America, performed in the years 1776, 1777, 1778, and 1779: illustrated with a chart shewing the tracts of the ships employed in this expedition* (Hartford: Printed and sold by Nathaniel Patten, 1783. [Chicago: Quadrangle Books, 1963]).

Lind, James, *A Treatise of the Scurvy. In three parts. Containing an inquiry into the nature, causes, and cure, of that disease, etc.* (Edinburgh: 1753).

Lyon, David, *The Sailing Navy List: all the ships of the Royal Navy: built, purchased and captured, 1688–1860* (London: Conway Maritime Press, 1993).

Lysaght, A M, *Joseph Banks in Newfoundland and Labrador, 1766* (London: Faber and Faber, 1971).

Macarthur, Antonia, *His Majesty's Bark Endeavour: the story of the ship and her people* (Sydney: Angus & Robertson, 1997).

MacBride, D, *An Historical Account of a New Method of Treating the Scurvy at Sea* (London: 1767).

McCormick, E H, *Omai: Pacific envoy* (Auckland: Auckland University Press, 1977).

McIntyre, Kenneth Gordon, *The Secret Discovery of Australia: Portuguese ventures 250 years before Captain Cook.* (Medindie, South Australia: Souvenir Press, 1977).

Mackay, David, *In the wake of Cook: exploration, science & empire, 1780–1801* (Wellington: Victoria University Press, 1985).

Mackeness, George, *The life of Vice-Admiral William Bligh, R.N., F.R.S.* 2 vols (Sydney: Angus & Robertson, 1931).

Maclean, Alistair, *Captain Cook* (London: Collins, 1972).

Magra (Matra), James Mario, *Journal of a Voyage round the world in HMS Endeavour, in the years 1768–1771*. Facsimile edition. Bibliotheca Australiana no 14. (Amsterdam: N Israel, 1967).

[Magra, James], *A Journal of a voyage round the world, in His Majesty's ship Endeavour, in the years 1768, 1769, 1770, and 1771: undertaken in pursuit of natural knowledge, at the desire of the Royal Society: containing all the various occurrences of the voyage, with descriptions of several new discovered countries in the southern hemisphere: to which is added a concise vocabulary of the language of Otahitee* (London: T Becket and P A de Hondt, 1771. Published anonymously).

Marquardt, Karl Heinz, *Captain Cook's Endeavour* (London: Conway Maritime Press, 1995).

[Marra, John], *Journal of the Resolution's voyage, in 1772, 1773, 1774, and 1775, on discovery to the southern hemisphere, by which the non-existence of an undiscovered continent, between the Equator and the 50th degree of southern latitude is demonstratively proved: also a journal of the Adventure's voyage, in the years 1772, 1773, and 1774* (London: Newbery, 1775. Published anonymously. [Facsimile edition. Bibliotheca Australiana, vol 15. Amsterdam: N Israel, 1967]).

Miles, John, *Infectious diseases: colonising the Pacific?* (Dunedin: University of Otago Press, 1997).

Mira, William J D, *James Cook, his coins & medals; some contemporary numismatic aspects of the life and voyages of Captain James Cook* (Sydney: Australian Numismatic Society, 1970).

Moorehead, Alan, *The Fatal impact: an account of the invasion of the South Pacific, 1767–1840* (London: Hamish Hamilton, 1966). (also Illustrated edition. London: Hamish Hamilton, 1987).

Morris, Aldyth, *Captain James Cook*. (Honolulu: University of Hawai'i Press, 1995).

Morris, Roger, *Pacific Sail: four centuries of western ships in the Pacific*. (Auckland: David Bateman, 1987).

Murray-Oliver, Anthony, *Captain Cook's artists in the Pacific, 1769–1779* (Christchurch, NZ: Avon Fine Prints, 1969).

Newfoundland Pilot: Containing A Collection of Directions for sailing round the whole Island (London: Thomas Jefferys, 1769).

Nordyke, Eleanor, *Pacific images: views from Captain Cook's Third Voyage* (Honolulu: University of Hawai'i, 1999).

Nutka: Captain Cook and the Spanish explorers on the coast (Victoria, British Columbia: Aural History, 1978).

Obeyesekere, Gananath, *The Apotheosis of Captain Cook: European mythmaking in the Pacific* (Princeton, New Jersey: Princeton University Press, 1992).

Orchiston, Wayne, *Nautical astronomy in New Zealand: the voyages of James Cook* (Wellington: Carter Observatory Board, 1998).

Ord, John Walker, *The History and Antiquities of Cleveland* (London: Simpkin & Marshall, 1846).

O'Sullivan, Dan, *The Education of Captain Cook* (Great Ayton, UK: Captain Cook Schoolroom Museum, 2000).

The Oxford Illustrated History of the Royal Navy (Oxford: Oxford University Press, 1995).

Pacific empires: essays in honour of Glyndwr Williams (Carlton, Victoria: Melbourne University Press, 1999).

Parkin, Ray, *H.M. Bark Endeavour: her place in Australian history; with an account of her construction, crew and equipment and a narrative of her voyage on the East Coast* (Melbourne: Miegunyah Press, 1997).

Parkinson, Sydney, *A Journal of a voyage to the South Seas, in His Majesty's ship, the Endeavour / faithfully transcribed from the papers of the late Sydney Parkinson: embellished with views and designs, delineated by the Author, and engraved by capital artists* (London: Printed for Stanfield Parkinson, the editor: and sold by Messrs Richardson and Urquhart; Evans; Hooper; Murray; Leacroft; and Riley, 1773).

_____, *A Journal of a voyage to the South Seas in His Majesty's ship, the Endeavour.* Facsimile edition, no A34 (Adelaide: Libraries Board of South Australia, 1972).

_____, *A Journal of a voyage to the South Seas* (London: Caliban, 1984).

Penrose, C V, *A Memoir of James Trevenen*, edited by Christopher Lloyd (London: Navy Records Society, 1959).

Perrin, W G, *Instructions to Captain Cook for His Three Voyages.* Reprinted from *The Naval Miscellany* (London: Navy Records Society, 1978).

Pisier, Georges, *Le Decouverte de la Nouvelle-Caledonie - Septembre 1774 – documents presentes, traduits et annotes.* (Noumea, Nouvelle-Caledonie: Societe d'Etudes Historiques de la Nouvelle-Caledonie, 1974).

_____, *Kunie or the Isle of Pines: a short history* (Noumea, Nouvelle-Caledonie: Societe d'Etudes Historique de la Nouvelle-Caledonie, 1978).

Portlock, Nathaniel, *A Voyage round the world; but more particularly to the North-West Coasts of America.* Bibliotheca Australiana, vol 43 (Amsterdam: N Israel, 1969 [London: John Stockdale, 1789]).

Prado y Tovar, Diego, *New Light on the Discovery of Australia as revealed by the Journal of Captain Don Diego de Prado y Tovar*, edited by Henry N Stevens, with annotated translations from the Spanish by George F Barwick. Second Series, no 64 (London: Hakluyt Society, 1930).

Rae, Julia, *Captain James Cook endeavours* (London: Stepney Historical Trust, 1997).

[Rickman, John], *Journal of Captain Cook's last voyage to the Pacific Ocean, on Discovery; performed in the years 1776, 1777, 1778, 1779, illustrated with cuts and a chart, shewing the tracts of the ships employed in this expedition. Faithfully narrated from the original MS* (London: Newbery, 1781. Published anonymously. [Facsimile edition. Bibliotheca Australiana, vol 16. Amsterdam: N Israel, 1967]).

Rienits, Rex and Thea Rienits, *The Voyages of Captain Cook* (London: Paul Hamlyn, 1968).

Rigby, Nigel and Pieter Van Der Merwe, *Captain Cook in the Pacific* (London: National Maritime Museum, 2002).

Robertson, George, *The Discovery of Tahiti. A Journal of the Second Voyage of H.M.S. Dolphin Round the World, under the Command of Captain Wallis, R.N., in the Years 1766, 1767, and 1768. Written by her Master, George Robertson.* edited by Hugh Carrington. Second Series, no 98 (London: Hakluyt Society, 1948).

Robertson, Jillian, *The Captain Cook myth* (Sydney: Angus & Robertson, 1981).

Robson, John, *Captain Cook's world: maps of the life and voyages of James Cook, R.N.* (Auckland: Random House NZ, 2000).

Rodger, N A M, *The Insatiable Earl: a life of John Montagu, 4th Earl of Sandwich.* (London: Harper Collins, 1993).

Rodgers, Paul, *To kill a God* (London: Heinemann, 1987).

Romancing the sea: Ship Store Galleries presents Voyages of the China Trade & Pacific Exploration: Raymond A, Massey, A.S.M.A. (Kapaa, Hawai'i: Ship Store Galleries, 1997).

Rose, Deborah Bird Rose, *Hidden Histories: Black Stories From Victoria River Downs, Humbert River, and Wave Hill Stations* (Canberra: Aboriginal Studies Press, 1991).

Rousseau, Jean Jacques, *Discours sur les origines et les fondements de l'inégalité parmi les hommes* (Amsterdam: 1754).

Sahlins, Marshall, *Historical metaphors and mythical realities: structure in the early history of the Sandwich Islands Kingdom* (Ann Arbor, Michigan: Univesity of Michigan Press, 1981).

_____, *How "natives" think: about Captain Cook, for example* (Chicago: University of Chicago Press, 1995).

_____, *Islands of History* (Chicago: University of Chicago Press, 1987).

Sainty, J C, *Admirality Officials, 1660–1870* (London: University of London, 1975).

Salmond, Anne, *Between worlds: early exchanges between Maori and Europeans 1773–1815* (Auckland: Viking, 1997).

_____, *The Trial of the cannibal dog: Captain Cook in the south seas* (London: Allen Lane, 2003).

_____, *Two worlds: first meetings between Maori and Europeans, 1642–1772* (Auckland: Viking, 1991).

Sampson, F Bruce, *Early New Zealand, botanic art* (Auckland: Reed Methuen, 1985).

Samwell, David, *A Narrative of the death of*

Captain James Cook. To which are added some particulars, concerning his life and character. And observations respecting the introduction of the venereal disease into the Sandwich Islands (London: G G J and J Robinson, 1786).

Sarychew, Gavrila A, *Account of a voyage of discovery to the North-East of Siberia, the Frozen Ocean and the North-East Sea.* 2 vols (Amsterdam: N Israel, 1969).

Les Sauvages de la mer Pacifique: manufactured by Joseph Dufour et Cie 1804–05 after a design by Jean-Gabriel Charvet (Sydney: Art Gallery of New South Wales, 2000).

Science and exploration in the Pacific: European voyages to the southern oceans in the eighteenth century, edited by Margarette Lincoln (Woodbridge, UK: Boydell & Brewer, 1998).

Seward, Anna, *Elegy on Captain Cook: to which is added An ode to the sun* (London: J Dodsley, 1780).

Sharp, Andrew, *The voyages of Abel Janszoon Tasman* (London: Clarendon Press, 1968).

The Significance of Cook's Endeavour voyage: three bicentennial lectures (Townsville, Queensland: James Cook University, 1970).

Sinclair, Shirley, *Elizabeth Cook: the captain's wife, 1741–1835* (Sydney: Maritime Heritage Press, 1995).

Skelton, Raleigh Ashlin, *Captain James Cook: after two hundred years* (London: for the British Library by the British Museum, 1969).

Skottowe, Philip, *The Leaf and the Tree: The story of an English family* (London: Research Publishing Co, 1963).

Slessor, Kenneth, *One hundred poems* (Sydney: Angus and Robertson, 1944).

Smith, Bernard, *European vision and the South Pacific, 1768–1850* (Sydney: Harper & Row, 1984).

_____, *Imagining the Pacific: in the wake of the Cook voyages* (Melbourne: Melbourne University Press, 1992).

_____, *Style, information and image in the art of Cook's voyages* (Christchurch: University of Canterbury, 1988).

Smith, Eric, *Clapham* (London: Clapham Society, 1990).

Smith, L Richard, *Captain James Cook: the Wedgwood portrait medallions* (Sydney: Wedgwood Society of Australia, 1979).

_____, *The Resolution & Adventure medal* (Sydney: Wedgwood Press, 1985).

_____, *The Royal Society Cook medal* (Sydney: Wedgwood Press, 1982).

Sobel, Dava, *Longitude: the true story of a lone genius who solved the greatest scientific problem of his time* (New York: Walker, 1995).

Söderström, Jan, *A. Sparrman's Ethnographical Collection from James Cook's 2nd Expedition (1772–1775)* (Stockholm: Ethnographical Museum of Sweden, 1939).

Solander, Daniel, *Collected correspondence, 1753–1782* (Melbourne: Miegunyah Press, 1995).

Sparrman, Anders, *Voyage to the Cape of Good Hope, Towards the Antarctic Polar Circle, and Round the world.* Originally published in 1785; 2 vols (New York: John Reprint Corp, 1971).

Spate, O H K, *The Pacific since Magellan. Vol. 1: The Spanish Lake* (Minneapolis: University of Minnesota Press, 1979).

_____, *The Pacific since Magellan. Vol. 2: Monopolists and Freebooters* (Canberra: Australian National University Press, 1983).

_____, *The Pacific since Magellan. Vol. 3: Paradise found and lost* (London: Routledge, 1988).

Studies from Terra Australis to Australia (Canberra: Australian Academy of the Humanities, 1989).

Sullivan, Robert, *Captain Cook in the underworld* (Auckland: Auckland University Press, 2002).

Suthren, Victor, *To go upon discovery: James Cook and Canada, 1758–1767* (Toronto: Dundurn Press, 1999).

Svet, Iakov Mikhailovich, *Dzhems Kuk* (Moscow: Mysl, 1979).

Sydney Parkinson: artist of Cook's Endeavour voyage, edited by D J Carr (London: Croom Helm, 1983).

Taillemite, Etienne, *Sur des Mers inconnues. Bougainville, Cook, Laperouse* (Paris: Decouvertes Gallimard, 1987).

Tanner, Julia, *From Pacific Shores. Eighteenth-century Ethnographic Collections at Cambridge. The Voyages of Cook, Vancouver and the First Fleet* (Cambridge: University of Cambridge Museum of Archaeology and Anthropology, 1999).

Taylor, Eva G R, *Navigation in the days of Captain Cook* (London: National Maritime Museum, 1980).

Taylor, Gordon, *The Sea Chaplains: A History of the Chaplains of the Royal Navy* (Oxford: Oxford Illustrated Press, 1978).

Terra Australis: the furthest shore (Sydney: International Cultural Corporation of Australia, 1988).

Terra Australis to Australia (Melbourne: Oxford University Press, 1988).

Thiéry, Maurice, *The Life and voyages of Captain Cook (Vie et les voyages du Capitaine Cook)* (London: Geoffrey Bles, 1929).

Thomas, Nicholas, *Discoveries: the voyages of Captain Cook* (London: Allen Lane, 2003).

Thompson, Hunter S, *The Curse of Lono* (New York: Bantam Books, 1983).

Thornton, Cliffford E, *Captain Cook in Cleveland: a study of his early years* (Middlesbrough: Middlesbrough Borough Council, 1978).

Treasures of the Pacfic: "Artificial curiosities" of the 18th century: being an exhibition and exposition of native manufactures collected on the three Pacific (Honolulu: Bernice P Bishop Museum, 1978).

Trevenen, James, *Notes concerning paragraphs in the 1784 Quarto edition of Cook's third voyage* ([typescript]. n.d.).

Urban, Manfred, *200 Jahre Göttinger Cook-Sammlung* (Göttingen: Universität Göttingen, 1982).

Vancouver, George, *A Voyage of Discovery to the North Pacific Ocean and Round the World, 1791–1795,* with an Introduction and appendices; edited by W Kaye Lamb. 4 vols. Second Series, no 163–166 (London: Hakluyt Society, 1984).

_____, *A Voyage of discovery to the North Pacific Ocean, and round the World.* Bibliotheca Australiana, vol 30–33. 3 vols + atlas (Amsterdam: N Israel, 1967 [London: Robinson, 1798]).

Vaughan, Thomas, *Captain Cook, R.N.: the resolute mariner: an international record of oceanic discovery* (Portland, Oregon: Oregon Historical Society, 1974).

Verner, Coolie, *Cook and the cartography of the North Pacific: an exhibition of maps for the conference on Captain James Cook and his times, April 1978* (Burnaby, British Columbia: Library Simon Fraser University, 1978).

Verzeichnis der Völkerkundlichen Sammlung des Instituts fur Völkerkunde der Georg-August-Universitat zu Göttingen, edited by Erhard Schlesier, and Manfred Urban (Gottingen: Institut für Völkerkunde Göttingen, 1988).

Views in the South Seas from Drawings by James [sic,] Webber (London: Boydell, 1808).

Villiers, Alan, *Captain Cook, the seaman's seaman: a study of the great explorer* (London: Hodder and Stoughton, 1967).

_____, *Captain James Cook: a tribute* (Oxford: Pitt Rivers Museum, 1970).

The Visual Encyclopedia of Nautical terms under sail (New York: Crown, 1978).

The Voyage of Governor Phillip to Botany Bay, Facsimile edition (Adelaide: State Library of South Australia, 1968 [London: 1789]).

The Voyages of Pedro Fernandez de Quiros, 1595 to 1606, translated and edited by Sir Clements Markham, 2 vols. Second Series, no 14–15 (London: Hakluyt Society, 1904).

Wales, William, *Astronomical Observations, made in the Voyages undertaken for making Discoveries in the Southern Hemisphere, and performed by Commodore Byron, Captain Wallis, Captain Carteret, and Captain Cook, in the Dolphin, Tamer, Swallow, and Endeavour. Drawn up from the journals which were kept by the several commanders, and from the papers of Mr. Charles Green* (London: Elmsly, 1778).

_____, *Remarks on Mr. Forster's account of Captain Cook's last voyage round the world, in the years 1772, 1773, 1774, and 1775* (London: J Nourse, 1778).

_____, and William Bayly, *The Original astronomical observations, made in the course of a voyage towards the South Pole, and round the world, in His Majesty's ships the Resolution and Adventure, in the years 1772, 1773, 1774, and 1775* (London: J Nourse, J Mount and T Page, 1777).

Wallace, Lee, *Sexual encounters: Pacific texts, modern sexualities* (Cornell University Press, 2003).

Warner, Oliver, *With Wolfe to Quebec: the*

path to glory (Toronto: Collins, 1972).

The Weidenfeld Atlas of Maritime History (London: Weidenfeld & Nicolson, 1986).

Whitehead, P J P, *Forty drawings of fishes made bythe artista who accompanied Captain James Cook on his three Voyages to the Pacific, 1768–71, 1772–75, 1776–80, some being used by the authors in the description of new species* (London: Trustees of the British Museum [Natural History], 1968).

Whiteley, William H, *James Cook in Newfoundland, 1762–1767* (St John's, Newfoundland: Newfoundland Historical Society, 1975).

Williams, Glyn, *Voyages of delusion: the Northwest Passage in the Age of Reason* (London: HarperCollins, 2002).

Withey, Lynne, *Voyages of discovery: Captain Cook and the exploration of the Pacific* (London: Hutchinson, 1987).

Woolf, H, *The Transits of Venus: A Study in the Organization and Practice of Eighteenth-Century Science* (Princeton: Princeton University Press, 1959).

Yarrington, W H H, *The Landing of Captain James Cook, Botany Bay, 1770 : as produced in connection with the Commonwealth celebrations at Kurnell, Botany Bay, New South Wales, Australia, on Monday, 7th January, 1901* (Sydney: Turner & Henderson, 1908).

Young, George, *A History of Whitby and Streoneshalh Abbey.* 2 vols (Whitby: Clark and Medd, 1817). [Republished Whitby: Caedmon of Whitby, 1976.]

_____, *The Life and voyages of Captain James Cook; drawn up from his journals and other authentic documents, and comprising much original information* (London: Whittaker, Treacher, 1836).

Zimmermann, Heinrich, *Heinrich Zimmermanns von Wissloch in der Pfalz, Reise um die Welt, mit Capitain Cook.* (Mannheim: C F Schwan, 1781).

_____, *Heinrich Zimmermanns Reise um die Welt mit Capitain Cook.* Bibliotheca Australiana, vol 73. (Amsterdam: N Israel, 1973 [Mannheim: 1781]).

_____, *The Third voyage of Captain Cook* (Fairfield, Washington: Ye Galleon Press, 1988).

JOURNAL ARTICLES, CHAPTERS, etc

Agnew, Vanessa, 'A Scots Orpheus in the South Seas: or, Encounter music on Cook's second voyage', *Journal for Maritime Research* (May 2001) (available at http://www.jmr.nmm.ac.uk/).

Anderson, William, 'A Journal of a Voyage Made in His Majesty's Sloop *Resolution*', in Cook, James, and James King. *The Journals of Captain James Cook on his Voyages of Discovery. Volume three: The Voyage of The Resolution and Discovery 1776–1780,* edited by J C Beaglehole. 2 vols (Cambridge: Hakluyt Society, 1967), pp723–986.

Bartholomew, M, 'James Lind and Scurvy: a revaluation', *Journal for Maritime Research* (January 2002) (available at http://www.jmr.nmm.ac.uk).

Bayly, William, 'Extract from the Journal Kept by William Bayly, Astronomer, on H.M.S. Adventure, Captain Furneaux, During Capt. Cook's Second Voyage', in *Historical Records of New Zealand. Vol. II.*, edited by Robert McNab (Wellington: Government Printer 1908), pp201–18.

Beaglehole, John Cawte, 'Cook the Man', in *Captain Cook: Navigator and Scientist,* edited by G M Badger (Canberra: Australian National University Press, 1970), pp11–29.

_____, 'Cook the navigator', *Royal Society of London Proceedings A*, no 314, (1969), pp27–38.

_____, 'The Death of Captain Cook', *Historical Studies*, Vol 11, no 43 (1964), pp289–305.

_____, 'Some problems of Cook's biographer' *Mariner's Mirror*, Vol 55, no 4 (1969), pp365–81.

_____, 'Some problems of editing Cook's Journals', *Historical Studies*, Vol 8, no ? (1957), pp20–31.

Bergendorff, Steen, 'Mythopraxis and history: on the interpretation of Makahiki', *J. Polynesian Society*, Vol 97, no 4 (1988), pp391–408.

Betts, J, 'The eighteenth century transits of Venus, the voyages of Captain James Cook and the early development of the marine chronometer', *Antiquarian Horology*, Vol 21 (1993), pp660–9.

Black, Jeanette, 'Too many Cooks', *The Map Collector*, No 34 (1986), pp10–15.

Borofsky, Robert, 'Cook, Lono, Obeyesekere and Sahlins', *Current Anthropology*, Vol 38, no 2 (1997), pp255–65.

_____, Reply. *Current Anthropology*, Vol 38, no 2, (1997), pp276–81.

Brenstrum, Erick, 'Cook and the weather', *Weather and Climate*, Vol 16, no 1 (1996), pp27–31.

Britten, James, 'The Collections of Banks and Solander', *Journal of Botany British and Foreign*, Vol 43 (1905), pp284–90.

_____, 'The Forster Herbarium', *Journal of Botany*, Vol 23 (1885), pp360–8.

_____, 'William Anderson and the plants of Cook's third Voyage', *Journal of Botany.* 1916. Vol 54 (1916), pp345–52; Vol 55 (1917), p54.

Burton, P J K, 'Two bird specimens probably from Cook's voyages', *Ibis*, Vol 1 11 (1969), pp388–90.

Carolin, R C, 'J.R. and J.G.A. Forster and their collections', *Proceedings of the Linnaean Society of New South Wales*, Vol 88, no 2 (1963), pp108–11.

Carr, D J, 'The Books that sailed with the *Endeavour*', *Endeavour*, Vol 7, no 4 (1983), pp194–201.

Collins, Roger D J, 'An Inside story: Dufour & Charvet's wallpaper of the South Seas', *Bulletin of New Zealand Art History*, Vol 9 (1985), pp5–13.

Connell, Mike, and Des Liddy, 'Cook's Bark *Endeavour*: did this vessel end her days in Newport, Rhode Island?', *Great Circle.* Vol 19, no 1 (date?), pp40–9. (Plus unpublished revised edition, 2003).

Cook, James, 'The Account of the flowing of the tides in the South Sea, as observed on board His Majesty's Bark', *Phil. Trans. of the Royal Society*, Vol 62 (1772), pp357–8.

_____, 'Method taken for preserving the health of the crew of His Majesty's Ship the *Resolution* during her late', *Phil. Trans. of the Royal Society*, Vol 66 (1776), pp402–6.

_____, 'An Observation of an eclipse of the sun at the Island of Newfoundland, August 5, 1766', *Phil. Trans. of the Royal Society*, Vol 58 (1767), pp215–16.

_____, 'Of the tides in the South Seas', *Phil. Trans. of the Royal Society*, Vol 66 (1776), pp447–9.

_____, 'Transitus veneris et mercurii in eorum exitu e disco solis, 4to mensis junii et iomo novembris, 1769', *Phil. Trans. of the Royal Society*, Vol 61 (1771), pp433–6.

_____, 'Variation of the compass, as observed on board the Endeavour Bark, in a voyage round the world', *Phil. Trans. of the Royal Society*, Vol 61 (1771), pp422–32.

Cook's Log, Quarterly Journal (Ipswich, UK: Captain Cook Society, 1976–)

Coote, Jeremy, Peter Gathercole, and Nicolette Meister, 'Curiosities sent to Oxford: The Original Documentation of the Forster Collection at the Pitt Rivers Museum', *Journal of the History of Collections*, Vol 7, no 2 (2000), pp177–92. [Also available at http://projects.prm.ox.ac.uk/forster/curios-sent.html.].

Danielsson, Bengt, 'They sailed with Captain Cook: Daniel Solander and Anders Sparrman', *Ethnos*, Vol 34, no 1–4 (1969), pp8–18.

David, Andrew, 'Captain Cook's first chart', *The Map Collector*, No 60 (1992), pp10–11 and No 61, p56.

_____, 'James Cook's 1762 Survey of St John's Harbour and Adjacent Parts of Newfoundland', *Terrae Incognitae.* Vol 30 (1998), pp63–71.

Davie, Donald, 'Trevenen', *Eighteenth Century Studies*, Vol 6 (1973), pp287–97.

Davies, William, 'David Samwell [1751–1798]: surgeon of the "Discovery", London-Welshman and poet', *Trans. Honourable Society of Cymmrodorian* (1926–7), pp70–113.

Edwards, Phyllis I, 'Sir Joseph Banks and the botany of Captain Cook's three voyages of exploration', *Pacific Studies*, Vol 1, no 2 (1978), pp20–43.

Freeman, J D, 'The Polynesian collection of Trinity College, Dublin; and the National Museum of Ireland', *J.Polynesian Society*, Vol 58 (1949), pp1–18.

Fry, Howard, 'Alexander Dalrymple and Captain Cook: the Creative Interplay of Two Careers', in *Captain James Cook and*

His Times, edited by Robin Fisher & Hugh Johnston (Vancouver: Douglas & McIntyre, 1979), pp41–57.

Furneaux, Tobias, 'Furneaux's Narrative', in Cook, James, *The Journals of Captain James Cook on his Voyages of Discovery. Volume two: The Voyage of The Resolution and Adventure 1772–1775,* edited by J C Beaglehole. (Cambridge: Hakluyt Society, 1961), pp729–45.

Garnock-Jones, P J, 'Kerguelen cabbage', *New Zealand Gardener*, Vol 45, no 1 (1989), pp57–8.

_____, Scurvy grasses. *New Zealand Gardener*, Vol 44, no 9 (1988), pp66–7.

Gathercole, Peter, 'Lord Sandwich's Collection of Polynesian Artefacts', in *Science and Exploration in the Pacific: European Voyages in the Southern Oceans in the Eighteenth Century,* edited by Margarette Lincoln (Woodbridge, UK: Boydell & Brewer, 1998), pp103–55.

_____, 'A Māori Shell Trumpet at Cambridge' *Problems in Economic and Social Archaeology* (1976), pp187–99.

Geraghty, Paul, Review of Captain Cook's South Sea island vocabularies. *J. Polynesian Society*,Vol 92, no 4 (1983), pp554–9.

Goldsmith, Michael, *Ressurecting James Cook* (Unpublished manuscript. 2004).

Green, C, and J Cook, 'Observations made, by appointment of the Royal Society, at King George's Island in the South Seas', *Phil. Trans. of the Royal Society*, Vol 61 (1771), pp397–421.

Groves, E W, 'Notes on the botanical specimens collected by Banks and Solander on Cook's first voyage', *J Soc Bibliography of Natural History*, Vol 4, no 1 (1962), pp57–62.

Hayman, Roger, 'Captain Cook's coat of arms', *Coat of Arms*, No 81 (1970), pp19–22.

_____, 'Captain James Cook's Armorial Bearings', *Coat of Arms*, No 82 (1970), pp97–8.

Herdendorf, C E, 'Captain James Cook and the transits of Mercury and Venus', *Journal of Pacific History*, Vol 21, no 1 (1986), pp39–55.

Hoare, Michael E, 'Cook the Discoverer, An Essay by George Forster', *Records of the Australian Academy of Science*, Vol 1, no 4 (1969), pp7–16.

_____, 'Johann Reinhold Forster: the neglected "philosopher" of Cook's second voyage [1772–1775]', *Journal of Pacific History*, Vol 2 (1967), pp215–24.

Hornsby, T, 'A discourse on the parallax of the Sun', *Phil. Trans. of the Royal Society*, Vol 53 (1763), pp467–95.

_____, 'On the transit of Venus in 1769', *Phil. Trans. of the Royal Society*, Vol 55 (1765), pp326–44.

_____, 'The quantity of the Sun's parallax', *Phil. Trans. of the Royal Society*, Vol 61 (1771), pp574–9.

Howse, D, 'The principal scientific instruments taken on Captain Cook's voyages of exploration, 1776–80', *Mariner's Mirror*, Vol 65, no 2 (1979), pp119–35.

_____, and A Murray, 'Lieutenant Cook and the transit of Venus, 1769', *Astronomy & Geophysics*, Vol 38, no 4 (1997), pp27–30.

'In Cook's wake: Donatien-Alphonse-François, Marquis de Sade', *Antipodes*, No 1 (1995), pp5–6.

Joppien, Rudiger, 'Cataloguing the drawings from Captain Cook's voyages: a task completed', *Australian Journal of Art*, Vol 3 (1983), pp59–78.

Kaeppler, Adrienne L, 'Concerning a Maori Shell Trumpet from Cook's Second Voyage and Some Implications', *J. Polynesian Society*, Vol 96, no 2 (1987), pp243–9.

_____, 'Cook Voyage Provenance of the "Artificial Curiosities" of Bullock's Museum', *Man, the Journal of the Royal Anthropological Institute.* 1974. Vol 9, no 1 (1974), pp68–92.

_____, 'Eighteenth Century Tonga: New Interpretations of Tongan Society and Material Culture at the Time of Captain Cook', *Man, the Journal of the Royal Anthropological Institute*, Vol 6, no 2 (1971), pp204–20.

_____, 'Die ethnographischen Sammlungen der Forsters aus dem Südpazifik: Klassische Empirie im Dienste der modernen Ethnologie', in *Georg Forster in interdisziplinärer Perspektive: Beiträge des Internationalen Georg Forster-Symposions in Kassel, 1. Bis 4. April 1993,* edited by Claus-Volker Klenke, Jörn Garber, and Dieter Heintze (Berlin: Akademie Verlag, 1994), pp59–75.

_____, 'Feather cloaks, ship captains, and lords', *Occasional Papers of Bernice P. Bishop Museum*, Vol 24, no 6 (1970), pp92–114.

_____, 'A Further note on the Cook Voyage Collection in Leningrad. *J. Polynesian Society*, Vol 92, no 1 (1983), pp93–8.

_____, 'The Göttingen Collection in an International Context', 'Tonga - Entry into Complex Hierarchies', 'Hawai'i-Ritual Encounters" (three chapters in) *James Cook, Gifts and Treasures from the South Seas* (Munich and New York: Prestel, 1998), pp86–93, 195–220, 234–48.

_____, 'Hawaiian Art and Society: Traditions and Transformations', in *Transformations of Polynesian Culture,* edited by Anthony Hooper & Judith Huntsman (Auckland: Polynesian Society, 1985), pp105–31.

_____, 'Pacific Culture History and European Voyages', in *Terra Australis* (Sydney: Art Gallery of New South Wales, 1988), pp141–6, 160–1, 164–6, 168, 181, 184, and 188.

_____, 'Polynesian Music, Captain Cook, and the Romantic Movement in Europe', *Music Educators Journal*, Vol 65, no 3 (1978), pp55–60.

_____, 'Preservation and Evolution of Form and Function in Two Types of Tongan Dance', in *Polynesian Culture History: Essays in Honor of Kenneth P. Emory,* edited by Genevieve A Highland, et al (Honolulu: Bishop Museum Press, 1967), pp503–36.

_____, 'A Study of Tongan Panpipes With a Speculative Interpretation', *Ethnos*, Vol 39, no 1–4 (1974), pp102–28.

_____, 'Tracing the History of Cook Voyage Artifacts in the Museum of Mankind', *The British Museum Yearbook*, No 3 (1979), pp167–97.

_____, 'Two Polynesian Repatriation Enigmas at the Smithsonian Institution', *Journal of Museum Ethnography* (Forthcoming).

_____, 'The Use of Documents in Identifying Ethnographic Specimens from the Voyages of Captain Cook', *Journal of Pacific History*, Vol 7 (1972), pp195–200.

Kame'eleihiwa, Lilikalā, Review [of Obeyesekere's *The Apotheosis of Captain Cook*], *Pacific Studies*, Vol 17, no 2 (1994), pp111–18.

Kāne, Herb Kawainui, Comments, *Current Anthropology*, Vol 38, no 2 (1997), pp265–7.

Kaye, I, 'Captain James Cook and the Royal Society', *Notes and Records of the Royal Society of London*, Vol 24, no 1 (1969), pp7–18.

Lamb, Jonathan, 'Social facts, political fictions and unrelative events: Obeyesekere on Sahlins', *Social Analysis*, No 34 (1993), pp56–9.

Lewthwaite, Gordon, 'Puzzle of Tupaia's map', *New Zealand Geographer*, Vol 26, no 1 (1970), pp1–19.

Marquardt, Karl Heinz, 'HM Bark *Endeavour*: what do we really know about the ship?', *Nautical Research Journal*, Vol 35, no 1 (1990), pp28–41.

Medway, D G, 'Some ornithological results of Cook's Third Voyage', *J. Soc. Bibliography Nat. Hist.*, Vol 9, no 3 (1979), pp315–51.

Morris, Robert J, 'Aikāne: accounts of Hawaiian same-sex relationships in the Journals of Captain Cook's third voyage', *Journal of Homosexuality*, Vol 19, no 4 (1990), pp21–54.

Obeyesekere, Gananath, 'British cannibals: contemplation of an event in the death and resurrection of James Cook, explorer', *Critical Inquiry*, Vol 18 (1992), pp630–54.

_____, 'How to write a Cook book: mythic and other realities in anthropological writing', *Pacific Studies* Vol 17, no 2 (1994), pp136–55.

Orchiston, Wayne, 'From the South Seas to the Sun: the astronomy of Cook's voyages', in *Science and Exploration in the Pacific. European Voyages to the Southern Oceans in the Eighteenth Century*, edited by Margarette Lincoln (Woodbridge: Boydell Press, 1998), pp55–72.

_____, and D Howse, 'From transit of Venus to teaching navigation: the work of William Wales', *Journal of Navigation*, Vol 53 (2000), pp156–66.

Palma, R L, 'Two bird lice (Insecta: Phthiraptera) collected during Cook's 2nd voyage around the world', *Archives of Natural History*, Vol 18, no 2 (1991), pp237–47.

Ravneberg, Ronald L, *The Hawkesworth Proof* (Unpublished manuscript. 2002).

_____, 'Searching for Captain Cook', PowerPoint presentation to Aldus Society, Columbus, Ohio, 24 January 2002.

Ritchie, George Stephen, 'Captain Cook's influence on hydrographic surveying', *Pacific Studies*, Vol 1, no 2 (1978), pp78–95.

Rose, Deborah Bird, 'The Saga of Captain Cook: morality in Aboriginal and European law', *Australian Aboriginal Studies*, no 2 (1984), pp24–39.

Ryan, Tom, '"Le Président des Terres Australes": Charels de Brosses and the French Enlightenment beginnings of Oceanic Anthropology', *Journal of Pacific History*. 2002. Vol 37, no 2 (2002), pp157–86.

St John, Harold, 'Biography of David Nelson, and an account of his botanizing in Hawaii', *Pacific Science*, Vol 30, no 1 (1976), pp1–5.

_____, 'The First collection of Hawaiian plants by David Nelson in 1779', *Pacific Science*, Vol 32, no 3 (1978), pp305–24.

Sahlins, Marshall, 'The Apotheosis of Captain Cook', in *Between Belief and Transgression: Structuralist Essays in Religion, History, and Myth*, edited by Michel Izard & Pierre Smith (Chicago: University of Chicago Press, 1982), pp73–102.

Saine, Thomas P, 'Georg Forster', In *Dictionary of Literary Biography, Volume 94: German Writers in the Age of Goethe: Sturm und Drang to Classicism*, edited by James Hardin (New York: Gale, 1990), pp36–45.

Skelton, Raleigh Ashlin, 'Captain James Cook as a hydrographer', *Mariner's Mirror*, Vol 40 (1954), pp92–119.

_____, 'Explorers' maps. X: James Cook and the mapping of the Pacific', *Geographical Magazine*, Vol 28, no 2 (1955), pp95–106.

_____, Introductory essay in *James Cook Surveyor of Newfoundland* (San Francisco: David Magee, 1965), pp1–32.

_____, 'Marine surveys of James Cook in North America 1758–1768 particularly the survey of Newfoundland', *Map Collector's Circle*, No 37 (1967).

Smith, A W, 'Captain James Cook; Londoner', *East London Papers*, Vol 11, no 2 (1968), pp94–7.

Smith, Bernard, 'Captain Cook's artists and the portrayal of Pacific peoples', *Art History*, Vol 7, no 3 (1984), pp295–312.

_____, 'Coleridge's Ancient Mariner and Cook's second voyage', *Journal of the Warburg and Courtauld Institutes*, Vol 19 (1956), pp117–54.

_____, 'Cook's Posthumous reputation', in *Captain James Cook and His Times,* edited by Robin Fisher & Hugh Johnston (Vancouver: Douglas & McIntyre, 1979), pp159–85.

_____, 'European vision and the South Pacific', *Journal of the Warburg and Courtauld Institutes*, Vol 13 (1950), pp65–100.

Snell, W E, 'Captain Cook's surgeons', *Medical History*, Vol 7 (1963), pp43–55.

Spate, O H K, 'The Literature of Cook's voyage', *La Trobe Library Journal*, Vol 11, no 41 (1988), pp25–9.

Stearn, William, 'Botanical results of Captain Cook's three voyages and their later influence', *Pacific Studies*, Vol 1, no 2 (1978), pp147–62.

_____, 'The Botanical results of the *Endeavour* voyage', *Endeavour*, Vol 27 (1968), pp3–10.

Steele, Joshua, 'Account of a Musical Instrument, which was brought by Captain Furneaux from the Isle of Amsterdam in the South Seas to London in Year 1774, and given to the Royal Society, and Remarks on a larger System of Reed Pipes from the Isle of Amsterdam, with some observations on the Nose Flute of Otaheite', *Philosophical Transactions of the Royal Society*, Vol 65 (1775), pp67–78.

Steinheimer, Frank D, 'Darwin, Ruppell, Landbeck & Co., Important historical collections at the Natural History Museum, Tring'. *Bonner Zoologische Beiträge*, Vol 51, no 2/3 (2003), pp175–88.

Stokes, John F G, 'Origin of the condemnation of Captain Cook in Hawaii: a study in cause and effect', *Hawaiian Historical Society Annual Report*, No 39 (1930), pp68–104.

Svet, Yakov M, 'Captain Cook and the Russians', *Pacific Studies*, Vol 2, no 1 (1978), pp1–19.

Taylor, Eva G R, 'Navigation in the days of Captain Cook', *Journal of Navigation*, Vol 21, no 3 (1968), pp256–76.

Thomson, J M, 'The significance of the voyage of the *Endeavour* to Botany and Zoology', in *The Significance of Cook's Endeavour voyage: three Bicentennial lectures* (Townsville: James Cook University, 1970), pp25–36.

Tonson, A E, 'The Arms of Captain James Cook, R.N., F.R.S.', *The New Zealand Armorist*, No 3 (1970), pp4–8.

Trask, Haunani-Kay, 'Cultures in collision: Hawaii and England, 1778', *Pacific Studies*, Vol 7, no 1 (1983), pp91–117.

_____, Review of Sahlin's "Islands of history". *American Ethnologist*, Vol 12, no 4 (1985), pp184–7.

Villiers, Alan, 'Captain Cook: the man who mapped the Pacific', *National Geographic*, Vol 140, no 3 (1971), pp297–349.

Wainburranga, Paddy Fordham, 'Captain Cook', in *Tyerabarrbowaryaou II: I Shall Never Become a White Man* (Sydney: Museum of Contemporary Art, 1994), pp8–9.

Wales, William, 'Journal of William Wales', in Cook, James. *The Journals of Captain James Cook on his Voyages of Discovery. Volume two: The Voyage of The Resolution and Adventure 1772–1775,* edited by J C Beaglehole. (Cambridge: Hakluyt Society, 1961), pp776–869.

Watt, James, 'Medical aspects and consequences of Cook's voyages', in *Captain James Cook and His Times,* edited by Robin Fisher & Hugh Johnston (Vancouver: Douglas & McIntyre, 1979), pp129–57.

Watts, John, 'Lieutenant Watt's narrative of the Reurn of the Lady Penrhyn Transport; containing an account of the death of Omai, and other interesting Particulars at Otaheite', in *The Voyage of Governor Phillip to Botany Bay; with an account of the establishment of the colonies of Port Jackson and Norfolk Island; compiled from authentic papers…to which are added the journals of Lieuts. Shorthand, Watts, Ball and Capt. Marshall with an account of their new discoveries* (Adelaide: Libraries Board of South Australia, 1968), pp222–48.

Whitehead, Peter J, 'Captain Cook's Role in Natural History', *Australian Natural History*, Vol 16 (1969), pp242–6.

_____, 'A Guide to the dispersal of material from Captain Cook's voyages', *Pacific Studies,* Vol 2, no 1 (1978), pp52–93.

_____, 'Zoological specimens from Captain Cook's voyages', *J. Soc. Bibliography. Natural History*, Vol 5, no 3 (1969), pp161–201.

Whiteley, William H., 'James Cook and British policy in the Newfoundland fisheries 1763–7', *Canadian Historical Review*, Vol 54, no 3 (1973), pp245–72.

_____, 'James Cook, Hugh Palliser and the Newfoundland fishery', *Newfoundland Quarterly*, Vol 69, no 2 (1972), pp17–22.

Williams, Glyndwr, 'Far more happier than we Europeans: reactions to the Australian Aborigines on Cook's Voyage', *Historical Studies*, Vol 19 (1981).

_____, 'Seamen and philosophers in the South Seas in the age of Captain Cook', *Mariner's Mirror*, Vol 65 (1979), pp3–22.

_____, 'To make discoveries of countries hitherto unknown: the Admiralty and Pacific exploration in the eighteenth century', *Mariner's Mirror*, Vol 82, no 1 (1996), pp14–27.

Williamson, Karina, 'John Hawkesworth', in *Dictionary of Literary Biography, Volume 142: Eighteenth-Century British Literary Biographers*, edited by Steven Serafin (New York: Gale, 1994), pp115–21.

RADIO PROGRAMMES

Agnew, Vanessa, and N A M Roger, *Music afloat*. Radio 4 series (London: BBC Radio, 2000).

INDEX

Page references in italics refer to illustrations, and those in bold to major articles. Colour plates are between pages 64 and 65.